Music Since 1945

Music Since 1945

Issues, Materials, and Literature

Elliott Schwartz/Daniel Godfrey

SCHIRMER BOOKS
An Imprint of Simon & Schuster Macmillan
New York

Prentice Hall International
London   Mexico City   New Delhi
Singapore   Sydney   Toronto

SCHIRMER BOOKS
An Imprint of Simon & Schuster Macmillan
1633 Broadway, New York, N.Y.   10019-6785

Library of Congress Catalog Card Number: 92-11959

Printed in the United States of America

printing number
   2   3   4   5   6   7   8   9   10

Library of Congress Cataloging-in-Publication Data

Schwartz, Elliott, 1936–
    Music since 1945 : issues, materials, and literature /
Elliott Schwartz and Daniel Godfrey.
       p.   cm.
    Includes bibliographical references, discography, and
index.
    ISBN 0-02-873040-2
    1. Music—20th century—History and criticism.
    2. Music—20th century—Analysis, appreciation.
    3. Music—Theory—20th century.
    I. Godfrey, Daniel. II. Title.
    ML197.S35   1992
    780'.9'04—dc20   92-11959
                     CIP
                     MN

To
Dorothy Schwartz
and
Diana Godfrey

Contents

Part II.　New Aesthetic Approaches

Preface

The literature of concert music composed since 1945 is rich and impressive, testimony to the brilliance of many distinguished composers, working within several important stylistic movements. Moreover, musical developments since the end of World War II offer unique challenges to listeners, forcing us to examine each of our aesthetic assumptions and cultural biases. For these and other reasons, more and more college and university survey courses are being devoted entirely to postwar music, rather than treating it as a mere addition to the study of earlier twentieth-century music.

Music Since 1945 is intended for use in such courses by students with a broad range of backgrounds: undergraduate music majors in both professional and liberal arts settings, as well as graduate music students specializing in a variety of areas, whether music history, theory, composition, performance, or education. This volume is, therefore, "introductory"; it proceeds from the assumption that virtually all readers will be unfamiliar with much of the material. We expect them to have a basic background in the history, literature, and structure of Western concert music, ideally including the earlier twentieth century, but nothing beyond that. Furthermore, *Music Since 1945* is general in its focus; it integrates aspects of music theory, history, literature, and aesthetics, rather than concentrating on only one of those dimensions. It is our hope that what analytical and historical detail we have incorporated will provide direction and impetus for more thorough study; titles of more specialized volumes, dealing with contemporary music from theoretical or musicological perspectives, are listed in the bibliography.

We also offer a set of nine factors to assist the student who may be confronting postwar concert music for the first time. Seven basic concerns—**pitch logic, time, sound color, texture, process, performance ritual,** and **parody** or **historicism**—shape the aesthetics of today's composers and influence their creative decisions. Two compositional tools—**technology** and **notation**—enable them to articulate those concerns. These nine factors, first presented in Chapter 4, function as informal reference guides in the remainder of the text.

Although the individual chapter titles seem to indicate an overall "topics" approach (rather than a historical one), the first three of the book's four parts follow a chronological line. Part I begins in the early years of this century and ends in the late 1950s. It concentrates on the origins of modernism, provides tools for further study (including an introduction to the "nine factors"), and brings the reader to the early postwar decade. Part II moves on to the early 1970s, and in so doing covers the peak years of postwar modernism. Individual chapters deal with issues of chance and control, texture as unique focus, multimedia explorations, the influence of non-Western culture, and the beginnings of electronic music.

The focus of Part III is the development of postmodernism from the 1970s to the early 1990s. Collage, quotation, minimalism, new views of ritual, the resurgence of tonality, and digital electronic systems are discussed in individual chapters. Part IV offers a new look at the material already discussed, from three specific vantage points: notation, national distinctions, and different approaches to such traditional genres as opera and concerto.

Apart from a sequential reading of the chapters, the student or instructor may wish to follow certain "tracks," or subplots, running from Part II to Part III. For example, the historical development of electroacoustic music begins in Chapter 8 and continues in Chapter 17; similarly, the discussion of multimedia in Chapter 9 could lead directly to a more extended look at performance ritual in Chapter 15; likewise, Chapter 7, devoted to serial and aleatoric/indeterminate processes, naturally relates to the discussion of repetitive, minimalist processes in Chapter 16.

Note, too, that certain chapters contain their own capsule chronologies, extending forward and backward to adjacent decades or even to previous centuries, where precedents provide a telling perspective. Finally, a particular concept or composer may reappear in a number of chapters. To give two examples: metric modulation is discussed in terms of its effect on perceived continuity (how *time* passes), and in another chapter is treated as an aspect of *texture*. John Adams's music appears in the chapter devoted to *tonality*, and then resurfaces in the chapter on *minimalism*. The seeming redundancy is deliberate; at each new point of discussion, the emphasis is different. If, to cite one further example, John Cage is discussed in terms of "chaos and order" (Chapter 7), multimedia explorations (Chapter 9), and non-Western influences (Chapter 11), it is because his work needs to be grasped in all three contexts. The inevitable repetition can only aid, rather than hinder, understanding.

In writing *Music Since 1945*, then, we have decided to present the changing nature of music from many perspectives: novel approaches to musical structure (materials, techniques, goals), important issues (social, aesthetic, technological), and firsthand acquaintance with composers and their works (recordings and scores). Our aim is that of fostering wider experience and greater understanding on the student's part—thereby, we hope, generating a sense of the excitement and adventure that naturally results from living fully in one's own time.

Acknowledgments

First and foremost, we must begin by expressing our deepest appreciation to Schirmer Books Editor in Chief Maribeth Payne, and her associate, Robert Axelrod, for their remarkable patience, understanding, and guidance in seeing us through this long project. Second, our special thanks go to Steve Long and Bruce Brooks, not only for their encyclopedic knowledge of the postwar music literature, but also for their willingness to lend us recordings from their extensive personal collections. Thomas Carranti, graduate composition student at Syracuse University, provided important assistance in compiling the discography and preparing the many musical examples. Work on the chapter dealing with non-Western music influences was greatly helped by Peter Westbrook's valuable input; similarly, in writing the chapters on electronic and computer music, we benefited from guidance offered by Michael Daugherty and Mark Drews. A number of colleagues provided important information and steered us in the direction of significant literature: Marshall Bialosky, Henry Brant, Brian Ferneyhough, Benjamin Folkman, Jonathan Kramer, Eric Lotz, Steven Stucky, Andrew Waggoner, and Steven Winick. In addition, the chapter on national styles owes a great deal to the help of Jeff Hamburg, Stephen Kelley, Byong-kon Kim, Max Lifchitz, Margarita Mazo, Tom Morgan, Rodney and Kryzstyna Oakes, Keith Potter, E. Michael Richards, Poul Rosenbaum, Leo Samama, Kazuko Tanosaki, Stephen Walsh, and Christopher Weait.

Many people were generous in helping us locate photos and artwork. In this regard, we are particularly grateful to Ralph Jackson and Barbara Petersen of BMI; Katharine Watson, Director of the Bowdoin College Museum of Art; Jon Appleton; and Tessim Zorach, who provided us with the book's cover art. Others who provided important contributions in this area include Iris Brooks, Rosalie Calabrese, the Finnish Music Information Centre, the studios of Western German Radio and Maison de Radio-France, Jacob Glick, Mary Klibonoff, Ronald Perera, Bertram Turetzky, and Glen Watkins. Our project inevitably entailed the use of many musical excerpts, and certain publishers were particularly helpful in sorting out our numerous permissions requests. Our special gratitude goes to Carol Metzker and the copyright department of European-American Music. Equally patient and generous with their time were Don Gillespie of C. F. Peters, Sally Groves of Schott (London), and Martha Cox of Theodore Presser Company. Our thanks also go to the permissions staffs of Boosey and Hawkes and G. Schirmer.

Various friends and colleagues have generously read parts of the manuscript; we have enjoyed an enriching exchange of ideas with many others as well. Especially noteworthy are Donald Aird, Margaret Barela, Barbara Lundquist, Paula Matthews, James McCalla, Robert Trotter, and Nick Humez, who also assisted us by compiling the index for this book. The contribution of libraries was invaluable; in particular, we would like to thank the Harvard, Cornell, and Ohio State University libraries, the music library of Bowdoin College, the American Music Center, and the Lincoln Center Library of the Performing Arts. Individual librarians, such as David Stamm and Donald Seibert, Head Librarian and Music Librarian respectively at Syracuse University, and Music Librarian Thomas Heck of The Ohio State University, also provided special help. Finally, we are indebted to our students at Bowdoin College, The Ohio State University, and Syracuse University, who read drafts of various chapters in manuscript, thereby helping us refine the text. We are grateful to them all.

E.S. and D.G.

Introduction

Anyone who has listened to a fair sampling of concert music composed since World War II, or studied some representative scores, has found the experience something of a revelation—immediately exhilarating for some, initially intimidating for others, and for all of us a profound departure from our previous encounters with music. Many compositions written after 1945 sound unlike any music we've ever heard before, and in their notation on the printed page, look quite unlike any music we have ever seen.

It would be entirely understandable, then, to assume that much post–1945 concert music is based on premises that seem distinctly new, even when compared with music of the earlier twentieth century. On one level, at least, that assumption is entirely correct. In studying this music, we will reexamine many of our ideas about fundamental elements, such as melody, harmony, and rhythm, and about larger topics such as "structure" or "performance."

In fact, new directions in style and techniques have proliferated so dramatically from World War II to the present that it would take volumes to approach them with real theoretical detail, or elucidate fully the cultural and political contexts of their development. Our task here, then, is one of getting acquainted, of identifying basic features and distinctions that suggest strategies for further listening and study. For that reason we will periodically refocus our discussions of postwar music, in all its diversity, around the nine factors described in the Preface. In our "Pieces for Study" chapters, and in certain other instances, those nine factors serve as a guide to the study of specific examples, and as a springboard for general discussion.

On another level, however, we should also realize that music composed since 1945 is not entirely "new." As we will discover in Chapter 2, the music of the early twentieth century provides many important clues and models for more recent developments. For that reason, we strongly suggest that, even before beginning Chapter 1, students acquaint themselves with as many of the works listed below as possible. This group of works by a baker's dozen of composers, all composed *before* 1945, should provide a useful background for the text to follow. Recordings of all of these pieces are listed in the discography.

Gustav Mahler: *Das Lied von der Erde*, final movement
Claude Debussy: Nocturnes for Orchestra; "La cathedrale engloutie" from Preludes for Piano, Book 1

Igor Stravinsky: *Le sacre du printemps; Symphony of Psalms*
Erik Satie: *Gymnopédies; Three Pieces in the Form of a Pear*
Edgard Varèse: *Octandre; Ionisation*
Béla Bartók: *Music for Strings, Percussion, and Celesta*; Sonata for Two Pianos and Percussion
Olivier Messiaen: *Quatuor pour la fin du temps*
Arnold Schoenberg: *Pierrot Lunaire*; Variations for Orchestra
Alban Berg: *Wozzeck*, Act III; Violin Concerto
Anton von Webern: Variations for Piano, Op. 27; Concerto, Op. 24
Charles Ives: *The Unanswered Question*; selected songs; Three Quarter-Tone Pieces
Henry Cowell: ''The Tides of Manaunaun''; ''The Banshee'' (piano)
John Cage: *First Construction in Metal; Imaginary Landscape No. 1*

Music Since 1945

PART

1

Precedents, Influences, and Early Postwar Trends

1

Composers and Audiences

The subject of this book is a body of art music composed since the end of the Second World War in 1945—often referred to by critics as "New Music." That label may have its drawbacks, but the alternatives are even more problematic. "Modern music" or "contemporary music" are terms that might well apply to the worlds of rock and pop, whereas the music to be studied here is closer in its aims to the "classical" stereotype: music created from personal conviction rather than the demands of the commerical market, and often intended for an elite audience rather than for mass appeal. Furthermore, such terms as "twentieth-century concert music," "modern serious music," or "contemporary art music" can be equally misleading. A significant number of the composers we will be discussing have rejected the notion of the "concert," or of music as "serious," or of high "art." The label "twentieth-century music" aims too wide of the mark. Now, at the end of the century, many of the art works produced during its first fifty years have become established masterworks. But "history" has not yet decided what the masterworks of the century's *second* half will be, or whether there will be any, or indeed whether the very idea of the masterpiece, as a vestige of romanticism, has become obsolete.

Perhaps we should begin our study of new music by confronting its supposed "inaccessibility." Most concertgoers regard recently composed music as difficult or unpalatable, even (in extreme instances) as "nonmusic" concocted by charlatans. Such a response isn't limited to music of the last few decades. On the contrary, much of the art music composed since 1900 has met with initial hostility or indifference. Many listeners simply wish to play it safe, finding their greatest satisfaction in the secure comfort of hearing familiar works. Others are made uneasy by the discord and fragmentation they find in new music; although they may realize that art inevitably reflects its times, they have no desire to be reminded that they live in an age of social conflict, violence, and rapid technological change. Still others are put off by the sheer diversity of stylistic options, perhaps interpreting these as an abnegation of "standards." (That sort of pluralism is not unique to music, of course: consider the stylistic range of other arts in our century, embracing cubism, futurism, the happenings movement, abstract expressionism, pop, op, realism, and the theater of the absurd.)

We should note that there was a time when even Wagner and Brahms were "modern" composers, generating controversy and hostility among audiences. In fact, a good deal of the tension between composer and listener had its origins in the nineteenth century, an era that witnessed the loss of court and church patronage; the development of a middle-class audience divided into many splinter groups; the model of Beethoven as the lonely, "heroic" figure deliberately creating difficult music; the rise of the virtuoso with special appeal to a mass public; and a fascination with history and the past. From the earliest years of the nineteenth century, art music has been composed in an increasingly fragmented social context, characterized by a sense of schism—a rift not only between concert music and popular genres but also between concert music of the past and the creations of living composers.

This situation has been even further complicated in the twentieth century, and for a variety of reasons—including, one must admit, the nature of the music itself. A good deal of music composed since 1900 can be described, even by its proponents, as angular, biting, and discordant. Some pieces even seem deliberately created to provoke the listener, as though the composer had set out to distort every traditional definition of "music."

Why have composers of such works chosen to create sounds that many listeners find disturbing? Oddly enough, we may find some answers by looking again to precedents set in the nineteenth century. Certainly the fascination that many composers have with novelty or uncharted territory is in itself a legacy from the romantic era, when "individuality" was paramount and when creative artists vied with one another to establish unique, even eccentric, profiles. For example, Franz Liszt is reputed to have said that any composition must contain at least one new chord, while figures such as Gustav Mahler or Richard Wagner cultivated highly personal sonorities in their handling of orchestral color. It is not too great a leap from such examples to that of Henry Cowell (1897–1965) exploring tone clusters and inner-string piano sonorities, or the explorations of birdsong and Hindu rhythms by Olivier Messiaen (1908–1992).

A romantic legacy of another sort can be heard in twentieth-century works whose composers are simply attempting to be "expressive" in the nineteenth-century sense. They may be concerned, however, with the depiction of "extreme" psychological or emotional states. Arnold Schoenberg (1874–1951), for example, was dealing with anguished, searing expressive

ILLUS. 1.1.

Arnold Schoenberg

Courtesy BMI Archives.

imagery (dreams, premonitions, guilt, fear, and the like) in such compositions as *Pierrot Lunaire* (1912). Similarly, Igor Stravinsky (1882–1971) was projecting a certain raw primitivism, the intensity of a prehistoric ritual, with the jarring rhythms of *Le sacre du printemps* (1913). In such music, composed against the backdrop of the prevailing tonal system, our responses of terror, pain, or relative uneasiness are entirely legitimate; the sonorities retain their emotive power, and are not meant to become pretty on repeated hearings.

Other composers of our century have taken a less overtly "expressive," more objective approach to their craft, although the results may be equally unusual. Such composers may enjoy exploring new techniques and materials for philosophical or acoustical reasons. Edgard Varèse (1883–1965), for one, based many of his musical forms and textures on scientific, rather than "expressive" or "dramatic," models. He was fascinated by the possibilities of translating the physical universe of matter and energy, vectors, masses, and trajectories into audible structures. Many of his titles, such as *Ionisation* or *Density 21.5*, reflect his special perspective. It is also revealing that he referred to his own work as "organized sound" rather than music; he once stated, "Don't call me a composer. Call me an engineer of rhythms, resonances, and timbres."

In his own way, Erik Satie (1866–1925) was equally antiromantic. Known for his dry wit and a talent for poking fun at the pompous, he affected aesthetic "distance," as opposed to romantic subjectivity, in his own work. In his attempt to deflate romantic pretensions, Satie developed a musical conception of curiously static understatement, a unique intermingling of ascetic mysticism, clarity, and even severity, as in his elegant *Gymnopédies*. It is no wonder that Satie's colleague Claude Debussy (1862–1918) referred to him as a "gentle medieval musician"; he does seem to have entered the modern world from another time and place.

There is one more important area in which the romantic tradition has influenced our own century. Appropriately enough, in the age of Darwin and Marx, nineteenth-century European intellectuals stressed the concept of art as evolution. Many creative figures of the period believed in a process whereby artistic languages must progress in certain predetermined directions (whether we or the artists like it or not), driven by an inner dialectic force that cannot be halted. Schoenberg, in moving from chromatic atonality to twelve-tone serialism, believed himself to be following a road that was inevitable. There are times when Schoenberg wished he didn't "have" to compose his kind of music; in one of his written statements he claims that "music is only understood when one goes away singing it, and is only loved when one falls asleep with it in one's head," half wishing that he might be permitted to create something a listener would love. We also have the story of the composer being asked, "Are you the famous Arnold Schoenberg?" and replying, "Someone had to be, and no one else volunteered." In

ILLUS. 1.2.

Edgard Varèse

Courtesy BMI Archives

fact, Schoenberg's career conforms to the romantic stereotype of Wagner, Berlioz, or even Beethoven: the artist who *must* follow his own path (or the predetermined path of historical necessity) in the face of public antagonism or indifference, who remains true to his own vision and avoids corrupting it at all costs.

Finally, we must consider the varying attitudes of twentieth-century composers toward their audiences. Occasions for composers to function as useful musical "citizens" in their communities—that is, to approximate the working conditions of a Haydn or Bach—have been rare. On the contrary, contemporary composers have developed relationships toward their listeners for which again, unfortunately, the nineteenth century has provided the models. Some composers, such as Stravinsky, have been assertive and outgoing. In this vein, Varèse's public statements created an image of self-confident assuredness. In denying that his pieces were "experimental," Varèse once stated, "I offer a finished product . . . it is for the audience to make the experiment of confronting a new work." On the other hand, figures such as Satie or Charles Ives (1874–1954) appear to have been withdrawn and puzzling, concealing their reticence behind a gruff or witty exterior. Ives's lack of interest in the practical side of music making is legendary. In fact, he once wrote, "why can't music go out in the same way it comes in to a man, without having to crawl over a fence of sounds, thoraxes, catguts, wire, wood and brass? Is it the composer's fault that man has only ten fingers?" His unconcern for performers as well as listeners reveals itself in such quirky practices as asking for a brief flute passage in the middle of a lengthy work for solo piano.

Still other composers have assumed an actively hostile, adversarial, stance toward the public. Schoenberg, in particular, developed such an attitude while working in the antagonistic, extremely conservative atmosphere of pre–World War I Vienna. (The Viennese concertgoers had made Gustav Mahler's life miserable, and Schoenberg was undoubtedly hardened by the painful experiences of his older colleague and friend.) To give some sense of the highly charged atmosphere of that setting: in 1913 Schoenberg conducted a concert including Anton von Webern's Six Orchestral Pieces and Alban Berg's *Altenberg Lieder*. The audience responded in a riot so chaotic that police had to be called in, making it impossible to complete the performance of Berg's composition.

Paradoxically, the premiere of Stravinsky's *Le sacre du printemps* (in the same year, 1913) resulted in an equally violent public reaction, even though Paris was—in contrast to Schoenberg's Vienna—a lively, sophisticated art center. During Stravinsky's early career he delighted in the challenge of composing for the Parisian listeners, who were remarkably modish, au courant, eager for the newest fashion. *Le sacre* simply went far beyond their expectations. In any event, public involvement, whether positive or negative, provided an important factor within the European creative climate; Stravinsky and Schoenberg flourished in the company of like-minded colleagues (a substantial artistic "community"), and an audience that—whether hostile, supportive, or curious—cared deeply about art music.

Conditions differed considerably in turn-of-the-century America, where eccentric, individual "maverick" personalities had to flower artistically with little or no support from colleagues and virtually no feedback from an audience of any size. Figures such as Ives developed in relative isolation, driven only by their own overwhelming desire to pursue an uncharted course. When Ives had occasion to reach audiences, either in person or by way of his writings, his zeal was remarkable, combining a romantic European belief in the artist's mission with a uniquely American sense of the moral "rightness" of change, challenge, and stretching one's limits. There is a refreshing honesty in his wanting music to provide "stronger meat for the ears and the mind," or in his response to hissing in the audience at a performance of music by Carl Ruggles: "You God-damn sissy! . . . get up and use your ears!"

A great many factors, then, contributed to the tendency for composers of the past hundred years to address their audiences in a "difficult" or "unsettling" language. A number of those factors, ironically, are by-products of the romanticism of the nineteenth century, the period that most concertgoers consider the antithesis of "difficult" modern music. This chapter has concentrated on composers active at the turn of the twentieth century because the problems of accessibility in post–1945 music have their roots in that earlier era. The next chapter attempts to isolate those features of the early twentieth-century literature that similarly foreshadow the special nature of recent "New Music."

Precedents and Influences: Music from 1890 to 1945

Because musical developments seldom fit the tidy divisions of the calendar, what we consider "twentieth-century music" may be said to have begun in the year 1890 rather than 1900. In fact, 1889 makes an even better starting point, since that was the year of the great international Paris Exposition celebrating the centennial of the French Revolution, and for which the Eiffel Tower was built. The exposition brought a variety of non-Western performing artists to Paris. European composers (Debussy and Mahler in particular), profoundly moved by the sounds of the Indonesian gamelan ensemble, began rethinking their concepts of sonority, texture, and musical time as a result. Many works composed in the 1890s, such as Debussy's *Prélude a l'après-midi d'un faune* and Schoenberg's *Verklärte Nacht*, have more in common with the "modern" music that followed than with the preceding decades' romanticism.

MUSIC FROM 1890 TO 1920

During the latter part of the nineteenth century, the Western system of major and minor key relationships known as tonality had become fundamentally weakened by ever-increasing levels of chromaticism. Traditional chromatic usage—that of "expressive" inflection within a solid tonal context—had given way to an incessant chromatic wandering, creating an unstable tonal flux. Many passages in the music of Wagner or Liszt, for example, pass rapidly through many keys without clearly confirming any of them; in a sense, they seem to have no key at all. This apparent breakdown of tonality led many composers to search for alternative musical languages.

Schoenberg chose to follow the implications of Wagernian chromaticism to their extremes; in a work such as *Pierrot Lunaire*, with its structure built on the linear interplay of brief motives and textural contrasts, rather than reference to a key center, he created a highly chromatic, atonal language. He apparently did so with a deep sense of responsibility and perhaps even some reluctance; he was convinced that his was the only true direction in which music, with Darwinian inevitability, should evolve. Stravinsky moved in a very different direction, however, as one can observe in *Le sacre du printemps*. The strongest, most daring forces in *Le Sacre* are its rhythms—asymmetrical, jagged, and unsettling—and the use of "primitive" pitch patterns drawn from folk music. Debussy's experiments in the use of free-floating sonority (relatively lacking in dissonant, chromatic tension), nondevelopmental form, and unusual scales present yet another approach.

Note, however, that as daring and innovative as these three composers were, they and most of their colleagues still held romantic assumptions about music's power to convey expressive or programmatic messages, and about the composer's impassioned, highly personal relationship to the act of creation. Given his later reputation as an overly cerebral, mathematically minded intellectual, it is important to realize how "romantic" Arnold Schoenberg really was in his compositional method. Many of his pieces were created in highly intense, virtually uninterrupted periods of a few weeks, as though in a single, impulsive white heat.

Other composers, in contrast, developed an antiromantic aesthetic. Erik Satie often allied his stark chord chains and mosaic formal patterns with low-key, introverted gestures of self-effacement, such as the creation of a "furniture music" intended to lie below the surface of conscious listening. Varèse's music of the early 1920s reflects another side of antiromanticism: the alliance of art with the worlds of science and technology rather than emotion and "feeling." Varèse's favorite definition of music was that given him by a physicist: the corporealization of the intelligence that is in sound. (Of course, one could argue that such fascination with science merely reflected another side of romanticism, especially in the early decades of this century, when technology symbolized glamour, power, and progress.)

In addition, Europe's growing awareness of the non-Western world was beginning to engender an expanded aesthetic, one that stressed isolated objects over "connections" and static situations over kinetic ones. We have noted the Balinese gamelan and its influence on Mahler and Debussy. It is interesting, in this context, to listen to Mahler's *Das Lied von der Erde* (1907–9) for its Chinese-derived text, its use of the pentatonic scale, its individual timbral "sound events," and in the final movement, its lengthy, slowly unfolding gestures.

On yet another front, experiments in the area of electronic music were just beginning. The extraordinarily perceptive composer Ferruccio Busoni (1866–1924), who accurately predicted an aesthetic swing toward a new classicism, also wrote of a musical future that would be dominated by electricity. Among the many devices invented early in the century, as if in response to Busoni's challenge, was an electronic keyboard instrument developed in the years 1904–6 by a Massachusetts inventor named Thaddeus Cahill; called the Telharmonium, it weighed over two hundred tons and transmitted its sounds over telephone lines.

MUSIC FROM 1920 TO 1945

The years between the two world wars witnessed the rapid rise of the movement known as neoclassicism, resulting from fundamental changes in the aesthetic attitudes of many composers. Those changes included a concern for systematic (rather than intuitive or impulsive) creative procedures, a fondness for problem solving, and the use of historical "models," with a special fondness for the linear textures of the pre–1800 era.

The neoclassic label became most frequently attached to the name of Stravinsky, and consequently to a stylistic language that was aggressively tonal. On the other hand, the label could also be applied to Schoenberg's development of the twelve-tone method as a way to systematize and control atonality. Schoenberg's 1923–24 Suite for Piano, Op. 25, his first consistently twelve-tone work, uses the dance forms of the early eighteenth century, such as the gavotte, minuet, and gigue; in this and later works the composer brings an objective discipline—and a certain aesthetic "distance" not unlike Stravinsky's—to bear upon his formerly impulsive, impassioned chromatic language.

The period between the wars also witnessed the growth of a uniquely American maverick style, along the lines of (although not necessarily related to) the model set by Ives. The frankly experimental music of John Cage (1912–92), Harry Partch (1901–74), and Lou Harrison (b. 1917) is especially noteworthy in its concerns for unusual intonation systems, instrumental resources, and performance rituals, all signs of a link to Asian rather than European sources.

PROPHETIC FACTORS ANTICIPATING POST-1945 DEVELOPMENTS

In studying all this diversity, some important trends emerge. This section summarizes these trends by describing several significant factors found in early twentieth century music that contributed to post–1945 developments.

The Interest in Non-Western Aesthetics and Musical Materials

There has, of course, been an undercurrent of "exoticism" in European music for many generations, with examples ranging from Beethoven's "Turkish" pieces to Rimsky-Korsakov's *Scheherazade*, and Puccini's opera *Turandot*. But from the 1890s onward, actual encounters with non-Western performing ensembles had a much more fundamental effect on Europeans. American composers, especially Pacific Coast figures such as Cowell, Cage, and Harrison, benefited from even closer personal contact with other cultures.

The Interest in "Noise" and Percussive Timbres

Precedents range from the 1909 Italian futurist manifesto (calling for an art to celebrate machines, urban life, and violence) to the 1913 "Art of Noises" of Luigi Russolo (postulating an "orchestra" of sirens, crashes, groans, and the like) and early works of Soviet realism celebrating the factory. There are other, less programmatic or political, reasons. Composers found percussion instruments exciting because their timbres are unique and special, or because they relate to the world of jazz, or for their connection to non-Western cultures, or for their focus on rhythm rather than pitch. It is particularly interesting, many decades after the fact, to read John Cage's amazingly prophetic "Credo" of 1937: "Wherever we are, what we hear is mostly noise. When we ignore it, it disturbs us. When we listen to it, we find it fascinating. The sound of a truck at fifty miles per hour. Static between the stations. Rain. We want to capture and control these sounds . . . we can compose a quartet for explosive motor, wind, heartbeat and landslide."

For three very different approaches to percussive sonority, it would be worth listening to Henry Cowell's piano pieces that exploit keyboard clusters or, like "The Banshee" (1925), the "noises" produced by playing directly on the strings; Varèse's *Ionisation* (1931) for percussion ensemble; and the Sonata for Two Pianos and Percussion (1937) of Béla Bartók (1881–1945).

Microtonal Experiments and New Intonation Systems

The division of the octave into twelve equally tempered pitches has been the norm in Western music since the mid-eighteenth century. A number of modern composers, however, have challenged that norm. Some call for more than twelve subdivisions, such as splitting each of the traditional twelve in half—creating a quarter-tone scale of twenty-four tones—or modeling a system on the scales of a non-Western musical culture, such as that of India or Indonesia. Other composers prefer retuning the twelve pitches within the octave to correspond to older intonation models. For example, Lou Harrison has been interested in just intonation, a system that flourished during the period of Western Renaissance polyphony.

The American Harry Partch—whose parents, significantly, had been missionaries in China at the turn of the century, and who developed a great love of Asian music and theater—began composing with a forty-three-tone division of the octave in the late 1920s. Any of his works would provide an excellent introduction to this area, as would Charles Ives's *Three Quarter-Tone Pieces* (1923–24) for two pianos tuned a quarter tone apart.

The Emancipation of Dissonance and Discord

Schoenberg coined the phrase "emancipation of the dissonance" to describe the highly chromatic harmony of both his early atonal and later twelve-tone works. The phrase is well chosen, since a dissonance—a sonority that in traditional tonal music is considered "incomplete," that is, in need of resolution to consonance—is now free to move to any other sonority, including another dissonance. As we can hear in Schoenberg's *Pierrot Lunaire* and in his later Violin Concerto (1934–36), states of "tension" and "resolution" still exist in atonal or twelve-tone music, but may be expressed through instrumentation, tempo, or dynamic levels rather than by the movement of pitches.

In other styles, one may detect a different sort of emancipation. Here a sonority traditionally considered "dissonant" may actually function as a consonance, either as a static element or as a point of resolution. The famous repeated chords of the ""Dance of the Adolescents" in Stravinsky's *Le sacre du printemps*, or the opening bass clusters of Cowell's "Tides of Manaunaun" (1912), can be said to function this way. Although biting or unsettling, they are not truly dissonant; the term *discord* describes them more accurately.

The Emancipation of the Consonance

Styles that stress percussive timbre, "noise," or unusual intonation systems have, in effect, defined their musical language as consonant by sidestepping the consonance and dissonance relationships associated with the traditional twelve-tone division of the octave. Other styles use the traditional pitch vocabulary but combine consonances in unconventional ways. In the music of Debussy or Satie, a particular chord type (say, a major triad in second inversion) may be used to harmonize every pitch of a melody, simply traveling up and down in parallel motion with the contours of the melody. The grand, hymnlike passage in Debussy's "La cathedrale engloutie" (1910) follows this pattern.

In other works, simple harmonic building blocks, such as major and minor triads, may follow one another without any dependence on key grammar. If carried to extremes, especially in the case of passages that use all twelve pitches, such nonfunctional use of triadic harmony can destroy the traditional sense of tonality as surely as any music by Schoenberg. It may also create an unpredictable overall form. But the very fact that the Western listener's ear finds triads so satisfying creates a curious, contradictory impression: while tonally unstable, the music may still seem innocent or "pretty," or perhaps meditative and distant. This allows Debussy's work in particular to project a quality summed up by Paul Griffiths as abandoning "the narrative mode, and with it the coherent linkage projected by the conscious mind; its evocative images and its elliptical movements suggest more the sphere of free imagination, of dream."

Simultaneity and Multiple Exposure

It seems only appropriate, during the century of film, that a musical texture akin to "multiple exposure" should have emerged. The creation of separate (often competing) musics, stated simultaneously at juxtaposed levels, goes beyond the traditional notion of polyphony, or even of polytonality, polymeter, and the like. For some composers such textures may be a way of celebrating the multiplicity and contradictions of existence. Ives was a significant innovator in this area, and his haunting piece *The Unanswered Question* (1908) remains a pioneer work; the *Octandre* (1924) and *Ionisation* of Varèse, using static blocks of sound, also create interacting levels.

Coloristic Orchestration

From the earliest years of this century, performers have been asked to explore novel aspects of instrumental technique—for example, *sul ponticello* bowings on the strings; fluttertongue and glissando effects for winds and brasses; plucking or scraping the strings of the piano; and the declamatory vocal technique, midway between song and speech, called *Sprechstimme*, which lends an expressionistic flavor to Schoenberg's *Pierrot Lunaire* and to the opera *Wozzeck* (1926) by Schoenberg's pupil Alban Berg (1885–1935). Mahler and Debussy both demonstrate a soloistic, color-oriented approach to the orchestra, with Mahler particularly interested in extracting intimate chamber textures from his gigantic ensembles. This technique, further explored by Schoenberg and then refined by another of his pupils, Anton von Webern (1883–1945), is known as *Klangfarbenmelodie* (literally, "tone color melody"); note the way brief motivic fragments are tossed from one instrument to the next in Webern's Concerto for Nine Instruments, Op. 24 (1934).

Mahler's orchestra uses instruments not usually associated with the world of art music: cowbells, alpine horns, mandolin, guitar. Other early twentieth-century composers were similarly interested in employing sleigh bells, automobile horns, anvils, wind machines, whips, and the like. The 1926 *Ballet mécanique* of George Antheil (1900–1959) employs an airplane propeller, doorbells, and buzzsaws; Varèse's *Ionisation* uses a pair of sirens.

Formal Stasis

The vivid, dramatic, expressive rhetoric of the nineteenth century and the forward-moving, goal-oriented grammar of tonal music in general were no longer considered the only norms. A number of composers, including Debussy, Stravinsky, Varèse and Satie, often preferred working with repetitive figures and blocklike mosaics, rather than "narrative" or dramatic forms. Although Webern's music is, in fact, highly developmental, his fascination with sound-silence relationships and symmetrical "palindrome" patterns lends his work an equally static, abstract quality. Bartók was also interested in palindromes and symmetries, as one can hear in the fugue of his *Music for Strings, Percussion, and Celesta* (1936). Musical *time*, too, is approached in fresh ways. A lack of concern with either Romantic expressive flow or goal-oriented "progress" is evident in the music of Webern, Varèse, and the neoclassic Stravinsky. Finally, by the late 1930s John Cage and Olivier Messiaen had both begun exploring the rhythmic patterns of non-Western cultures, evidence again of a turning away from traditional musical rhetoric.

New Views of Compositional Process and Problem Solving

Beginning in the 1920s, composers grew more interested in the actual processes of the creative act, especially the manipulation of limits, materials, and strategies during precompositional stages. (That interest was probably conditioned by a distaste for the self-indulgent impulsiveness they associated with romanticism.) Schoenberg, working within the discipline of the twelve-tone technique, provides an excellent model from the viewpoint of one particular aesthetic. From a different position, we could look to the neoclassic example of Stravinsky. His provocative statement that "rhythm and motion, not the element of feeling, are the foundations of musical art" exalts the role of composer as manipulator of abstract materials and as supreme problem solver.

Creative Use of Performance Space and Performer Placement

Charles Ives, perhaps drawing on childhood memories of his father's legendary experiments (performers on hilltops or in rowboats on a lake, or two bands marching "against" each other with different musical materials), was interested in the placement of musicians in performance spaces. Such concerns overlapped Ives's above mentioned fascination with musical simultaneities. Other twentieth-century composers have worked with problems of performer placement. Some, like Bartok specifying the stage layout of his *Music for Strings, Percussion, and Celesta*, have been concerned with acoustical phenomena, and others primarily with theatrical (dramatic or visual) effect.

Altered Instruments and New Instruments

We have already noted a stretching of traditional instrumental resources, such as Ives's tuning of pianos in quarter tones and Cowell's use of piano clusters in "The Tides of Manaunaun." John Cage went even further in altering the nature of the piano; in 1938 he composed his first work for a grand piano with various objects inserted between its strings, thereby modifying the timbres to create the equivalent of a miniature percussion ensemble. This instrument became known as the prepared piano.

Others have gone beyond the alteration of existing instruments to the creation of new ones. For such composers, instrument building has become a critical aspect of the creative act. In the early 1930s Harry Partch began designing his own instruments to facilitate performances of music using his forty-three-tone intonation system. In Europe a number of electronic instruments, such as the Theremin and the Ondes Martenot, had been developed by the 1940s. In addition, Cage had begun using objects from the "media" world of sound reproduction, in particular radios and phonograph turntables, as performance instruments.

FOUR WORKS COMPOSED BEFORE 1945

The four representative works singled out here, all composed before 1945, contain fascinating "prophecies" of later concerns. None was immediately influential (i.e., within the first few years after its composition); each, however, would eventually make a great impact.

Charles Ives: The Unanswered Question

This 1909 piece for string orchestra, solo trumpet, and four flutes presents the listener with multiple levels of activity. In fact, the entire work involves the juxtaposition of many different "musics"—tonal versus atonal, highly consonant versus dissonant, smooth versus angular, quiet versus shrill. These levels are so individualized that they proceed simultaneously in different meters or at different tempi. In Example 2.1, note that the strings and trumpet are moving very slowly, but that the flute ensemble is much faster (and begins to accelerate at its *allegro* entrance). The musical strands

EXAMPLE 2.1.

Charles Ives: *The Unanswered Question*

have also been separated spatially, so that the sounds of strings, flutes, and solo trumpet emerge from different parts of the hall. The spatial arrangements, and the notated instructions for unsynchronized overlappings, ensure that no two performances will ever sound exactly alike.

The performers are, in fact, enacting a "program," one that endows them with unique role-playing personalities. The strings play very quietly throughout, representing the silence of the seers; the trumpet, which repeats its one jagged phrase at staggered intervals throughout the piece, asks "the Perennial Question of Existence"; the third element, which Ives terms "the Fighting Answerers (flutes and other people)," grows increasingly dissonant and angular with each reappearance. A trait of the entire work that amazes European listeners, but that Americans may be more likely to take for granted, is its unabashed combination of stylistically incongruous elements, without any attempt made to "integrate" them. For many composers, it also represents an important attempt to bring the multiplicity—the contradictory juxtapositions and the competing antiphonal stimuli—of real life into the world of art.

Anton Webern: Variations for Piano, Op. 27, Second Movement

Unlike the preceding piece, this 1936 work is a model of integration on an astonishing number of different levels. To begin with, one can hear it either as a piece in three brief movements, or as an unbroken series of variations on a tone row. The all-pervasive use of the row, along with the presence of palindrome or mirror patterns in each movement, reinforces the close relationship among the three movements. The tone row for the Variations contains symmetries within itself. (An introduction to the tone row may be found in "A Brief Look at the Twelve-Tone Set" in Chapter 7.) In Example 2.2, note that pitches 6 and 7 of the original row (C and F#) are duplicated as pitches 6 and 7 of the retrograde inversion; moreover, the pitches E♭ and

---

EXAMPLE 2.2.

The row, and basic permutations, for Webern's
Variations for Piano, Op. 27

A occur at same points. Webern frequently chooses a different row form for each of the two hands, so that these "identities" and mirrors are highlighted.

In the amazing middle movement (Example 2.3), Webern seems to have organized not only his pitch relationships, but also register, rhythm, articulation, and dynamics. The movement consists of a strict two-part canon between the hands, at the eighth note, in contrary motion and at a very rapid tempo. The two "lines" cannot be heard independently, given the great leaps and constant hand crossing. Instead, the listener perceives a single "line" of two-note (or two-chord) cells. Each cell has its own dynamic level (chosen from the three possibilities *f*, *p*, and *ff*) and articulation (from a choice of four); moreover, the dynamics and articulations form larger units, such as [*f p f*], [*p f p*], and [*f p ff*], which then recur in retrograde order. The result is a state of constant variety, in that no two cells are ever exactly the same in all details.

The movement consists of two similar sections, each repeated. (Some analysts, noting a resemblance to Baroque binary dance form, have suggested that if we think of the entire Variations as a suite, this middle

EXAMPLE 2.3.

Anton Webern: Variations for Piano, Op. 27, second movement

movement might be considered a gigue.) During each of the two sections, different row forms are presented in each hand, chosen to either begin or end with a G# or A. The pitches of each row are strictly assigned to fixed registers, equally distributed above and below the central pitch, A. Note, too, how the As from each row line up as a repeated two-note cell on A at measures 1, 9, 13, and 19. (In fact, we may sense a curiously "tonal" quality to the movement, although it is impossible to tell whether the "key" is A, B♭ or G#.)

Olivier Messiaen: Quatuor pour la fin du temps

This 1940 work for violin, clarinet, cello, and piano is an outstanding example of Messiaen's work in the late 1930s and early '40s. Certain aspects of the style are reminiscent of Debussy, particularly the "coloristic" (rather than functional) harmony and a flexible, through-composed sense of form. To these Messiaen added unique concerns of his own, and by the decade of the *Quatuor* he had developed a number of highly personal traits: (1) palindromic rhythms and rhythmic patterns derived from Hindu models, as well as a fondness for rhythmic ostinati that repeat continuously, although their pitches may change; (2) birdsong as a source of melodic and programmatic inspiration; and (3) the use of special scales called "modes of limited transposition," drawn from similar Balinese and Javanese precedents. The familiar wholetone scale of six pitches, which can be transposed only once is such a mode; in fact, Messiaen refers to it as Mode 1. Example 2.4 shows the next two modes in his series: Mode 2, an octatonic (eight-pitch) scale with two possible transpositions, and Mode 3, with nine pitches and three possible transpositions.

EXAMPLE 2.4.

Two of Messiaen's "modes of limited transposition"

In the first movement of the *Quatuor,* "Liturgie de cristal," a number of these concerns operate simultaneously. In the brief excerpt of Example 2.5, note the evocation of birdcalls in the violin and clarinet parts. They are set against a seventeen-unit rhythmic ostinato (coupled with a repeated series of twenty-nine chords) in the piano part, and a similar pattern of fifteen durations for a five-pitch cello ostinato. (Elsewhere, Messiaen has noted "comme un oiseau" above these parts.)

EXAMPLE 2.5.

Olivier Messiaen: *Quatuor pour la fin du temps,*
first movement, "Liturgie de cristal"

A mystical, deeply felt religious quality imbues much of Messiaen's music; a devout Catholic, for decades he was the organist of the Church of the Holy Trinity in Paris. The title *Quatuor pour la fin du temps* comes from the Apocalypse, and is dedicated to the angel "who lifts his hand towards the heaven saying, 'There shall be no more time.' " The quartet, composed during Messiaen's imprisonment in a German war camp, was first performed there by the composer and three other prisoners in January 1941. It is certainly one of the most moving musical documents to have come out of World War II.

John Cage: First Construction in Metal; Imaginary Landscape No. 1

In these two early compositions, both composed in 1939, Cage moves away from the traditional Western absorption in pitch, to a point where "pure" (i.e., nonpitched) timbre and rhythmic structure dominate his thinking. The *First Construction* is scored for an ensemble of six percussionists, who perform on such instruments as brake drums, oxen bells, large "thundersheets" of metal, gongs, Turkish cymbals, and a "string piano" (that is, the strings of a grand piano struck directly). The entire work is based on units—rhythmic and formal—of sixteen; for example, there are sixteen sections, each consisting of sixteen measures. These units, at every level, subdivide into the proportions 4-3-2-3-4. (Note that Cage, like Webern and Messiaen, works with palindromes.) In the earliest stages of the work's creation, Cage also wanted to assign sixteen sounds to each player, but eventually abandoned that plan.

Example 2.6 shows the opening page, with units of four measures, three measures, two, and then the repeat of three. The bracketed figures—labeled *a*, *b*, and the like—recur in different combinations throughout.

There may seem to be a contradiction here between Cage's careful structuring of his material—a natural outgrowth, perhaps, of his study with Schoenberg—and the actual material itself, so far removed from the tempered Western scale. But there is no paradox if we consider non-Western models: Cage's structural logical seems related to the rhythms of India, and his percussive, gonglike sonorities are evocative of the gamelan.

In the *Imaginary Landscape No. 1* for mixed quartet, the underlying rhythmic principles are similar: the work contains four sections, each consisting of fifteen measures (further subdivided into five times three), with the sections separated from one another by "interludes" of increasing duration. The most provocative feature, though, is the instrumentation of Cage's quartet: two phonograph turntables (playing recordings of sustained oscillator

EXAMPLE 2.6.

John Cage: *First Construction in Metal*

frequencies), cymbal, and inner piano. Like the "found sounds" of his prepared piano, the "found" electronic sounds on the records permit Cage to extract novel timbres from a familiar object. These two early Cage works, then, foreshadow at least two future directions: the growth of electronic music and the wedding of Western and non-Western traditions.

New Ways of Listening: The "Loudspeaker Revolution"

Along with the shaping forces discussed in the preceding chapters, another, equally important concern has influenced our present musical climate. Unlike those noted earlier, this one is truly the product of the postwar era. It is also a technological, rather than an artistic, development: an aesthetically neutral "tool" that nonetheless has vast aesthetic implications. Simply by fostering greater communication among composers and a heightened awareness of experimental trends, this concern has been a prime force in accelerating the pace of musical change. It has also altered many cherished assumptions about composition, performance, and listening. Finally, it has led to the creation of a totally new medium called "electronic music."

We are referring to the development of the long-playing record (LP) and the tape recorder shortly after the end of World War II. These two inventions, which became commercially available in the late 1940s, transformed the nature of the musical experience in profound ways. Today we may consider them part of a larger phenomenon—evidenced by the increased use of amplification and electric instruments in live performance, the explosive growth of radio and television, and such recent develop-

ments as the compact disc, videocassette recorder, and personal stereo—
that which may be termed the loudspeaker revolution.

Certain aspects of this revolution have their roots in the past. Recordings, electrical amplification, and even instruments for the performance of
"electronic music" were well known before the 1940s, and mechanical
means for the reproduction of live sound can be dated as far back as 1877,
when Thomas Edison invented the cylinder phonograph. Early phono-
graphs—like their latter-day offspring, the LP record unit and magnetic
tape deck—were designed to be aesthetically neutral. One simply assumed
that the new medium would be used to "freeze," store, and play back the
sounds of musical performance, functioning as a substitute for the live
concert. The potential for the recording medium to alter the musical experience was not immediately apparent; even today, many listeners tend to
regard the recording as an impartial observer. (Similarly, the camera and
the photograph were originally intended to capture visual images of the
physical "real world," but not to intrude upon that world.)

Even if the assumption of aesthetic neutrality were true, we could still
argue that the postwar existence of LP records and tape, simply as vehicles
for the preservation and transmission of concert music, has had an enormous impact on composers. The study of Western music history reveals
that styles have been changing at an ever-increasing rate since the eighteenth century. One reason for this accelerated pace is a heightened degree
of interaction among composers, thanks to improved communications and
transportation, greater access to scores, and (in our own century) the presence of recordings.

The rate of stylistic change has increased even more since 1945, primarily due to the development of long-playing records and tape facilities.
For the first time in history, composers have had virtually unlimited access
to a great variety of musical stimuli, including the works of their fellow
creative artists. In this regard, the tape-recording medium, with its ease of
storage and editing, has been even more important for composers than the
long-playing disc. A new piece might be premiered in New York, and a
tape of that premiere performance heard, studied, and avidly discussed by
colleagues in London, San Francisco, Tokyo, or Stockholm within a matter
of days. By this process, stylistic developments and entire movements could
become influential among composers well in advance of their acceptance
by the average listener.

Twentieth-century music has by no means been the only beneficiary of
the new technology. On the contrary, factors of convenience, reasonable
cost, and wide availability combined to create an unprecedented expansion
of public taste for *all* recorded music. The first few decades of the long-
playing record saw a remarkable growth of interest in the music of Vivaldi
and other Baroque composers, Berlioz, Bruckner, ethnic and folk musics,
Medieval and Renaissance motets and masses, the entire opera literature,

and twentieth-century "classics" by such figures as Mahler, Satie, Paul Hindemith, Aaron Copland, Stravinsky, Bartók, and Webern—the latter two having died in 1945, three years before the LP was introduced on the market.

Thanks to the recording industry, then, we have all come into contact with a greater range of musical styles—historically, ethnically, and geographically—than any preceding generation could have imagined. As we will discover later (Chapter 13), some composers use their own eclectic backgrounds as starting points for their work, and capitalize on their audience's broad listening experience as well. They create pieces that draw freely from different stylistic sources, juxtaposing incongruous elements together or quoting fragments from recognizable works of the past to create musical collages.

CHANGES IN LISTENER PERCEPTION

In estimating the full effect of the loudspeaker revolution on postwar musical developments, an influence that goes beyond any of the above examples, we should bear in mind that recording technology has never really been neutral with regard to its subject. From Edison's 1877 invention to the present, machines originally designed for the preservation, storage, and retrieval of live performances have affected music in unexpected ways. Even in the early years of recording, some creative artists realized that one could use recording technology to compose a sort of music that would be impossible otherwise. In this regard, they resembled colleagues in the visual arts, working with photography, in their perception of a new medium as a vehicle not merely for extending the familiar but for doing something truly new. By 1930 Paul Hindemith and Ernst Toch had begun experimenting with the distortion of recorded sounds and the mixing of patterns on variable-speed turntables. Bauhaus artists played records backward and scratched into grooves to create the sound of repeated fragments. John Cage, as we noted earlier, discovered in his *Imaginary Landscape No. 1* that he could use records and variable-speed turntables as performance instruments in a chamber ensemble.

After World War II, an ever-growing number of creative artists, influenced by such experiments and aided considerably by the development of the tape recorder, began to use unique features of recording and playback media to compose an unusual brand of music. Their efforts at bending or stretching the technology for specific creative purposes (usually termed *electronic music* or *tape composition*) will be discussed more fully later, beginning with Chapter 8.

On a different level, however, the new technology has outgrown its neutral role and intruded upon our musical perceptions in ways much less specific than those employed by electronic-music composers. In fact, at this level the influence of recordings is subconscious, and thereby more pervasive. To begin with, our constant exposure to the recording media forces us to reconsider the essentials of musical performance—the traditional association with visual stimuli, theatrical gesture, the acoustics of performing space, and the immediacy of "real time." It is significant, in this regard, that Cage conceived his *Imaginary Landscape No. 1* with the possibility of a radio broadcast performance in mind. With characteristic foresight, Cage recognized that loudspeaker performance, even the broadcast of a chamber work being played "live," might have unique qualities.

Over half a century has elapsed since Cage composed *Imaginary Landscape No. 1*, and during that period listening habits have altered to the extent that many people now regard "recorded music," or "loudspeaker music," as synonymous with "music." As a result, our perceptions have changed; we have all made subtle, subconscious adjustments to our definition of *performance*. For example, the visual stimulus and physical setting of the original ("real") performance have been eliminated, creating a peculiar ambience for the music: sounds that were intended for cathedrals or for eighteenth-century drawing rooms can be heard in our kitchens or automobiles.

With the removal of visual factors, one could argue that sound has become the sole focus of loudspeaker performance. But to complicate matters further, the new medium has altered even sound itself. Balances and timbres can be adjusted by microphone placement in recording or broadcast, so that the mechanical action of a harpsichord or the click of a guitarist's fingernail may become excessively audible or totally suppressed. Furthermore, if one is listening to a record or tape, the succession of sounds may be an artificial construction: what appears to be a natural flow of phrases and passages may be, in fact, a highly selective assemblage of edited "takes," removing the spontaneity of a live, real-time interpretation.

When we listen to a live performance in the concert hall, our attentiveness to the music may vary between intense concentration and daydreaming. By contrast, loudspeaker performance permits attentiveness to be "controlled" in a variety of ways. At one level, Muzak™ and other purveyors of background music have created a species of recorded sound designed solely as ever-present ambience, affecting listener responses subliminally. At the opposite extreme, records and tapes permit us to listen to a single performance many times, to study a symphony (or its interpretation) as though it were as "fixed" in time and space as a novel or painting. Just as we use the recording media to freeze sound patterns, we can manipulate playback technology to freeze time, or at least control it. We may achieve that end by altering speeds, playing records or tapes backward, changing the order of movements, or repeating sections of a work. Any of those situations places us in the unique position of "performing" the record, or "composing" a new work from isolated fragments of an existing one. By choosing a specific ordering of records or tapes, we can program a succession of works according to our preferences. In short, we can summon up command performances of incredible stylistic variety, far beyond those available to princes and potentates in the not-too-distant past.

The changes wrought by the loudspeaker revolution suggest a world in which musical performance is indistinguishable from electronic illusion. Musical form, content, duration, or direction can be altered in microseconds. The logic of musical continuity, one of the hallmarks of the Western concert tradition, is torn apart as we hear radio or television performance of popular songs with no endings, only gradual fade-outs or instant cuts to other tunes, news flashes, or commercials. In addition, the increased use of electronics in live performance, whether by way of electronic instruments or amplified traditional ones, create illusions of a different sort. The "directionality" of sound can now be a function of microphone and loudspeaker placement; consequently, a sound may not necessarily emerge from the same location as its original performing source. Finally, from a purely visual standpoint the newer electronic instruments contradict all our traditional assumptions about the "look" of sounding objects in their size, shape, bulk, portability, and relationship to the sounds they produce.

Composers have been observing the loudspeaker revolution, with its illusions and altered perceptions, and have shaped their music as a response. Some composers have asked themselves, perhaps subconsciously, What sort of musical experience could we create that *cannot* be captured on a recording? Their ideas may take them into areas of improvisation and chance in an attempt to create spontaneous situations that could never be duplicated, or perhaps into a focus on the visual, spatial aspects of performance. Other composers of a very different temperament might ask, What sort of musical experience would *benefit* from existence in reproducible, recorded form? They would be more likely to create a music of highly complex sound relationships, one that requires repeated hearing for comprehension and that stresses permanence—the pleasures of perceiving finely wrought structural connections—rather than immediacy.

To sum up: the twin inventions of the long-playing record and the tape recorder may well be the most important developments of our century. In overall significance, they certainly rival the creation of the printing press in the fifteenth century and the pianoforte in the eighteenth. The post–1945 loudspeaker revolution has created subtle subconscious changes in our musical thinking: about continuity, immediacy, structural complexity, and the nature of "performance" itself. As we will see, much of the music composed since the 1940s exploits these changes.

New Concepts and Tools

In the introduction we suggested that the innovative character of post–1945 music might require a new vocabulary, if only to facilitate the listener's understanding and discussion. As we will see when we examine specific works composed in recent decades, the range of influences on composers in our century, their aesthetic aims, and the techniques they employ are remarkably diverse. For many such works, older terms that have served well when applied to the music of Mozart, Bach, or even Schoenberg and Stravinsky—terms like *harmony*, *counterpoint*, or *meter*—may no longer be entirely adequate.

The art music of our century's second half, or at least a significant portion of it, reflects a unique gamut of priorities and concerns. These may reflect the special province of composers or more general concerns of today's culture. They may even be largely subconscious, to the degree that many are not yet fully aware of their existence—any more than Bach was aware of using I-IV-V-I progressions or Beethoven of writing in "sonata form." But the new priorities and concerns necessitate the use of a new terminology—a set of concepts by means of which we may focus our listening, analysis, discussion, and musical enjoyment.

For our purposes, nine such concepts may be identified. Referred to throughout the rest of this book as the "nine factors," they will often be highlighted by boldface type when they are mentioned. Seven of them— **pitch logic, time, sound color, texture, process, performance ritual,** and **parody** (or **historicism**)—refer directly to aspects of the musical "experience," that is, the act of hearing or witnessing a work. We hope that, as each term is considered, the listener's attention will focus on that particular aspect of the experience, thereby—when they are all integrated—making the whole more manageable. (This is what usually occurs in the study of traditional repertoire, when amorphous "sounds" in the air become perceptible in terms of scales, rhythmic patterns, fugal entrances, and the like.)

The other two terms refer to important compositional "tools," **technology** and **notation**. Although the listener does not always perceive these as part of the experience, they make the experience possible.

Let us consider each of the nine factors in turn—referring to the four works discussed at the end of Chapter 2 and examining their implications for post–1945 music.

SEVEN CONCEPTS FOR THE STUDY OF NEW MUSIC

Pitch Logic

Every composer today has to make decisions about how (or whether) to use musical pitch. Until the late nineteenth century, the need for such decisions would never have occurred to most composers. Western music, by definition, involved the twelve notes of the chromatic scale, within a system of tonal harmony whose basic principles were taken for granted. But ever since Wagner, Debussy, and others began to move beyond those tonal principles, composers have discovered more and more radical ways to challenge long-standing assumptions about the role and behavior of pitch.

Consider, for example, the strict twelve-tone procedures used by Webern in his Piano Variations, Op. 27. Although the octave is divided according to standard equal temperament, traditional hierarchies of scale and key center are replaced by a row and its permutations. As listeners, we sense—whatever our experience (or lack of it) in serial analysis—that a careful, precise manipulation of pitches and intervals lies at the heart of the music; to this degree, the "subject" of the work *is* its **pitch logic.** By contrast, Cage's *First Construction in Metal* reveals little concern for specific pitch. In fact, Cage often obscures our recognition of pitch by his use of diffuse percussion sonorities. Similarly, Henry Cowell's innovative use of inner-string piano sonorities and keyboard clusters relegates pitch to a low hierarchical position. Pitches in Messiaen's *Quatuor pour la fin de temps* form scales, but the scales themselves are unusual, and they are employed in nondirectional, nonfunctional cycles and sequences.

ILLUS. 4.1.

Henry Cowell performing directly on the strings of the piano. With this single act, the composer challenges our traditional perceptions of pitch logic, texture, sound color, and performance ritual

Courtesy BMI Archives

Today's composers, then, work with possibilities that would scarcely have been imaginable a century ago. They may use any intonation system within the octave and may fashion a scale from any arrangement of pitches they wish. One pitch may function as a key center, or all pitches within the collection might be of entirely equal significance. Alternatively, a composer may choose to give little or no priority to pitch logic, or may decide to compose with sounds that have no identifiable pitches. One might even choose to create music for which no sounds of any kind are specified.

Time

Another essential requirement for the composer is to determine how pitches or other sounds are to be located in time. For most Western music written between 1600 and 1900, this meant creating rhythmic shapes or patterns that relied on an unchanging meter. The role of meter, along with the use of simple rhythmic relationships within it, was generally taken for granted.

The works studied in Chapter 2, however, raise new questions about time. The opening of Ives's *The Unanswered Question* appears to be devoid of meter. In fact, the entire work conveys a "timeless," spacious quality. As it proceeds, however, we become aware of three different time worlds experienced simultaneously, all but the flute choir existing "out of time." Messiaen's *Quatuor* establishes an isorhythmic relationship between time (rhythm) and pitch, so that both aspects appear to be slowly revolving in different orbits; in its own way, it is as timeless as the Ives. The second movement of Webern's Piano Variations, in contrast, conveys the impression of compressed time, a highly complex argument racing past in a trajectory of only a few seconds. Some listeners, left breathless by the experience, may wish that they could slow it down, but unless one can study the score and thereby freeze the structure, the music will be forever locked in fast forward—which is, presumably, the intended effect. Note, too, that Webern creates a special sort of *continuity*—jagged, unsettling, unpredictable, dotted with rapid-fire alternations of sound and silence— quite unlike the two works by Ives and Messiaen. Cage, however, provides a series of highly stable, even predictable continuities for *First Construction*, subdividing time into palindromic, symmetrical units (small-scale and large-scale divisions mirroring one another). In fact, Cage's concern for carefully calibrated time relationships is analogous to that of Webern in dealing with pitch.

During the postwar decades composers have become even more fascinated not only with new rhythmic possibilities, but with time itself, and with its potential as an experiential and artistically malleable phenomenon. Metric and rhythmic patterns can be organized in any number of elaborate ways: complex meters such as $\frac{7}{16}$, $\frac{11}{32}$, or $\frac{6}{4} + \frac{3}{8}$ (instead of the usual duple and triple meters), changing meters, and irrational subdivisions of the beat—into units of 7 or 11, for example—have all become standard. Or, if one wishes, rhythmic events need not adhere to any metrical pattern. The composer can structure events in time to any degree of spontaneity, irregularity, or complexity, or encourage performers to take the responsibility for decisions about the temporal placement of sounds.

New ways of *perceiving* time—new, at least, to typical Western audiences—may be explored by the composer. As in *The Unanswered Question*, time can be experienced as passing by at more than one rate simultaneously. The events of a work may be reordered, fragmented, or interwoven in an effort to liberate the experience of time from a strictly linear, past-present-future orientation. Time may also be "suspended" or "stretched" through the use of static or gradually evolving harmonic or rhythmic material, this possibility being particularly reflective of non-Western influences.

Sound Color

Traditionally it has been common to think of melody and harmony (which are functions of pitch logic) and rhythm (a function of time) as being the primary defining elements in the character of a musical composition. But in recent decades composers have been led to reexamine other elements as well—elements once considered peripheral but now elevated to higher levels of importance. For example, many composers have turned to timbre, or tone color, as a primary field of exploration. The formal structure and extramusical program of *The Unanswered Question* hinge upon the distinct timbral contrasts among the three forces; in fact, one might claim that timbre articulates form in this instance. Similarly, Cage's employment of percussion timbre in the *First Construction* is wedded to formal structure; moreover, the unusual sonorities themselves are primary to our experience of the work. Not that one needs unusual or special instruments to produce unique sonorities; in the second movement of the Piano Variations, Webern creates a remarkably individual sound world with a familiar, traditional instrument. The piano is explored in an unfamiliar playing style—what post–1945 composers would call "extended technique"—calling for sharp registral extremes, sudden dynamic shifts, and changes of articulation, all at dizzying speed.

Today a vast range of sound color is open to the composer, made available by the discovery of new possibilities: further "extended techniques" for traditional instruments, playing styles drawn from the worlds of jazz and rock, electronic amplification and modification, and the use of relatively unfamiliar instruments—either from other cultures (such as the sitar, koto, gamelan, santur, shakuhachi), the early periods of Western music (the shawm, sackbut, recorder, viol), or the composer's inventive mind (the instruments by Harry Partch being a notable example).

The electronic technology of the late twentieth century enables environmental sounds—birdcalls, motors, running water, explosives—to be amplified, electronically or acoustically modified, sampled and manipulated digitally, or recorded and played back using a variety of tape editing techniques. All of these possibilities, then, have made sound color one of the most important frontiers to be explored by the modern-day composer.

Texture

Texture in music is usually characterized in pictorial or tactile terms, perhaps with such words as "heavy," "light," "dense," "transparent," "busy," or "simple." (Such descriptions tend to focus on density or mass, rather than the traditional textbook view of texture in terms of vertical-horizontal organization.) The resources with which today's composer can create various kinds of texture have expanded vastly, yielding remarkable new possibilities—and leading certain composers to give texture a role of even greater importance than pitch and time in the progress and structure of a work.

Compare the dense, massive fabric of John Cage's *First Construction in Metal*, produced by the percussion ensemble, with the dry, brittle quality of Webern's Piano Variations. In both cases, texture itself has become a positive feature of the work, and in both cases the texture is a focused, monolithic entity: it is *one*. The tapestry of Messiaen's *Quatuor* is much more complex, in that it can be heard on many levels; each of its four instrumental parts is rich in information, and each combines with the rest to create a larger, complex web. In contrast, the three levels of activity introduced in Ives's *The Unanswered Question* always seem to exist in separate worlds, more of a juxtaposition—a multiple exposure—than a polyphonic whole.

It may be increasingly apparent that many of our "nine factors" are interdependent. Various choices that composers may make with regard to pitch, time, or sound color inevitably have implications in the realm of musical texture. For example, when many instruments are closely packed together with only a semitone between parts, the result is a dense ensemble cluster. The use of microtones—a pitch-related decision—would allow a large number of parts to be placed even less than a semitone apart, creating a virtual wall of sound. The character of that wall—its density—would also depend on choices made in the domain of sound color. Imagine a tone cluster played *sul ponticello* by fifteen muted violas, and then those same pitches being sustained by fifteen trombones, all playing *molto vibrato* while opening and closing plunger mutes continuously at different rates.

Similarly, textural possibilities might also result from certain approaches to time. To create an unlimited degree of rhythmic freedom in individual parts, and in the relationship between parts, would allow for a huge range in contrapuntal textures, from the simple and transparent—only a few brief notes, perhaps—to the densely elaborate and impenetrable. A fabric of precisely determined rhythms, strictly coordinated, would project a different textural identity.

Recent compositional thinking has emphasized the exploration of very light or sparse textures as well as massive ones. Here, too, sound color and texture are closely intertwined, as we will find in so-called post–Webern works (see Chapters 7 and 10), in which individual "dots" of instrumental color appear on a background of silence. In fact, we will find the use of silence itself, pioneered in the music of John Cage, to play a significant role in the exploration of musical texture.

Process

The concerns we have dealt with so far in this chapter pertain to the basic fabric of a musical work, elements that affect the actual sound of the music as we experience it from one moment to the next. The larger design of a musical work—or more accurately, the process through which a work is brought into being—has itself been a major focus for exploration and innovation by many of today's composers.

Think again about ways both Cage and Messiaen employed carefully calibrated rhythmic series in their works; in Cage's *Imaginary Landscape No. 1*, the temporal proportions at every level, from small rhythmic units to overall form, are based on the number sixteen. Recall, for example, the middle movement of Webern's Piano Variations, in which all the vital aspects of the musical fabric—pitch, rhythm, register, articulation, dynamics—are related to the symmetrical properties of a single tone row, or Ives's scenario for *The Unanswered Question*, which not only determines the quasitheatric roles but also predetermines much of the music.

These are relatively straightforward examples of music as the playing out of a process or scheme devised by the composer. Many, often more elaborate examples lie in the chapters ahead: processes that govern the placement and duration of events in time, processes based on numerical series, on mathematically generated relationships, on aspects of natural phenomena, on chance. Such systems may govern the entire range of time spans from the smallest level (moment to moment) to the largest (encompassing the entire composition). They are not necessarily restricted to pitch, but may relate to tempo, dynamics, register, instrumentation, texture, formal succession of events or degrees of improvisation.

Why have so many composers become so preoccupied with compositional process? One answer may have to do with the enormous range of possibilities they face. Stravinsky, in his *Poetics of Music*, probably spoke for many composers when he remarked: "I experience a sort of terror when, at the moment of setting to work and finding myself before the infinitude of possibilities that present themselves, I have the feeling that everything is permissible to me." Indeed, composers have often found this "infinitude of possibilities" as intimidating as it is exhilarating, especially those who have felt that music must continue to be artfully and coherently crafted, as in previous eras.

It is perhaps in response to this situation that many creative artists of our century have chosen to focus on the development of their own set of guidelines, principles, and methods. One important trend, particularly after World War II, has been to treat composing as problem solving, and to treat the musical work as the realization of a predetermined or "precompositional" scheme, designed to address self-imposed issues or "problems."

Performance Ritual

By now it is clear that no aspect of the musical experience has remained exempt from scrutiny and reevaluation. Particularly in the latter part of the twentieth century, many composers have looked deeply into music as it traditionally manifests itself in our culture and found it replete with axioms and assumptions that, for them, are too confining artistically.

One area in which such assumptions are pervasive is that pertaining to the circumstances and routines of performance. For most concertgoers, it goes without saying that music is performed on a stage or in some other space set apart from the audience. A certain etiquette is attached to the tuning of an orchestra; it is assumed that audience members may converse only at certain times, must remain silent at other times, and are expected to applaud only at certain junctures. All these constitute an artistic and sociological ritual that, although it is taken for granted, fundamentally influences our relationship with the music.

Even within the traditional context, composers can choose to highlight certain aspects of that ritual. It is an inescapable fact—or at least it was before the loudspeaker revolution—that musical performances are *visual* events. To see a performance of Webern's Piano Variations, as opposed to merely hearing one, is a breathtaking experience. Anyone who has observed the pianist's "extended technique"—the agility required to extend his or her arms to both ends of the keyboard, and then suddenly cross hands (as one must do to play the second movement)—will not easily forget it. A performance of Cage's *First Construction in Metal* is a special experience of another sort. Percussion instruments (and the "choreography" entered into by anyone playing them) are exciting, and an ensemble of many players activating a large body of such instruments is doubly so.

It is entirely possible, though, that a composer may wish to escape the traditional concert format. For some, it seems only natural, when creating a musical composition, to create, or re-create—the ritual through which it is presented. Others might wish to argue that our Eurocentric art-music concert "tradition," while seemingly venerable and inevitable to us, represents only one of many options practiced around the world. In any case, new relationships between audience, performer, and composer may be conceived. Performers may surround, be surrounded by, or be located in the midst of audience members. Ives's *The Unanswered Question* uses wide spatial placement of its forces in such a way that the audience is confronted by multiple stimuli—sounds coming from many directions—and receives the full import of the different levels as eternally separate.

As we will see, many ways of disrupting the traditional ritual have been explored in the past few decades. Audience participants may be asked to perform, improvise, or even compose part or all of the work. Members of the audience may be encouraged to come and go as they please, to converse with performers, or to display approval or disapproval. Unconventional performance spaces may be envisioned: streets, public buildings, private homes, public transportation vehicles, and natural outdoor settings.

Composers may also rethink the placement of a performance in time. A performance may begin and end at any time of day or night, and may be of any length (seconds, hours, days—even months or years). It need not be temporally defined by a discreet beginning or ending, or by clear structural divisions in between. The end of a work by one composer may overlap with, or transform itself seamlessly into, the beginning of a work by another composer—or the music of two or more composers may be performed at one time.

Finally, we should consider new forms of interaction between music and the other arts—sometimes referred to as *mixed media* or *multimedia* performance, moving beyond the traditional formats offered by ballet, opera, and theater. This is a major area of innovation, with possibilities too numerous to mention here. For a thorough discussion see Chapters 9 and 15.

Parody (Historicism)

Many people think of parody exclusively in terms of satire. Some examples of musical parody happen to fit that limited definition: Debussy's biting use of Wagner's *Tristan* Prelude in his "Golliwogg's Cake Walk" is certainly one. But in a larger sense *parody* may refer to any refashioning of already existent material, often quite serious (or emotionally neutral), such as Renaissance "parody masses," which often used love songs as cantus firmi, or Haydn's quotation of the Austrian national anthem for the slow movement of his String Quartet in C, Op. 76, No. 3.

Parody is related to the broader concept of "historicism," in which entire styles (rather than specific works) are examined, appropriated, fragmented, and then recollected in new guises. Historical awareness has often surfaced in a composer's work in the form of references that serve as homage to or commentary on an earlier style. The references are often deliberate, devices to evoke certain associations in the minds of listeners.

For example, note the use of different styles in *The Unanswered Question*. The strings are always triadic and consonant; they create a sense of serenity and wisdom, perhaps drawn from the language of church music, which Ives knew well. The flutes, by contrast, are unstable and eventually overwrought, using the language of late nineteenth-century dramatic music. As a different example, Webern's Piano Variations works within the nineteenth-century "recital piece" tradition—and offers some dazzling virtuosic fireworks in the process. The second movement also uses the strict binary dance form associated with the Baroque era and makes reference to the concept of terraced dynamics.

In both cases, the historical models had come from the composer's own tradition. "Historicism" of another sort occurs when entirely different traditions meet, to create a new and highly personal amalgam. Debussy's encounter with the music of Indonesia at the 1889 Paris Exposition turned out to be a dramatic moment in the history of Western music. It was the first significant instance in which a Western composer was inspired to go beyond the surface characteristics of "exotic" music to adapt some of its basic technical features (in Debussy's case, pentatonic and wholetone scales) for his work. Cage's *First Construction in Metal* reveals that he, too, has been drawn to the gamelan, as Messiaen (in *Quatuor pour le fin de temps*) has been to meditative Indian music.

On another level, each of the four *titles* just mentioned makes an overt reference to tradition. Cage draws upon the world of the visual arts (his title sounds as though it might be more appropriate to a piece of sculpture), and Webern upon the European tradition of abstract art music; Ives links his work to philosophical speculation, while Messiaen connects his to scripture.

We will observe many more instances of historicism, and some of outright parody, in post–1945 music. Eclectic stylistic mixes continue to flourish, as composers become more conscious of music—and performance rituals—from other cultures, other genres (jazz, folk music, popular music), and other periods in Western music history. This awareness is, in turn, tied to the growth of communication technology; recording and broadcasting have made music from almost anywhere in the world immediately accessible.

TWO COMPOSITIONAL TOOLS

Of our nine factors, two more remain: **technology** and **notation.** We have set these two apart because they are not always primary to the composer or immediately perceptible to the audience. A concertgoer experiencing a given work might not even be aware of the presence, or the unique contribution, of either factor, just as we rarely stop to consider the cultural impact of the printing press or the tensile properties of steel and concrete while enjoying literature and architecture.

For centuries, highly sophisticated artifacts have made, preserved, and disseminated music: pianos, guitars, clarinets, pens, paper, staves, clefs, radios. The history of musical style invariably reflects changes among these inventions, including the creation of new ones. The latter half of the twentieth century is no exception. The radically new approaches to many of the preceding seven factors would not have been possible without (a) the mutually reinforcing link to a rapidly developing technology and (b) an expanded repertoire of visual symbols for notating these new approaches.

Developments in technology are highlighted in Chapters 8 and 17 (concerned with electronic and computer music), as well as Chapters 9 and 15 (on multimedia and performance ritual); similarly, specific issues pertaining to notation are discussed in Chapter 19. But on a more general level, these compositional tools stand behind *all* the innovations of the new music.

A PERSPECTIVE ON NEW APPROACHES

The nine factors are not themselves new; all music is shaped by these elements. What is new is the way composers may now isolate these various aspects of music so that each may be examined and explored individually for its untapped potential. In other musical traditions, such elements as rhythm, harmony, instrumentation, and performance ritual are often inseparable. They evolve, if at all, in an integrated fashion. In many societies, the music changes only as the culture changes, and the composer's individual genius—and any unorthodox views he or she might have about particular aspects of music—are of little relevance. By contrast, the symmetrical pitch schemes of Webern's Piano Variations, Op. 27, like the rhythmic series in Messiaen's *Quatuor*, represent a much more self-conscious effort to reexamine every aspect of musical expression, and how those aspects interact, in order to seek out new possibilities.

A look back over past millennia at the writings of such figures as Pythagoras, Boethius, Guido, Zarlino, Rameau, and Busoni will show that a penchant for scrutinizing and debating every element in the art of music making is not new; nor is the tension between the maintenance of tradition and the impulse toward change and progress. Those concerns have long been a vital part of music in the Western world. The very nature of post–1945 experimentation has made most modern-day composers—and those who study their music—more conscious of the many specific facets of music that are open to experimentation. Focusing our attention on these specific areas as we discuss the work of various composers will provide valuable insight and take much of the mystery out of understanding new music.

The Early Postwar Years

By any standards, the year 1945 can be regarded as a critical turning point in the history of Western music. Most obviously, it witnessed the close of World War II. The Allied victory in Europe ended a lengthy period of strict artistic censorship; modernist music, which had been banned by the Nazis, could once more be heard in Europe's concert halls and radio broadcasts. As if to compensate for this previous lack, special concert series and symposia devoted to innovative music, such as the Darmstadt, Donaueschingen, Royon, and Gaudeamus festivals, began to spring up in Germany, France, the Netherlands, and elsewhere.

In the United States, the artistic climate was perhaps closer to one of celebration. During the 1930s and '40s, while Europe's cultural life was reduced to a shambles, the United States had gradually assumed a position of musical leadership. A distinguished collection of European composers had crossed the Atlantic; by the war's end, Schoenberg, Stravinsky, Bartók, Darius Milhaud, Sergei Rachmaninov, and Paul Hindemith were all residing in the United States. Moreover, the "radical" American composers somewhat removed from the Western mainstream—not only Cage, but Varèse and Ives as well—were beginning to become influential on the European scene.

America entered the postwar era with great confidence and energy, and a certain degree of prosperity as well. Newfound interest in the arts resulted in an unprecedented blossoming of symphony orchestras and opera companies. There was also a surge of interest in building—especially plans for "fine arts centers" (from which such complexes as New York's Lincoln Center, the Chandler Pavilion of Los Angeles, and Houston's Jones Center would ultimately materialize). The first signs of a population boom appeared, followed by a corresponding expansion of educational facilities, including an increase in the size and scope of arts programs at colleges and conservatories.

SOCIAL CONTEXTS FOR STYLISTIC CHANGE

For many younger composers in the United States and Europe, the tonal language of neoclassicism, which had entered the mainstream, no longer held interest. In a search for alternatives, many were led to the rediscovery of two contrasted principles, each highly controversial, that had developed many decades earlier: "rational" serialism and "irrational" Dadaism. A number of critical social factors fueled the search for new styles.

The Aftermath of World War II

Earlier in the century, a period of free, untamed experimentation, somewhat naïve and even a bit romantic in its optimism, had come to a bitter end during World War I. The resulting neoclassic style represented a sober, conscious pulling back, dictated in equal parts by the trauma of the war itself (shattering the earlier optimism), by the economic realities of the Great Depression, and by a desire to communicate with the large concert-going public. The close of World War II, however, brought with it a more daring, extroverted attitude, a longing to wipe the slate clean, and a stronger economic base within which experimentation might flourish.

The Less Urgent Need for Mass Communication

Many composers were convinced that the previous generation's attempts to bridge the schism between creator and the larger public had failed. The era of greatest social consciousness—of *Gebrauchsmusik* in Europe, the Works Progress Administration in the United States, and a reaching out to audiences generally—had passed. Many artists now felt that in an increasingly pluralistic, electronic, mobile society, audiences had become more fragmented than ever. There seemed to be no mass public left, in fact: just a variety of small but intense fringe audiences.

Technology and the Avant-garde

Composers began once again to proceed from a position of enthusiastic faith in the future (as they had before 1914) and a fearlessness about new, unknown worlds to be conquered. They were bolstered by their sense of alliance with the many staggering developments in technology—from television, to lasers, to the splitting of the atom and unleashing of nuclear power.

The Growth of New Patrons

In Europe, government-supported radio networks and major international festivals supported the furtherance of experimental music. The United States, in contrast, witnessed the growth of greatly expanded university facilities for the arts, including the creation of campus-based new-music ensembles. On both continents, dance companies became active in commissioning and performing new works. Many of these newly emerging patrons encouraged composers to explore and experiment freely.

THE INFLUENCE OF WEBERN AND MESSIAEN

Of all the international new-music festivals organized after World War II, perhaps the most influential was the annual summer course at Darmstadt, Germany. Almost immediately after its founding, Darmstadt became a center for the study of Schoenberg and his school. In this regard it reflected the interests of the younger European composers, who were intrigued by the prospect of controlling pitch relations along the systematic, nontonal lines advanced by Schoenberg. In addition, for many composers the concern with control went beyond the domain of pitch. Their study of Debussy, Webern, Varèse, and non-Western musics had opened up a new sound world of isolated (or rapidly shifting) timbres, registers, and dynamic levels. The rediscovery of Debussy was, for example, a revelation to the young Pierre Boulez (b. 1925)—not Debussy the creator of sentimental, "pretty" salon music, but Debussy the "radical" innovator, exploring uncharted areas of form and instrumentation, taking for himself the freedom to be antisystematic, the Debussy who supposedly replied to his professor when asked what rules he followed, "My pleasure."

Many composers of the postwar generation wished to combine the rigor and discipline of Schoenberg (without his romantic gestures), the timbral sound world of Debussy (without his harmonic language or programmatic leanings), and Stravinsky's objective approach to music as problem solving or as process fulfillment (without his neoclassic tonality). This aesthetic seemed to be embodied in the music of a single composer, that of Anton von Webern: structurally brilliant, intense in its brevity, virtually non-Western in its whispered, self-effacing gestures. Some of the younger generation found that they preferred Webern to Schoenberg. Their number included Boulez, who after Schoenberg's death wrote a 1951 article appropriately entitled "Schoenberg est mort," perhaps in the spirit of the ancient cry, "the king is dead, long live the king." Boulez praised Webern as the new king, the major influence on postwar music. Less tied to the "expressive" gestures of nineteenth-century romanticism than his teacher, Webern seemed to point the way to the future. In a 1958 article, Boulez repeated the same argument, but this time also linking Webern with Debussy:

> [W]hereas Schoenberg and Berg ally themselves to the decadence of the great German Romantic tradition . . . Webern—via Debussy, one might say—reacts violently against all inherited rhetoric, in order to rehabilitate the powers of sound. . . . There is indeed only Debussy whom one can compare with Webern.

The works of Schoenberg and Webern, although obviously important, were by no means the sole topics of study at Darmstadt. It was also here that major postwar compositions were premiered and analyzed. René Leibowitz (1913–72), a disciple of Schoenberg, and Olivier Messiaen, who conducted similar classes at the Paris Conservatoire, served as leaders at the Darmstadt sessions. Messiaen's influence, in particular, was profound. Students were inspired not only by his use of unusual modes (controlling pitch in a manner entirely different from Schoenberg's), isorhythmic overlays, and irregular Indian and Greek rhythms, but also by his restless curiosity and all-embracing attitude toward every variety of sound source.

During the Darmstadt summer of 1949 Messiaen composed an étude for piano entitled "Mode de valeurs et d'intensités"; he showed it to his Darmstadt students, including Boulez and Karlheinz Stockhausen, the following year. In this novel piece, Messiaen divides the piano's range into three overlapping areas, assigning a series of twelve pitches to each division (see Example 5.1). In addition, Messiaen has devised a rhythmic series

EXAMPLE 5.1.

The three series used by Messiaen in "Mode de valeurs et d'intensités"

© 1949 Durand S.A. Used by permission. Sole Representative U.S.A. Theodore Presser Company

of twenty-four durations, a seven-level dynamic series (from *ppp* to *fff*), and a series of twelve articulations. The pitches at the highest register are assigned brief durations and quieter dynamics, while those at the bottom of the keyboard are longer and louder. Note that each of the thirty-six pitches is associated with one unchanging attack, register, and dynamic level, a feature referred to by some critics as "consistent pitch individuality." Example 5.2 shows the first few measures of the actual piece, set out in three-part polyphony.

The étude is quite effective, with sounds that range from the delicate to the clangorous, spacing that allows individual lines to stay out of each other's way, appropriately dramatic gestures, and a shrewd use of the piano's sympathetic resonances. Messiaen's handling of pitch is not strictly serial; the actual succession of notes within the three levels is unsystematic. It was his ordering of the other musical dimensions that constituted a daring stroke. Although Messiaen apparently never intended the piece to be more than an experiment, it made an enormous impression on those who first heard it at Darmstadt; as such, it was an important harbinger of *integral serialism*, the application of twelve-tone technique to musical elements other than pitch.

EXAMPLE 5.2.

Olivier Messiaen: "Mode de valeurs et d'intensités"

© 1949 Durand S.A. Used by permission. Sole Representative U.S.A. Theodore Presser Company

THE GROWTH OF INTEGRAL SERIALISM

The model of Messiaen's piano étude, along with specific Webern works in which rhythmic and dynamic values, though not serialized, seem to assume the same primacy as pitch, led a number of European composers to explore their own brand of integral serialism. This number included Pierre Boulez, Karlheinz Stockhausen, Karel Goeyvaerts, Henri Pousseur, and Luigi Nono. In his *Structure 1a* for two pianos (1952), Boulez borrowed the highest of the three pitch series from Messiaen's "Mode de valeurs" to create a tone row (see Example 5.3a). In transposing the row, Boulez retained the original number assigned to each pitch—for example, taking the opening E♭–D–A (1–2–3) down a half step to D–C#–G# results in a new number pattern, 2–8–4—thereby creating the potential for twelve different number series, one for each row transposition. Any of these numerical patterns could then be applied to "rows" of duration, dynamic level, and articulation, as shown in Example 5.3b.

Serialism developed along different lines in the United States, primarily through the work of Milton Babbitt (b. 1916). Messiaen's experiments are not relevant to Babbitt's thought; in fact, Babbitt composed the first strictly twelve-tone music to serialize rhythms and dynamics, his *Three Compositions for Piano* (1947), at least a year before Messiaen's studies. Rather than attempting a correspondence of "row" numbers to twelve specific durations or volume levels, as in the Boulez example above, Babbitt

EXAMPLE 5.3A.

Tone row derived by Boulez from Messiaen's "Mode de valeurs et d'intensités"

EXAMPLE 5.3B.

Twelve-element sequences ("rows") for rhythm, dynamics, and articulation in Boulez's *Structure 1a*

created rhythmic patterns through the use of an "attack set." This set, 5–1–4–2, dictates the position of attack points or durations within the regular flow of traditional meter, such as even sixteenth notes in $\frac{3}{4}$ time.

In the opening two measures of Example 5.4b we can perceive a twelve-pitch series in each of two polyphonic strands. Both lines use the same row (that of Example 5.4a), transposed to begin on pitches a tritone apart, B♭ and E). But note that all twelve pitches are stated *within* each measure as well, as the composite of both lines. The tritone transposition of the opening hexachord provides the "missing" six pitches of the complete row; in other words, Babbitt has created a tone row with *combinatorial* properties (see Chapter 7).

In these same two measures, each voice states the attack set (indicated by brackets) in its original form. In measures 3 and 4, the pitch row is stated in retrograde (R) for the right hand and retrograde inversion (RI) for the left; the attack/duration series is similarly transformed by the same operations, to 2–4–1–5 in the right hand and 4–2–5–1 in the left. (To create the "inversion" of the basic 5–1–4–2, one subtracts each of these numbers from 6, creating the pattern 1–5–2–4. For the R and RI, simply read the appropriate pattern from right to left.) Finally, note that Babbitt has assigned *mp* dynamics for all statements of the original, or prime, row, *mf* for the R form, *f* for I, and *p* for RI.

These controlled, deterministic aspects of Babbitt's rhythmic continuity may not necessarily be apparent to the listener. At the surface level, in fact, the *Three Compositions for Piano* provide an unassuming, easily flowing narrative, with offbeat accents closer to the syncopated world of jazz than to that of Webern or Messiaen.

OTHER POSTWAR DIRECTIONS

Although serialism rapidly became a major influence on younger composers, it was certainly not the only important postwar development. Other

EXAMPLE 5.4A.

Babbitt's tone row for *Three Compositions for Piano*

EXAMPLE 5.4B.

Milton Babbitt: *Three Compositions for Piano*

composers, especially in the United States, decided to bypass issues of "total control" entirely in favor of a more open-ended approach. Webern's compositions were certainly studied and discussed as avidly in America as in Europe, yet many Americans found their structural precision less significant than their novel timbres and fleeting, epigrammatic gestures. This is not to minimize Webern's influence on American composers. He had to share the American stage, however, with three other equally powerful figures. *Edgard Varèse* was known for his aggressive, extroverted, high-voltage sonorities and boldly clashing *fortissimo* textures, within a structure that favored the balancing of weights and densities (much as a physicist would) over the traditional European values of pitch manipulation, polyphony, or motivic development. Although *Charles Ives* had ceased composing in the 1920s, his music became widely known only in the decade before his death in 1954; his juxtapositions of many different musics in collage textures, with apparent disregard for stylistic consistency, would prove to be influential. *John Cage,* in renouncing such European concerns as the twelve-pitch division of the octave, harmony, and the distinction between musical tone and noise, had become deeply involved with non-Western aesthetics and techniques and a universe of "found sounds."

Given this variety of influences, a good deal of postwar American music moved in uncharted directions. In the 1950s there simply were no European counterparts for someone like Lou Harrison, exploring ancient intonation systems, aspects of Medieval polyphony, and the use of Asian instruments; or Harry Partch, creating a highly personal language of forty-three microtones to the octave, as well as special instruments and notational symbols to articulate his language in performance; or Conlon Nancarrow, akin to Partch in his need to wed a unique music to special instruments and notation—in this instance, the player piano and its paper rolls.

Moreover, it was in the United States that the philosophy of composition by way of chance procedures and indeterminate notation, diametrically opposed to the strict discipline of total serialism, began to take hold in the early 1950s. The emergence of a New York school of composers led by Cage coincided with the advent of equally open-ended multimedia events and "happenings." Cage's own music had begun changing in this direction, in such works as the 1951 *Imaginary Landscape No. 4* for twelve radios and the 1952 "silent" piece 4'33". Many Europeans, Stockhausen and Boulez among them, had begun to explore improvisatory, open-ended techniques by the close of the 1950s.

ILLUS. 5.1.

A number of composers at the Brussels World's Fair
(1958). John Cage is lying on the floor; kneeling
directly above him are Mauricio Kagel, Earle Brown
(glass in hand), Luciano Berio, and Karlheinz Stockhausen (holding a sheet of paper)

Photo: Faider, Brussels. Courtesy John Cage

STYLES IN TRANSITION

The remarkable degree to which many older composers changed their outlook offers another yardstick for measuring the upheaval, ferment, and tremendous excitement of newness in the air during the first postwar decade.

The most visible figure in this group was Igor Stravinsky, who moved from a position as champion of neoclassic tonality and arch opponent of twelve-tone music to that of embracing serial technique. His last major work that can be termed tonal was the opera *The Rake's Progress* (1948–51), related in spirit and material to Mozart's Italian opera style. It was first performed in September 1951, only a few months after Arnold Schoenberg's death. Perhaps with his great rival gone, Stravinsky felt less constrained about studying his works. Perhaps he now viewed the twelve-tone method in a historical perspective, that is, ripe for neoclassic borrowing. For whatever reason, Stravinsky gradually began to adapt serialism to his own purposes and became especially interested in Webern. (When the International Webern Society was formed in 1962, Stravinsky was listed as a founding director.)

Other composers felt a similar need to strike out in new directions. Elliott Carter (b. 1908) gradually moved from a folklike tonal, neoclassical style, reminiscent of Copland, to an essentially nontonal language of great rhythmic and polyphonic complexity. The Italian Luigi Dallapiccolla (1904–75), who had been regarded by the Mussolini government as a cultural traitor for his tentative exploration of chromatic pitch rows, blossomed into a fully twelve-tone composer of great lyric strength. Roger Sessions (1896–1985), after having approached the technique very gradually, produced in 1953 his first twelve-tone piece, the Sonata for Solo Violin, and was pleasantly surprised to find the creative process "flowing easily and without constraint." Benjamin Britten (1913–76) and Aaron Copland (1900–1990) also began to work in a modified serial style. Copland's first attempt was his 1957 Piano Fantasy, built on a ten-note row; the composer explained his fascination with the technique by stating that "I began to hear chords that I wouldn't have heard otherwise."

Not all established composers in search of new paths turned to serialism. In his *Rural Antiphonies* (1952) and *Antiphony I* for orchestra (1953), Henry Brant (b. 1913) began creating works for large ensembles, using antiphonal separation of the forces throughout the entire area of a concert hall. At the same time, Lukas Foss, having achieved distinction in a solid Hindemithean, neoclassic style, began moving into areas of group improvisation and free atonality. In 1951–52, Otto Luening, with hundreds of pieces in a tonal, neoclassic idiom behind him, embarked on a collaborative venture with Vladimir Ussachevsky (1911–90) to explore the newly discovered medium of tape music.

In surveying these experiments and stylistic transitions among postwar composers, we can begin to sense their spirit of adventure and concern for certain characteristic issues:

1. The search for alternatives to tonality as a viable language for most young composers

2. The degree of one's creative "control" over the final musical product, within a spectrum bounded by the extremes of totally controlled serialism and improvisatory chance music
3. A growing fascination with areas beyond pitch—texture, rhythm, register, color, mass, and density—as primary structural and expressive elements
4. The uses of new technology, especially the recently developed tape recorder, in composition and performance

These concerns will be studied more carefully in Part II. First, however, let us examine a few specific compositions—each created during the 1950s, and each marking a significant turning point in its composer's style—in some detail.

Pieces for Study I

The seven compositions in this chapter, composed between 1948 and 1959, constitute a cross section of postwar musical styles. The analyses here are guided by the nine factors set out in Chapter 4. Please note that, in examining these—or any other—works, we should not assume that each of the nine factors will be equally significant either from moment to moment or from one composition to another. (Similarly, when studying eighteenth- or nineteenth-century music of the tonal mainstream, we would hardly expect every passage to provide examples of "counterpoint" or "chromaticism.") Consider the nine factors, then, as a checklist of concerns, priorities and perspectives, to be used as an aid to greater understanding of late-twentieth-century music.

Karlheinz Stockhausen: Kreuzspiel

Kreuzspiel by Karlheinz Stockhausen (b. 1928) is scored for oboe, bass clarinet, piano, and three percussionists (playing six tomtoms, two conga drums ["tumbas"], and four suspended cymbals). It was composed during

ILLUS. 6.1.

John Cage (left) and Karlheinz Stockhausen, in a
"souvenir" photo, about 1958

Courtesy John Cage

Stockhausen's period of study at Darmstadt, and was premiered there
during the summer of 1952. The influence of Messiaen's "Mode de valeurs
et d'intensités" was still fresh at Darmstadt, and Stockhausen (along with
his fellow student Boulez) was intrigued by the concept of extrapolating
pitch successions to such other musical dimensions as duration and volume. *Kreuzspiel* ("Crossplay") can be studied as an early example of total
serialism. But its special significance lies elsewhere, primarily in its attempt
to place serial technique within the context of large-scale dramatic narrative.

The first serial works of the early 1950s, in their extension of twelve-
tone procedures to musical areas other than pitch, would often create rapid
successions of widely contrasted registers, volume levels, and articulations,
all occurring simultaneously. Although the resultant "pointillist" textures
could be brilliant or evocative, they might also appear to be overly disjunct
or fragmented. Moreover, the busy, actively changing details often seemed
to cancel each other out, paradoxically creating a static quality with little

audible shape or direction. Dissatisfied with these aspects of serial texture, Stockhausen tried to reconcile them with a sense of continuity.

Kreuzspiel consists of three main sections, framed by an introduction and coda. Sectional divisions often occur at points in time that are multiples of thirteen; for example, section I begins after an introduction of thirteen bars. Example 6.1 shows the opening measures of the introduction. Note the registral placement of notes for the piano: either very high or very low. The twelve pitches are initially stated as three-note chords, equally divided between the extremes of the piano keyboard. At the same time, the conga drums articulate the rhythmic series 2–8–7–4–11–1–12–3–9–6–5–10, the beginning of each unit marked by the upper drum. Percussion ostinati of this sort create a driving backdrop for the entire piece.

As section I progresses, the high and low pitches gradually exchange places; they are picked up by the wind instruments as they reach midrange. At the midpoint of section I (m. 52, or 13 × 4), the process "unwinds" in retrograde inversion, so that by measure 91 (or 13 × 7) the pitches are distributed again at the extremes of the keyboard. To complete the "cross-

---

EXAMPLE 6.1.

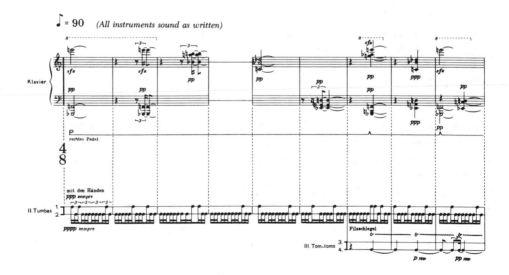

Karlheinz Stockhausen: *Kreuzspiel*

play," pitches that were very high at the outset are now in the deep bass register, and vice versa.

Section II begins with woodwinds in midregister, branches out to the extremes of the keyboard, and then returns to the wind timbre. The duration series formerly heard in the conga drums is now played by cymbals. Finally, for section III both of the preceding processes take place simultaneously, each in retrograde.

Stockhausen's aesthetic intent is, paradoxically, both radical and conservative. The composer was concerned with integral serialism's tendency to create aggregates of seemingly disassociated particles, and he felt a need to construct audible processes or shapes that would provide dramatic context for such textures. For the ten-minute span of *Kreuzspiel*'s duration, one can perceive a number of "crossplay" operations occurring simultaneously—on the levels of pitch, duration, register, volume, and instrumentation. These operations, and their serial permutation (such as retrograde or inversion) create the form of the entire work. On another level, one can hear *Kreuzspiel* as an energetic toccata, dominated by its hypnotic, steady percussion rhythms in a way that may recall non-Western ritual or American jazz, rather than the European models of Messiaen or Webern.

In discussing *Kreuzspiel* with reference to the "nine factors," one is immediately struck by the predominance of **pitch logic** as primary, assuming the division of the octave into twelve equally tempered units, and the carefully calibrated relationships among them. (On the other hand, one should not overlook the striking use of nonpitched percussion or quasi-percussive sonorities at extremes of the keyboard register.) Serial process is equally important, especially in areas where pitch series are correlated with aspects of **time**. Stockhausen's concerns with **texture** and **sound color**, however, result in a more traditional sense of gradually changing continuity (or "narrative"), overlaid against the serial process. It is the interaction of these multiple concerns and processes, in fact, that results in the audible musical "form."

Elliott Carter: Sonata for Flute, Oboe, Cello, and Harpsichord

The stylistic development of the American composer Elliott Carter underwent great changes during the decade following World War II. As he describes it, he became "preoccupied with the time-memory patterns of music, with rethinking the rhythmic means of what had begun to seem a very limited routine used in most contemporary and older Western music." When compared with his earlier neoclassic compositions, his Sonata for Cello and Piano (1948) and String Quartet No. 1 (1951) are notable for their new harmonic freedom—a more flexible use of dissonance, and the

ILLUS. 6.2.

Elliott Carter (left) and Pierre Boulez

Courtesy BMI Archives

disappearance of key signature—and the "extreme disassociation" (to use Carter's phrase) between individual instruments. In a manner possibly related to the model of Charles Ives, whom Carter had known well for many decades, these postwar works reveal a personalization of instruments. The written scores are conceived as "auditory scenarios for performers to act out with their instruments, dramatizing the players as individuals and as participants in the ensemble."

If the idea of individualizing chamber roles may have derived from Ives, the rhythmic innovations of Carter's postwar pieces represent a unique synthesis all his own. In considering the rhythmic dimension, Carter studied Indian talas, Arabic systems, and subtle tempo changes in Balinese gamelan music. Eventually he devised a way of controlling and articulating gradual changes within rhythmic continuities; this technique is often called *metric modulation*. Carter also noted that "in considering change, process, evolution as music's prime factor," he wanted to "make [materials] interact in other ways than by linear succession." It is significant that the 1952 Sonata for Flute, Oboe, Cello, and Harpsichord has a personal, highly flexible approach to form based on a fluid sense of discourse and response, rather than motivic development.

Apart from temporal considerations, the sonata is notable for its light, playful spirit, perhaps related to the presence of the harpsichord. Although

Carter had no desire to write a "neobaroque" piece, the sonata still retains a decorative, ornamental, even elegant quality. And there is no doubt that the harpsichord dominates the sonata's texture. In the composer's words, the three other instruments are used as "a frame for the harpsichord," with woodwind and cello figures frequently emerging from the harpsichord's resonant upper partials. For example, the first movement begins with a loud, dramatic gesture in which the harpsichord figures prominently, triggering responses, imitations, and extensions by the other players. Carter suggests that the subsiding ripples of this opening "splash" constitute the rest of the movement, and critics have interpreted the movement's overall form as a slow motion analogue of the harpsichord attack-decay pattern, eventually dying away to silence.

It is possible, however, to perceive the work in a very different way: as a scenario in which the players function as "actors." On this level, Carter exploits the four unique timbres as equally important characters in a minidrama. Soon after the beginning, in which the opening flurries overlap and interrupt one another, the regular, even beats of the harpsichord collide with the lyric, quasi-improvisatory gestures of the other players. Thus is established a pattern recurrent throughout the sonata of simultaneous levels of rhythmic activity—rigid, clockwork regularity against fluid, impulsive bursts of "commentary."

The second movement, *Lento*, begins quietly on a single pitch, G, passed from one instrument to another and then chromatically inflected to a lyric motive. (The idea of focusing on one note with changing timbre has origins in Viennese *Klangfarbenmelodie*, and in Carter's own earlier *Eight Etudes and a Fantasy*. In this particular piece, it could also be perceived as "commentary" on a characteristic of the harpsichord, the ability to vary a single note with changes of registration.) Although much of the movement is slow and meditative, there is a sudden, rapid burst of tutti figurations near the close, reminiscent of the "splash" with which the first movement had begun. It also prefigures the sonorities and gestures of the movement to follow.

During this dramatic passage, we may perceive a unique temporal flow in which different pulses interact—that is, where one level of metric regularity meshes with, or merges into, another. Carter, devoting special attention to that particular experience, has created an accurate notation technique that would allow one tempo or meter to change to another. This procedure is known as metric modulation. In Example 6.2, an excerpt of the flute part, the sixteenth notes of a $\frac{4}{4}$ measure are first grouped traditionally in fours, then in threes for the $\frac{6}{16}$ bar, and then renotated as triplets in $\frac{2}{8}$. The $\frac{2}{8}$ bar equals a single beat of the ensuing $\frac{4}{4}$ passage, which moves at a slower tempo than the $\frac{4}{4}$ measure with which the excerpt began.

At times Carter's gestures—metric modulation, the superimposition of impulsive, quasi-improvisatory rhythms on a regular beat, and the virtuosic ornamentation of lines—combine to create an oddly jazzlike effect.

EXAMPLE 6.2.

Elliott Carter: Sonata for Flute, Oboe, Cello, and Harpsichord (flute part)

These fleeting references to the world of popular dance music are heightened even further in the last movement, *Allegro*, which begins with the rhythms of a forlana, a Venetian gondolier's dance. The forlana fades into other dance rhythms, with frequent "crosscuts" (Carter himself likens this to movie editing) or the superimposition of one dance rhythm on another. Metric modulation is employed most often in this movement, as various tempi and rhythms appear in different states of interaction.

The Sonata for Flute, Oboe, Cello, and Harpsichord, in its avoidance of traditional classical development, seems to follow the example of the late Debussy sonatas. In discussing his own piece, Carter speaks of his concern "with contrasts of many kinds of musical characters . . . with filling musical time and space by a web of continually varying cross references," and with his goal of "a fluid, changeable continuity." Even though the work is precisely notated in great detail, its effect in performance seems spontaneous.

Let us place the Carter Sonata in perspective, with special attention to the nine factors. The harpsichord conveys a certain **historicism**: associations with eighteenth-century music in general, and a quality of rhythmic propulsion and dance in particular. The breadth of **sound color** is striking, especially when the harpsichord, with its combination of delicacy and percussive bite, combines with other, contrasting colors. The sonata's unusual **texture** is partly influenced by these sharp timbral contrasts. Extended individual lines, rather than Webernian "points," predominate; the lines are often set against one another, however, so that a collision of disparate elements (in the spirit of Ives's *Unanswered Question*) results. That disparity, heightened by the overlay of many different rhythms and tempi, reflects Carter's concern with musical **time** and varieties of continuity. A major outgrowth of that concern, "metric modulation," may be considered an example of a **process** for which the composer has devised an innovative **notation**.

Lukas Foss: Time Cycle

During the 1950s Lukas Foss (b. 1922) began to move in creative directions that offered alternatives to his former neoclassic style. His experiences as a professor at the University of California at Los Angeles proved to be especially significant, since it was there in 1955 that Foss first explored improvisation. In an attempt to wean his students "away from the tyranny of printed notes," he organized an ensemble devoted to nonjazz group improvisation. The group devised systems of elaborate ground plans, charts, and diagrams, and also studied the improvisatory traditions of various cultures. Their early performances, in a fairly tonal idiom, proved unsatisfactory; the improvisations, in Foss's words, sounded like "music badly remembered." But Foss and the other group members then began to explore materials—rhythmically jagged, freely dissonant, and often nontonal—more naturally suited to the medium. These stylistic changes also exerted a profound effect on Foss's written-out, fully composed music.

Time Cycle (1959), which the composer regards as the beginning of a new phase in his creative development, consists of four movements for soprano and orchestra, each based on a text by a different author, the first two in English (his adopted language) and the last two in his native German. The juxtaposition of four authors and two languages might be considered a form of collage on one level (and Foss would, in later works, use fragmented word groupings literally as collage elements, requiring performers to assemble their own texts). But on another level the four are tightly integrated by their obsessive concern with the subject of time. Foss's musical setting of the words attempts to reflect those obsessions.

The first movement sets a poem, "We're Late," by W. H. Auden: "Clocks cannot tell our time of day . . . because we have no time until we know what time we fill." The music, like the text, confronts and questions our Western sense of forward-moving clock time. Both the vocal and orchestral lines consist of short melodic cells, often treated polyphonically in strict canon. The singer's declamation is robotlike, mechanical, even childish. The splintered, fragmented quality of the vocal line is imitated in the strings, then followed by the "ticking" of many overlapping clocklike fragments. Some of the musical gestures recall Webern, especially the extensive use of seconds, sevenths, and ninths, the ever-changing textures, and asymmetrical alternations of sound and silence. But the music is essentially pitch-centered: strongly articulated D♭s at the end of sentences (e.g., on the words "time" and "was").

In the second movement the clock imagery is replaced by that of bells: the text uses A. E. Housman's lines: "When the bells justle in the tower / The hollow night amid / Then on my tongue the taste is sour / of all I ever did." The "justle" is created by overlapping, clashing lines, using a series of all twelve tones in rapidly changing meters, and the "sourness" by a brilliantly orchestrated series of glissandi. The third movement, based on an entry from the diaries of Franz Kafka, opens with the lines: "The last week was like a total breakdown . . . impossible to sleep, impossible to wake, impossible to bear life, or, more accurately, to bear the continuity of life. The clocks do not synchronize." Here the collapse of time is directed inwardly, as a mirror of psychic mental breakdown; the music is appropriately expressionistic, reminiscent at times of Alban Berg.

The final movement, at a very slow tempo, is set to the watchman's midnight warning in Nietzsche's *Also sprach Zarathustra*—a recitation of the numbers one through twelve, alternating with solemn maxims and prophecies. Foss, once again treating his material in canonic imitation, punctuates the twelve numbers by "bell" strokes (signifying the twelve bells of midnight) produced by such instruments as glockenspiel, triangle, harp, and piano. In addition, players in the orchestra are instructed to whisper the numbers one through twelve (or their equivalent in the language of the performance site), growing louder with each successive statement. ("Twelve," then, would be a *fff* stage whisper.) The rhythmic flow of the movement, a steady $\frac{3}{2}$ meter, is disturbed by each appearance of a number. As seen in Example 6.3, "five" occurs as the fifth beat of a $\frac{5}{4}$ measure, "six" the sixth beat in $\frac{6}{4}$, and so on, the beats articulated by triangle, glockenspiel, and (for "six") harp. The extension of instrumental resources into the domain of theater, by having orchestra players whisper or speak, is a direction that Foss and many other composers would explore more fully in the following decades.

The premiere of *Time Cycle* with the New York Philharmonic Orchestra included performances, between the movements, by Foss's UCLA Improvisation Ensemble. In retrospect, Foss compares this use of an improvisation group to that of "a commedia dell'arte group of clowns [who would] improvise between the songs" in earlier centuries.

In discussing Foss's work with reference to the nine factors, one could easily begin with **time**, since its importance is evident throughout (beginning with the title). "Time" is contemplated in many of its aspects: experiential time versus clock time, the juxtaposition of different time worlds, time as cumulative duration. Each aspect inspires a novel approach to **texture**; the variety of which is one of the work's most notable features. Foss moves easily among post–Webernian *Klangfarbenmelodie*, Ivesian mul-

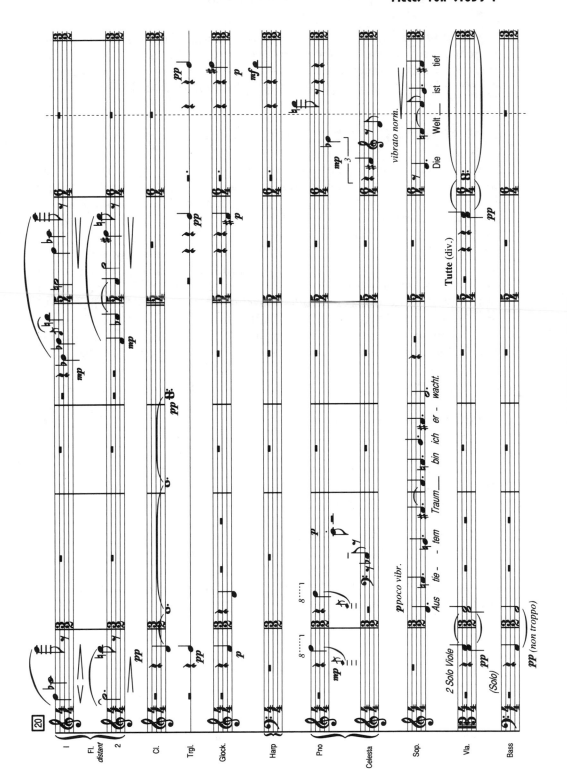

EXAMPLE 6.3. Lukas Foss: *Time Cycle,* fourth movement. Copyright © 1960, 1962, 1964 by Carl Fischer, Inc., New York. Used by permission

tilayered juxtaposition, and lush, romantic gestures reminiscent of Mahler or Schoenberg. The unusual **performance ritual** includes the addition of an improvisatory chamber ensemble between movements and the use of orchestra players as chanting, whispering "actors" during the final section.

Igor Stravinsky: Agon

The emergence, late in his life, of Igor Stravinsky as a serial composer was, in the opinion of the critic Hans Keller, "the most profound surprise in the history of music." Stravinsky's growth in this direction was gradual. As early as 1952, in his Cantata, he first introduced a row. *Threni* (1958) was his first completely twelve-tone and nontonal piece. The ballet score *Agon* occurs midway in this development; it was begun in 1953 (when Stravinsky's interests were primarily tonal), postponed twice while other compositions were attended to, and finally completed in 1957. As a transitional work, then, *Agon* offers fascinating aspects of both the "old" and "new" Stravinsky. In fact, the ballet begins diatonically in C major, then adds chromatic elements, gradually moves toward the use of twelve-tone rows, and eventually returns to its original diatonic statement in the key of C.

Agon is one of the first works in which Stravinsky used sets of twelve pitches (as opposed to a smaller number). Significantly, the use of serial technique makes his music no less "Stravinskian." The motives generated by tone rows are still articulated with his characteristically lean, athletic energy. Furthermore, neoclassic references are as prominent as ever: canonic and fugal passages, traditional French dance forms, and extended passages reminiscent of Renaissance polyphony abound. Although the score calls for a large instrumental ensemble, Stravinsky often uses it in smaller chamberlike subdivisions.

The word *agon* can be translated as "contest," and the ballet, as dance and music, was conceived as a series of games concerned (significantly) with aspects of the number twelve. Accordingly, there are twelve short movements (four groups of three) and twelve dancers (four males and eight females). On only two occasions—the close of the first movement and the end of the entire ballet—do all of the dancers appear together. The choreography and costuming (rehearsal clothing and a bare stage) underline the abstract nature of Stravinsky's music. Many of the dancers in the original production referred to *Agon* informally as the "IBM ballet" for its precision and coolness, and the composer compared it to the paintings of Piet Mondrian.

The ballet opens with four male dancers onstage, their backs to the audience. The remaining movements of section 1 add four more dancers at a time, until all twelve are introduced. Stravinsky then adds a "Prelude" linking sections 1 and 2. The opening C-major fanfare, and the modal, neorenaissance "cadences" of the Prelude, lend a strong sense of key center. And since the very opening returns as the Finale, and much of the Prelude recurs in the Interludes preceding the third and fourth sections, the entire score is characterized by an alternation of tonal and serial pitch languages.

Pitch rows are important building blocks of the three remaining sections. Stravinsky uses a great many rows, rather than a single set for the entire ballet. They are most frequently used in a linear manner; two or more set forms are superimposed in the context of traditional, often canonic, part writing. Stravinsky is also fond of taking six-pitch groupings (hexachords) and treating them as motivic fragments. Example 6.4a shows a canonic brass figure, stated at the outset of the "Bransle simple." This passage is built on a hexachord pattern, noted in Example 6.4b. (For the meaning of "P" and "I9," see "A Brief Look at the Twelve-Tone Set" in Chapter 7.) The complementary hexachord—that is, the remaining six pitches of the twelve-pitch set—provides the material (in transposition) for the "Bransle gay" number that immediately follows.

Stravinsky also employs seventeenth-century French dance forms— sarabande, bransle, and galliard—as starting points for the individual movements of sections 2 and 3. But their angular contours and steely timbres are distinctly modern. In fact, one critic remarked that they recall court dances "as much as a cubist still-life recalls a pipe or guitar." The unusual instrumentation is noteworthy, especially that of the Sarabande (for solo male dancer), scored for xylophone, solo violin, and two trombones, and a Galliarde (two female dancers) for low strings, harp, mandolin, and three flutes.

Section 4 moves away from the world of French courtly dance to relatively "pure" abstraction. The individual numbers—reminiscent of Webern in their spare, pointillistic texture—consist of a theme, variations, and refrain. Solo male and female dancers are featured, and each succeeding number brings more dancers onstage until the full company reappears at the end. The music, too, comes full circle, with an altered—and oddly subdued—"recapitulation" of the opening C-major brass fanfare.

The interaction of the twelve-tone **process** and tonal ideas points to **pitch logic** as central to the ballet's overall concept. Two other areas, however, stand out in particular: the transparent, cleanly etched **textures** (articulated by a unique palette of **sound color**), and fascinating references to **historical** models—not only musical ones, but those of balletic **performance ritual**. These concerns had characterized Stravinsky the neoclassicist for much of the century; significantly, they remain intact even though the surface language has changed.

EXAMPLE 6.4A.

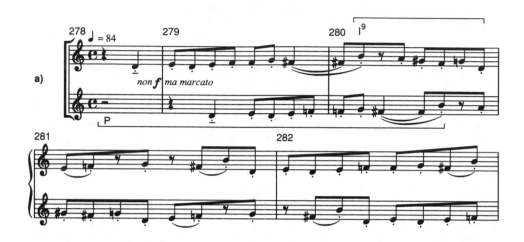

Igor Stravinsky: *Agon*, "Bransle Simple"

© Copyright 1957 by Boosey & Hawkes, Inc. Copyright
Renewed. Reprinted by permission

EXAMPLE 6.4B.

Hexachordal set and inversion used in "Bransle
Simple"

John Cage: Sonatas and Interludes;
Music of Changes

During the 1940s John Cage heightened his pursuit of two strong interests,
both related to his fondness for non-Western music. He became convinced
that the essence of musical structure was duration—ratios and measurements of time—which would allow for sound and silence, or "tone" and
"noise," to function as equally useful materials. He had also developed a

preference for percussive sounds, which could free the ear from conventional Western notions of equal temperament and harmony.

On another, more pragmatically American level, Cage had also been actively "inventing" or redesigning instruments to suit his needs. The idea of the prepared piano had originated as early as 1938, for a Seattle performance occasion where Cage wanted the sounds of a percussion ensemble but had only a piano. He discovered that the insertion of various objects between the piano's strings would radically alter the instrument's timbre; it could, in effect, transform piano sonorities into bell, gong, woodblock, and drum sounds. Traditional staff notation, though adequate for directing the performer, cannot begin to convey the actual sonorities of this music in performance. In "preparing" the piano, the performer alters not only timbre, but intonation and pitch as well.

Between 1946 and 1948 Cage composed the *Sonatas and Interludes*, his most elaborate work for the prepared piano. (The actual preparation of the piano strings is more complex and time-consuming than one might suspect. Detailed instructions, applying to almost every key of the instrument, specify which materials are to be used, along with their exact distance from the dampers.) Sixteen sonatas—single-movement works in binary form, closer in proportion to those of Scarlatti than those of Beethoven—are grouped in fours, with each group separated by an interlude, the whole spanning a duration of some seventy minutes. They reflect the composer's serious interest in Eastern philosophy. As Cage notes, the entire cycle is intended to express "dramatic and contemplative states, both traditional and private, particularly the so-called permanent emotions of traditional Indian aesthetic theory—the heroic, erotic, wondrous, mirthful, odious, sorrowful, fearful, angry, and their common tendency towards the tranquil."

The rhythmic aspects of the sonatas are crucially important: not only the number of measures and beats, but their structural divisions into proportions. In comparing Sonata I and Sonata V, for example, we might be most immediately struck by their differences in mood, sonority, and level of rhythmic energy. But note that internal subdivisions in each are dictated by strict ratios. In Sonata I (Example 6.5) the significant proportion is 4:3. The focal point of the sonata's first section (everything before the first repeat sign) is a $\frac{7}{4}$ measure; 28 quarter-note beats precede that measure and 21 follow it, forming the ratio 4:3. The 28-beat passage, the 21-beat passage, and the central $\frac{7}{4}$ bar are themselves subdivided into groupings of 4 + 3; moreover, the duration of the entire first section exceeds that of the second section by a factor of 4 to 3 (56 beats to 42).

Sonata V is constructed similarly on the ratio 4:5. This ratio determines not only the relative lengths of the two sections (18 and 22½ measures) but also the internal subdivisions within the sections. Thus, the 18 measures of

EXAMPLE 6.5.

John Cage: *Sonatas and Interludes*, Sonata I

the first section are grouped as two units of 9, each with a 4 + 5 subdivision.

Cage's non-Western aesthetic goal, what he termed the "objectifying of feelings," can be heard in the *Sonatas and Interludes'* relatively distant quality of ritual ceremony rather than intense, personal involvement. During the late 1940s and early '50s, Cage gradually found this antiromantic stance leading him to the "objectifying" of music itself, through the use of chance operations in the process of composition. He was drawn to chance procedures as a means of reducing the influence of his own will upon the act of composition. That idea was a natural outgrowth of his absorption in Eastern philosophy and religion—in particular, the Indian aesthetic principle that art should imitate nature in its manner of operation, and the Zen Buddhist belief that there should be no separation between art and life.

Cage's piano piece *Music of Changes* (1951) reflects this new interest. For this work, his selections of pitches, nonpitched percussive sounds, durations, amplitude, tempo, and other variables are not dictated by conscious choice or what Cage might term "human will," but rather are derived from the tossing of coins, which in turn refer to a carefully prepared list of possibilities. The procedure derives from that of the ancient Chinese oracle book *I Ching*, in which sixty-four sets of texts are used for consultation after a similarly random selection process.

There are two similarities to the earlier *Sonatas and Interludes*. First, a traditional Western instrument has been transformed in such a way that its European bias is mitigated. Second, Cage maintains his fascination with predetermined time structures. His sounds, rhythmic figures, and dynamic values, though arrived at randomly, are paradoxically placed within a strict framework of proportions: $3:5:6\frac{3}{4}:6\frac{3}{4}:5:3\frac{1}{8}$, for a total of $29\frac{5}{8}$. Within each section—for example, $29\frac{5}{8}$ measures of $\frac{4}{4}$ time—that series determines the number of measures before a tempo change occurs. The series also controls structural divisions on a larger level, bringing the entire work to a total of $29\frac{5}{8}$ sections, grouped into four movements.

Although Cage's notation for *Music of Changes* includes metronome markings, bar lines, and meter, there are no note values or rests. Rhythms and durations are "measured" directly on the page; each $\frac{4}{4}$ measure, no matter what its tempo or degree of activity, occupies the same graphic space. The placement of musical events within that space is to be judged by the pianist. As with the *Sonatas and Interludes*, the notation reflects a compromise between a traditional norm and the new demands of Cage's concept.

Let us examine the Cage works with special attention to the nine factors. **Pitch logic** is severely limited in the *Sonatas and Interludes* and virtually nonexistent in *Music of Changes*, where it has been replaced by concern for a broader spectrum in which "noise" and "tone," sound and silence, coexist. On the other hand, Cage's interest in **process** is paramount. His strict durational series and consultation of random "oracles" are as deeply committed to the idea of precomposition as any serial technique of Webern or Babbitt. The primary difference lies in the tendency of Cage's processes to subject **time** to strict control while leaving pitch relatively flexible.

While evidence of Cage's multicultural **historicism** may be found in his application of Asian aesthetic principles, his **textures** often seem surprisingly allied to Webern, both in their rapidly shifting **timbres** (which are virtually guaranteed by use of the prepared piano) and in the positive role played by silence. At the same time, the incongruous effect of exotic sounds emerging from that most Western of instruments, the grand piano, creates a striking **performance ritual**. Finally, Cage's modifications of standard **notation** reflect these performance features.

Benjamin Britten: The Turn of the Screw

Benjamin Britten's use of a tone row in the chamber opera *The Turn of the Screw*, though not as shocking as Stravinsky's conversion to serialism, must have come as something of a surprise, nevertheless, to the operatic establishment. Twelve-tone writing is not what one would expect of a conservative composer specializing in a traditional stage genre. At one level, the language of *The Turn of the Screw* may indicate the degree to which Schoenberg's techniques had become absorbed into the mainstream. On another level, it also reveals a fascination that Britten had always felt for the music of the second Viennese school. (Even as a youngster, he had wanted to study abroad with Alban Berg, but was not permitted to. As a student at the Royal College of Music, he had led a peaceful "rebellion" to have the scores of Anton Webern purchased for the college library, which at that time had none.)

In composing *The Turn of the Screw*, based on the well-known short novel by Henry James, Britten had a number of dramatically powerful elements to work with: the presence of ghosts, the psychology of characters under ever-increasing pressure, the confrontation of evil with innocence, and—most important—the sheer ambiguity of the entire tale. (One never knows whether the ghosts are real or imagined, or where the evil actually resides.) Britten's opera consists of two acts, divided into many short scenes. Each brief scene adds a new twist to the complex plot—as one critic noted, "an instant of the screw's turn." Moreover, the scenes are separated from one another by orchestral interludes, with each scene linked to its own interlude. The interludes are themselves variations on a twelve-tone motive (Example 6.6a), Britten's statement of the complete row. The row itself (Example 6.6b), appropriate to this tale of multiple meanings and interpretations, is ambiguous: it may be heard as a chain of falling fifths, a chain of rising sixths, or a pair of interlocking wholetone scales separated by a fifth.

A different level of ambiguity colors the tonality of the individual scenes. As each scene moves to the next, the key center shifts through all twelve pitches, beginning with A and proceeding along an ascending Aeolian scale. The first "black key" tonality, A♭, is reserved for the final scene of Act I—appropriately, for the first entrance of one of the ghosts. The

EXAMPLE 6.6A.

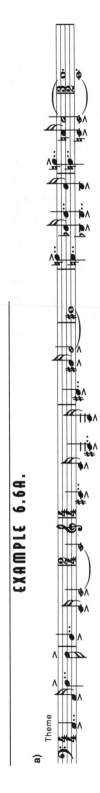

The "theme" from Britten's *The Turn of the Screw*. © Copyright 1955 by Hawkes & Son (London) Ltd. Copyright Renewed. Reprinted by permission of Boosey & Hawkes, Inc.

EXAMPLE 6.6B.

Britten's twelve-tone row for *The Turn of the Screw*. © Copyright 1955 by Hawkes & Son (London) Ltd. Copyright Renewed. Reprinted by permission of Boosey & Hawkes, Inc.

scenes of Act II appear in keys outlining the transposed inversion of the Aeolian succession, beginning on A♭ and ending with a finale that hovers between A and A♭, depicting the struggle for the soul of the little child on stage.

Each of the variations presents the row in a new guise, related to the dramatic situation of the scene to come. Variation IV appears as a grotesque march, in which the theme is gradually revealed in bass part; variation VIII is a series of cadenzas, each of which begins on a note determined by the row; in variation XI a canonic duet for alto flute and bass clarinet reveals first six notes of the row, then eight, and finally all twelve. In the final Variation (XV), all twelve pitches form a repeated chord, scored differently in each statement.

The brief excerpts in Example 6.7 show Britten's use of row fragments and implications to create the opera's important themes and motives. Examples 6.7a and 6.7b invert the row's ascending fifths into descending fourths, which now move down by a whole step. Example 6.7c, associated with the evil "ghost" Quint, makes use of the row's opening trichord, in both original and inverted forms. Example 6.7d, sung by the young boy Miles, inverts the row's interlocking sixths to form thirds but at the same time is also curiously related to Quint's motive. Example 6.7e combines thirds, fourths, and wholetone movement. Finally, the passacaglia that dominates the last scene is a direct statement of the row itself. This intricate organization contributes to the taut, remarkably tense quality of *The Turn of the Screw*; one feels that not a note has been wasted.

Britten's tonal approach to serial **process**, though unorthodox, reflects concern with the theatrical implications of **pitch logic**, linking the tone row to large-scale unfolding of dramatic conflict and changing key relationships among scenes. **Timbre** and **texture** contribute to the drama through the association of specific tone colors with characters—the celesta with Peter Quint, for example). Britten's **historicism** is evident in references to other music—folk song and dance, nursery tunes, church bells, operatic traditions from Wagner to Puccini and Alban Berg. In the fusion of tonal and serial languages, comparisons with Berg are especially apt. *The Turn of the Screw*'s musical language—tight and disciplined, tonal on the surface and darkly ambiguous beneath—parallels Henry James's language remarkably and forms a perfect setting for one of the great suspense tales of English literature.

EXAMPLE 6.7

Benjamin Britten: *The Turn of the Screw.* a. Act I, scene I; b. Act II, scene I; c. Act I, scene IV; d. Act I, scene VI; e. Act I, scene V; f. Act II, scene VII

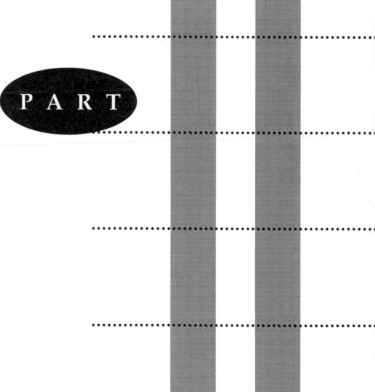

PART **II**

New Aesthetic

Approaches

"Order" and "Chaos"

By the late 1950s two distinctly contrasted poles of thought had evolved regarding issues of rationality, conscious control, and "order" in art; by the 1960s the gulf between them was regarded as a major split within the musical avant-garde.

At one pole, which we might call "order," is integral serialism, typified in the music of those years by Stockhausen, Babbitt, and Boulez. Serial music attempts to articulate highly calibrated distinctions within individual musical parameters (pitch, duration, register, dynamic level, phrasing), as well as detailed, complex relationships among them. Notation, highly specific and often daunting, assumes a position of preeminent importance; the score may well be regarded as "the work" itself, and performance as an ephemeral, imperfect realization of the work. A hierarchical pyramid of composer-performer-listener is assumed from the outset; the composer's role is to control events, to be "in charge."

At the other pole is the music of John Cage and the composers influenced by his example, advocating a very different approach to "order"— one that values spontaneous, immediate, and even unpredictable aspects of the musical experience. Those composers have sought to minimize their control over surface details of any given performance. Instead, chance factors often replace the influence of the composer's personal "will" on the act of music making. Because the result—often a seemingly uncontrolled juxtaposition of random events, most of them antimusical by any familiar standards—has engendered controversy, even outrage, among many listeners, we might label this pole "chaos." Although that term is misleading, it is used here for its polemic value, as a reminder of the intense, often passionate hostility felt toward Cage during the first postwar decades.

Cageian composers who encourage spontaneity and unpredictability tend to approach music as an "activity" rather than a finished "product." They are less likely, therefore, to regard the notated score as primary. On the contrary, notation is approached as a series of instructions for making performances, no more and no less. Because performances of the same composition could vary drastically from one occasion to another, one would hardly refer to the written score as "the work" in the serialists' sense of a fixed, permanent art object that demands repeated hearings for complete comprehension. And unlike the serialists' view of music as a composer's art, the Cageian focus on the changeable, temporal, perhaps even theatrical aspects of live music making stresses music as a performer's art—or perhaps as a listener's art, since the composer may be no less surprised at the moment-by-moment events in his or her pieces than anyone else. Cage has stated, "I have become a listener and the music has become something to hear."

Ironically, the underlying assumptions of "chaos" and "order" are each solidly grounded in traditional values. Music is often considered the most mathematical, most logical, and most precise of the arts—an "orderly" art of measurements, ratios, and proportions. For example, the full range of audible frequencies is divided into specific pitches and intervals, just as time is divided into proportional rhythmic and metric values. Moreover, those intervals and proportions are linked to one another with rigorous logic and precision by intricate "grammatical" relationships. At the same time, music has also played a vital role in our celebration of the irrational and the unknowable. The most mystical of the arts, linked to magic and ceremonial ritual, music in performance offers the most immediate, perishable and sensual of experiences, a few fragments of sound in the air, heard and then gone. Subtle shadings of pitch and rhythm, elusive to notation, characterize both the interpretations of Western classical performers and the improvisatory traditions of jazz and the vast body of non-notated music around the world.

Degrees of musical "order" and "chaos," as complementary approaches to musical experience, have coexisted for centuries. During the 1950s, however, they became separated. Let us consider these two extremes separately before discussing their relationships.

When Schoenberg established the concept of a twelve-note row or series, he also devised a method of varying and expanding upon the series while maintaining its essential structure. Central to the method are four "operations" to which the row can be subjected: transposition, retrograde, inversion, and retrograde inversion—operations that remain a basic resource for serial composers today. They are explained below with reference to the following row, from Webern's Concerto for Nine Instruments, Op. 24 (1934), first movement:

$$\text{B} \quad \text{B}^\flat \quad \text{D} \quad \text{E}^\flat \quad \text{G} \quad \text{F}^\sharp \quad \text{G}^\sharp \quad \text{E} \quad \text{F} \quad \text{C} \quad \text{C}^\sharp \quad \text{A}$$

This unaltered form of the row can be called P_0. *P* stands for "prime," and *0* means not transposed.

Transposition is effected by shifting the entire series up a given number of semitones. If, for instance, we transpose the row by a major third—that is, four semitones—the following results:

$$P_4 \quad = \quad \text{D}^\sharp \quad \text{D} \quad \text{F}^\sharp \quad \text{G} \quad \text{B} \quad \text{A}^\sharp \quad \text{C} \quad \text{G}^\sharp \quad \text{A} \quad \text{E} \quad \text{F} \quad \text{C}^\sharp$$

Retrograde presents the row in reverse sequence. A retrograde of P_0 would be labeled R_0, and that of P_4 would be called R_4. Hence:

$$R_0 \quad = \quad \text{A} \quad \text{C}^\sharp \quad \text{C} \quad \text{F} \quad \text{E} \quad \text{G}^\sharp \quad \text{F}^\sharp \quad \text{G} \quad \text{E}^\flat \quad \text{D} \quad \text{B}^\flat \quad \text{B}$$
$$R_4 \quad = \quad \text{C}^\sharp \quad \text{F} \quad \text{E} \quad \text{A} \quad \text{G}^\sharp \quad \text{C} \quad \text{A}^\sharp \quad \text{B} \quad \text{G} \quad \text{F}^\sharp \quad \text{D} \quad \text{D}^\sharp$$

Inversion entails replacing each upward interval with its downward equivalent and vice versa. Again, this could be done to P_0 or to any transposition of it, such as P_4. Hence:

$$I_0 \quad = \quad \text{B} \quad \text{C} \quad \text{A}^\flat \quad \text{G} \quad \text{E}^\flat \quad \text{E} \quad \text{D} \quad \text{F}^\sharp \quad \text{F} \quad \text{B}^\flat \quad \text{A} \quad \text{C}^\sharp$$
$$I_4 \quad = \quad \text{D}^\sharp \quad \text{E} \quad \text{C} \quad \text{B} \quad \text{G} \quad \text{G}^\sharp \quad \text{F}^\sharp \quad \text{A}^\sharp \quad \text{A} \quad \text{D} \quad \text{C}^\sharp \quad \text{F}$$

Retrograde inversion presents the inversion in reverse order. Thus:

$$RI_0 \quad = \quad \text{C}^\sharp \quad \text{A} \quad \text{B}^\flat \quad \text{F} \quad \text{F}^\sharp \quad \text{D} \quad \text{E} \quad \text{E}^\flat \quad \text{G} \quad \text{A}^\flat \quad \text{C} \quad \text{B}$$
$$RI_4 \quad = \quad \text{F} \quad \text{C}^\sharp \quad \text{D} \quad \text{A} \quad \text{A}^\sharp \quad \text{F}^\sharp \quad \text{G}^\sharp \quad \text{G} \quad \text{B} \quad \text{C} \quad \text{E} \quad \text{D}^\sharp$$

The four operations yield forty-eight variations of the original twelve-note series. Importantly, however, while each row form offers a new pitch sequence, the intervals of P_0 are preserved, even though their order or direction (up or down) may be reversed. Inherent in this system, then, is the power to generate variety while maintaining cohesion.

Milton Babbitt's refinement of this system through the language of modular arithmetic and set theory enhanced its power and ease of use for the composer. Babbitt viewed the twelve-note row as a *set* and each note as an *element* of the set.

He recognized that every pitch in a set really represents a whole class of pitches, a *pitch class* comprising itself and all its octave equivalents (e.g., B represents all Bs, high and low). To reflect this more general identity, Babbitt numbered the chromatic scale from 0 to 11, starting with the first note of the set, and then assigned each pitch class its corresponding number rather than letter name. Actually, each element of the set could be identified by two numbers, its *order position* (also labeled 0 to 11) and its pitch class number. Thus, our row from the Webern concerto might be labeled as follows:

	(0,0)	(1,11)	(2,3)	(3,4)	(4,8)	(5,7)	(6,9)	(7,5)	(8,6)	(9,1)	(10,2)	(11,10)
P_0 =	B	B♭	D	E♭	G	F#	G#	E	F	C	C#	A

More commonly, however, the set would simply be identified by pitch class numbers:

$$P_0 = 0 \quad 11 \quad 3 \quad 4 \quad 8 \quad 7 \quad 9 \quad 5 \quad 6 \quad 1 \quad 2 \quad 10$$

Modular arithmetic, with a modulus of 12, allows one to carry out the four basic operations on a set more easily and still remain within the same twelve (0–11) pitch classes. For instance, to transpose P_0 to P_4, one simply adds 4 to all the members of P_0, modulo 12 (e.g., 0 + 4 = 4, 11 + 4 = 15 - 12 = 3, 3 + 4 = 7, etc.). Thus:

$$P_4 = 4 \quad 3 \quad 7 \quad 8 \quad 0 \quad 11 \quad 1 \quad 9 \quad 10 \quad 5 \quad 6 \quad 2$$

To arrive at the inversion of P_0, one finds the *complement* of each pitch class number, modulo 12 (e.g., 11 inverts to 12 - 11 = 1, 3 inverts to 12 - 3 = 9, etc.). Thus,

$$I_0 = 0 \quad 1 \quad 9 \quad 8 \quad 4 \quad 5 \quad 3 \quad 7 \quad 6 \quad 11 \quad 10 \quad 2$$

If we divide P_0 into four *subsets* of three elements (0 11 3 / 4 8 7 / 9 5 6 / 1 2 10), we see at a glance that each of these four *trichords* contains a minor second down and major third up or vice versa. In fact, each trichord is a transposed retrograde, inversion, or retrograde inversion of the other three. (If the first trichord were labeled P_0, the other three would be RI_4, R_9, and I_1.) Set theory, however, allows us to look deeper. One simple discovery, in this case, would be that each trichord can be reordered, transposed, and/or inverted into a *prime form* of [0,1,4]. (Brackets and commas are standard for labeling sets.) The first trichord, for example, can be reordered as [11,0,3] and then transposed by 1 to become [0,1,4]. For both composer and analyst, the [0,1,4] trichord is then revealed as a source of harmonic integrity built into the set. Highly symmetrical twelve-tone sets of this kind, as well as those with similarly related subsets of four elements (*tetrachords*) and six elements (*hexachords*), are pervasive in both pre- and postwar serial repertoire.

"ORDER"

Milton Babbitt

In an essay of the 1950s Pierre Boulez made a controversial statement: "Every musician who has not felt—we do not say understood, but indeed felt—the necessity of the serial language is USELESS!" The intense emotional fervor of that utterance certainly contradicts the commonly held notion of integral serialism as cold or cerebral. On the contrary, the growth of European serialism is directly related to the need felt by Boulez, Stockhausen, and others to make a "new world" after the devastation of World War II. At the same time, they may have perceived the serial technique—pulverizing, fragmenting, and then reassembling musical parameters—as an artistic analogue to the splitting of the atom. Some of their most prominent stylistic features (the erasure of pulse regularity, the eruptive gestures, the showers of rapid figurations) may, for some listeners, carry provocative subtexts associated with the birth of nuclear fission.

Milton Babbitt has consistently taken an altogether different approach. Whereas his European counterparts suddenly "discovered" Schoenberg and Webern after the end of World War II, Babbitt, as an American, had been steeped in their music even before beginning study with Roger Sessions in the mid-1930s. In addition, he was well versed in mathematics (in fact, the son of an actuary) and during the war years taught mathematics as well as music at Princeton University. Babbitt was quick to recognize the potential for applying logical processes to Schoenbergian pitch techniques; to this end, he advocated the adoption of a new terminology, including words and concepts borrowed from the world of mathematics and logic, especially set theory.

He preferred using the term *set* rather than tone-row, and *pitch class* rather than pitch. The concept of pitch class allows one to represent all octave (registral) varieties of a single pitch—a high C# and a low C#, for example—as equivalent, in fact, as a single number within a set. Babbitt also called attention to subsets, by referring to these as *trichords*, *tetrachords*, and *hexachords* (three-, four-, and six-pitch groupings, repectively).

Babbitt has shown great interest in a special property of certain sets termed *combinatoriality*. If a set is hexachordally combinatorial, for example, then permutating the set (through transposition, inversion, retrogression, and retrograde inversion) will create a new series whose first hexachord has no pitches in common with the first hexachord of the original. Stated somewhat differently, the original hexachord can generate its own complement through traditional serial processes. If two combinatorial sets are stated simultaneously, therefore, a complete aggregate of all twelve pitches will be available horizontally as well as vertically. Example 7.1 displays one form of Schoenberg's row for the Variations for Orchestra, Op. 31, and beneath it, the row inversion transposed down three semitones. The two forms are combinatorial with regard to each other: a combination of the two hexachords marked *a*, or the two marked *b*, will produce a new collection of all twelve pitch classes.

EXAMPLE 7.1.

Two forms of Schoenberg's combinatorial row for
the variations for Orchestra, Op. 31

Babbitt also standardized the numbering of pitches within a set. Whereas (as noted in Chapter 5) Boulez had numbered the pitches of his row from 1 to 12, in order of their initial appearance, Babbitt numbers pitch classes 0 to 11, in order of their distance—in semitones—from a basic, referential pitch class. This system allows inversions, transpositions and other permutations of the set to be generated by simple mathematics. In Example 7.2, the referential pitch class (0) is F, the first member of the series. To arrive at the inversion, subtract each number from 12; for transportation, add the appropriate number (of semitones) to each number.

One may also represent a set by pairs of numbers. The first number of each pair indicates that pitch class's ordering within the set, while the second number represents the pitch class itself. Thus the series of seven pitch classes, shown in Example 7.2, could be renumbered as seven pairs. In Example 7.3, the referential pitch class—numbered 0— is C. Serial operations could be performed upon each element of the number pairs.

Both Boulez and Babbitt explored ways of "serializing" durations and other nonpitched elements in their ground-breaking post–war compositions, and both are regarded rightly as pioneers in this area. Babbitt's works, however, are much more thorough in establishing a direct relationship between time and pitch. As we observed in his early *Three Compositions for Piano* (see Chapter 5), Babbitt has explored ways of serializing duration as well as pitch. But Babbitt's continuing interest in time-

---

EXAMPLE 7.2.

	(F	C	B	A$^{\#}$	C$^{\#}$	E	F$^{\#}$)
P$_0$	0	7	6	5	8	11	1
I$_0$	0	5	6	7	4	1	11
I$_4$	4	9	10	11	8	5	3 (15 minus 12)

The prime and two permutations of a seven-note set

EXAMPLE 7.3.

	(0,5)	(1,0)	(2,11)	(3,10)	(4,1)	(5.4)	(6,6)
P$_0$	F	C	B	A$^{\#}$	C$^{\#}$	E	F$^{\#}$

Representing pitch classes of the set in Ex. 7.2 by pairs of
numbers

---

pitch relationships soon led him in new directions. In the opening clarinet
solo of his 1948 *Composition for Four Instruments* (Example 7.4), the numerical series 1–4–3–2 is used to control not only individual durations (and
consequently the rhythm), but also a changing metrical reference: the
rhythm is first stated with the sixteenth note as the basic unit, then with the
quarter note (four sixteenths, then the dotted eighth (three sixteenths), and
finally the eighth note (two sixteenths).

In Babbitt's 1954 *Composition for Twelve Instruments*, a set of twelve
durations is derived from a transposition of the work's basic twelve-pitch
set. Example 7.5a shows this set; the second number in the parenthetical
pair above each pitch, originally meant to represent pitch class, determines
relative duration. In Example 7.5b the sixteenth note is the fundamental
unit. During the course of the *Composition for Twelve Instruments* this durational set is manipulated by means of the numerical operations described
here in "A Brief Look at the Twelve-Tone Set." The importance Babbitt
attaches to the rhythmic domain is confirmed by the surface gestures of the
work: not only the gradual accretion of textural levels from isolated events
to chordal masses, but also a corresponding linking of fragmented duration
patterns, which eventually create (at the end of each of its three movements) a complete rhythmic set.

In his later writings and compositions, Babbitt has offered another
method for unifying durational and pitch structure: the representation of a
numerical series as *time points* within a bar. The measure, when subdivided

EXAMPLE 7.4.

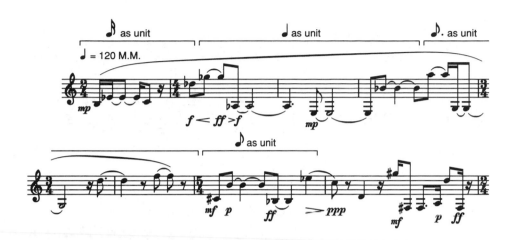

Milton Babbitt: *Composition for Four Instruments*

© 1949 Merion Music, Inc.
Used by permission

into twelve units (for example, sixteenth notes in $\frac{3}{4}$ meter) acts as a temporal analogue to the octave. The same set of integers therefore denotes pitch placement within the octave and attack placement within the bar. (See Example 7.6 for a simple illustration.) Furthermore, one can apply the standard numerical operations on this set of integers to create permutations. The result is not only a controlled vocabulary of durations but a way of generating surprising, offbeat accents against a steady pulse. In contrast to the "atomic," explosive sound world of Boulez, then, Babbitt's music often conveys a strong sense of traditional meter and rhythm with unusual syncopations, perhaps reminiscent of a swinging jazz beat—not surprising, given Babbitt's love of American popular music. (His catalog includes music for an off-Broadway musical and a serial work for jazz ensemble with the punning title *All Set*.)

Like Schoenberg before him, Babbitt has felt his musical language to be a logical outgrowth of the great tradition of Western art music, a tradition that places high priority on the careful calibration of materials, the manipulation of these to generate forward motion, and the idea of "development"—varying and extending a limited body of ideas, anticipating and encouraging relationships that gradually unfold in time. Also rooted in tradition, specifically in post–Beethoven Germanic music, is Babbitt's belief that great works are difficult, revealing their secrets only after careful study,

EXAMPLE 7.5.

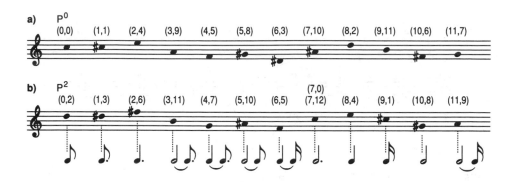

Prime set and derived rhythmic series for Babbitt's
Composition for Twelve Instruments

EXAMPLE 7.6.

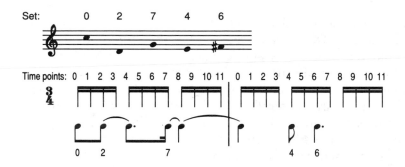

Time points derived from a five-note set

and that those secrets have more to do with structure than with the sounds of any single performance. To this tenet, he has added a uniquely twentieth-century American conviction equating the work of the serious composer with that of the research scientist or university scholar.

Nowhere has this philosophy been expressed more succinctly than in an outspoken article called "The Composer as Specialist" (also published under the more provocative title "Who Cares If You Listen?"). In this 1958 essay Babbitt championed the right of artists working at the cutting edge to pursue their "research" regardless of popular taste or comprehension, and the obligation of society to treat artistic innovation with the same respect accorded scientific advances. Measuring artistic achievement by "success" in the concert hall was not a fair index, wrote Babbitt, since the Western art music establishment—in his terms, the "right wing of the entertainment industry"—is resistant to experimental, serious thinking. In his view, performing a complex serial composition at Lincoln Center would be akin to having a professor of philosophy or physics read a learned paper on a late-night TV talk show. In either case, members of the audience would turn to one another and murmur, quite appropriately, "I don't understand it." Babbitt has suggested that performances of difficult new music at general concerts for the lay public are inevitably underrehearsed, inaccurate, and misunderstood; they are a disservice to all concerned. He suggests, rather, that recorded studio performances of his music, carefully edited, be distributed (together with copies of the score) to universities and research libraries.

Milton Babbitt has been a seminal figure on the American musical scene. By the nature of his professorship at Princeton and codirectorship of the Columbia-Princeton Electronic Music Center (see Chapter 8), he has come into contact with many student composers and has played an important role in developing wider acceptance of serial music within the academic community. For some of the younger composers, Babbitt's technique and methodology have been most influential; for others, however, including many who choose to compose in altogether different styles, he has served as an admirable model of intellectual discipline and academic integrity.

Other Composers Concerned with Serial Order

A list of younger American composers strongly influenced by Babbitt would include Charles Wuorinen, Donald Martino, and Mario Davidovsky. Each of these has developed a strong personal profile; each has won the Pulitzer Prize in composition. (Davidovsky is discussed in Chapter 12.) Charles Wuorinen (b. 1938) has extended Babbitt's time point technique to areas of large-scale structure: the relative durations of broad sections form proportions analogous to the intervals of a pitch set. As with a tone row or a time point series on the microrhythmic level, a series of durations on the macrorhythmic level can be manipulated by the standard numerical operations. A typical use of macrorhythmic time points to generate the proportions of measure groups is given in Example 7.7, which uses the number series of Example 7.6. Within the macrorhythm of twenty-four (two times twelve) measures, each measure is analogous to a sixteenth note in the two

EXAMPLE 7.7.

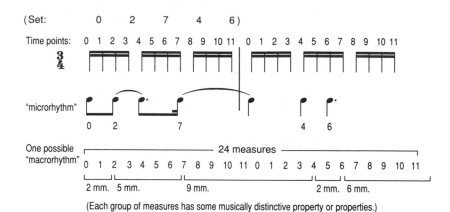

(Each group of measures has some musically distinctive property or properties.)

Microrhythm and macrorhythm derived from the
same set

measures of $\frac{3}{4}$ time; in an actual composition, each group of measures would have some musically distinctive property or properties.

Wuorinen likens this nesting process (where different structural/durational levels mirror each other) to the Schenkerian notion of tonality. The small-scale rhythmic reflection of the tone row occupies the role of foreground (surface level) of a tonal composition, while the larger proportions assume roles of middle ground and background (*Ursatz*). As if to emphasize the Schenkerian analogy, he employs greater spontaneity on the surface level, injecting melodic and rhythmic embellishments not tied to the row, while adhering to its structure more simply on larger levels.

Donald Martino (b. 1931) was a graduate student of Babbitt's at Princeton and, like Babbitt, had grown up with a strong interest in jazz. He is a skilled clarinetist, and a passion for idiomatic, often virtuosic and bravura instrumental writing pervades much of his work. His concern for unique instrumental persona, both melodic and timbral, lends an intensely dramatic quality to the rhetoric of his solo lines; even in the music for larger ensembles, the sense of solo "soliloquy" is never long absent. Martino's own description of Notturno, his chamber sextet that won the 1974 Pulitzer Prize, is that of "twenty people talking about the same thing, each from a new viewpoint. . . . ."

Martino's interest in serial technique began in the late 1950s. He credits twelve-tone studies with having "opened up so many possibilities," and notes that serial technique has been especially useful "as a means of defining your world, of helping to organize that world." Far from lessening

ILLUS. 7.1.

Donald Martino

Courtesy BMI Archives

his fascination with mercurial, extroverted, ultraromantic gesture, serial ordering has led Martino to correlate many details of performance, including extended instrumental technique, phrasing, and articulation, with large-scale formal design and pitch structure.

Other composers who became known in the 1950s had strong ties to Schoenbergian principles, but were not linked directly to either Babbitt or Princeton. Two of the most prominent were Stefan Wolpe (1902–72) and George Perle (b. 1915). Wolpe was a rising young figure of the German avant-garde, but as a Jew and an outspoken socialist, he left Germany upon the Nazi accession to power in 1933. He eventually settled in New York in 1938, where he exerted considerable influence as a teacher; Morton Feldman (1926–87), David Tudor (b. 1926), and Ralph Shapey (b. 1921) were among his students. Perle, American by birth, became interested in the

Second Viennese School during the 1930s and has written extensively on the music of Alban Berg. Both Perle and Wolpe have been concerned about the seemingly static quality of much serial music; in their own compositions they have attempted to reconcile the systematic control of atonal material with the hierarchical levels and distinctions of tonal music. To this end they have created concepts analogous to consonance, dissonance, and key centers. They, too, have used pitch rows to generate the proportions and large-scale formal design of compositions.

"CHAOS"

John Cage

The term *chaos*, though less accurate in many ways than its opposite, *order*, has been applied as a pejorative by many listeners to the seemingly anarchic compositions of John Cage. The composer himself, though, was known to use the term with positive associations, as in his statement: "Here we are. Let us say Yes to our presence together in Chaos." Cage has also written:

> our intention is to affirm this life, not to bring order out of chaos or to suggest improvements in creation, but simply to wake up to the very life we're living, which is so excellent once one gets one's mind and one's desires out of the way and lets it act of its own accord. (*Silence*, p. 12)

Throughout his career, Cage chose to undertake a thorough re-examination of the raw materials of music: sound, silence, and performance ritual. In contrast to the serialists, who consider themselves heirs to the great Western art music tradition, Cage preferred to explore alternative but equally venerable musical traditions, in particular those of the non-Western world, and earlier twentieth-century American mavericks such as Ives and Cowell.

We have noted his increasing absorption in the use of chance operations, inspired by his serious study of Zen Buddhism. In such early 1950s' works as *Music of Changes* (see Chapter 6) and the *Imaginary Landscape No. 4* for twelve radios, the creative process was dictated by a complex series of chance operations. The aim of allowing compositional decisions to be made by tossing a coin was to remove Cage's will and personality from the operation—in his words, "letting sounds be themselves." But the results were precisely notated and permanently fixed, suggesting faithful, accurate realization by a performer along traditional lines. By the late 1950s Cage had come to believe that such control over performers was virtual enslavement and inconsistent with his philosophy. Motivated by the desire to see performers enjoying the same freedom he had won for himself (and for sounds), he began to extend his idea of *indeterminacy* into the domain of performance.

A critical step in this direction was his 1952 work 4'33", consisting of four minutes and thirty-three seconds of silence, subdivided into three movements and usually performed by a pianist (although the score permits other realizations as well). Although many may simply dismiss 4'33" as a notorious example of nonmusic, it deserves our serious attention, and for three reasons. First of all, it presents us with nonintentionality at its most extreme: a situation in which the three activities of composition, performance, and listening are equally chance-derived. Second, by his focus on duration rather than sound Cage suggests that music can be redefined as a *time art*, a structured vehicle for articulating the passage of time. Third, the piece forces us to acknowledge that there is really no such phenomenon as "silence." There are simply those sounds that are intended and those that are unintended. A performance of 4'33" provides a frame within which unplanned, accidentally produced environmental sounds—a cough, a ticking of a clock, an airplane overhead, the room's ventilation system—emerge as primary content. Perhaps Cage was alluding to such an experience in his statement that "the music I prefer, even to my own or anyone else's, is what we are hearing if we are just quiet."

His compositions of the later 1950s and beyond have maintained the same unpredictable, iconoclastic quality. (A number of examples are discussed in later chapters.) Many works are intended for performance in a virtually infinite variety of formats. The 1958 *Concert for Piano and Orchestra* consists of parts for piano and thirteen other instruments, any or all (or none) of which may be used for a given playing; in addition, other works of Cage may be freely superimposed upon the *Concert* material(s). Performances frequently involve elements of theater and dance, engaging the eye as well as the ear. The *Water Music* (1952) for piano, radio, blowing whistles, decks of cards, and pouring water is not atypical. Cage often delights in an Ivesian collision of multiple stimuli, reminiscent of a three-ring circus: a situation in which music and environment become one.

Obviously, a vast gulf separates the notated "score" for Cage's music and any specific event resulting from a reading of that score. Furthermore, the written music itself is frequently based on randomly arrived-at sources, such as astronomical charts (the 1970 *Etudes Australes*) or the imperfections on the manuscript paper. While these experiments have endeared Cage to many fellow artists, particularly those engaged in theater, poetry, or dance, they have also provoked great hostility. For the premiere of *Atlas eclipticalis* (in 1964) under Leonard Bernstein and the New York Philharmonic, contact microphones were attached to each instrument and fed to an electronic system for "scrambling," timbral alteration, and loudspeaker placement. But the performance was most memorable for the sight of the audience walking out, virtually en masse, while members of the orchestra hissed and smashed their microphones.

All of these compositions, performances, and violent reactions have been occasioned by an idea that Cage called *indeterminacy*. Simply stated, a musical factor is indeterminate if it is dictated by chance and operates without any links to other factors. As we observed with regard to 4'33", a notated score may be indeterminate—unpredictable and unspecified—with respect to its composition or its performance. Various performances of the same work are similarly indeterminate with respect to one another. In any event, the musical experience is meant to be immediate, spontaneous, and unique: a ritual celebration, not a fixed art object bounded by predetermined relationships or notational straitjackets. (In a much different sense, however, many of Cage's scores might well be regarded as "objects" of visual art. One might find Example 7.8, a portion of an *Atlas eclipticalis* page, stimulating on the level of calligraphy alone.)

Cage's indeterminacy should be distinguished from improvisation, in that the latter is directed to a known end. When musicians improvise in jazz playing or Baroque figured-bass realization, they have a well-defined context or grammar as a constant reference point. Much of the fascination of Cage's indeterminacy lies in its avoidance of such known context. There are no models, precedents, or ideals of "correctness" to guide the players. In essence, the composer has willingly relinquished control over the finished musical "product," the performance we hear, by supplying materials—often ambiguous—for players to assemble as though working with a kit of building blocks.

That act of relinquishing is much more revolutionary than any mere fondness for noise or dissonance. For some critics it may bring into question the composer's sense of responsibility or seriousness of purpose. Cage rejects the very idea of responsibility, since it is predicated on a definition of art as an act of will. As for purpose, he once wrote that he wanted "sounds, not purposes." He has also stated:

> nothing is accomplished by writing a piece of music
> nothing is accomplished by hearing a piece of music
> nothing is accomplished by playing a piece of music
> our ears are now in excellent condition. (*Silence*, p. xii)

A work for narrator and live electronics that both describes and embodies Cage's aesthetic is appropriately entitled *Indeterminacy*. It is divided into a number of sixty-second units, each unit acting as boundary for the narration of an anecdote, superimposed against a limited number of elec-

EXAMPLE 7.8

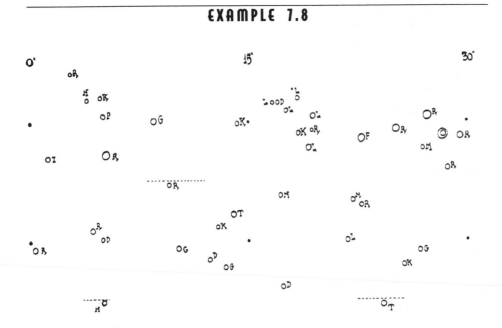

John Cage: *Atlas eclipticalis*

tronic sounds. (Stories with many words are read at an *allegro* tempo, while those with relatively few words necessitate a slower-paced delivery.) On one level, then, *indeterminacy* can be perceived as an extended "duet" for unsynchronized forces, indeterminate of one another. But it is particularly interesting to focus on the anecdotes themselves as they illustrate and exemplify nonintentionality. To paraphrase two briefly: (1) The narrator (Cage) is sitting in an indoor lodge at a winter resort, listening to a jukebox and looking out the window. He watches people outside, skating to the music of the jukebox even though they're not aware of it. (2) The narrator (Cage) looks into a shop window containing a special display. The display is meant to demonstrate a sophisticated machine for automatic writing, but it has malfunctioned and is totally out of control, its paper roll askew and ink spattering in all directions. The activity has become sinister, even "romantic," and infinitely more interesting.

Other Composers Concerned with Chance

Among the composers of the postwar era interested in the use of chance and relative performer freedom is the small group who worked closely with Cage in New York City during the 1950s: Morton Feldman, Earle Brown (b. 1926), Christian Wolff (b. 1934), and David Tudor. Feldman explored a number of notational formats, each devised to control certain areas of musical discourse while leaving others free. For his series of works called *Intersections* (1951–53) he created a graphic notation that dictated texture, overall durational flow, and pitch register (high, medium, or low) while asking his performers to choose specific pitches and rhythms. In his later *Durations* series, however, Feldman attempts a different mix of control and freedom: here all the pitches have been written out, but their coordination and synchronization is intentionally unspecified. A highly complex polyphony of color and line inevitably results, although different in its internal details with every performance. Consistency at another level is maintained by the unchanging dynamic—always very quiet, forcing the ear to focus on subtle relationships and interactions.

Whereas many of the serialists feel a kinship to the methodology of science and mathematics, the composers of the 1950s New York school were inspired by contact with *visual artists*. Cage felt strong affinities to the work of Marcel Duchamp, Jasper Johns, and Robert Rauschenberg, while Feldman knew such figures as Willem de Kooning, Philip Guston, and Mark Rothko. One can perceive similarities between Cage's method and the "action painting" technique of Jackson Pollock, or, perhaps, between Feldman's essays in static equilibrium, the paintings of Mondrian, and the subtle color field experiments of Josef Albers.

Similarly, Earle Brown's ensemble music is inspired in part by the mobile sculptures of Alexander Calder. Two such works have the title *Available Forms,* the first for chamber ensemble, its successor scored for large orchestra divided into two groups, each with its own conductor. One page of *Available Forms II* is shown in Example 7.9. The passages labeled with large numbers are rehearsed individually, and then combined in any order, successive or simultaneous, determined by the conductor(s) during the performance.

The proportional notation of elongated noteheads to represent relative duration (a format in which Brown pioneered) is ideally suited to the work's unsynchronized ensemble textures. In contributing to these textures, musicians are asked to make sensitive, informed musical choices within a stylistically agreed-upon context—closer to personal, romantic gesture than to the value-free, context-free indeterminacy of Cage. The roles of the work's two conductors are even more directly "involved"; during rehearsals, each conductor concentrates on the nuances of ensemble textures and gestures, discussing their possible employment in performance. During the performance itself, each of the two conductors selects events, their succession, and simultaneous juxtaposition, indicating those choices by holding up the fingers of one hand.

Christian Wolff is best known for his works that explore the responses

ILLUS. 7.2.

Alexander Calder, *Red Fossils* (steel and wire mobile). Note the flexible form; although the components are fixed, their relationship is variable. A similar approach can be found in musical works by Brown, Stockhausen, and Boulez

Courtesy Bowdoin College Museum of Art

of players in quasi-improvisatory chamber settings. Each of Wolff's performers works with an array of optional musical gestures, without knowing which ones will be called upon at any moment. Elaborate cues, calling for immediate decisions, are dependent upon the decisions of others. Players must always be prepared to make instantaneous changes of direction in response to unpredictable cues from their partners. As with many Cage and Brown pieces, then, the form of the music is changeable—in this case, the result of close player interaction and cooperation. Wolff himself likens the performance of such chamber works to "taking a walk with friends." In a similar vein, Cage has written of Christian Wolff's *Duo II for Pianists* that the function of each performer is "comparable to that of a traveler who

EXAMPLE 7.9.

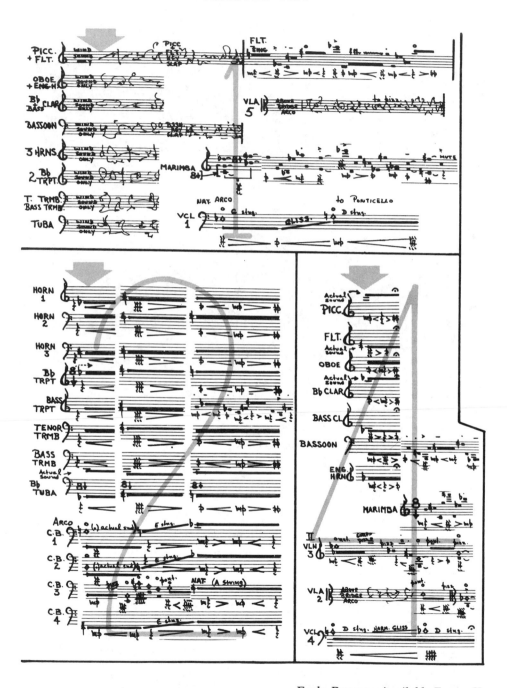

Earle Brown: *Available Forms II*

must constantly be catching trains the departures of which have not been announced but which are in the process of being announced."

INTERMEDIATE POSITIONS BETWEEN "ORDER" AND "CHAOS"

Cage and Babbitt are special figures: dedicated, even isolated, in their roles as teachers and prophets. Each has been unique in his single-minded loyalty to a particular aesthetic and methodology, as committed to his uncompromising principles in the 1990s as he was in the 1950s. Virtually all other composers have found positions somewhere between these two poles. Some, originally grounded in ideas of "order," have moved to positions of greater flexibility, as a reaction to the overspecificity (and the resultant performance difficulties) of strict serialism. Others may savor the explosive potential of juxtaposing one kind of creative impulse against another, the equivalent of a musical balancing act. This may be the same love of "danger" that infuses the act of improvisation (which Lukas Foss has defined as "chance corrected by the will"). Some composers with backgrounds in jazz accept the idea of performers sharing responsibility for the making of a work, and the collective chamber context of jazz (like commedia dell' arte) in which known performer "personalities" become protagonists in spontaneous, unplanned narrative. Still others take a practical, performance-oriented stance in the aesthetic midrange. For example, Henry Brant frequently works with unsynchronized group textures in order to make the antiphonal effects of his spatially separated large ensembles more practicable in performance and more audible to the listener (see Chapter 15).

Witold Lutosławski (b. 1913) and Lukas Foss also deal with issues of improvisation and performer freedom with an eye for the practical, and both share a prewar background in tonal neoclassicism. Their interests are not in Cagean relinquishing of control but rather in realizing complex ensemble textures with relative performer ease. Lutosławski's *Trois poemes d'Henri Michaud* (chorus and orchestra, 1963) offers a succession of busy, intricate textures created by overlays of rapidly moving improvisatory gestures. Similarly, Foss advocates flexible notation as a means of encouraging performer spontaneity. He questions the serialists' "need to notate every minute detail," and suggests that traditional *accelerando, ritardando,* and *rubato* indications are preferable to rigidly notated rhythms. He states:

> . . . a rigid rubato; contradiction in terms. Imagine asking the performer to feel a moment "out of time," as it were, when it is notated slavishly "in time." Similarly, an effect of, say, chaos, must not be

notated in terms of a subtle order. To learn to play the disorderly in orderly fashion is to multiply rehearsal time by one hundred. (Schwartz and Childs, p. 329)

Foss's use of the word *chaos* is revealing here. An especially effective example of Foss's stimulating his players to engage in vivid, occasionally shocking or "chaotic" performance gestures is his *Paradigm,* discussed in Chapter 15.

Pierre Boulez and Karlheinz Stockhausen

After the completion of *Structures 1a,* Boulez began to adopt a style that incorporates degrees of freedom, even chance approaches, within the language of serialism. This change came about after his 1949 meeting with John Cage. Although greatly impressed by Cage, Boulez could not surrender his creative personality to the ideals of total indeterminacy, and coined a new term to describe his own approach: *aleatory music* (from the Latin *alea,* related to games of chance with dice). Significantly, he developed a similarly skeptical view of those composers who work from a position of total control. In his view, such composers feel that if they "apply . . . a certain scientific environment to their music and writings, they achieve security. They think they are safe." By contrast, Boulez stated, "I want that uncertainty. I find it necessary to discover my own way of imagination."

Before embracing aleatory techniques, Boulez had begun to depart from a strictly serial approach in *Le marteau sans maître* (1953–54, revised 1957), a setting of poems by René Char for contralto voice, alto flute, viola, guitar, vibraphone, xylophone, and unpitched percussion. Of the nine movements, only four are vocal (the third, fifth, sixth, and ninth), and in fact only three poems are set (the last movement is a variant or reprise of the fifth movement). Moreover, the instrumentation varies from one movement to next, with the complete complement of players heard only twice.

Parallels to the historical model of Schoenberg's *Pierrot Lunaire* abound: the dreamlike, intense (but obscure) imagery of Char's text, the kaleidoscopic focus upon subgroups within the total instrumentation (and especially the flute-voice duo of the third movement), even the occasional use of *Sprechstimme* vocalization. But one can also perceive, in Boulez's choice of nonpercussive instruments, a uniquely "French" ensemble sonority, totally unlike that of the Schoenberg. There are also distinctly non-Western influences; Boulez has commented on the connections between the xylophone and African music, the vibraphone and Balinese gamelan, the guitar and Japanese koto.

It is virtually impossible to analyze the structure of *Le marteau* from a position of strict integral serialism. Pitch rows and durational correlates have shaped the overall language of the work, but are then bent to meet

Boulez's compositional needs of the moment. He reserves the right to break with the system, use his own judgement, and make creative choices. As he has written about the work, " there is in fact a very clear and very strict element of control, but starting from this strict control . . . there is also room for what I call *local indiscipline* . . . a freedom to choose, to decide and to reject."

An example is the relation between pitch and duration in the sixth movement, "bourreaux de solitude." As the analyst Steven Winick has noted, Boulez establishes a durational series of rising sixteenth-note increments, from a single sixteenth note to a dotted half note (or twelve sixteenths), corresponding to the placement of pitches within a row. But as the row itself undergoes continual transposition, the pitch corresponding to a single sixteenth continually changes. During the course of the first few measures (see Example 7.10), the pitch "base" shifts from its starting point, D, to G$^\#$, A$^\#$, C$^\#$, A, and E. In addition, the durations and rhythms grow distorted and stretched for extended passages. Furthermore, there are numerous pitch repetitions, not generated by the serial processes, perhaps allied to the importance of the word *imitation* in the text. None of this suggests a rejection of serialism. On the contrary, Boulez acknowledges that the technique has generated the work's melodic, chordal, and rhythmic material; it thus provides a basic grammar and syntax with which he could then explore different ideas.

In later works, Boulez channels his interest in heightened flexibility in the direction of large-scale form. The Third Piano Sonata (1957) is conceived as an open-form "mobile" of five movements, with eight different ways of ordering these in performance. Only two of the movements, entitled "Trope" and "Constellation-miroir," have been published; each of these, in turn, contains mobile subsections to be realized in a variety of orderings. For example, "Trope" consists of a "text," which in turn serves as the subject of a "commentary," "parenthesis," and "gloss," the successions of which are aleatory. (A similar concept underlies the ordering of *Le marteau sans maître*, movement 1 acting as prelude to movement 3, and movements 2, 4, and 8 as commentaries on movement 6. In that case, however, the order is fixed.) In "Constellation-miroir," episodic sections offer possibilities for combination, forming pathways to and from fixed points, much like a road map with alternate routes.

The Third Piano Sonata raises three additional points: (1) Although a modicum of free choice exists for the performer, it concerns only large-scale form. The details of the work are strictly determined and carefully notated. (2) That only two of the sonata's five movements exist in a finished state is itself revealing. Other Boulez works are similarly open-ended and perpetually "in progress"; the composer feels a certain reluctance in bringing a work to closure, either in its composition or in its realization. (3) The notation of opening up formal boundaries by adding "routes" and-

EXAMPLE 7.10.

VI

«bourreaux de solitude»

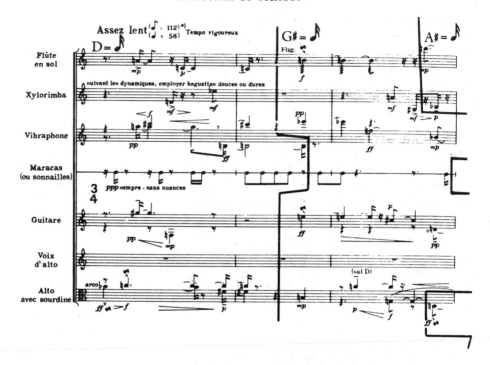

Pierre Boulez: *Le marteau sans maître*, sixth movement, with additional segmental markings by Steven Winick

"commentaries" seems characteristically European and can be directly related to the poetry of Stéphane Mallarmé and the novels of James Joyce. Whereas Cage, Feldman, and other American composers are inclined to relate their use of chance to developments in the *visual* arts, Europeans such as Boulez and Stockhausen have apparently been motivated more by *literary* concepts.

Almost from the very beginning, Karlheinz Stockhausen's approach to serialism has been tempered by the use of dimensions outside the controlled "system." (As we have already seen in his early *Kreuzspiel*, timbre is treated as an independent variable, not subject to the work's serial organization.) By the late 1950s Stockhausen, like Boulez, had begun to combine the precisely articulated sound world of serialism with greater emphasis on open form and performer choice. His *Klavierstücke XI* for piano (1956) consists of nineteen extended passages, unconnected and visually scattered about a very large single sheet. A section of the score is shown in Example 7.11.

Passages are highly specific as to pitch and duration, but completely-open with respect to articulation, tempo, and dynamics. A group of instructions for these open elements is given at the conclusion of each passage; the pianist is asked to apply these to whichever passage his or her eyes randomly light upon next. Not only will the ordering be variable, but a given passage played twice will probably have widely differing surface characteristics. A performance of *Klavierstücke XI* is considered complete when a single passage has been heard three times.

EXAMPLE 7.11.

Karlheinz Stockhausen: *Klavierstücke XI*

Chance plays a more important role here than in the Boulez sonata, where performer choices are always conscious, deliberate, and routed through fixed channels. *Klavierstücke XI* is, in fact, closer to Earle Brown's *Available Forms* series in its unusual merger of detailed pitch notation with unpredictable, spontaneous articulation and dramatic gesture. Stockhausen carried this paradoxical merger further in two works of 1959. To perform *Refrain* for keyboards and percussion, a transparent plastic strip containing musical material is placed over the score, in a different position for each performance. By this means the relatively contemplative surface of the piece is disturbed by a series of flurries, clusters, and trills at unpredictable moments. *Zyklus* is composed for solo percussionist, surrounded by a literal circle of instruments. The circle is not only physical but musical as well. The percussionist plays from a spiral-bound score that can be placed either upside down or right side up on the music stand and, beginning at any page, read through in either direction until the sequence returns to the starting point.

SIMILARITIES BETWEEN THE PHILOSOPHIES OF "CHAOS" AND "ORDER"

The seemingly opposed musical philosophies of serialism and indeterminacy, which polarized a generation of composers in the 1950s and '60s, reveal a surprising number of common ties. Here are a few:

The Influence of the Second Viennese School

That Babbitt and Boulez should consider their work a direct continuation of the Schoenberg-Webern lineage is obvious. But ironically, Cage, profoundly influenced by his studies with Arnold Schoenberg, also has ties to that tradition. According to Cage, it was his teacher's "emancipation of the dissonance," with its rejection of hierarchies and insistence on the equality of musical building blocks, that led the younger figure to consider a similar "emancipation" of his own, one that would free noise from pitch and

ILLUS. 7.3.

Percussionist Steven Schick, surrounded by a circle
of instruments, in a performance of Stockhausen's
Zyklus

Photo: Grace Bell

sound from silence. One can also hear reminders of Webern's pointillistic
textures, already a feature of Cage's earlier work for percussion ensemble
and prepared piano, in the work of Brown and Feldman.

Interestingly, Pierre Boulez was among the first to notice that the prepared piano, by loosening the relationship among the individual notes of
the keyboard, is a heterogenous timbral collection rather than a traditional
"instrument."

The Influence of the Loudspeaker Revolution

It is no coincidence that both philosophies came to prominence in the early 1950s, after the invention and dissemination of the long-playing record and magnetic tape recording and playback facilities. The fine-tuned measurements, materials, syntax, and complex relationships of serial music require—in fact, virtually demand—many repeated hearings at the highest level of attention. Since composers of serial music believe that its essence resides in such relationships, the visual stimulus of "live" performance is not necessarily a benefit. On the contrary, live performance is problematic, since it will inevitably be flawed by errors. Because inaccurate notes, rhythms, or dynamic levels throw an entire network of relationships into disarray, serialist composers might well prefer to have their music exist in the form of spliced and edited recordings.

Paradoxically, the phenomenon of recording may have inspired a very different response among composers more concerned with spontaneity, improvisation, and the ritual and visual aspects of performance. Those composers, with John Cage in the vanguard, have frequently created music that stresses experiental aspects other than sheer sound and that effectively resists recording.

Distance from the Mass Audience

Figures such as Babbitt or Cage are not creating music to please the typical music lover. On the contrary, both have frequently outraged, even scandalized, the musical establishment. This seems only appropriate for figures who take on the role of "prophet" (or have that role thrust upon them). As the political analyst Garry Wills has noted in an entirely different context, "prophets are a scandal in democracies. They are not 'representative.' They cannot be controlled or called off by their 'constituents,' because no constituency sent them. They create their audience, and compel it. They do not follow or submit to it."

The highly personal view of artistic creation shared by Babbitt and Cage, which some might term "elitist," is a fairly recent by-product of Western high culture. If asked to think of other musical "prophets," we would probably name Beethoven, Wagner, Schoenberg, but certainly no one who lived before the nineteenth century. In fact, the notion of the lonely, misunderstood artistic genius is a creation of the romantic era, using Beethoven as the prototype.

It may seem that such composers are no longer concerned with communication, either within a traditional Western "expressive" language or in the larger social, ritual sense. But both Babbitt and Cage deny that. Babbitt would simply remind us that any kind of communication requires a "suitably equipped receptor." To the degree that we refine our listening apparatus, we discover that he has much to say. And much of Cage's work is ceremonial and ritual at heart. He has stated that one prime function of music is "to celebrate," and the need to engage the attention of a large public, whether by shocking it or by other means, is most important to him.

Challenges for the Performer

Much of Webern's music, although admittedly difficult to realize in performance, does not spotlight individual players in an extroverted manner, or suggest that the limits of performability are being taxed. (His Piano Variations, studied earlier, may be considered an exception.) By contrast, Boulez's and Stockhausen's scores contain innumerable passages of virtuosic brilliance. The pages of *Le marteau sans maître* or *Klavierstücke XI* are filled with angular leaps, rapid figurations, sudden dynamic contrasts, and jagged contours. Similarly, the demands of Cage's *Water Music* or the ensemble gestures of Brown's *Available Forms* call for flamboyant, daring performances. Pieces by Brown and Feldman, and certainly the more elaborate indeterminate works of Cage or the graphic scores of Christian Wolff, ask performers to go beyond technical virtuosity; in such works the players often collaborate with the composer in "creating" the surface of a given realization. Their choices, both large-scale or small, made before the fact or spontaneously in real-time performance situations, may be crucial to the unfolding of a work.

Proponents of extreme "order" may have a very different view of performance, of course. While Cage's work celebrates the very act of performance, Milton Babbitt has stated that performers are simply executants, occupying the same role with respect to music that printers have to literature. But what phenomenal executants they can be! Anyone who hears top-flight soloists and chamber ensembles projecting the quirky, impetuous rhythmic and dynamic shifts of Babbitt's music is in the presence of unparalleled virtuosity. That factor is equally important for Babbitt's electronic music composed for (and on) the RCA synthesizer (see Chapter 8), in which both the machine and the composer demonstrate virtuoso skills.

PROCESS AND TEXTURE

Two remaining points of comparison between "order" and "chaos" are so important that we must discuss them separately. Significantly, these are two of the nine factors so critical to our study of recent music: **process** and **texture.**

The post–1945 philosophies of musical "chaos" and "order" are both deeply concerned with compositional **process.** For Cage, Babbitt, Stockhausen, Brown, and a host of other composers, musical creation involves the realization of a precompositional scheme: a matrix of twelve pitch classes and forty-eight forms, a durational series derived from a pitch set, a map of the heavens superimposed on manuscript paper, the *I Ching,* or (as in *Klavierstücke XI*) a performance regulation that controls the outcome of a highly mobile form. In each instance the act of composing is one of problem solving. This concern points up again the inadequacy of the term *chaos,* to describe indeterminate music. Many chance-derived works are just as disciplined in their own way as "orderly" serial compositions. The controls are applied, however, to different aspects of the musical experience—constraints and guidelines for the creative act, or for performance, rather than for details of pitch, rhythm, or other quantifiable components of musical grammar. Moreover, many aleatoric works of Stockhausen and Boulez, created to break free of rigid systems, succeed by substituting *other* systems. In Morton Feldman's words, "What music 'rhapsodizes' in today's 'cool' language is its own construction. In the music of both [Boulez and Cage], things are exactly what they are—no more, no less. . . . what is heard is indistinguishable from its process. In fact, process itself might be called the Zeitgeist of our age."

Musical **texture** will be discussed separately in Chapter 10. For the present, though, we might note that, as with process, the philosophies of "order" and "chaos" share surprisingly similar texture traits. Two extremely different textures seem to predominate. One focuses on isolated pitches and rapidly shifting timbres, strongly influenced by the pointillistic model of Webern: the sound world of both Babbitt's *Composition for Twelve Players* and Feldman's *Durations.* The opposite texture, as heard in Brown's *Available Forms,* the *Venetian Games* of Lutosawski, and Stockhausen's *Refrain,* is a relatively dense wall of shifting, diffuse sonority, the equivalent of keyboard clusters scored for an ensemble. For listeners more attuned to traditional concert or popular music, either texture may seem puzzling or even irrational. Webern himself, after hearing a rather underrehearsed performance of his music, is said to have commented, "A high note, a low note, a note in the middle—like the music of a madman." Whatever "madness" one hears in the texture of serial music, it is equally appropriate to indeterminate or aleatoric compositions.

The Electronic Revolution I: Tape Composition and Early Synthesizers

The ongoing quest for new sounds and new ways to organize them has demanded resources that reach beyond the limits of acoustic instruments and voices. Modern technology has provided such resources in the form of tape machines, mixers, microphones, analog and digital synthesizers, and the computer. More than any other development since the turn of the century, electronics have expanded the techniques and materials available to composers, revolutionizing their approach to the basic factors we have stressed, especially **pitch logic, time, texture,** and **sound color.**

PRECEDENTS

The postwar years affirmed the remarkable prophecies of Ferruccio Busoni, whose famous "Sketch of a New Esthetic of Music" (1907) predicted the widespread use of electronic musical machinery half a century in advance.

But the vision of a sonic art inspired by technology and reaching far beyond human limitation is centuries old. As early as 1624 Francis Bacon's *New Atlantis* imagined a music of "quarter-sounds," "rings," "warblings," and "artificial echoes," of voices made "shriller," "deeper," or "louder" by artificial means, and of sounds conveyed over distances through "trunks and pipes"—a startlingly accurate foretelling of such phenomena as microtones, reverberation, filtering, amplification, and electrical sound transmission. Such possibilities were expressed many times in the three centuries that followed, and occasionally actual mechanical devices were constructed, although their purpose was usually to imitate familiar instrumental sounds rather than to suggest new ones. Some of these were powered by electricity, others by springs, weights, or pneumatic pressure; among them were Abbé Delaborde's electric harpsichord of 1761, perhaps the earliest musical device to use electricity, and Johannes Maelzel's panharmonicon, a mechanical orchestra for which Beethoven wrote his *Wellington's Victory* in 1813.

By the late nineteenth century the link between electricity and sound was firmly established with the development of the telephone and phonograph. Those inventions were designed to transmit, store, or reproduce sound; the actual generation of sound, at least for musical purposes, began in 1906 with the Telharmonium (also called the Dynamophone) of Dr. Thaddeus Cahill. A gigantic keyboard instrument weighing over two hundred tons and capable of a diverse array of electronically controlled timbres, this was probably the first device that could be called a synthesizer. It was designed to transmit live performances of traditional repertoire over telephone lines, to be monitored by listeners even hundreds of miles distant from the live performer. It was news of the Telharmonium that inspired Busoni's predictions.

A number of more practically sized instruments appeared in the following decades, including the Theremin in 1919, on which a sliding pitch continuum was controlled by moving one's hand toward or away from a rodlike antenna; an "automatic musical instrument" invented by E. Coulpeus and J. Givelet in 1929 that used perforated paper rolls to control four oscillators; and many others with names such as Vivatone (1932), Novachord (1938), and Clavioline (1947). Two electronic instruments developed in the late twenties, the Trautonium and the Ondes Martenot, were used by established composers, the former by Richard Strauss and Paul Hindemith, the latter by Honegger, Milhaud, Varèse, and Messiaen. The best-known work to call for an Ondes Martenot is Messiaen's *Turangalîla-Symphonie* of 1948.

Optical soundtracks on film also provided an early outlet for electrical sound synthesis. In the midthirties, for example, the German engineer Oskar Fischinger began drawing wave forms and other shapes on optical tracks to produce unique timbres; ten years later the Whitney brothers,

John and James, photographed moving objects to create wave shapes on optical film, resulting in unusual sound effects.

While the above devices concern the electronic synthesis of sound, other pre–1945 activities focused on the electronic manipulation of sounds already extant. In the 1930s, for example, Ernst Toch and Paul Hindemith both experimented with distortion and collage using phonograph recordings and variable-speed turntables. In John Cage's *Imaginary Landscape No. 1*, discussed in Chapter 2, turntable speed was varied to manipulate laboratory test signals, and the results were mixed with instrumental sounds for live radio broadcast.

MUSIC AND NOISE: EXPANDING PHILOSOPHIES

Although technology has become crucial in opening up new realms of sound, the electronic idiom would never have evolved without a revolution of attitude about what sounds are admissible as "musical." The earliest, most vociferous revolutionaries were a group of Italian artists and writers known as the "futurists," especially Filippo Marinetti, Francesco Pratella, and Luigi Russolo. Although only Pratella was a musician, all three wrote manifestos between 1909 and 1913 insisting that all imaginable sounds, whether human, animal, or artificial, should be the true musician's resource. Traditional instruments and musical practices were regarded as elitist, cowardly, and divorced from real life. (A few years later a comparable trend, Dadaism, emerged in the visual arts.) Russolo's 1913 manifesto, "The Art of Noises," proposed a series of new instruments such as "rumblers," "thunderers," "crushers," "whistlers," "gurglers," and "screamers"; he organized a series of concerts featuring ensembles of such instruments.

That any sound, real or imagined, might be shaped into a musical experience proved an irresistible concept to some composers. One was George Antheil, who gained international notoriety for his *Ballet mécanique* (1923); the American premiere in 1927 called for a pianola, sixteen pianos, eight xylophones, electric doorbells, anvils, buzz saws, automobile horns, and an airplane propeller. Another was Edward Varèse, whose *Ionisation* (1933) for thirteen percussionists incorporated an unprecedented variety of hitherto less common instruments, most of them unpitched (e.g., sleighbells, sirens, anvils, giuros, temple blocks, whip). The radical idea of an entire work for such instruments epitomized Varèse's approach to sound as raw, physical material to be sculpted into abstract but dynamically interacting shapes and masses. Although the noise element in Varèse's music might remind one of Russolo, his interest in subjecting "blocks," "planes," and "beams" of sound to his artistic will, including sounds not yet heard or imagined, was inimical to the futurists' anti-intellectual, antibourgeois emphasis on the sounds of everyday life.

John Cage eventually formulated an ethos similar to but more persuasive and influential than the futurists' creed, and by the late 1930s he was asserting that music must expand to incorporate noise and all other "nonmusical" sounds. Cage predicted before the war that electronic instruments would be fundamental in composing with extramusical sound. Like Varèse, however, he first explored this frontier through the use of percussion, including such "instruments" as thunder sheets, automobile brake drums, and tin cans.

The earliest beginnings of electronic music, then, were rooted in two separate approaches: the emancipation of real-life acoustic sounds through electronic manipulation, and the creation of entirely new sounds by electronic means. Both eventually flowed into full-scale, competing movements, but found themselves linked by common dependence on a single electrical device—the magnetic tape recorder.

THE FIRST MAJOR DEVELOPMENTS

The combination of fidelity, durability, and plasticity provided by magnetic tape was ideally suited to compositional needs, far surpassing the wire recorder and phonograph in the ease and quality with which both acoustic and electronic sounds could be stored, manipulated, and reproduced. The first magnetic tape recorder, the AEG Magnetophone, was manufactured in Germany and publicly demonstrated in 1935. Refinements during the next fifteen years culminated in the commercial availability of tape machines around 1950, offering many composers practical and affordable access to the electronic medium.

The first important developments in electronic music took place independently on two continents, Europe and North America, following separate paths of evolution. In Europe, funding and equipment for experimentation were supplied gratis by national broadcasting facilities, in keeping with a European pattern, still evident today, of large-scale state and corporate sponsorship for new music and art. Given the scope and complexity of such facilities, a division of labor eventually emerged (one still operative in European studios today) between the composer and the technician, the former voicing his musical intentions and the latter manipulating the equipment to realize them. The early to middle 1950s saw a different picture take shape in the United States. Composers had to rely on their own funding strategies, or at best, on the generosity of colleges and universities where they taught, to equip themselves for experimentation. (This is where commercial access to the tape recorder really became invaluable.) In typically American fashion, they also became "do-it-yourselfers," finding whatever space they could for their activities, piecing together whatever devices they or their host institutions could afford, and serving as their own technicians.

In the early 1950s two major centers of activity emerged in Europe, one French and the other German, based in the state-funded broadcast studios of Paris and Cologne respectively. Each became a highly visible focus for its own particular aesthetic and technical approach to electronic music. From the Paris studio came *musique concrète,* which focused on everyday acoustic sounds of the environment, suggesting historical ties to the futurist movement; from Cologne came *elektronische Musik,* which, in its focus on the actual creation of sound by electronic means, recalls the Telharmonium, Trautonium, and other early synthesizers.

Musique Concrète

Musique concrète, the first approach to electronic music composition that yielded a substantial repertoire, began in 1948 with a series of brief études by Pierre Schaeffer (b. 1910), a broadcast engineer working in Paris at the studios of the Radiodiffusion-Télévision Française (RTF). Working initially with phonograph discs, Schaeffer used recordings of machines, running water, thunder, footsteps, breathing, and other environmental sources. (His first essay featured the noises of a steam locomotive.) Sounds were assembled in collages, isolated in continuous loops, subjected to changes in speed and playback direction, and otherwise altered much as Hindemith and Toch had done in the 1930s. Schaeffer, however, broke new ground by carefully structuring the sequence of events and recording the result. He thereby created a permanent artifact that, like a musical score, could be "performed" (in this case, played back) repeatedly and listened to critically. In October 1948 Schaeffer broadcast a "Concert of Noises" over French radio, featuring five studies in this genre. He termed his music *concrète* because it was fashioned from the real, or concrete, sounds of the external world and because the method of composition was also concrete, molding sound materials directly into a finished work without the intermediate steps of music notation and live performance.

In 1949 Schaeffer was joined in the RTF studios by composer Pierre Henri (b. 1927). The following year they presented the first public concert of electronic music in Paris, and by 1951 they had formed the Group for Research on Musique Concrète, establishing the first real electronic music studio intended solely for compositional use. Other noted figures who worked in this facility include Pierre Boulez, Luc Ferrari, Olivier Messiaen, and Karlheinz Stockhausen. Henri and Schaeffer collaborated on a number of compositions that became classics of their type, including *Symphonie pour un homme seul* (1950) and the opera *Orpheus*, which stunned and outraged the public at its 1953 premiere in Donaueschingen, West Germany.

Out of their association emerged tape techniques that became standard for decades to follow: montage (superimposing two or more sounds), reverse playback, variable-speed playback (which changed the pitch level of recorded material), continuous sound loops, and intercutting (splicing together unrelated or reordered fragments of sound). These were all subject to changes in dynamics, and in later years, to other electronic transformations such as reverberation, filtering (attenuating selected frequencies to change the timbre of a sound), and tape delay (creating a feedback loop between playback and record heads so that a sound echoes or overlaps with itself). Two of Henri's later and oft-cited works in the *concrète* genre include *Le voyage* and *Variations for a Door and a Sigh*, both of 1963.

Perhaps the most striking aspect of this music is its ability to mine a startling wealth of material from limited sources. When the beginning, middle, and end of a familiar sound are recorded, or when a fragment of it is isolated and repeated continuously (possibly with changes in playback speed and direction), a whole new body of sounds emerge, many bearing little resemblance to the original. *Variations for a Door and a Sigh*, for instance, is fashioned from only three constituents: the creaking and closing of a door, breathing sounds, and a musical saw; from these, however, Henri generates a diverse series of no less than twenty-five variations.

One other sound-processing mechanism made possible by magnetic tape, subtler than the others but none the less vital, is spatial location. After 1950 one could obtain both stereophonic (two-channel) and quadraphonic (four-channel) tape machines; these allowed recording and playback on two or four separate but simultaneous channels, permitting sounds to alternate between speaker locations or move gradually through space. Most of the post–1950 compositions mentioned in this chapter are at least stereophonic and explore spatial location to some degree. Some composers, however, have pursued this to an extreme. The most formidable instance from the 1950s is Edgard Varèse's *Poème électronique* (more thoroughly discussed in Chapter 9), in which a variety of electronic and *concrète* sounds were routed to over four hundred speakers, causing sounds to soar across vast spaces.

elektronische Musik

In 1951 *elektronische Musik* had its genesis in the studios of the Nordwest-deutscher Rundfunk (Northwest German Radio), or NWDR, in Cologne. Composer Herbert Eimert (1897–1972) and physicist Werner Meyer-Eppler joined forces with Robert Beyer of the NWDR to form the Cologne studio. Although their work involved tape techniques similar to those used by Schaeffer and Henri, it applied them exclusively to sounds of electronic origin. The primary source for these sounds were sine wave generators, or *oscillators*, and there was much exploration of a process known as *additive synthesis*, whereby sine waves of different frequencies are combined to generate a pitch with particular overtones, and thus a particular timbre. (A pure sine wave itself, or rather the tone it produces through a loudspeaker, has no overtones.) The Cologne studio also had noise generators (capable of producing a thick band of frequencies within a given range), ring modulators, filters, and reverberators. The ring modulators allowed one tone to modulate the amplitude of another, producing complex *sidebands* (sum and difference tones), and the resulting sonority could then be filtered to control timbres.

Eimert allied these procedures with serial composition, which he considered the only meaningful pursuit for creators of new music. He saw *elektronische Musik* as pure, "authentic" composition (his term), because it entailed actually building the sounds themselves from scratch, as distinct from *musique concrète,* where sounds were recorded from the environment. This Cologne approach was deemed all the more superior because it appeared to promise complete control of pitch, rhythm, timbre, and other elements from the very point of sound formation on. (With recorded material, much of this was dictated by the sound source.) Such control was regarded as the ultimate solution to the complexities of writing and performing serial music. Eimert's public forum for these views was the periodical *Die Reihe* (or "The Row," referring, of course, to the twelve-tone row), which he founded in 1955.

Naturally, the RTF studio in Paris seemed antithetical to serialist composers like Boulez and Stockhausen, who soon turned away from it. The Cologne studio, on the other hand, became an emblem of post-Webern serialism in Europe. Stockhausen became the studio's artistic director in 1953. Other renowned figures who worked there include Karel Goeyvaerts, Gottfried Michael Koenig, and Henri Pousseur.

Stockhausen's first significant electronic work, *Studie II* (1954), epitomizes the theoretical stance prevailing at the NWDR during this period. Example 8.1 shows a page from the score with which Stockhausen documented the content of this work. (*Studie II* was, in fact, the first electronic

EXAMPLE 8.1.

Karlheinz Stockhausen: *Studie II*. © Copyright 1956 by Universal Edition (London) Ltd., London. © Copyright Renewed. All Rights Reserved. Used by permission of European American Music Distributors Corporation, sole U.S. and Canadian agent for Universal Edition London

composition to be formally notated.) The score suggests the precision with which every element was controlled. The pitch range of sonic events is shown overhead, with shading to indicate overlapping of sounds; the exact timing of events appears on a horizontal scale in the middle; and a corresponding loudness contour for each event is shown in decibels below. The score only hints at the precompositional rigor underlying the sonorities and their combinations. Every aspect of the work, from sounds to structural proportions, is based on calculations using the number five and its square root. Stockhausen applies these in such a way that frequency and pitch relationships diverge completely from the harmonic series and the equal-tempered scale, yielding timbres, intervals, and "chords" utterly foreign to traditional expectations.

Combining Resources

Activities at the Paris and Cologne studios became well known throughout Europe, partly through exposure at the major German new-music festivals in Donaueschingen and Darmstadt. Within a few short years other important studios were established in which both electronic and *concrète* approaches were freely accommodated, sometimes within a single composition. One such facility was the Studio di Fonologia Musicale at the Radio Audizione Italiane (RAI) broadcast station in Milan, founded in 1955 by Luciano Berio (b. 1925) and Bruno Maderna (1920–73). Other important figures who worked there during the next decade include Luigi Nuno (1924–90), Henri Pousseur, and John Cage.

The more open attitude at the Milan studio, where method and style were considered matters of personal preference rather than ideology, is apparent from three significant and contrasting works created there: Pousseur's *Scambi* (1957), Berio's *Thema: Omaggio a Joyce* (1958), and Cage's *Fontana Mix* (1958).

Pousseur (b. 1929) created *Scambi* from a single electronically generated source: white noise, containing all audible frequencies at the same amplitude or loudness. He divided the noise spectrum into select frequency bands, meticulously filtered and combined in a variety of ways. These were recorded onto tape loops, whose playback was further transformed through changes in sequence, tape speed, and reverberation. All this was carefully contrived to produce an entirely fresh, completely abstract musical experience. The aim was to avoid any familiar points of reference, using sounds that bear no likeness to any known acoustic phenomena (e.g., musical instruments, voices, environmental noise), organized to avoid any periodicity or pitch focus suggestive of music in its usual sense.

By contrast, familiarity plays a crucial role in Berio's *Omaggio a Joyce*, which depends for its stunning effect on the tension between a known element, the human voice, and the astonishing transformations it undergoes. This work, too, has a limited sound source, the voice of Cathy Berberian reading from the eleventh chapter of James Joyce's *Ulysses*. Berio subjected her words to the entire gamut of tape manipulations (montage intercutting, speed and direction change, looping, tape delay), employing them in remarkable ways. Montage, for example, was used to superimpose the same sounds many times, so that they seem to be uttered by a roomful of identical voices. In a unique use of intercutting, fragments of the word *blooming* were spliced together repeatedly, beginning with *bl* and then lengthening to *bloo*, eventually culminating in repetitions of the entire word. In other places, Berio exploited the onomatopoetic and alliterative properties of the text, especially the consonant *s*; the word *hiss,* for example, appears in many guises, isolated, repeated, and prolonged.

The most noteworthy aspect of the piece is not the startling constellation of sonic affects but rather the new dimension electronic technology brings to the marriage of music and text. For Berio it meant not simply putting words to music, but rather finding music in the words and bringing it to the fore. In this regard, the choice of *Ulysses* as a source is especially apt; Berio has transformed Joyce's words in a way comparable to Joyce's own manipulation of everyday language.

The Milan studio, which produced the all-electronic and all-*concrète* works just mentioned, was also the staging ground for Cage's *Fontana Mix,* a work discussed at greater length in Chapter 13. It is enough to point out here that it unites both electronic and prerecorded sources, and that Cage's methods, which leave the final realization completely open-ended and unpredictable, are quite divergent from the painstaking strategies behind either *Scambi* or *Omaggio a Joyce.*

Paradoxically, though Cologne continued to represent serialism throughout the 1950s, it was here and not Milan that the first widely influential European work to reconcile electronic and *concrète* materials was produced. That work, Stockhausen's *Gesang der Jünglinge* ("Song of Children," 1956), was also one of the first to explore the transformation of human speech. It is indeed serially organized, but it also represents an amalgam of many electronic techniques developed up to that point.

The *concrète* source in *Gesang,* a boy's voice reading from the Book of Daniel, undergoes the entire range of tape manipulations. Particularly stirring are passages where it is multiplied, superimposed, and otherwise transformed to create sweeping gestures with eerie crowdlike and choruslike effects. The purely electronic material into which all this is integrated involves both additive synthesis (as in *Studie II*) and the opposite process, *subtractive synthesis,* which begins with a complex sound (e.g., white noise or ring modulation) and filters out unwanted frequencies to achieve the desired timbre. Neither subtractive synthesis nor the common presence of *concrète* and electronic sound sources met with Stockhausen's purist standards when he first arrived in Cologne. But *Gesang der Jünglinge* marks the beginning of a broadening process for Stockhausen, later leading to the incorporation of live performance with tape music, elements of indeterminacy, and mixed media.

Both *Gesang der Jünglinge* and *Omaggio a Joyce* heralded what was to become a long-lasting fascination, still alive today, with electronic explorations of language and phonetics. (Also pivotal in this regard was György Ligeti's *Artikulation* of 1958, realized at Cologne and based on a "language" of electronically generated "phonemes" modeled after those of real speech.) During the 1960s transformations of the human voice continued to depend on the same recording and tape processing methods used by Stockhausen and Berio. But as we will find in Chapter 17, the field opened up dramatically during the next two decades, thanks to computer technology.

American Pioneers

Also during the early 1950s, but quite independently of events in France, Germany, or Italy, the electronic medium made its appearance in North America. It began neither with the ideological divisions that at first took hold in Europe, nor with such august facilities as the RTF or NWDR. In fact, Vladimir Ussachevsky, among the earliest pioneers in the United States, started with an Ampex 400 and assorted other hardware purchased at his own expense.

This necessary self-sufficiency gave Americans an advantage over their European counterparts: they were compelled to play a hands-on role in discovering what new sounds electronics could produce. In Europe the composer might typically conceive of sound events first and then hope that equipment and personnel could achieve them (much as in instrumental writing). But the composer in America tended more to explore the technology with an open mind, hoping to discover sounds and methods he or she might never have imagined, determining afterward how such discoveries might be integrated in a musical context.

Unlike composers of electronic music in Europe, those in the United States did not initially divide up into aesthetic movements or factions, given the small scale and individual nature of their enterprise. Ironically, by the 1960s, when a division between the West Coast avant-garde and the East Coast academic mode of thinking became apparent in America, many studios in Europe had begun to entertain a more catholic mix of attitudes and technologies.

Ussachevsky's explorations began in 1951, and he was joined a year later by his Columbia University colleague Otto Luening. Experimenting with whatever equipment they could afford or borrow, and working in whatever space they could find (including Ussachevsky's living room and

ILLUS. 8.1.

Vladimir Ussachevsky (left) and Otto Luening in
the Columbia-Princeton Electronic Music Studio: a
photo from the late 1950s

Courtesy BMI Archives

Arturo Toscanini's basement), they prepared works for what was to prove
a historic concert of tape music in New York City's Museum of Modern Art
in October 1952.

Luening and Ussachevsky relied primarily on tape manipulation of
recorded sounds, using the same techniques—arrived at independently—as their Parisian counterparts. But although they used a small
amount of electronic modification as well, what really distinguished their
activities from *musique concrète* was the exclusive reliance on musical instruments for raw material. Their idea was to extend the output of instruments beyond their physical capabilities and into uncharted realms. In his
Fantasy in Space and *Low Speed,* for example, Luening conjured a surrealistic

world of unfamiliar sounds (such as tones below playable range) from an ordinary flute. In *Sonic Contours* Ussachevsky expanded the sonorous possibilities of the piano with reverberation, filtering, and various tape techniques; one technique was to mix together rhythmically distinct passages, all occurring within the same pitch range, to generate a contrapuntally dense and intricate texture unattainable in live performance. The above three works were among those presented at the October 1952 concert.

Among Luening and Ussachevsky's individual works, the best known is the latter's *Of Wood and Brass* (1965), whose instrumental sources include trombone, trumpet, xylophone, and Korean gong, aided by a filter, ring modulator, and electronic oscillator. But the two men also composed many works in collaboration, including *A Poem in Cycles and Bells* (1954) and *Concerted Piece* (1960), both interesting because they combine tape music with live orchestral performance (the former being one of the earliest live-plus-electronic pieces written), fusing normal instrumental playing with the extension of instrumental sonorities in the same work.

Tape music with instrumental sounds did not remain the sole province of Americans. One of many examples is the oft-cited *Orient-Occident* (completed in 1960 but revised in 1968) of Iannis Xenakis (b. 1922). This piece incorporates Xenakis's own orchestral music, gongs (and other objects) sounded by a cello bow, and amplified electrical disturbances of the ionosphere, all transformed by tape manipulations. On the other hand, use of environmental sources was not a purely European phenomenon either; among the more impressive works in the *concrète* repertoire is *Dripsody* (1955) by the Canadian engineer Hugh Le Caine (b. 1914). This engaging polyphonic essay is concocted from only one sound source, a single drip of water, which was rerecorded again and again at different speeds to create droplike sounds with pitches ranging over seven octaves.

Another pair of collaborators, Louis and Bebe Barron, are deserving of mention. They had actually been the first to explore creative uses of magnetic tape, before either Ussachevsky or Schaeffer. (Schaeffer was still working with phonograph discs at the time.) But their real claim to fame was that in 1951 they began to construct their own electronic sound generators and processors, thus providing an American correlate to Eimert and Meyer-Eppler in Cologne. Their aesthetic concerns, however, were quite opposite to those of *elektronische Musik*; they emphasized the random, unpredictable output of electronic circuits—and the new sonic discoveries that might result—rather than the absolute control sought by Eimert and Stockhausen. Being more interested in singular effects rather than fully wrought compositions, the Barrons ultimately turned in a more commercial direction, becoming best known for their film music, which includes soundtracks for *Bells of Atlantis* (1953) and *Forbidden Planet* (1956), among many others.

The Barrons were also part of yet another private musical endeavor, lending their expertise to the Project of Music for Magnetic Tape, a consortium of composers that included Earle Brown, John Cage, Morton Feldman, David Tudor, and Christian Wolff, assembled in 1951. It was among this group that the connection between electronics and the radical avant-garde first took root in the United States, ultimately leading to such phenomena as live electronic performance and multimedia composition.

The pivotal work to ensue from the Music for Magnetic Tape project was Cage's *Williams Mix* (1952), drawing from electronic sounds, urban and rural sounds (natural and man-made), instrumental and vocal sounds, and small sounds audible only with amplification (a possibility that fascinated Cage from that point on). This work stands apart for three reasons. First, it was one of few works to combine *concrète* and electronic sounds before *Gesang der Jünglinge* was made. Second, it was Cage's first use of chance methods in the electronic medium, relegating compositional choices to tosses of a coin. Third, unlike most *concrète* works, its purpose was not to change familiar sounds into something surprising or unfamiliar, although this was sometimes the result; rather, Cage wished to approach sounds without bias, and so left the question of how much to distort, and in what way, to chance mechanisms.

ELECTRONIC MUSIC COMES OF AGE

By the early 1960s a large number of fully equipped, fully operational electronic music studios had been established in Europe, the United States, and Japan. These facilities relied on what have come to be known as "classical" techniques, techniques that involved piecing a work together, sound by sound, splice by splice, without the time-saving benefit of automation that newer technology was to bring a few years later. By 1960 *elektronishe Musik, musique concrète,* and all other practices from the 1950s could be equally well accommodated within the classical studio.

The Classical Studio

The basic hardware in the classical studio, along with the methods of its use, had become standard by the mid-1950s and was to remain so for the next decade. Studio facilities included a mixer (to combine sounds and route them to selected tape channels), two- and four-channel tape machines, microphones, reverberation units, oscillators, pulse generators, noise generators, ring modulators, and a variety of sound filters (with capabilities too numerous to mention). Among other devices often found were envelope shapers, to control the contour of a sound (attack, duration, and release), and frequency shifters, which shift the partial frequencies of a sound up or down, often mutating it beyond recognition. By the late 1950s the standard oscillator could produce more than just a simple sine wave; also built in were outputs for square waves, ramp (or sawtooth) waves, and triangle waves, each wave shape having its own basic timbre (see Figure 8–1). Although much of this circuitry was originally adopted from scientific laboratories for musical use, it had been cleverly adapted and now appeared to offer the composer inexhaustible riches.

As of the early 1960s, both the NWDR studio in Cologne and the RAI studio in Milan exemplified the above format. Others to evolve in this mode include the Radio Nippon Horo Kyokai (NHK) studio in Tokyo, founded in 1954 by Toshiro Mayazumi, and the Studio of Experimental Music at the Polish Radio in Warsaw, established in 1957. Similarly, the Institute of Sonology in Utrecht, Holland, was established in 1964 by Philips Laboratories as an outgrowth of its studio in Eindhoven, founded eight years earlier by Henk Badings. (It was in the Eindhoven studio that Varèse composed his *Poème électronique*.) The Paris studio, on the other hand, continued on its own path throughout the 1950s and 1960s, maintaining its focus on primarily *concrète* materials.

The first major centers in North America also fit into the classical mold, and as indicated earlier, space and support were provided by academia rather than government or business. Among these centers were the University of Illinois's Experimental Music Studio (set up in 1958 with Lejaren Hiller as director), the Columbia–Princeton Electronic Music Center (established by Luening, Ussachevsky, and Milton Babbitt in 1959), the University of Toronto studio (founded in 1959), and the Yale Electronic Music Studio (instituted in 1960 by Mel Powell).

Both the Yale and the Columbia–Princeton studios became associated in the early 1960s with a certain compositional aesthetic, also dubbed "classical," characterized by subtly manicured sounds and intricate gestures. Given the limits of the classical studio, these had to be constructed detail by detail, with every sound, no matter how brief, synthesized individually, recorded on its own piece of tape, and spliced to other such pieces to form a musical continuum. The most celebrated examples of this are the *Synchronisms* of Mario Davidovsky (b. 1934), a series of works for tape and various live instruments composed in the Columbia–Princeton studio between 1963 and 1974. (His *Synchronisms No. 1* receives a fuller discussion in Chapter 12.) Davidovsky's instrumental writing, with its typically kaleidoscopic articulations, dynamics, rhythms, and pitch shapes, is interwoven with equally supple, exactingly wrought electronic material into an integrated whole.

FIGURE 8-1.

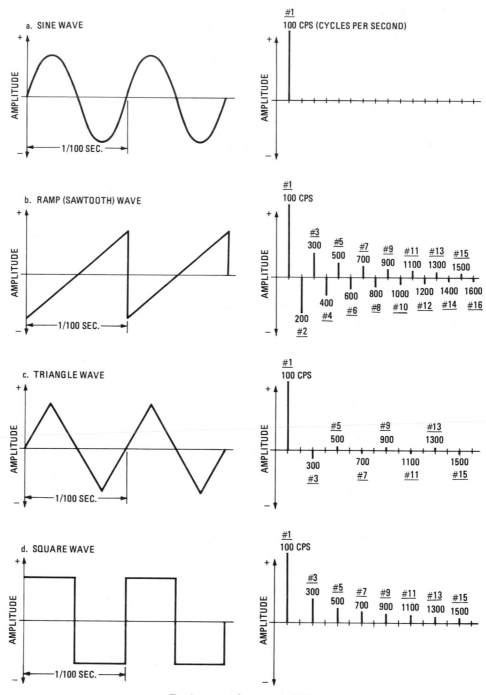

Basic waveforms and their component frequencies
("harmonic partials") for a tone of 100 cycles per
second

ILLUS. 8.2.

The studio of the Group for Research on Musique
Concrète, Paris, with its director François Bayle c.
1970

Also similar in idiom, although purely electronic, is the *Second Electronic Setting* (1962) of Mel Powell (b. 1923); it is truly a "classic" in that not only does it depend on the labor-intensive recording and splicing already described, but its sounds are structured primarily from additive synthesis with sine waves, much as in the early days of *elektronische Musik*.

The RCA Synthesizer

In addition to its traditional equipment and techniques, the Columbia–Princeton studio had one unique asset of historic significance: the RCA Mark II Synthesizer. Derived from an earlier and smaller model built in 1955, the Mark II was installed at Columbia in 1959. Enormous and complex (for many years, Milton Babbitt was the only composer to master its idiosyncracies), it occupied an entire wall and embodied features hitherto

ILLUS. 8.3.

A mid-1960s view of the Electronic Music Studio
of the NWDR (Nordwestdeutscher Rundfunk),
Cologne

unavailable. It eliminated not only the need for tape manipulation but also the laborious necessity to interconnect various electronic components manually. Instead, information regarding the pitch, timbre, duration, envelope, and dynamics of every sound, along with all desired combinations of sounds, was specified in advance and stored as perforations on paper tape. All the hardware necessary to achieve the hoped-for result (oscillators, filters, and so on) were contained and integrated within, so that when the paper tape was fed back into the system, the synthesizer "performed" according to instructions. Once satisfied, the composer's only need for a tape machine was to record the final product.

For Babbitt the RCA synthesizer was a dream come true for three reasons. First, the ability to pinpoint and control every musical element precisely—not just pitch and rhythm, but timbre, dynamics, and articulation as well—permitted him to realize a **process** of total organization (i.e., integral serialism) with a degree of refinement and precision unavailable in live instrumental performance. Second, the time needed to realize his elaborate serial structures with classical techniques would have been incalculable, whereas the RCA synthesizer brought them within practical reach.

ILLUS. 8.4.

Milton Babbitt seated at the RCA Synthesizer (late 1950s)

Courtesy BMI Archives

Third, this machine raised a new issue regarding the challenges and complexities of contemporary music; the question now was no longer "What are the limits of the human performer?" (easily surpassed by the synthesizer), but rather "What are the limits of human hearing?" (which the synthesizer could also exceed). To Babbitt, the latter was a more worthy frontier, and he considered his own electronic works to be, in part, a vehicle for exploring it. His *Ensembles for Synthesizer* (1964) is one such composition, and although first exposure may be confusing to the unaccustomed listener, a well-informed hearing based on familiarity with the work and its procedures can be revealing and rewarding.

The Voltage-controlled Synthesizer

From today's perspective, the technology and techniques of the classical studio seem primitive and inefficient, and the kind of automation offered by the RCA synthesizer appears tantalizing by comparison. But because the RCA machine was huge, expensive, and difficult to master, it was not a viable alternative for most composers. A more affordable solution became possible in the mid-1960s with the easy availability of solid-state circuitry, including the transistor, which supplanted the ungainly and less reliable vacuum tube. Such devices as oscillators, filters, envelope shapers, and amplifiers could now be contained in small, self-contained modules. These modules could, in turn, be made to interact through a process known as *voltage control.*

For instance, the frequency of one oscillator might be made to fluctuate at the frequency of another, a process called *frequency modulation* (or FM). Or the pitch of an oscillator (or the setting of a filter, or the loudness of an amplifier) might be controlled by other sources of changing voltage such as an envelope shaper, random voltage generator, or electronic keyboard. Countless such permutations were possible; they made complex sequences of highly varied sounds easy to attain without endless hours of recording, splicing, or rapid-fire twisting of knobs by an army of assistants. Further, since modules could be compactly arranged, a composer could experiment conveniently with different interconnections (or *patches*) and hear the results at once.

Voltage-controlled synthesis was introduced to the musical world by three different inventors, all working independently of one another. In 1966 Donald Buchla installed his first integrated console of voltage-controlled devices, the Electric Music Box, in the San Francisco Tape Music Center. By that same year, in upstate New York, Robert Moog had perfected his Moog Synthesizer System of voltage-controlled modules, which could be custom organized in arrangements of varying size and capability. Two years earlier, the Italian audio engineer Paolo Ketoff had already built the Syn-Ket, a relatively small and inflexable arrangement of voltage-controlled units whose highly portable console made it uniquely suited to live performance.

By the late 1960s other commercially manufactured units could be obtained, including the ARP 2500 and the Synthi 100. By 1970 Moog, Buchla, ARP, or Synthi systems, in both large- and small-scale incarnations, had become standard equipment in studios throughout the United States and, to a lesser extent, in Europe.

It was in 1968 that the power of this technology burst into the limelight with release of the album *Switched-on Bach*. Created on a Moog synthesizer by Walter Carlos and Benjamin Folkman, this recording renders electronic transcriptions of J. S. Bach's music with a scintillating, multitimbred virtuosity that opened everyone's eyes to the potential, both artistic and commercial, of the electronic medium. But the first newly composed work relying on voltage control to gain widespread attention—and the first such work intended specifically for a recording—was *Silver Apples of the Moon* by

ILLUS. 8.5.

The Electric Music Box series 200 of the late 1960s,
created by Donald Buchla

Morton Subotnick (b. 1933), commissioned by Nonesuch Records and realized on a Buchla synthesizer in 1967. This was followed by two other
record-length Subotnick pieces created on a Buchla, *The Wild Bull* (1968)
and *Touch* (1969).

The Subotnick works highlight a basic design philosophy behind the
Buchla, one with clear musical implications. *Switched-on Bach* could not
have been realized on the Buchla because, unlike the Moog, it had no
piano-style keyboard and no reliable way to tune oscillators to the chromatic (or any other) scale. What the Buchla lacked in precision, however,

ILLUS. 8.6.

Joel Chadabe operating the CEMS System at the State University of New York, Albany (c. 1970), custom configured with voltage-controlled modules by Robert Moog

it made up for in the flexibility with which modules could be interfaced and controlled. This allowed Subotnick to achieve a dazzling variety of timbres and dramatic percussion effects in real time (i.e., without having to stop the tape and rearrange connections between modules).

The multilayered, impulsively accented ostinatos that surface repeatedly in this music were made possible by the ultimate in voltage-controlled automation, the sequencer. (Sequencers, in fact, were found on the Moog, ARP, and Synthi as well.) This device can trigger a steady stream of events from other modules while modifying their output simultaneously; at the same time, its own output can be controlled by other devices or by the composer. In short, the sequencer made instantly possible a multifarious series of rhythms and textures that might have taken weeks to accomplish with classical techniques.

ILLUS. 8.7.

Peter Zinovieff and the Synthi 100, at the EMS Studio in London (c. 1970)

Tape Music with Live Instruments

In some respects, the tape studio would seem to offer an ideal work situation for a composer. Every last detail of a piece can be finely honed, tested, and refinished if necessary, until the composer is pleased with the end product; moreover, once the work is on tape, the composer can be guaranteed a flawless performance every playback, without concern for human performers' mistakes or inadequacies. But some composers would find that situation lacking in immediacy or drama; and for anyone sitting in an audience, the prospect of facing two or more inanimate loudspeakers while a tape simply plays itself out may have limited appeal. When live performances and tape music are combined, however, the riches of the electronic medium can be had without sacrificing the vitality—and uncertainty—of the human element. Indeed, the tension between the fixed (i.e., recorded) and live aspects of the performance can add to that vitality.

Two obvious challenges confront the composer of this venture: how to relate sounds on tape (in terms of pitch, timbre, rhythm, or other elements) to music played by the live performer, and how to coordinate timing between the two during performance. To the latter question, at least, different answers can be found in three of the earliest significant works in this genre.

Edgard Varèse's *Déserts* (1954), for winds, percussion, and prerecorded tape, presents the easiest solution: instrumental and tape sections simply take turns—when one finishes the other begins. But although there is no simultaneous interplay between live sonorities and those on tape (which are derived mainly from factory noises and other *concrète* sources), both are built into violent blocks and layers of texture typical of Varèse, offering two alternating perspectives on his concept of music as "organized sound." In his Capriccio for Violin and Two Soundtracks (1952), Henk Badings (b. 1907) takes an opposite strategy, suitable to his musical style. Both the violin and the tape part were written out primarily in traditional notation, appropriate because the work is tonal and because most of the tape material, generated electronically, is clearly delineated in pitch and rhythm. During performance, the tape is played nonstop, and the violinist has only to read from score, as if he were playing instrumental chamber music. (A later work to adopt this strategy, although hardly tonal, is Lejaren Hiller's *Machine Music* of 1964, for piano, percussion, and tape; each of two tape channels has its own traditionally notated staff.)

A third approach, one that became common in later years, is found in *Musica su Due Dimensioni* (1952) for flute and tape by Bruno Maderna. Performance of this work requires two people, one playing the flute and one operating the tape machine, starting and stopping it at various times according to cues given in the score. By following the score, the tape operator can respond flexibly to the flutist, whose relationship to events on the tape (a mixture of electronic and *concrète* material) is only loosely coordinated. The first three of Davidovsky's *Synchronisms,* written between 1963 and 1965, require this kind of start-and-stop tape operation.

There is yet another possibility, found in John Cage's *Aria with Fontana Mix:* no relationship between tape and live performer is attempted or even contemplated. But this represents an exception; usually, some degree of coordination between human and machine is considered desirable. One important link between the two is usually provided by **notation,** allowing the musician to time entrances and activities appropriately. Since electronic music so often involves complex sonic gestures and textures for which conventional notation was never intended, the composer must devise other symbols or cues that suggest what is happening on tape, and some form of graphic representation is most common.

A trendsetter in this domain was Stockhausen's *Kontakte* for piano, percussion, and electronically generated tape (1960). As seen at the top of Example 8.2, dots, ligatures, wiggly lines, and other shapes are meant to give the players some visual semblance of what the tape part sounds like,

EXAMPLE 8.2.

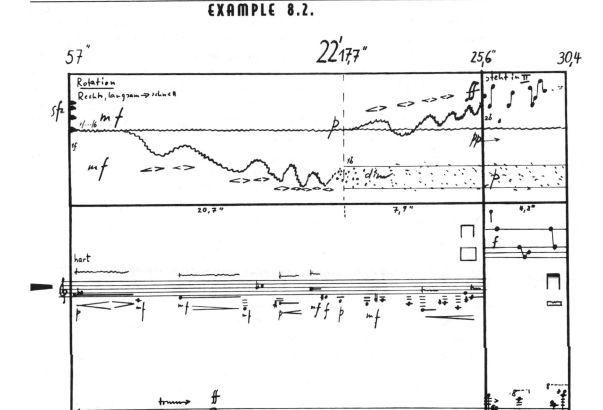

Karlheinz Stockhausen: *Kontakte*

and timings are given to show where these events and textures begin and
end. Higher sounds are nearer the top, lower sounds nearer the bottom.
The visual and temporal references are crucial to the players, who must
determine the placement and duration of their notes with reference to the
given time frame and the electronic sounds within it. This is an example of
proportional or *spatial* notation.

There seem to be as many solutions to coordinating the live-plus-tape situation as there are pieces, and the repertoire is not limited to the use of only a few instruments as in the examples just cited. Important early works for tape and orchestra, apart from those by Luening and Ussachevsky already mentioned, include Henri Pousseur's *Rimes pour différentes sources sonores* (1959), the "different sound sources" including tape and varying groups within the orchestra, and Roberto Gerhard's *Collage* (1960) for orchestra and tape. In such works, the conductor must serve as a mediator between tape, score, and instrumentalists.

Another compositional challenge hinted at earlier is the musical integration of live and prerecorded material. Probably the most common response is an effort to match or otherwise relate electronic and instrumental timbres. Davidovsky's *Synchronisms,* for example, contain passages (often dominated by percussive attacks in both instrumental and electronic parts) where the timbre and texture of live and prerecorded sounds are so well matched as to become almost indistinguishable. In Morton Subotnick's *Laminations* for tape and orchestra (1970), extended performance techniques such as fluttertonguing, keyslapping, and blowing into the mouthpiece alone are used to associate instrumental sonorities with electronic ones. The tape–performer relationship can also be extended into other elements such as pitch and rhythm. Donald Erb's *In No Strange Land* (1968), for example, involves not only timbral correspondences but also melodic imitation between trombone, double bass, and tape, further blurring the distinctions between them.

One possibility exploited by many is to use the same instruments both in live performance and on the accompanying tape, often with the latter conceived as an electronic extension of the former. Meyer Kupferman's *Superflute* (1971) for flute and tape demonstrates this principle, except that, while the live soloist plays an ordinary flute, the tape part consists of prerecorded and transformed material from alto flute and piccolo, so that the totality represents a "superflute" spanning lowest to highest registers.

Electronics in Live Performance

Electronics in live performance have commonly been favored by the more extreme avant-garde, given its preoccupation with theater and multimedia endeavors. All this will be dealt with extensively in Chapter 9, but it would be useful here to place this phenomenon in context with other developments in electronic music.

Among the important studios to have emerged in North America during the 1960s, one has been mentioned only in passing: the San Francisco Tape Music Center. This decidedly nonacademic undertaking (although it was reconstructed in 1966 at Mills College) was established in 1959 by Morton Subotnick and Ramon Sender, who were joined soon after by Pauline Oliveros and Terry Riley. Just as the Columbia–Princeton studio came to symbolize for many the East Coast, cerebral or "academic" viewpoint, the San Francisco Tape Center became the symbol of West Coast, unbridled experimentalism, dedicated to improvisation, mixed media, and live or "real-time" use of electronics. (It is probably no accident that the Buchla synthesizer, which is better suited to real-time composition, originated in California, whereas the Moog, more useful for work scrupulously prepared in the studio, originated in New York.)

In Europe such polarities were less acute by 1960; the continent's most visible composer, Karlheinz Stockhausen, had himself gone from one extreme to the other, beginning the 1950s with an emphasis on strict control and total organization, but ending that decade with a shift toward live electronics and indeterminacy, influenced in part by John Cage. Even in the United States, the perception of an East Coast versus West Coast dichotomy was oversimplified. At the University of Illinois, for example, facilities were shared during the 1960s by such diverse figures as the computer-oriented Lejaren Hiller, the serialist Herbert Brün, the microtonalist Ben Johnston, and the wildly experimental Salvatore Martirano. Many performing groups specializing in live electronic performance also turned up throughout North America during this period. (These are described in Chapter 9.)

From an auditory standpoint, live electronics can function in two basic ways: as an alternative to conventional instruments and voices, or as an extension of them, much as in the tape-plus-live situation. The first possibility is straightforwardly represented by John Eaton (b. 1935), who has played the easily portable Syn-Ket synthesizer in a conventional performance format, as with his *Concert Piece* for Syn-Ket and Orchestra (1967). Electronic instruments also were used by John Cage and David Tudor in their legendary collaborations with the dancer and choreographer Merce Cunningham (from 1953 through the 1960s). In this case, however, the performances were chance-based and improvisational, each one requiring its own idiosyncratic configuration of equipment, pieced together by the composers themselves.

Before the 1980s and the advent of digital technology, the second category (electronics and extensions of ordinary voices or instruments) involved tape manipulation and/or electronic processing of live input. Tape delay was a favorite among composers, since it could be easily engineered and controlled, instantly transforming even a single instrument into manifold layers and sustained textures. On the other hand, electronic modification could subject instruments or voices to countless timbral or other acoustical mutations not possible with tape techniques alone. Filters, modulators, frequency shifters, and other such devices could reshape sonic input in innumerable ways, and the possibility of automating and proliferating these changes with voltage control offered a still richer palette.

Among the first in the United States to explore these possibilities during the 1960s were Larry Austin, Alvin Lucier, David Behrman, and Gordon Mumma. In England, Cornelius Cardew was a leader in this field, and on the continent, Karlheinz Stockhausen was the foremost innovator. For all these composers, however, the use of real-time electronics was consistently coupled with a strong theatrical element, as is explained further in Chapter 9.

CONCLUSION: LOOKING AHEAD

The word "revolution" in the title of this chapter suggests a fundamental upheaval in assumptions or values. As we have seen, what was revolutionary about the electronic medium was not merely that it was new and offered something never heard before. More than this, it was grounded in two previously unthinkable suppositions.

One had been promulgated earlier in the century by Cage, Varèse, and the futurists before them: that composers could assert, willy-nilly, what sounds they regarded as legitimate in a musical vocabulary, no matter how remote from anything the ear might have considered musical in the past. Any sound whose organization could be envisioned, and thus any sound at all, was fair game. (Of necessity, this not only suggested but required revolutionary concepts of organization as well.) The other extraordinary notion was that the human intermediary between composer and audience, the performing musician, could be either transmogrified (in the case of live electronics) or supplanted entirely by a machine, by **technology.** (The electronically generated piece for tape alone is the extreme instance of this, fabricated in the studio and performed unerringly by a tape machine.) And of course, it was that very technology that made the unrestricted universe of sounds, now legitimized as musical, accessible to the composer.

As promising as all this may seem, however, it became apparent by the 1970s that the electronic medium had far from lived up to its heralded potential. In actuality, none of the techniques or hardware developed up to that point offered the degree of control and versatility many hoped for, and one of the basic problems was that, unlike living performers, tape machines and voltage-controlled synthesizers were not intelligent and could not always respond with subtlety or sensitivity to the composer's demands. Furthermore, there were annoying limitations—surprising in light of all the above—to the variety and character of what could be coaxed from existing hardware, including an artificiality of sound that was often difficult to avoid.

As we will discover in Chapter 17, the response to these challenges, still developing apace, has been the exploration of computers and other digital systems for musical purposes. Although computer music was born in the 1950s, it was not until the mid-1970s that digital technology began to rival *concrète* techniques and voltage-controlled synthesis in widespread usage. The decades that followed saw an exponential growth in computer science and an equally remarkable expansion of its musical applications.

Multimedia and Total Theater

The two important concepts in this chapter—theater and multimedia—are interrelated. Every live musical performance, whether avant-garde or traditional, is to some extent both a theatrical and multimedia event. This is obviously true of such genres as opera, ballet, and the Broadway musical. But even an orchestral or chamber music performance involves movement, physical space, and in some cases, singing or speaking. Instruments, music stands, or any other material requirements might even be regarded as ''props.''

Nevertheless, our culture has long since developed a **performance ritual** that isolates music from extraneous visual and aural stimuli, and from any outward physical expression not required to perform it. In instrumental music especially, the sounds encrypted in the score are of overriding importance, divorced from any ritual, gesture, dance, or vocalization. Both the musical work and its performance are typically presented as artifacts, to be admired at a distance, set apart from the audience by the stage and, in recent times, by the recording process.

Electronic developments noted in the previous chapter, along with questions raised in Chapter 7 about order and freedom, have intensified many composers' concerns about performance ritual. Now that sounds can be created directly on magnetic tape or disk, bypassing live human participation, are we to accept musical experience as one of perceiving sound relationships exclusively? How vital are the nonaural stimuli—visual, spatial, and social—that once were embedded in musical discourse (and still are in many cultures)? How important are human factors and other unpredictable aspects of live performance? Should a musical composition, like a painting or sculpture, be a permanent object, exactly the same every time one encounters it?

Such questions have led many composers to focus attention on the theatrical dimension inherent in all music. To do this, they have often gone radically beyond the experience and expectations of the average concertgoer, exploring more flexible relationships between music, its physical surroundings, and the people who perform and listen to it. In large part, theirs is an effort to overcome the isolation, ossification, and abstraction of music as traditionally presented in the concert hall.

For our purposes, the terms *theater* and *multimedia* apply to any composition that in an innovative or experimental way involves more than the sonic material itself to achieve its artistic goals. Works of this kind may incorporate one or more of the following extramusical elements:

1. Visual stimuli, such as lighting, film, slides, or video
2. Motion or speech on the part of dancers, actors, or the musical performers themselves
3. Physical objects or props, ranging from everyday items to sculpture, painting, and other forms of visual art
4. The creative use of physical space, such as the unusual placement or movement of sound sources—performers or loudspeakers—throughout a performance area
5. Audience participation in the performance and/or composition of a work

Electronic **technology** is frequently associated with such compositions; this may involve the playback of prerecorded (not necessarily musical) material, the electronic modification of live acoustic sources, or actual real-time performance on electronic musical instruments.

A musical event becomes increasingly theatrical as it moves further beyond direct presentation of the music itself to incorporate extramusical elements such as those outlined above. As the scope and influence of a composition reach out to encompass the widest possible range of activities, participants, spaces, and spans of time, it approaches what might be called *total theater*. The discussion below ranges from works in which the theatrical element is more limited, centered around the actions of individual performers, to those aimed at an experience of total theater, employing an extensive variety of multimedia resources.

THE EXTENDED PERFORMER

During the past half century composers have tried to extend the expressive resources of the individual performer through two basic approaches: (1) by broadening the range of activities—movement, gesture, vocal utterance—required as part of the performance, and (2) by augmenting the range of sounds that may be produced by an instrument or voice. While the first is relevant to this chapter and the second seemingly more pertinent to discussions of **texture** and **sound color**, they are in fact closely associated. Theatrical departures during performance may, as a by-product, give rise to highly unorthodox (and sometimes appropriately evocative) sounds; on the other hand, educing unusual sounds from an instrument may necessitate or inspire anomalous physical gestures.

In any case, works involving multimedia or theatrical elements often make unusual demands on the individual performer, so much so that certain performers have gained widespread recognition for their daring and expertise in tackling this repertoire: among the many are bassist Bertram Turetzky, trombonists Vinko Globokar and Stuart Dempster, clarinetist Phillip Rehfeldt, saxophonist John Sampen, oboist Heinz Holliger, pianists David Tudor and Yvar Mikhashoff, percussionists Max Neuhaus and Jan Williams, and sopranos Jan DeGaetani, Phyllis Bryn-Julson, and Neva Pilgrim. Musicians like these are known above all for widening the natural resources, both acoustic and physical, of their instruments, and for expanding their activities into theatrical realms. Many of the works they perform involve techniques they themselves have developed, often in direct collaboration with composers. (Composers often prove to be skillful performers of their own music. Conversely, some of the performers listed have also gained recognition as composers.)

The relatively small amount of experimentation with unconventional performing techniques before 1945 was primarily centered on the voice. The most important and influential example is surely Arnold Schoenberg's *Pierrot Lunaire*, Op. 21 (1912). The element of theater arises largely from the incongruity between what one expects from a vocalist and the seemingly half-sung, half-spoken *Sprechstimme* one actually hears. In the opera *Wozzeck* (1921) Alban Berg expanded further on vocal technique by often requiring performers—particularly male members of the cast—to sing at pitch levels far above their normal tessitura, using either *Sprechstimme* or a deliberately raucous falsetto. The effect is disturbing, underscoring the libretto's dark expressionism and emotional brutality.

As extraordinary as these developments may have seemed at the time, they were only the beginning of a search for new dimensions in vocal and instrumental practice, a search that accelerated greatly after World War II. Where voice is concerned, Luciano Berio was one of the most important pioneers, greatly aided by the uncanny vocal agility and theatrical intensity of soprano Cathy Berberian (1925–83), his wife, for whom he wrote many important works. In her collaborations with Berio, and also with John Cage, she inspired an entire generation of vocalists who came to prominence during the 1960s and '70s, establishing a new body of techniques and sonorities. She also introduced a highly extroverted, uninhibited approach to performance rarely witnessed on the nonoperatic stage.

Berberian perfected many unorthodox and vocally demanding modes of sound production, including half-sung words, whispered words, raspy tones, tones without vibrato, singing while inhaling, tongue rolls, tongue clicks, shouting, humming, groaning, gasping, laughing, and coughing, among others. As in Example 9.1, from Berio's *Circles* for female voice, harp, and two percussionists (1960), these techniques are typically associated with fragmented text or nonsense syllables and are made more challenging by sudden, rapid, unpredictable shifts between contrasting sounds at different dynamic levels. Such practices by their very nature transform vocal performance into a theatrical event. The extraordinary effort they require creates both an aural and visual spectacle; moreover, they project inner experiences such as anger, anguish, ecstasy, and sensuality with a

EXAMPLE 9.1.

Luciano Berio: *Circles* (voice part)

visceral power unattainable in ordinary performance. The volatile and prismatic character of Berio's vocal lines achieves its greatest extreme in two historic works, *Thema: Omaggio a Joyce* (mentioned in the previous chapter) and *Visage*, where Berberian's voice undergoes striking transformations through the use of electronic technology.

The composer-soprano Joan La Barbara (b. 1947) has furthered the legacy of Cathy Berberian while also incorporating newer techniques of her own. These include circular breathing (allowing one to prolong a tone or line indefinitely), glottal clicks, high flutters, yodels, and multiphonics (sounding two or more pitches at once). While these techniques can all be found in various ethnic cultures, their appearance in a formal concert setting has an extraordinary effect. In many cases, La Barbara intensifies that effect theatrically by involving spatial and visual elements, often with the help of electronics. The visual element may involve slide or video projections, or in the case of *"as lightning comes, in flashes"* (1981), the use of heavy costumes that are to be left behind as environmental sculpture after the performance.

More radical still is the German composer Dieter Schnebel (b. 1930), whose conscious focus has been to make extrinsic those theatrical elements that are already intrinsic to performance. His *Maulwerke* (literally, "mouth works") for three to twelve vocalists (1968–74) emphasizes ordinarily peripheral aspects of performance to the almost total exclusion of musical sounds as we normally think of them. Schnebel redirects the attention away from the usual source of vocal expression, the singing voice, and toward its contributing parts—lungs, larynx, mouth, and tongue. These become vehicles of expression in their own right, sonically and visually magnified using microphones, amplifiers, loudspeakers, and video equipment. The amplification of breathing sounds, laryngeal contortions, and tongue noises has a novel, sometimes comical or vulgar effect; equally important, however, is the visual effect of these activities, which are graphically "choreographed" in the score and highlighted on video. In the fourth and final section, for instance, entitled "Zungenschläge und Lippenspiel" ("tongue strokes and lip play"), the score consists not of notes but of drawings in which various motions of the tongue and lips are pictorially displayed.

As with the voice, the resources of virtually any instrument may be broadened to encompass elements of music theater and multimedia. Unconventional modes of sound production (tapping the wood of a violin, rattling the keys of a clarinet, or shouting into the mouthpiece of a trombone) inevitably have a theatrical effect not equaled by more traditional methods. During *Spillihpnerak* for solo viola by David Bedford (b. 1937), written in 1972 for Karen Phillips (whose name is spelled backwards to form the title), the violist slacks the bow hairs, inverts the bow, and plays so that the wood passes underneath the instrument while the hairs pass above it, sounding all four strings simultaneously. Aurally, the result is unique, since sustained quadruple stops are rarely to be heard on a stringed instrument; visually, the effect of "deforming" and relocating the bow is startling, even disorienting. The performer's actions are unavoidably theatrical, but also necessary to achieve the musical result.

A similar relationship between the aural and visual exists in such works as *Rainbows* (1981) for bowed piano strings by Stephen Scott (b. 1944) and *Unisonics* (1976) for alto saxophone and piano by Curtis O. B. Curtis-Smith (b. 1941), both of which involve bowing the piano strings. "Bows" are fashioned from long bands or cords, each of which is led around one or more strings in the piano; when the damper is released and the bows are moved back and forth, deeply resonant sounds emerge from inside the instrument. At times the pianist may be called upon to alternate or combine bowing the strings with strumming or plucking them, or with playing the keyboard. In live performance, watching the carefully choreographed motions required to coordinate these activities is as much a part of the experience as hearing the rich array of resulting sonorities.

In the works just mentioned, the exploitation of new sonorities is the first priority, while the dramatic ingredient is a welcome but inevitable outgrowth. In other instances, however, the emphasis is shifted from new sounds to the element of drama involved in producing them. The compositions of Heinz Holliger (b. 1939), for example, often seem contrived to exploit the theatrical impact of doing the unexpected with one's instrument, as in his *Pneuma* for wind ensemble, organ, percussion, and radios (1970). Here the wind players are asked to elicit a variety of nonpitched sounds from their instruments by rattling keys or valves and by blowing or singing into mouthpieces and other apertures. This is as much theater as it is music, and its provocative quality seems to have primarily one dramatic purpose: to shock jaded concert audiences out of their complacent views of performance.

While nonstandard practices can transform music into theater, theatrical effects may also result from the ordinary physical gestures of performance when exaggerated beyond the point of auditory consequence. Thus, for example, in *frog pond at dusk* for three to twelve musicians (1975) by Malcolm Goldstein (b. 1936), string players are told at one point to continue an upbow "off into space"; similarly, in *Vox Balaenae* ("Voice of the Whale") for three masked performers (1971) by George Crumb (b. 1929), the pianist is called upon to repeat the final figure more and more quietly until the last repetition is pantomimed in complete silence. Both instances are unequivocally theatrical in their intent, relying ultimately on purely visual stimuli.

One composition built entirely around this idea is *Antiphony VIII (Revolution)* for solo percussion and two-channel tape (1984) by Kenneth Gaburo (b. 1926). Written for percussion virtuoso Steven Schick (who has performed it in the former Soviet Union and elsewhere around the globe), the work is meant to reflect a variety of emotional responses to the possibility of nuclear war, represented by changes in the soloist's behavior. As the performance progresses, the player begins to tap his mallet stems nervously together between musical passages, to strike the instruments clumsily or miss them altogether, and in general to appear increasingly disoriented by the elaborate percussion set-up that surrounds him. In the ominous conclusion, he loses his grip on the mallets, which fly from his hands as he tries to use them, leaving him physically and psychologically disabled. Here again, the ordinary actions of performance become transformed into theater through exaggeration or distortion.

Vocalization by instrumentalists (rather than singers) is another way of generating dramatic intensity, since it departs so startlingly from conventional practice. One approach is for performers to sing and play the same line simultaneously, as in *Jack's New Bag* for ten players (1966) by Barney Childs (b. 1926). Another possibility is to sing, hum, whisper, or speak one line (with its own melody and/or rhythm) while playing another simultaneously on one's instrument; all are demonstrated in Elliott Schwartz's 1966 *Dialogue No. 1* for solo contrabass. In his 1963 *Pajazzo* for eight jazz musicians, the Swedish composer Folke Rabe (b. 1935) combines the above techniques with improvisation and interaction between performers, who mumble and hum while playing, imitate instrumental sounds vocally, and even sing into each other's instruments. Vocalization by instrumental players is common in the music of George Crumb, even where a vocal soloist is featured. The effects are not only novel but also specifically relevant to the dramatic conceit of a given passage. For instance, in his *Songs, Drones, and Refrains of Death* for baritone and five instrumentalists (1968), the latter are called upon to whisper, "sing hauntingly," and "shout brutally"; these and other such effects powerfully underscore the stark mysteries of Federico García Lorca's text.

Another example, *Voices* for orchestra (1971) by Olly Wilson (b. 1937), involves a nonstandard resource not yet mentioned: whistling. In perhaps the most dramatic moment of the piece, the entire string section whistles a sustained tone in unison while also playing lush, gradually shifting sonorities with the rest of the orchestra. The drama of the moment emerges when all string players, in one unified motion, move their heads slowly from one side to the other as they whistle, so that the tone seems to swell, diminish, or sweep across acoustic space, depending on where one is seated in the hall. The aural and visual imagery are not only interdependent but perfectly matched: the sight of forty heads gradually turning together vividly reinforces the aural effect of shimmering sound moving through space.

ELECTRONICS IN LIVE PERFORMANCE

Chapter 8 introduced a uniquely postwar genre: music for live acoustic performers and prerecorded tape. In addition, electronics can also be employed in real time, either as a means of extending a live performer's capabilities or as a sound source in their own right. This "human versus machine" scenario has a built-in theatricality. The uncommon appearance of electronic devices in a concert hall and the movements required to employ them draw attention to the visual, kinetic, and spatial aspects of performance. Further, the unusual sound world of electronics suggests other less conventional experiences as well, especially those offered by experimental music theater and multimedia. Reinforcing this theatricality is the compatibility of musical and visual electronics (e.g., lighting, slides, film, or video), whose technologies often overlap.

Interaction with a Prerecorded "Clone"

The simple combination of live performer and prerecorded tape can be an interactive and theatrical one, particularly where the instrument or voice is accompanied by its own prerecorded "double." Landmark works in this genre include *Transición II* for piano, percussion, and two tape machines (1959) by Mauricio Kagel (b. 1931), Lukas Foss's *Echoi* for four instruments and tape (1963), and two pieces by Robert Erickson (b. 1917): *Ricercar à 5* for trombone and tape (1966), written for Stuart Dempster, and *Ricercar à 3* for double bass and tape (1967), written for Bertram Turetzky.

In all these works, as in innumerable pieces written since, the performers are asked to record passages before the performance, and then to perform with, and in many cases respond extemporaneously to, the sounds of their own "clone" as they are played back in concert. This confronts the listener/viewer with new justapositions: in particular, a "frozen" past (recorded music) set against a volatile present (music performed in real time), and the sight of one performer or small ensemble contrasted with the sound of many such performers or ensembles coming from different locations.

The Electronically Empowered Musician

When we think of using technology to boost a performer's capabilities, we normally envision a conventional amplification system: microphone, amplifier, and speakers. But this relatively primitive technology can be put to extraordinary use. Robert Ashley (b. 1930) pushes it to its limits in his theater piece *The Wolfman* for voice and tape (1967). The singer plays the part of a "sinister nightclub vocalist," performing a variety of nonverbal sounds with the microphone right next to his or her mouth. Both the tape and voice parts are amplified to excruciatingly high levels, and feedback is phased in and out by manipulating the voice, the microphone, and feedback levels. The outcome is vehemently iconoclastic and satirical.

The basic microphone-amplifier-loudspeaker arrangement has also been put to ground-breaking use by John Cage. Cage introduced the possibility of using contact microphones (which pick up vibrations directly from their physical source) in live performance. These can be affixed to any object, not necessarily musical, and then routed through amplifiers to loudspeakers. Once amplified, tables, chairs, clothes, anything can be scraped, struck, or otherwise "played." In *Cartridge Music* (1960) Cage instructs an unspecified number of players to elicit sounds from a variety of objects with the help of contact mikes and phonograph cartridges. In even less structured situations, Cage has simply "monitored" the use of objects; contact mikes may be attached to pen and paper as he writes a letter, or to his throat as he drinks a glass of water. Thus, where other composers have used physical elements to bring out the theater in musical activity, Cage uses sound to bring out the theater (and sonic richness) in everyday physical existence.

In a live electronic setting, the microphone is usually part of a more elaborate system in which the sounds of performance are subjected to a variety of transformations (filtering, reverberation, ring modulation, etc.) as well as "classical studio" manipulations of magnetic tape (tape delay, looping, etc.). More recently, digital technology has made these and other effects such as "chorusing" and detuning instantly accessible in live performance.

Live transformation through tape techniques first became common in the 1960s, through such works as *Casta (insert the performer's name here)* by Ben Johnston (b. 1926). One recorded realization performed by bassist Bert Turetzky, *Casta Bertram,* illustrates the complexity of dealing with tape recorders in a live situation. The recording engineer must work quickly and accurately during the performance, recording and mixing the player's sounds (instrumental and vocal) and forming the resulting tapes into loops. These are then played back on three different playback systems, generating a fabric of sound that grows in density and complexity until the soloist is ultimately buried in a sonic landslide of his own making. Certainly the frantic activity of the recording engineer, if visible, creates an element of theater; but more dramatic, perhaps, is the sensory discrepancy between the sight of a solitary instrumentalist on stage and the barrage of sounds he or she has created.

In *ABM (Anti-Bass Music)* for speaker and bass player (1960) by Daniel

Lentz (b. 1942), tape delay is used to transform vocal and instrumental sounds into violent, explosive textures. These are the outgrowth of a "war" waged by the two performers in which the speaker attempts (symbolically) to destroy the bass player and his instrument—the latter representing, in the composer's words, "deadly weapons used and justified as the protectors of our musical culture." The conflict, often at near-unbearable volume, presents a perfect example of the genre referred to by David Cope as "antimusic." It eventually results in the destruction of both protagonists, followed by any of several optional endings, one of which includes reading a list of Vietnam War dead.

It was not until the early 1980s that any new technologies comparable to live recording, tape manipulation, and playback became available. These and other related developments are explored more fully in Chapter 17. It is enough to say here that a variety of powerful, inexpensive, and easily portable devices, made possible by refinement of the microchip, have largely supplanted the tape machine in live electronic performance.

More efficient and flexible than live recording and subsequent manipulation, and more often employed in a real-time context, is the direct processing of sound. A performer's output can be filtered, modulated, and otherwise reshaped in innumerable ways, or it can be transformed into signals that modify other sound sources.

In Europe the dominant figure in the early development of such possibilities was Karlheinz Stockhausen. Very much influenced by John Cage during the late 1950s and early 1960s, Stockhausen embraced live electronics, multimedia, and indeterminacy together as vehicles for developing a more flexible and organic relationship between composer, performers, and their visual, spatial, and acoustic environment. His *Mikrophonie I* for tam-tam, electronics, and six performers (1964) stands as a benchmark among works that employ electronic processing of instrumental sounds. During the performance, sounds from the tam-tam are produced and transformed by two groups of three musicians simultaneously (see Figure 9–1). In each group, one player activates various parts of the tam-tam with glass, wood, metal, rubber, and other materials, another moves a directionally sensitive microphone around the instrument, and a third operates a filter and amplifier, which process the microphone signal. The three players in each group may respond to or act independently of one another, but the sonic result of any action by one player is entirely dependent on actions of the other two. The two groups engage in a highly volatile relationship, variously imitating, ignoring, supporting, or undermining one another's activities, all according to a series of scenarios whose order is chosen by the performers ahead of time. This interplay is given theatrical immediacy by the variety of physical movements required in performance. The result is less a composition in the traditional sense than it is an opportunity, ingeniously structured by the composer, for a dynamic complex of interactions

FIGURE 9-1.

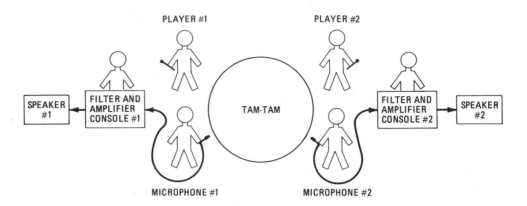

Basic setup for Stockhausen's *Mikrophonie I*

to take shape before the ears and eyes of the listener. This complex may vary considerably from one performance to the next.

Apart from the work of Stockhausen, most experiments in live electronic performance during the 1960s and early '70s were carried out by American composers. One such pioneer is Gordon Mumma (b. 1935), who has composed a series of works revolving around a "cybersonic console"—a complex of circuitry, designed and built by Mumma himself, that can be set up onstage or actually worn by an instrumentalist. In works like *Mesa* with bandoneon (1966) and *Hornpipe* with horn (1967), sounds from the instrument trigger certain responses from the cybersonic unit; these in turn modify the instrumental sounds electronically, sometimes beyond the point of recognition, while also influencing further responses from the performer. This feedback loop between technology and human participant results not so much in a performance as in a **process,** a drama between performer, machine, and sound that unfolds in real time.

While preassembled units such as the cybersonic console may remain unchanged from one performance to the next, another approach has been to create a new electronic set-up for each piece, so that "composing" the electronics is very much a part of creating the work. One of the earliest and foremost explorers in this territory was pianist and composer David Tudor, whose multimedia collaborations with the Merce Cunningham Dance Company (and frequently with John Cage) were pivotal in the development of mixed-media composition. One such work is *Bandoneon!*, in which sounds from the bandoneon (an accordianlike instrument) are used to control electronic sound sources, video images, moveable loudspeakers, and lighting, thus extending a single performer's resources beyond instrumental sound to encompass a whole range of media.

A similarly unique arrangement is found in *L'sGA* (1968) by Salvatore Martirano (b. 1927). Written for "gas-masked politico, helium bomb, three movie projectors, and two-channel tape," this work achieves utterly bizarre deformations of human speech. The "politico" wears a gas mask filled with helium while narrating a tortuously fragmented reconstruction of the Gettysburg Address. The helium causes wild pitch fluctuations in the narrator's voice, which is then picked up by microphone and subjected to further electronic distortions, all set against a backdrop of film and prerecorded tape. The narration becomes increasingly contorted and chaotic, finally reaching a climax of total entropy and devastation.

Another twist, explored by Pauline Oliveros (b. 1932), is to create music theater not just of instrumental activity but of physiological activity as well. In *Valentine* (1968), composed for the Sonic Arts Union, she uses contact mikes to amplify the heartbeats of four performers who are playing a game of hearts on stage. Although the work also incorporates narration, projections, and various disassociated activities onstage, the real musical-theatrical focus is the card players' loudly audible heartbeats, which fluctuate as their fortunes change during the game, creating an intimate link between sound and drama.

Electronic extension of the live performer saw little philosophical or technological development from the mid-1970s to the early 1980s. Since then, the most useful development in this area has been the Musical Instrument Digital Interface or MIDI (described more fully in Chapter 17). Dexter Morrill's MIDI Trumpet and Gary Nelson's MIDI Horn are examples of instruments whose live input triggers a variety of responses from a computer and associated electronics. Recent efforts by Salvatore Martirano and by jazz trombonist George Lewis also rely on microcomputer technology. During the late 1980s both Martirano and Lewis began to perform using their own software, which functions as a robot (Martirano's term) or a sideman (jazz terminology), digitally interpreting live improvisational input and then responding with output to other electronic devices. The result is a real-time, mutually interactive duet between musician and machine.

Live Electronic Instruments

As in so many other areas, John Cage was first in the use of electronic devices as live performing instruments in their own right. The earliest important example is his *Imaginary Landscape No. 4* of 1951, in which twenty-four players perform on twelve radios. It was not until the 1960s, however, that electronic sound sources other than the tape machine were

---

ILLUS. 9.1.

Pauline Oliveros and Stuart Dempster, two important figures in the creation and performance of multimedia works

Photo: Gisela Gamper. Courtesy of the Pauline Oliveros Foundation

employed consistently in concerts, happenings, experimental theater and other mixed-media events. A number of composers, such as David Tudor, David Behrman, Max Neuhaus, Salvatore Martirano, and Stanley Lunetta, designed and built their own equipment. Both Martirano's Sal-Mar Construction and Lunetta's Moosack Machine (the latter as much sculpture as instrument) used digital logic to control a variety of sound sources; both were visually imposing in and of themselves, and both provided a theatrical and musical basis for numerous multimedia adventures. Other composers, not as interested in building their own equipment, preferred to use premanufactured instruments—usually smaller, more portable and practical units—created by Moog, Buchla, and ARP.

More recently, digital synthesizers like those by Yamaha, Roland, Casio, and Korg have proved highly versatile in multimedia and music theater settings. They are used, for example, by Yehuda Yannay (b. 1937) in a genre he calls "synthesizer theater." Preprogrammed pitch sequences and other basic elements are run from a Macintosh computer while the composer uses synthesizers and other equipment to shape this material in real time, also coordinating it with visual media. Michael Daugherty (b. 1954) has employed a cornucopia of such devices in elaborate set-ups that also incorporate lighting and projections. Daugherty has traveled throughout the United States and abroad as a kind of one-man multimedia band, playing music that fuses avant-garde, popular, and jazz styles into a vibrant collage. He is one in a generation that has treated the portability and commercial availability of high-tech audio electronics as an opportunity to take avant-garde music "on the road."

A trend to watch for in the future is a growing reliance on artificial intelligence, which will become increasingly important in the real-time interface between artist and machine, as composers look for more sophisticated, "intelligent" responses from computers. A current leader in this trend is composer/performer Top Machover, whose experiments are described in Chapter 17.

Experimental Ensembles

It is worth noting that the Ashley and Mumma works mentioned earlier were first presented by improvisational groups of which the composers were performing members. Beginning in the 1960s, such groups were among the first to make consistent use of live electronics as part of multimedia presentations. Among the earliest and most influential were the ONCE Group of Ann Arbor, Michigan (founded by Robert Ashley, David Behrman, Alvin Lucier, and Gordon Mumma), and the San Francisco Tape Music Center (Pauline Oliveros, Morton Subotnick, and Ramon Sender), both of which began performing in 1960. The two most prominent ensembles overseas were AMM of London (directed by Cornelius Cardew) and Musica Elettronica Viva of Rome (featuring expatriate American composers Frederic Rzewski and Alvin Curran, among others). Other live electronic improvisatory groups who became active during the 1960s and early 1970s include the California Time Machine (founded by Daniel Lentz), Mother Mallard's Portable Masterpiece Company, and the German group Feedback.

Characteristically, these ensembles would come to the performance space equipped with a battery of synthesizers, microphones, mixers, and other electronic equipment, along with a collection of musical instruments (particularly percussion) and nonmusical objects from which sounds could be coaxed. Also typical was the inclusion of lighting and projection equipment, in addition to any other objects that might serve as props. While works by individual composers were often featured, just as common were presentations in which many or all members shared in both the conception and performance.

Beginning in the early 1970s, much of the live electronic and multimedia collaboration in the United States became allied with academic institutions. Three of the most important have been the California Institute of the Arts, Mills College, and the University of California at San Diego. Two other institutions, Stanford University and the Massachusetts Institute of Technology, already reknowned for important research in computer music, became increasingly involved in the application of digital technology to multimedia explorations during the 1980s. In a fiercely antagonistic response to this trend, composers such as Laurie Anderson, Philip Glass, Pauline Oliveros, Joseph Celli, and Paul Dresher, along with electronic ensembles led by Michael Gordon, John Zorn, Glen Brancha, and others, have resisted any ties to academia. They have chosen instead to appear in such alternative performance spaces as the Knitting Factory in New York City or the Painted Bride in Philadelphia.

In Europe, Karlheinz Stockhausen was the dominant force in improvisatory and theater-oriented live electronics from the early 1960s through the 1980s, traveling all over the world with an ensemble of collaborators. The distinction between this and other such ensembles is that the music performed was exclusively Stockhausen's. His home base for these operations was the radio station in Cologne (West Deutsche Rundfunk), reflecting once more—as with the founding of electronic studios—a basic difference between support for artistic innovation in the United States and in other countries.

SOUND AND SIGHT

As we have emphasized, music becomes increasingly theatrical as its activities extend beyond the production of sound itself, thus focusing more attention on **performance ritual.** Up to this point we have explored these extensions as though looking from the performer's point of view outward, showing how various innovations expand his or her resources. But from the audience's perspective, an even more obvious aspect of theatricality is the radical integration of music with other media. From that point of view, music appears as only a part—albeit a central one—of a more comprehensive performance art, directed at a broad range of perceptual and intellectual sensibilities. Our discussion here, as before, emphasizes developments up to about 1975, since the following years have been characterized more by variation and refinement than by major innovation.

Contemporary efforts to fuse music with other media are not new. Apart from the marriage of music with dance, stage drama, or both—long extant in traditions around the world, from Wagner's *Gesamtkunstwerk* to Japanese Noh drama—perhaps the most significant forerunner of recent trends was Alexander Scriabin (1872–1915). Like Wagner, Scriabin envisioned the possibility of a total artwork directed at all the faculties of perception. Unlike Wagner, however, but very much like many of today's composers, he sought to shape nonmusical events in the same abstract, non-narrative way as music. His only real attempt to realize this dream was in *Prometheus (The Poem of Fire)*, Op. 60, for orchestra, chorus, and color organ (1911), in which colored light projections were "orchestrated" with the same specificity and rhythmic precision as pitches, each color being associated with a certain type of chord.

As with Scriabin, recent attempts to incorporate visual media almost always involve technology of one kind or another: slide projections, film, video, electronically controlled lighting, and lasers, which can be readily manipulated or made to change and evolve during performance. Lighting is a basic visual resource in multimedia composition and can completely alter one's sensory response to the environment, affecting perception of color, depth, and texture. Stockhausen exploits the psychological power of lighting in his *Trans* for strings, winds, percussion, and amplified weaving machine (1971); the audience sees only the silhouette of a string orchestra playing behind a softly lighted scrim, an image that underscores the haunting, otherworldly atmosphere of the music.

Musicians have taken a particular interest in the interaction of light and sound. This is often found in rock concerts, where pitch and amplitude followers or threshold devices have been used to control lighting intensity, color, direction, and strobe rate. Since the 1980s digital interfacing between electronic musical instruments and lighting control units has simplfied this kind of integration, a descendent of Scriabin's correlation of color and chord type.

Lighting can do more than manipulate the observer's psychological response; it can also serve as a directly expressive medium in its own right. Lasers achieve particularly interesting results, since they can be programmed to shift in response to changes in audio variables, permitting live musicians literally to "play" the resulting patterns of light and color. The foremost pioneer in this area is composer Lowell Cross (b. 1938), whose 1970 *Video Laser II* for laser, audio system, televisions, translucent plastics, and electronic sound sources (in collaboration with Carson Jeffries and David Tudor) was one of many ground-breaking musical events presented at Expo 70 in Osaka, Japan. Morton Subotnick has also been a leading figure in this area; during the early 1970s he worked with lasers as well as other light projection devices in his Sound Light Studio at the California Institute of the Arts.

Slide projections are familiar components of multimedia composition, often involving images that are abstract or have no explicitly rational sequence or significance. Richard Felciano's *Signs* for four-part chorus, electronic tape, and three projectors offers an interesting twist. Felciano (b. 1930) calls for images to be projected from film strips and move frame by frame from one image to the next, thus allowing the sequence and duration of images to be timed with the same precision as other events in the work (see Example 9.2.). The images consist of everyday signs and symbols (e.g., "stop," "exit," "keep out," etc.) that take on a rhythm and significance of their own as the work progresses, while reflecting the apocalyptic "signs" in the choral text with a mundane irony.

Film has also proved a vital resource for mixed-media composers. Since film is ordinarily thought of as a primary medium of focus, incorporating it into an event that involves other media of equal significance offers a challenge to our perceptions, as when film accompanies music, instead of the reverse. For instance, in the precedent-setting *Ballet mécanique* (1923) by George Antheil, assorted keyboard and percussion instruments (along with two electric doorbells and an airplane propeller) may be performed with an optional abstract film by Fernand Léger; no coordination between sounds and filmed images is specified. If this indeterminate layering is extended to other media, then film may play only one part in an environment of sensory stimuli (lights, slides, artwork, movement, sounds), typically coordinated—if at all—by improvisational guidelines. Such events may also use two or more film projectors at once, creating separate and competing images or a collage of overlapping material. Early innovators in this domain include Morton Subotnick, members of the ONCE group, Salvatore Martirano, and Mauricio Kagel. Others, Reynold Weidenaar chief among them, have explored film and sound as inextricable parts of a single expressive medium.

One example of the many unorthodox uses of film is found in *Ping* by Roger Reynolds (b. 1934). Written in 1968, it calls for three instrumentalists, live electronics, slides, mirrors, colored lights, and projector, and is based on a text by Samuel Beckett. The film consists solely of a bald male figure, clad only in briefs, attempting to remain motionless while standing in a box for twenty-two minutes. The projector is located so that the filmed image is enormous, dominating the observer's field of vision throughout the performance. This imposing image, obviously alive but unmoving, stands in eerie contrast to other elements, which are constantly changing (including

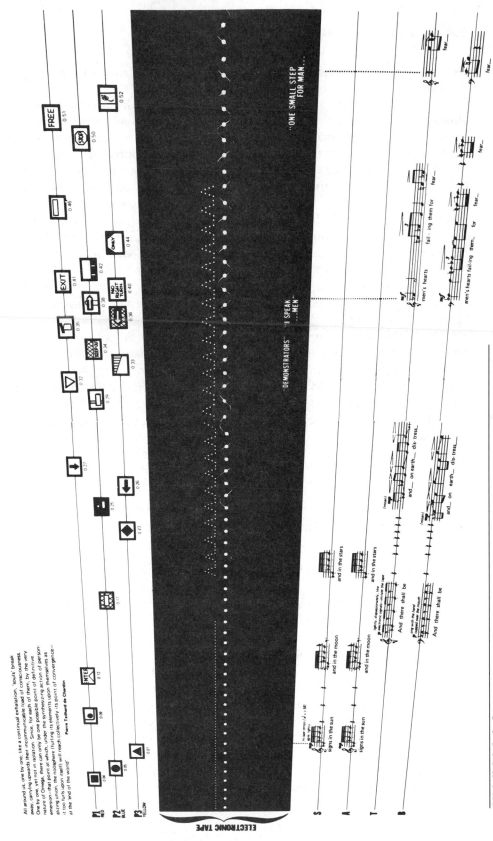

EXAMPLE 9.2. Richard Felciano: *Signs.* Used by permission of E. C. Schirmer Music Company, Inc., Boston

the amplitude and location of sounds, which are controlled by passing a light pen over groups of photoresistors).

Video, the successor to film as an electronic visual medium, allows alteration, transformation, and synthesis of visual imagery in much the same way that electronic devices allow the synthesis and manipulation of sounds. It is also far more susceptible to real-time control than film. The uncontested pioneer of video as a medium for visual art and experimental performance is Nam June Paik (b. 1932), who as early as 1963 presented a one-man exhibition in West Germany entitled "Exposition of Music–Electronic Television." (Paik's views as a composer were radicalized by his encounters with Cage and Stockhausen in Europe during the mid-1950s.) His most famous musical projects were often carried out in collaboration with cellist Charlotte Moorman, who in various works played a cello made of television screens while wearing miniature screens with active imagery on various parts of her body. Examples include *TV Bra for Living Sculpture* (1969), *TV Glasses* (1971), and *TV Cello* (1971).

The 1980s have seen the development of highly flexible real-time interaction between video images and musicians. In Joan La Barbara's *Voice Windows* (1986), for example, digital technology allows large-scale projections of phantasmal video images to be controlled by the voice. The acoustic-video interface is so sophisticated that even minute shifts in pitch or timbre can effect complex, instantaneous permutations of color, shape, and texture; the vocalist literally performs the imagery.

MUSIC AND MOVEMENT

Movement, an inherently theatrical aspect of musical performance, may also function as a separate, self-contained medium in an experimental performance setting. It was, in fact, an essential component of the earliest full-fledged "happenings," carried out jointly by John Cage, Robert Rauschenberg, and Merce Cunningham in the early 1950s. These large-scale multimedia events broke new ground by discarding all assumptions about content, meaning, or the necessity for a shared design between dance, music, and any other medium in a collaborative event. Just as Cage sought to eliminate all intention or logical sequence, to "get out of the way of" sounds, Cunningham sought to divest movement of any direction, continuity, or mimetic value. Frequently chance was employed to ensure a noncoordination of activities, in order to permit the sensory amalgam and individual events within it to be appreciated directly and openly, with minimum prejudice from the artists.

Charlotte Moorman, performing Nam June Paik's *Concerto for Cello and Videotapes* at New York's Whitney Museum, 1982

Photo: Catherine F. Skopic

One spectacular result of this partnership was *Variations V* (1965), in which choreography by Cunningham and music by Cage were accompanied with film images by Stan VanDerBeek and video images by Nam June Paik. This work did involve some coordination of movement and music: electronic sensors were placed around the stage, so that the dancers' movements triggered sounds from a bank of synthesizers, sounds that were further modified by John Cage, David Tudor, and Gordon Mumma at the synthesizer controls. Space, in other words, became a musical instrument on which dancers performed with their movements.

A special attraction of working with mixed media has been that, by decentralizing music and elevating other elements to a comparable status, one is equally free to "compose" for visual media, movement, architectural, or even environmental resources. In his abstract theater piece *Pas de cinq* (1965), Mauricio Kagel serves as his own choreographer and set designer, creating a performance complex of five fifteen-foot walkways in the shape of a pentagon, with four other walkways connecting the angles. Five actors traverse these walkways, each carrying a wooden staff or umbrella; they follow graphically notated routes through the pentagonal maze, while walking and pounding the floor according to musically notated rhythms, all of which have to be memorized. Example 9.3 shows a typical page of the score.

The uneven terrain and varied materials of the walking surface not only affect the dynamics of rhythmic events, but also cause inevitable entanglements between performers, making an accurate performance of the notated instructions impossible. The resulting tension is heightened by the behavior of the performers; although mute throughout, they project different relationships with one another, manifested through "glances, sudden turns, bent carriage, unfair use of walking stick, gallant gestures," and such. In the resulting totality, distinctions between music composition, choreography, dramaturgy, and set design are obliterated; each aspect is inextricably dependent on the others in determining the outcome.

Real-time interaction between sound and the movement of performers through space has led to a variety of ingenious technological schemes, involving photosensors, radio telemetry, and, more recently, high-tech digital mechanisms. One recent innovation, known as MIDI Hands and devised in 1985 by the Dutch composer Michael Waisviscz, allows hands and arms to perform simply by moving, without the intermediary of bows, keys, mallets, or their associated instruments. Elaborate wiring converts the hand motions to MIDI signals, which in turn control the output of various synthesizers.

EXAMPLE 9.3.

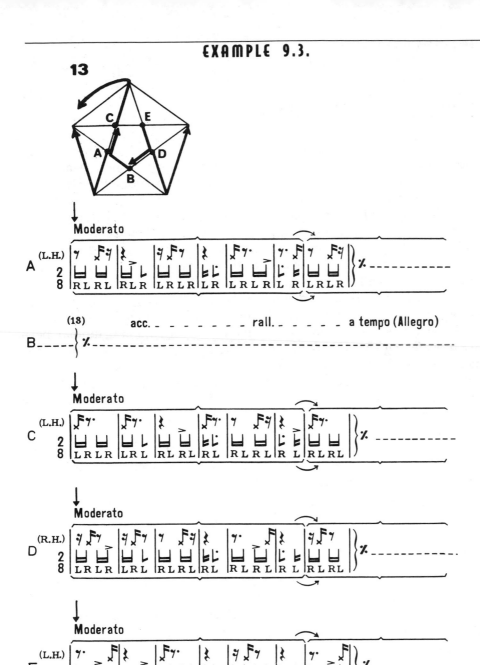

Mauricio Kagel: *Pas de cinq*

AUDIENCE PARTICIPATION

Audience involvement represents yet another step in the experimental composer's effort to reach beyond the boundaries of the concert stage and Western performance traditions. *Chortos II*, a 1972 work by Richmond Browne (b. 1940), is notable for its participatory theater. The work begins with a bitterly ironic word piece using biblical images to depict the wartime destruction of the Vietnamese countryside, performed by a chorus in drab military clothing. As the speech ends, there is a sudden and total blackout in the hall, at which point menbers of the chorus suddenly turn on small, previously hidden flashlights and head out into the audience. They move with silent determination through the aisles and rows, brushing or bumping against audience members and occasionally shining lights at them, while chaotic sounds from an amplified musical saw and tubular bells reach deafening levels onstage. At no time is this "SWAT team" of chorus members clearly visible; their movements through the hall can be sensed only through the motion of many small lights, through the sounds they make, and through touch as they push brusquely past the seats. The bodily movement of performers, although not clearly seen, is powerfully felt nonetheless.

Another, more ominous instance of passive rather than active participation—as yet unrealized—is postulated by Phillip Corner (b. 1933) in a work whose title and performance instructions are the same: "One anti-personnel type-CBU bomb will be thrown into the audience" (1969).

Audience participation is usually a more voluntary affair. In Gordon Mumma's *Cybersonic Cantilevers* (1975), for instance, the audience is invited to provide the sound material. A number of monitor stations equipped with microphones and headsets are spread around in a large space. Audience participants bring prerecorded sounds (on cassette machines) or any other sound-producing objects they like. Their sounds are routed from the microphone to an electronic processing device designed by the composer. The processed sounds are then played back through the headsets and over loudspeakers that ring the area. The monitor stations are also equipped with switches that allow participants to influence the processing of sounds, while oscilloscopes visually display the results. Similarly, the 1971 *Ecology of the Skin* by David Rosenboom (b. 1947) entails "group dynamic brain-wave encounters" between members of the audience, who control lighting effects at will by pressing electrodes to their temples. Both the Rosenboom and Mumma examples are cybernetic in the sense that audience and technology interact to create the event.

This kind of audience involvement is often predicated on the principle that composers should not function as dictators, and that music should not be "done to" an audience. The ideal is a musical event in which all participants share the opportunity to express themselves creatively. The improvisation group Musica Elettronica Viva was among the first to espouse this philosophy. MEV was known in the late 1960s for its "Sound Pool" concerts, in which audience members were invited to bring any instruments they chose and play along with members of the group. The invitation sometimes resulted in hundreds of performing participants.

In recent years one of the more persistent advocates of audience participation has been Pauline Oliveros, a number of whose pieces from the early 1970s to the present consist of open-ended scenarios, outlined verbally, that minimize her own influence on the outcome. In much of this work she has bucked current trends by playing down the role of technology, perhaps viewing it as a barrier to ready and open involvement by all. Her *Horse Sings from Cloud* is one example. Members of the audience, along with any musicians who might be participating, are encouraged to prolong any sound they wish until they no longer feel the need to change it, at which point they are to follow with another sound. Inevitably, each participant's choice is influenced by the choices of others, so that the continually shifting sonic web that results is dependent both on individual personalities and on spontaneous group interaction.

MUSICIANS AS ACTORS, MUSIC AS POLEMIC

In most of the works looked at so far, the theatrical content has been abstract or implicit; no teleology or narrative content is verbally or gesturally conveyed, as it is in traditional theater, opera, and ballet. This is not to suggest that avant-garde composers have dispensed with recognizable words and actions; on the contrary, those elements are commonly present, but frequently in a way that challenges the assumptions and attitudes of conventional audiences.

Animus III for clarinet and tape by Jacob Druckman (b. 1928) is a representative example. Druckman summarizes the dramatic shape of the work on the first page of the 1969 score: "The clarinetist enters in the person of the arch-virtuoso, self-confident almost to the point of arrogance. During the 16 minutes of the work there is a gradual dissolution of the personality of the player. The person who leaves the stage at the end of the work is dissociated and hysterical to the point of insanity." This gradual unraveling is exhibited partly by interruptions in the highly demanding solo line, during which the player lectures the audience—confidently and engagingly at first, but later with a growing sense of uncertainty and distraction—on the technical vagaries of performing on his instrument. The tape part, consisting of prerecorded and processed clarinet sounds, along with live microphone feedback, participates in the ultimate destruction of the soloist's personality. Related to this is Pauline Oliveros's *Two Double Basses at Twenty Paces* (1968), in which the performers lecture the audience on the history and construction of their instruments while performing excerpts from the bass literature. As the work nears its conclusion, their performance is abruptly halted by a series of cataclysmic sonic (electronic) and visual events, eventually culminating in the projected image of Beethoven's death mask. A more recent work in this vein is the 1979 *Catalogo Voce* by Larry Austin (b. 1930), in which the singer delivers a lecture on the physiology of the voice with the help of an anatomical model, illustrative slides, and a thoroughly incompetent lab assistent. The presentation becomes gradually more incoherent until it unravels completely at the end.

All three of the foregoing examples require the performer to talk about the mechanics of performing, leading in each case to dire results. While it may seem natural for experimental works to challenge, defy, even ridicule established cultural precepts, these works attack tradition through a more explicit and openly sardonic form of commentary: in each, the pedantry and self-importance of the Western musician is first lampooned and then symbolically obliterated.

From this one might conclude that (1) when the theater in experimental music is acted out more explicitly, its inherently polemical nature often rises to the surface and (2) the thrust of this polemic is typically one of cultural self-analysis, self-criticism, and reevaluation. Along these lines, many experimental composers have cast a critical eye not just on our musical culture but on Western society as a whole. For instance, much of Berio's music from the 1960s and early 1970s has an explicitly social and political message, as in *Passaggio* for narrator, chorus, instruments, and tape (1965), and *Opera* (1971, revised 1977). All three pit the helpless individual against an oppressive society. Another pivotal work from this period is Luigi Nono's *Intolleranza 1960*, a brazenly political opera indicting postwar civilization for its inherent fascism. In each case, a challenge to society and government is represented, in part, by a performance format intended to challenge the musical establishment. *Intolleranza*, for example, was one of the earliest works to include electronic tape, film, slides, and innovative lighting effects in an otherwise conventional operatic setting.

In contrast are three important European works of the 1960s that either eliminate or obscure explicit verbal content, although each definitely involves theater and acting. Stockhausen's *Momente* (1964), for soprano, four choral groups, and thirteen instrumentalists, consists of entirely independent fragments or "moments" in sequence, each one unrelated to any other. The resultant sense of discontinuity pervades the choice of vocal "texts" as well; these include a deliberate overlap of different languages, meaningless nonsense syllables, handclaps, laughter, foot stamping, and outbursts from the audience.

Two theater works by György Ligeti (b. 1923), *Aventures* (1962) and *Nouvelles Aventures* (1965), explore a similarly uncertain realm. Both pieces are scored for three singers and seven instrumentalists; in each, the "words" cannot be found in any language, as they have been "composed" phonetically by Ligeti. They do impart, however, a broad range of human emotions and responses such as (quoting the composer) "understanding and dissension, dominion and subjection, honesty and deceit, arrogance, disobedience," and the like. The interpersonal dramas projected by this abstract language of sounds are so convincing in performance that many attempts have been made to stage the work fully, complete with set and props, even though the work was only intended as a theater piece for chamber musicians. Uniquely, these works do manage to covey a narrative content while still maintaining their abstract, nonverbal character.

TOWARD TOTAL THEATER

Since the late 1950s many works have aspired to the all-embracing status of "total theater," and various terms such as *happenings* or *environments* have arisen to categorize them. One common characteristic of such works is that in addition to including sound, visual media, movement, improvisation, and audience involvement, they often explore more expansive performing spaces, reaching out into an entire auditorium, an entire building, an entire neighborhood, or beyond.

A landmark in the genre was the collaboration between Le Corbusier, Iannis Xenakis, and Edgard Varèse, resulting in the Phillips Pavilion at the 1958 Brussels World's Fair. Through an installation of over four hundred loudspeakers, Varèse's *Poème électronique* swept repeatedly across the building's high, angular spaces while projected images illuminated the walls. This work established a number of important ideas: (1) that such an event could proceed continuously, with no beginning or end; (2) that it could involve vast spatial dimensions; and (3) that the listener/viewer could walk in, out, around, or through at will, regulating or modifying the experience by choice. That same year, an American pioneer in mixed media, Milton Cohen, began to present a series of freely structured events in Ann

Arbor, Michigan, under the rubric of Space Theater, involving visual art, projections, movement, sound and audience improvisation (eventually leading to formation of the ONCE group). Perhaps the most famous outgrowth of these developments came a decade later with the John Cage–Lejaren Hiller collaboration, *HPSCHD* (1969), a sonic and visual "walkthrough" environment described more fully in Chapter 12.

The spatial openness in such works can be extended to create large-scale theater "environments," as in the historic 1972 production at Yale University of Stockhausen's *Hymnen* (1967) under the direction of the conductor John Mauceri. The staging ground for that event spanned the entire central portion of the Yale campus, requiring that several blocks be closed to traffic. "Themes" of the presentation—nationalism, war, and peace—followed from the nature of Stockhausen's tape (which is described more fully in Chapter 13). The quadraphonic tape formed the skeleton of the work, played back through enormous speakers installed on rooftops. Live performing forces included amplified orchestra, a haranguer, a variety of choral ensembles, a mock military police troop, three airplanes, aerial searchlights, and projections on the walls of buildings.

The environmental scope of that production was an optional aspect of the composition, but for some works by Stockhausen, huge spaces are a must. His 1984 opera *Samstag* ("Saturday")—one of a series of operas for each day of the week, begun in 1977 and collectively entitled *Licht*—had to be premiered in the sports stadium of Milan because of its size and complexity. Robert Moran's monumental *39 Minutes for 39 Autos* required the entire city of San Francisco for its execution in 1969. Moran (b. 1937) called for automobile horns and lights, home and office lights (performed by "audience participants"), and live and prerecorded electronic sounds, all aided by television and radio facilities.

As some of the examples above suggest, large-scale multimedia works may be temporally as well as environmentally extended. La Monte Young's performances with his Theater of Eternal Music, which include slowly evolving sound and light environments lasting for many hours or even days, will be discussed in Part III.

CONCLUSION

We have emphasized that unorthodox performance practices necessarily have a theatrical impact, and that the element of theater becomes stronger as traditional expectations and experimental activities diverge. Departures from the norm achieve their dramatic power in part by surprising, shocking, or cajoling observers into a more attentive or receptive state. An audience that has been shaken loose from its bearings, uprooted from its habitual patterns of response, may be moved more easily in the direction intended by a composer or performer. Just as important, experimental works may serve to push performers, audiences, and the culture as a whole beyond what some see as an outdated attachment to nineteenth-century European ideals. Those who create such works are combating what composer Edwin London has called a "masterpiece psychosis," embodied by the rarefied ritual of concert performance, the worshipful attitude toward "great composers," the isolation of musicians on a "pedestal" (i.e., the stage), and treatment of the precisely notated score as inviolable scripture.

Texture, Mass, and Density

The words *texture, mass,* and *density* provide visual and tactile analogies for an experience of sound that is difficult to describe in purely acoustic terms. The experience ranges from silence on one end of the spectrum to high-intensity noise from the highest to lowest audible frequency on the other, with literally infinite possibilities in between. This entire spectrum has opened up to composers during the past half century, owing to new freedoms in the exploration of **pitch logic, time, sound color,** and compositional **process,** all of which interrelate to create **texture.** The possibilities are so rich and varied that many composers have made texture a focal element in the structure of their music.

PRECEDENTS

Once the boundaries of traditional tonality began to fall away in the late nineteenth century, musical texture was no longer limited by the strictures of tonal voice leading and counterpoint. In Debussy's music, one result was an extended use of parallel chords; the complete sameness of motion from one chord to the next represents a degree of homophony—a uniformity of texture—not possible when voices are working, coordinated but individually, toward a tonal goal.

Schoenberg, in totally abandoning any semblance of tonality whatsoever, opened up a vast array of textural opportunities. One widely noted example is "Summer Morning by a Lake (Colors)," the third of his Five Pieces for Orchestra, Op. 16 (1909). The opening chord in this movement (C–G#–B–E–A) has a completely static, neutral quality, made possible by its lack of tonal implications and barely discernible rhythmic motion. With little distraction from tonal or rhythmic momentum, the ear becomes more alert to sound color and texture, which fluctuate subtly as the chord alternates between two timbrally distinct groups of instruments. (This is the most famous instance of *Klangfarbenmelodie*, Schoenberg's term for a "melody" of successive tone colors, analogous to that of successive pitches.)

The twelve-tone technique, which Schoenberg later developed, often played a crucial part in generating texture. Webern's idiosyncratic use of the technique gives rise to lean, transparent textures, exposing the intervallic consistencies and symmetries in his pitch material. The spare opening of his Concerto for Nine Instruments, Op. 24 (1934) is a classic illustration; it plainly and economically highlights the structure of the row, which is made up entirely of trichords related by inversion and retrograde. This, too, is an instance of *Klangfarbenmelodie*, each trichord being played by a different instrument.

The freer use of dissonance allowed by expanding or abandoning tonality greatly liberated the composer's approach to counterpoint, since polyphonic voices were no longer obliged to gravitate toward triadic relationships. Whole new realms of contrapuntal texture were discovered, as can be heard in the music of Stravinsky, Bartók, and Ives. In Bartók's music, for example, a densely packed counterpoint of seconds, tritones, and sevenths often arises from a literal, interval-for-interval imitation or symmetry between complex lines that would be impossible if traditional relationships held sway.

For Stravinsky, in contrast, harmonic freedom more often meant the ability to generate contrapuntal textures from highly *dis*similar lines of counterpoint. The introductory section of the *Rite of Spring* (1913), for example, culminates in a densely complex orchestral fabric woven from a variety of melodically and rhythmically distinct instrumental lines. Diatonic yet harmonically conflicting strands are superimposed, at times representing eight different and simultaneous subdivisons of the beat (triplet eighths, quintuplet sixteenths, septuplet thirty-seconds, etc.). But where Stravinsky apposes contrasting individual lines, Ives superimposes entire musical passages with conflicting rhythm, tempo, and tonality. An oft-cited instance is the second movement ("Putnam's Camp") of his 1914 *Three Places in New England,* which depicts two separate marching bands converging from opposite sides of town as they play different marches.

In these examples both Ives and Stravinsky achieved bristling textures of massive weight and complexity by generating a highly dissonant collage from otherwise relatively familiar elements. Edgard Varèse, however, went entirely beyond the familiar; in such works as *Intégrales* for woodwinds, brass, and percussion (1925) and *Arcana* for orchestra (1927), he deals directly with dissonant and disparate blocks of sound, clashing and contending with one another to create a highly charged polyphonic web. In both his instrumental and electronic music Varèse anticipated the achievements of Ligeti, Penderecki, and others by treating aggregates of sound—defined by timbre, texture, register, and rhythm—as basic components of musical structure, much as a traditional composer might treat melody or harmony.

The above-mentioned examples by Debussy, Schoenberg, and Webern offer uniquely simple, sustained, or transparent textures, while those of Bartók, Stravinsky, Ives, and Varèse represent textures of unprecedented density and intricacy. But perhaps the boldest exploration of texture before 1945 was by Henry Cowell, who pioneered the use of tone clusters. In a tone cluster, all possible notes between a specified upper and lower limit are sounded at one time, resulting in a texture whose density and vibrational complexity come as close to noise as acoustic instruments can. (Noise contains all frequencies within its upper and lower limits). Clusters may be notated in complete detail, such as ♩, or with only the outer limits specified: ▌ or ▎ .

Cowell originated the use of clusters in his early piano music with such works as "The Tides of Manaunaun" (1912) and "The Hero Sun" (1922). The performer uses fists, palms, or even forearms, and the effects range from thunderous masses of sound and frenetic splashes of color to quiet, expansive, ethereal textures. Ives's song "Majority" (1921) is another well-known early example employing clusters in the piano accompaniment.

Another important concept originating with Cowell is that of performing on an instrument using techniques for which it was not designed, thereby evoking new timbres and textures. Again, he turned to the piano. "Aeolian Harp" (1923) and "Sinister Resonance" (1925) require the performer to reach in and sweep, strike, strum, or mute the strings with one hand while manipulating the keys with the other. Perhaps the most notorious example is "The Banshee" (1925), during which the pianist plays only on the strings, never touching the keyboard, while an assistant holds down the damper pedal. The entire work is played in the lowest register of the piano, where the strings are swept continuously in various ways. (Periodically, fingernails stroke the strings lengthwise, producing an eerie "scream" suggestive of the title.) The result is a work shaped entirely by fluctuations in its texture, dominated by rumbling, howling, richly resonant waves of sound with no clearly discernible pitch (except for an occasional pizzicato).

As with works of Varèse, Cowell's music embodies the remarkable notion that a composition may be structured or "sculpted" not from discreet pitches, chords, or rhythms but from raw, abstract sound. That notion anticipates not only the music of Penderecki, Górecki, and other Eastern European "sound mass" composers of later decades, but also the basic achievements of electronic music.

TEXTURE AND INSTRUMENTAL COLOR

Instrumentation and Orchestration

As a general paradigm, we might say that the number of simultaneous pitches within a given interval span (density), their registral placement (high or low, wide or narrow), and their rhythmic relationship (e.g., homophonic, contrapuntal, etc.) provide the basic quantitative substance of a musical texture; sound color, dynamics, and articulation—the way a tone is shaped, including the quality of accent and release—transform that basic substance and give it further distinctive qualities.

Countless examples of evocative textures in pre–1945 orchestral and chamber music literature spring from innovative use of instrumental color. Hector Berlioz's *Symphonie fantastique* (1830) was perhaps the earliest work to employ unorthodox methods of orchestration. But frequent, sometimes drastic departures from "good" or "acceptable" orchestration in the service of timbre and texture became more common in the early twentieth century, particularly in the works of Mahler, Debussy, Stravinsky, Prokofiev, and Copland, among others. These departures might involve imaginative instrumental doublings, placement of instruments in their extreme high or low registers, rarely used chord voicings, or the creative use of flutter-tonguing, muting, string harmonics, multiply divided strings (*a 3* or more) or other less common effects.

After 1945 the relationship between instrumental color and texture became an ever more fruitful basis for innovation, even within relatively traditional approaches to instrumentation. Stefan Wolpe, for example, picks up the technique of *Klangfarbenmelodie* where Webern left off and extends it to soaring dimensions in his *Chamber Piece No. 1* for fourteen instruments (1964). This is evident in Example 10.1, which shows two brief melodic

lines arching from low to high and back again, both spanning more than two octaves. By comparing the fragments in boxes with the reduction underneath, one can see that single lines are projected through a constantly changing series of doublings. The color and sweep of these lines brings an ecstatic and kinetically charged quality (one found throughout Wolpe's music) to a texture that is otherwise sparse and economical. (Earlier in this passage, Wolpe acknowledges his debt by inscribing "Oh, Webern . . ." between the staves.)

While *Klangfarbenmelodie* offers a kaleidoscope of timbre that is melodic or *horizontal*, an equally rich variety of color may be arrayed harmonically or *vertically*. For example, passages in Messiaen's *Chronochromie* for orchestra (1960) employ every type of instrumental color simultaneously, each with a distinctly individual line, thus forging a huge, prismatic contrapuntal landscape. Elsewhere in this work, timbrally distinct groups (instead of individual instruments) are similarly layered, each having its own durational scheme and chordal characteristics.

The departures from conventional instrumentation mentioned earlier—unusual doublings or combinations, extremes in register, fluttertonguing, and so on—had become more common in new music by the 1960s and 1970s; today, they must be accepted not as signs of originality but as part of an established timbral and textural reservoir that has grown inevitably richer with time. To these might be added one more instrumental technique that has emerged since World War II, that of *timbral modulation* or transformation. Although related to *Klangfarbenmelodie,* it is perhaps more akin to amplitude and frequency modulation in electronic music, since its focus is on transformation of a single, sustained sonority from one timbre to another. In its simplest manifestation, two instruments of different timbre sustain one chord or pitch, but one swells while the other diminishes; pitch remains constant while sound color shifts from the timbre of one instrument to that of the other. In Example 10.2, from Daniel Godfrey's *Scrimshaw* for flute and violin (1985), this exchange takes place repeatedly, with a pattern of swelling and diminishing staggered between the two instruments. (The violin not only alternates color with the flute but also modulates its own timbre with a gradual change in bow position.)

Transmutations of this kind are frequent in the music of Steven Stucky

---

EXAMPLE 10.1.

Stefan Wolpe: *Chamber Piece No. 1*

EXAMPLE 10.2.

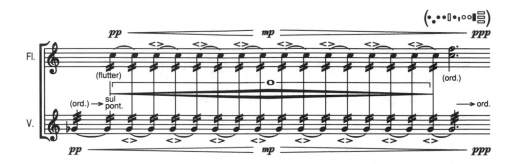

Daniel Godfrey: *Scrimshaw*

Reprinted by permission of American Composers
Alliance, New York

(b. 1949). Example 10.3 is an illustration from his *Sappho Fragments* for
mezzo-soprano and chamber ensemble (1982). Cross-rhythms and overlapping entrances yield a texture that modulates both timbrally and rhythmically. Two strands are transformed, one involving the pitches D and F
(flute, violin, and piano), the other involving E and F# (vibraphone and
cello). Note the shift in timbre and rhythm between the flute's sixteenths
and the piano's quintuplet sixteenths, set against continuous triplets in the
violin. Also note that the crescendo and initial decay of the vibraphone's E
mask the pianissimo entrance of the cello, whose oscillation between E and
F# emerges seamlessly as the vibraphone dies away.

New Performance Techniques

Previous chapters have touched on a variety of performing techniques that
bring forth new and unusual sounds from traditional instruments. We have
had a glimpse of this versatility from experiments with the piano by Cage
and Cowell, but virtually every other instrument offers a comparable
wealth of novel capabilities.

George Crumb's *Vox balaenae*, for instance, opens with an elaborate
melisma for electric flute, which the flutist doubles, note for note, by singing at the same time. Other startling effects that can be elicited from woodwind and brass instruments include rattling or slapping the keys or valves,
percussive effects with the tongue, biting the reed (creating a harsh or
"pinched" sound), blowing without lip pressure (creating a wind sound),

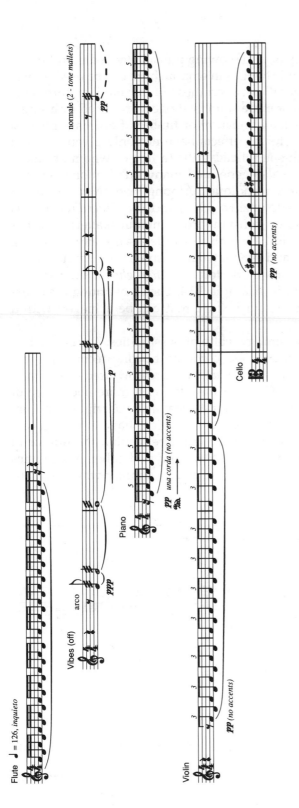

EXAMPLE 10.3. Steven Stucky: *Sappho Fragments*, second movement. © 1988 Merion Music, Inc. Used by permission

tapping with knuckles or fingers, and blowing into a detached mouthpiece. Also, alternative fingerings and changes in embouchure can be used to produce microtones (pitches that fall between those of our familiar chromatic scale) and multiphonics (two or more sounds at once, produced by a single fingering), as well as to alter the intonation or timbre of ordinary pitches.

The novelty and variety of such effects have not only given rise to a new class of performers with specialized skills (a few of whom are mentioned in Chapter 9) but have also generated many publications devoted exclusively to new performance techniques. Among them, *New Sounds for Woodwind* (1967) by Bruno Bartolozzi (b. 1911) and *The Other Flute* (1974) by Robert Dick (b. 1950) outline nonstandard techniques, alternative fingerings, and specialized **notation;** they also include a score and recording of music, composed by the author, that demonstrate these innovations (*Collage* for four solo woodwinds by Bartolozzi, *Afterlight* for flute solo by Dick). As is visually apparent in Example 10.4, Dick's haunting essay exemplifies the opulence of color and texture that can be achieved with a single instrument.

String instruments offer a similar wealth of possibilities. A great variety of generally accepted but hitherto less common bowing techniques (*sul ponticello, flautando, col legno battuto, ricochet,* etc.) are now used extensively in contemporary scores. The recent past has also seen more liberal use of harmonics, left-hand pizzicato, wide vibrato, *non vibrato,* triple and quadruple stops, *scordatura,* and *glissando.* New practices have also emerged, such as bowing behind the bridge, on the tailpiece, behind the nut, or in fact, anywhere on the instrument. These and myriad other possibilities cause the instrument to resonate in unique and unfamiliar ways.

EXAMPLE 10.4.

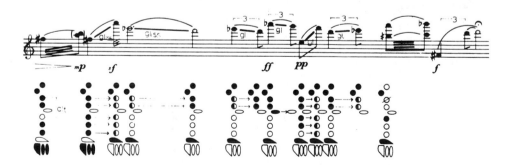

Robert Dick: *Afterlight* for solo flute

One of many contemporary works abounding in such procedures is Jacob Druckman's *Valentine* for solo contrabass (1969). As seen in Example 10.5, Druckman also incorporates a rare departure, that of using a timpani mallet (as well as bowing and pizzicato) to activate the strings.

The square noteheads in this example indicate use of the timpani mallet, open notes being struck with the mallet head, filled notes with the wooden handle. In addition to the usual five-line staff, the brace contains other lines below the staff to indicate playing on various parts of the bass (bridge, tailpiece, body front or side, etc.). The line above the staff is for vocal sounds ("pa"). This passage offers a richness of texture surprising for a solo instrument, generated by startling effects in rapid-fire sequence. In the first gesture, for example, a z through the stem indicates "buzzing" (made by ricocheting the wooden handle closely on the strings). As indicated by the steplike notehead, this is to be executed while making a rapid arpeggio across the strings between bridge and tailpiece. At 7'42" the x-ed noteheads indicate a downward pizzicato arpeggio with all four strings "choked" (prevented from resonating by the left hand). In the next figure, the mallet handle is beaten rapidly from side to side between the A and E strings, moving from the bridge to the fingerboard.

Much of the groundwork for all this innovation was laid by Luciano Berio, who is widely acknowledged as a pioneer in experimenting with instrumental color. His *Sequenzas* for solo instruments (beginning with *Sequenza I* for flute in 1958) are widely inventive explorations of timbre, and although less radical in technique than the above examples, they continue to influence and inspire the work of many others.

EXAMPLE 10.5.

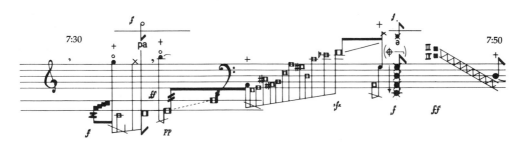

Jacob Druckman: *Valentine* for solo contrabass

Given that a single instrument can produce such a broad spectrum of sounds, one can imagine the potential of such techniques when applied to *many* instruments at once. This realm is explored repeatedly and with great experimental fervor by the American composer Donald Erb (b. 1927). In his works for band and orchestra, conventionally notated and performed passages are often juxtaposed with others that deviate drastically from ordinary practice, with results that words cannot convey. Erb's *The Seventh Trumpet* for orchestra (1969) is recognized as a classic in this respect. It includes, for example, a gradually ascending glissando for strings, articulated by rapid (and unsynchronized) pluckings; in other passages, groups of wind instruments are asked to perform percussive "tremolos" with keys alone (i.e., without blowing), or to play solely upon their reeds.

One area particularly ripe for timbral and textural exploration is percussion. Dramatic differences in attack, resonance, and timbre can be achieved depending on where, how, and with what a given instrument is struck. Percussionists are not even limited to mallets or sticks; for example, metal instruments like gongs, tam-tams, cymbals, or vibraphone will produce unique resonances when activated by the fingertips, metal rods, or the bow of a cello. Beyond this, present-day ensembles routinely employ a dazzling assortment of percussion instruments. In addition to the usual display of drums, timpani, cymbals, tam-tams, xylophone, glockenspiel, triangles, and other instruments owned by most orchestras, today's scores often call for wood or temple blocks, castanets, tambourine, guiro, maracas, crotales, almglocken, wind chimes, bongos, tabla, marimba, vibraphone, or other instruments too numerous to mention. Before 1945 many of these were considered exotic when they appeared in such scores as John Becker's *The Abongo* for percussion orchestra and dance troupe (1933), Varèse's *Ionisation*, Antheil's *Ballet mécanique*, or Cage's *First Construction in Metal*.

The instruments just listed have long been extant in one culture or another, but other percussion resources are new. Among them are everyday objects with resonant properties attractive to the composer: brake drums, iron pipes, tin cans, wine glasses, whistles, auto horns, and pistols, to name a few. (The conjuring of new "instrumentation" from improbable sources has been taken to comical extremes by composer/performer David van Tiegem.) Some instruments have been refined or developed specifically for contemporary scores; included are the musical saw, vibra slap, lion's roar, whip, ratchet, thunder sheet, wind machine, and waterphone. Harry Partch and David Moss are among composers who have designed and built their own instruments from scratch, emphasizing sculptural elegance as well as acoustical innovation.

Since about 1960 this staggering wealth of acoustical resources has inspired the formation of ensembles devoted exclusively to percussion, such as the Percussion Group Cincinnati, Zeitgeist, and the Netherlands Percussion Ensemble, among many others.

New Instrumental Combinations

During the eighteenth and nineteenth centuries instrumental combinations such as the orchestra, woodwind quintet, string quartet, and piano trio became standard, while other formats such as the symphonic band, big band, and saxophone quartet have become common only during the twentieth century. (Widespread recognition of the saxophone quartet as a concert ensemble is credited to Sigurd Rascher, a legendary advocate of new music for the saxophone.) But among the freedoms enjoyed by today's composer is the freedom to select and combine instruments purely according to imagination. One resulting phenomenon is the mixed chamber ensemble, typically consisting of any combination of string, woodwind, brass, percussion, or keyboard instruments, with or without voice, and usually with no more than one or two of each kind. Early twentieth-century examples may be found in Stravinsky's *L'histoire du soldat* (1917) for clarinet, bassoon, cornet, trombone, violin, double bass, and percussion (with narrator and dancers) or Varèse's *Octandre* (1923) for flute, oboe, clarinet, bassoon, horn, trumpet, trombone, and double bass, to single out just two.

Since 1945 scores for mixed ensembles of this kind have become so common, written by composers of every stylistic persuasion, that countless groups specializing in this repertoire have come into being. A list of the more prominent ones would include the Ensemble InterContemporain, the Ensemble Modern, the Fires of London, the Melos Ensemble, "Die Reihe" Ensemble, Speculum Musicae, Boston Musica Viva, the Pittsburgh New Music Ensemble, and the California Ear Unit.

Of course, creative instrumentation may involve any imaginable combination, as in Jo Kondo's *Sight Rhythmics* for violin, electric piano, banjo, steel drum, and tuba. An opposite strategy is followed by Gunther Schuller (b. 1925) in his *Five Moods for Tuba Quartet* (1972), and by Paul Chihara (b. 1938) in his *Tree Music* (1966) for three violas and three trombones.

Another trend is the use of early instruments or instruments from other cultures (the latter to be explored in Chapter 11) as new sources of color and texture. Twentieth-century works for one or more recorders are numerous, ranging from Paul Hindemith's relatively straightforward *Trio* (1932) to the maniacally innovative *12.5.83* for alto recorder by Drake Mabry. More noteworthy, perhaps, is the use of the sackbut, shawm, crumhorn, rebec, viol, and other less familiar instruments from the Medieval and Renaissance eras. These are still strange to concertgoers not familiar with early music; in an avant-garde setting they are totally anomalous, a notoriously irreverent example being Mauricio Kagel's *Music for Renaissance Instruments* (1965).

TEXTURE AND PROCESS

In previous chapters we have already encountered in the music of Stockhausen, Boulez, Babbitt, and Wuorinen vividly elaborate textures resulting from a rigorous compositional **process.** Although total organization tends to produce in their works a textural surface of galactic complexity, an important distinction separates their music from that discussed in the following paragraphs. Babbitt and Stockhausen did not aim chiefly at generating and manipulating complex polyphonic textures, but rather at achieving a cohesion or integration of all compositional materials (pitch, duration, dynamics, etc.). In the works discussed below, however, texture is a primary focus of the compositional process.

A straightforward illustration is offered by the player-piano studies of Conlon Nancarrow (b. 1912), an American expatriate in Mexico whose eccentric artistry remained little known until the late 1960s. The control and precision possible in punching piano rolls have allowed him to achieve elaborate polyphonic relationships and virtuosic extremes utterly beyond the reach of any live performer. These result from layering rhythmic strands of different *tempos,* often employing such ratios as 12:15:20 (Study No. 17), 2 to the square root of 2 (Study No. 33), or 60:61 (Study No. 39). Some studies superimpose voices that accelerate or decelerate in differing ways. In Study No. 21 (*Canon X*) the upper of two voices begins at an extremely fast tempo and then gradually decelerates, while the lower voice does the opposite simultaneously. Thus, the upper register moves from extreme density to utter sparseness, while the lower register gradually builds to a thunderous mass of sound. In other words, a pattern of changing tempos creates a pattern of changing densities. The music's texture is shaped by a temporal process.

To some extent, the same can be said of Elliott Carter's music; but where Nancarrow views opposing layers of rhythm and tempo in mathematical terms, Carter associates them with the contrasting dramatic roles or personalities he assigns to instruments. Often the protagonists consist of instrumental groups, each with its own characteristic form of behavior. For example, his Double Concerto for harpsichord, piano, and two chamber orchestras (1961) might crudely be described as two concertos played simultaneously, each identifiable by its own distinctive rhythms and intervals, but just as importantly, by its own entirely distinct tempos. In fact, at one point in the middle movement, the piano and associated instruments accelerate from very slow to very fast while the harpsichord and its group do the opposite, the tempos coalescing and diverging much as in Nancarrow's *Canon X.* The two ensembles do influence and interact with one another (in Carter's words, "interrupting" or "commenting" on each other's activities) much as two actors in a play. The textural outcome, however, is a kaleidoscopic and continuously evolving polyphony of contrasting tempos and playing styles.

In many of his other works Carter fashions the same kind of richly layered contrapuntal textures by assigning divergent dramatic roles to individual instruments (rather than instrumental groups). In the String Quartet No. 2 (1959) Carter views these "roles" or "personalities" in plainly anthropomorphic terms: the first violin is impetuous, mercurial, and virtuosic; the second violin is stubborn and rhythmically rigid throughout; the viola is prone to maudlin, melancholy behavior; and the cello tends to be romantic and effusive. In summarizing their roles, Carter has explained: "Each player, in turn, dominates a movement while the other three mimic the leader, translating his phrases into phrases from their own vocabularies. In between the movements, there are three cadenzas, solos for first violin, viola, and cello, during which the other members oppose the cadenza player as if they were disenchanted by his actions." Example 10.6 from the cello cadenza exemplifies the way Carter uses tempo and rhythmic detail to differentiate between these instrumental personalities. What appear to be elaborate cross-rhythms are really to be played and heard as independent rhythms, relatively simple in themselves, proceeding at different tempos. The first and second violins play regularly spaced attacks, each at its own speed, with occasional rests; the viola plays—in effect—a rubato line of sustained but somewhat irregularly spaced pitches; and the cello, in keeping with its soloistic role, begins with its own regular pulse but then shifts suddenly (in m. 254) to longer durations from which it accelerates dramatically, as if breaking away from the others in defiance.

To combine and coordinate completely individual streams of musical activity is a complex challenge; but in achieving it, Carter has eschewed the mathematical precision of electronic technology or other artificial means (as developed by Nancarrow, for example). Instead, he has evolved his own process of manipulating time, working purely within the bounds of traditional music notation. Cross-rhythms, involving many ways of subdividing the beat, are one resource used to project and control independent tempos. Another such tool, pervasive in Carter's scores, is *metric modulation,* already introduced in Chapter 6. Example 10.7 offers a simplified illustration of how this technique is used to achieve the simultaneous accelerando and ritardando found in works like the above-mentioned Double Concerto.

Carter's highly fluid and variegated polyphonic textures, then, are the outgrowth of a temporal process characterized not simply by polyrhythm but, as Charles Rosen has suggested, by "polytempo." This term could also apply to Stockhausen's *Zietmasse* ("Tempos") for five winds (1956), which achieves as many as five temporally independent streams of activity through the combination of strict and aleatoric notation, the latter allowing

EXAMPLE 10.6.

Elliott Carter: *String Quartet No. 2*, first movement

separate parts to establish or change their own meter and tempo autonomously.

In live performances of Carter's Double Concerto and Second String Quartet mentioned above, as well as his *Symphony of Three Orchestras* (1976), the polyphony is spatially enhanced by separating dramatically and temporally distinct instruments or groups of instruments onstage. Stockhausen's *Gruppen* for three orchestras (1957) and *Carré* for four orchestras and four choruses (1960) also depend on spatial separation to clarify the textural, timbral, and rhythmic identity of each ensemble. Both are works

EXAMPLE 10.7.

A simplified illustration of metric modulation

whose central concern is the polyphonic interaction of distinct sound masses or textures.

In the preceding examples by Nancarrow, Carter, and Stockhausen, texture is the product of counterpoint generated by durational processes involving multiple tempos. The music of Iannis Xenakis is also governed by process, and as with Nancarrow, the process is mathematically conceived. But Xenakis's textures are not contrapuntal, that is, they do not result from the combination of independent lines or layers of counterpoint to yield a composite texture. For Xenakis, the basic substratum of music *is* texture, even though it may be the product of many smaller sonic components. The only counterpoint one might speak of meaningfully in such works is a "counterpoint" of textures or sound masses.

Xenakis's background in architecture and engineering informed his approach to composition, inspiring him to establish the Center for the Study of Mathematical and Automated Music in Paris in 1966. During the 1950s and '60s his music grew out of mathematical processes derived from calculus, game theory, and scientific principles such as the Kinetic Theory of Gases and Bernoulli's Law of Large Numbers. Many works from this period rely on what Xenakis has called the *stochastic* method, in which sound masses are shaped by mathematical probability (as expressed in Bernoulli's Law). The stochastic approach allowed Xenakis to calculate, as a function of probability, the shape and behavior of composite masses of sound made up of many brief sound events. Thus, his music is often dominated by enormous clusters or "clouds" of small sound "particles," beginning, ending, and fluctuating in density as rain or hail does when striking against a hard surface (Xenakis's own analogy). Two early and highly influential works to exhibit this approach were *Metastasis* for sixty-one-piece orchestra (1954) and *Pithoprakta* for fifty-piece orchestra (1956).

In *Pithoprakta*, for example, the entire string section is divided into individual parts. For Xenakis, the use of as many separate parts as there are orchestra players is a logical outgrowth of the stochastic process, since large sound masses built of many small events require many individual participants. This practice became common for other texture-oriented composers as well (especially Ligeti, Penderecki, Serocki, and Lutosławski), making it possible to generate massive sonorities that saturate a given register or span of time.

Exactly how the stochastic process translates into actual rhythms and pitches is beyond the scope of this chapter, but the musical outcome is fascinating. In *Pithoprakta* alone one can perceive a great range of orchestral sound masses, including "cloudbursts" of rapid but imprecise percussive noises—made by tapping the bodies of stringed instruments, as cross-rhythms create the impression of innumerable randomly spaced attacks—and dense fabrics created when pitch is introduced into the equation. With regard to the latter, maximal density is often achieved by ensuring that any two instruments sharing the same register have different pitch contours, rhythms, or both; consequently, no two instruments play the same pitch at the same time. Furthermore, the registral span traveled by each instrument overlaps that of its neighbors such that every part of the ensemble's range is traversed in various ways by four or five instruments at a time. Moreover, pitches are chosen so that every note within a four- or five-octave span is represented at least once in every beat.

By varying states of articulation as well, Xenakis has created textures of remarkably contrasted character. One can hear in *Pithoprakta*, a string orchestra sonority during which every instrument plays a forced pizzicato (*arraché*), a passage in which all strings play a continuous glissando while moving at different rates in different directions, and another featuring *col legno battuto* (*frappé*) for every player. What is apparent when experiencing the entire work is the overall shape of these gestures, the fluctuation of their densities, and the sometimes sudden, sometimes subtle shift from one texture to the next—all these qualities being vital to the work's structure.

Like Carter, Xenakis has added a spatial dimension to the unfolding of texture in some of his works. Among them are *Terretektorh* for eighty-eight-piece orchestra (1966), *Polytope de Montréal* for four chamber orchestras (1967), and *Nomos Gamma* for orchestra (1968), in all of which the musicians are spread out among the audience.

The relationship between texture and compositional process takes on a different aspect in Berio's *Chemins II b/c* for nine woodwinds, six brass, percussion, electric guitar, electric organ, piano, and strings. This work began as *Sequenza VI* for solo viola (1966); a chamber ensemble was then added to the viola part, resulting in *Chemins II* for viola and nine instruments (1967); the instrumentation was then further expanded to include full orchestra in *Chemins II b* (1970), after which a part for solo bass clarinet was added to create *Chemins II c* (1972). *Chemins II b/c* is yet another version, replacing the bass clarinet with a tenor saxophone. With each incarnation the music gained a new stratum of texture, the totality being compared by Berio to an onion with many layers, the outer layer providing a new surface and the older layers changing in function. "Process" in *Chemins II b/c*, then, refers to the composer's way of working: revision and/or accretion of material through successive versions of the composition.

Texture is an outgrowth of process in the music of Brian Ferneyhough (b. 1943) as well. On a purely surface level, his scores are fabulously ornate, characterized by a dense succession of highly variegated gestures and effects, which present immense challenges to the performer. Underlying this is a labyrinthine system of thought, as much guided by the composer's views on phenomenology and epistemology as by purely musical concerns. (Ferneyhough's *Carceri d'Invenzione I* is discussed in Chapter 21.)

SOUND MASS: VARIABLE DENSITY AND COMPLEXITY

Instrumental Music

We return again to the discovery made by Cowell, Ives, and Varèse that blocks or masses of sound can serve just as well as chords or individual notes in shaping a musical discourse. For our purposes, a "sound mass" is a sonority liberated from being heard in terms of specific pitches or chords, allowing it to serve as more abstract and in some ways more versatile material. Not only is sound mass just as malleable as notes or chords with respect to rhythm, register, timbre, dynamics, and other variables, but it can also be manipulated in terms of its apparent "weight" or "density" and the relative simplicity or complexity of its surface. Sound-mass textures, however, are fundamentally different from genuinely contrapuntal ones in that individual lines of music, perhaps represented by individual instruments or instrumental groups, have no significant identity of their own, being indistinguishable parts of a larger fabric. Thus, the texture in Xenakis's *Pithoprakta* cannot be usefully regarded as contrapuntal; even though it contains an enormous amount of counterpoint, each part is only one of very many similar parts contributing to a single massive, composite texture.

An instrument or ensemble may be approached not as a vehicle for pitches and rhythms but as a source of raw sound from which textures can be erected or sculpted. This is illustrated in the *Organbook 1967* of William Albright (b. 1944), who as a composer and performer has been a leader in exploiting new sounds for the organ. Two types of texture are featured in one passage, one generated by tone-cluster glissandos and the other by very rapid thirty-second note patterns , both textures ranging wildly and unevenly over the compass of the keyboard. The rapidity and unpredictable contour of the thirty-seconds obviates any perception of specific pitch or rhythmic content; what we perceive instead is a blurred totality, identified by its overall shape and duration. The sliding clusters are perceived in a similar way, measured by their width, speed, range, and contour. This passage is without any clearly defined sense of rhythm; its rhythm unfolds on a more abstract plane, formed by the relative durations of the two textures and by the pacing of their registral peaks and valleys. (Sound color is also a factor; there are frequent changes from one manual to another, and hence changes in timbre.)

Two composers, György Ligeti and Krzysztof Penderecki, came to prominence during the late 1950s and 1960s as pathfinders in using sound masses of varying color, density, and complexity. Like Xenakis, but without the aid of any mathematical system, they treated these as the primary constituents of their music, superseding melody, harmony, and any immediately discernible rhythm (or *microrhythm*). Typically, the structure of their works from this period unfolds in a large-scale rhythm (or *macrorhythm*) shaped by durations and rates of change within and between bands or blocks of sound.

Ligeti's *Atmosphères* for orchestra (1961) is among the most renowned compositions in this genre. All eighty-eight instruments of the ensemble play a separate part, with only rare instances of doubling during the nine minutes of the work. (As one would expect, nearly every page of score is huge, often dominated from top to bottom by strings *divisi a 56.*) The opening sonority typifies Ligeti's technique. Fifty-six muted strings, all playing *sul tasto*, quietly sustain a gigantic semitone cluster spanning five octaves, parts of which are filled in or doubled by winds and bass. Ligeti forms masses or blocks of sound by saturating a given register, but does so in many ways and with many timbral transformations. In one well-known passage (mm. 23–28), the saturation results from minor-third tremolos spaced a semitone apart; the string tremolos begin slowly and then accelerate rapidly, while woodwind tremolos in the same register begin rapidly and slow to a standstill. Thus, even though the overall texture remains quiet and the pitch content remains static, the shifting relationship between winds and strings creates a subtle metamorphosis of color and surface activity.

Example 10.8—showing only the winds and first violins—illustrates

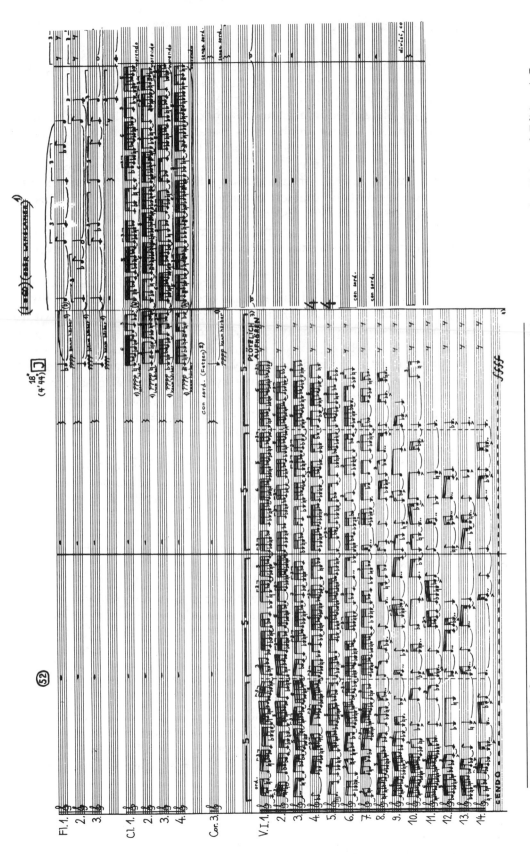

EXAMPLE 10.8. György Ligeti: *Atmosphères* (winds and first violins only). © Copyright 1963 by Universal Edition A.G., Wein. © Copyright Renewed. Used by permission of European American Music Distributors Corporation, sole U.S. and Canadian agent for Universal Edition Vienna

another way of saturating a fixed range of pitches while transforming color and texture within it. During the first two measures shown, all fifty-six string instruments are following separate routes over the same four notes (b♭ to d♭) while executing a giant crescendo. (The complex interlacing of parts to generate a dense, highly active surface is referred to by Ligeti as *micropolyphony*.) The enormous tension of this moment, which has been building for many measures, is suddenly and remarkably released by a dramatic shift to what in effect is the same texture, with the same pitches, only now played at the quietest possible dynamic by eight wind instruments. The cessation of strings occurs a split second after the winds have already entered; thus, the wind entrance is masked, leaving the impression that the abrupt disappearance of one layer has exposed another layer already present.

This passage represents only one of Ligeti's many varied approaches to creating, transforming, and juxtaposing textures in this piece. At times, entire blocks of sound enter or cut off abruptly, while elsewhere, textures develop or dissipate gradually. Differing textures may abut, overlap, or interlace in a variety of ways. Throughout the work, instrumental color plays a vital part in articulating the behavior of sound masses. The simultaneous use of nonstandard techniques by many players also has a role. In measure 76, for example, all fifteen brass players blow softly into their instruments without producing any tone, and in measures 88–101 the entire string section plays nothing but glissando harmonics, with constant changes in speed and contour.

In later works Ligeti's exploration of texture embraces a more expanded harmonic palette and a greater identity for the individual performer. *Lontano* for orchestra (1967), for instance, goes beyond semitone clusters, opening its vocabulary to wider intervals and more open sonorities. Furthermore, the many individual lines are no longer mere "particles" in a sound mass but more distinct voices—albeit in very large number—canonically interwoven into a vibrant tapestry.

The most important works by Krzysztof Penderecki (b. 1933) are also dominated by the manipulation and interaction of textures with varying density and complexity, emphasizing a broader spectrum of sound than that offered by clearly defined pitches, chords, or rhythmic sequences. The alternative notation in his scores makes this immediately apparent. Swaths of sound—rising, falling, growing, diminishing, overlapping, and colliding—are graphically depicted. Special symbols also appear, calling for unconventional sounds on conventional instruments (scraping, hissing, rattling, knocking, etc.). The most striking and widely acclaimed example of this is *Threnody for the Victims of Hiroshima* for string orchestra (1960), which is discussed in Chapter 12. Other orchestral works exemplifying this approach include *De natura sonoris* (1966) and the Capriccio for Violin and Orchestra (1967).

The dense orchestral textures we have seen are commonly associated with Eastern European composers, especially Ligeti and members of the so-called "Polish School" (Penderecki, Lutosławski, Kazimierz Serocki, Henryk Górecki, and Tadeusz Baird). In the aforementioned works by Ligeti and Penderecki, however, the harmonic, rhythmic, and timbral elements that contribute to such textures are means to an end, significant mainly in terms of the overall sound mass to which they contribute. By contrast, the music of Witold Lutosławski is multidimensional in its concerns. In the fourth movement of his *Venetian Games* for orchestra (1961), for instance, the harmonic and rhythmic features of individual polyphonic "cells," the ever-changing contrapuntal relationships among those cells, and the continually evolving totality of timbres and densities that results are all of interest and importance.

This is visually evident in Example 10.9, which also shows Lutosławski's characteristic fusion of precise control and aleatoric methods. Winds, brass, pianos, and strings (and elsewhere percussion) are treated as separate timbral groups, each performing brief cells of material unique to itself (here labeled f_1, g_1, h_1, etc.). While the entrance of each cell is precisely timed, bar lines are not used, thus eliminating any rigid interpretation of tempo or any attempt to coordinate parts within a given cell. This practice yields a high degree of rhythmic intricacy and spontaneity, but with no significant change in timing from one performance to the next.

The difference between cells is marked by more than contrasts in rhythm, interval, register, and timbre; different cells involve different forms of interplay between parts—different "games" (one of several connections between the title and the music). In the cell labeled f_1, for example, all three parts play seven notes from a repeated four-note pattern, all with similar spacing and articulation; but there are no notes in common between the three pitch patterns and the actual rhythm is different for each instrument, creating an elaborate interplay from relatively simple materials. In h_1 a different sort of "game plan" is involved. The twelve string instruments enter on a semitone cluster spanning a major seventh ($f^{\#}$ to f) and wend their way downward by whole or half steps, continually interweaving to maintain registral saturation. As an additional twist, however, each subgroup of instruments—violins, violas, cellos, and basses—represents a scale of lengthening durations (e.g., sixteenths, dotted sixteenths, eighths, and dotted eighths in the violins). Each of the other cells in the example also has its own idiosyncratic design, yielding its own unique textural surface. The excerpt displays a polyphony of disparate textures, from the sparse and pointillistic f_1 to the dense and involuted h_1. As with Ligeti and Penderecki, the structure and macrorhythm of this movement flow from the sequence, pacing, and continuously varied juxtaposition of these materials. More like Carter, however, each timbral group also projects its own internal set of relationships, its own polyphonic personality.

EXAMPLE 10.9.

Witold Lutosławski: *Venetian Games*, fourth movement

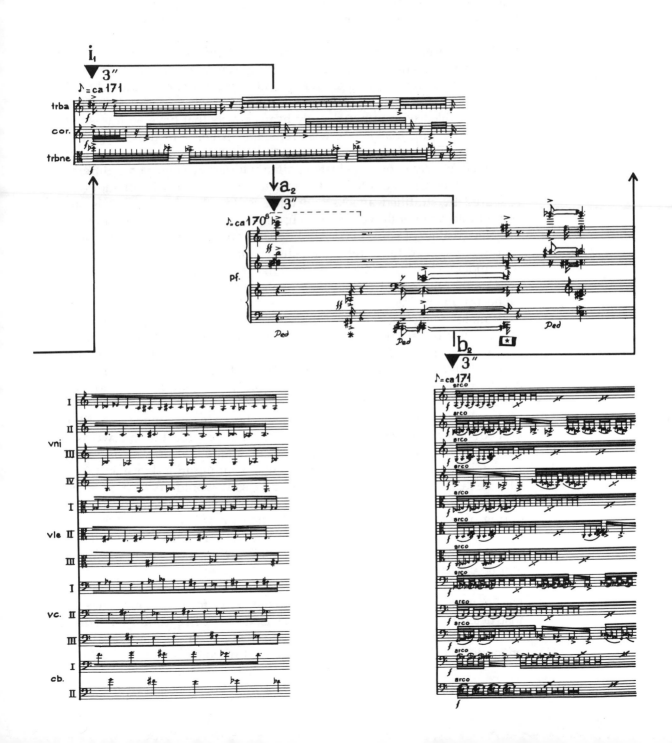

The music of Karel Husa (b. 1921) also entails the buildup of mammoth instrumental constellations from individual, rhythmically independent strands of material (motives or melodic fragments). Husa dovetails these aleatoric passages with more conventionally notated ones. Widely known examples are his *Apotheosis of This Earth* for concert band (1971) and *Music for Prague* (1968) for band or orchestra. (The latter is discussed in Chapter 21.)

Vocal ensembles have proved an especially versatile resource for texture-oriented composition. Trend-setting examples include Ligeti's *Requiem* for two soloists, two choruses, and orchestra and Penderecki's *St. Luke's Passion* for narrator, solo voices, and orchestra, both of 1965. These works are filled with hitherto rarely heard effects that have an immediate appeal, attracting many otherwise reluctant listeners to the avant-garde experience. Particularly beautiful are those sonorities that involve long, sustained, slowly evolving clusters, often with every singer on a different note. In many instances the text is too drawn-out to be discerned, or too obscured by stratified attacks and releases. In other instances it is subsumed into an overall web of asynchronous murmuring or pattering.

New realms of sound mass and density open up when aleatoric techniques are applied to choral composition; a broad sampling of such effects is found in *The Whale* (1966) by the English composer John Tavener (b. 1944), a biblical fantasy for speaker, two vocal soloists, chamber choir, and orchestra. In one instance, six voices rapidly but freely chant a line of text, each maintaining a given pitch but with no specified rhythm or effort to synchronize parts. The result is a random, murmuring texture of indistinguishable consonants and vowels, harmonically flavored by the six-note chord it outlines. Another passage, seen in Example 10.10a, calls for a continuously wavering glissando in all voices. The simplicity of notation belies the complexity of the resulting aural impression. Since pitch, rate of glissando, and rhythm of text are all freely chosen, every singer's rendition will be slightly different, yielding a weft of many separate but interweaving parts. In other words, the free aspect of the notation ensures an asynchronous relationship between all participants, resulting in a dense and complex textural surface. To notate this precisely would require as many written-out parts as there are singers, with a rhythmically intricate staggering of contours between all parts. In the case of Example 10.10b, however, it is hard to imagine *any* exact notation that could produce the violent, elaborate flood of sounds effected here by giving the performers a few simple choices and instructions.

Aleatoric methods can also produce prolonged, subtly shifting tapestries of vocal sound. In *The Whale*'s final moments, for instance, singers are instructed to "choose any note" and to sustain it for five minutes in a quiet monotone. The random pitch choices and inadvertent fluctuations of tone engender a veiled, shimmering entwinement of voices.

EXAMPLE 10.10.

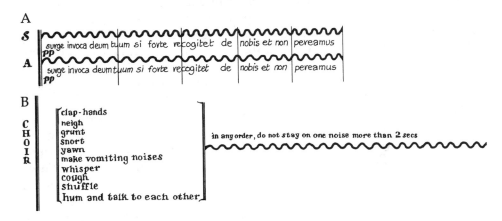

John Tavener: *The Whale*

When discussing texture, mass, and density in recent music, the tendency is to focus, as we have so far, on maximally weighted sonorities—dense clusters, massive "walls" of sound, surfaces glittering with detail—because they make such an immediate impression, being so markedly at odds with traditional Western practice. But the opposite extreme, large temporal spans containing *very little* sound, also represents a remarkable departure, stimulating new ways of thinking about the experience of time and the relationship between sound and silence. Such sparsity of material draws one's awareness to the subtlest qualities of sound itself (color, attack, amplitude shape, etc.) and to one's innermost responses to it. This was a vital consideration for Morton Feldman, unquestionably the leading figure in the use of spare, contemplative instrumental textures.

The primacy of a sound's color and other intrinsic qualities, and the relative unimportance of narrowly defined pitch and rhythm, are expressed through Feldman's use of indeterminate notation. Example 10.11 shows an excerpt from *The King of Denmark* for solo percussionist (1964). The graphic score provides only general guidelines for choosing pitch and rhythmic placement; the three horizontal levels signify high, middle, and low (for pitch), and the boxes indicate approximate increments of time within which notated sounds are to occur. Other symbols indicate general categories or amounts of activity, leaving more specific choices to the performer. (The *R*, for example, represents a roll on any instrument, and the large *5* means that five sounds may be played on any instrument in any register within the time frame.) The work's rarified atmosphere stems not just from its minimal density but also from two startling performance directives prefacing the score: (1) the dynamic must remain uniform and extremely quiet throughout, and (2) no sticks or mallets are to be used—instruments must be played only with fingers, palms, or parts of the arms.

During the past three decades, texture and timbre have continued to be an exploratory focus for many composers, but the avoidance of harmonic and rhythmic definition found in the foregoing examples has since lost its revolutionary appeal. (Penderecki himself began writing quasi-tonal "neo-romantic" music during the 1970s.) The new attraction to rhythmic and harmonic immediacy, however, has not precluded the use of large instrumental sound masses. For instance, in *The Surma Ritornelli* for eleven musicians (1983), American composer Christopher Rouse (b. 1949) deploys weighty instrumental textures with electrifying rhythmic urgency and force. Harshly dissonant chords played by the entire ensemble proceed with an impulsive, strongly accented, highly energized rhythm, while remaining homorhythmic throughout. The impression is one of large, unyielding, blocklike sonorities charging along unpredictably. In general, the work is a modern-day evocation of the primitivism in Stravinsky's *Rite of Spring* or *Les noces,* and of Varèse's enthusiasm for the raw, kinetic power of sound.

Another trend, begun in the 1960s but reaching full momentum in the 1980s, has been to adopt a less dissonant, more transparent harmonic idiom while pursuing a radically slowed treatment of time. In this music, rhythm, melody, and harmony evolve gradually in repetitive patterns, yielding sustained textures in which any immediate sense of change is minimized. The works of the Americans Steve Reich, Terry Riley, and Philip Glass (discussed more thoroughly in later chapters) are regarded as classics in this respect. But striking examples can also be found among the works of

---

EXAMPLE 10.11.

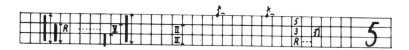

Morton Feldman: *The King of Denmark*

Copyright © 1965 by C. F. Peters Corporation. Used by permission

Karel Goeyvaerts, Louis Andriessen, Gavin Bryars, and others from Europe and the British Isles. Although these composers reduce the quantity of musical information in a way very different from that of Morton Feldman, a similar purpose is served in that the listener is left with—and drawn into the heart of—the sounds themselves, their acoustical properties, their physiological and emotional resonances, and their unfolding in time.

Electronic Music

An extended treatment of electronic music, including its significance as a virtually unlimited resource in the realm of texture and timbre, is found in Chapters 8 and 17. It is only necessary here to outline a few points of particular relevance. Most important is that electronic technology offers the composer a direct link to creating texture and sound mass without the intermediation of instruments or voices. The electronic composer works directly with the basic stuff of sound—wave shapes, frequencies, loudness contours, noise—either generated in the studio or recorded in the environment. Also important is that electronics permit a flexibility and precision not attainable by live musicians. All of the effects discussed earlier in an instrumental context (densely elaborate counterpoint, timbre modulation, interaction of sound masses, etc.) can be directly engineered through such expedients as tape manipulation, sequencing, multitracking, sound processing, and computer control.

The control afforded by electronics is obviously valuable when complex compositional processes are involved in realizing texture and color. It is not surprising, then, that both Stockhausen and Xenakis turned to this technology to realize their concepts. Stockhausen, for instance, could not have given sonic form to his esoteric theories about sound color (developed in the late 1950s) without the electronic medium. His idea was to place rhythm, pitch, and timbre on a single continuum by choosing a pattern of pulses—that is, a rhythm—and speeding it up hundreds of times to become a pitch with its own distinctive waveform and resulting timbre. This could only be done electronically, of course. Since the waveform would be a replica of the original rhythmic pattern in miniature, an integral relationship between rhythm and timbre would be achieved. Stockhausen applied this concept in *Telemusik* for magnetic tape (1966).

The intricate counterpoint that results from stratifying independent and contrasting strands of activity, as noted in instrumental works by Carter and Nancarrow, is standard fare in the electronic repertoire. Such layering can be easily achieved with multitracking on tape recorders or multisequencing with digital equipment (although the removal of human striving and interaction renders this uninteresting to some composers). Moreover, the spatial separation needed to highlight individual layers of sound is easier to engineer electronically than with live musicians, being primarily a matter of speaker placement. In fact, distinct textures or streams of polyphony can even be *panned* (gradually shifted from one location to another), moving through and interacting in space in ways inconceivable with live instruments or voices. (Varèse's use of over four hundred speakers in *Poème électronique* remains the most impressive instance of this.)

Even in live performance, electronic instruments have been advantageous to composers working with texture. Pauline Oliveros was an early pioneer in this respect, using multiple tape decks as a real-time medium during the 1960s. Her many works in this genre include *Lightpiece for David Tudor* (1965), *I of IV* (1966), *C(s) for Once* (1966), and *Beautiful Soop* (1967), the last of which involves no fewer than four tape decks. *I of IV*, in particular, is emblematic of her meditative, intuitive attitude toward sound. Slowly changing combination and difference tones are fed through an elaborate tape echo and tape delay system, producing a dreamlike, oceanic wash of timbres.

New realms of sound mass and density also open up when live and electronic means are combined, especially where orchestral performance is involved. To cite just one example of particularly monumental scope, "... *inwendig voller figur* ..." (1970) by Swiss composer Klaus Huber (b. 1924) combines a large chorus, a gigantic orchestra, seven amplified vocal soloists, and a quadraphonic tape derived from prerecorded choral, brass, and percussion sounds. Not only does every member of the orchestra play a separate part, as in other sound-mass compositions we have seen, but the chorus of at least sixty singers is similarly divided. Most significant here, however, is that choral and instrumental sounds are still further proliferated and timbrally extended by their electronically modified counterparts on tape. These forces combine to create a sonic environment ranging from titanic clusters and splashes of sound to delicately surreal and hushed sonorities.

CONCLUSION

Having examined the phenomenon of texture and color in new music from many perspectives in this chapter, we have still only scratched the surface. Nearly every musical innovation mentioned in other chapters has implications in this area. For example, collage techniques (discussed in Chapter 13) offer unique possibilities in the realm of texture not dealt with above. The inclusion of non-Western instruments among the composer's resources —an important feature of Chapter 11—brings entirely new timbral possibilities barely touched on so far. The list goes on. What is important here, however, is the newfound importance of these issues among today's composers, and the willingness of some to make texture, density, color, and related concerns a primary focus in shaping their music. This development, perhaps more than any other, suggests the degree to which freedom from a traditional orientation toward pitch and rhythm has evolved in the past half century. Out of that freedom has grown a new and robust enthusiasm for sound itself and all its aspects.

Non-Western Musical Influences

Debussy's encounter with the music of Indonesia was a rare opportunity for a composer in the Western hemisphere in 1889. By contrast, in today's world of instantaneous global communication, Westerners have ready access to broadcast or recorded music from all over the planet. Rapid travel has made the live experience of most kinds of music more accessible as well, both in Western concert halls and in its places of origin; moreover, the emergence of ethnomusicology as an academic discipline has brought such music to university campuses. As a result, many have come to realize that music rooted in the traditions of Western civilization, perhaps the only music they have ever known, really constitutes a tiny fraction of the musical world in its totality.

By "Western" we are referring not so much to a geographical locality as to an established set of musical practices and expectations; these include jazz, popular idioms, and most important here, the so-called classical or concert music that prevails in the metropolitan centers of Europe, North America, and Westernized areas of South America today. In this sense, the music of native American or other ethnic cultures in the Western hemisphere can be considered non-Western for our purposes.

As many have discovered, the musics of non-Western cultures offer not only a vast treasury of sounds that are still fresh but also a broad range of alternative perspectives on the ritual and societal contexts of music. Thus, they provide an attractive field of exploration for performers, scholars, listeners, and composers, especially those who view the concert music tradition, even in its more avant-garde guises, as a calcified residue of nineteenth-century European thinking. (In fact, some prefer to label it "Eurocentric" or "European-derived" rather than "Western.") Many composers consider that thinking to be outdated and lacking in vitality, not only in the actual sounds produced but also in the lifeless formality (from their standpoint) of the usual concert setting, which reflects a detached and limited view of music as either fine art or entertainment.

To a great degree, non-Western influences address these concerns. They also suggest fresh perspectives on many of our nine basic factors. **Pitch logic** and **time** are treated very differently in some traditions. Also, instruments unfamiliar to Western listeners may be used, offering new experiences in **sound color**. And **performance ritual** in vernacular traditions often has a primacy it lacks in Western practice. In exploiting these possibilities, composers sometimes imitate or quote melodies and other materials directly, making **historicism/parody** an important concern.

EMBRACING SOUNDS FROM OTHER CULTURES

Two aspects of music from other parts of the globe have influenced the course of Western music: (1) distinctive melodic, harmonic, or rhythmic practices, and (2) the quality of sound produced by instruments, tuning systems, and methods of performance not found in the traditional Western mainstream. Both possibilities have proved significant.

Non-Western Influences on Style and Method

In the traditional repertoire there are many instances where composers have incorporated superficial characteristics of music from foreign lands, perhaps beginning with Mozart's use of Turkic melodies and rhythms (e.g., the Rondo *alla turca* from the Piano Sonata in A major, K.331). Later examples include the Hungarian dances and rhapsodies of Brahms and Liszt, the pentatonic melodies (evoking Chinese music) in Mahler's song cycle *Das Lied von der Erde* (1908), the Indian-influenced scale formations in Albert Roussel's 1914 opera-ballet *Padmâvatî*, and the strains of Brazilian rhythm and melody in Milhaud's ballet *Le boeuf sur le toit* (1919) and his *Saudades do Brasil* for piano (1921).

For other composers in the standard repertoire, another and more deeply influential interest has been the folk music of their own homeland. Although this music is not "non-Western" from a geographical point of view, its vigor, directness, spontaneity, and variety have suggested refreshing alternatives to the conventional limitations of art music. Illustrative of this are Schubert's adaptation of the German *Ländler* (a waltzlike folk dance), Mussorgsky's derivation of melodies from Russian folk tunes, the assimilation of Hungarian folk elements by Zoltán Kodály and Béla Bartók, Heitor Villa-Lobos's emulation of Brazilian dance rhythms, and the borrowing of American folk materials by Aaron Copland and Virgil Thomson. In the late nineteenth and early twentieth centuries, the rhythms and melodic patterns of Spanish dance music were exploited by such Spaniards as Isaac Albéniz and Manuel de Falla, as well as by other Europeans such as Maurice Ravel, Claude Debussy, and Jacques Ibert.

Although less frequently programmed, a number of composers in the Americas were very involved in the music of their own lands. Around 1910, for example, Charles Wakefield Cadman began a long series of works inspired by American Indian traditions. Beginning in the 1930s, Alberto Ginastera drew from the gaucho dances of his Argentinian homeland, and Carlos Chávez turned to the music of Indian cultures in his native Mexico, cultures predating his own Hispanic forebears. During the same period, William Grant Still began to draw upon the work songs, spirituals, and blues of his African-American heritage.

After 1945 the search beyond Western art music intensified, and among the most important participants were those whose music was shaped both by conventional Western practice and by their own non-Western roots. Alan Hovhaness (b. 1911), born of Armenian and Scottish parents, has been by far the most prolific representative of this trend; since the late 1930s and up to the present he has generated an enormous body of work, including fifty symphonies, much of which reflects his enthusiasm for the music of Armenia as well as that of India, Korea, and Japan. Refusing to borrow directly from extant material, his approach has instead been to study other music cultures in great depth, and then allow their characteristics to emerge naturally in his own writing.

Two concerns dominate Hovhaness's thinking: Eastern melody and Western counterpoint. A straightforward illustration is found in the finale of his Symphony No. 21, *Etchmiadzin*, of 1970, named after the religious capital of the Armenian Church. Example 11.1 shows four lines of counterpoint moving simply but independently, much as they would in a mass

EXAMPLE 11.1.

Alan Hovhaness: Symphony No. 21, *Etchmiadzin*,
third movement (strings only)

by Palestrina. But here, individual lines have the character of Armenian folk and religious melodies, proceeding mainly in stepwise motion, with occasional grace notes, over a mode containing two augmented seconds. The exotic linear harmonies that result are especially evocative of choral music in Armenia.

Unlike Hovhaness, whose music usually remains rhythmically and harmonically straightforward, Chou Wen-Chung (b. 1923) has incorporated the instrumental music of ancient China into a distinctly modern Western idiom. His first major success was *Landscapes* for orchestra (1949), which creates a sparse, delicately impressionistic sound world from brief oriental melodies. His intensive research into classical Chinese music, poetry, dance, and art, together with composition studies under Varèse and Otto Leuning, eventually led in the late 1950s to a more dissonant style, incorporating not only elements of traditional music but principles of Chinese poetry and calligraphy as well. Example 11.2, from *The Willows Are New* for solo piano (1957), shows the economy and subtlety of his approach. The piece is dominated by a melody, appearing here in the right hand, of an eighth-century composition for the ch'in (the Chinese long zither). Sixteenth-note

EXAMPLE 11.2.

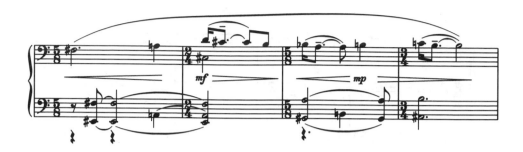

Chou Wen-Chung: *The Willows Are New*

Copyright © 1960 by C. F. Peters Corporation. Used by permission

ornaments, octave doublings, and a minor-ninth underpinning evoke the character of ch'in music and approximate—to the extent equal temperament will allow—its subtle pitch inflections.

Similarly, Chinary Ung (b. 1942) has blended the music of Cambodia with Western practice. Ung's intimacy with this music grows out of his active involvement as a performer in native Cambodian ensembles. His writing for Western musicians draws upon both religious and popular traditions, featuring richly elaborate vocal and instrumental lines and exotic percussion timbres. Examples include *Mohori* for soprano and chamber orchestra and *Spiral* for cello, piano, and percussion (1987).

Other composers, originally from non-European backgrounds, who have fused Eastern elements with Western instrumentation and technique include Toru Takemitsu, Toshiro Mayuzumi, and Toshi Ichiyanagi of Japan, Isang Yun of Korea, Ravi Shankar of India, Halim El-Dabh of Egypt, Ilhan Mimaroglu of Turkey, and Paul Ben-Haim of Israel. As with Chou and Ung, these composers have built upon familiarity with their own musical roots, either through intensive research, performance activities (with indigenous instruments), or both.

In a sense, the composers just mentioned represent the East looking west, seeking ways to give their ethnic heritage modern, European-based forms of expression. An equally vital tradition, however, is that of the West looking east, searching for fresh sound material and alternative aesthetic viewpoints. Movement in this direction first gathered momentum on the West Coast of America, instigated in large part by Henry Cowell. From the 1930s to the 1950s Cowell traveled throughout Asia and the Middle East, and much of his music incorporates the sounds and in some cases the instruments of Asian cultures, as in his two Koto Concertos (1962 and 1965) and his Symphony No. 13 (*Madras*) for orchestra and the Indian jalatarang and tablatarang (1958). During the late 1940s and 1950s Cowell's fascination with this uncharted sound world spread to his former students Lou Harrison and John Cage, whose enthusiasm for Oriental music and philosophy in turn changed the course of musical thought for many others.

Another West Coast figure to emerge before the war but to influence generations of composers afterward was Harry Partch. His exploration of new tuning systems and instruments began with a wildly eclectic appetite for music of every description, including Chinese lullabies, Congo puberty

ILLUS. 11.1.

Harry Partch, performing on two of his instruments
(the gourd tree and cone gongs)

Courtesy BMI Archives

rites, Yaqui Indian rituals, and Christian hymns, among others. His most important student was Ben Johnston, who has subsequently become a major figure in the use of alternative tunings.

Many composers have adapted non-Western musical elements to a framework of Western instrumentation, tuning, and performance setting, using the less familiar material to enhance their already established vocabulary. For example, Olivier Messiaen's rhythmic approach naturally inclined him to Hindu music; in addition, his exotic, metallic percussion timbres were inspired partly by the Indonesian gamelan. Both influences are reflected in his massive *Turangalîla-symphonie* (1948). Other Messiaen works focus more specifically on a given culture. His *Sept Haïkaï* for piano and small orchestra (1962) is modeled on elements of *gagaku* (Japanese court music from the eighth through twelfth centuries). His two most prominent students, Stockhausen and Boulez, have also written works with exotic resonances from the East. The percussion writing in Boulez's *Le marteau sans maître*, for example, followed from his exposure to music from Africa and the Far East, and parts of Stockhausen's electronic *Telemusik* involve prerecorded ethnic music from the Sahara, the Amazon, Bali, Vietnam, Japan, and elsewhere.

A classic in this context, illustrative because it draws from so many diverse sources, is George Crumb's *Ancient Voices of Children* for soprano, boy soprano, oboe, mandolin, harp, electric piano, and three percussionists (1970). Crumb injects subtle references to American Indian song, Hispanic folk idioms, Japanese court music, and Indonesian gamelan music at various points, along with fragmentary quotes of Bach and Ravel. (*Ancient Voices of Children* is discussed more fully in Chapter 12.)

Steve Reich (b. 1936) has adapted non-European thinking to standard instruments of the West with a special enthusiasm; his love for African drumming, the Indonesian gamelan, and Hebrew cantillation grow out of a natural propensity for repetitive patterns and subtle, slowly unfolding transformations. La Monte Young and Terry Riley (both born in 1935) also discovered an innate compatibility between their own thinking and that of Eastern traditions, particularly from India. Non-Western influences played a different role, however, in the development of Philip Glass (b. 1937). Rather than reinforcing existent tendencies, they were for Glass a new and life-changing force. His association with the Indian sitarist and composer Ravi Shankar and his tabla accompanist, Alla Rakha, beginning in 1964, started him on the path he has traveled since.

The music of Riley, Young, Reich, and Glass, devoted to cyclical, harmonically static—or *minimalist*—structures, has engendered considerable controversy (see Chapter 16). It is worth noting here, though, that suggestions of minimalism—in particular, the use of repetition and transparent textures—had already appeared before the 1960s in works by Harrison, Hovhaness, and other composers interested in non-Eurocentric musics.

ILLUS. 11.2.

Steve Reich and Musicians in a performance of
Drumming, a work influenced by African techniques
and aesthetics (see Chapter 16). Reich is the fourth
player from the right

Photo: Peter Moore. Courtesy BMI Archives

Colin McPhee (1901–64), for example, lived in Bali during the 1930s. In
such works as his 1936 *Tabuh-Tabuhan* for orchestra, McPhee explored the
use of static harmony, intricate but essentially repetitive rhythm (reminiscent of the gamelan), and heterophony (in which a number of instruments
play different variations on the same melodic pattern simultaneously, a
noted trait of music from many Asian cultures).

   While the music of ethnic populations represents something new—a
looking outward or beyond—for many composers, it is for others a way of
looking inward at themselves and their own history. This is especially true
of those who have turned to their own Jewish, Hispanic, or African roots
for inspiration. Those roots have played a formative role in much of Western culture, but—except for the Hispanic—are nevertheless largely unrep-
resented by the nineteenth-century European musical tradition. African
music is, of course, at the core of all jazz and jazz-related idioms, whose

evolution began around 1890 with the black musicians of New Orleans. But it was not until the 1960s that Afro-American jazz musicians began to emphasize a connection between jazz and its African lineage. One of the most energetic proponents of this trend, important here because their music was as much "serious" or avant-garde music as jazz, was the Art Ensemble of Chicago. Their performances have encompassed not only musical (especially rhythmic) features of Sub-Saharan African cultures, but authentic instruments and ritual elements as well. Other black jazz/avant-garde figures to reestablish ties with African culture during this period include saxophonist John Coltrane and trumpeter Don Cherry.

A number of Jewish composers have directly incorporated elements of their heritage. Stefan Wolpe's exposure to Semitic dance, song, and instrumental music in Palestine during the 1930s helped shape his approach to rhythm and melody in later works, although the influence is beneath the audible surface. In Steve Reich's music, the links are more obvious; one particular work, *Tehillim* (1981), is based entirely on the vocal style of Hebrew cantillation, adapted to Reich's own hypnotic, cyclical approach. The 1986 *Yerusha* by David Stock (b. 1939) is a high-energy pastiche of

ILLUS. 11.3.

The Art Ensemble of Chicago

Courtesy of the Ensemble

klezmer tunes, synagogue melodies, and contemporary dissonance, scored for solo clarinet and large chamber ensemble. For other composers, Jewish culture and history have had a less direct but no less significant impact. Thus, a number of works by Richard Wernick (b. 1934), such as the *Kaddisch-Requiem* (1971) and *Prayer for Jerusalem* for soprano and percussion (1971), grow out of an intense awareness of his heritage. On the other hand, they contain little trace of liturgical style or ethnic musical practices. Similarly, Yehudi Wyner (b. 1929) has written many works for the synagogue, but primarily in his own contemporary, Western mainstream idiom.

Hispanic music also has stimulated new thinking among the avant-garde, particularly in North America, where the integration of South and Central American cultures within the United States and Canada is an urgent and visible issue. Among the most recent composers in this arena are Cuban-born Tania Léon and Puerto Rican William Ortiz, both of whom write in a style enlivened by Latin influences. Ortiz (b. 1947), for example, has sought common ground between the sophisticated resources of experimental composition and the raw, untamed power of street music in urban Hispanic communities, a synthesis found in his *124 East 107th Street* for percussion (1979).

Instruments from Other Traditions

Non-Western classical and ethnic traditions not only suggest unconventional ways of using Western instruments and technologies but also bring to light what to Westerners are unfamiliar sounds. The average Eurocentric concertgoer, for example, might be shocked to learn that there are literally thousands of instruments being played around the world today, each with its own history and performance practice. Even those acquainted with somewhat better-known instruments, such as the Chinese ch'in or the Indian sitar, would be surprised to hear that there are over 150 types of instruments played in China and over 200 in India. Some cultures, such as those in the more remote republics of the former Soviet Union, use instruments rarely heard by Western ears. To the composer in search of fresh sonic material, the dizzying scale of this global resource rivals that of the electronic music studio.

Public awareness of instruments from other lands took hold with tours to Western countries by sitar player Ravi Shankar and sarod player Ali Akbar Khan in the 1960s, and the wide exposure given the sitar by George Harrison of the Beatles, beginning with the song "Norwegian Wood" (1965). During the same period, groups such as the Paul Winter Consort began to popularize percussion instruments and playing styles from Latin America, Africa, and India. The 1960s also saw a flood of new releases, especially on the Nonesuch and Monitor recording labels, featuring live field recordings of ethnic music from Eastern Europe, the Middle East, West Africa, Indonesia, Japan, and the South Pacific. Among the avant-garde, as well, the 1960s brought the first serious and consistent attempts to compose with Eastern instruments in a Western context, although composers such as Henry Cowell, Alan Hovhaness, and Colin McPhee had begun investigating such instruments since before World War II.

Hovhaness has written numerous works incorporating instruments from all over the Orient, including those of Japan, Korea, Indonesia, South India, and the Middle East. Hovhaness's Symphony No. 16 (1963), for example, calls for an assortment of East Asian instruments, including pyunjong (bronze bells) of Indonesia and the kayakum (twelve-stringed zither) of Korea. His interest in such instruments has been more broad than deep, inspired by their evocative eloquence rather than by any deep-seated affinity with a given tradition. Thus, in his *Firdausi* for clarinet, percussion, and harp (1976), percussion instruments may be chosen freely from a culturally diverse array, including Laotian drum-gongs, deep gongs from Java or Bali, and various drums from the Near, Middle, and Far East. In some of his works, Eastern and Western instruments are interchangeable, as in *Khorhoort Nahadagats* for oud (a Middle Eastern lute) and strings (1976), where the oud may be replaced by a Baroque lute or guitar.

Lou Harrison has been perhaps the most prominent and indefatigable advocate of a global approach to instruments and intonation systems. In contrast to Hovhaness (apart from his devotion to Armenia), Harrison has immersed himself deeply in the music theory and practice of various cultures. In 1961 he embarked on a two-year pilgrimage to Japan, Korea, and China, studying with musicians of the region and subsequently becoming an expert collector and builder of, and performer on, instruments of oriental heritage. (In 1977, for example, he designed and constructed two Javanese gamelan orchestras in collaboration with William Colvig.) More important, he composed major works for these instruments, such as *Pacifika Rondo* for Western and oriental instruments (1963) and *La Koro Sutra* for chorus and gamelan (1972). In these works, as in many others, melody and harmony are straightforward and transparent (and generally modal), bringing the unique instrumental sonorities into relief. In such works the exotic gongs, metallophones, and drums of the gamelan yield resonant percussive timbres unlike anything normally heard in the concert hall, although many composers have emulated them through creative use of Western instrumentation. (Both Cage and Harrison himself achieved similar sounds as early as the 1940s with the prepared piano and with a variety of improvised percussion instruments—brake drums, cooking pots, garbage cans, and the like.)

The interface of cultures gains a special intensity when instruments from both East and West are combined. We have already mentioned works by Harrison, Cowell, and Hovhaness that explore such a synthesis, and

ILLUS. 11.4.

Lou Harrison, standing next to two metallophones
of his gamelan

Photo: Betty Freeman. Courtesy Peer-Southern Music Co.

other composers such as David Amram, David Loeb, and Ingram Marshall
have followed this trend. Many Asian composers have done likewise, and
November Steps for biwa (a Japanese lute), shakuhachi (a Japanese bamboo
flute), and orchestra, written in 1967 by Toru Takemitsu (b. 1930), is an
often-noted example. The soloists' notation in Example 11.3 really gives no
hint of the biwa's strangely fluid twang or the continuously shimmering
harmonics in the shakuhachi's rich, breathy tone. As unearthly as these
sounds may seem to Westerners, they are to Japanese ears deeply reflective
of earth, nature, and spirit. On the other hand, the impressionistic orchestral sonorities accompanying them—particularly the delicate interlacing of
rapid string figures interspersed with harmonics, and the resonances of

EXAMPLE 11.3.

Toru Takemitsu: *November Steps* (solo parts)

gongs, bells, and tam-tam—communicate that same sense of wonder and nature to occidental listeners.

Interestingly, Takemitsu is not eager to resolve these two ways of hearing, stating in his program note that he prefers to "vivify the foreignness of the sound" that distinguishes Eastern from Western timbres. The distinction is more than accoustic, as the Japanese instruments require a different attitude on the listener's part. Takemitsu exhorts listeners to open their awareness entirely to what they hear: "Before long," he states, "you will understand the aspirations of the sounds themselves."

The human voice, too, can be regarded as a non-Western instrument, depending on how it is used. For example, the vibrato and rounded tone that Westerners associate with "good" singing would be regarded as weak and inexpressive in remote peasant communities of Bulgaria, whose ideal of vocal production involves an unwavering, knife-edged tone. The supple, nasal timbres of various Asian singing styles may seem whiny and unappealing to some occidental listeners. On the other hand, Western listeners are often incredulous at the virtuosic ornamentation of which Asian voices are capable.

One composer, David Hykes (b. 1953), has dedicated his career to a subtle form of vocal control previously mastered only by Tibetan Buddhist monks and the *hoomi* (throat singers) of Mongolia. From these sources Hykes learned that a single voice can produce many sounds at once by exact control of all the muscles and other physiological factors that contribute to vocal output. For example, the voice can sustain a fundamental tone while simultaneously bringing out one or more of that tone's harmonics, thus creating a chord; in fact, the skilled practitioner can move quickly from one harmonic to the next to create, in effect, a drone (the fundamental) with a melody on top (the harmonics). The techniques depend on stillness and concentration, as quietly sustained vocal sonorities are subtly transformed. The musical outgrowth, therefore, inevitably reflects the mystical, deeply meditative ambience of its Tibetan and Mongolian origins.

Hykes's best-known work, developed during the late 1970s, is *Hearing Solar Winds*, a delicate, gentle study of uninterrupted sound lasting an hour or more; it is sung by his own six-voice Harmonic Choir, which typically performs in dark, acoustically resonant spaces illuminated only by candlelight.

When it comes to experimentation with unusual instruments, the greatest innovator was Harry Partch, who from the 1930s until his death in 1974 exclusively composed for and performed on instruments that he had either adapted or designed and built himself. Many of these are suggestive of instruments from other times or cultures, as in the Kitharas I and II (resembling large Greek or Roman lyres), an Mbira Bass Dyad (a giant derivative of the African mbira or thumb piano) and various marimbalike bamboo instruments such as the Boos I and II and the Eucal Blossom (evoking both African and East Asian precedents). Their sound is unique, as much a result of tuning (discussed below) as of timbre, but equally distinctive is their appearance, which also brings to mind cultures far removed from our own. Partch's Gourd Tree, for example, an arrangement of temple bells with gourd resonators spread out along a eucalyptus branch, would appear as natural in a Japanese garden as on the performing stage.

As we move into the twenty-first century, it seems likely that the mixing of East and West will lead to a Westernization of ethnic instruments. To cite just one of many existing attempts, the young Indian composer Priti Paintal has designed and built a two-octave chromatic set of tablas, dubbed the Kromatabla, as part of her effort to integrate Asian and Western techniques.

An ironic footnote to all this is that, while non-Western instruments present the classical concertgoer with an unfamiliar (and not always welcome) challenge, they have been embraced warmly by more popular, commercially oriented performers and their audiences. Since the Beatles began the process by popularizing the sitar and tabla in the mid-1960s, a number of groups have attempted to fuse jazz, avant-garde, and ethnic ingredients; they use instruments, rhythmic and melodic ideas, and even elements of ritual from indigenous cultures around the globe. Apart from its purely sonic interest, the music played by these ensembles (which include the Paul Winter Consort, Oregon, and the West German group Einsteig, among others) has arisen as a kind of cultural antidote to the artificial, materialistic, ecologically destructive trends in Western civilization, evoking instead the nature-oriented spirituality often associated with the tribes, villages, and outbacks of less high-tech societies.

The reverse process is unfolding in Eastern countries, where ethnic music occasionally exhibits some of the musical traits of jazz, rock, and other popular Western genres, including the use of traps and electric guitars, while culling out the rituals and subtleties of performance that endured through many previous generations. This has led to such phenomena as highlife (a pop genre in Nigeria) and the rise of popular recording artists in Turkey, India, Japan, and elsewhere whose songs share many qualities with American "Top 40," while superficially tinged with the rhythmic, melodic, and instrumental trappings of their own musical heritage.

Tuning Systems

The average Western listener is probably unaware that the twelve-note, equal-tempered scale we are accustomed to—the so-called chromatic scale—represents only one of literally countless possible ways to tune notes within the octave. Many of these possibilities, such as just intonation and various meantone temperaments, are part of our own history, predating equal temperament. Other systems of intonation—some radically different from our own—continue to flourish around the world today: the Indian system of twenty-two *śrutis*, for example, or the five-note *slendro* scale of Java. (To musicians steeped in these traditions, our equal-tempered system often seems quite out of tune!)

Equal temperament became a permanent underpinning of the Western tradition by the early nineteenth century and has since dominated not only the standard and avant-garde repertoire of concert music but even jazz, folk, and rock idioms as well. Those composers who have turned away from this tradition to other systems of intonation have fundamentally challenged our listening habits, opening up a treasury of very different sonorities arising from intervals or frequency ratios among tones that cannot be found in the Western chromatic system.

In this area, as with instrument design and construction, Harry Partch has been the twentieth century's foremost innovator. (In fact, instrument tuning and design were inseparable issues for him.) He felt kinship with ancient Greek, Arab, and Chinese musical scholars who delved deeply into the intrinsic properties of tones and their vibratory relationships, and he was drawn to the natural integrity in many scale systems of antiquity. By contrast, he regarded nearly everything about music in modern-day civilization as vacuous and contrived, and part of his skepticism was focused on equal temperament and its twelve, precisely even divisions of the octave, which he considered arbitrary and inherently lifeless.

To Partch, the natural system from which scales and intervals can meaningfully be derived was the harmonic or "counting number" series (1, 2, 3, 4, 5, . . .), which governs overtone structure, resonance, and other acoustic phenomena. Example 11.4a shows the intervals formed by the simple frequency ratios in the lowest part of the harmonic series. Example 11.4b shows some of the intervals that appear in a "just" major scale, formed by these and other simple ratios from the first sixteen numbers of the series. Example 11.4c shows equal temperament's approximation—a crude one, in Partch's view—of the same scale. (Except for 2/1, the ratios over the staff in Example 11.4c are themselves only approximations of

EXAMPLE 11.4A.

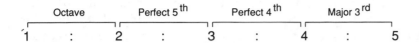

Octave   Perfect 5th   Perfect 4th   Major 3rd

$$1 \quad : \quad 2 \quad : \quad 3 \quad : \quad 4 \quad : \quad 5$$

Intervals formed by simple vibratory ratios

EXAMPLE 11.4B.

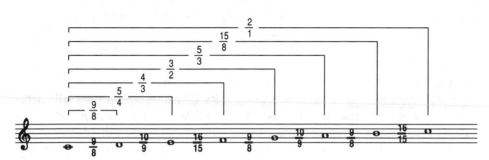

Vibratory ratios in a "just" major scale

EXAMPLE 11.4C.

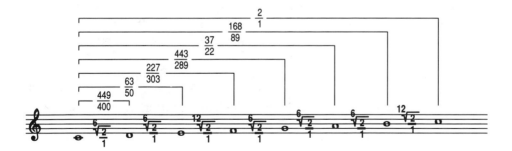

Vibratory ratios in an equal-tempered major scale

lengthy decimals.) Whereas the pure intervals of just intonation are linked to the natural sound world by the harmonic series, the intervals of equal temperament are based on increments of semitones formed by the artificial ratio of $12/\sqrt{2}$, resulting in complex vibratory relationships that cannot be found naturally in the acoustic world. To Partch, therefore, the equal-tempered scale seemed a fraudulent and sterile basis for music making.

It is indeed true that the ear can easily appreciate the difference between the "cleaner" sound of justly tuned intervals (particularly the major third and perfect fifth) and the more jangling quality of their equivalents in our equal-tempered system. But Partch also recognized the expressive nuances that varients of the same interval could achieve, as in the just scale of Example 11.4b, for example, where whole steps of two sizes (9/8 and 10/9) are found. (In equal temperament, a given interval type is always tuned exactly the same, no matter where it occurs in a scale.) Partch's exploration of this, however, went far beyond simple scales like that in the example. Instead, his instruments were tuned to scales extracted from his own system of forty-three tones to the octave. (His Chromelodeon uses all forty-three.) Although this system is based primarily on simple ratios like those of just intonation, some of these produce intervals quite unlike any in the chromatic scale, such as 11/6 (halfway between a minor and major seventh) and 9/7 (almost halfway between a major third and perfect fourth).

Two notable figures, Lou Harrison and Ben Johnston, have followed staunchly in Partch's footsteps, arguing for a broad view of intonational possibilities and against the present-day practice of squeezing every kind of music into the same immutable system of twelve equidistant scale degrees. Both have composed with various forms of just intonation and have also experimented freely with many other tuning schemes. But while Johnston freely devises new systems to suit new works, Harrison's music has evolved from his study of existing systems from other times and cultures. He is an expert as much on just tunings and meantone temperaments in preclassical Europe as on the tuning systems of Asian musics. His works range in influence from Medieval church music to Schoenberg and to the ethnic sources already mentioned, and these influences are often reflected by his choice of tunings as much as by instrumentation or other elements of style.

This attention to intonation means that Harrison often has Western instruments retuned or, in the case of strings or voices, performed with modified intonation, as in *Three Pieces for Gamelan with Soloists*, for retuned horn, viola, and suling (Javanese bamboo flute), or his *Concerto in Slendro* (1961) for retuned celesta, two pianos with tack hammers (also retuned), and an assortment of triangles, gongs, and metal garbage cans. (The Javanese *slendro* refers to any pentatonic tuning with three large seconds and two small thirds, these being roughly equivalent to our major second and minor third respectively.)

The lengthy, contemplative works of La Monte Young and Terry Riley, and their interest in alternative tunings, are at least partly a response to the raga music of the Hindustani tradition in Northern India. A remarkable tenet of this tradition is that the physiological, psychological, spiritual, and environmental affects of melodic patterns are governed in part by the vibratory qualities of intervals. The Indian system has twenty-two scale degrees, or *śrutis*, which allow for many subtle but precise variants on one basic seven-note scale; these subtle inflections are considered essential to the music's harmonious influence on listener and surroundings.

Here are refreshing implications: that music's power may reside as much in the sounds themselves as in what is done with them; that music can be absorbed on a directly emotional, intuitive, and even physical level, without dependence on the intellect (although such music may be intellectually satisfying as well); and that the notion of boredom, which might be defined as restlessness of the intellect, can be rendered meaningless (even for performances lasting hours on end) if the music succeeds in nourishing and sustaining the listener on a much deeper level. (The unbroken attention that a two- or three-hour raga can elicit from audiences in live performance—with no change in harmony—seems ample demonstration of this possibility.)

Works by Young and Riley from the 1960s already reflect this distinctly non-Western outlook, even though they had yet to begin their study with Pandit Pran Nath. Along with their cyclical and temporally expansive approach, they also started during this period to work with just intonation, whose acoustically pure intervals naturally lend themselves to the same kind of mystical absorption in the inner life of tones that attracted both composers to the music of India. Young's ultimate exploration of the effects of pure intervals was *The Well-Tuned Piano*, an extended composition for piano retuned to just intonation. Beginning in 1964, this work was performed by Young in many versions, varying in length, order of events, and improvisatory detail, culminating in the five-hour version of 1981. Riley's 1984 composition *The Harp of New Albion* is also a protracted work (nearly two hours) for piano tuned to just intonation. (By the 1980s just intonation became a consistent feature of his piano performances.) In both *The Well-Tuned Piano* and *The Harp of New Albion* the just scale produces many sonorities that sound strangely out of tune to ears conditioned by equal temperament, but it also yields intervals or chords whose unique, shimmering resonances cannot be achieved on a normally tuned piano.

New tuning systems have not always been linked to non-Western influences; their development is often motivated purely by an urge to break free of the twelve-note limit. Around 1920, for example, Alois Hába built a quarter-tone piano, dividing the semitone into two equal parts to form twenty-four tones to the octave, and Charles Ives wrote his *Three Quarter-Tone Pieces* for two pianos tuned a quarter tone apart. In 1911 Ferruccio

Busoni had already proposed a "sixth-tone" system (dividing the semitone into three equal parts, rendering thirty-six tones to the octave), and Joseph Yasser proposed a nineteen-tone equal temperament in his 1932 treatise *A Theory of Evolving Tonality.*

Since then, many so-called microtonal scale systems have emerged (the term *microtone* referring to scale steps smaller than the semitone in our chromatic system), although none has gained consistent or widespread usage. Experimentation with such systems, however, has become much easier with the help of electronic music technology, as demonstrated in the *Microtonal Etudes for Electronic Music Media* by Easley Blackwood (b. 1933), with tunings that range from thirteen to twenty-four divisions of the octave.

RITUAL AND FUNCTION

As explained in Chapter 9, many composers have challenged the artificiality and complacency they see in Western music by questioning its habitual settings and routines—its rituals of performance—and non-Western music has offered them enlightening perspectives. For example, the Western view of music, poetry, visual art, dance, and theater as separate and distinct forms of expression, to be exhibited by some and observed by others, is foreign to many peoples around the world. In Native American rites, for instance, chanting, dance, ceremonial props, and elaborate dress are inseparable parts of a single experience in which all participate directly (with no concept of "performer" and "audience").

But many ethnic traditions raise an even broader issue: the very function of music in society. Westerners are parochial in their view of music as art and entertainment; in many other cultures it is an integral element of daily life. In parts of Africa, for example, music is essential not only to funerals, weddings, and religious functions, but also to hunting, planting, harvesting, and other day-to-day activities. (Rarely is this music notated in any form, being passed on orally from generation to generation.) Many composers have pointed to all this as if to say, "See? The nineteenth-century European way is not the only way—and not necessarily the most interesting or meaningful one—to make music."

There have been attempts within the Western repertoire to unify the arts, as in the *Gesamtkunstwerk* (total artwork) of Wagner's later operas, and to integrate music into day-to-day living, as in the *Gebrauchsmusik* (music for use in homes, factories, schools, and the like) espoused by Paul Hindemith and Kurt Weill in the 1920s and '30s. But the first composer to act out a truly radical vision of music's rituals and functions was, again, Harry Partch, who early in life became frustrated by the inertia of Western thinking and inspired by the exuberant power of ethnic traditions.

In the 1920s Partch began to draw a distinction between two types of music that he termed "corporeal" and "abstract." Art music of the West is abstract, he argued, because its symphonies, quartets, and other codified genres—even its vocal forms—are structured according to instrumental, primarily nonverbal principals. Conceived purely in the mind for appreciation by the mind, music in modern civilization has become a highly specialized activity, divorced from the everyday speech, song, movement, visual artistry, and social milieu to which it was inextricably bound in ancient times. By contrast, the music of many other peoples, both past and present, is corporeal, in that the voice and the body are always essential vehicles of expression. Corporeal art is fundamentally rooted in the physical and emotional realities of life, conveyed through singing, chanting, storytelling, poetry, acting, and dance, some or all of which may be interwoven into a single, vital enterprise.

Partch aspired to this same physicality, immediacy, and integration in his own works, and the apotheosis of his effort was *Delusion of the Fury* (1966). Subtitled "A Ritual of Dream and Delusion," this music theater piece features singers, dancers, actors, and a stage set dominated by an imposing array of Partch's own visually striking instruments. The first act is based on a Noh play of eleventh-century Japan and the second on an African folk tale, both acted out with mime, dancing, and singing. But the overall feel is less reminiscent of Africa or Japan than of ancient Greek drama; in fact, the instrumentalists sometimes function in the manner of a Greek chorus, acting, singing, and dancing when not playing their instruments. Subject matter rooted in folk legend, a musical score that is stark, primitive, and rhythmically insistent, and staging that requires vigorous physical involvement from the entire cast all make *Delusion of the Fury* a convincing exemplar of the corporeal concept.

Partch's infectious brand of iconoclasm has inspired many younger composers to reexamine Western culture from the ground up. Chief among these has been the composer and author Peter Garland (b. 1953), who has traveled throughout the Americas, documenting and absorbing native traditions in search of a new connection between modern-day culture, America's indigenous peoples, and the natural world in which they are rooted. Beginning in 1973, he published twelve volumes of the journal *Soundings*, which like Cowell's *New Music Quarterly* before World War II has given greater visibility to highly significant but relatively obscure figures, especially Partch and Conlon Nancarrow.

No one has challenged modern-day assumptions about music's function or purpose more fundamentally than John Cage, whose impatience with Western habits of thinking and hearing led to what he called "purposeless music." Non-Western influences were crucial to his development, and their role was more philosophical than musical. During the late 1940s Cage studied the traditional principals of Indian aesthetics, as expressed in the writings of Ananda Coomaraswamy, and he became interested in Zen Buddhism, which he encountered while attending Daisetsu Suzuki's lectures on oriental thought at Columbia University. The Indian influence was limited, most notably expressed in his *Sonatas and Interludes* (discussed in Chapter 6).

Zen, however, proved a life-changing force for Cage, leading directly to his emphasis on silence and on chance procedures. The Zen philosophy of Japan teaches that what is not expressed is as significant as what is expressed, and that knowledge and truth are most purely to be found in the gaps between expression. Thus, silence and the subtle outlining of a part to intimate the richness of the whole have long been vital to Japanese art and music. Zen also teaches that the ultimate truths can be realized only when one's individuality is no longer a factor.

Both these lessons—the value of silence and the need to free one's actions from individuality—are embodied in what Cage considered his most significant piece, *4'33"*. This work is "purposeless" in the sense that nothing is expressed during the four and half minutes of silence, representing the ultimate renunciation of individual creative input from composer and performer. But the purposelessness here has a serious purpose, because this period of silence or nonexpression does allow ultimate truths to be realized, bringing into high relief what Cage considered to be the true essence of music—sounds as they really are (in this case the random sounds of audience and environment), not subjugated to the theories, emotions, or activities of musicians.

In general, Cage's use of chance is Zen-inspired, providing a way to end the tyranny of the individual ego over sound. Thus, his works from about 1950 on really constitute opportunities for sounds to "be themselves," as he often expressed it. Improvisational schemes are devised not only to minimize the composer's role but even to exclude the personal preferences of performers. In both *Fontana Mix* and *Cartridge Music*, for example, Cage provides materials to be freely chosen by performers to form a "score" (for unspecified instruments), but his guidelines for assembling and interpreting the score ensure that there is no way for the participants to anticipate the aural outcome of their choices. In *Music of Changes* chance procedures eliminate any freedom of choice whatsoever, since every decision in composing the work, apart from its basic set-up, is made on the basis of coin tosses, and since the pianist must respond precisely to the resulting notation. Although based on the Chinese *I Ching*, this work, too, aspires to the Zen ideal by attempting to remove all human contrivance from the creative act, simply allowing sounds to come into being.

Since about 1970 Pauline Oliveros has developed a similar aesthetic with works that are as much conceptual art as they are music composition, emphasizing an open, uncritical, meditative relationship between sounds, musical participants, and the environment. Generally, audience members are the performers. Her *Sonic Meditations*, for example, a series of twenty-five pieces "for everybody" (1971–74), consist entirely of prose instructions—sometimes no more than a sentence—that suggest ways of making, listening to, and/or thinking about sounds. A few of the many possibilities explored are remembering or imagining sounds; communicating sounds telepathically to other participants; making vocal or instrumental sounds that start, stop, or change according to intuitive criteria; contemplating sounds in the environment and/or in one's own body; and responding vocally to external or internal sounds. Oliveros emphasizes an awareness of breathing and turning the attention inward, the work's avowed purpose (stated in the score's introduction) being to expand consciousness by exploring the depths of what already exists within and around us. In fact, the purposes, methods, and attitudes of Western music are eschewed completely in favor of what Oliveros calls "ancient forms," in which such divisions as individual and environment, sound and sound source, observer and observed (i.e., audience and performer) have no place.

Another manifestation of the same outlook has been group composition, a phenomenon fundamentally at odds with the nineteenth-century European aesthetic but common in various other cultures around the world, where the concepts of attributing authorship or ownership of a musical idea to any individual would seem preposterous. Perhaps the first tentative step in this direction was taken by John Cage and Lou Harrison in their *Double Music* (1941). A more recent and ambitious effort in this direction was a 1982 thirty-five-minute piece called *Gamelan N.E.A.* (its title acknowledging support from the United States National Endowment for the Arts), composed collectively by Barbara Benary, Philip Corner, Daniel Goode, and Peter Griggs.

CONCLUSION

Looking back over this chapter, we can see that composers have approached non-European-derived music from two general points of view. First, for composers like Crumb and Stockhausen, it is a treasury of fresh sounds and musical philosophies that add breadth and scope to what nevertheless remains a thoroughly Western approach to music making. From this standpoint, the inherent properties and minute details of other traditions are less important than their otherness, their capacity to lead

Western ears beyond the limits and assumptions of an essentially European nineteenth-century aesthetic. The second approach, perhaps carried furthest by Lou Harrison and Harry Partch, is to delve deeply into and absorb the theory, philosophy, and performance practice of other traditions, to some extent adapting Western thought to Eastern principles rather than the reverse.

Whatever the approach to non-Western idioms, their influence has represented a force for change in music—and therein lies an irony. Many of the sources from which composers typically draw (such as North Indian ragas, West African tribal rites, or Indonesian gamelan music) stem from cultures that are *synchronic*—a term coined by anthropologist Claude Lévi-Strauss—in that they attach no value to concepts of cultural and societal change or progress, often dedicating themselves instead to the purity and longevity of established traditions. By contrast, occidental civilization and its arts are *diachronic* (also Lévi-Strauss's term), tending to regard change and development as positive and necessary for cultural health and well-being. Musics that have resisted change, therefore, are helping to change music in the Western world. (The influence is two-way, of course; as already noted, Western influence has begun to affect the music of ethnic groups throughout the world.)

Ultimately this is all a result of the growing interconnectedness, creating what Marshall McLuhan called a "global village," inescapably created by communication technology. While some may find this regrettable, others see the emergence of a unified global culture as a worthy ideal for the coming age—a culture enriched by what Lou Harrison, in using instruments from the world over, calls "transethnic" or "planetary" music.

Pieces For Study II

Many of the issues that acquired a special urgency in the first few decades after World War II overlap: developments in electronic music, for example, are directly related to the intensification or relaxation of **pitch logic**. Paradoxically, the electronic revolution greatly aided the pursuit of both "order" and chance (or "chaos"), offering unprecedented control for those seeking the former while opening up new ways of exploring and automating unpredictable or uncontrolled events for those interested in the latter. Chance procedures, in turn, played a vital role in experimental music theater, multimedia, and other novel extensions of **performance ritual**. Similarly, unusual ways of approaching **sound color** and **time**, including developments in the electronic medium, have yielded new **textures**. We can focus our study of these issues by concentrating on a few individual works, the earliest composed in 1960, the latest in 1974. The eight pieces discussed in this chapter represent a variety of styles, but all can be related to the same broad range of concerns.

Krzysztof Penderecki: Threnody for the Victims of Hiroshima

Penderecki's Threnody (1960), scored for string orchestra, was recognized instantly as a major, ground-breaking contribution to the twentieth-century repertoire. More than any other such work from this period (including those by Ligeti and Xenakis), it has come to exemplify the use of **texture** as the primary basis for musical ideas and their organization. For virtually all of its eight-minute duration, *Threnody* consists exclusively of textural blocks, clusters, and densely intersecting polyphonic strands.

Penderecki's single-minded attention to textural "fabric" can also be observed in his treatment of **pitch logic** and **time**, an approach that ensures that no rhythmic pulse or pitch sequence can be discernible at any given moment. In place of rhythm in the ordinary sense, we have temporal proportion between continuous textures that adjoin or overlap one another; the timing and duration of the works' events are notated in seconds of clock time. In place of note-by note pitch relationships (intervals or harmonic progressions), there are mainly two kinds of material: (1) pitch clusters and (2) various unorthodox sounds of indefinite pitch, such as playing the highest notes possible, arpeggiating the strings behind the bridge, tapping the soundboard, or bowing on the wood, the bridge, or the tailpiece.

Example 12.1 is representative of the former. Each section of the orchestra plays its own cluster, one instrument to a note, filling up a given pitch range with every possible chromatic and quarter tone therein. These five sound masses of maximum density begin at separate moments (almost imitatively), and then shift pitch level either abruptly or by glissando (with or without tremolo) in a sequence shown by the dotted lines, forming what one might call a texture melody or sound-mass gesture that spans thirty-eight seconds. As to the second category above, nonstandard instrumental techniques, their most astonishing use occurs just over a minute into the piece, when all fifty-two members of the orchestra alternate among these effects in rapid sequence with no consistent ordering or synchronization, resulting in an impenetrable, overwhelming clatter.

Although *Threnody* is not dependent on any kind of calculated precompositional scheme, a large-scale intuitive **process** shapes the interaction of the two fundamentally different sonic phenomena noted earlier (pitch clusters, usually sustained for at least ten seconds and unpitched effects, usually heard in quick succession or brief outbursts). The pathos of the title is reflected in this process, which centers on the brutal contrast and conflict between these materials. About five minutes into the piece, held notes and unpitched attacks do become interwoven and integrated for a time (the only passage, in fact, with conventionally notated rhythm). Ultimately,

EXAMPLE 12.1.

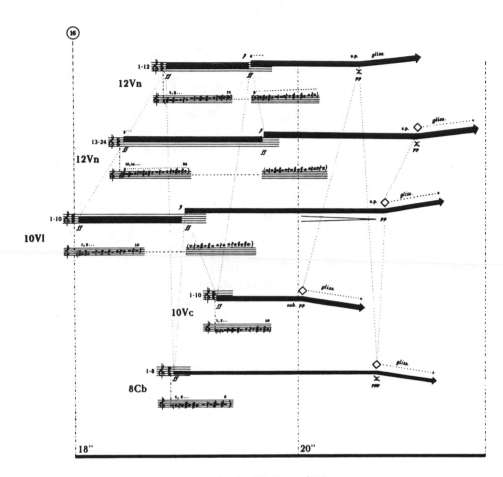

Krzysztof Penderecki: *Threnody for the Victims of Hiroshima*

however, this gives way to a series of nonpitched percussive attacks, played by whole sections of the orchestra in rhythmic unison. In the end, cluster sonorities attain a grim victory, with the entire orchestra holding out a two-octave, microtonally saturated wall of sound for thirty seconds as it fades from *fff* to *pppp*.

All of this calls for radical methods of **notation**, and the two bars in Example 12.1 are typical. Here the exact pitches in each cluster are given with conventional noteheads, but other aspects of notation are graphic and aleatoric. For example, entrances and other activities are shown only in approximate relation to segments of time, and the actual timing depends on cues from the conductor. Individual performers also have latitude, since the rate and extent of the glissandi are not specified. The Z-like figures in measure 17 indicate a rapid, unevenly bowed tremolo and are one of a dozen esoteric-looking symbols used throughout the score for nonstandard techniques.

On first experiencing *Threnody*, many listeners react most strongly to the work's extraordinary palette of **sound color**: sonorities may be haunting one moment and frightening the next. These are all the more remarkable when one realizes that they are being produced by a traditional (and unamplified) "classical" string orchestra. It may be especially jolting, in fact, to see the work played in the concert hall; there, the shocking discrepancy between our expectations (the visual "cues" of familiar instruments and musicians in formal dress) and hard-edged reality may upset our assumptions regarding **performance ritual**. Finally, we might note that Penderecki's concern with cluster sonorities, and his chosen range of experimental timbres, reveal the influence of **technology**—perhaps subliminal rather than direct—on his aesthetic. The sound world of *Threnody* emulates that of the tape studio. The composer creates the equivalent of white noise, filter effects, percussive envelopes, multitracked repeating loops, and the like, in a brilliant use of string ensemble resources to produce sounds much like those of electronic music.

Milton Babbitt: Vision and Prayer

Composed for soprano voice and synthesized accompaniment, Milton Babbitt's *Vision and Prayer* (1961) uses Dylan Thomas's poem of the same title as its text. The tape component of the work was realized at the Columbia–Princeton Electronic Music Center on the RCA synthesizer. Babbitt's compositional **process** for this work is intricately linked to the sound and structure of the poetry.

Each of the twelve stanzas in Thomas's poem has seventeen lines, shaped in an unusual fashion. Each of the first six stanzas begins with a one-syllable line and grows by one syllable per line until the ninth line, then shrinking by one syllable per line until a final line of one syllable, thus forming a diamond shape on the page. The last six stanzas all do the opposite, beginning and ending with nine syllables and having a one-syllable line in the middle, each forming an X shape on the page. In both cases the ninth line forms an axis of symmetry (Example 12.2).

This mirrorlike structure resonates throughout Babbitt's composition; it is apparent, for example, in his approach to **pitch logic**. All the pitch

EXAMPLE 12.2.

W h o
A r e   y o u
W h o   i s   b o r n
I n   t h e   n e x t   r o o m
S o   l o u d   t o   m y   o w n
That I can hear the womb
O p e n i n g   a n d   t h e   d a r k   r u n
Over the ghost and the dropped son
Behind the wall thin as a wren's bone?
In the birth bloody room unknown
To the burn and turn of time
And the heart print of man
B o w s   n o   b a p t i s m
B u t   d a r k   a l o n e
B l e s s i n g   o n
T h e   w i l d
C h i l d .

In the name of the lost who glory in
The swinish plains of carrion
U n d e r   t h e   b u r i a l   s o n g
Of the birds of burden
Heavy with the drowned
And the green dust
A n d   b e a r i n g
The ghost
F r o m
The ground
L i k e   p o l l e n
On the black plume
And the beak of slime
I pray though I belong
Not wholly to that lamenting
Brethren for joy has moved within
The inmost marrow of my heart bone

Stanzas 1 (top) and 7 (below) from Dylan Thomas's
Vision and Prayer

From Dylan Thomas: *Poems of Dylan Thomas*. Copyright
1946 by New Directions Publishing Corp. Reprinted by
permission of New Directions Publishing Corp.

material is generated from a twelve-tone row, one that embodies a high level of symmetry. This is most directly exhibited by the opening gesture of the work, in which four versions of the row—prime (P^0), retrograde inversion transposed by ten semitones (RI^{10}), retrograde transposed by five semitones (R^5), and inversion transposed by 11 semitones (I^{11})—are heard in four simultaneous lines of continuous sixteenth notes. The resulting pitches are spelled out in Example 12.3.

Although they start on different pitches, the intervals of the outer two row forms in Example 12.3 (P^0 and I^{11}) mirror each other, since they are related by inversion, and the same is true of the inner two row forms (RI^{10} and R^5). The four together, then, are emblematic of the way stanzas in the text are shaped, since they mirror each other out from the middle, as though there were an invisible axis of symmetry between the RI^{10} and R^5.

The kind of intervallic symmetry found in the opening gesture pervades the entire work, although its rhythmic treatment is far more complex thereafter. The properties of the set that enable this are evident in Example 12.3. P^0 and its permutations divide into three-note groups (or *trichords*), all of which can be reordered, inverted, or both to form either a minor second and a minor third or a minor second and a major third. The synthesizer accompaniment uses almost exclusively these two basic trichord types from beginning to end. Nevertheless, Babbitt generates from them a continual abundance of melodic and harmonic material without the pitch doublings and redundancies foreign to the serial idiom.

What really makes this possible is the property of combinatoriality (introduced in Chapter 7); in this regard, note that the row in *Vision and Prayer* is a remarkable instance of hexachordal combinatoriality. Any given permutation of the row can be transposed, inverted, retrograded, or retrograde-inverted in any of twelve different ways such that the first

---

EXAMPLE 12.3.

P^0:	F	E	C#		G#	C	A		E♭	D	G		B	F#	B♭
RI^{10}:	E♭	G	D		F#	B	B♭		E	C#	F		C	A	G#
R^5:	B♭	F#	B		G	D	E♭		A	C	A♭		D♭	E	F
I^{11}:	E	F	A♭		D♭	A	C		F#	G	D		B♭	E♭	B

Opening pitch material from Milton Babbitt's *Vision and Prayer*

hexachord of the resulting series has no pitch in common with the first hexachord of the original, and likewise for the second hexachords. In Example 12.3 Babbitt superimposes two such combinatorial row pairs, P^0-RI^{10} and R^5-I^{11}. As one can see, the result, here and throughout the work, is maximal pitch variety, in terms not only of melodic succession but of note-against-note combinations as well, even though the trichord types and mirrorlike relationships mentioned above remain continually present.

Babbitt links pitch even more directly to the sound and structure of the poem in places such as verse 2, where an approximate rhyme scheme works symmetrically in from the beginning and end toward the middle (the vowels of lines 1 and 2 rhyming with those of lines 16 and 17, the vowels of lines 3 and 4 rhyming approximately with those of lines 14 and 15, etc.). Babbitt echoes this scheme in the voice part by having lines that rhyme end on the same pitch. On a larger temporal scale, Babbit also uses vocal pitch definition to imitate the mirrored shape of stanzas: the voice part begins the work with spoken text in verse 1, followed by *Sprechstimme* in verse 2 (with its approximate sense of pitch), followed by the main body of the piece (verses 3–11), in which definite pitches are sung; at the work's end, this sequence is reversed, with the pitched singing changing first to *Sprechstimme* in verse 11 and then to spoken text in verse 12.

Babbitt also employs **time** in reflecting the mirrored structure of stanzas. This can be seen, for example, on the largest temporal scale of the work, as Example 12.4 illustrates. The composer divides the music into seventeen sections, corresponding to the seventeen lines in each verse. The twelve sung verses are framed by an introduction, three interludes, and a brief coda, all for synthesizer alone. The totality forms a more or less symmetrical arrangement centering on the ninth section, the middle interlude, just as each stanza of the text centers on the ninth line. The introduction and coda, both lasting only a few seconds, suggest the one-syllable beginning and ending of the earlier verses. In terms of number of beats, verses 5–6 and 7–9 span a relatively short duration (147 and 213 beats respectively), while verses 1–4 and 10–12 span a longer duration (392 and 378 beats respectively), so in this sense also the proportions of the work are mirrored out from the middle.

The **notation** of *Vision and Prayer* is significant in its high degree of

---

EXAMPLE 12.4.

Intro.│1│2│3│4│inter.│5│6│inter.│7│8│9│inter.│10│11│12│coda

Structural outline of Milton Babbitt's *Vision and Prayer*

specificity for the singer. The vocal part is quite detailed in its dynamic and articulation markings; as one might expect, its melodic contours, asymmetric rhythmic patterns, and complex beat subdivisions present formidable nchallenges for the soloist. The detailed vocal notation is contrasted, however, with a relatively simplified, shorthand approach to the synthesized material, providing only enough information for the singer to follow the electronic part.

These synthesizer "cues" are written in traditional notation. From them, one might surmise that the tape part functions primarily as a modest accompaniment; in fact, there are many subtle relationships between the two forces, and intricacies within the electronic part, that are impossible to glean from the printed page. For example, Babbitt uses his pitch series as the basis for time pointing in both electronic and live parts. He also associates varieties of **sound color** in the synthesizer part—from bell-like sonorities to percussive attacks to rapid-fire articulations of "woodwind" colors—with syllables in the poetry. Once again, the notation provides no clue to this. But even with a more complete score, the intricate links between pitch, time, and other dimensions (this piece being an instance of integral serialism) would be difficult to trace without an advanced understanding of the composer's working methods.

The aural effect of these links, however, is unmistakable, particularly in relation to the work's **texture**. Voice and synthesized tape offer a fascinating interplay of isolated lines, pointillistic flurries, and the dense polyphony of melodic contours and cross-rhythms—a tortured but iridescent complexity strikingly appropriate to Dylan Thomas's poetry. Indeed, all the aspects of *Vision and Prayer* discussed above are parts of an expressive whole, wherein the fantastical, ominous pathology of the text is brilliantly conveyed by the music.

Of course, this intricate and precise web of associations between music and text is dependent on **technology**, specifically the RCA synthesizer and its capacity for precise control. Finally, a by-product of that technology is the listener's experience in live performance (especially novel in the 1960s) of witnessing the interaction of human vocal soloist and loudspeaker sharing the concert stage—a uniquely postwar **performance ritual**.

Mario Davidovsky: Synchronisms No. 1

The live-plus-electronic performance format noted above has been a predominant element in much of Mario Davidovsky's music. Between 1963 and 1977 Davidovsky completed a total of eight *Synchronisms*, compositions for electronic tape and one or more instruments. *Synchronisms No. 1* for solo flute and tape (1963) exemplifies the fluidity and clarity of gesture, as well as the intricate interplay of acoustic and electronic timbres, for which all these works are known.

Davidovsky's aesthetic and technique are those of the serialist, as one may gather from the Cologne-influenced character of his tape part (a highly sophisticated assemblage of electronically generated sounds, carefully spliced to form kaleidoscopic continuities) and the mercurial, equally dazzling shifts within his solo line. More significant for our purposes, however, is his successful integration of the two performing forces, often creating the illusion of a single seamless fabric. The "synchronism" between the flute and tape part hinges chiefly on how their inherent differences vis-à-vis **pitch logic, time**, and **sound color** are reconciled. For instance, the electronic medium is capable of producing any pitch, microtonal or otherwise, whereas the flute customarily plays (as in this piece) only the twelve chromatic pitches. The same applies to sound color, with the electronic medium capable of infinite variety and the flute limited to its own characteristic timbres. In the temporal domain the situation is reversed, the flautist being capable of constant adjustments in tempo and rhythm, whereas the speed and duration of electronic sounds is fixed on tape.

Davidovsky's goal was a single, evolving **texture** within which these personality traits are preserved but integrated into a coherent relationship. Nearly all the pitches in the tape part are nontempered, as against the equal-tempered pitches of the flute, but electronic pitch successions are usually so rapid (a possibility dependent on **technology**), and the flute and electronic gestures so artfully dovetailed or intermeshed, that one senses an expansion rather than a discrepancy of vocabularies. The timbre and articulation of sounds on tape are painstakingly crafted to complement those of the flute, using the classical studio techniques referred to in Chapter 8. As seen in Example 12.5, the flute part meets the tape sounds halfway, with its own expanded repertoire of color and articulation, as in the fluttertonguing, the high, forced attacks (accented Xs), and the breathy, percussive notes (⊕s).

Here, as in Babbitt's *Vision and Prayer*, the interface of electronics with a live soloist necessitates an unusual approach to **notation**. As with Babbitt, the tape part here is notated only insofar as coordination with the flute requires; unlike Babbitt, however, Davidovsky has the tape taking cues from the performer as well as vice versa. (The tape operator follows the score, and starts or stops where indicated.) In some places the tape and flute are precisely in sync (as in the thirty-second-note outburst in Example 12.5), but in others (e.g., the figure immediately following) they are more freely aligned, making notation of the tape part unnecessary. In other words, only the minimal graphic approximation needed to cue the performer is offered.

EXAMPLE 12.5.

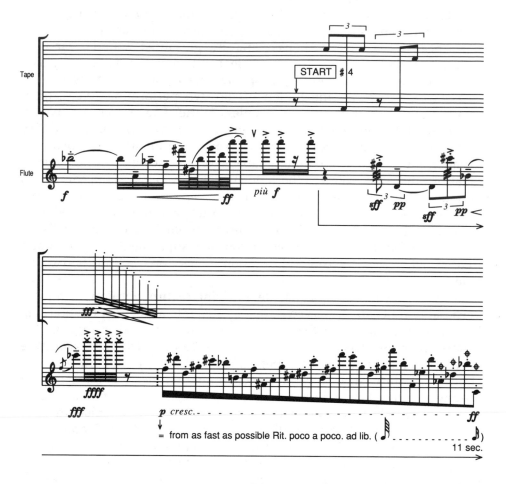

Mario Davidovsky: *Synchronisms No. 1*

Copyright © 1965 by Josef Marx. Used by permission of
McGinnis & Marx Music Publishers

John Cage and Lejaren Hiller: HPSCHD

Like Babbitt's *Vision and Prayer* and Davidovsky's *Synchronisms*, *HPSCHD*
unites electronic resources with live performance. In other respects, however, these works are as dissimilar as could be. Whereas Babbitt, in particular, has used the electronic medium to maintain strict control over
moment-by-moment details of **pitch logic**, **time**, and **sound color**, Cage

and Hiller (b. 1924) concern themselves only with large-scale choices in such areas. Responsibility for specific details has either been left to chance or delegated to performers, giving them wide latitude in the selection, combination, and timing of electronic and other materials. In short, while Babbitt wishes to ensure an outcome as close to his predetermined ideal as possible, Cage and Hiller choose rather to set the stage for a limitless variety of possible outcomes, leaving the listener unfettered by the composer's intentions, free to make his or her own sonic discoveries.

While a guest artist at the University of Illinois, Cage worked with Hiller on *HPSCHD* between 1967 and 1969. Their resultant composition represents a unique integration of both composers' interests: a work for computer-generated sounds, using as its "model" a well-known musical spoof by Mozart, an eighteenth-century indeterminate game of sorts entitled *Introduction to the Composition of Waltzes by Means of Dice*. (Mozart created a minute-long, sixty-four-measure waltz in four eight-measure sections of music, each section to be repeated, and each measure to be selected by a throw of the dice from a series of alternatives he had composed.) One imagines that Mozart's game, which is notated in keyboard format, might have been played by a harpsichordist. In fact, *HPSCHD* derives its title from the word *harpsichord*, reduced to six capital letters in the manner of 1950s computer printout titles.

To translate their ideas into performance, Cage and Hiller devised an elaborate ground plan, a compositional **process** that combines controlled and indeterminate elements. *HPSCHD* was designed to have two essential **sound color** sources: computer-generated tapes (from one to fifty-one of these) and one to seven harpsichords. The electronic material employs fifty-one different tuning systems, each tape containing music composed with a different equal-tempered division of the octave, ranging from five to fifty-six tones per octave, excluding the usual twelve-note division. Further, the music on these tapes is computer-composed by programs designed to generate (with data influenced by the *I Ching*) a variety of musical states, ranging from loud to soft, from silence to densely concentrated activities, and from sustained sounds or simple rhythmic patterns to highly agitated and irregular gestures.

The implications for **texture** are extraordinary: when all fifty-one tapes are playing simultaneously, the listener is hearing fifty-one different tuning systems at one time, effectively saturating the span of frequencies heard. The electronic parts and harpsichord passages are all concatenated or superimposed to produce endlessly varying textural combinations. Thus, all tapes played together encompass, for practical purposes, all textural conditions as well as all frequencies.

Although the superficial result, ironically, is one undifferentiated, chaotic mass of sound, any number of distinct sonic experiences may emerge at any time, depending on how and where the listener's attention is di-

ILLUS. 12.1.

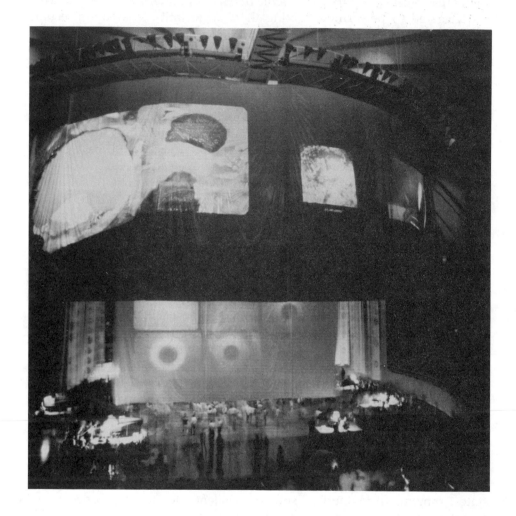

HPSCHD by Cage and Hiller, in performance at the
University of Illinois, 1969

Bruce Dale, © 1970 National Geographic Society. Used by
permission

rected. For example, the first of the seven harpsichord parts (Solo I) is
composed by the same computer programs that composed the electronic
sounds, except that the harpsichord is tuned to the twelve-note scale, the

only scale not represented among the fifty-one tapes. The other harpsichord solos stem from Cage's preoccupation with chance procedures. Except for Solo VII, the point of departure for this is Mozart's musical dice game, repeated twenty times; Solos III–VI begin with one realization but then proceed to include other keyboard music by Mozart and, in Solos V and VI, works by composers found at roughly equal intervals along the subsequent historical continuum (Beethoven, Chopin, Schumann, Gottschalk, Busoni, and Schoenberg, as well as Cage and Hiller themselves). In some places the right- and left-hand parts are coordinated as in the original compositions, but elsewhere they are moved out of sync with one another. In Solo VII the performer chooses any Mozart work and plays it in any way desired. This borrowing and scrambling of past material is an instance of **historicism/parody**; as with the electronic material, its aim here is a sound surface saturated with a full range of possible musical experiences, any one of which might come into focus, depending on the listener's location in space and time.

The premiere of *HPSCHD* took the form of a massive multimedia environment, staged in and around the University of Illinois's enormous, circular Assembly Hall on the Urbana campus in May 1969. The sound, including the highly amplified harpsichords, was distributed by fifty-eight speakers placed throughout the hall. A gigantic collage of slide, film, and light projections (involving eight film projectors, eighty slide machines, and some eight thousand slides of both real and abstract images) covered the interior of the hall, around and through which an audience estimated at six thousand moved unrestrictedly during the five-hour production.

Obviously, *HPSCHD* offers a radical contrast to traditional **performance ritual**, in its mode of presentation over a lengthy period of time in a large public space—not a concert hall—within which people may come and go freely. Ideally, sounds, visual stimuli, and theatrical elements are meant to surround the listener at 360 degrees, creating a sense of visual as well as aural saturation and leaving audience members open to countless possible experiences, depending on how they move through the space. At the Illinois premiere, listeners felt free to stay in the performance space for any duration of time, to sit or to walk around, to dance with partners, eat their lunch, or read newspapers.

One other well-known mode of presentation for *HPSCHD*—one involving a vastly different **performance ritual**—is the Nonesuch long-playing record of the work that appeared around the time of the multimedia premiere. The recorded version, involving all fifty-one tapes but only three soloists, invites performance participation in the home by including a "score" (also composed by the computer) for the frequent alteration of volume and stereo balance dials.

Peter Maxwell Davies: Eight Songs for a Mad King

Peter Maxwell Davies (b. 1934) composed *Eight Songs for a Mad King* in 1969 for his own ensemble, the Pierrot Players (later renamed the Fires of London). On one level the work may be regarded as a song cycle intended for a conventional concert setting, with an ensemble of conventional forces (baritone voice, flute/piccolo, clarinet, violin, cello, piano/harpsichord, and percussion) led by a conductor. (Its instrumentation, in fact, is similar to that of Schoenberg's *Pierrot Lunaire*.) On another level, though, it radically disrupts traditional expectations of **performance ritual** within the concert setting, and in this sense is regarded as a milestone in the evolution of chamber music as theater, following in a tradition which extends back to *Pierrot Lunaire* itself.

Maxwell Davies collaborated with the poet Randolph Stow, who wrote for him a series of eight poems in the form of a monologue by King George III of England, a monarch known for the loss of the American colonies during his reign and for severe nervous and psychological disorders (regarded at the time as "madness") during his last ten years. Stow's poems, which include fragments of the king's own recorded words, depict his decline into madness through a series of incidents: (1) The King flatters, then rants at a gatekeeper who confines him to palace grounds. (2) He imagines a walk in the country, during which pleasant woods distort into "strangling ivy" and "pythons." (3) He imagines conversing with an attractive young woman. (4) He sees himself floating down the Thames, escaping his people. (5) He cries out for his fictional queen, Esther, believing that he has divorced Queen Charlotte. (6) He denies his illness, accusing others of dishonesty. (7) He warmly encourages his people to make merry, then suddenly vilifies them for their vices. (8) He announces his own death (as though in the past), then bemoans the history of his madness and coming demise ("He will die howling").

The inspiration for these poems came from a small mechanical organ once owned by George III, with which he attempted to teach birds to sing. (The king himself was unsuccessful in learning flute and harpsichord.) It was here that Maxwell Davies found the impetus for a theatrical twist to traditional performance ritual. The baritone soloist, wearing a monarch's robe and crown, plays the role of George III, while the percussionist can be perceived (certainly at the work's terrifying conclusion) as the gatekeeper. The flute, clarinet, violin, and cello, seated inside giant bird cages, are the bullfinches George is teaching to sing, serving also as characters in his illusionary world and reflections of his own imprisoned personality.

Certain songs are, in fact, conceived as dialogues between the monarch and the instruments: in No. 3 the flute is the "lady-in-waiting" of the song's title; in No. 4 the cellist represents the River Thames; in No. 6 the clarinet mocks the king's demented chatter; in No. 7 the violin represents the king's tortured psyche, which he symbolically destroys by grabbing the instrument from the player and shattering it; and in the finale, No. 8, the percussionist/gatekeeper, beating a drum with leather whips, drives the shrieking, cowering king offstage.

This dramatic effect is reinforced by the voice part, which calls for startling departures in vocal technique (with precedents in Schoenberg's *Pierrot Lunaire*, Berg's *Wozzeck*, and Berio's *Visage*). These include registral extremes (up to an octave or more above treble clef), clusters and multiphonics (inaccessible to most singers), trills, slides, shouts, groans, and noises. Their effect is deeply disturbing and lends a jarring pathos to the king's madness. The other instruments employ wildly extended techniques as well, which combined with the rich vocal palette often yield a **texture** and **sound color** almost implausibly at odds with one's expectations from such an ensemble. The resulting air of irrationality is further underscored by Maxwell Davies's approach to **pitch logic** and **time**, with bizarre swings in style, ranging from mock-Baroque clarity to violent dissonance and improvised rhythmic chaos.

As Example 12.6 illustrates, imaginative visual symbols are used to specify this atmosphere of dementia. Here, in an extraordinary link between text and **notation**, the score resembles a bird cage in which the flute (representing both a bullfinch and a young woman) is entrapped by the words of the king. The latter, in a free recitative, alternately urges the bullfinch on with twittering noises and pleads grotesquely for the woman's attention. The flute replies by mimicking the voice part freely and interjecting the notated figures in any order at will. (The second figure from the right is one of the work's central motives.)

As implied above, **historicism** is also crucial to the air of insanity and irony. All the movements have eighteenth-century titles (e.g., "Minuet," "Allemande," "Recitative & Air," "Spanish March"), and the entire work is peppered with parodies of Baroque style that quickly run amok. No. 7, in fact, borrows directly from Handel's *Messiah*, whose text George III was fond of quoting. Labeled "Country Dance," this song begins with the instrumental obbligato to the *Messiah*'s first aria, rhythmically slewed into a barroom vamp for the soloist's contorted rendering of "Comfort ye, comfort ye my people." The instruments then revert to a foxtrot as the king raves at his subjects, leading to another rendition of the obbligato, this time beginning with the authentic eighth-note pulse but soon degenerating into furious, pounding clusters.

As the instruments deride and torment the king, as styles blur, and as everyone's virtuosity is pushed to improbable limits, we are left to wonder, according the composer's program note, who it is that is truly mad.

EXAMPLE 12.6.

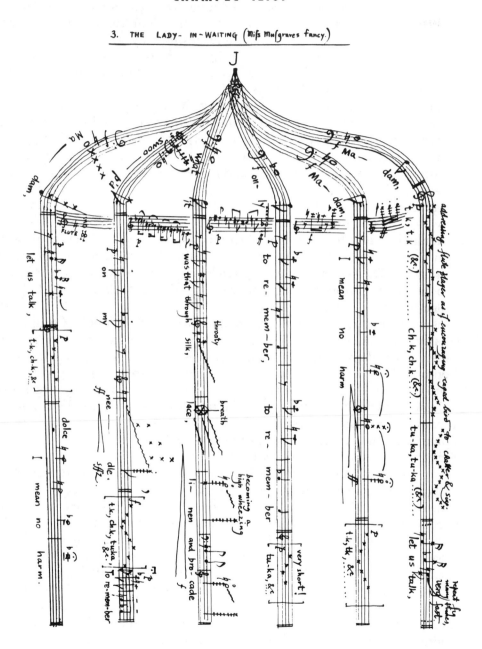

Peter Maxwell Davies: *Eight Songs for a Mad King*,
third movement

George Crumb: Ancient Voices of Children

George Crumb's *Ancient Voices of Children* (1970) is composed for soprano, boy soprano, oboe, mandolin, harp, electric piano, and three percussionists. As in many of his vocal works, the text is from the darkly primitive and fantastical poetry of Federico García Lorca. In Crumb's music **pitch logic**, **time**, **texture**, and **sound color** all contribute to a stark, phantasmal sound-scape that seems ideally matched to Lorca's words. Melodic lines, typically drawn from simple but unusual scale patterns, generate a constant sense of harmonic ambiguity. (Note the pitch vocabulary of Example 12.7a, E–F–G–A♭–B–C♯–D♯.) The supple, changeable rhythm and the many pauses and silent spaces contribute to the music's primeval aura.

The prevailing texture is sparse, with few chordal sonorities and rarely more than two or three instruments at a time, but from these Crumb elicits an extraordinary array of exotic timbres, effected by such techniques as threading paper through strings of the harp, using a chisel inside the piano to create glissandi, and playing the mandolin with a glass rod and metal plectrum (resembling "bottleneck" style on a guitar). The rhythmic and instrumental practices found here call for specially devised **notation**. One particular hallmark of Crumb's scores, seen in Example 12.7b, is the use of visual alignment rather than meter to allow eccentrically shaped rhythm while maintaining a well-coordinated ensemble.

What really stands out in *Ancient Voices*, however, is the variety of allusions to the music of other cultures. For instance, the soprano line in Example 12.7a (sung into the piano to generate a distant, mysterious res-onance) is reminiscent of melodies found among indigenous American tribes, with their grace-note inflections, asymmetrical phrasing, persistent emphasis on a few notes, and—to unaccustomed ears—peculiar intonation, suggested here by cross-relations (E with F, G with A♭). Tongue clicks and meaningless syllables augment the primitive ambience of the line. In a section entitled "Dances of the Ancient Earth," an austere intensity sug-gestive of Chinese or Japanese court music is created by the zitherlike doubling of harp and mandolin (with pairs of mandolin strings tuned a quarter tone apart) and by stark rhythmic unisons punctuated with per-cussion and voice. Example 12.7b evokes a taste of flamenco, both with the supple voice line and with a simple triad which is "strummed"—not by anything resembling a guitar but by the percussionists' voices. The sharply percussive, bell-like sonorities that open the final movement have the ex-otic clangor and ceremonial flavor associated with religious rites of the Far East. None of these are meant by Crumb to be specific, erudite references, representing instead a free **historicism**, adapting and mixing many sources to create a vivid palette of sound color and texture. **Parody** also plays a

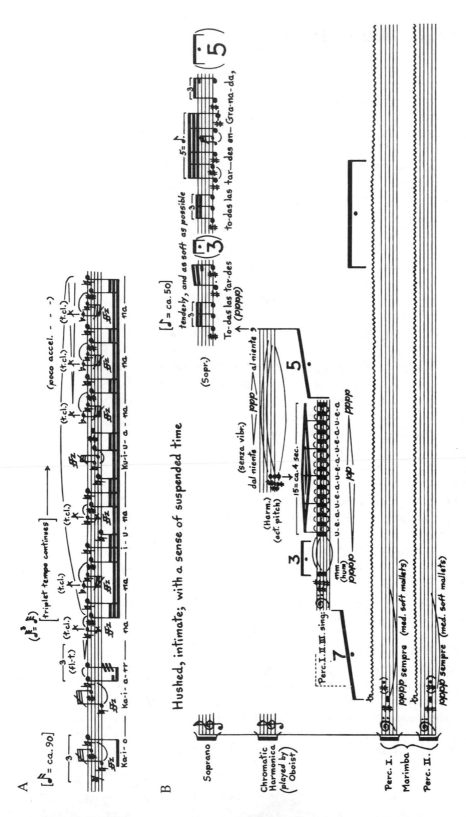

EXAMPLE 12.7. George Crumb: *Ancient Voices of Children.* a. Part I; b. Part IV. Copyright © 1970 by C. F. Peters Corporation. Used by permission

part, with a rhythmic quote from Ravel's *Bolero* and a toy-piano passage from Bach's "Bist du bei mir." Most remarkably, the many different borrowings create not the musical hodgepodge one might expect but a single, evocative language beautifully wedded to the enigmatic and primal quality of the text.

Peter Schat: To You

To You was composed in 1972 by the Dutch composer Peter Schat (b. 1935) under the auspices of STEIM (Studio for Electro-Instrumental Music), a major center for experimental music in the Netherlands. It is scored for solo vocalist, six giant humming tops, and four instrumental groups: (1) piano, three guitars, and bass guitar; (2) piano, organ, guitar, and bass guitar; (3) piano, guitar, and bass guitar; and (4) piano, organ, and guitar. All of these sound sources are to be amplified electronically.

The work is an intensely iconoclastic and theatrical setting of bitterly political poetry by Adrian Mitchell. (In the initial Amsterdam performances, the space was intersected by ceiling-high projections of Mitchell's poetry.) The text directs its outrage at the brutality of World War II, but the music also takes its cue from present-day social injustice and hypocrisy, exemplified for Schat by the Dutch government's practice (c. 1970) of confiscating electric guitars, regarding them as vehicles of rebellious self-expression. Schat's response was to include nine guitars in this work; the **sound color** and **texture** are largely governed by their output, which varies between clearly etched counterpoint, frantic scurrying about, ping-pong-like antiphonal exchanges, monstrous percussive attacks, and barrages of sound that overwhelm the rest of the ensemble.

An ironic approach to **pitch logic** and **time** projects the text: musical "madness" (disjunct fragments, overlapping nontonal flurries, and percussive jabs) is established as the norm, but with each occurrence of the refrain "My love, they are trying to drive us mad," the music takes a sudden turn towards the traditionally "normal," with triadic chord successions and coordinated chorale-like ensemble rhythms.

The most striking theatrical touch is the placement of large humming tops, five feet high, at the corners and perimeters of the bizzarely lighted performance space. The tops seem to embody the futility and insanity decried in the text; at the end of each stanza (marked by the refrain) one or more tops are heard from various locations. At the end of the work, all of them are activated, a **performance ritual** that engulfs the audience with a sound mass on every side, swimming and spinning from all directions. In its early performances by the Amsterdam Electric Circus, Schat envisioned the hall itself as a madhouse, representing in microcosm the madhouse of society.

Pierre Boulez: Rituel in Memoriam Bruno Maderna

Like Penderecki's *Threnody*, Boulez's *Rituel in Memoriam Bruno Maderna* is shaped by its **texture**, but unlike the former, the latter's textural evolution is the intended outcome of a carefully thought-out compositional **process**. *Rituel* was written in 1974 in memory of Boulez's fellow composer and conductor Bruno Maderna, and its ritualistic severity results from the relentless unfolding of a single motivic idea, gradually expanded as time goes on and presented by successively more varied instrumental combinations, all accompanied by incessant, dirgelike percussion.

The orchestra is divided into eight groups of increasing size: one oboe, two clarinets, three flutes, four violins, wind quintet, string sextet, wind septet, and fourteen brass. Each group has its own percussionist, except the last group, which has two. Because each group is homogeneous, the work's texture develops in clearly defined layers of **sound color**, as more groups become involved.

The basic motive referred to above can best be described as a cell of variable size in which a held note is preceded and/or followed by one or more thirty-second notes. Cells of this kind are the only pitched material for most of the work, but they do change and grow, from long notes with only a single thirty-second note before or after at the beginning, to held notes of widely varying duration with larger adjoining groups of thirty-seconds by the work's midpoint.

Two types of texture, illustrated in Examples 12.8a and 12.8b, are created with these cells and alternate to make fifteen sections. All odd-numbered sections have the kind of sustained homophony seen in Example 12.8a. They always employ the brass group, but other groups are gradually added until in sections XIII and XV all eight groups of the orchestra play together. In even-numbered sections, continuously changing versions of the basic motive are strung together as in Example 12.8b, forming lines that are rhythmically distinct for each group and that, except in section II (for oboe solo), are superimposed contrapuntally. Here, too, the number of groups expands, adding layers of contrapuntal density, until groups 1–7 are heard together in section XII. As section XV progresses, the overall growth process of the work is reversed, as first the oboe and then progressively larger groups are eliminated, concluding with only groups 7 and 8.

Odd-numbered sections offer a stark "refrain" (Boulez's word) against the more elaborate even-numbered sections, and **time** is a critical element in this distinction, not only because odd and even differ in rhythmic complexity, but also because they organize time in two different ways. Odd-numbered sections, as seen in Example 12.8a, require the conductor to cue in the percussion and other groups at unspecified, irregular intervals. After that, however, the percussionists are on their own, while the other instruments follow the conductor, who gauges the length of held notes in loose coordination with the percussion. By contrast, even-numbered sections, as in Example 12.8b, entail strictly notated rhythm; in this case, however, the conductor gives only entrances (in any order), after which each instrumental group and associated percussion have their own rhythm and establish the tempo independently. Thus, neither odd nor even sections will ever be predictable in exact detail, but their textural and temporal personalities—bold homophony versus independent, freely layered contrapuntal strands—are assured.

In addition to the ubiquitous basic motive described earlier, a subtler unifying element also guides the compositional process and effects both **time** and **pitch logic**: the number seven. Pitch material is derived from a seven-note pattern of three tritones plus one note, and although transpositions, inversions, reorderings, and pitch duplications mask this pattern in the score, it is clearly heard, giving the work a harmonic and melodic identity that is consistent and unmistakable throughout. More obvious manifestations of seven are: the seven instrumental groups of up to seven instruments (excepting brass and percussion); the seven pairs of odd and even sections up through XIV; the growth of odd-numbered sections from one motivic statement in section I to seven such statements in section XIII; and the progressive tendency toward longer thirty-second-note figures, the longest having seven thirty-seconds. Section XV, spanning the last third of the work, reverses and balances preceding developments, with seven subparts that become progressively smaller, from seven expanded variants of the motivic cell in the first subpart to one simple version at the end. The thirty-second-note figures also tend to become shorter in this section, until the work concludes with a single thirty-second note *ppp*.

In *Rituel*, then, the unrelenting pursuit of one motivic idea through a seven-based process yields music that is richly varied in texture and yet monumentally austere.

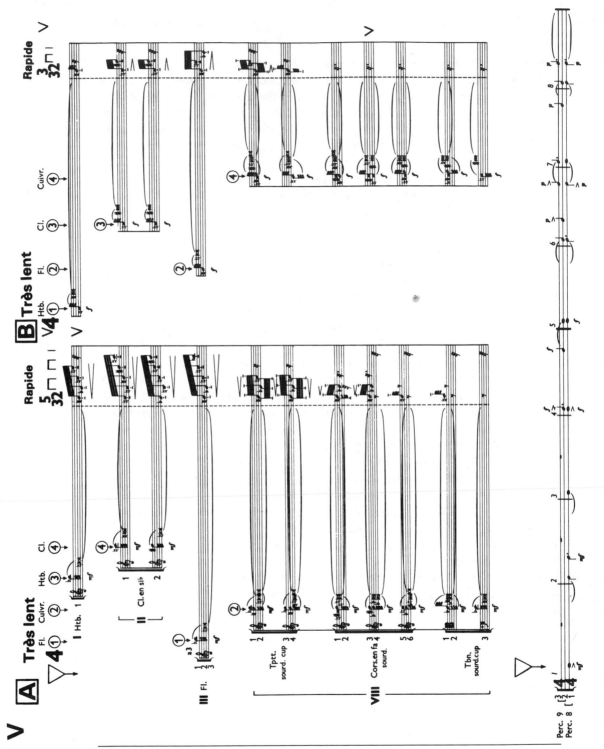

EXAMPLE 12.8. From Parts V (12.8a) and VI (12.8b) of Pierre Boulez's *Rituel in Memoriam Bruno Maderna.* © Copyright 1975 by Universal Edition (London) Ltd., London. All Rights Reserved. Used by Permission of European American Music Distributors Corporation, sole U.S. and Canadian agent for Universal Edition London

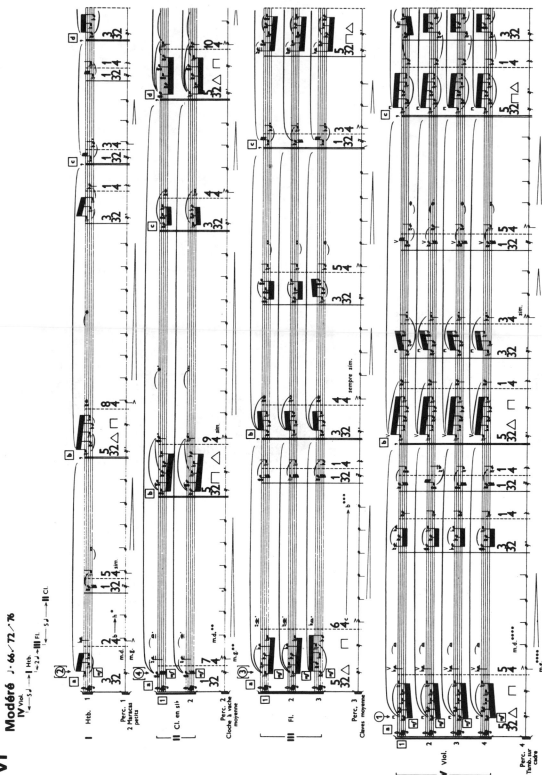

PART III

More Recent
Developments

Collage and Quotation

The new approaches to musical discourse (control, chance, texture, "theater") of the 1950s and 1960s, whatever their differences, share two features: (1) Each is nontonal, marked by a strong reluctance to use the scales, triads, melodic contours, and tonal centers of the common practice period. (2) Each is internally *consistent*; a particular sound world or musical language tends to pervade the total fabric of a given work or body of work. In the late 1960s and early 1970s those two features became greatly weakened, at times even giving way to their exact opposites, eclecticism and a fresh use of tonality.

We will begin discussing both trends in this chapter, which is devoted to the aesthetics and techniques of stylistic imitation, *collage* textures, and the use of *quotations* from fragments of other music. These may be regarded as special instances of **historicism or parody**. The use of found materials is not new, of course. Renaissance parody masses by Dufay and Josquin incorporate secular tunes of the day; J. S. Bach made use of Lutheran hymns and stylistic borrowings from his Italian and French contemporaries; the "Dies irae" appears in works of Berlioz and Liszt; and a well-known nursery tune was a resource for Mozart. Among twentieth-century works consider Berg's incorporation of Wagner in his *Lyric Suite* and Stravinsky's inspired re-creations of Gesualdo, Pergolesi, and Tchaikovsky.

In each of these cases, however, the borrowed material has been "translated" into the language of the composer and treated in a manner consistent with that language, thus maintaining a sense of stylistic uniformity. By contrast, recent decades have seen a proliferation of works in which borrowed materials are deliberately treated as isolated fragments from the "outside world" that clash with the prevailing style rather than conform to it. Such pieces serve as commentaries on memory, time, history, and taste. In fact, *style itself*, usually taken for granted, may be the subject of a work's content.

PRECEDENTS AND INFLUENCES

Examples of deliberate style clash are virtually impossible to find before the turn of the century. Style juxtaposition becomes important, however, after 1900. Its first three major proponents—Mahler, Ives, and Berg—represent a creative period of only forty years, roughly from 1890 to 1930. That era seems to have presented composers with an unusual stylistic crossroads: our first conscious awareness of so many alternative, competing musical traditions and languages. The musical universe is even more pluralistic and open-ended now than in 1900. Today's musicians (and audiences) are surrounded by a multiplicity of traditions, musical languages, and performance rituals. These are not just abstract footnotes and paragraphs in textbooks, but living experiences for many, thanks to international travel, performing ensembles dedicated to specific repertories, radio broadcasts, and sales of records by the millions.

The loudspeaker revolution, then, not only has contributed to the broadening of our musical tastes but also has made us more familiar with the very act of *style juxtaposition*. Listeners are accustomed to mixing styles—leaping from one century or continent to another—when placing discs on their record changers. When hearing popular music on the radio, we often deal with leaps of another sort: beginnings and endings of tunes are slapped together or cut directly to commercial advertising, just as composers working in electronic studios splice together snippets of tape, snippets that may include sounds (even other music) from the "real world" outside the concert hall.

By the mid-1960s experiences of this sort, brought about by the loudspeaker revolution, had begun to effect a collective change in the way we perceive all music—a change that composers were bound to explore in new works. Many composers were also drawn to style juxtaposition in response to developments in the relatively rarefied domain of postwar concert music. Three factors are worth noting here. First, developments in the area of **texture,** whether resulting from serial, indeterminate, or stochastic processes, had accustomed the ear to *discontinuity* as a legitimate musical fabric. Second, a number of composers had come to regard the orthodoxies of the 1950s as closed systems. In the area of **pitch logic,** they were anxious to break down the isolated compartments separating tonal and nontonal languages, just as their colleagues had bridged the barriers between serial control and improvisatory freedom. The earlier concern for stylistic consistency now seemed repressive: an artificial hothouse atmosphere, elegant and perhaps beautiful in its integrity, but stifling. Finally, many younger composers of the 1960s, although schooled in academic avant-gardisms, could not suppress a longing for a return to their musical roots. These composers, like the rest of us, had developed their early love for music as the result of exposure to some relatively "popular" genres: perhaps jazz, or classical Western art music, or ethnic and folk musics, Broadway musical theater, rock. Whatever the sources, they wanted to find a way of using them in their creative work.

It may be more than coincidental that the 1960s, the decade during which the idea of style juxtaposition first excited composers, also witnessed the beginnings of great public interest in Ives and Mahler. (In 1961, to commemorate the fiftieth anniversary of Mahler's death, Leonard Bernstein and the New York Philharmonic staged a major retrospective and issued commercial recordings of his symphonies.) For many reasons, the time was ripe for musical *eclecticism,* and many landmark examples of style juxtaposition were composed during the second half of the 1960s: George Rochberg's *Contra mortem et tempus* and *Music for the Magic Theater* (1965); Bernd Alois Zimmermann's *Musique pour les soupers du Roi Ubu* (1966); Foss's *Baroque Variations* (1967); Stockhausen's *Hymnen* (1967); Berio's *Sinfonia* (1968); and Maxwell Davies's *Eight Songs for a Mad King* (1969).

The close of that decade, the year 1970, coincided with the bicentennial of Beethoven's birth. Given Beethoven's ranking as a major Western cultural icon, it was singularly appropriate that celebrations connected to his name would foster "stylistically" adventurous works. Stockhausen's *Opus 1970,* also known as *Stockhoven-Beethausen,* consists primarily of recorded fragments not only of Beethoven's music but also of spoken passages from Beethoven's writings (including the famous Heiligenstadt Testament), which are designed to be manipulated in a live electronic, quasi-improvisatory situation. By contrast, Mauricio Kagel's *Ludwig Van* is intended for live, rather than electronic, performance. It may strike the ears of many listeners as a surrealist fantasy. Every note, phrase, and extended

ILLUS. 13.1.

Mauricio Kagel, seated in a room lined throughout with Beethoven score fragments. This space was created for the motion picture version of *Ludwig Van*

Reproduced by kind permission of Universal Edition A. G. Wien Archiv.

passage of *Ludwig Van* has been taken directly from Beethoven's music. Although the original pitches have not been transposed, Kagel has made great alterations in dynamic levels, articulation, and tempi, as well as simultaneous, overlapping statements of unrelated excerpts; the music is, consequently, both highly familiar and strangely alien. Kagel, concerned with the inevitable distancing between contemporary listeners and the "classics," wants to provoke the opposite response—to make audiences aware of Beethoven's *modernity*. Similarly, he wants musicians to interpret Beethoven as "new music." In his words, *Ludwig Van* "seeks to say to the interpreter that music of the past should also be performed as music of the present." Second, Kagel's technique of piecing together unrelated Beethoven phrases is designed to eliminate the boundaries between individual works. He would prefer that we associate the name Beethoven not with isolated compositions but with one collection of sonorities and gestures—that the entire Beethoven *ouevre*, in fact, be regarded as one single piece.

COLLAGE

The approach to "history" exemplified by the Kagel and Stockhausen works is a far cry from 1920s Stravinskian neoclassicism. Today historical models are more likely to be fragmented, isolated, and thrown into utterly foreign contexts—to be subjected to a collage technique. In the visual arts, the term *collage* refers to the use of snippets of cloth, newspaper clippings, and the like within the frame of paintings and drawings. Three provocative results are noteworthy. First, the art work literally takes on a new *dimension,* in that a flat surface has acquired depth. Second, the *textural* contrasts are now explicit, rather than suggested within a single medium. Third, physical objects from the "real world" have penetrated the artificially closed system bounded by the picture frame.

Collage Technique

One use of collage in recent music is adapted literally from the corresponding procedure in the visual arts: musical fragments are actually snipped and placed so that they abut or overlap one another. This can easily be done in the classical electronic studio with magnetic tape and splicing block. Collage was, after all, the first basic technique of the Paris *musique concrète* school, and in John Cage's *Williams Mix* and *Fontana Mix* tapes of the 1950s, street sounds, country sounds, electronic sounds, small sounds requiring amplification, and the like are curiously linked together.

But the splicing can be metaphorical rather than physical. That is, a composer might wish to create a score, intended for traditional acoustic performance, in which the rapid-fire juxtapositions are written out. The German composer Bernd Alois Zimmermann (1918–70), fascinated by questions of historical pluralism, became noted for a technique in which dozens of seemingly unrelated musical quotations are symbolically "spliced" to create odd, often unsettling, mosaics. One of his most provocative examples is the ballet *Musique pour les sòupers du Roi Ubu.* At first glance it appears to be a crazy quilt of associations and references; one critic likens it to a musical crossword puzzle. Example 13.1 shows a typical passage. The first two score pages alone include brief references (all of them clearly labeled) to Hindemith's *Mathis der Maler,* Wagner's *Tristan* Prelude, Mussorgsky's *Pictures at an Exhibition,* and a Beethoven sonata, all dovetailed into one another, and all against a backdrop of Renaissance dances. Later on, Berlioz's *Symphonie fantastique* and Wagner's *Die Walküre* are used as well.

Collage technique pervades much of Zimmerman's music, especially

ILLUS. 13.2.

Marcia Marcus, *Walter Gutman* (collage and painting). The background for this portrait is an assemblage of fragments taken from other art works and
from commercial advertisements

Courtesy Bowdoin College Museum of Art

his *Requiem* and the opera *Die Soldaten*. Although it may strike one as
humorous, even nonsensical, collage actually reflects Zimmermann's serious concern with the phenomenon of **time**. In his words: ''A composer
must above all expose himself to time. In composition (which is: organization of time) time is in a certain sense 'overcome'; it is brought to a
standstill ... what we call present is only the barrier between past and
future.''

    For John Cage, metaphorical splicing had its origins in entirely differ-
ent concerns and experiences, including his early background in creating

EXAMPLE 13.1.

Bernd Alois Zimmermann: *Musique pour les soupers du Roi Ubu*

tape studio "mixes." His fondness for electronic assemblage was channeled into purely acoustic terms on a number of occasions. One of the most elaborate and ambitious is *Europera* (1988), a monumental theater piece, in Cage's words, "intended to be a collage, of a pulverized sort, of European opera." Given access to the music library of the Metropolitan Opera House, Cage collected the instrumental parts of many standard-repertory operas. Individual pages of these were photocopied at random and distributed to instruments other than the ones for which they were originally intended. Costumes were similarly selected from the opera company's wardrobe department and assigned randomly to members of the cast. The singers choose their arias from a list of vocal prototypes, but do not know when and where (or if) these arias will be sung until the night of performance. Arias might very well overlap or be cut off in midphrase, and would almost certainly be set against entirely unrelated instrumental material. There is no conductor; all of the activity onstage and in the pit, much of it colliding in unpredictable simultaneities, is cued by digital time displays.

In recent years Cage developed a literary genre called the *mesostic*, which permits the creation of *verbal* collage from snippets of preselected writings. In his 1988–89 series of six Norton Lectures at Harvard University (published in book and cassette form under the title *I–IV*), Cage draws upon phrases and sentence fragments from Henry David Thoreau, Marshall McLuhan, Ludwig Wittgenstein, James Joyce, and Buckminster Fuller, among others, to create a multilayered assemblage of images, abstract syllables, and strangely moving poetry.

Found Sources

From another standpoint, we may approach collage not so much as a technique of snipping and splicing, but as a unique collection of materials: preexisting sound objects analogous to the scraps of newspaper or tablecloth employed by visual collage artists. These may consist of taped or recorded music, mechanical devices such as music boxes or calliopes, and objects that make limited "musical" sounds (automobile horns, dinner bells, sirens, ringing telephones). Once again, John Cage was a major pioneer, not only in assembling studio pieces from tape fragments, but in his use of flower pots, brake drums, and thunder sheets in his percussion ensemble music and twelve radios in his *Imaginary Landscape No. 4.*

During the late 1960s Stockhausen, in his continuing concern for embracing opposites (as his *Gesang der Jünglinge* unified *musique concrète* and *elektronische Musik*), became interested in the use of shortwave radio signals as source material for transformation in the manner of *Mikrophonie*; the result was a work called *Kurzwellen*. Stockhausen also developed an interest in the integration of electronically generated sounds with recorded sources; in his *Telemusik* (1966) recorded folk and ethnic musics from around the globe function as his source.

Stockhausen's 1966–67 *Hymnen* presents a more elaborate scenario, lasting roughly two hours. To symbolize world unity and interdependence, Stockhausen uses recorded national anthems, sometimes using one to modulate another electronically, resulting in a strangely distorted but almost recognizable intermixture of the originals. The rhythm of one anthem may be modulated by the harmony of a second, and the result modulated by the dynamic envelope of a third. Fragments of anthems may be heard in what Stockhausen calls their "raw, almost unmodulated form," while others will lose their initial character entirely. In the composer's words, "aside from the national anthems, certain 'found objects' have been added: scraps of speech, sounds of crowds, recorded conversations, a Chinese marketplace, the christening of a ship."

Hymnen is subdivided into four movements, or "regions," each of which concentrates on specific anthems and nations. Region 1, for example, is dedicated to Boulez and centered on the "Internationale" and "La marseillaise"; its other sound sources include Morse code signals, children's cries, and military band fragments. Stockhausen prescribes varying performance formats for *Hymnen*: as a radio piece, on record, produced in a church, or—as noted in Chapter 9—performed outdoors. One version calls for live soloists and tape; in 1969 Stockhausen expanded on Region 3 (dedicated to Cage and featuring the Russian, American, and Spanish anthems), recasting it as a work for orchestra responding to events on tape.

STYLE JUXTAPOSITION AND QUOTATION

Musical collage can also be thought of as a *metaphor* for a broad creative aesthetic. From this more general standpoint, we may consider as examples of collage any compositions that include eclectic style juxtapositions or fragments of music borrowed from the "outside world." Let us discuss each of these two sub-categories separately.

Style Juxtaposition

Different musical languages, tonal and nontonal, may weave in and out of focus, either successively or simultaneously, engaging in interaction or conflict with one another, often generating a distinctive **texture.** Quotations from other music may be brief and fleeting, drawn from relatively obscure works, or so carefully disguised that immediate recognition is unlikely. In any event, the quotations are not necessarily central to the primary argument of the work, which is that of relationships between supposedly incompatible musical worlds.

George Crumb often juxtaposes tonal and nontonal fragments with great psychological and associative effect. His 1971 *Vox balaenae* ("Voice of the Whale") for amplified flute, cello, and piano draws its motivation, and some of its material, from the sounds of humpback whales. These sounds are not used directly (by means of recordings), but are subtly suggested by extended performing techniques and electronic reverberation. Crumb also establishes a sensitive equilibrium among three stylistic levels: an unsettling, atonal fabric; melismatic, virtually static, solo cadenzas; and an ethereal, shimmering celebration of B major. The latter, a direct evocation of mainstream romanticism, projects a heightened sense of expressivity. Note,

ILLUS. 13.3.

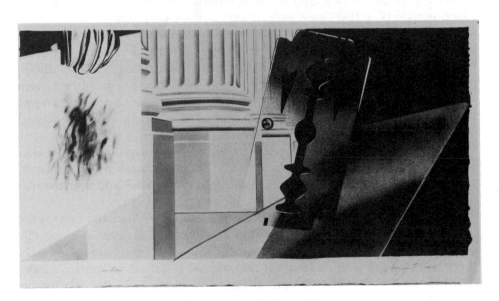

James Rosenquist, *Chambers,* 1980 (lithograph). An example of style juxtaposition: note the classic column, razor blade, highway stretching into the distance, and (in the upper left) a cartoonlike gloved hand

too, Crumb's fleeting quotation of Strauss's famous *Also sprach Zarathustra* opening—related, in most listeners' minds, not to a concert work but to a film, Stanley Kubrick's *2001: A Space Odyssey*. In many ways, the entire technique of musical collage is similarly "cinematic." Composers who work frequently with collage techniques may refer to their musical discourse in terms of flashback, quick cuts, multiple exposures, and the like.

Although Crumb's quotations tend to be drawn from the common-practice tonal tradition and especially from the romantic era, other periods of music history are equally favored by other composers. Music of the Middle Ages and Renaissance may be especially suitable for borrowing, partly because those periods provide sufficient "distance," and also because pre–1600 and post–1945 musics share many common traits in such areas as rhythmic process, the creative use of performing space, and a penchant for unusual (to our ears) sonorities. Significantly, the loudspeaker revolution fueled not only the 1960s development of the collage aesthetic but also, and at the same time, a period of phenomenal growth for the *early music movement*. As much as anyone, composers were excited by the availability on records of new and unusual repertories, and many have tried to capture aspects of this "new" old music in their own work.

Mauricio Kagel's *Music for Renaissance Instruments* (1965), explores the timbres, although not the musical gestures, of early music. By going directly to the sound sources, the instruments themselves, he immediately enters into the sonorities of another era, and then attempts to subvert them. Lukas Foss, in his 1986 *Renaissance* Concerto for Flute and Orchestra, attempts to evoke both earlier timbres and gestures—ironically, in a work scored for a modern symphonic ensemble. The concerto, which Foss terms "a handshake across the centuries," incorporates whispered fragments of Monteverdi and Rameau and makes stylistic references to seventeenth-century madrigal and intrada. A duet between soloist and Renaissance drum occupies a prominent place in the final movement.

In his 1969 *Saint Thomas' Wake* for orchestra, Peter Maxwell Davies has taken a sixteenth-century pavan and transformed it into a twentieth-century foxtrot. Instrumental timbres delineate what he considers to be the three levels of the work: a harp for the original Elizabethan source, a 1930s dance band for the foxtrot derivations, and large orchestra for further transformation, commentary, and synthesis of the other two. Similarly, his *Antechrist* (1967) begins with a strongly rhythmic medieval tune, then proceeds to dismember it in an expressionistic, nightmarish manner—perhaps reminiscent of the paintings of his English contemporary Francis Bacon. The distorted fragments, fractured syntax, and complex cross-rhythms convey great expressive power.

Baroque style references are equally plentiful in late twentieth-century compositions. Jacob Druckman's orchestral *Prism* (1980) uses material from operas by Charpentier, Cavalli, and Cherubini based on the myth of Jason and Medea; each of Druckman's three movements draws material from a different opera, so that the ancient myth is observed and retold from different angles. The elegant, stylized gestures and chord progressions of the seventeenth and eighteenth centuries are incorporated into a web of angular, atonal lines and diffuse, often dense textures.

Similarly, the Russian composer Alfred Schnittke (b. 1934) employs fleeting Vivaldi-like passagework, fragments of continuo cadences, and flowery cadenzas in his 1977 Concerto Grosso No. 1, scored for two solo violins, strings, continuo, and amplified prepared piano. Schnittke's movements are entitled Toccata, Recitativo, Cadenza, and the like; the spirit of Baroque courtly dance and flowing aria continually brush against polyrhythmic interruptions arhythmic textural wash, and massive cluster dissonances. As with Druckman's *Prism*, the identifiability of specific quotes is subordinate to the larger interaction of late twentieth-century rhetoric and distant, almost archaic gestures and sonorities.

Source materials for eclectic borrowing are not limited to art music. Jazz, popular, and vernacular styles are just as likely to become part of a collage texture, especially in the hands of American composers who know those traditions well. Because these particular styles have wide currency, their use in collage may well draw listeners into the process and lend a work greater accessibility. The compositions of William Bolcom (b. 1938)—who as a pianist has recorded Ives, Scott Joplin, George Gershwin, and Stephen Foster—move with fluency and grace from one language to another, including Western art music, parlor songs, and contemporary avant-gardisms. The blending and fusion of these languages has been a strong concern of his for many years. (In an interview, Bolcom recalls his student years at the Paris Conservatory in the 1960s, and his failure to win first prize because his string quartet contained an unexpected reference to a black American spiritual. Henri Dutilleux, one of the judges, came up to him and said, "C'est une rupture de style.")

The four movements of Bolcom's *Second Violin Sonata* (1979) run the stylistic gamut from violent, hard-edged post–Webernian gesture to jazz, blues, and ragtime, and to unmeasured quasi-improvisatory textural wash. The final movement, dedicated to the memory of the jazz violinist Joe Venuti, is especially moving, its lyric, nostalgic idiom drawn directly from American popular culture. Similarly, Bolcom's *Black Host* (for organ, percussion, and tape) brings together many styles: strangely appropriate for a work that the composer considers a study in fear, despair, and the violent dualisms of modern life. So many of the stylistic shifts (often wrenching) seem "right" because they confirm the work's subliminal program. Also, they derive from our experience of the organ itself; in this case, Bolcom has drawn his material—clichés of the carnival merry-go-round, the roller skating rink, the grand European cathedral, the Gothic horror movie—from the social history of the instrumental protagonist.

Vernacular styles act as a foil for the European post–1945 avant-garde in a 1967 work for clarinet and piano by Sydney Hodkinson (b. 1934), *The Dissolution of the Serial*. The work begins with the gestures of Pierre Boulez at his most severe: changing meters, extremes of register and dynamics, "pulverized" rhythms, even performance directions in French. Gradually, however, the listener begins to notice an increasing use of unsynchronized gestures, seemingly random snatches of *almost* familiar tonal music—was that Wagner? or Tchaikovsky?—and unexpected triads. The dry, pointillistic textures and tight clarity of the opening are now buried beneath a rush of romantic gestures: lush chords, crescendos, expansive passagework. A glance at the notation (as in Example 13.2) confirms our sense that the earlier rigid scaffolding has literally collapsed. The heavy numbers representing meter change, once so precise and formidable, are now in danger of falling off the page. A few moments later the disintegration of serial rhetoric brings us not to Western art music but to a collage of improvised pop, rock, and jazz fragments. Shorthand chord changes and suggestions of performance styles have replaced the overly fussy notation of the beginning. Eventually (and imperceptibly) *The Dissolution of the Serial* moves to one more dimension of performance: the introduction of a prerecorded tape, against which the two live performers *speak* in nonsense dialogue. The ultimate dissolution of total control has become, appropriately, theater.

Quotations from Other Works

These are intended to be perceived, and perhaps even recognized, by the listener. Once more we find an obvious parallel in the visual arts: reproductions of other—often famous—works, originally created by, for example, Rembrandt, Reubens, Michelangelo, Van Gogh, and the like, placed in an unfamiliar context.

In music of this category, quotation goes beyond the use of a few fleeting, half-hidden references. Extended quotations can, in fact, generate substantial multimovement pieces. One of the earliest examples, Lukas Foss's 1967 *Baroque Variations,* is discussed at length in Chapter 18. Other examples may be found in the music of George Rochberg (b. 1918).

An established serialist in the 1950s, by the mid-1960s Rochberg had come to find "the palette of constant chromaticism increasingly constricting." He also chafed at the insistence of the then-current avant-garde(s) that music must always be "new"—that composers must sever all ties with their tonal tradition. By contrast, Rochberg felt the need to effect (in his words) a "rapprochement with the past."

In Rochberg's early attempts to forge a new, eclectic style, the music of

EXAMPLE 13.2.

Sydney Hodkinson: *Dissolution of the Serial*

Used by permission of the composer

Charles Ives—similarly inclusive rather than closed, and open to a multiplicity of experiences and influences—served as a model. It is significant that one of Rochberg's first works using style juxtaposition, the chamber quartet *Contra mortem et tempus* (1965), includes an extended quotation from Ives's Largo for clarinet, violin, and piano, as well as references to Varèse, Berio, and others. In his *Music for the Magic Theater* (also 1965) for large chamber ensemble, the approach to collage technique is extended further. Against a backdrop of late twentieth-century angularity and diffuse texture, one perceives an overlay of stylistically diverse quotations (Mozart, Beethoven, Mahler, Webern, Stockhausen), as though Rochberg, like Bernd Alois Zimmermann, were forcing the listener to reexamine notions of "past." Even more immediately striking is Rochberg's use of one single extended quotation, virtually an entire movement of a Mozart divertimento, as a focal point or foil for other borrowings. (As noted in Chapter 18, Luciano Berio carries this idea even further in his 1968 *Sinfonia*, placing the scherzo movement atop a preexisting Mahler scherzo.)

Rochberg has since become less interested in outright quotation and more in creating his own original style juxtapositions. His first major work of this nature was the Third String Quartet (1972), featuring a Bartók-like movement, a Beethoven-like movement, the sensual chromatic language of Mahler, and a biting Stravinskian primitivism. Whether quoting specific pieces or making more general references to earlier styles, Rochberg's works pit styles against one another, exploring their relationships as composers of earlier times might have manipulated themes or key centers—as agents of dramatic conflict, integration, and reconciliation.

Programmatic and Theatrical Aspects of Quotation

Although a sense of history and an awareness of the expressive power of style may stand behind the use of quotation, other, equally compelling, reasons for using borrowed material exist. For George Crumb, quotation may have strong programmatic, even deeply symbolic connotations. The borrowed materials at the center of his 1970 string quartet *Black Angels* may, on one level, simply reflect the composer's "urge to fuse unrelated stylistic elements and juxtapose the seemingly incongruous." But because the quartet dates from the height of the Vietnam War, and because its exposition of opposing forces and its dramatic confrontations are explicitly presented in terms of good and evil, a high degree of symbolism attaches to Crumb's quotations: the funereal plain-chant "Dies Irae," a famous Paganini passage known as the "devil's trill," and Schubert's *Death and the Maiden* string quartet. Crumb transforms the last of these—ironically, itself borrowed from one of Schubert's own songs—into a strangely moving pseudo-Renaissance "Pavana Lachrymae" by minimizing its romantic, "expressive" qualities.

Finally it is difficult to discuss a Crumb work without referring to its **performance ritual**—the use of lighting, robes, masks, percussion instruments, crystal glasses, electronic amplification, and distortion. In Crumb's case, the notion of reaching out to the "world beyond" the source—which motivates so many collage/quotation works—may spill over into other dimensions.

Other composers have taken a more extroverted, outgoing approach to musical borrowing. During the 1970s Joan Tower (b. 1938) began a gradual move away from serialism, incorporating triads and tonal gestures into her musical language. In the course of planning new works, she found that certain composers and pieces of the tonal tradition could serve as springboards for her own invention. Tower's 1985 Piano Concerto, conceived as a homage to Beethoven, makes prominent use of three Beethoven piano sonatas. Similarly, her *Petroushskates* for chamber quintet (1980) combines the ostinato gestures important to Stravinsky's ballet *Petrushka* with the imagery of figure skating. As seen in Example 13.3, these aspects are apparent even in the work's opening measures. Stravinsky, a composer who delighted in parody, perhaps more than anyone else, becomes himself a subject of parody. The graceful gliding of skates and the multiple imagery of two "carnival" settings result in an unusually engaging work of high energy—at times a twentieth-century toccata, at other times lyric, and always sparkling.

William Bolcom's 1973 *Whisper Moon* offers a study in memory: dreamlike, nostalgic, gentle. Its textures are diffuse, and its motion leisurely, even static at times. During the course of its ruminations, mysterious references suddenly emerge and just as unexpectedly disappear: familiar Tchaikovsky and Mahler phrases, a hint of ragtime, and (most prominently) lengthy quotes of the popular songs "Blue Moon" and "Louise." Example 13.4 (p. 260) demonstrates the overlay of different styles against one another, the discontinuities and quick cuts. A brief, throwaway phrase from the Tchaikovsky violin concerto appears just before rehearsal number 18, followed by a lengthier reference to "Louise" at number 19. Bolcom's footnote for the violinist indicates the respect with which he approaches and incorporates "low" vernacular music.

Some European Examples

A number of European composers have made extensive use of quotation. An important work by the Danish composer Karl Aage Rasmussen

EXAMPLE 13.3.

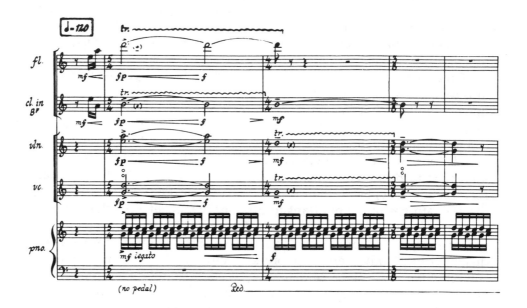

Joan Tower: *Petroushskates*

(b. 1947) is the 1972 chamber work *Genklang* ("Echo"), scored for celesta and three pianos: one prepared, one played by two performers, and one mistuned to create a honky-tonk effect. The entire composition is built on fragments from the Adagietto movement of Mahler's Fifth Symphony, transformed into the sonority and sensibility of a giant music box. In Peter Schat's 1977 opera *Houdini* the amalgam of styles has political overtones similar to those of *To You* (discussed in Chapter 12), making symbolic reference not only to shackles, imprisonment, and escape but also to issues of truth, fraud, and the relation of art to "magic." On the most obvious level, though, *Houdini* is a circus opera—raucous, vulgar, and with all the exuberance of popular entertainment.

The English composer Sir Michael Tippett (b. 1905) has a long history of employing borrowed material to great dramatic effect; for example, his use of black spirituals is a striking feature of the oratorio *A Child of Our Time* (1939–41). In his 1970 opera *The Knot Garden* Tippett includes a Schubert song and original music in American popular, rock, and folk-protest styles, all set within an uncompromisingly angular idiom. Similarly, at an intense moment in Tippett's Third Symphony (1972), we hear a surprising, *fortissimo* statement of the opening of the finale of Beethoven's Ninth Symphony, leading to an extended section for soprano and orchestra in blues style.

David Bedford, an English composer of a younger generation, studied in Italy with Luigi Nono and developed a thorough grounding in strict serial technique. But he is also an experienced rock performer, having played with Kevin Ayres and the Whole World and written music for the guitarist Mike Oldfield. In addition, he enjoys working musically with children and has composed works using nontonal, unsynchronized textures for them to perform. All of these interests meet in his 1971 theater piece *The Garden of Love,* in which two very different performing groups, a "new music ensemble" and a rock band, confront and imitate one another. Aleatory and metrically notated sections collide, and theatrical effects abound: for example, all of the players are asked to make sounds on toy whistles and bird warblers. By the end of the work, a pop setting of William Blake's poem "The Garden of Love," female page turners have become go-go dancers, the audience is invited to join the dancing, and the formal concert atmosphere is now that of a nightclub.

Style juxtapositions are integral to the work of H. K. Gruber (b. 1943), an Austrian composer whose best-known work is *Frankenstein!!* for narrator and chamber orchestra. Equipped with slide whistle, kazoo, and other noisemakers and props, the narrator is asked to bluster, croon, and frolic his way through a satiric text based on classic tales of horror, turning an ordinary performance scenario into a madcap vaudevillian affair. The outrageous behavior of the soloist is underscored by the music, which caroms from one stylistic extreme to the next, ranging from jazzlike passages to hard-edged atonality and to Viennese schmaltz.

Russian composer Alfred Schnittke, who refers to his music with the term *polystyle*, insists that it is "not merely blind eclecticism," but rather "the conscious collaboration of different styles upon each other." His Concerto Grosso No. 4/Symphony No. 5 carries the sense of intentional ambiguity even to the domain of genre. The slow movement derives its material from *another* slow movement, that of a very early (1876) unfinished piano quartet by Mahler, of which only twenty-four measures have been preserved. At the very end of Schnittke's movement—a fabric of string clusters, massive sound walls, melodic fragments, and reverberating gongs—all twenty-four measures of the Mahler quartet are played in the original instrumentation by four musicians grouped around the piano within the orchestra.

CONCLUSION

Why have so many composers become attached to the technique and esthetic position of collage and quotation in recent years? There are as many answers as there are creative figures. Some, agreeing with Karl Aage Rasmussen, may feel that "originality" in the late twentieth century is virtually an impossible order. If all the cards have been dealt, so to speak, the job of the creative artist is to keep shuffling the deck. "Newness," then, may be reinterpreted as a matter of syntax and grammar, the *rearrangement of existing material*. Many would cite the neoclassic Stravinsky as the prime source for such an opinion. In this vein, Rasmussen quotes the seventeenth-century philosopher Blaise Pascal: "There are no new thoughts. There are only new ways of combining the thoughts we know."

For other composers, collage is *time travel*. Lukas Foss has stated that "composing is like making love to the future." But for many the *past* may be more important than the future. Composing might be redefined as an evaluation of the past—reverence for the past or disdain for it, a feeling that history is dead or that history is everything. In Bernd Alois Zimmermann's view, collage represents the unity of past, present, and future. Alfred Schnittke sees his "polystylistic" technique as confirmation that *all* music is contemporary music. Still other composers might interpret the collage aesthetic as a way of confirming the vitality of tradition, or a nostalgic look backward at an elusive past that cannot be recaptured, or (if one is pessimistic) sifting through the ruins of a shattered tradition.

Finally, collage technique can be a way of commenting on modern *listening* habits. Modern culture is nothing if not wildly eclectic; thanks to the loudspeaker revolution, twentieth-century audiences have more varied tastes and experiences than any comparable group in history. Since Webern, Vivaldi, Tibetan chant, and Dixieland jazz are all available in record shops, and all inescapably part of our century, why not use them all?

Composers themselves can provide us with answers. In the words of Lukas Foss:

EXAMPLE 13.4.

William Bolcom: *Whisper Moon*

What I did in the *Baroque Variations* was to present my own nightmare—Adam and Eve driven out of paradise. My home is Bach, Beethoven, Mozart. But you see: man has a double need, to return to his past, which is home, and to discover the future. Then he feels that he is living in the present.

or Karl Aage Rasmussen:

What makes our situation a new one is the very realization that materials are not infinite (a mysterious counterpoint to exactly the same realization in many other areas of life). . . . Maybe it is possible by experimental condensing and combining to discover commonly shared experiences and communications in the language of music. *Not* concentrating on its atoms (notes, etc.) but on its molecules. And thus construct new patterns or "patchworks" of musical meanings.

or George Rochberg:

My search has led to an ongoing reconsideration of what the "past" (musical or otherwise) means. Current biological research corroborates Darwin: we bear the past in us. . . . We are filaments of a universal mind; we dream each other's dreams and those of our ancestors.

It is obvious, then, that the ideal of stylistic consistency, so important in the history of Western art music (even including the first decades after 1945) has given way to a much broader concept. With regard to our nine factors, **historicism** is the most easily recognizable feature of many collage-oriented works. But it is useful to remember that collage and quotation also create uniquely fascinating **textures** and bring into question many issues concerning the nature of **time.**

It is possible to argue that the origins of the collage aesthetic are related to perceptual changes caused by new **technology** and the increased, open-ended freedom in many areas of **performance ritual**, coupled with a disenchanted response to post–1945 **process**. It would be tempting to consider style juxtaposition as "antiprocess," were it not for the fact that some examples are created by processes of their own. In the same vein, it is ironic that an approach intended to refute the ideal of unified style is now practiced so frequently that it may be considered a style of its own: eclecticism.

The Resurgence of Tonality

As musical radicalism reached a plateau in the late 1960s and early 1970s, a different trend began gathering momentum, one that emphasized directness of expression, untrammeled by any theoretical or philosophical agenda, and unconcerned with challenging the status quo. Certain composers began to rebel against what seemed to have become an inviolable code, one requiring that every piece should be innovative, iconoclastic, or "difficult" for the average audience. There was a growing feeling that the outer trappings of originality (dissonance, complexity, experimental instrumentation, etc.) had ironically become predictable, institutionalized features in much of the contemporary repertoire. To write straightforward, accessible, or outwardly beautiful music seemed as much an apostasy—at least within the avant-garde establishment—as the abandonment of tonality had been early in the century. Liberating themselves from the need to be self-consciously "modern," many composers turned with new enthusiasm to materials normally associated with the tonal past.

The word *tonality* applies traditionally to the so-called common-practice period of Western music, roughly from 1700 to 1900, in which an established hierarchy of pitch or chord relationships centers on a tonic. In practice, however, and for our rather broad purposes of definition, any new music that encompasses even fleeting or superficial features of traditional tonality may be considered tonal simply by association. Such features include a persistent and discernible pulse, clear rhythmic patterns, consonant sonorities, lyrical melodic phrasing, and diatonic scale relationships (as found in modes or keys). During the 1970s and 1980s this return to familiar musical materials gained widespread professional acceptance, as may be judged, for example, by the success of such American figures as Dominick Argento, Ned Rorem, Joseph Schwantner, David Del Tredici, Ellen Taaffe Zwilich, Stephen Albert, and John Harbison, all of whom have received Pulitzer Prizes for works with a strong tonal presence and considerable audience appeal.

The evolution of this trend presents a curious picture. From the words of critics and annotators it would appear that such composers offered something "new" and hitherto unavailable to the average listener who had become disenchanted with the avant-garde. In actuality, they were turning in a direction that other composers on both sides of the Atlantic had followed *all along*. After World War II many chose to compose independently of "respectable" avant-garde circles, working in styles that found favor with traditional audiences while remaining highly original. Among the most prominent were Dmitri Shostakovitch of the Soviet Union, Henri Dutilleux of France, Carl Orff of Germany, Allan Pettersson of Sweden, the Polish expatriate Andrezej Panufnik, and a number of British composers, including Benjamin Britten, Sir Michael Tippett, Ralph Vaughan Williams, and Sir William Walton. Also in this group is a long list of Americans greatly liked by the public but (until the mid-1970s) regarded by their fellow composers to be outside the mainstream of progress. Most notable were Samuel Barber, David Diamond, Howard Hanson, Roy Harris, Vincent Persichetti, Walter Piston, William Schuman, and Virgil Thomson. (The concert works of Leonard Bernstein also apply here.) In addition to these, Steve Reich, Terry Riley, Philip Glass, and other early minimalists of the 1960s were plainly tonal in orientation, and until later, they too were considered—mistakenly—to be on the fringes of history in the making.

Why, if such widely programmed composers as Barber, Britten, and Shostakovitch had been writing with tonal materials all along, may we speak of a "return to tonality" in the 1970s? Why would a composer like George Rochberg be lauded as a history maker by turning to a kind of sonic material long since handled with great expertise by many of his contemporaries? The difference is that Rochberg and others like him had first established considerable reputations in an *atonal* language and then—to the delight of audiences but the horror of many colleagues—did an about-face toward a more accessible idiom. Rochberg became the most visible "defector" in the United States, particularly with his String Quartet No. 3. Penderecki and Henryk Górecki (b. 1933) later shocked European audiences by abandoning their radically modern sound-mass aesthetic in favor of an openly lyrical and harmonically approachable style, Górecki with his Symphony No. 3, *Symphony of Sorrowful Songs* (1977), and Penderecki with his Symphony No. 2, *Christmas* (1980). Górecki's work, for soprano and orchestra, does offer a new listening experience, with its sustained unfolding of quiet modal harmonies and gently shimmering diatonic clusters, but the Rochberg and Penderecki works are unabashed in their emulation of nineteenth-century practice. All three, however, reflect the same underlying impulses: an impatience with the obligation to be modern or original, an eagerness to embrace (rather than resist) the ear's natural affinity for tonal clarity and rhythmic periodicity, and a yearning to share beauty and emotion with the listener. The fact that established members of the vanguard were responding to such impulses encouraged younger, as yet less established composers to do the same. It also stimulated more serious interest in composers like Barber, Schuman, Tippett, and Dutilleux.

Other factors reinforcing this turn of events include non-Western musical influences, the influence of jazz and popular music, and the use of collage and quotation, especially quotation of music from the past. (As explained in related chapters, all these introduce tonality in some form or other directly into the compositional process.) Not surprisingly, major figures whose music embraced such varied concerns, notably Gunther Schuller and Lukas Foss, actively encouraged the new climate of change during the 1970s. Schuller, for example, as a composer, conductor, author, public speaker, and administrator, wielded considerable influence in advocating more pluralistic attitudes among programming committees and granting institutions. By the early 1980s tonality had become, albeit in many guises, a widely accepted and vital resource on the new music scene.

REVISITING THE PAST

Rochberg's music is a valuable starting point, not only because he was pivotal in the resurgence of tonality but also because he represents an extreme, sometimes adopting older styles directly. In many of his works after the late 1960s, such as the Violin Concerto (1975), the harmony moves through a world bordered by the acrid but still transparent sonorities of Bartók at one end and the lushness of Mahler's symphonic writing at the other, with excursions into simpler, more plainly triadic music redolent of the classical era. (At times, Rochberg even ignores the modern-day disdain for such things as key signatures and antecedent-consequent melodic phrasing.) Some passages are openly derivative, as in the impish,

ILLUS. 14.1.

George Rochberg

Photo: Larry Sandberg. Courtesy Theodore Presser
Company

march like tune found in the Oboe Concerto (1984) or the quirky sequential
motive that opens the Violin Concerto's second movement, both of which
could as easily have been written by the Prokofiev of *Love for Three Oranges*
or the *Classical* Symphony sixty years earlier.

Rochberg's success paved the way for many others. David Del Tredici
(b. 1937) has also adopted traditional tonality for his own, and like Roch-

Three Pulitzer Prize–winning composers, David Del
Tredici (left), George Crumb, and Stephen Albert

Photo: Mike McCloy. Courtesy Bowdoin Summer Music
Festival

berg, he often intermingles this kind of music with twentieth-century dissonance. Unlike Rochberg, however, his approach is more one of parody
than of emulation, motivated less by a high-minded sense of mission to
restore music's greatness and more by a sense of playfulness and irony,
even mischievousness, as he revels in the freedom to be traditional or
modern—or anywhere in between—according to his expressive needs. His
whimsical, often humorous relationship with tradition evolved in response
to the subject that occupied him in a series of works from 1968 until 1981:
Lewis Carroll's *Alice in Wonderland*. The best known of these works are
Final Alice for soprano, folk ensemble, and chorus (1976) and *In Memory of
a Summer Day* (1980).

For many composers, then, there has been a shift of emphasis since the
mid-'70s: it is no longer important that musical material be new or original, only that it be used creatively and effectively. Our discussion of Rochberg would seem to suggest that derivation from earlier music requires

sublimation of a composer's own musical identity, but this has proved untrue. Even without the wild eccentricities of Del Tredici's *Alice* pieces, borrowing directly from past styles may still achieve results that are individual and unmistakably contemporary. As one small illustration, consider the oddly dissonant approach to an A-major triad in Example 14.1, from the opening of the Chamber Symphony (1979) of Ellen Taaffe Zwilich (b. 1939). These measures would sound entirely at home among Stravinsky's neo-classical works, but Zwilich's extensive development of this idea throughout the piece is contrary to Stravinsky's treatment of such material. In Zwilich's Symphony No. 1 (1982) some passages, if isolated, might easily be mistaken for Mahler, others for Shostakovitch, yet none of this music sounds like imitation nor does it appear as a hodgepodge of borrowed ideas. Instead, Zwilich manages to forge a coalescence of these and other materials that is very much her own.

CREATING NEW LANGUAGES WITH "OLD" MATERIALS

Composing with tertian harmonies or a clear sense of pulse does not necessarily require appropriation of stylistic elements from the past. For one thing, all the composers mentioned in this chapter have freely explored not only alternatives to the traditional tonal forms—rondo, sonata form, variation form, and the like—but also new syntactical relationships among triadic sonorities and between harmony and rhythm. New ways of establishing consonance and dissonance and new concepts of repetition and phrasing have also been a concern. Perhaps the most radical demonstration of this appears in the works of Reich, Glass, and the other minimalists discussed in Chapter 16. Their gradual metamorphosis of continuously reiterated musical ideas entails an extreme level of repetition, protracted harmonic rhythm, and at times, a complete absence of dissonance unprecedented in Western music. But there are many other ways to handle tonal matter that diverge from conventional practice.

The music in Example 14.2, from the chamber opera *Full Moon in March* (1979) by John Harbison (b. 1938), conveys a traditional sense of harmonic flow. At the same time, little in this passage resembles the so-called functional harmony (i.e., harmony involving chord functions such as tonic and dominant) of the eighteenth and nineteenth centuries. Each measure is based on a tonal sonority, the dominant eleventh (e.g., G–B–D–F–A–C$^\sharp$ in

EXAMPLE 14.1.

Ellen Taaffe Zwilich: Chamber Symphony

© 1979 Elkan-Vogel, Inc. Used by permission

m. 26, or E–G#–B–D–F–A#[B♭] in m. 27), but the chords are not arranged to form a conventional progression, and their identity is clouded by tightly spaced voicing in a low register. Nevertheless, there is a convincing sense of tonal continuity, created in part by voice leading, which behaves here much as it might in a Bach chorale, some notes being repeated from one chord to the next while others change by a minor second. Another traditional device, the harmonic sequence, also plays a role, as the chord pattern in the first two measures (G^{11} [inverted]–E^{11}) is repeated and then twice transposed by a half step ($A^{♭11}$–F^{11}, A^{11}–$F^{#11}$).

Among Harbison's better-known works are the Piano Concerto (1978), *Miribai Songs* (1982), and the ballet *Ulysses' Bow* (1984). All these demonstrate a similarly individual approach to familiar tonal materials, although they also have a traditionally crafted feel suggestive of Britten, Walton, Schuman, Barber, and others already involved with tonality before it became a trend in the 1970s.

One specific characteristic Harbison shares with those older composers, and with most others rooted in the tonal tradition, is the preference for an obvious beat. But the presence of tonal elements does not require a conventional sense of rhythm, and traditional sonorities can take on a new perspective in a more progressive, less pulse-oriented rhythmic context.

EXAMPLE 14.2.

John Harbison: *Full Moon in March*, Swineherd's
Arioso

Example 14.3, from the second of the *Three Short Fantasies* for Piano (1973) by Yehudi Wyner, shows one of innumerable guises this might take. An inverted D dominant-seventh chord is incorporated in an unmetered and asymmetrical series of rapid sixteenths; the chord is heard in groups of four and three, which alternate with a pattern of three pitches dissonant to the D chord, arranged in an angular, widely leaping palindrome. This placement of a conventional chord in rhythmically and tonally unconventional surroundings forms a unique stylistic blend. The past and the present are difficult to separate in Wyner's music, which assimilates both modern compositional technique and the composer's experience as a keyboard performer of jazz and concert music.

Another equally novel confluence between old and new can be found in the music of the Danish composer Poul Ruders (b. 1949). Much of his music is triadic, but with a quirky energy that is distinctly contemporary yet strangely evocative of ancient or primitive musics. Typical is his *Vox in Rama* (1984) for clarinet, electric violin, and piano, in which a relentless eighth-note pulse and vigorous accentuation transform a relatively simple harmonic texture into something ritual and austere, not clearly influenced by any other culture present or past, but chillingly reflective of the pathos in the biblical passage that inspired it, in which Rachel mourns her children.

Many young composers, especially in the United States, have risen to prominence in the 1980s by forging fresh, highly personal idioms from otherwise familiar tonal and rhythmic elements. Notable among them are Nicholas Thorne, Stephen Hartke, Augusta Reed Thomas, Steven Paulus, and Aaron Jay Kernis. Their development will be especially interesting to watch in the decades ahead.

EXAMPLE 14.3.

Yehudi Wyner: Three Short Fantasies for Piano, second movement

Used by permission of the composer

ILLUS. 14.3.

Poul Ruders

Photo: Jesper Høm. Courtesy Wilhelm Hansen Editions

MELDING PAST AND PRESENT

One phenomenon discussed in Chapter 13 is also relevant here: the juxtaposition of disparate styles and materials. Our emphasis before was on
either a borrowing from or parody of existing literature. Some composers,
however, have gone beyond eclecticism, striving to fuse tonality and atonality, East and West, past and present into a unified and more broadly
communicative language.

The two most prolific figures in this regard (although direct quotation
does appear in their music) are Hans Werner Henze (b. 1926) of Germany
and Gunther Schuller of the United States. Henze's gigantic *oeuvre* encompasses a broad cross-section of materials, although serial organization and

conventional form surface repeatedly within them, and different musical languages often converge in a single work. A much celebrated instance is his *We Come to the River* (1976), a politically charged, operatic extravaganza reflecting the composer's Marxist convictions. Lyrical *bel canto* singing, raucous vocal extremes, gentle diatonicism, harsh dissonance, rigorously structured passages, and freely experimental ones are all part of one musical discourse.

Schuller's equally diverse sources include jazz, musics from around the world, and all aspects past and present of the Western concert tradition. His popular *Seven Studies on Themes of Paul Klee* (1959) touches on these

---

ILLUS. 14.4.

Gunther Schuller

Photo: Bachrach. Courtesy John Gingrich Management

individually, but later works such as the 1978 *Deaï* ("Encounters") for assorted voices and three orchestras strive more ambitiously for a genuine synthesis. Schuller's voluminous output in recent decades has been dedicated with growing urgency to finding an integrated language, one that benefits from modern advances but whose many dimensions might reach a broader listenership. (Schuller's *Abstraction* for string quartet and jazz ensemble is discussed in Chapter 21.)

Similar concerns have led Warren Benson (b. 1924) toward what he calls an "inclusive" music, encompassing tonality, free atonality, serialism, ethnic elements, and other strains. At times one of these may predominate, at others they may intermingle; throughout, however, the material is very much of Benson's creation rather than derivative of others. His *Songs for the End of the World* (1980) for mezzo-soprano and chamber ensemble offers an especially poignant mélange of simple tonality and forceful dissonance. The same could be said for the music of John Corigliano (b. 1938), whose scores conjoin functional tonality, lyrical diatonicism, and simple rhythmic structures with twelve-tone passages, tone clusters, complex rhythmic gestures, and avant-garde performance techniques. Corigliano's Oboe Concerto (1975) and Clarinet Concerto (1977) are characteristic.

TONALITY AND SERIALISM

Another approach to creating new languages with old materials is that of generating tertian harmony through serial methods. Alban Berg pioneered this development in such works as the Violin Concerto (1935) and the *Lyric Suite* for string quartet (1926), where twelve-note rows are employed to project definite tonal centers. Henze continued this exploration in his Violin Concerto No. 1 (1947) and *Boulevard Solitude* (1951), an opera in seven scenes. In the latter, the composer uses a single tone row as a source for consonant lyricism, brutal chromaticism, references to jazz, and allusions to Puccini. During the 1950s, both Copland and Stravinsky began to incorporate elements of twelve-tone practice in their vocabularies. Copland's Piano Quartet (1950) and Stravinsky's *Threni* for six voices and orchestra (1958) are well-known examples of how serial technique enriched each composer's language without disguising it.

In each case, a pitch series is selected and manipulated so that consonant intervals (thirds, fourths, and fifths) are prominent. Whether transposed, inverted, or retrograded, such a row consistently generates tonal-sounding chords and melodic sequences. However, the syntax governing the connections between them may differ altogether from that of conventional tonality, guided instead by properties of the row and how the composer chooses to manipulate it.

Sophisticated extensions of this basic idea are found in the music of George Perle, much of which represents concepts advanced in his 1977 book *Twelve-Tone Tonality*. Examples include his String Quartet No. 7 (1973) and Six Etudes for Piano (1976). More recently, the British composer Alexander Goehr has become noted for his application of serial technique to the symmetrical scale patterns favored by Messiaen (his teacher), and the American John Peel has used twelve-tone technique to generate sometimes Wagnerian, sometimes Debussy-like harmonic textures.

SIMPLICITY, STASIS, AND SLOW MOTION

Perhaps the most striking of recent departures in the use of tonality have been those that suspend or drastically retard harmonic motion, isolating chords from any immediate sense of sequential flow, often shifting the emphasis to the rhythmic and timbral exploration of a single chord, and in general, to the experience of tertian sonorities as sounds in and of themselves.

George Crumb, for example, often relies on a highly idiosyncratic use of static harmony. The wispy, transparent feeling of tonality in his music is engendered by harmonically ambiguous combinations of fourths, fifths, and tritones and by melodic fragments drawn from wholetone and diatonic scale patterns; but these sounds typically appear as though suspended in time, appearing in sparse, fleeting gestures devoid of any harmonic context and often surrounded by more dissonant material. Their evocative potential is explored with flighty rhythms, delicately exotic embellishments, and fantastical instrumental effects (strumming inside the piano, whistling into wind instruments, rubbing wine glasses, etc.).

Crumb's ephemeral, impressionistic hints of a motionless tonality, which first appeared in the early 1960s, proved influential to many younger American composers; perhaps most notable is Joseph Schwantner (b. 1943), who draws more consistently on tonal resources than Crumb, but incorporates them in a fanciful and ecstatic idiom highly reminiscent of the latter's music. This idiom is illustrated in Example 14.4, from Schwantner's *Wild Angels of the Open Hills* (1977) for soprano, flute, and harp, where a single G-major sonority is embellished with added tones and ornately arpeggiated. The harmony is static, with no sense of tonal progression between these measures and those that precede or follow; we hear G-major as it is rarely heard, with superimposed, delicately contrasting strands of

EXAMPLE 14.4.

Joseph Schwantner: *Wild Angels of the Open Hills,*
first movement

Copyright © 1978 by C. F. Peters Corporation. Used by
permission

activity in the flute and harp supported by a Crumb-like vocal line, diatonic but impulsively ornamented and rhythmically unpredictable. Such overtly and continuously triadic music, however, is rare in Crumb while pervasive in Schwantner (although the final measures of Crumb's *Vox Balaenae* anticipate this aspect of Schwantner's style).

As eccentric as they sometimes are, the works of Crumb and Schwantner still bear the tint of an American–European concert music aesthetic, being thoughtfully conceived, cleverly wrought, consciously individualistic, and obviously intended as "high art." Other composers who have embraced a dramatically simplified tonal language have done so in rebellion against this very aesthetic, regarding the self-conscious artifice of most new music as elitist, overly cerebral, and—paradoxically—conservative. From this point of view, the sophisticated, technically advanced music of Schoenberg, Webern, Boulez, Babbitt, Carter, and other such figures epitomizes the old order, while extended, boldly unadorned explorations of tonality represent the new avant-garde.

In earlier chapters we saw this attitude beginning to take hold in the mid-1960s among minimalists and those inspired by non-Western cultures. Another focus of rebellion against modernism during that period was the London-based Scratch Orchestra, founded in 1969 by Cornelius Cardew (1936–81). This wildly experimental ensemble stressed theatrical elements, public participation, and music as a group-oriented, nonegocentric phenomenon. John Cage was a major influence, but Cardew's Marxist political views led toward acceptance of sounds more easily digestible by the public than Cage's. The Scratch Orchestra promoted the music of fellow British composers such as Brian Eno (b. 1948), Gavin Bryars, and Christopher Hobbs, known for their relentlessly straightforward, sometimes deliberately artless brand of tonality.

Eno's "ambient music," represented by a series of electronic albums including the appropriately titled *Music for Airports,* is especially antithetical to the Western composer's usual bias, being openly intended as background listening (Erik Satie advanced a similar notion, early in the twentieth century, with his "wallpaper music"). Any notions of meaningful content or structure, artfully devised for attentive audiences, are snuffed out. At the same time, despite its immediate, naïve appeal, this is not music fairly categorized as "commercial." It lacks the formulaic, stylistically predictable aspects of such popular genres as rock, jazz, easy listening, or new age. (On the other hand, it is rarely listed as "classical" in record catalogs.) Nor does it have the patterned or repetitive structure associated with minimalism. Rather, it is a music whose harmonic progressions and timbral fluctuations, however simple and slow to evolve, are carefully conceived and through-composed.

The force of politics has been equally significant in shaping the tonal revival in the United States. Such works as Steve Reich's *Come Out* (1966) for tape, or Frederic Rzewski's *Coming Together/Attica* (1972) for narrator and instruments, use simplicity and repetition to throw a highly charged statement on racial inequality into relief. Anthony Davis's 1985 opera *X* (or *The Life and Times of Malcolm X*) is a more recent example, a work musically and dramatically intensified by the influence of African-American culture. This trend, anticipated in the 1920s and 1930s by the *Gebrauchsmusik* of Paul Hindemith and Kurt Weill, has resurfaced in Europe in more recent decades as well. Henze's 1976 collection of essays *Musik und Politik,* for instance, propounds a music suitable for the mass public while vilifying the vested avant-garde.

One important coterie of composers to thumb its nose at the complexity and sophistication of new music took shape in California during the early 1970s. Harold Budd (b. 1936) emerged as its informal leader, spearheading a trend—a seemingly reverse iconoclasm—that came to be known as "pretty music": rhythmically simple, often very quiet music with uncomplicated melodies and uncompromisingly straightforward tonal harmony. Other composers in this loose group included John Adams, Ingram Marshall, Paul Dresher, and the once brutally avant-garde Daniel Lentz. These composers were very much aware of their counterparts in London; in fact, Budd and Eno eventually collaborated on two albums, *The Plateau of Mirror* and *The Pearl,* and Adams's early *American Standard* was recorded for Gavin Bryars's Obscure Music label.

The radically sparse approach of this California group partly reflects the influence of Morton Feldman and Pauline Oliveros, prominent since the 1960s for their intuitive, anti-intellectual emphasis on spare, barely active textures and an inward absorption in sound and temporal space. But the tonal element, not yet present in either Feldman or Oliveros, was, ironically, greatly facilitated by another child of musical modernism: electronics. The works by Terry Riley mentioned in other chapters (such as *In C* or *A Rainbow in Curved Air*) demonstrate the logic of this: the electronic medium has given rise to feedback, tape delay systems, tape loops, and other such techniques for creating sound textures—techniques that lend themselves naturally to building, sustaining, and gradually transforming tertian harmonies.

Eno, Budd, and most others in the "pretty music" group are best known through their recordings, which continue to rely heavily on electronic synthesis and are more often marketed in the popular, jazz, or new-age category than as "serious" music. Moreover, there is a sameness among these composers; an absence of any distinctive musical dialect. However, one figure among them, John Adams (b. 1947), has achieved a highly personal voice that, despite its outwardly simple harmonic and rhythmic resources, has a momentum and emotive power quite unlike other approaches to tonality.

We consider the minimalist, repetitive aspects of Adams's music in Chapter 16; for the present, it will suffice to note certain features of his harmonic language. That language typically consists of unembellished triads and seventh chords played homophonically and repetitively with a rapid, relentless pulse. Although lengthy spans of time may be devoted to just one, two, or three chords, the harmony has a definite flow and direction, sometimes dramatically articulated by abrupt key changes but more often brought about by a modulatory process so stretched out in time as to be almost indiscernible, a process described by Adams in the program notes to his *Harmonium* (1981) as "moving over vast stretches of imaginary terrain" or as "a kind of celestial gear shifting." Even the more rapid harmonic motion on the music's surface has a peculiar, nontraditional twist idiosyncratic to Adams's style. For instance, the passage excerpted in Example 14.5 oscillates repeatedly between E♭ major and E minor, chords linked by a common G but having no functional relationship in the traditional sense. As seen here in the choral part, Adams's simple harmonic surfaces are enriched by a constant, often mercurial shift in rhythmic accent.

Other composers, with no connection to London or California circles, also began creating entirely distinct idioms out of simple harmonic resources during the late 1960s and early '70s. The Estonian composer Arvo

Pärt (b. 1935), for example, has become known for seemingly endless chains of simple modal progressions, often to be played slowly at a mystical, whisper-soft dynamic. (His work is discussed further in Chapter 20.) Many passages in music by the German Wilhelm Killmayer (b. 1927) rely entirely on simple consonances. Killmayer's work of the late 1960s, in fact, has an airy paucity much like that of Morton Feldman, with isolated, often brief moments of sound separated by periods of silence. The orchestral Sinfonie No. 2 (1969), for example, apart from one rare moment of dissonance, consists predominantly of unaccompanied single notes or two-note melodic fragments, played solo or in unison, separated by rests of varying length and with brief two- or three-note consonances occasionally interjected. The sounds themselves are entirely straightforward, yet their disposition is strangely austere and disjointed, an odd synthesis not found elsewhere in either traditional or contemporary repertoire.

Yet another unmistakable stylistic identity has been forged by Japanese composer Somei Satoh (b. 1947), even though Satoh's harmonic palette is even more drastically limited than that of any composer mentioned thus far. Typical is his *Birds in Warped Time II* (1980) for violin and piano, which continues for over eleven minutes without changing (except for a few brief measures) its E-minor harmony (Dorian mode) or its shimmering piano texture. This texture underlies a sustained, wistful violin line that unfolds in an improvisatory, ever-changing manner, though it never strays from the mode. Satoh's music is much like Japanese calligraphy: spare, atmospheric, and expressing much with few means, reflecting the influence of Shinto and Zen Buddhism in his thinking.

None of these developments is entirely "new," and it is only fair to point out a number of precedents. Lou Harrison and others associated with East Asian musics prior to the 1960s (see Chapter 11) anticipated more recent developments in rhythmic simplicity and tonal transparency, as did Carl Orff (1895–1982). The brazen straightforwardness of Orff's popular stage cantata *Carmina Burana* (1936) seems mild when compared to the overpowering, monolithic severity of his later theater works *Antigonae* (1948), *Oedipus der Tyrann* (1958), and *Prometheus* (1968).

Every composition cited in this chapter relies on long-familiar sounds, sounds that, taken out of context, might just as easily be found in jazz, new-age music, or earlier concert repertoire. Because originality depends less on what sounds are used than on *how* they are used, however, composers such as Adams, Pärt, Killmayer, and Satoh, for example, are easily distinguishable from each other and from their contemporaries, though they all rely on simple, essentially similar materials.

280

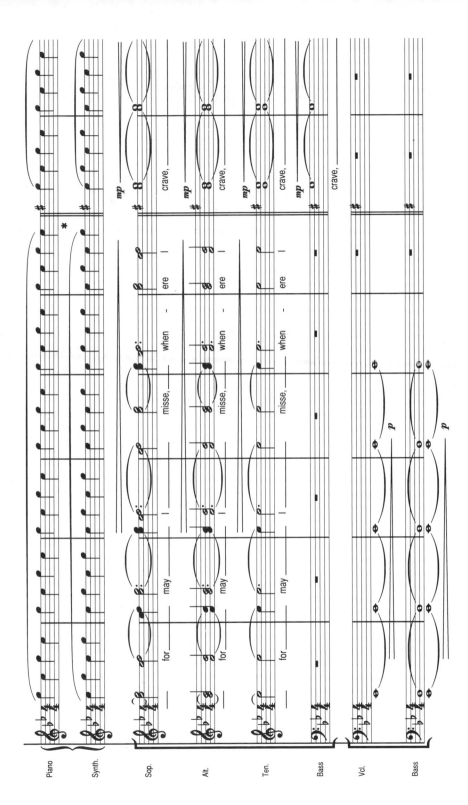

EXAMPLE 14.5. John Adams: *Harmonium*, Part I. Copyright © 1981 Associated Music Publishers, Inc. International Copyright Secured. All Rights Reserved. Used by permission

THE REAL VANGUARD OF MODERN TONALITY

The new acceptance of tonality has brought greater recognition to the music of older composers once thought too traditional to matter. Beginning with the 1980s, it has become increasingly common for new-music programs to include composers like Walter Piston, Aaron Copland, and Ralph Vaughan Williams along with more dissonant and experimental ones, and major orchestras have begun programming music of this kind with greater frequency. David Diamond, for instance, found his major symphonic works getting more attention during this period than they had received when written thirty years earlier, and it was the Chicago Symphony's 1982 performance of Andrezej Panufnik's *Sinfonia Sacra* that first earned him major recognition in the United States, even though the work was completed in 1963.

In the United States, the first evidence of this attitude change came with the awarding of the 1975 and 1976 Pulitzer Prizes, respectively, to Dominick Argento (b. 1927) and Ned Rorem (b. 1923). Until then, Argento had been little known, and Rorem had been dismissed as too conservative by much of the new-music community, even though he was already the most prolific and widely performed American composer of art songs, having written nearly three hundred of them. Like Gian Carlo Menotti (b. 1911), whose 1951 *Amahl and the Night Visitors* is probably the most-performed twentieth-century opera, Argento and Rorem had adhered all along to a lyrical, singable melodic ideal that naturally served their love of vocal music. For Rorem, the Pulitzer brought peer recognition for working in an idiom, with its distinctive mix of modality and chromaticism, that he had pursued consistently for the previous thirty years. Argento's success was still more notable, because few other composers had employed the traditional syntax of functional tonality as openly as he. But his work showed that even this is possible while still maintaining a modern-day identity. Much of his music is persistently triadic, with little dissonance and few changes in meter or other rhythmic complexities. This is evident in Example 14.6, from his *Six Elizabethan Songs* (1958). Here, a simple F-major melody is supported by a thoroughly common harmonic progression: I–I⁶–II⁶₅–V⁷–I. The jauntiness reminds one more of Stravinsky than anything from an earlier century, though these songs are far more consonant and rhythmically straightforward than any music by Stravinsky.

Other figures of a tonal bent who once flourished in the immediate postwar era but then became lesser known—Ingolf Dahl, Arthur Bliss, Paul Creston, Norman Dello Joio, Alec Wilder—are now becoming more widely

EXAMPLE 14.6.

Dominick Argento: *Six Elizabethan Songs*, No. 1

© Copyright 1970 by Boosey & Hawkes, Inc. Reprinted
by permission

programmed. These composers have been treated lightly by historians and
critics, and their work is often branded as conservative or derivative. But
while pioneers like Babbitt, Carter, and Cage have been upheld as major
forces in our musical culture, it is the composers of the tonal mainstream
who have been played and heard most frequently, especially by performers
and audiences seeking a change from standard literature but having little
patience for the new or experimental. This was true in the 1960s, before the
current resurgence of tonality, and is even more so today.

Nearly all the composers noted above established their reputations and
their musical style before World War II, and many of them are dubbed
rather loosely as neoclassical. But *neoclassicism* is a term more appropriately
applied to the music of Stravinsky, Prokofiev, Poulenc, and other composers between the world wars—expressively somewhat aloof, clearly defined
in its rhythms, cleanly etched in its chordal and contrapuntal textures, and
offering a twentieth-century twist on traditional tonality and form. This
brand of neoclassicism became more limited after 1945. While a number of
composers persisted in an unequivocally neoclassical vein—Carlos Chavez,
Irving Fine, Bohuslav Martinů, Walter Piston, and Alexander Tcherepnin,
among them—Stravinsky and Copland, once considered exemplars of the
aesthetic, began moving toward serial procedures.

A number of practices have emerged from this style, however, that
continue to attract a variety of more conventionally minded composers.
The prewar neoclassicist had required a harmonic language with the same
clarity, consistency, and sense of a tonal center as found in traditional

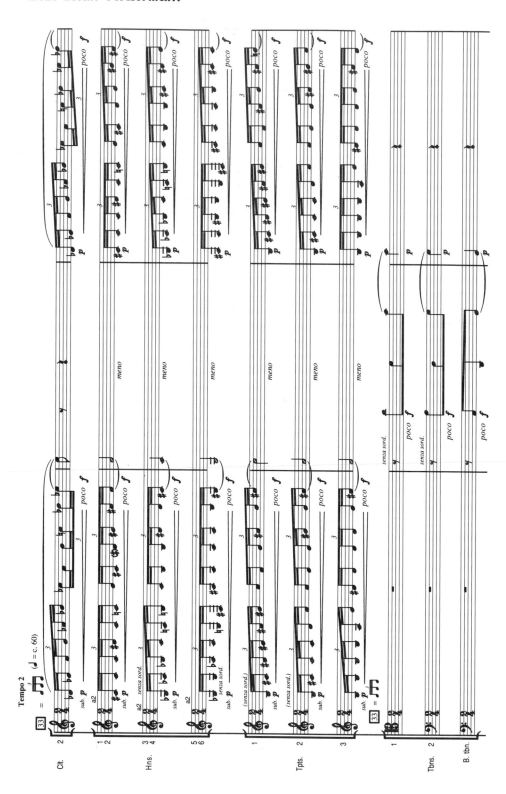

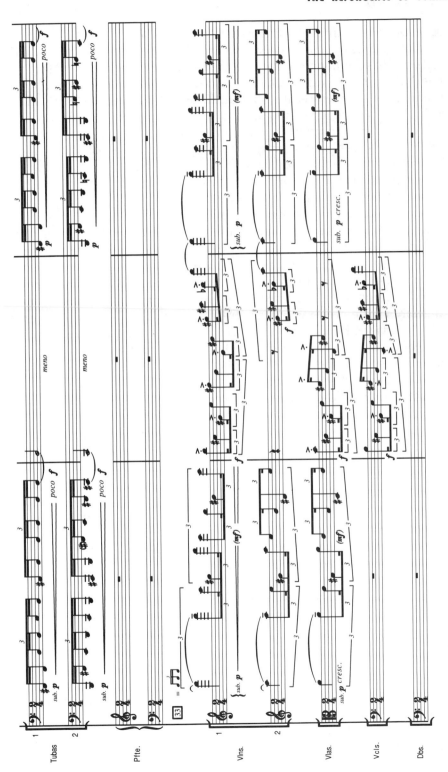

EXAMPLE 14.7. Sir Michael Tippett: Symphony No. 4. © 1977 Schott and Co., Ltd., London. All Rights Reserved. Used by permission of European American Music Distributors Corporation, sole U.S. and Canadian agent for Schott London

practice, but one with something new to offer. Some of the resulting techniques and names commonly associated with them include modality (Vaughan Williams), pandiatonicism (Stravinsky), polytonality (Bartók, Milhaud, Stravinsky), quartal harmony (Hindemith), and the use of octatonic and other synthetic scales (Bartók, Stravinsky). Space does not allow us to explore the above techniques in any detail, but an analysis of works by Barber, Britten, Schuman, Walton, and other such composers will often reveal a variety—and sometimes a creative admixture—of these, along with other forms of extended tonality and chromaticism.

To single out just one such synthesis from this vast repertoire, Example 14.7, from the Symphony No. 4 (1977) by Sir Michael Tippett, displays three layers of activity: (1) a giguelike motion in the strings; (2) a repeated three-note motive in the trombones; and (3) sextuplet chords in the clarinet, horns, trumpets, and tubas (the clarinet and horn parts are transposed). These layers are distinguished by more than rhythm; each one occupies its own tonal area, making this an instance of polytonality. But pandiatonicism and a chromatically altered scale also have a role. The strings play diatonically within an E-major scale (disregarding one B♭), but they maintain the intervallic freedom—with wide leaps, dissonant intervals, and an absence of traditional voice leading—characteristic of pandiatonicism. The clarinet, horns, trumpets, and tubas play within a scale based on B major but sometimes enriched by various alterations (C♮, D♮, F♮, and A♮); although the result cannot be called diatonic, nontertian chords are formed freely within this tonal orbit, much as they would be in pandiatonic harmony. The trombones play a simple diatonic motive centered on G. Thus, a variety of tonally derived methods interact to create a scintillating, multilayered, multidimensional texture.

The monumentality and complexity of this single-movement symphony is in keeping with its subject—the journey from birth to death—and demonstrates that those already connected with tonality before it returned into vogue have produced music as powerful, imaginative, and even unorthodox as any by more recent converts. This applies not only to harmonic vocabulary but also to elements such as instrumentation and structure. In Tippett's Symphony No. 4, for example, the structure is novel, consisting of four main sections and three developmental interludes that juxtapose and interweave the work's three principal motives in various ways. (The recurring sounds of "breathing" from a wind machine add an unusual instrumental touch as well.)

The music of Samuel Barber (1910–81), like that of Tippett, Britten, and Shostakovitch, provides healthy perspective on the supposed "newness" of neoromanticism and the new tonality. From the mid-1930s to the end of his life, Barber continued to pursue his own fusion of tonal methods, one that reached beyond such labels as *neoclassical* and *neoromantic* to encompass an enormous expressive and emotional range. Consider Barber's Concerto for

Piano and Orchestra, Op. 38 (1962). The opening melody of the second movement, for example, is simple, lyrical, and mostly diatonic, with the same kind of memorability (and the same traditional antecedent-consequent structure) as the well-loved themes in his 1936 Adagio for Strings or the 1947 *Knoxville: Summer of 1915* for soprano and orchestra.

In contrast, the first and third movements feature an aggressive, hard-edged chromaticism that becomes at times demonic in its intensity, as illustrated by the piano's rising torrent of dissonances in Example 14.8, from the third movement. While the B♭ pedal and the relentless metrical pattern clearly reinforce a sense of tonality, there is an extraordinary disparity between the stridency of this passage and the quiet delicacy of the second movement's opening measures. Nevertheless, this and other diverse material in the concerto's three movements seem neither fractured nor eclectic, but emerge convincingly from the same idiom.

In retrospect, one wonders how the remarkable tonal explorations and formal innovations of Barber, Tippett, and others mentioned here could have been treated lightly by so many academics and opinion makers before the 1970s. One explanation for the conservative impression once made by this repertoire lies in its more regular *rhythm*. In nearly all of this music the beat is discernible, whereas in more avant-garde repertoire eliminating

EXAMPLE 14.8.

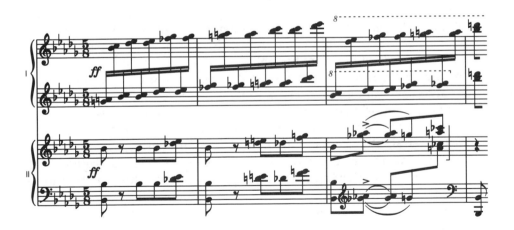

Samuel Barber: Piano Concerto, Op. 38, third movement (two-piano score)

tonality has usually meant eliminating any audible meter or pulse. Generally, the concept of atonality suggests that not only all sonorities but all moments in time are inherently equal in weight and directional focus, obviating any clear perception of beat or meter. It is no surprise, therefore, that so many composers participating in the recent revival of tonality have also returned to a clearly defined pulse (and to the rhythmic accentuation made possible thereby), something composers like Barber and Tippett never abandoned.

CONCLUSION

If there has been any common goal among twentieth-century composers it is one of freedom: freedom from assumptions about what music should sound like and how, where, and when it should be performed, and freedom to explore all sonic possibilities, whatever their source. But some have felt in retrospect that, before the mid-1970s, the institutions of new music seemed to replace one set of assumptions with another, recognizing avant-gardisms and obvious departures from the past as assertions of creative freedom while dismissing anything more familiar or approachable as reactionary. Ironically, this can be understood as a remnant of the nineteenth-century vision of the artist as a lone romantic figure, daringly inventive, faithful only to his own inner voice, courageously unaffected by the whims of public response, but ultimately revered by society for having braved uncharted realms of creative thought.

In the 1970s, however, tonality and music of the past began to gain wider acceptance among composers as a vast resource that could be tapped without compromising one's individuality or integrity. Compositional freedom now meant freedom to choose *any* kind of material, including tertian sonorities, straightforward rhythmic patterns, obvious repetition, or anything else that might once have been pigeonholed as conservative. This development, more than any other, has paved the way for a more pluralistic environment in the 1980s and thereafter, one in which a broad spectrum of approaches and influences is viewed with greater interest and in which the rhetoric between factions (through-composed versus aleatory, tonal versus atonal, uptown versus downtown, etc.) has lessened.

New Views of Performance: Space, Ritual, and Play

At first glance this chapter may appear to be a continuation of material begun in Chapter 9, "Multimedia and Total Theater." But the two are different, in emphasis and, to a degree, in chronology. In Chapter 9 we dealt with the expansion of music into "theatrical"—especially visual and technogical—dimensions during the 1960s, which can be seen as a natural consequence of the tape studio experience with its focus on multiple stimuli, novel textures, and discontinuity (the latter leading to collage technique as well).

Although we consider multimedia works in this chapter, our primary concern is **performance ritual** itself. Many composers who delight in isolating and exploring individual components of performance ritual have converted the ritual into an object of attention and conscious manipulation (analogous to composers of earlier eras focusing on "harmony"). Their pieces need not involve multimedia presentation, and they are not necessarily theatrical. In fact, they may be uncostumed and unstaged, perhaps performed by a concert pianist or the members of a woodwind quintet.

There are many good reasons why a fascination with performance ritual should flourish just now. We have become acutely aware of many different cultures and alternative performance traditions, including rituals related to the late twentieth-century loudspeaker revolution. Moreover, many have begun to view "performance" as an integral component of *all* the arts. A painter or sculptor engages in physical activity during the creation of a work; those of us who perceive the work have to follow visual patterns with our eyes or move around the sculpture or walk about the picture gallery. Similarly, people "perform" works of architecture by moving around or within them, or by reading blueprints (if we have the skill to decipher them). Poetry is performed by reading aloud or by reading silently to oneself. By the same token, we may perform music by making sounds with our voices or instruments, by reading the printed score, or by activating a playback machine and causing loudspeakers to vibrate. These examples may seem extreme. But they remind us that in any performance, even at the level of four people sitting down to play a string quartet, complex factors are at work.

In recent decades, a number of composers have decided to use these factors as positive creative stimuli, and in so doing touch on issues that go beyond the overtly theatrical. Let us discuss the individual components that constitute all performances in order to see how different composers have attempted to alter them.

COMPONENTS OF PERFORMANCE

Space

A musical performance takes place not in the abstract but in a physical, architectural, and acoustical setting: a small room, a large hall, a cathedral, a gymnasium, a town square, or some other. Each space not only causes sound to reverberate and resonate in a unique way, but also offers special architectural challenges, visual reference points, and built-in cultural associations. Composers have always made use of these: Gregorian chants, for example, were created with the resonances, echoes, and sights of a cathedral or monastery in mind. A Haydn string quartet was designed for performance in a rather large living room, a Mozart divertimento for outdoor entertainment, a Gabrieli canzona for antiphonal question–answer dialogue across the vast interior of San Marco in Venice (with brass groups situated in distant balconies or alcoves).

ANTIPHONAL SEPARATION

The last example suggests one use of performance space encountered fairly often in Western music: the spatial separation of players for antiphonal effects. Well-known models include Beethoven's *Leonore* Overture No. 3 (with its offstage trumpet), the placement of cannon effects for Tchaikovsky's *1812* Overture, Berlioz's use of multiple brass bands in his *Requiem*, and *The Unanswered Question* by Charles Ives. The interplay of monologues, dialogues, and asides among instrumental "characters" in Elliott Carter's music makes the spatial separation of players essential to the performance of his Second and Third String Quartets, for example, or his Double Concerto for Piano, Harpsichord, and Two Chamber Orchestras.

Two of Stockhausen's orchestral works of the late 1950s are notable for their use of spatial separation to achieve unique **textures.** *Gruppen* for three orchestras (1957) grows out of the composer's experience in spatial placement of sounds (see the discussion of his *Gesang der Jünglinge* in Chapter 8) and also reflects his interest in unifying disparate elements—apparently contradictory tempi, timbres, or densities—by treating them as related manifestations of periodicity (vibration and impulse). One might regard this interest as an attempt to formulate an all-encompassing **process** for perceiving and manipulating the world of sound at its most microscopic and macroscopic. Stockhausen's later work *Carré* (1960) for four orchestras and four choirs has a more homogeneous surface. Here the composer is concerned with subtle changes of articulation and timbre within dense clusters and with movement of these sound masses around the performance space.

Whereas Stockhausen wants to find common grounds for reconciling and ultimately unifying multiple stimuli, the Canadian-born Henry Brant wishes to underscore, even celebrate the very fact of diversity. Brant has always been a "radical" composer, at first concerned with wildly imaginative instrumental combinations, and in his later music (beginning with the 1953 *Rural Antiphonies*) with the separation of performing forces. His antiphonal works, with their semisynchronized Ivesian textures and controlled group improvisation, often feature utterly contrasting ensembles and/or styles—such as circus band, orchestra, and organ for his 1970 *Kingdom Come*—placed in different locations. Brant has also explored the use of light projections in performance (many years before pop and rock groups discovered their value) and spatial deployment in areas outside the concert hall, such as an outdoor park with players sitting on tree branches. One can easily trace Brant's fondness for such juxtapositions to Ives, but at a much higher "voltage" befitting the uniquely hysterical quality (as he sees it) of the late twentieth century. In Brant's words,

. . . single-style music, no matter how experimental or full of variety, could no longer evoke the new stresses, layered insanities and multi-directional assaults of contemporary life on the spirit. Perhaps if music itself were layered and hammered together out of irreconcilable elements, it could speak more expressively of the human predicament.

NEW SPACES

Just as Brant's antiphonal ventures often explore settings outside the concert hall, other composers are similarly engaged with "alternative" spaces. Max Neuhaus (b. 1939) is especially active in this area. The sounds of his 1967 *Drive-In Music* can only be heard on a car radio while driving along a specially prepared route with sound generators placed in trees and light fixtures along the roadway. A computer conversion system was used in Neuhaus's *Telephone Access* (1968), in which one could activate a unique, personal "piece" by telephoning a designated number and then speaking; sounds would be made in response to specific words and vocal characteristics. Various Neuhaus installations—electronic sound "sculptures" set up in public spaces and often designed to take listeners by surprise—can be found in New York's Times Square (the sounds come through a sidewalk grating), the Museum of Modern Art sculpture garden, and a stairwell at the Chicago Museum of Contemporary Art. Neuhaus also has a long-standing interest in underwater sounds (a number of installations have been designed for swimming pools) and radio works that encourage listener phone-in participation, such as his 1977 *Radio Net*.

Other composers share Neuhaus's interests. To mention but a few: Michel Redolfi's hour-long underwater *Sonic Waves* attracted large audiences—many with snorkels or face masks—to its 1982 presentation at the Dartmouth College swimming pool. The *Freeway Concerto* by Robert Suderberg (b. 1936), scored for solo trombone and an ensemble of fifteen automobiles, received its 1986 premiere in the California Institute of the Arts parking lot; its "orchestral" activities include the sounds of car horns, car radios and tape decks, and flashing headlights. *Elevator Music* (1967) by Elliott Schwartz places the audience (ten at a time) within an elevator, moving up and down in a building of at least twelve stories while performers remain situated in the vestibules outside the doors on each floor. Morton Subotnick's *Ritual Game Room* installations of the early 1970s, featuring audience interaction with synthesizers in a simulated arcade or pinball-game setting, were most often set up in university student unions. On a more serious level, Charlie Morrow has created ritually symbolic ensemble works, many of them involving the audience, for New York's Central Park.

Sounding Bodies

Music-making objects that occupy (and often dominate) the space are usually referred to as instruments. Although we usually think of these objects in terms of their distinctive timbres, they may also dominate performances simply by their silent presence. To begin with, they are often *visually* commanding—impressive, even beautiful, when viewed as sculpture or furniture. They may complement or contradict the architectural setting in which they are placed. Certain instruments, such as a cathedral organ, are literally part of the architecture; others have been designed for specific spaces—the modern grand piano meant to resonate in a vast public space, and the tiny Baroque clavichord in an intimate, private one.

Beyond their intrinsic visual fascination, instruments have the capability of forcing the humans who operate them into equally fascinating shapes. Observe the gestures and muscular operations of anyone playing the piano, trombone, sitar, clarinet; each instrument creates its own "dance" (if only as a by-product) and its own choreography. The human performer may come to develop a personal relationship with his or her instrument, almost regarding it as an animate being.

new instruments

In other cultures, music-making objects are regarded with reverence, as if they were indeed "beings" blessed with magical powers. Percussion instruments, so crucial to many ceremonial rituals, certainly have this mythic status. (Whatever force can make a hollowed tree limb—or animal skull, or tautly stretched hide—"speak" must be treated with profound respect.) The twentieth century's explosion of interest in percussion has many causes: a desire to avoid decisions regarding pitch while shifting primary focus to *timbre,* a link to non-Western or jazz elements, and the instruments' visual and ritual appeal.

Many composers create their own bells, gongs, drums, chimes, and the like from household or industrial objects and group them into collections or percussion ensembles, along non-Western lines. Cage's early percussion ensembles are noteworthy, as are the groups of mixed percussion—at times referred to as "American Gamelan"—organized in recent decades. One of these, known as Gamelan Son of Lion, became fairly influential in the northeastern United States during the 1970s and stimulated a great many composers (among them Daniel Goode, Peter Griggs, and Philip Corner) to use non-Western sensibilities and traditions in their work.

For some composers, the fusion, or perhaps confrontation, of East and West is an important factor in their work. For example, Lou Harrison has composed a concerto for Western violin, and Vincent McDermott a concerto for grand piano, both with gamelan accompaniments. The Chinese-American composer Tan Dun creates a ritual music in which traditional instruments (such as the koto and shamisen) interact with specially designed ceramic bowls, gongs, globes, chimes, and stringed instruments, all of these scattered antiphonally throughout the performance space.

The construction of original instruments is not restricted to percussion, of course. Harry Partch was a prolific inventor of string as well as percussion instruments, and in San Diego, where he last settled and where his instruments have been permanently housed, his influence is still strong. San Diego is home to the improvisational KIVA Ensemble, which uses a battery of "found objects" as instruments, and an active community of people whose interest in microtonal intonation almost invariably suggests instrument building.

Many newly constructed instruments, like Partch's, are visually stimulating. The Italian composer Mario Bertoncini has created a striking assemblage of wires, tubing, and potentiometers capable of producing delicate, sustained gestures in a variety of timbres for his 1977 *Chanson pour instruments á vent*. Bertoncini considers his performing resource not a new instrument, which should ideally be capable of realizing a variety of musical styles and events, but rather, a sound sculpture, especially built to play only one sort of piece, not unlike Max Neuhaus's installations.

Instrument building as a compositional activity is closely linked to an interest in **process,** to the degree that the musical gestures one envisions and the new instrument one builds are twin aspects of a single creative impulse. In some cases the instrument *is* the piece. Recent developments in electronics have led to increasingly sophisticated installations, such as the one for David Behrman's 1978 *Cloud Music*. Behrman wanted to see whether "light from the sky would trigger some kind of system, and trigger changes as clouds went by." He has devised a photosensing circuitry that responds to changes in the cloud cover; these changes, in turn, control electronics sound generators.

Appropriately, unorthodox instruments and alternative performance spaces are often linked together. Sound installations have been set up in schools, gymnasiums, libraries, parks, airports, and planetariums. Museums are frequently used as sites. One especially memorable show of eight installations, The Magic Theater, was organized in 1968 by the Nelson Gallery of Art in Kansas City; the show included a walk-in environment by Terry Riley within which participants activated tape loops of their own just-completed conversations.

new Views of Traditional Instruments

Many composers who don't wish to build new instruments from scratch have taken traditional instruments and radically altered their playing technique. This affects not only timbre but the performance "choreography" and the visual experience of the audience as well. Some of these alterations are related to the influence of specific performers: for example, the cellist Frances-Marie Uitti is unusually adept at playing her instrument with two bows simultaneously, while the trombonist Stuart Dempster has created a new instrument from a mouthpiece and a length of garden hose; some composers have then used these techniques in their own works.

In other cases, alterations grow out of the instrument's very nature. The grand piano, for example, because of its imposing size and its culturally sanctioned position as an icon of Western art music, virtually *demands* (at least in the minds of certain composers) to be considered freshly.

We have already noted Cage's prepared piano; Cowell's tone clusters (and use of inner strings); Conlon Nancarrow's creative use of player piano technology; Stephen Scott's "Bowed Piano" ensemble music (see p. 314). Ben Johnston's *Knocking Piece*, for instance, requires an ensemble of musicians to play on the insides—the wood case and metal frame—of the grand piano. Cornelius Cardew's *Memories of You* for piano solo treats the instrument as a theatrical prop rather than a sound source. His score consists of multiple

"piano" symbols, arranged on a crosshatched grid:

The small circles, placed inside or near the piano symbols, represent the placement of sound events—any sounds, which may or may not include piano sonorities—within that performance area. The order in which the events are performed is only partially controlled by the composer.

The human voice—like percussion, a primal and inherently ritualistic instrument (perhaps the first)—can also be used in fresh ways. The composer Joan La Barbara has a remarkable singing voice: an unusually extensive range, and a virtuosic command of multiphonics, circular breathing, and extended techniques. She has created a number of works that capitalize on her performing gifts. Her *October Music: Star Showers and Extraterrestrials* (1980) explores spatial sound distribution, as four channels of prerecorded vocal material are played back on speakers placed throughout the hall. Against this overlay, La Barbara reacts to the antiphonal, prerecorded material improvisationally, producing sometimes similar, sometimes contrasting gestures in what might be called a "theater of sounds." A different but equally powerful effect emerges from the ethereal, sustained consonances of Stockhausen's *Stimmung* (1968). Six singers contribute to an interactive texture of great subtlety: primarily one chord made up of harmonics (which are produced by reducing vibrato to a minimum, very low dynamic level, and the use of amplification), whose surface is varied by individual incantations.

Many new approaches to the use of the *speaking* voice in performance rely upon electronic manipulation: for example, the use of amplication makes the gentle, whispered timbres of John Cage's mesostic readings audible. The "text-sound compositions" of the San Francisco composer Charles Amirkhanian use recorded words and tape-studio techniques to create ingenious works of audible concrete poetry. A more sophisticated digital technology has aided Charles Dodge (b. 1942) in the creation of concrete poetry of another sort; he composes witty, moving "songs" by means of computerized speech synthesis.

Traditional electronic hardware may also be regarded as a collective "instrument," and treated as a compositional resource. For example, Stockhausen's *Mikrophonie* series makes special use of the microphone, just as Cage's *Cartridge Music* "liberates" the phonograph pickup. Similarly, Alvin Lucier (b. 1931) turns the phenomenon of room "distortion" to advantage in his magical *I Am Sitting in a Room* (1970). This piece is made by a performer recording a brief spoken passage (beginning with the words of the title and, in essence, explaining the composition), then copying the recording and recopying each copy, using room distortion, until only the rhythms and inflections of the original statement remain.

Finally, an entirely new genre of altered instruments has resulted from the computer development known as musical instrument digital interface, or MIDI (described more fully in Chapter 17). In Greg Fish's *A Little Light Music* (1987), for example, mallet handles alter or break the paths of light beams as they strike percussion instruments, thus triggering a variety of responses from the computer and associated electronics, and providing a strong visual and theatrical element.

RITUAL

People exhibit a certain kind of socially sanctioned ritual behavior while participating in ceremonial "celebrations"—whether a wedding, funeral, halftime at a football game, or High Mass. Most likely, the ceremonial occasion is itself a "multimedia" affair in which architecture, costuming, color, poetry, music, dance, food, and drink intermingle. But in many Western situations musical performance also acquires the status of a self-sufficient, independent ceremony. When people assemble for this activity—listening to music or concert going—they also behave in culturally approved ways.

From the *listener's* standpoint, consider some of the variables involved in attending a concert of Western art music: advance knowledge of the date, time, and possibly the works to be performed; tickets and printed programs; the performance space with its raised platform, permitting a view of the sounding objects; the audience seats all facing the same direction; and the ban on moving about, speaking, applauding, eating, or drinking while the music is in progress. Performers, too, have rituals of their own: the obligation to present the works in a predetermined order at the advertised time and place; the ban of speaking or walking about while playing; specified moments for tuning up and so on. Some of these factors are specific to certain ritual occasions and not others. Note how many would change if our musical performance were to take place at a Pops concert, a jazz club, a parade down Main Street, or an Italian opera house.

Changes in Performance Behavior

Symphonic or chamber music performers are unlikely to speak, walk, or move about onstage during the playing of a work. The rarity of such occasions—and consequently their potential for expressive effect—has led some composers to explore their use. An example is George Crumb's *Echoes of Time and the River* (1968) for orchestra. In this work, groups of musicians march to and from their positions while playing. These processionals, which also include the whispering of chanted vocal material, intentionally highlight the ritual aspect of the performance, transforming the activity onstage into a symbolic enactment of some arcane, mysterious ceremony.

In his 1973 *Poebells*, Edwin London (b. 1929) has set Edgar Allan Poe's monumental poem "The Bells" for amplified narrator and large percussion ensemble. The instruments, themselves commanding from a visual and theatrical standpoint, include gongs, chimes, thunder sheets, celesta, sleigh bells, cow bells, and mallet instruments, to create an overwhelming bell-like sonority. A surprise bell instrument, put to inspired use in the most agitated stanza of Poe's poem, is an ominous, ringing telephone at the speaker's rostrum. London further augments the visual panorama with the figures of a man and woman onstage. The two act in ritual stylized pantomime, sing wordlessly, and scream ("Terror! Horror!"). They can be seen rushing among the ensemble instruments as though through a forest, or moving in stately fashion as part of a wedding ceremony while members of the percussion section call out congratulations and throw rice at them.

Lukas Foss makes more extroverted use of speech and movement in his *Paradigm* (1968) for percussion, guitar, and three additional instruments. Loud, violent declamation, amplified whispering, and isolated fragmented syllables all become part of a single textural language. Spoken words are particularly riveting during *Paradigm's* slow movement. Words chosen at random (but uttered in a set sequence) by individual players create strangely evocative sentences related to the condition of late twentieth-

ILLUS. 15.1.

Edwin London's *Poebells* in performance. Note the presence of two actors among the percussionists— in this section, as "bride" and "groom"—and the telephone (lower center), which plays an important role in the work

Photo: Roland Paolucci. Courtesy University of Akron

century music. Example 15.1 shows the chart of words used by the players to create these sentences. (Each sentence begins with the phrase "Bury your . . ." spoken by the percussionist/conductor.) Since columns are grouped by parts of speech, any succession from left to right (passing from one player to the next) will result in a grammatical sentence—even a poetic "image"—no matter what the aleatoric permutation. Physical gestures are an equally prominent feature of *Paradigm*. The percussionist often "conducts" with one of his instruments, or punctuates his own speech with rhythmic drum beats. At the very end of the work, a furious *tutti* texture, the percussionist "cuts off" each player by rapping sharply on his or her music stand. Only one performer refuses to stop, continuing to play rapid

EXAMPLE 15.1.

Fold this sheet out so it can be referred to while playing pages 8 through 13.

Percussion/Conductor	High Instr.	Middle Instr.	Low Instr.	El. Guitar
[W]	[W]	[W]	[W]	[W]
nostalgic *wehmütigen* *prétentions*	pretention, *Gelüsten,* *nostalgiques*	devious *hinterhältige* *fantaisies*	fantasies *phantasien* *sinueuses*	. . . not for me. . . . *nix für mich.* . . . *pas pour moi.*
therapeutic *thereputischen* *attitudes*	attitudes *Attitüden,* *thérapeutiques*	political *politische* *manoeuvres*	maneuvers *Manöver* *politiques*	, waste. , *Leerlauf.* , *a priori.*
secret *geheimen* *coquetteries*	ornaments, *Flausen* *secrètes*	calculated *ausgeklügelte* *caresses*	caresses *Liebkosungen* *calculées*	with 12 tones. *mit 12 Tönen.* *avec 12 tons.*
polite *vornehmen* *rêveries*	sentiment, *Gefühlen,* *volages*	routine *routinierte* *plaisanteries*	games *Spiele* *routines*	ad nauseam. *ad nauseam.* *jus qu'à là nausée.*
sophomoric *unreifen* *insultes*	abuse, *Schimpfwörtern,* *juveniles*	timid *ängstliche* *recettes*	recipes *Rezepte* *timides*	of yesterday. *von vorgestern.* *d'avant hier.*
idle *faulen* *propositions*	applause, *Lorbeeren,* *superflues*	indiscreet *indiskrete* *façades*	detours *Umwege* *indiscrètes*	. . . but, is it art? . . . *ist das noch Musik?* . . . *mais, est-ce de la musique?*
hidden *vesteckten* *sonates*	sonata, *Sonaten,* *laborieuses*	virtuous *keusche* *erreurs*	mistaken *Verirrungen* *vertueuses*	of fashion. *der Mode.* *à la mode.*
pen heavy with *längst überholten* *belles lettres*	scruples, *Skrupeln,* *scrupuleuses*	gratuitous *pedantische* *actions*	choices *Methoden* *gratuites*	et cetera, *und so weiter.* *et cetera.*

Any expression from one column can be followed by any expression from the next one.

Lukas Foss: *Paradigm,* word list for second movement

passagework even as the other players acknowledge the final applause and bow to the audience.

The American composer Tom Johnson (b. 1939), now living in Paris, has developed a "self-reflexive" approach to performance ritual. In many of his works the performers speak or sing directly to the audience, explaining (sometimes with great irony) what they are doing. The libretto of Johnson's *The Four Note Opera* consists entirely of statements by the singers about the difficulty of their tasks, the social snobbery attached to their individual vocal registers, and the implausibility of various plot clichés. For his *Lecture with Repetition,* the solo performer reads a formal text that begins, "I call this Lecture with Repetition because I normally read each sentence three times." After reading that sentence twice more, he or she goes on to explain that audience members may extend or shorten the number of repetitions by calling out the words "more" or "enough." The remainder of the lecture is a straightforward, often perceptive disquisition on the many possible scenarios that could result, the nature of audience participation, and the aeshtetic qualities of repetition. In performance, each sentence could be stated any number of times, punctuated by individual, often overlapping, shouts from the audience.

In a similar vein, Mauricio Kagel's chamber work *Sonant* (1961) requires each of the players to speak directly to the audience, reading sentence fragments aloud during performance. Example 15.2 consists of an

---

EXAMPLE 15.2.

00" / 11" *mf* **rall.** FIRST, WOULD YOU GIVE A SIGN TO THE OTHER PLAYERS TO MAKE SURE THAT THEY'RE WITH YOU ? AND THEN PLAY chords composed of tones sounding close together, in the middle register, separated by relatively large leaps.

11" / 11" *f* ↓ *pp* (I WOULD LIKE TO CONVINCE MYSELF – WHATEVER ONE'S INTERPRETATION OF THE EXISTENCE IN THE WORLD OF PROBABILITY LAWS – THAT THE SAME PROBLEMS PLAY A PART NOT ONLY IN COMPOSITION, BUT ALSO IN LISTENING.)

22" / 32" *mf* *p* *f* Might I be so bold as to ask you to play the chords strictly periodically, but in such a way that the vertical density – continually varied – suggests to the listener an aperiodicity of the intervals of attack. WHY NOT BRING THE TONE-CONTROL INTO IT ? Have a try. THAT'S RIGHT. A BIT MORE TO THE LEFT . . . and then suddenly way over to the right. Meanwhile keep playing the chords more narrowly and irregularly, till you reach a monodic articulation in low register. Play each note "on the fret". HOW ABOUT A FAST SEQUENCE OF HARMONICS ? If that doesn't appeal to you, slide with fingernail or plectrum slowly along the 6th string. You know that the glissando is brightest when approaching the bridge, and you can emphasize this with the tone-switch, turned to maximum treble.

Mauricio Kagel: *Sonant* (guitar part)

excerpt from the electric guitar part. Careful timings, dynamic levels, and rhythmic flow are indicated at the left, running from top to bottom. The capitalized words must be made audible by means of speaking, chant, loud whispering, or shouting.

Speech or movement are only two areas in which performing rituals may be altered. A number of compositions may begin with all the trappings of traditional performance, but then move in surprising and often ambivalent directions. At one point in Stockhausen's *Momente,* for example, the ensemble of musicians breaks into applause, seemingly clapping for the audience. At the opening of Morton Subotnick's *Play! No. 1* (1966) for woodwind quintet and piano, the musicians tune up to the note A, just as we might expect. Only after many seconds do we realize that the A is itself part of the work, being bent to other inflections and imitated, and eventually leading to the use of film, electronic tape, and a free-for-all conclusion of controlled chaos. Subotnick also choreographs the players' movements (arm extended, head turned, leg raised, and so on) to heighten the association of ritual with physical gesture.

Pauline Oliveros is also careful to specify physical gesture (in this instance, the choreography of conductors' motions) in her ensemble piece *To Valerie Solanos and Marilyn Monroe in Recognition of Their Desperation* (Example 15.3) Lighting cues are also specified with great care; on the other hand, **pitch logic** occupies a lower hierarchical position, in that Oliveros uses verbal instructions rather than traditional musical symbols.

Physical gesture is perhaps the most important element of *Metamusic* (1964) for violin, saxophone, piano, and conductor by Toshiro Mayuzumi (b. 1929), as most of it is pantomimed. Elaborate but silent performing gestures are interrupted, at unpredictable moments, by outbursts of sonority; individual parts are unrelated to one another, producing a unique "polyphony" of physical gestures. In Example 15.4, a portion of the piano part, note that only the gestures enclosed in rectangular boxes are sounded; all others are seen but not heard.

In two provocative European works, the aural component has been eliminated altogether. Dieter Schnebel's *Nostalgie* (1962) is scored for a solitary conductor as the only performer, creating a purely visual experience, apart from any musical content inferred by the viewer's imagination. Mauricio Kagel attempts something similar in his *Solo* (1967), a film in which a conductor performs in silence, directing his gestures to lifeless instruments stationed without their players on the stage.

In the examples just noted, the physical evidence offered to our eyes seems to contradict what we hear (or fail to hear). We may have a similar sensation in seeing and hearing one of Morton Subotnick's "ghost electronic" pieces. In such works live onstage musicians are "accompanied" by a tape that emits silent electrical signals rather than sounds. The signals activate devices that may alter the pitch, timbre, or directionality of the

EXAMPLE 15.3.

CONDUCTORS' SIGNALS: Conductors may use any combination of right hand and left hand signals.

Left Hand: Pointing at individual player means solo cue.
- 1 finger   means strings
- 2 fingers   means winds
- 3 fingers   means brass
- 4 fingers   means percussion
- 5 fingers   means all

Right Hand:
Circle made with thumb and first finger means long tones, unmodulated.
Fist means long tones, modulated.
Palm out with arm straight up means fade out slowly.

Downbeat means attack.
Cutoff means release.

LIGHT CUES (all performers):
Red Light–introduce pitch number 1 on cue from conductor. Continue independently unless fadeout cue is given.
White Light Flash–gradually introduce pitches 2, 3, 4, and 5 in any order.
Yellow Light–borrow pitches and modulation techniques from other players.
Also continue your own selected pitches and modulation techniques.
Blue Light–return gradually to your own five pitches.
White Light Flash–return gradually to your own pitch number 1. Fade out extremely slowly when there is no more blue light.

Pauline Oliveros: *To Valerie Solanas and Marilyn Monroe in Recognition of Their Desperation*, portion of instruction page

instrumental passages, creating an ambiguous relationship between the players' physical actions and the music they produce.

Ambiguity also colors our response to Alvin Lucier's 1965 *Music for Solo Performer*, a pioneering use of electronics to extend not just the outer but also the inner activity—the neurophysiology—of the performer. The soloist has his or her scalp wired with electrodes that pick up alpha brain waves; these are processed by filters and amplifiers and then led to speakers placed throughout the hall, which in turn cause adjacently located percussion instruments to resonate. Since alpha waves are present only

EXAMPLE 15.4.

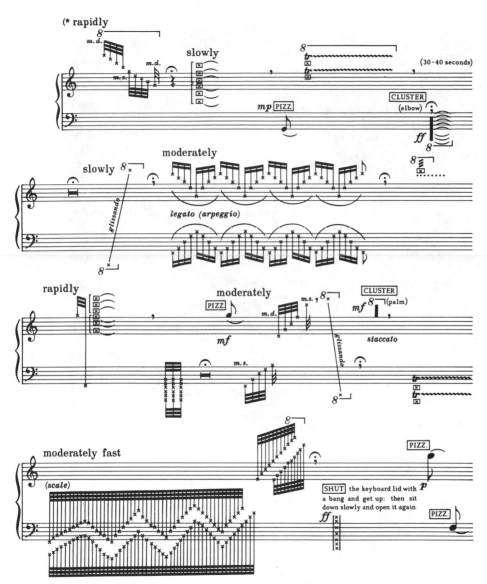

(* Everything must be performed as written but only with animated gestures and without any sound. Exceptions are the tone clusters, the pizzicati, and the banging of the keyboard lid which have to be heard. Their indications in the music are enclosed in boxes.

Toshiro Mayuzumi: *Metamusic* (piano part)

ILLUS. 15.2. Alvin Lucier, in a realization of his *Music for Solo Performer.* Photo: Phil Makanna

during nonvisual activity in the brain, the performer can control events by opening and closing the eyes: paradoxically, the act of opening them, a "positive" physical gesture, causes all sounds to cease. *Music for Solo Performer* is highly theatrical on another level as well, in that the entire ritual of setting up the performance—including scalp preparation, electrode installation, and the like—is carried out silently and deliberately before the audience.

Finally, rituals of one genre may crop up in another. A well-known historical precedent is Schoenberg's *Pierrot Lunaire*, originally designed for cabaret, not concert, performance. Robert Erickson's *General Speech* (1969) for solo trombone is a phoneme-by-phoneme "transcription" of General Douglas MacArthur's farewell address to the cadets at West Point; like Tom Johnson's *Lecture with Repetition*, it is presented at a lectern. The "speaker" (trombonist) wears the brimmed cap, sunglasses, white gloves, and broad epaulets of a military hero; the surrealist effect is heightened by the use of black light. Another work for solo trombone, Berio's *Sequenza V* (1966), is based on the composer's childhood memory of a famous European clown, known for aiming a mock rifle at imaginary birds; during the piece's opening minutes, the soloist aims his trombone high at the balcony or ceiling. The performance space of Elliott Schwartz's 1972 *Telly* for winds, brass, and percussion is intended to resemble a darkened movie theater. Aided by uniformed "ushers," audience members are led to their seats in the dark. The only flickering light is that of three television sets—at first seen only by the players, and later by the audience as well.

A different sort of genre "translation" is achieved in Charles Dodge's *Any Resemblance Is Purely Coincidental* for piano and tape. The tape part for this piece has been digitally synthesized from a 1907 recording of Enrico Caruso singing the aria "Vesti la giubba" from *I pagliacci,* with the hisses and scratches—as well as the orchestra—electronically removed. With the remaining sonic material (i.e., Caruso's voice, magically cleaned up and available for manipulation) Dodge extends the original Leoncavallo in surprising ways, creating dense "choral" passages and new melodic shapes. For example, a series of rising and falling chromatic runs (for both tape and piano) is drawn from one of the most poignant moments of the aria: the clown's tragic, hollow laughter.

Theatrically, the piece operates on many levels. To hear a legendary aria (and voice) transmuted digitally is fascinating. In addition, there is an inherent, ironic ambiguity in witnessing the piano soloist—whose part varies from a parody of the original opera to angular, post–Webernian flurries—being placed in the role of "accompanist" for an invisible singer who never appears onstage (and who died many decades ago). Significantly, *Any Resemblance Is Purely Coincidental* begins with a fragment of the original 1907 recording, complete with orchestra, scratches, and hiss, and eventually dies away with the original recording as well. The effect is ineffably sad, as though the spirit that had been momentarily freed at a séance—or the genie let out of the magic lamp—is returning home, perhaps reluctantly.

Changes in Listener Behavior

Just as performers observe certain rituals, listeners have their own rituals or expectations, which composers may enjoy manipulating for creative purposes. For some, space can be a critical factor—whether the listeners occupy a single focused location, facing the same direction, or are scattered about, and whether they stand or sit, speak or remain silent or become creative participants in the activity. Some composers may confront—or confound or contradict—the traditional concert format, while others may prefer to avoid that format entirely by creating works for parks, plazas, concourses, and other public spaces. Such pieces may discourage "attentive" listening, or fixed seating/standing positions, since they assume the existence of multiple (even competing) stimuli in the vicinity. Works designed for public spaces may be as dissimilar as the highly focused, almost single-minded, installations of Max Neuhaus are from elaborate multimedia works like the Cage-Hiller *HPSCHD*.

What we might term "conscious" and "subconscious" modes of audience interaction also distinguish such works. Overtly theatrical extravaganzas, from *HPSCHD* to the *Freeway Concerto*, are offered and presented as "performances," at a scheduled time, to an audience well aware of their existence. Other installations operate as a "continuous show," designed to reach a transient audience of people going about their business who have *not* entered the space for artistic reasons. Such works succeed by catching their listeners unawares, or contributing to a larger ambience. One of the most imaginative installations of this sort exists at a particularly well-known (and well-traveled) public space: the underground passage between the two United Airline concourses at Chicago's O'Hare Airport. The composer William Kraft and the designer Michael Hayden have combined bell-like electronic sonorities and a brightly colored overhead display of jagged, shooting neon lights to create a magnificent multimedia environment that is being "performed" around the clock. People—chatting, laughing, walking, or standing on moving walkways going in opposite directions—are an essential component of the work; they make the experience complete.

Many recent works involve audience members as participants in various ways. The audience might participate in only one carefully specified aspect of performance: the composer and performance artist Alison Knowles uses beans as elements of counting rituals in her piece *Gem Duck*; at the work's end, she may cook the beans and ask the audience to eat them. At the conclusion of Leonard Bernstein's 1971 *Mass*, performers leave the stage and spread out into the hall, linking arms with audience members in an expression of brotherhood and whispering, "Pass it on." Or audience members may influence a composition's form. In Henri Pousser's opera *Votre Faust* (1967), the audience is invited to determine by vote which of several directions the plot will take. (Similarly, a 1964 work by Xenakis called *Strategie* sets two orchestras and two conductors in competition, working from a set of ground rules; the results are shown on a large electronic scoreboard clearly visible to the audience.) Or listener participation can be more all-pervasive. David Bedford's *With 100 Kazoos* is scored for orchestras and kazoos played by members of the audience. For the 1966 Brandeis University premiere of his *Rozart Mix,* John Cage created a virtual avalanche of tape loops and invited anyone present to place these on playback decks situated around the large performance/listening area; the resulting experience was notable not only for its random collage of multidirectional sounds but also for its participatory, open-ended visual and social "theater."

Audience involvement is nowhere more intense than in Robert Ashley's *Public Opinion Descends upon the Demonstrators* (1961), a work ostensibly for soloist operating a battery of equipment for the production of electronic sound. The soloist, surrounded onstage by an array of electronic gear, produces sounds that correspond directly to specific actions and reactions from individuals in the audience—coughing, shifting position, whispering, glancing at a wristwatch, and the like. Because the audience members initially have no knowledge of their role in the musical outcome, the piece typically begins rather quietly: audiences tend to be respectfully silent during the opening moments of a performance. More and more participants eventually catch on, at first experimenting with various types of behavior in an effort to decode the performer's responses, then deliberately playing the situation—some with wild gesticulations, as they compete for the soloist's attention. Meanwhile, the soloist (in trying to keep up) reaches a feverish level of activity onstage. The overall form—from virtual silence to utter pandemonium—is nearly always the same from one performance to the next, perhaps because the same social **process** is always being enacted. Armchair psychologists might enjoy studying the fascinating exchange of power roles during the course of the work, as the answer to the question of *who performs on whom* varies from moment to moment.

A similar question, always implicit in discussing graphic scores, or improvisational performance, is, *Who has composed this music?* When audience members participate directly in performance, a degree of improvisation (i.e., real-time composition) is inevitably involved. Audience participants serve as both composers and performers. In a larger context, however, the question becomes irrelevant. Many ethnic and folk traditions include forms of collective music making, often created for ceremonial occasions and unusual performance spaces. In such situations participants from every walk of life engage in community "performances" in the streets, parks, and village squares; music, dance, and art are often inseparable, and the roles of composer, performer, and listener are merged into one.

New Rituals and All-inclusive Rituals

Although traditional rituals usually provide sufficient material for extension and confrontation, composers may occasionally wish to devise their own, often massively large-scale, rituals in which music plays a significant role. These may be the work of one individual or a collaboration; the latter category would include the first Happenings at Black Mountain College in 1952 (with input from John Cage, the choreographer Merce Cunningham, the artist Robert Rauschenberg, and others) or the later Cage–Hiller *HPSCHD*.

A leader among individual figures is La Monte Young, who in his early career—as a student of North Indian music, inspired by Cage's ideas—began presenting performances at Yoko Ono's loft in 1960. Shortly afterward he banded together with a group of artists, musicians, and poets including Ono, Alison Knowles, Dick Higgins, Nam June Paik, and George Brecht to sponsor multimedia performances (many involving audience participation), exhibits, and publications. This loose collective became known as the Fluxus movement. Although its members could hardly be called a "school"—each prizing his or her independence—they shared a belief in indeterminacy, the necessity of blurring artistic categories, and awareness of one's environment.

Since the 1970s La Monte Young's works, many in collaboration with his wife, Marian Zazeela, have called for lengthy improvisations over sustained drones (both electronic and acoustic), in a highly ritualistic context. For an extended work such as *The Tortoise: His Dreams and Journeys*, the visual and physical setting are integral to the experience. Performances at Young's Theater of Eternal Music, with their slowly evolving transformations of sound and light, might last for many hours or even days.

Young has attempted to create special environments (which he calls Dream Houses) for the presentation of his ritualistic work. Other composers, however, are more excited by the prospect of enhancing or subverting the already existent rituals of a known environment. In this vein, the 1977 *Bonn Feier* by Pauline Oliveros, lasting a full week, was designed to make use of the entire city of Bonn, Germany. Over a seven-day period, subtle alterations occurred within the everyday life of the town center: musicians performing in the city square but not making any sounds, pickets marching about with blank signs, a man undressing and applying makeup to his face in very slow motion, and eventually a bonfire in the large market square on the evening of the final day.

Such '"all-inclusive" pieces stress the interaction of sound, sight, physical space, and activity, at times tightly focused and controlled, but more often diffuse and chaotic in its multiplicity of conflicting images. We might be reminded of Ives's use of independent, even contradictory layers of material to evoke the jumble and collisions of real-life experience. A comment of John Cage also comes to mind; Cage, when asked why he composed music, replied: "Well, the first thing you have to do is not ask the question 'why.' Look at your environment, which you are enjoying, and see if it asks why. You'll see that it doesn't." The function of art, in this sense, is to remind us that the sounds of reality, their clash and their harmony, are inherently exciting. (Pauline Oliveros has wondered why tourists send *visual* documents, in the form of picture postcards, to friends back home, when they could be recording the *sounds* of the location on tape.)

Similar all-inclusive involvement may occur whenever a musical composition, perhaps even one intended for an enclosed auditorium, is performed in a "real world" space: a stadium, outdoor public plaza, or shopping mall. In Chapter 8 we noted one such presentation, the 1972 realization of Stockhausen's *Hymnen* as an outdoor "happening" on the Yale University campus. Consider also a summer performance of Tchaikovsky's *1812* Overture in a public park, or chamber music played aboard a cruise ship. In such situations, the self-enclosed ritual of the work may underscore, contradict, invade, repel, or interact with the larger real-world ritual action outside.

Although the environmental scope of the Yale production of *Hymnen* is optional rather than essential to a performance of the work, other compositions by Stockhausen require huge spaces. Because of its size and complexity, his 1984 opera *Samstag* ("Saturday") had to be premiered in the sport stadium in Milan. Works on this scale can resemble a circus, and appropriately, the Canadian R. Murray Schafer (b. 1933) has composed a work entitled *Patria III: The Greatest Little Show on Earth* (1987). He calls it "a hybrid between a real carnival and an artistic one"; in addition to musicians and visual artists, the show includes magicians, fire eaters, tightrope walkers, freak shows, and other trappings of a country fair.

PLAY: MUSIC AS "GAME"

We have been discussing "alternative spaces" as though they were uniformly vast, public plazas. A different sort of space for the performance of new music, relatively intimate and private, is the classroom. Since the mid-1960s English schoolchildren have been introduced to new music in their classrooms by means of brief pieces created by leading British composers. Experience with traditional notation is not necessarily required of the youthful performers. One such venture is *Sound Patterns I* by Bernard Rands (b. 1934). Example 15.5 shows the opening of the work. The numbered arrows indicate equally spaced cues from a conductor, directed to the four groups A, B, C, and D. Hand claps are indicated by ⊗, finger snapping by ⬭, tongue and cheek pops by ⦁.

More challenging is David Bedford's *Fun for All the Family* (Example 15.6), which calls for diverse instrumental timbres and requires some prior performing experience. All players begin on the square marked "start"; each player makes four short sounds, choosing any pitches, either *pp* or *mf*, during the duration of the square (each square lasts twenty seconds). The performers split off into two groups, then four, and finally eight distinct parts, eventually joining again at the very end.

Bedford's score and title are both reminiscent of board games, and

EXAMPLE 15.5.

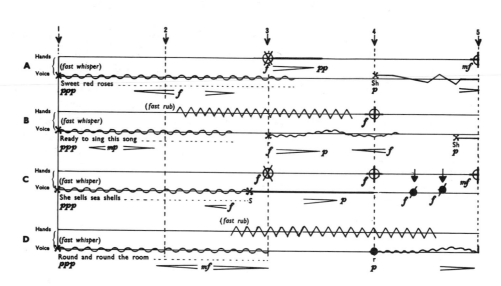

Bernard Rands: *Sound Patterns I*

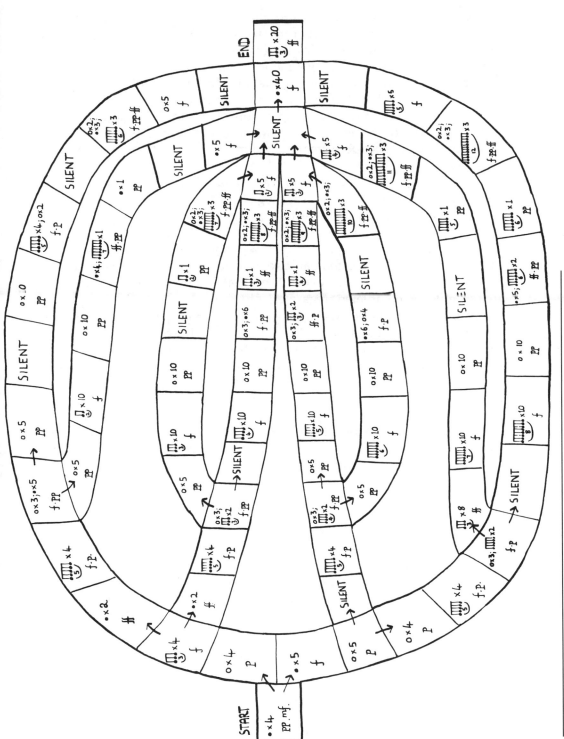

EXAMPLE 15.6. David Bedford: *Fun for All the Family.* © Copyright 1970 by Oxford University Press. Reproduced by permission of the publisher

perhaps such music should be approached in that spirit. The game-playing aspects of new music grow out of the nature of performance itself: human beings with certain interests or skills, goals to achieve, and the pressures of time and coordination. Though these considerations have always been present in the realization and interpretation of a musical "object," they can now *become* the object. There is a certain antiromanticism in this view. Music is conceived not as the expression of grand feelings, but as the concrete activity of people making sounds, testing their responses, reflexes, skill, and intelligence: performance as a game, even in some instances as **process.**

Making a game of music in no way trivializes it. For mathematicians, statisticians, economists, and sociologists, games are serious business. Games may be especially interesting to creative artists in music, theater, and dance, since they all share the problem of distributing and combining fixed activities in time. For example, we might learn about varieties of "form" from comparing football and basketball (where the clock determines the number of activities) with baseball (in which all prescribed activities must be completed, regardless of time).

In *Any Five* by Barney Childs, the work's mobile form derives from the players' responses and actions. As Example 15.7 shows, various cues from individual performers, such as stating the current month aloud, trigger ensemble gestures (which have been rehearsed in advance). Specific timings are most important—an important prop is a large clock with a sweep second hand, visible to the players—but the duration of the work is not predetermined. Any group "event" initiated by player cue may be performed only once. Two of these events are especially effective in performance: the spoken word *STOP*, producing a solo cadenza on the part of the person who utters the word; and dropping a tennis ball, which results in an elaborate *tutti* passage.

As most of the examples above indicate, game pieces frequently explore unusual features of **performance ritual** to arrive at ensemble **textures** of varying degrees of complexity. A fairly specific musical texture may arise naturally from the premises of the "game," as in Charles Hamm's *Rounds* (1964). The score, a lengthy strip with ends joined together to form a huge loop, is placed on a turntable or revolving stage so that a continuous band of notated music moves past stationary players, who read the music when it comes around to them; conversely, a parade of musicians might move around the circle. In either event, a canonically imitative texture results. Or game pieces might evince, as in Christian Wolff's music, a concern for coordinating relationships among instruments: answering, initiating, or anticipating a colleague's activity may become the subject of an improvisatory game of reflexes and responses.

A critic could argue that game pieces, while fun for the players, are lost on an audience. But this is not true of pieces that involve the audience

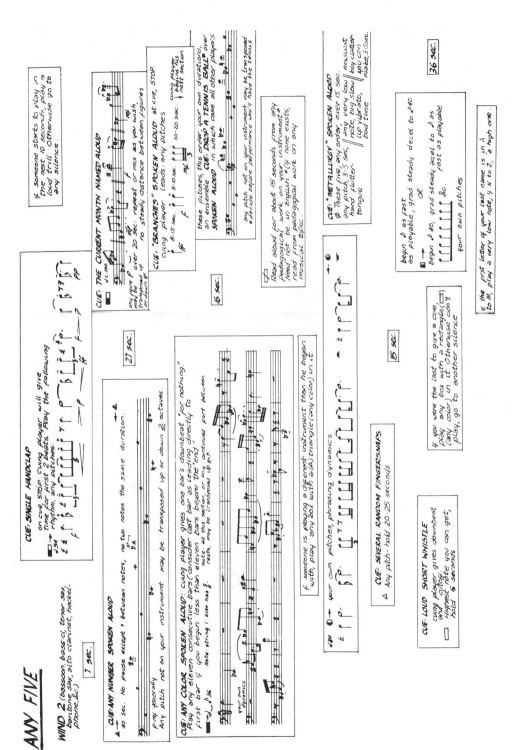

EXAMPLE 15.7. Barney Childs: *Any Five* (Woodwind II part). © Copyright 1967 by Smith Publications, 2617 Gwynndale Ave., Baltimore, MD 21207. Used by permission of Smith Publications.

directly (as does Pousseur's *Votre Faust*) or whose surface gestures offer an immediate musical, theatrical, and visual appeal. With other pieces, leaving the audience out is not necessarily a defect. Many game pieces do not assume the presence of listeners at all: they are intended for performance in a classroom or living room, solely for the enjoyment of the people making the music, and they assume that everyone present will participate. Such pieces, then, share in the tradition of the Renaissance madrigal, the Indonesian village gamelan, or the string quartet of Haydn's time—as performers' music, first and foremost.

ILLUS. 15.3.

The Colorado College Bowed Piano Ensemble, performing a work by Stephen Scott, upper left

Courtesy Stephen Scott

Process and Minimalism

16

In this chapter we focus on compositional **process,** which, as we know, has played a significant role in the development of twentieth-century music, especially in the last half of the century. Although process has been referred to earlier, the subject is discussed here in greater detail, not least because we are considering it from an entirely new aspect.

PROCESSES, INAUDIBLE AND AUDIBLE

We have noted that many composers, perhaps influenced by Stravinsky and Schoenberg, tend to view artistic creation as an act of problem solving —the "working out" of a precompositional scheme. Certain schemes can generate large sections or entire dimensions (such as pitch or rhythm) of music; they obviously are very powerful compositional tools, and composers may regard the sounding object (the work) and the processes of its construction as one and the same. They may hope, or even insist, that listeners identify with process to the same degree as they do.

We have also noted that the concept of process is broader than any single musical style. Processes may be natural (acoustical or biological, for example) or artificially calculated; they can generate random, unexpected sounds or tightly integrated, carefully controlled relationships. In fact, we have observed "processes" in twelve-tone pieces, examples of integral serialism, indeterminate and aleatoric music, and multimedia works.

In recent decades we have also witnessed the creation of music that reflects "statistical" and "biological" processes. The compositional use of statistics is noted in Chapter 10 with regard to the music of Xenakis, whose textures are built on mathematical premises of probability and project a quality of ever-shifting density, analogous to such natural phenomena as sand storms or swarms of insects. Along similar lines, electronic technology enables Pauline Oliveros and Alvin Lucier (among others) to translate bodily rhythms and fluctuations into sounding patterns.

The processes noted above have one feature in common: all are distinguished by virtue of being inaudible. Although the processes may be important during the act of composing, the listening ear cannot follow them.

Since the mid-1960s, however, the musical world has shown great interest in an alternative approach to process. Many composers are now interested in working with processes that are audible. These processes involve extended repetitions of deliberately limited material, within which a series of minute changes slowly and gradually evolve; as a result, the listener can hear the process unfolding. A great many terms have been coined to describe this phenomenon (perhaps a measure of its impact). One of its chief practitioners, Steve Reich, refers to it as "pulse music." Others apply such labels as "phase music," "trance music," "process music," and "pattern music." Most people, however, use the term *minimalism*.

For our purposes, we define minimalism as music for which materials, or their working out, are deliberately limited. At the same time, we should recognize that the term, which originated in the visual arts, is fairly ambiguous. It can describe a number of specific approaches that are *not* necessarily "process"-related. We will consider a number of the latter before returning to the main subject of this chapter—minimalist repetitive (and gradual) process.

DIFFERENT APPROACHES TO MINIMALISM

Silence

Silence perhaps the most explicitly minimalist musical gesture of all. John Cage's *4'33"* is, of course, the prototype for music that aims to focus listener attention on unintended sounds. The esthetic aims of this activity may vary from absorption in the everyday (recognizing beauty in the "commonplace"), to self-knowledge, to a sense of religious oneness. But it does open our listening sensibility to a vast range of sounds all around us. In fact, David Cope has coined the term *silounds* for those very quiet sounds that are revealed only when we are trying to be silent.

Conceptual Music and Theatrical Sound Events

Conceptual works may infer, rather than specify, sounds; their realization is intentionally ambiguous, and may often be closer to internal (imagined) or silent theater than to actual sound production. La Monte Young's works created within the Fluxus movement are representative examples. In Young's *Composition 1960 #4*, the performer turns off the lights for the duration of the composition (after having announced this fact and the predetermined duration to the audience). For *Composition 1960 #5*, a butterfly is turned loose in the performance space; when it flies away the piece is assumed to be ended. Verbal scenarios such as these can be construed as instructions for action or for contemplation.

Minimalist tendencies are also evident in brief, highly theatrical, sound events that aim for specific sonic or visual effects. At an April 1979 Fluxus concert in New York, as reviewed by Tom Johnson, two such works were performed. For *Constellation No. 11* by Dick Higgins, everyone in the audience was instructed to think of a word and a number from one to ten. Then, beginning with a downbeat and continuing for ten beats, they all performed their chosen words on their chosen counts. The program also included Nam June Paik's *One for Violin*, in which a performer—in exaggerated slow motion—raises a violin above his or her head and smashes it on a wooden block.

Drones and Continuities

The reverse side of Cagean silence is a continual sound—a drone or other sustained fabric—of lengthy duration, either unchanged or undergoing subtle alterations. Ligeti's *Atmosphères*—like two of his other works of the 1960s, *Continuum* for harpsichord and *Volumina* for organ—focus on cluster sonorities in this way. In Stockhausen's choral work *Stimmung,* a single chord is sustained for seventy-five minutes; James Fulkerson asks that a C-major chord be maintained for many hours in his *Triad;* Harold Budd's *Lovely Thing* consists of a single chord repeated again and again, each time more quietly than before. At their extremes of performability, such works may well evolve into conceptual pieces.

Drones and sustained sonorities are at the heart of La Monte Young's monumental, ongoing work-in-progress, *The Tortoise: His Dreams and Journeys.* This infinitely extended composition consists of instrumental and vocal elaborations, stressing pure intonation and upper partials, above given fundamental-pitch drones, in a sustained context of great duration. As with Cagean silence, the longer a single sustained event lasts, the more likely that the ear will perceive (or imagine it is perceiving) great diversity or complexity. If the duration is extremely long—a matter of hours rather than minutes—the single event can become enveloping and all-encompassing. Jonathan Kramer refers to such experience as *vertical music,* inducing a sense of timelessness, an "eternal now."

Limited Materials

Some composers may employ an unusually limited body of material to create an entire work, but with the intention of generating a great variety of textures, gestures, rhythms, and tempi from a circumscribed number of sources—in other words, the use of minimum means to achieve maximum results. For the 1971 text-sound tape composition *Just* by Charles Amirkhanian (b. 1945), four brief words in the composer's voice—"rainbow," "chug," "bomb," and "bandit"—constitute the total material. These words are multitracked and superimposed so that the single recorded voice appears on all channels. The net effect may be minimalist, but it also projects a sweeping variety of relationships. Amirkhanian has created, in effect, a narrative of many different rhythms, tempi, and textures.

Tom Johnson's *Four Note Opera* is built on only four pitches, which are manipulated so inventively that the listener hears different key centers, a variety of ostinato patterns, sudden shifts of tempo, and the broadest possible range of emotional states—the full expressive gamut of a mock grand opera. Similarly, Jonathan Kramer (b. 1942), in a number of pieces spanning the years 1972–84, limits the material for each composition to only six pitches. In Kramer's words, "the reason for this restriction is to provide a slow-moving harmonic background to the rapid motion of surface notes and rhythms, and to lend a family resemblance to the very different materials of the piece." In Kramer's 1980 *Music for Piano No. 5,* the listener can perceive a shifting sense of key center, textural variety, extremes of register, tempo, and rhythmic contrast, and different levels of consonance and dissonance. The two excerpts in Example 16.1 illustrate the range of "maximal" contrast.

Repetition and Gradual Change

Finally, we return to the phenomenon that began this discussion, the one most frequently associated with the term *minimalism*—a **process of repetition and gradual change**. Philip Glass calls this "music with repetitive structures," and listeners are undoubtedly struck first by its static surface: ostinati carried to great lengths, or perhaps another approach to the concept of "drone." The material undergoing repetition is usually simple to begin with (a melodic contour, a brief chord series), often limited in pitch content. It may be repeated with no changes at all, or with gradual and process-driven changes that may reveal themselves only after many minutes. Paradoxically, this technique, while simple on the surface, can lead to great complexity—and often great length—in performance.

EXAMPLE 16.1.

Jonathan Kramer: *Music for Piano No. 5*

MINIMALISM AND AUDIBLE PROCESS

Highly repetitive passages, extended periods of harmonic stasis, and lengthy ostinati can be found throughout the history of Western art music: the Notre Dame organum of Leonin and Perotin, lengthy stretches of Beethoven's *Pastoral* Symphony, the finale of Schubert's Symphony No. 9 in C Major, the opening of Wagner's *Das Rheingold* (an E♭-major chord held for more than three minutes). Twentieth-century examples include Ravel's *Bolero,* the third movement of Schoenberg's *Five Pieces for Orchestra* (a single chord with changing timbres), and Elliott Carter's *Eight Etudes and a Fantasy* for wind quartet, in which one étude is built on a single major triad and another on only one pitch. Especially notable is the remarkable achievement of the English composer Kaikhosru Shapurji Sorabji (1892–1988) integrating Western and Indian influences in works whose dense fabrics and complex chord structures undergo little or no change over lengthy time spans.

But these examples are quite different from the minimalism of Philip Glass and Steve Reich. To begin with, minimalist repetitions may last for thirty minutes, an hour, or even longer. Secondly, minimalist ostinati and their gradual changes are systematic—that is, linked to a *process.* Finally, even the lengthiest ostinati in mainstream Western literature function within a larger context of progression and direction. The patterns of Terry Riley, Reich, or Glass, by contrast, become virtually immobile aesthetic objects in their own right. A more suitable Western precedent for minimalism is Erik Satie's *Vexations,* a work for piano in which a brief phrase is subjected to a **process** of 840 literal repetitions, for a duration of some eighteen hours.

The most appropriate precedents, though, are found in the performance traditions of *non*-Western music: the Indonesian gamelan, African drumming, the classical music of India. In these and other varieties of world music, time is often "vertical" rather than directional. Certain musical vocabularies—such as those of pitch or rhythm, which offer great variety in the post-Renaissance Western tradition—may be reduced in order to focus on *other* areas: spacious durations, repetition, and the idea of very gradual change.

This particular ordering of priorities is especially interesting, given the great emphasis placed on direction and goal orientation in Western tonality—and beyond that, the aesthetic positions of Schoenberg and Webern, which place high value on brevity and arhythmic gesture and frown on repetition (except that of inaudible processes). In many respects the minimalist approach can be regarded as an overwhelmingly negative reaction to some of the most cherished ideals of the mainstream, and to those of the postwar avant-garde in particular.

In studying minimalism, then, it is important to consider not only the idea of *process*, but also that of *audibility*. In this regard, the following statements from Steve Reich's 1968 essay "Music as a Gradual Process" are revealing.

> I do not mean the process of composition, but rather pieces of music that are, literally, processes. . . . I am interested in perceptible processes. I want to be able to hear the process happening throughout the sounding music. . . . Performing and listening to a gradual music process resembles: pulling back a swing, releasing it, and observing it gradually come to rest . . . turning over an hourglass and watching the sand slowly run through to the bottom . . . placing your feet by the ocean's edge and watching, feeling and listening to the waves gradually burying them.

These words disclose a great sensitivity to the cyclic rhythms of the natural, physical world (and to human experience) and certainly reveal one of the motivating forces behind Reich's position on minimalism.

Other motivating forces for minimalism have come from the tape studio (loops and multiple tracks); from music outside the standard repertoire (non-Western musics, the Notre Dame school, rock); from the worlds of dance and theater (the experimental choreography of Merce Cunningham, Lucinda Childs, and Laura Dean; the plays of Samuel Beckett such as *Waiting for Godot* and *Endgame*); from the visual arts (Sol LeWitt's paintings of solid colors, Andy Warhol's multiple images of Marilyn Monroe or tomato soup cans, or his films of people sleeping); and from Eastern religion and philosophy.

Finally, minimalism can be regarded (as we regarded the collage and quotation movement, or multimedia) in the context of major aesthetic issues that emerged during the 1950s and '60s: the relative importance of **pitch logic,** "control" versus "freedom," form, complexity of **texture,** and **performance ritual.** In confronting these issues, certain composers were led to reject the sound world held dear by the avant-garde of the immediate postwar era (Webernian kaleidoscopic timbral fragments, textures of extreme discontinuity etched against silence, and nontonal sonority) in favor of other cultural models.

MINIMALIST TECHNIQUES

A study of minimalist scores reveals the following basic techniques for effecting gradual melodic, rhythmic, and textural change within a steady, repetitive ostinato fabric.

ILLUS. 16.1.

Detail of Sol LeWitt, *Lines and Color Straight, Not Straight and Broken Lines Using All Combinations of Black, White, Yellow, Red and Blue,* 1977 (silkscreen). Although repetitive process is important here, subtle changes in pattern and color, creating great textural variety, are also critical

Photo: Multiples, Inc. Courtesy Bowdoin College Museum of Art

Additive Melody

As practiced by Philip Glass, this technique extends or reduces a repetitive melodic pattern by increments of the smallest rhythmic value. In Example 16.2, from Glass's *Music in Similar Motion* (1969), each measure is repeated many times at a very rapid tempo. Incremental changes affect not only the melodic contour but the rhythms and durations as well.

EXAMPLE 16.2.

Philip Glass: *Music in Similar Motion*

© 1973 Dunvagen Music Publishers, Inc. Used by permission

Rotation

By beginning successive statements of a melodic or rhythmic pattern at different points within the pattern, the order of elements can be rotated. (As Tom Johnson has described it: "Then there are. Rotations then there. Are rotations then. There are rotations . . .") Example 16.3 shows the first four masures of Steve Reich's *Clapping Music* (1971), a work that employs *phase shifting*. From the unison opening, player 2 rotates the rhythmic pattern by shifting one eighth note "to the right" with each new measure while player 1 continues the unaltered pattern. Each shift creates a canon at a new time interval and generates a new composite rhythmic pattern.

EXAMPLE 16.3.

Steve Reich: *Clapping Music*

© Copyright 1980 Universal Edition (London) Ltd., London. All Rights Reserved. Used by permission of European American Music Distributors Corporation, sole U.S. and Canadian agent for Universal Edition London

Texture Construction

An ostinato fabric of multiple voices may gradually grow more (or less) complex as individual members enter (or leave) the texture during repetitions. In Example 16.4, from Elliott Schwartz's *Dream Music with Variations* (1985), the ostinato texture grows more complex until, at its most filled-in state, it projects a complete twelve-tone row. This may also occur in a single-line context as the outcome of a systematic "substitution"; beats are substituted for rests, or vice versa, within a constantly repeating ostinato cycle. Steve Reich refers to this as *construction*. In Example 16.4 the construction begins and ends at the points marked *.

EXAMPLE 16.4.

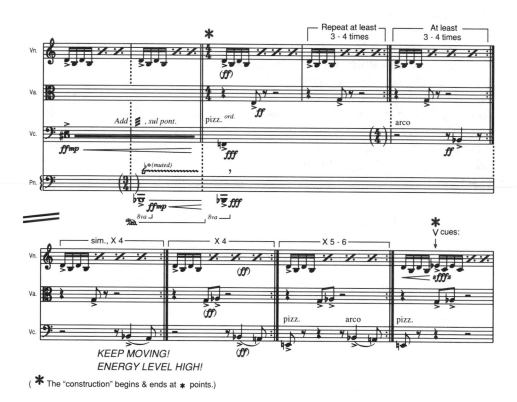

(✱ The "construction" begins & ends at ✱ points.)

Elliott Schwartz: *Dream Music with Variations*

© 1984 by Theodore Presser Company. Used by permission

Isorhythmic Overlap

One can create an isorhythmic overlap of patterns in which ostinati of varying lengths are stated simultaneously. In a prominent texture of Glass's opera *Einstein on the Beach* (1976), a rhythm of four beats ♩ ♪ ♪ ♪ ♪ ♪ ♩ is heard three times, while in another part a pattern of three beats ♩ ♩ ♩ is sounded four times. It takes twelve beats, then, for the composite texture to come full cycle, that is, for the two beginning points to coincide again.

MINIMALIST COMPOSERS: THE EARLIEST GENERATION

The first composers to be concerned with repetitive process share a number of common traits. All were born between 1935 and 1937. In their student days and early careers, all were involved with electronic tape studios and jazz, rock, or improvisation. They also share similiar influences: Cage (especially his focus on the individual sound for its own sake, and non-intentional processes), Morton Feldman's spacious approach to sonority and duration, La Monte Young's interest in drones, and non-Western cultural models.

Terry Riley

Terry Riley came to repetitive structures from a background in jazz performance (on saxophone and keyboards) and early immersion in the West Coast experimental-music scene. In the late 1950s Riley met La Monte Young, when both were students at the University of California at Berkeley. He then joined Young's Theater of Eternal Music ensemble and worked with Pauline Oliveros during the earliest years of the San Francisco Tape Music Center. From all of these sources, Riley developed a strong interest in loop effects and drones. His jazz improvisations (a number of which have been written down in shorthand form) reveal his fascination with the effects of overlapping repeated ostinati.

This technique is expanded further in Riley's monumental ensemble work of 1964 *In C*, for any number of players on any melody instruments. There is no "score," only parts distributed among the players. Moreover, the parts are all alike; it is on this premise that the work's entire logic is based. A repetitive note C ♪♪ ♪♪ heard in the piano's very highest register provides a rhythmic reference—and a pedal point—for the duration of the piece. Against this ostinato, each player performs a succession of fifty-three melodic phrase fragments in order, starting with number 1, and in strict tempo and precise rhythm. (The first eleven fragments are shown in Example 16.5.)

The rigorous performance format is tempered, however, by an infinitely flexible approach to repetition. Each player may perform a given fragment any number of times before moving on to the next, may rest at any time, and does not need to synchronize entrances of new fragments with performing colleagues. In most performances, each phrase fragment is repeated for about one minute or so. (To perform eleven fragments of *In C* shown in Example 16.5 would most likely take between ten and fourteen minutes—that is, the time it takes for all performers to have reached phrase number 11.) The piece seldom runs for fewer than forty-five minutes, throughout which one continues to hear the repeated high C of the piano ostinato. The use of an obsessive rhythmic pulse, established in Riley's work, soon became a trademark of the minimalist movement.

Because each player moves through the score at a separate pace, the entire ensemble tends to spread out gradually, playing several fragments simultaneously in a dense canonic **texture.** Paradoxically, though, *In C* may present a different textural message each time we hear it, since its extended canon produces a slowly moving chord series—basically triadic, although not goal-directed. Note, too, that if the performing ensemble contains mixed timbres, the foreground–background relationship will change as solo colors emerge from the overall fabric.

Riley's approach to **pitch logic** is almost exclusively diatonic, producing (as canonic resultant) a succession of major and minor triads. But one

---

EXAMPLE 16.5.

Terry Riley: *In C*

cannot really call it "tonal," since long-term goals are so distant that they appear nonexistent. (The long-term tonal goals are there, however; Riley's sparing use of F$^{\#}$ and B$^{\flat}$, the only accidentals in the piece, set up slow-moving modulations.) A similar ambiguity exists with regard to **time.** Is *In C* a "slow" piece or a "fast" one? One could legitimately hear it as both: its extremely rapid surface gestures are couched in a context of very slow pitch change and almost imperceptible harmonic motion.

Minimalist works frequently suggest a variety of approaches to **performance ritual.** The presentation of *In C*, with its absence of narrative events and its lengthy duration, poses special challenges. The work is often presented as an antiphonal, spatially separated concert-in-the-round, or as an "environment" within which listeners are invited to come and go, talk, move about, even eat, drink, dance, or speak with the performers. In any event, its flexibility invites theatrical performances. Many critics have approached it as an elaborate game piece rather than a fixed art object. Given its semi-improvisatory nature, overlaid against a fixed drone and rigid harmonic scheme, it could even be considered a Western form of raga.

Other works of Terry Riley, such as *A Rainbow in Curved Air* and *Poppy Nogood and the Phantom Band*, are more overtly jazz-oriented. They often feature lengthy, electronically altered improvisations by the composer on saxophones, keyboards, or both; tape delay systems provide the same canonic textures and regular rhythmic pulses that dominate *In C*. In recent years, Riley has composed pieces that evoke the sonorities and techniques of Indian music. (He and LaMonte Young both studied with the Indian vocalist Pandit Pran Nath, and he has frequently joined forces with tabla players and sitarists for performances and recordings.) Conversely, he has also begun to write for such standard Western ensembles as the string quartet and symphony orchestra.

In fact, Riley was one of the first composer-performers since George Gershwin to thread his way between categories of classical, popular, and ethnic music—a phenomemon the record business calls *crossover*. This blurring of lines, which continues to characterize minimalism, may pose problems for critics, scholars, performers, and record companies. (In Philip Glass's words, "there's a dichotomy of music in the U.S. Everything has to be either classical or popular. . . . Classical music always has been academic music, so if you're not classical and you're not pop, then what *are* you?") Fortunately, listeners tend not to be overconcerned with categories. In fact, by the late 1970s Glass and Reich had achieved a celebrity rivaling that of rock artists.

Steve Reich

Steve Reich was initially trained in Western art music and counts Bach, Stravinsky, and jazz as his earliest influences. He took a philosophy degree at Cornell University, but later concentrated on music exclusively at Juilliard. Reich then moved to California, where he studied with Berio and Milhaud at Mills College and developed a strong interest in loop and ostinato effects while working in tape studios. His experiments with *phase shifting* emerged directly from the studio experience; in two 1965 works using the human voice—*It's Gonna Rain* and *Come Out*—loops containing identical sound material, running slightly out of sync with each other, create effects of gradual change during the course of their simultaneous repetitions.

To begin with, they produce a canonic **texture,** somewhat similar to that of Riley's *In C,* but with the shifting relationships now under precise control. (Reich claims that minimalism's roots in Western tradition can be traced back to canonic technique, beginning with the twelfth-century Notre Dame school.) As with Riley, the repetitions extend over a very long duration, creating an ambiguous sense of time passing either very rapidly *or* very slowly, enabling the listener to study the musical fabric as though it were an object in space.

Beginning in 1967, Reich's interest in phase shifting began to move away from the electronic studio and increasingly in the direction of instrumental live performance. In *Piano Phase* (1967) two pianists play the same ostinato in slightly different tempi, so that the second player moves farther ahead of the first. *Violin Phase* (also 1967) extends this device to four players, though it is more commonly played by one live violinist with the other violin parts on tape. There are no electronic sounds, only a single twelve-beat melodic pattern for violin, heard at many overlapping, imitative levels. (See Example 16.6. In the solo–tape performance format, the soloist gradually increases his or her tempo here, so that the live part becomes one

♪ ahead, then two, and so on.) As the relationships among the four parts gradually shift, "resultant melodies"—a product of the hocketlike interaction of parts—emerge and recede.

Reich's gradual processes are an outgrowth of his fascination with timbral, melodic, and rhythmic aspects of a preexisting "subject" or source. For *It's Gonna Rain,* the subject is the voice of a street preacher in San Francisco, telling the biblical story of the great flood. In the composer's words, "I was extremely impressed with the melodic quality of his speech which seemed to be on the verge of singing. . . . I began making tape loops of his voice which made the musical quality of his speech emerge even more strongly" (*Writings about Music,* p. 49). For *Violin Phase,* Reich's phase-shifting treatment similarly highlights the violin's rhythmic drive, accented

EXAMPLE 16.6.

Steve Reich: *Violin Phase*

double stops, and subtleties of bowing. Little or nothing is done to disturb the natural working-out of the process; Reich simply assumes that, over a long time, the processes themselves—and the resultant changes in pattern, tempo, and timbre—will be audible to the listener.

Later works increase in both ensemble size and formal complexity. In *Drumming*, composed in 1971 (after Reich's study of African drumming in Ghana), Reich introduces a number of new techniques, including the processes of construction and reduction described earlier. *Music for Eighteen Musicians* (1976) offers a much broader palette at all levels—rhythmic, textural, and (perhaps most notably) harmonic. In the composer's words, "there is more harmonic movement in the first five minutes of *Music for Eighteen Musicians* than in any other complete work of mine to date." The music reflects Reich's intensive study of gamelan: a cycle of eleven chords, heard at the beginning and end of the work, serves as the material for the whole, and the interplay of constant rhythmic blocks (pianos and mallet instruments) against variably shifting "breath" pulses of winds and human voices is fascinating.

Other important changes have enriched Reich's technique: a freer use of registral placement, the human voice as a timbral resource (often imitating the sounds of other instruments), the gradual changing of sound color while maintaining constant rhythm and pitch, and a delight in relationships among instrumental groups of different timbres. Significantly, these stylistic developments, which open up greater textural variety, parallel a growing number of commissions from mainstream concert ensembles, such as *Tehellim* (1981) for four sopranos and symphony orchestra. *Tellehim*, set to excerpts from the Book of Psalms (the title means "praises" in Hebrew) is often jubilant, close to the ecstatic quality of Perotin and the thirteenth-century Notre Dame school that Reich loves so much. The overall language of *Tehellim* is more chromatic in its harmony, broader in its overall melodic shape, and surprisingly traditional in its approach to form. In fact, its large-scale tempo contrasts offer a "symphonic" narrative. Although *Tehellim* was composed after the composer's study of Hebrew cantillation, and may suggest the Middle East in its use of tambourines and hand clapping, it is not meant to evoke ethnic or religious music. Just the opposite, in fact: Reich chose psalms for his text precisely because the oral tradition for singing psalms has been lost. As he puts it, "this meant that I was free to compose the melodies for *Tellehim* without a living oral tradition to either imitate or ignore."

Different Trains (1988) presents a stark contrast to the glowing tone of *Tehellim*. Reich, when asked to create a work for the Kronos Quartet, had initial difficulties with the string quartet medium, since it did not offer the matched sets of identical instruments on which his earlier ensemble pieces had relied. (That reliance, dating back to *Piano Phase*, grew out of the early tape pieces' use of multiple loops of identical recorded material.) He then hit on the idea of creating a piece for electronically "multiplied" quartets, and carried one aspect of that idea—the use of recorded samples—into other dimensions: thus, *Different Trains* employs a collage of taped speech samples, train whistles, and air-raid sirens. The work's programmatic, semiautobiographical subject matter is often sober, drawing on Reich's childhood memories of family trips by train between New York and Los Angeles during the years 1939–42, and contrasting these with the experiences of European Jews—including other children—taking very different trains to concentration camps, and their deaths, during the same years.

Philip Glass

Like Steve Reich, Philip Glass received formal conservatory training, which included the experience of composing music in the accepted twelve-tone academic avant-gardisms of the 1950s. Many years later, he would state, "people sometimes tell me my problem is I don't know Schoenberg. On the contrary, I know him too well." He and Reich were students together at Juilliard. At the end of his formal training, when Reich decided to travel westward to California, Glass headed to France and worked with Nadia Boulanger. He has positive memories of that experience and credits her counterpoint teaching (and her devotion to Baroque music and Stravinsky) with helping shape the course of his career. Glass also met the great Indian sitarist Ravi Shankar in Paris and began his ongoing absorption in musical traditions outside the Western European canon.

Even in his earliest repetitive music, Glass shows a special fondness for *additive processes*. At the very opening of his 1967 *Strung Out* for amplified violin (Example 16.7), the two-note and three-note groupings are subjected to additions and deletions of one or two eighth notes. The accumulating cells, both melodic and rhythmic, may seem directionless; by Western standards they lack qualities of development or climax. But they are also rich in subtle changes, which grow more complex as the cells expand and contract. Additive processes may also be applied to chord series, creating arpeggiated patterns that resemble traditional cadence formulas. *Another Look at Harmony* (1974–78) takes familiar chord patterns (such as vi–ii–IV–V–I) and transforms them in unexpected ways.

The shifting play of brief relative durations over a very long time span is an important aspect of Glass's additive style. Pieces such as *Music in Twelve Parts* (1971–74), lasting more than four hours, encourage listeners to focus on **time** and the perception of gradual unfolding. Glass hopes that, in his words, one can "discover another mode of listening—one in which neither memory nor anticipation (the usual psychological devices of programmatic music, whether Baroque, Classical, Romantic, or Modernistic)

EXAMPLE 16.7.

Philip Glass: *Strung Out* for amplified violin

have a place in sustaining the texture, quality, or reality of the musical experience." Jonathan Kramer, in his study of *vertical* time, suggests that we hear highly repetitive compositions by Glass and Reich as we might hear Cage: perceiving the sounds directly, without making any assumptions about purpose, direction, symbols, or goals.

Many of Glass's interests came together in the 1976 opera *Einstein on the Beach*. When he and Robert Wilson began their collaboration on *Einstein*, they agreed that the opera would serve as a vehicle for extreme lengthenings of time, that music would be provided by the Philip Glass Ensemble, and that—although singing and dancing (or stylized movement) would be important—there would be no "libretto" or "lyrics." In the opera, numbers and solfège syllables, that is, the rhythms and pitches being performed, are the sole texts for singing. (*Einstein on the Beach* is discussed at greater length in Chapter 21.) Glass's later operas are equally monumental in scope and subject matter: *Satyagraha* deals with political and religious issues in the career of Gandhi, and *Akhnaten* concerns the life of an Egyptian pharoah who advocated monotheism. Like Reich, Glass has taken an increased interest in working with mainstream instrumentation. Music for the later operas is no longer provided by the Philip Glass Ensemble; the composer now uses a conventional opera pit orchestra, supplemented by electric keyboards.

REICH AND GLASS: A PRELIMINARY COMPARISON

During the years when repetitive process music was first attracting attention, the names of Glass and Reich were invariably linked together, perhaps giving the impression that their musical languages were all but identical. In truth, each composer has evolved a highly personal, distinctive approach. Three basic areas of stylistic difference can be noted:

1. Steve Reich seems primarily concerned with shifting relationships among polyphonic levels; these in turn produce textural and timbral changes. Glass is especially interested in applying additive processes to melodic contours and arpeggiated chord series.

2. Reich often begins with "found objects," a preference that extends back to his early tape loop works. In the words of the critic Thomas DeLio, "the subject of Reich's music is the presentation of multiple views of a single gesture within the context of gradual transformation." By contrast, Glass is more inclined to work from scratch, creating a more self-contained musical environment.

3. More abrupt changes occur in Glass's music: almost willful, arbitrary, not necessarily related to or dictated by an external system.

Reich is more inclined to see (or hear) a process through to its logical conclusion.

In the music of *both* composers, though, two important factors are at work: high-voltage and fast-paced *repetition,* and the use of **process** to initiate *change.* A pattern may itself undergo change, or the relationships among constituent parts of a pattern may change; subtle dynamic, registral, or timbral shifts may occur as well. Both Glass and Reich have perfected a sense of knowing *when* changes should occur, and *how* to affect them gradually (even imperceptibly). A typical page of score—for either composer—may show certain parts in an ensemble texture (or certain registers, since parts are often stratified by register) gradually dropping out and being replaced by others. In this way textural transitions are accomplished with relative ease.

Both Glass and Reich, like Terry Riley and La Monte Young, have pursued the serious study of non-Western music. Glass studied tabla and sitar with Ravi Shankar; Reich (expanding upon his early background in jazz percussion) has spent extended periods exploring African drumming and Indonesian gamelan. Moreover, Glass and Reich each formed a performing group, the Philip Glass Ensemble and Steve Reich and Musicians. For a long while, they did not make their written scores available to other performers. In this regard they have followed the examples of Harry Partch, LaMonte Young, and the Theater of Eternal Music, the standard practice of jazz and rock groups, and the ensemble traditions of gamelan and African drumming.

Non-Western influences have led Reich and Glass to foster an unusual approach to performance difficulty, at least by Euro-American standards. In their own groups (and the music composed for these groups), they have sought a brand of *"ensemble virtuosity"* rarely found in the West: a combination of technical brilliance with the suppression of individual ego. Reich, when asked about difficulty in his work, has written about the "arrangement of people within an ensemble where the parts are all exactly equal and extremely simple. . . . The virtuosity is in their ensemble relationship to each other." That quality is the result of great discipline (a highly concentrated attention on the part of every player) and precise response to detailed instructions. There is *no* improvisation or use of chance elements—a point, incidentally, where both Reich and Glass would part company with Terry Riley.

The composer-ensemble format has also evoked the sonorities and gestures of rock/pop music. Philip Glass, in particular, loves the qualities of the electric organ, amplified winds and human voices, and hard-driving rhythmic beat; Glass is increasingly seen as a crossover figure bridging the gap between classical and popular musics. He is hardly alone, however. David Byrne (of the Talking Heads) has, like Glass, collaborated with

Robert Wilson on spectacular theatrial productions and written scores for experimental choreographer Twyla Tharp. Brian Eno and David Bowie are also active in creating music with strong minimalist overtones.

Frederic Rzewski

After studies at Harvard and Princeton universities, Frederic Rzewski (b. 1938) traveled to Rome in 1960 as a Fulbright scholar. There he became known as founder, pianist, and chief composer-member of the Musica Elettronica Viva improvisation ensemble, a group noted for its use of eclectic "collage" assemblage and audience participation. He has also spent extended periods in France and Belgium. Rzewski's compositions often use deceptively simple means for generating sophisticated, complex structures. A prime example is *Les moutons de Panurge* for a flexible, indeterminate ensemble of melody instruments. (In this regard it resembles Terry Riley's *In C.*) All of the players work from identical copies of a surprisingly simple-looking score, consisting of a single melody and instructions for performance. The melody comprises sixty-five pitches in an undulating, repetitive contour and complex rhythm; all members of the ensemble are required to play it together at a rapid tempo. (Example 16.8a shows the opening, up to pitch number 15.) It would be very difficult to maintain precise coordination of such a tune for very long. Rzewski complicates the players' job even further by requiring that the line be played in an additive sequence of pitches (1, 1 2, 1 2 3, 1 2 3 4, 1 2 3 4 5, 1 2 3 4 5 6 . . .) until all the notes are performed. (See Example 16.8b for a realization up to pitch 9.) At the point where all sixty-five pitches are "in," the entire melody is played minus pitch 1 (that is, 2 through 65), then repeated again minus 1 and 2, and so on, until only the last note is sounded as a final "tonic" pedal tone.

At the rapid tempo required, the **process** is laden with pitfalls and booby traps. Inevitably, the single line breaks up into prisms, fragments, and overlapping canons during performance. Rzewski's instructions to the players are revealing: "In the melody above, never stop or falter, always play loud. Stay together as long as you can, but if you get lost, stay lost. Do not try to find your way back into the fold." The process and the instructions conspire to create a situation in which failure is virtually assured—a process in which distortions and "error" play an important role, as they do in the physical universe.

In the work's early stages the repetitions grow in duration, since one note is being added each time; paradoxically, though, as Jonathan Kramer points out, the rate at which we hear new notes decreases eventually to zero. This factor, along with the dense canonic texture of *Les moutons de Panurge* (not entirely unlike that of *In C*), results in a static sound object—an example of *vertical time.*

EXAMPLE 16.8A.

a)

Frederic Rzewski: *Les moutons de Panurge*

EXAMPLE 16.8B.

b)

Realization of Example 16.8a (through pitch 9) according to performance instructions

THE MIDDLE AND YOUNGER GENERATION OF MINIMALISTS

The ground-breaking efforts of Young, Riley, Reich, Glass, and Rzewski have helped to establish repetitive process as a viable aesthetic and compositional technique. As with many other novel approaches to musical sensibility and structure, what once appeared to be radical and self-contained is now a tributary in music's mainstream. An increasing number of younger composers feel free to use elements of minimalist technique in larger contexts, or to overlap repetitive elements with more directional, goal-oriented ones.

John Adams

In this regard, the music of John Adams, born a decade or so later than the five pioneering figures noted above, is worthy of study. A fine clarinetist (he premiered Walter Piston's Clarinet Concerto [1967]), Adams studied composition at Harvard with Leon Kirchner, but also developed early outside interests in experimental music, rock, and jazz. Ironically, Adams's experience in acoustical phenomena in the electronic studio caused him to question atonality. He had what he terms a "diatonic conversion" when he realized (in his words) "the resonant power of consonance. . . . there's such a lack of resonance in atonal music, with all the upper partials clashing against each other."

Adams's move to California in 1972 brought him in closer contact with the ideas of Riley and Reich, and helped move him farther in the direction of minimalism. His first work was *Phrygian Gates* (1977) for piano solo, followed by the 1978 *Shaker Loops.* The latter work, originally for string septet and expanded for string orchestra, reveals the influence of Steve Reich, which was strong at that time, and it quickly brought Adams's work to the attention of the musical community.

The title refers to the religious sect known for their quiet, simple lifestyle and (in vivid contrast) their wildly quivering dances celebrating union with God. But Adams's composition is also concerned with "shakes" in the Baroque sense: trills, melodic figurations, and filigree decorations. The other word in the evokes images of tape loops; they are represented by melodic "modules" that repeat until a signal from the conductor to change. (This degree of conductorial freedom holds true for the original septet; for the orchestral version Adams has written out all the "loop" patterns.)

The outer two movements are primarily concerned with "shaking" rhythmic patterns, and the middle two with very slow, almost stationary sonorities (in movement II, *senza vibrato*). Even at this early stage in his develoment, Adams's work is notable for its integration of surface minimalism with overtly "expressive" dynamics and phrasing, even chromatic dissonance for emotional effect. The influence of Copland and Bartók can be felt as much as that of Reich or Riley.

In the 1980s Adams began to show a special affinity for large instrumental forces. His 1981–82 *Grand Pianola Music* for wind band, two pianos, and wordless sopranos creates the ambience of joyous, even bombastic music circus, an eclectic, irreverent mix of Sousa marches, Beethoven, and gospel hymns, all riding above a vibrant, repetitive ostinato. *Harmonium* for chorus and orchestra (1980) covers a much broader expressive gamut. The texts, by John Donne and Emily Dickinson, range from the terrifying to the delicate and are mirrored exceptionally well. Adams enjoys using all of the standard gestures of European romanticism: crescendo, diminuendo, the sudden *sforzando*, and long arching phrases, all against pulsing patterns. The minimalist side of Adams's work has been thoroughly absorbed into the mainstream—so thoroughly, in fact, that it may strike some listeners as a special use of traditional ostinato. (It is also most important to note, in this context, that Adams does not wish to be regarded as a minimalist or have the term applied to his music.)

Given Adams's fondness for the long melodic line and expressive gesture, it seemed only natural for him to compose a stage work. His 1987 opera *Nixon in China* is brilliantly effective in its integration of repetitive technique with broad solo aria, dance, and dramatic confrontation. Within this unique synthesis of styles—seemingly uniting Reich with Puccini—Adams plays with standard operatic formulas: the introspective soliloquy, crowd scene, love duet, drinking song, large ensemble number, and the like. Moreover, he has created forceful and sympathetic onstage characters, positively *verismo* in comparison to the stylized rituals of Glass. Richard Nixon, Pat Nixon, Mao Tse-tung, and the others take on distinctive musical profiles; at the final curtain, we realize that an old-fashioned narrative ("maximal") drama has been played out. Repetitive process has simply provided the textural underpinning.

Laurie Anderson

Like Adams, Laurie Anderson (b. 1947) is a decade younger than the first generation of minimalist composers. She, too, has adapted its techniques to her own purposes—in this case, a unique genre midway between rock, ballad singing, performance art and social commentary. Of all the "crossover" artists, Anderson may have achieved the most significant successes. She straddles lines not only between serious and popular music but also between music, art, and theater; she has also managed to earn the high regard of her peers as well as the larger public.

Anderson has a degree in art history and experience as a professional violinist and performance artist. Her compositions are often brief—many last no longer than a pop song—and are designed for two different media: commercial recording *and* multimedia presentation. (Her song "O Superman" is discussed in Chapter 18.) As part of her multimedia approach, Anderson frequently plays a violin that may glow in the dark, or have a bright neon bow, or a bow made of magnetic tape drawn over the tape heads installed in the body of the instrument. Or she may perform as vocalist, singing, chanting, or simply speaking, her timbres transformed by a battery of sophisticated technological gear. Laurie Anderson has been known to refer to herself as a mere storyteller or even a stand-up comedian,

ILLUS. 16.2.

Laurie Anderson in performance. Each of the microphones in front of her effects a different timbral alteration of her voice

Photo: Jeffrey Mayer. Courtesy Warner Brothers Recordings

but her themes are often quite serious, even poetic. They reveal her concerns about the paradoxes, the ambiguities, the technological nightmares, and the wonders of life in the late twentieth century.

The Youngest Generation: Michael Torke

The youngest composers working with repetitive structures take their cue as much from the generation of Adams and Anderson as that of Reich and

Glass. If anything, they are even more eclectic in appropriating different styles—including minimalism—for different purposes. One representative American composer, Michael Torke (b. 1961), first studied music in his native Wisconsin, then came to New York for further training at the Juilliard School. By his admission, Torke discovered jazz, rock, and pop music at a relatively late stage, but found that he could incorporate them easily into his language. His music is extroverted and eclectic, freely mixing classical and rock models with the repetitive thrust of minimalism. *The Yellow Pages*, composed in 1984 for mixed chamber quintet, presents a synthesis of neoclassic gestures (especially those of Copland and Stravinsky) with pop music and repetitive patterns. *Vanada* (also 1984) adds the instrumentation of rock: piano, electric piano, synthesizers, bass guitar, brass trio, and a large percussion battery. Torke's handling of instrumentation in *Vanada* is remarkable; he also manages to create a fine balance of varied textures, especially when dense cluster sonorities are balanced against subtle chamber timbres.

CONCLUSION

Having examined the techniques of minimalism and the musical traditions that inspired the minimalists (or conversely, caused them to search for alternatives), we may now ask what *statements* minimalist composers and their works may be trying to make. One might argue that these composers are trying to tell us:

1. About **pitch logic,** arguing for greater simplicity, limited materials, and the presence of a tonal center. Most repetitive music is diatonic, its patterns often restricted to only a few pitches. Although pitch materials can be chromatic—more recent works by Steve Reich provide good examples—or even employ all twelve tones systematically, the very act of constant repetition creates the impression of central focus.

2. About the machine. Steve Reich's term "pulse music" is especially apt: we live in a world surrounded by pulses and steady-state frequencies; automobiles, refrigerator motors, vacuum cleaners, our own body rhythms. Significantly, each approach to musical **process** discussed in this chapter has been influenced by an aspect of technology. Earlier in this century, creative artists were excited by machines' sleek beauty, speed, or raw brutal power and viewed

them as glamorous. Today artists may be more fascinated by the efficiency, or the perverse randomness, of the machine's internal workings, or by the cyclical throbbing hum of its motorized sounds. Some creative artists may be attracted by the predictability of machines (their "boredom"), or by their fallibility: perhaps, as suggested by Rzewski's *Les moutons de Panurge,* they are at their most interesting when they break down.

3. About the use of *everyday, even banal materials* as the subject of art. This concept, so important to visual artists from Duchamp to Warhol, may be reflected in the minimalists' use of simple triadic chords, the instrumentation of popular music, or predictable canonic processes.

4. About *time* and memory. Philip Glass believes the experience of repetitive music can free the listener from notions of remembrance, expectation, or direction—traditional ways of imposing our thought processes on external material. On another level, minimalism allows each listener to explore his or her threshhold of interest. When time merely slows down to a crawl, we may grow impatient; "boredom" reflects our desire to speed up the pace of events. On the other hand, *vertical time* or timelessness may engage our interest in an all-consuming way, allowing us to focus on details or to perceive phenomena that have been previously unnoticed. If the music indeed puts us in a trance, the experience will be anything but boring.

5. About joy. The effect of much minimalist music is often exuberant, euphoric, perhaps even mystical in a uniquely gripping way. If it speaks to us (i.e., if we can move beyond boredom) we may recognize an expressive kinship with the unswerving patterns, semicanonic imitation and "frozen" durations of African ritual drumming, or the ecstatic organum of the Medieval church. At its best, minimalist music can be unparalleled in the intensity of its expression, not to mention the brilliance of its colors: the sounds of electric instruments, amplified instrumental and vocal timbres, and electrically modified sonorities. One paradox of repetitive process music is its ability to be austere and sensuous at the same time.

6. About accessibility and reaching a new constituency in a pluralistic age. Beginning in the mid-1960s, minimalist composers have literally created a new audience. Their work has attracted people with a great range of musical tastes, from Perotin to Webern, rock music to Cage, Italian opera to Stravinsky. It has also struck a responsive chord with people active in other arts, and people who

have been disenchanted with the postward avant-garde and welcome an alternative. Philip Glass expresses the sentiments of most composers of this persuasion when he states, "There was a time when there wasn't this tremendous distance between the popular audience and concert music. And I think we're approaching that stage again."

The Electronic Revolution II: Computers and Digital Systems

17

Although the tape machine, classical studio, and voltage-controlled synthesizer had revolutionized the way many composers approached their art, this technology began to seem rather dated as the 1970s progressed. Even with the help of filters, envelope shapers, ring modulators, and other sound processors, the palette of sounds one could ultimately coax from a bank of oscillators had its limits, and lacked the natural subtleties and complexities of acoustic instruments and voices. Moreover, composing with a Moog or Buchla synthesizer still required a good deal of manual labor—patching modules together, adjusting inputs and outputs, dubbing, splicing, synchronizing tape channels—all of which came to seem rather primitive. During the same period, the musical potential of computers and other digital devices became increasingly apparent. Given that computer technology was known still to be in its infancy, it appeared to hold a long and promising future for the composer.

ANALOG VERSUS DIGITAL

To understand the advantages and advancements that computer music and related developments encompass, we must distinguish between **analog** and **digital** technology.

Tape manipulation, voltage control, and all the other resources introduced in Chapter 8 depend on *analog* circuitry, which produces varying levels of voltage, corresponding directly to varying levels of amplitude or frequency in the sounds being generated. The waveform in Figure 17–1 will help in visualizing this correspondence. The waveshape depicted might represent a sound wave—a rapid fluctuation of air molecules whose pattern is perceived by the ear as a tone with a particular frequency, amplitude, and timbre. As the vertical axis shows, however, the same waveshape could just as accurately represent the motion of a loudspeaker cone creating that sound wave, and it could also represent equally well the fluctuation of voltage in a synthesizer inducing that motion in the speaker cone. There is, in other words, a direct analogy between the acoustic sound and its electronic source.

On the other hand, *digital* hardware (of which the computer is an example) deals not with voltage levels but with numbers. The basic steps in digital sound synthesis are depicted in Figure 17–2. A computer generates a waveshape not with continually rising and falling voltage but with a

FIGURE 17-1.

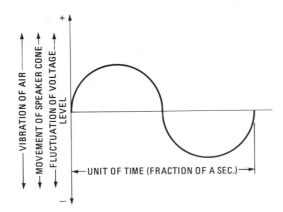

Three guises of a simple waveform

FIGURE 17-2.

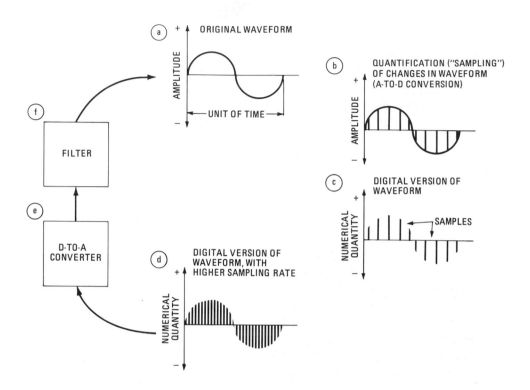

Digital conversion of a simple waveform

series of numbers that go up and down to approximate the desired wave-form. Figure 17–2a is a hypothetical waveform to be generated; as Figure 17–2b illustrates, the computer constructs it by representing its amplitude instant by instant with a number or quantity (each quantity shown here as a vertical bar). As seen in Figure 17–2c, the result is a series of such quantities that approximates the intended shape of the wave.

Each quantity is called a *sample,* and the higher the sampling rate (i.e., the number of samples per time unit), the more closely this series of quantities will represent its acoustic goal. This can be seen in figure 17–2d, where the higher number of samples (suggested by the more frequent vertical bars) outlines a smoother shape, one closer to the desired wave-form. (In large mainframe computers, sampling rates of fifty thousand cycles per second are common.) In any case, the digital form of the wave, as we can see, is really just a string of numbers stored in the computer's memory.

To be realized in sound, however, this string of numbers must be transformed into an electrical signal—an analog fluctuation of voltage that can move the speaker cone. A *digital-to-analog* (or D-to-A) *converter* (Figure 17–2e) is used to accomplish this transformation. The typical computer music facility of the 1960s and 1970s required both a mainframe computer and a large bank of such converters. Ideally, the conversion process should transform discrete increments of change like those in Figure 17–2d into a continuous waveform like that in Figure 17–2a. In reality, however, the quantifying and converting processes produce acoustical by-products— unwanted partials and other extraneous noise—which must be filtered out (Figure 17–2f) to achieve acceptable results.

The advantages of *digital synthesis* over analog synthesis are easy to see. A string of numbers can be modified and manipulated with much more precision and flexibility than voltage-controlled devices or magnetic tape, especially considering that a single tone may be represented by as many as fifty thousand numbers (samples) for every second of its duration. Digital hardware and software can manage these numbers to simulate (but with greater sophistication) all the sound processing functions we have already encountered with older, analog technology—timbral modification, envelope shaping, sequencing (i.e., ordering), mixing, and the like.

Note, however, that the practice of converting digital information into sound can be reversed. Once acoustic sounds are turned into analog electrical signals by means of a microphone, they can then be digitized (i.e., changed into numbers) by *analog-to-digital* (or A-to-D) *converters*. This process is called *digital sampling*, and as with digital synthesis, it too depends on very high sampling rates for the best results. Figure 17–2 could be used to visualize digital sampling as well, the only difference being that the analog wave form sampled (Figure 17–2a) would be produced by a real sound rather than the composer's imagination.

In either case, however, the result is a string of numbers that can be stored in computer memory, manipulated at will, and then transformed into sound by digital-to-analog conversion. Hence, digital sampling makes possible a kind of high-tech *musique concrète* wherein sounds can first be digitally recorded, then fragmented, reordered, timbrally altered or otherwise varied through sophisticated computer programming, and finally reconverted into a remarkable transmutation of the original.

As we shall soon note, the musical power of digital technology has not been limited to large mainframe computers. Since 1980 the musical community has seen a proliferation of smaller, more efficient, and more affordable digital equipment—devices that can be installed in small studios (or even used on the concert stage) and that require little or no computer know-how, while surpassing the musical capabilities of their mainframe ancestors.

THE DISCOVERY OF COMPUTER MUSIC

In Chapter 8 we encountered two inventions that bore some resemblance to computers—the automatic music synthesizer of Givilet and Coulpeus (1929), and the RCA synthesizer (1955). In both cases, punched paper rolls were used to "program" instructions and enter them into the synthesizer, much as punched IBM cards were once fed into large computers. (The perforated paper also functioned as a kind of memory apparatus, storing data and instructions that could be recalled and implemented again and again.) These early synthesizers were really analog instruments, however, using oscillators as sound sources: they were able to respond only in mechanically prescribed ways to a limited range of instructions. A computer, on the other hand, is capable of actually generating sounds digitally—with the help of a D-to-A converter—as well as processing them, and it can even be programmed to make compositional choices. All these capabilities first came to light in the mid-1950s.

Bell Laboratories

In 1957 Max Mathews (b. 1926), an engineer at Bell Telephone Laboratories in New Jersey, began experimenting with the computer to generate and manipulate sound. By 1962 he had created MUSIC4, the first computer music language to gain widespread use among composers. By today's standards, computers of that era were big, awkward, slow, and expensive to operate, and early computer music languages like MUSIC4 were primitive and time-consuming to master. In spite of these technical challenges, Mathews managed to arouse the enthusiasm of several composers, including James Tenney (b. 1934), Jean-Claude Risset (b. 1938), Hubert Howe (b. 1942), J. K. Randall (b. 1929), and Godfrey Winham (1934–75).

Tenney was the first composer to work with Mathews at Bell Labs, beginning in 1961, and he completed his computer-generated *Noise Study* that same year. The first significant contributions in computer-synthesized music, however, were works by Mathews himself. Although not a composer by training, he produced a number of pieces—such as *Numerology* (1960), *May Carol II* (1960), and *The Second Law* (1961)—which, when released on the Decca recording label, gave the medium its first real publicity.

By 1964, using a modified version of MUSIC4, Howe, Randall, and Winham had started up a computer music facility at Princeton University, which owned a large IBM computer similar to the one at Bell Labs. Princeton quickly became one of three major university-based computer music centers in the United States during the 1960s (the other two being the University of Illinois and Stanford University), and most of the significant works involving computer-generated sound to emerge during those years were created at either Princeton or Bell Labs.

Out of this early period evolved a basic set of procedures that remained standard in computer composition for the next decade and a half. In most cases, the large computers required were located at universities, intended to serve the diverse needs of an entire campus. Thus, the electronic music studio and the computer were commonly in different buildings—or even different parts of town. Typically, a composer would begin by entering numerically coded commands on punched computer cards, thereby specifying pitch, timbre, duration, loudness, and other variables for each note. A computer operator would then feed these into the computer for "batch processing," meaning that the composer's "job" would be processed in sequence behind other jobs already entered. This might take anywhere from hours to days. The computer's output would be another set of numbers, just like those in Figure 17–2d, representing the sound waves desired. The composer would then play the digital tape back through D-to-A converters and filters and record the resulting analog output on ordinary magnetic tape. Once back in the studio, the results could be auditioned, but if the composer was even slightly dissatisfied, he or she would have to prepare a new set of cards with any changes and start all over again. This protracted—and now mercifully outdated—ordeal remained a common *modus operandi* for computer music synthesis from the early days at Princeton until the late 1970s, although many innovations allowing for more immediate feedback began to appear during those years.

Lejaren Hiller: The Computer as Composer

At the same time that Max Mathews was learning to coax sounds from the computer, the scientist and composer Lejaren Hiller was exploring its potential in a very different way. In 1955, while working at the University of Illinois, Hiller postulated that a computer could be "taught" the rules of a given musical style and then called upon to compose accordingly. Hiller's first attempt at this was the *Illiac Suite* for string quartet, completed in 1957 in collaboration with Leonard Isaacson. Named after the high-speed Illiac computer on which it was realized, this work resulted from notes, rhythms, and dynamics chosen by the computer, whose output was then transcribed into traditional notation. Hiller and Isaacson programmed the computer to make random choices within varying sets of restrictions, ranging from traditional rules of counterpoint and harmony to compositional schemes based on chromaticism, twelve-tone procedure, and probability theory. The supposition behind this experiment, only partially borne out, was that as the program altered or narrowed these restrictions over time, there would be an audible, stylistically recognizable shift in the computer's musical output.

Hiller's goal was not simply to automate the composition of music in any chosen style, but also to explore a model scenario for human composers in which one could define the limits of a composition, make any aesthetically crucial decisions, and then let the computer work out the remaining details. Although not a musical success, the *Illiac Suite* led him to further research focusing primarily on the laws of probability and on information theory (a field of mathematics pertaining to the balance between redundancy and the unexpected, applicable to language, music, or other systems of communication). Among later works to result were *Computer Cantata* (1963) for voice, computer-generated tape, and chamber ensemble, and *Algorithms 1* (1968) for tape and nine instruments.

Hiller was not the only one to assign composing chores to the computer during the mid-1950s. It was often used by Iannis Xenakis to help calculate the massive complexities of his instrumental textures. As explained in Chapter 10, Xenakis was known for his "stochastic music"—compositions that relied, like Hiller's, on laws of probability, as well as on game theory, Markoff chains, Boolean algebra, and other mathematical systems. The clouds or clusters of activity in his music sometimes comprised literally thousands of individual sounds; mathematical formulas permitted Xenakis to specify the shape, density, and behavior of the overall texture, leaving the innumerable notes, durations, and articulations within it to be calculated by the computer. Xenakis's earliest work to be assisted by the computer is the 1954 *Metastasis* for sixty-one-piece orchestra; as in Hiller's case, the resulting sounds are to be produced by instruments rather than the computer itself.

While Hiller experimented with giving the computer an active (although never exclusive) role in making compositional decisions, Xenakis saw the computer more simply as a tool for helping with difficult but essentially routine tasks of composing, especially those that required massive calculations. Both approaches, however, are variants of what has come to be known as computer-aided composition or computer-composed music (the first term is preferable, since few composers completely abdicate a decision-making role.) Heightened interest would develop in this area a decade or so later, during the late 1970s, with advances in artificial intelligence (or AI) software, enabling a computer not only to calculate, organize, and store data but also to make judgments, deductions, and predictions (and therefore more "intelligent" choices).

Hybrid Systems

A third way to make music with computers emerged during the mid-1960s—one encompassing both analog and digital technology. This required a so-called hybrid system, in which sound was generated and processed by analog devices (oscillators, filters, amplifiers, etc.) while the control settings for these devices (e.g., the frequency of an oscillator or the output level of an amplifier) were dictated by a computer. The idea of controlling analog devices with preprogrammed input had been anticipated, again, by the early RCA Synthesizer, as well as by the British musical inventor Daphne Oram. In 1959 Oram had developed a system (called "Oramics") in which analog sound synthesis was governed by an arrangement of coded film strips and photoelectric cells.

It was with voltage control, however, that computer-driven setups became more practical. Instructions could be programmed and stored in memory (usually in the form of digital tape); then, when it was time to execute the piece, the composer's instructions would be "played back" by the computer through a bank of digital-to-analog converters, whose output could be made, like any other voltage, to "turn the knobs" (electrically, of course) in the voltage-controlled modules. A simple diagram of this scenario is shown in Figure 17–3.

FIGURE 17-3.

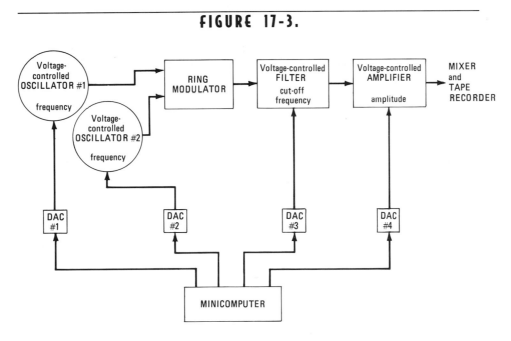

Example of a simple "hybrid" (digitally controlled) analog setup

Lejaren Hiller, and Gustav Ciamaga (b. 1930) at the University of Toronto, were among the earliest to investigate this area, beginning around 1965. But the first full-fledged hybrid facilities were Max Mathews's GROOVE (Generated Real-time Output Operations on Voltage-Controlled Equipment) setup at Bell Labs and Peter Zinovieff's privately owned and developed MUSYS III system in London. Both of these were fully operational by 1970, and by 1972 the EMS (Elektronmusikstudion) in Stockholm had also developed a hybrid facility. All three depended on a self-contained minicomputer located in the studio itself. This made possible a more efficient working environment for the composer, in particular the longed-for advantage of immediate feedback. Since the minicomputer, unlike larger mainframes, was used by only one person at a time (the composer), and since analog equipment could respond immediately without the lengthy calculations involved in computer-generated sound, the composer could enter a set of commands and hear the results directly afterward.

Among the earlier important works to result from this technology were two 1971 compositions: *Phosphons* by Emmanuel Ghent (b. 1925), realized on the GROOVE system, and *Chronometer* by Harrison Birtwistle (b. 1934), realized on the London-based MUSYS III system. The latter is notable because the sounds were actually nonelectronic (clock noises), while timbral processing of these sounds was governed by the computer. Chronometer, then, is a digitally controlled *concrète* work.

One other example of a hybrid approach (already mentioned in Chapter 9) is the Sal-Mar Construction, built in 1973 by Salvatore Martirano, which was an important early step in bringing digital technology into a live performance setting. To make that possible, Martirano had to build the circuitry himself, linking together computer functions, D-to-A converters, and analog devices (oscillators, filters, etc.) in one integrated, transportable unit.

Developments on the Continent

The foregoing would seem to imply that Europe played no important role in the first two decades of computer music, and indeed, apart from isolated endeavors by Xenakis, Koenig, and a few others, little happened there until Jean-Claude Risset returned to France in 1969. In the ensuing years he joined forces with Pierre Boulez to battle the skepticism and indifference of colleagues and bureaucrats; by 1975 their struggles had led to the founding of IRCAM (Institut de Recherche et Coordination Acoustique/Musique) in Paris. From then until the present, IRCAM has remained one of the most prestigious and richly endowed centers for computer music research and composition in the world (with analog synthesis and instrumental music also among its activities), and one of the few not aligned with a major university. IRCAM is a world center in every sense: composers from many countries have worked there. Americans in particular, such as John Chowning and Max Mathews, played a central role in the institute's founding, using U.S.-built PDP-10 and PDP-11 computers (from Digital Equipment Corporation), and MUSIC4 and MUSIC5 programming languages. Since then, composers from North America have continued to be a sizable presence at IRCAM.

MUSIC FROM THE MAINFRAME

Until about 1980, when microcomputers and small digital synthesizers began to take hold, the term *computer music* chiefly denoted music generated by large mainframe computers. Much of this repertoire has a consistent, characteristic quality, attributable in part to a certain sameness among the programming languages employed. Although a variety of languages existed, designed to meet different requirements, those most widely used, such as MUSIC4 and its derivatives (e.g., MUSIC4BF, MUSIC5, and MUSIC 360), were conceptually similar.

One aspect of this "computer sound" is timbre. With a few exceptions, the programming languages in question were grounded on *additive synthesis*, wherein each sound is formed by combining sine waves of different frequencies, resulting in a particular spectrum of harmonics and therefore a particular timbre. This additive process offers a high degree of control over sound color, but it is also an inherently artificial phenomenon, producing the unnatural, sometimes rather sterile quality typical of pre-1980 computer-generated sound. Its opposite, *subtractive synthesis*, eliminates selected frequencies from a complex sound while reinforcing others to get the desired timbre. This process parallels the way most sounds are formed in the natural, acoustic environment. (A wind instrument, for example, takes raw vibratory input from a reed and sends it through an air column that attenuates some frequencies and emphasizes others to produce a characteristic tone color.) In the electronic sphere, however, subtractive synthesis has been primarily an analog technique, as when electronically generated sounds are "pared down" or refined by filters.

Another attribute common to many pre–1980 computer works, encouraged by the nature of languages like MUSIC4, is their use of traditional instrumental textures. To program a large computer with unrestricted flexibility—to fine-tune every gesture, every nuance, with a fresh, uniquely tailored set of instructions—a composer would need expertise in machine code or assembly language, along with unlimited time and an unrestricted user expense account. Responding to the need for a more practical—if more restricted—alternative, MUSIC4 and its successors standardized programming functions by turning the computer into an "orchestra" of imaginary "instruments," generally constraining composers to an orchestra-and-instruments mode of thinking. (The instruments, of course, were really just data-manipulating routines.) Compared with the analog studio repertoire, then, computer-generated music—even works by otherwise very different composers—often tended toward a similar and rather narrow range of textures, characterized by a polyphony of distinct voices with distinct pitch material. The attractive side of this was that an orchestra of newly conceived, timbrally unique instruments could be conjured up, and yet the activity of these instruments could be controlled in precise and predictable ways.

In addition, a great many mainframe-generated works have been "complex" in style: harmonically dissonant, rhythmically intricate, and highly systematized. The labor- and time-intensive activity involved in computer composition clearly favored process-oriented composers—those using serial, statistical, or other structured methods where choices in pitch, duration, and other elements were guided largely by preestablished rules. (Such choices could be largely finalized before attempting computer realization, thereby minimizing the need for repeated trial-and-error cycles.) One work that embodies the timbral and textural qualities just discussed is the 1973 *Group Variations* by Benjamin Boretz (b. 1934), prepared in the Princeton University Computer Center and converted to sound at Bell Labs. That this piece was conceived as a kind of instrumental polyphony is aurally apparent, and in fact, versions for both computer-generated tape and chamber orchestra were prepared.

Some computer works from this period, however, did manage to get beyond the generic personality of the medium. *Earth's Magnetic Field*, composed by Charles Dodge in 1970, was realized at Princeton University and Bell Labs, using the same kind of hypothetical instruments, contrapuntal textures, and distinct timbres noted above. But Dodge took the extraordinary step of basing pitch selection on fluctuations of magnetism in the Earth's outer atmosphere caused by solar winds, as recorded during 1961 on geophysical charts known as Bartels diagrams.

The melodic and rhythmic outcome, although technically random, yields supple gestures that Dodge further clarified by a judicious use of sound color. In the first half of the twenty-nine minute composition, only the diatonic scale is used, producing a strangely transparent quality unusual to the computer medium; in the second half, however, a correspondence is set up between fluctuating magnetic indices and the twelve pitches of the equal-tempered scale, yielding relatively dissonant results. Like Xenakis, Dodge created here a musical expression of natural phenomena, using the computer to handle the huge quantity of data involved; but whereas Xenakis's music grew out of scientific formulae intended to predict or explain natural occurrences, Dodge's work was derived from such occurrences directly. Thus, as Dodge has explained in his notes to the recording, this music truly represents "the sun playing on the magnetic field of the Earth."

Another mainframe work with a distinctive complexion is Barry Vercoe's *Synthesism* (1970). Vercoe (b. 1937), originally from New Zealand, completed his training in the United States. In 1968, while a researcher at Princeton, he began developing a variant of the MUSIC4B language known as MUSIC 360, designed for the IBM 360 computer. His goal was a high-speed language that would be easier to use, offer a more flexible range of operations, and reduce turnaround time between computer input and sound output, all this in order to make computers more practical and attractive to the average composer. *Synthesism,* although created with an early version of MUSIC 360, already exhibited features that set it apart. To achieve its peculiar harmonic flavor, Vercoe took advantage of the computer's microtonal capabilities, dividing the octave into sixteen equal steps. (For the computer, formulating new scale systems is merely a matter of numerical specification.) He also employed routines for filtered noise, a rare instance at that time of subtractive synthesis in computer music. Moreover, while rhythm was arrived at systematically using ratios from the sixteen-note scale, pitch choices were based on random number functions, often resulting in rapid, mercurial sequences that contribute to the work's unique harmonic and gestural personality.

A later work to exploit MUSIC 360 in a different way is John Melby's 1979 *Chor der Steine* ("chorus of stones"). This bold, evocative essay, like so many computer-generated works, entails the serialization of both pitch and rhythm. It is also singular for combining additive, subtractive, and FM synthesis (explained below) within a single composition, thereby engendering a rich diversity of timbres that have an almost lifelike presence. Furthermore, in keeping with past practice at the University of Illinois, where the piece was realized, Melby (b. 1941) called upon the computer to make compositional choices, relying on its computational power to work through the complex serial operations by which much of the musical detail was determined.

INTERACTIVE DIGITAL COMPOSITION AND PERFORMANCE

The Responsive Computer

Digital systems have continually been made smaller, faster, more afford-able, and easier to use, spurred by efforts to broaden their usefulness and appeal and by the miniaturization of electronics from vacuum tubes to transistors to microchips. By 1971, when Barry Vercoe had moved to the Massachusetts Institute of Technology as founder and director of its Ex-perimental Music Studio, the need to bring computer music in line with this trend was acutely apparent. The inconvenience and procedural arcana of realizing digital sound were stifling to some composers and intimidating to others. Vercoe was determined to bridge the gap between familiar mu-sical concepts and the numerical abstractions interpretable by the com-puter, in hopes that the technology could be made more immediately responsive to the composer's input—perhaps quickly enough for intuition and spontaneity to play a greater part. His response to this challenge was MUSIC 11, a more "user-friendly" version of MUSIC 360, which could be run on smaller, less expensive computers like the PDP 11, bringing digital synthesis within the means of smaller studios. Further, now that video display terminals (VDTs) were standard, he devised a system of computer graphics responsive to input from a musical keyboard, wherewith the com-poser could interact more directly with the computer. It was with this newly interactive arrangement that Vercoe composed his *Synapse* (1976) for viola and computer-synthesized tape.

In Paris, Xenakis also pioneered such "interactive" possibilities. In 1966 he founded the Center for the Study of Mathematical and Automatic Music (Centre d'Etudes de Mathématique et Automatique Musicales, or CEMAMu), and it was here that he evolved a computer-based, highly interactive installation known as the Unité Polygogique Informatique du CEMAMu, or UPIC. By the early 1980s this had been perfected to the point where users could draw shapes representing waveforms, pitch contours, or other specified elements directly onto a screen and hear the result played back right away. Xenakis's *Mycenae A* (1978) for tape was created on the UPIC system.

By 1980 instantaneous interaction and response had been achieved in some studios. At Colgate University, for example, Dexter Morrill experi-mented with a configuration that allowed one to "play" the computer on drumlike surfaces. The sound output was immediate upon impact, its character depending on where and how hard one struck the surface and how the computer was programmed to respond. From 1977 to 1983 William Buxton ran the Structured Sound Synthesis Project at the University of Toronto, which featured a video graphics display and large plastic rings to be rotated by hand; these helped the user to enter and modify musical data in a physical, intuitive way.

A demand for interactive technology was also felt at IRCAM in Paris during the late 1970s, leading to a series of machines (the 4A, 4B, 4C, and 4X) driven by a PDP-11 computer. The young American composer Tod Machover (b. 1953), Director of Musical Research there at this time, used the 4A and 4C to realize two of his better-known works, *Light* (1979) for two computer-generated tapes and fourteen instruments, and *Soft Morning, City!* (1980) for soprano, double bass, and computer tape. In spite of the complexity and power of these machines, built by Italian physicist Giuseppe di Giugno and comprising a huge array of computer-driven digital oscillators and envelope shapers, they were well suited to Machover's penchant for subtle inflections and intuitively shaped gestures, providing for ease of input, sensitive real-time control, and immediate aural feedback.

Systems like those devised by Vercoe, Xenakis, Morrill, and Giugno were a far cry from the keypunch machines, punch cards, and lengthy turnaround times of early computer music. But they were still expensive and highly specialized, available only in the location where they were custom built, and useful only to composers happy with their musical and technical idiosyncrasies. The early 1980s, however, ushered in an entirely new family of digital musical instruments that changed the relationship between composers and technology forever. The miniaturization of digital circuitry made it increasingly possible to integrate the functions of many electronic music devices on one tiny microchip.

Among other things, microchips could contain digital oscillators and noise generators, which now made it unnecessary to convert digitized waveforms through D-to-A converters. (By 1990, what once might have been an entire roomful of equipment, including a whole bank of digital synthesizers, could be embodied on a silicon chip the size of a dime, an example of what is known in the computer trade as "very large-scale integration.") All this gave rise to fast, low-cost, relatively portable instruments—from table-top digital keyboard synthesizers and sound processors (like those in Illustration 17.1) to multifunctional, microcomputer-driven music systems like the synclavier—whose many advanced capabilities could be mastered without lengthy technical indoctrination.

The following outline represents the capabilities that such instruments boasted in varying combinations during the 1980s, capabilities that only a decade before necessitated massive mainframe computer power and a highly trained user.

ILLUS. 17.1.

A typical MIDI studio arrangement (at Syracuse University). Keyboard units on left A (top to bottom): Yamaha DX-7 synthesizer, Roland Jupiter-6 synthesizer, Yamaha DX-7IIFD synthesizer, E-Mu Emulator II digital sampler. On the table (left to right): Macintosh computer and MIDI switching console, Roland Super Jupiter synthesizer, Casio CZ-101 synthesizer, video cassette machine and monitor. Left of keyboards (not shown): Yamaha SPX-90 digital effects processor. Computer, synthesizers, sampler and effects unit are all interconnected with MIDI cables

Photo by Tom Prutisto

1. Easy design and storage (on floppy or hard disk) of "patches," sounds whose timbre and envelope are tailor-made by the composer, to be readily recalled from memory for performance or further modification.

2. Versatile piano-style keyboards, whose capabilities include non-standard (even custom-devised) tunings; division into two or more parts for playing different voices simultaneously; alteration of timbre, attack, and/or loudness according to finger velocity or key location; and assignment of separate sound events to separate keys so that, for example, one could play an "octave" of twelve disparate activities, in any order and at any rate.

3. Digital envelope generators, filters, and other sound processors, including "effects" modules, which produce reverb, echo, and other more exotic transformations such as pitch shifting, chorusing, and time compression. (Pitch shifting shifts all the component frequencies of a sound by the same quantity, creating new harmonic ratios and hence new timbres; chorusing makes a single voice sound like an ensemble of such voices in unison; and time compression speeds music up without changing its pitch, something a tape recorder cannot do.)

4. Real-time sound-processing options such as pedals, control wheels, or wind controllers (into which the performer breathes), used to create glissandos or alter tempo, loudness, timbre, modulation, vibrato, and other variables.

5. A multichannel sequencer, which can memorize lengthy series of keystrokes (entered through the computer or played directly on the keyboard) and play them back on demand.

6. Additive synthesis, whereby the timbre of each voice can be easily programmed using sine-wave harmonics (up to thirty-six per voice on the Synclavier).

7. FM (frequency modulation) synthesis, whereby the frequency of one oscillator is modulated by one or more others according to user-adjustable algorithms, resulting in sidebands (sum and difference frequencies) that function as harmonics of the sound in question and yield strangely lifelike timbres.

8. Sampling to disk, whereby brief fragments of sound are "recorded" in digital form, after which they can be looped, reversed, multiplied, transposed, filtered, modulated, or otherwise transformed, stored on a hard or floppy disk in their modified form, and thereafter recalled at the touch of a button or key.

9. Interactive video display for music notation, and for graphic analysis and editing of waveforms.

10. MIDI (Musical Instrument Digital Interface), a communications system that allows any number and all manner of digital

synthesizers, samplers, effects units, and microcomputer terminals to be interconnected and to respond to or control each other remotely.

Initially, the more impressive products to appear on the market around 1980 were the self-contained music systems, encompassing a broad range of the resources just outlined within one versatile package. In practice, however, it turned out that most such instruments, like the Fairlight Computer Music Instrument and the Con Brio ADS 200, were not really flexible enough for serious innovation and were popular primarily in commercial studios, where they offered producers a large, obedient ensemble of instrumental sounds at a fraction of what it would cost to hire live studio musicians.

The Synclavier, however, which composer Jon Appleton (b. 1939) began to develop in 1975 at Dartmouth College, was an exception. During the 1980s it was manufactured and marketed by New England Digital Corporation for a variety of users, from commercial to experimental. It truly was an entire computer music system unto itself, transportable anywhere and easily set up for live performance. By about 1985 the Synclavier II had evolved into a state-of-the-art machine, incorporating every feature listed above, with the exception of MIDI. *Syntrophia* (1977), among Appleton's first compositions for Synclavier, has passages that became typical of his music for the instrument, with simple triadic sonorities colored by surrealistic, shimmering timbres and sometimes layered into a more complex polyphony. Larry Austin's *Canadian Coastlines* (1981) also used the Synclavier. In this work a four-voice "computer band" joins forces with eight musicians in a diatonic but increasingly elaborate canon whose melodic, rhythmic, and textural shape is derived from the coastal contours of Canada. While the electronic sounds in the above works were recorded on tape, the Synclavier, like so many other digital keyboard instruments, was also intended for live performance, not just in the jazz and pop idioms but in concert halls as well. Niel Rolnick, Joel Chadabe, and Jon Appleton himself are among those who have performed with it frequently.

For either the popular musician or the serious electronic composer of the 1980s, the least expensive way to get involved with digital composition was to purchase a keyboard synthesizer like those made by Yamaha, Korg, Roland, or Casio, of which there were countless varieties. Sound generation ranged from microprocessor-controlled analog oscillators in the Roland Jupiter, to FM synthesis in the Yamaha DX-7, to sine-wave phase distortion in the Casio CZ-1. All had a double attraction: for the popular performer or songwriter, the better machines created a realistic sound that could be made nearly indistinguishable from live instruments, while for the more experimentally inclined, they allowed for the design of new timbres, elaborate attack-and-decay profiles, and other unusual sound properties.

Digital samplers like those made by Ensoniq, Akai, or the Emulator series by E-mu, had a similar two-sided appeal. The commercial musician could sample (i.e., digitally record) a live trumpet, for instance, and then produce a realistic trumpet part from the keyboard. The experimental composer, on the other hand, could graft together the initial attack from a sampled trumpet sound, the sustain of a sampled vocal sound, and the decay of a sampled piano sound, possibly filtering or otherwise modifying the results, thus creating a lifelike but unique trumpet-voice-piano instrument that could be played back in chords or melodic sequences on the keyboard. (Around 1975, less than ten years before, this same kind of sample-to-disk procedure would have required massive "number crunching" on large computers.)

It became quite common for a young aspiring rock or jazz musician of the 1980s to assemble a number of such devices (usually including a digital sequencer and drum machine) in his or her home and produce a polished recorded product that sounded like a band of accomplished professionals. The orchestral sounds for many film scores and popular albums were produced with similar equipment. It was equally common, however, for college-based electronic music studios to build versatile, custom-designed, experimentally oriented facilities around these same instruments. The studio pictured in Illustration 17.1 represents this trend and embodies every feature touched on in the above outline.

The greatest power and adaptability of an arrangement like that of Illustration 17.1, however, resides in a feature that cannot be seen in a photograph. Remarkably, all of the studio's features can be exploited fully at one time by just one person, thanks to the most revolutionary development in low-cost digital electronics to date: MIDI. This technology allows a single keystroke, control-wheel motion, pedal movement, or command from a microcomputer (e.g., an Apple Macintosh) to activate every device in the studio remotely and in synchrony, with each device responding according to conditions predetermined by the composer. At the very least, it enables a musician to sit at a single keyboard and play an entire roomful of MIDI-connected digital instruments at one time. Moreover, with easily acquired software, note sequences played on a keyboard or other performance inputs can be digitally recorded by the computer. Many channels (up to sixteen or more) of these performance commands can be superimposed, repeated, fragmented, and reordered through simple computer input, and then played back (at any tempo) again and again at the touch of a button; with each run-through the composer may reassign channels, change instrumental configurations, or adjust the balance and spatial location of sounds. All these channels of MIDI information may be stored on disk, to be replayed at any time much as magnetic tape may be replayed. Unlike the signals on tape, though, they contain no actual sound, but only a coordinated set of instructions as to how sounds should be produced by electronic instruments in the studio or on stage. Figure 17–4 is a simple

FIGURE 17-4.

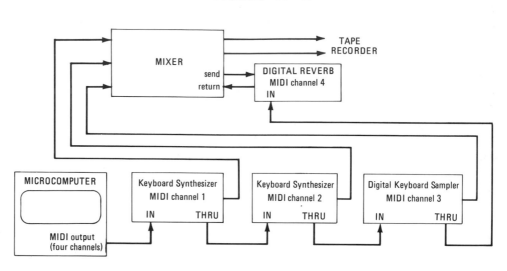

Example of a MIDI setup, with two keyboard synthesizers, a digital keyboard sampler, and a digital reverberation unit, all activated and controlled by a microcomputer via four MIDI channels.

illustration, among literally countless possibilities, of the kind of interfacing just described.

By the late 1980s, nearly every digital sound instrument on the market had MIDI inputs and outputs. Thanks to industry-wide norms for MIDI systems, a studio could be continually updated with new equipment or software in full confidence that older and newer hardware could be fully integrated.

While MIDI technology has come to play a vital role in live performance as discussed below, it does have limitations as a compositional resource in the studio, the main one being that commercially manufactured products necessarily lack some of the malleability needed for true sonic innovation. In particular, both hardware and software—designed to be highly interactive and easy to use—inevitably entail standardization of choices and some compromise of freedom. Another limitation is that MIDI itself may soon be obsolescent, as technology continues to accelerate exponentially. As of the early 1990s, fast and powerful computers like the NeXt and the SUN have already begun to proliferate, and it has recently become possible to compress an entire "studio" of sampling, synthesis, and sound processing instruments—along with all the software to manipulate them—onto a single, easily installed microchip. This has given rise to the "virtual console," wherein everything takes place within the computer itself and the composer/performer, working with graphic displays, conducts all activity seated in front of a video monitor.

Even in the realm of MIDI, however, recent advances in hardware and software have brought the virtual console nearer to reality on PC-compatible and Macintosh computers. Turbosynth, for example, a product of Digidesign, Inc., compresses a variety of MIDI synthesizers onto an audio board that fits into one's personal computer; included are analog, FM, and additive synthesis modules, and a sample editor. The software allows modules and patch cables to be represented and configured graphically on the computer monitor. The resulting patch can be linked with another program, Digidesign's Pro Tools, which offers sequencing, digital mixing, "non-destructive" editing (permitting unlimited edit attempts without losing the original), CD-quality sixteen-track recording (of either electronic or acoustic sources), and SMPTE time code functions (for coordinating sound with film or video), all in one potent, highly flexible package. In short, given a computer with sufficient memory and disk space, it is possible to produce even a large-scale, complex electronic work from start to finish while seated before the computer.

Even more advanced is MAX, an artificial intelligence (AI) program developed at IRCAM for the Macintosh and marketed by Opcode Systems, Inc. Perhaps the only MIDI resource ideally suited to experimental composition, MAX allows even musicians with no programming expertise to create an infinite variety of custom-made MIDI output devices and routines (automated patching units, sequencers, real-time controllers, etc.) using simple on-screen graphic displays. One can continually invent and reinvent a studio full of phantom hardware at will (except for the synthesizers themselves), limited only by the composer's imagination.

Computers in Live Performance

In some respects the computer is the "performer," offering control, precision, and the ability to render even complicated passages predictably and flawlessly. As such, a computer-generated tape is the conceptual antithesis—perhaps even more so than analog tape—of the inherently fallible live musician. In fact, many early computer works were designed exclusively for phonograph recordings. The audible product of J. K. Randall's *Lyric Variations* for violin and computer (1968), for example, entails no live performance at all, since both the computer and the violin parts are designed for recorded playback. Ironically, though, the automated, impersonal aspect of digital sound makes it an even more fascinating resource in the context of live performance, since it heightens the tension between "perfection" and human frailty. (Actually, the recent search for real-time, interactive systems and "intelligent" software is an effort to humanize technology, to obscure the boundary between humans and machines.)

Apart from the theatrical and multimedia issues considered in Chapter 9, it is important to consider the nexus between digital circuits and live performers, since it represents the apogee in interactive electronics. An early example is the digital system known as Daisy, developed in the early 1970s by Joel Chadabe (b. 1938) to control analog sound processors and spatial location. In a number of Chadabe's compositions, the performer is asked to interact with Daisy's transformations of his or her own sounds, transformations that are automated and constantly changing in unpredictable ways. (Chadabe's interest in live performance applications, especially those involving artificial intelligence and microcomputers, led to the formation of his Intelligent Music Company in the mid-1980s.)

In more recent years, as one might expect, MIDI has become the dominant force in this area. Among other things, it has made it possible for composer-performers literally to *play* the computer and its associated hardware. Dexter Morrill (b. 1938) has concocted what he calls the MIDI Trumpet (although his methods can also be applied to other instruments of the orchestra). A frequency detector is placed in the mouthpiece, and various switches are mounted in the valves and elsewhere on the body of the instrument. These are routed through a MIDI interface to the computer, which has been programmed (using an AI language called LISP) to translate pitches and switch movements into MIDI instructions for various synthesizers and effects boxes. Morrill is thus able to trigger electronic events—including spontaneous ones that respond to preprogrammed criteria—at the same time that he improvises on trumpet. *Sketches for Invisible Man* (1989) for solo MIDI Trumpet and digital electronics, created at the Colgate University studio, was one of Morrill's first vehicles for this system.

Gary Nelson (b. 1940), codirector of the TIMARA (Technology in Music and Related Arts) program at the Oberlin Conservatory, anticipated Morrill by several years, developing the MIDI Horn in 1985 (see Illus. 17.2). While Morrill's approach has been to alter existing instruments, Nelson and his partner John Talbert have built their instruments from scratch; they are designed to be played by brass players (Nelson was formerly a professional tuba player) and interfaced with a Yamaha DX-7. Since then, a variety of similar instruments, all easily interfaced with any MIDI-controllable synthesizer, have appeared on the market, including the Akai EWI (Electronic Wind Instrument), available in either trumpetlike or saxophonelike versions, and the Yamaha WX-7, a wind controller resembling a clarinet. One group, the Prism Saxophone Quartet, sometimes performs as an entire ensemble of WX-7s.

Unlike Morrill's instruments, Nelson's MIDI Horn makes no sound itself; rather, as the performer blows into the mouthpiece, moves the keys, and manipulates pedals, wheels, and sliders, these actions are converted to

ILLUS. 17.2.

Gary Nelson, playing a MIDI Horn

Courtesy Oberlin Conservatory of Music.

MIDI data and "read" by a Macintosh computer. In Nelson's standard configuration for interactive improvisation, a DX-7 synthesizer functions as the soloist's voice, responding directly to the MIDI horn, while another synthesizer (the Yamaha TX-816) serves as an accompanimental "orchestra" of 128 players. Guided by preprogrammed algorithms, the computer interprets the soloist's actions in the form of instructions to both the solo and accompanimental synthesizers and to an effects unit that further processes their output. A simple illustration is found in *Warps in Time* (1987). This improvisatory piece includes a variety of accompanimental sequences already composed and stored on disk, along with an algorithm for how and when they are to be activated; in performance, each time the soloist changes from one note to the next, his keystrokes trigger a new sequence, which continues to play until the next note change. As in Morrill's approach, the improvisational, interactive element here ensures that no two performances of the work will be the same. The work does have a clear identity, though, defined not only by the soloist's predetermined range of activities but also by the computer's preprogrammed response to them.

Morton Subotnick has become one of the most avid proponents of real-time interactive composition. His *Hungers* (1987), for instance, uses the

Yamaha Computer-Assisted Music System (or YCMAS), comprising a variety of synthesizers and sequencers and a digital mixer. In this work, these are all driven by MIDI commands from a Macintosh computer, as are lighting and video displays; the computer responds in turn to real-time input from a MIDI keyboard. Subotnick's *In Two Worlds* (1987) for solo saxophone, orchestra and WX-7 wind controllers takes the live/interactive element to an extreme. Here, the computer music system serves as an electronic "orchestra," controlled by a conductor with the same movements that direct the real orchestra. What makes this possible is a MIDI "Air Drum," which translates baton movements into MIDI signals, the latter being fed to a Macintosh that controls an array of synthesizers. Still in the forefront of computer music research, Max Mathews has updated this concept with his Radio Drum; stick movements are sensed by antennae and converted to MIDI signals, whose effects on electronic instruments are freely defined by the performer through the MAX program.

A younger innovator in this area is Tod Machover, director of the Experimental Media Facility at the Massachusetts Institute of Technology. Machover developed the "hyperinstrument" concept, involving a Macintosh computer run by HyperLisp (an AI programming language) and a "data glove" manufactured by Exos—the "Wrist Master," worn by instrumentalists, and the "Hand Master," worn by conductors. The latter is modeled by Machover in Illustration 17.3. The concept is richly emplified by his 1991 *Begin Again Again . . .*, a solo work written for cellist Yo-Yo Ma (wearing the Wrist Master) and digital electronics. The data glove is connected via analog-to-digital converters and signal processors to the computer, as are acoustic sensors and sensors on the cello and bow. The computer interprets this input, using it to formulate control signals sent to sound processors that affect the cello's output, to a rack of Yamaha TX-816 synthesis modules, and to a sample processing unit containing samples of the soloist playing his instrument. Yo-Yo Ma does more than simply perform the printed music; through his musical inflections and spontaneous physical gestures he affects the response of the whole system, which transforms his playing into a galaxy of electronic textures.

Although microchips and MIDI seem like the ultimate solution to the challenges of live electronics, attempts have been made to interface larger, more expensive computer systems with live musicians. Perhaps the most significant one is Pierre Boulez's *Repons,* realized at IRCAM with the 4X machine mentioned earlier. His most celebrated composition of the 1980s, it was begun in 1981 and subsequently matured over a period of years (as has much of Boulez's repertoire). Performing forces include the 4X machine itself (basically a high-powered digital effects box); a mixer for balancing, combining, and spatially distributing sounds; a 68000 VME computer, which drives both the 4X and the mixer; and Boulez's Ensemble InterCon-

ILLUS. 17.3.

Tod Machover modeling the Exos Dexterous Hand
Master data glove

Photo by Peter Menzel

temporain, known for its astonishing virtuosity and precision under his direction.

In performance, twenty-four members of the ensemble are seated in the center of the hall, and six soloists (cymbalom, glockenspiel, harp, vibraphone, and two pianos) are placed around the hall's perimeter, as are six loudspeakers, through which the soloists' modified output is heard. Transformations of soloist's sounds include time and pitch shifting, modulation (by each other), and rapid spatial movement, among others. The idea of "response" conveyed by the title is central: the twenty-four-member ensemble and soloists respond to each other, and the soloists and computer system do likewise. To fully appreciate this nearly hour-long work, whose effects range from supple shifts in color to cataclysmic outbursts, and to experience in particular the spatial aspect of response between ensembles and loudspeakers, one would have to be present at a live rendition.

During the 1980s the 4X was touted by some as the most advanced sound-processing device ever engineered, although it was so specialized and expensive that its influence in the live electronics arena was limited. Its successor is the smaller, more portable, and equally capable 5A, whose versatility and power are made possible by very large-scale integration.

ACOUSTIC VERSUS DIGITAL SOUND: A VANISHING BOUNDARY

For the more commercially inclined, one lure of computer technology has been its potential to analyze acoustic instrumental and vocal sounds and to recreate them with complete dictatorial control over the outcome and without the vagaries—or expense—of live performance. To those with purely artistic motives, however, the computer as sonic imitator has provoked some interesting questions: Is there a new region of sounds, somewhere between the acoustic and electronic, the natural and artificial? Can familiar sounds be transfigured digitally into something entirely new and yet retain a true-to-life character? (Or conversely, is this a way to contrive new sounds without the synthetic quality common to the electronic medium?) Can the expressive power of familiar sounds be augmented through digital transformation? Can we gain a new perspective on our sonic world through its electronic metamorphosis?

Of course, the phenomenon of *musique concrète* revolves around similar issues, as do analog filtering, modulation, and tape manipulation in live electronic performance. But breakthroughs in digital sampling and synthesis since about 1975 have brought new meaning to such questions. The extent of this is apparent in a work like *Dreamsong* (1978), composed by Michael McNabb (b. 1952). This work, created at Stanford University's Center for Computer Research in Music and Acoustics (CCRMA), features FM-synthesized sounds and acoustic sources—speech, crowd noises, and a soprano voice—that have been digitized and reprocessed. The quantum leap in musical powers brought by digital technology is most strikingly epitomized in *Dreamsong* when vocal melody metamorphoses into and out of electronic melody, with no perceptible point of transition between the two. In this instance and others mentioned below, the computer becomes a kind of supermedium, capable at once of both hi-tech virtuosity and human lyricism.

Recreating Acoustic Phenomena

The musical alchemy in works like *Dreamsong* became possible through years of research in the computer music field, and especially through attempts to fathom all the subtleties of psychoacoustics and enlist them in composition by recreating them digitally. The leading center of such research, from the mid-1960s until the founding of IRCAM a decade later, was in fact Stanford University's CCRMA, under the leadership of John Chowning. Using powerful computer programs for analysis and synthesis, Chowning and his colleague James Moorer delved deeply into the way we perceive spatial location and movement of sound, and the ways in which our sense of pitch definition and color relate to attack transients (how sounds begin), formant structure (the frequencies that a given instrument or voice tends to reinforce or attenuate), and vibrato. Chowning's most significant discovery, however, was FM synthesis, which made it easy to achieve sounds with a realistic, acoustic character, using simple algorithms to control modulation sideband ratios. This process, eventually built into many portable synthesizers such as the Yamaha DX-7, was a major step in overcoming what had seemed the innate artificiality of electronically generated sound.

Chowning sometimes illustrated his findings in his own works. *Turenas* (1972), for example, uses quadraphonic speaker placement, variable reverb, and simulated Doppler effect to create a two-dimensional sound field through which clearly defined sonic entities, some of them made with FM synthesis, move about at various speeds.

Research has been central to IRCAM's mission as well, with similar emphasis on links between the acoustic and electronic worlds—a concern we have already noted in Boulez's *Repons*. As at Stanford and other major centers, many of the experiments at IRCAM could be carried out only with the heavy capacity of larger computers, remaining far beyond the reach of MIDI synthesizers to this day. A prominent instance is *Mortuos plango, vivos voco* (1980) by the British composer Jonathan Harvey (b. 1939). The material in this piece is derived from the acoustic properties of two sounds: the tenor C bell of Winchester Cathedral and the voice of a chorister (the composer's son) singing the words inscribed on it (from which the title is taken). Digital analysis provided Harvey with the harmonic spectrum of the pealing bell and the fluctuating resonances and noise transients (by which words are recognized) of the boy's voice. He then fashioned a dazzling and moving synthesis of the two, with vocal tones heard in bell-like clusters and bell sounds filtered by patterns of speech, so that the bell seems to be "ringing" the boy's voice and vice versa.

Digital Sampling and Transformation

The alternative to recreating the characteristics of live sound is working with that sound directly, sampling it (i.e., digitizing it through A-to-D converters) and then using computer software to alter chosen aspects of it while leaving the rest as is. Once reconverted to analog sound, those properties of the original that are preserved lend realism to what is otherwise new and unfamiliar.

As the most natural and personal of instruments, the human voice has proved to be a favorite subject for digital sampling and resynthesis. Among earlier examples are Max Mathews's *Bicycle Built for Two* (1962), realized with A-to-D and D-to-A converters on Bell Laboratory's IBM mainframe, and Alvin Lucier's *North American Time Capsule* (1967), a live performance piece realized with the Vocoder, a digital voice encoder and processor built by Sylvania Electronic Systems.

Charles Dodge, however, was the first to bring significant attention to speech sampling and resynthesis. Dodge's first works in this vein include *Speech Songs* (1973), realized at Bell Laboratories, and *In Celebration* (1974), realized at Columbia University and Nevis Laboratories. In both works, poetry was read into a microphone, recorded digitally, subjected to a variety of startling alterations, and then restored (through D-to-A conversion) to analog sound. The resynthesized voice retains its clear pronunciation and unmistakably human character, but also does things no human voice could do. At times, single syllables are isolated and repeated on a rapid succession of pitches; at other times, they are sustained and projected through chromatic flourishes spanning up to two or more octaves. Elsewhere, words are multiplied and resynthesized as chords, chord progressions, clusters, contrapuntal textures, or a chorus of glissandos. The rhythm of declamation often varies drastically without affecting intelligibility, and the inflection of a given word or sentence is sometimes changed repeatedly in quick succession—heard now as an affirmation, now as a question, now as a contorted melody.

The success of Dodge's work depended in part on "synthesis by analysis," a process whereby the resynthesis of digitized speech sounds is guided by the computer's analysis of the original voice, thus ensuring greater realism. Dodge used a form of analysis that determined the changing formants of the voice as it spoke or sung. But by the late 1970s there emerged a new analytical approach called "linear predictive coding," in which the computer constructs a filter modeled after the speaker/singer's vocal tract and its behavior from one instant to the next. Resynthesis based on linear predictive coding allowed pitch, rhythm, and timbre to be manipulated with even greater flexibility, while retaining the realism and clarity of the voice far more convincingly than earlier methods. (One of the outstanding compositions using this technique, Paul Lansky's 1979 *Six Fantasies on a Poem by Thomas Campion,* is discussed separately in Chapter 18.)

As of the early 1990s, the Herculean mathematics needed to execute linear predictive coding still precludes adaptation to microchips, but the so-called sample-to-disk units available on the market since the 1980s are still a powerful and flexible resource, both in the studio and on the stage. In fact, since these are MIDI instruments, they can be interfaced with a microcomputer, so that sampled sounds can be transferred to the computer for analysis and modification. By about 1985 inexpensive software could be purchased (such as Digidesign's *Sound Designer*) that allowed a sampled waveform to be reversed, fragmented, redrawn, or merged with other waveforms, then to be replayed in its new guise by the sampling instrument. Also readily available were tools for waveform analysis such as "fast Fourier transforms," which graphically display the harmonics of a sound and their change in amplitude over time.

FUTURE DEVELOPMENTS

Beginning with the earliest oscillators and tape machines, every stage of development in electronic music has seemed truly revolutionary until rendered obsolete by the next. At present, store-bought equipment and the operation of a few controls can accomplish what a studio full of technicians and electronic hardware could not have rivaled three decades ago. As this trend persists, music technology will continue to become smaller in size, easier to use, more interactive, more automated, more versatile, and more "intelligent." What this means for the future of music composition, however, is unclear, since better technology does not in itself mean better music, and since even the most far-reaching advances are of merely technical interest where artistic vision is absent. Further, there is a small but growing trend, in both artistic and commercial sectors, away from what is perceived as the cold, hard, sterile precision of digital sound and toward the warmer, richer quality (to the ears of some) produced by analog circuits. In a larger context, there is also a growing reaffirmation of acoustic instrumentation and live, nontechnological performance—a return to human music making.

It is likely, though, that the electronic medium's endless treasure trove of sonic shapes and colors, and the opportunity to compose directly with harmonics, formants, acoustic space, and other such phenomena, will always prove an irresistible temptation to many composers.

Pieces for Study III

The ten works to be studied in this chapter were composed between 1967 and 1984. In them, the concerns of Part III are manifested and underscored. The chapters in this section have dealt with important, often provocative issues: the quotation of existing music, the revival of tonal materials, alternative concepts of performance, minimalism, and the evolution of high-tech sound synthesis. Although a number of these issues are hinted at in Part II (reflecting a certain chronological overlap), they acquired particular force and influence during the late 1960s and beyond.

Lukas Foss: Baroque Variations

One of the most influential compositions of the late 1960s, *Baroque Variations* (1967) presented a confluence of many currents in Lukas Foss's thinking at that time: a reverence for the classics; a fondness for Ivesian collage; a fascination with the "time warp" possibilities of electronic technique (tape delays, loops, and echo effects); and an interest in improvisation, chance, and performer choice. These concerns led to a three-movement orchestral work in which unfocused fragments and dream images, drawn from Baroque sources, combine to create a surrealistic montage. Here Foss makes use of dense cluster **textures,** improvisation by the orchestral players, and a novel approach to **performance ritual,** including the visual shock of radical "theater."

It is also a celebrated instance of **parody/historicism,** in that its materials are drawn directly from eighteenth-century sources. The first of Foss's three movements is based on the *Larghetto* from Handel's Concerto Grosso, Op. 6, No. 12, the second on Scarlatti's Sonata K. 380 for harpsichord, and the third on the *Preludio* from Bach's Partita in E Major for solo violin. In his program note, Foss has described the work as "dreams about" rather than "variations on" the three pieces in question. Indeed, Foss does not so much vary the original music as allow it to blur, refocus, fade, reappear, and overlap with itself, in a manner that suggests free association or stream of consciousness. **Pitch logic** is tied to the tonality of the music quoted, which remains recognizable, though sometimes distorted, from beginning to end. (All three movements are in E major, and Foss's transformations never lose the sense of E as tonic. In this sense, perhaps, his model is, appropriately, the suite rather than the symphony.) But **time** and **texture** are approached more radically.

In the first movement, Handel's *Larghetto* is performed as written and without pause, except that most of it is played *inaudibly*. Fragments of melody, an inner line, or a harmony may emerge unpredictably between moments of silence. The memory of this well-known music provides a fixed temporal and textural framework, but Foss manipulates our perception of time and texture by allowing only sparse, fleeting glimpses of the original. We sense the presence of something familiar yet curiously obscured by a Webern-like discontinuity.

Even these brief fragments are distorted at times, emerging in more than one key and tempo simultaneously. This is underscored by **sound color,** with electric organ, virbraphone, and electric guitar adding an alien cast to what might otherwise pass for a Baroque ensemble. Those witnessing a live performance would also be confronted with a strangely theatrical variant on **performance ritual:** the sight of many musicians bowing, fingering, and puffing—but silently—on their instruments, as many of the notes not played are pantomimed. Both aurally and visually, then, it is as if the listener were experiencing Handel while drifting in and out of a delirium.

In the second moment, the Scarlatti sonata is played in its entirety on a harpsichord within the orchestra, surrounded and obscured by orchestral "commentary": clusters, *glissandi,* rhythmic distortions, and echoes of the original.

The third and most elaborate variation had been originally composed as a separate orchestral piece entitled "Phorion"—Greek for "stolen goods."

As in the first variation, the Baroque original—a rapid, rhythmically driving display piece for solo violin—is the only source of material. The element of theater also returns; as fragments of Bach emerge and submerge in and out of audibility, bowing and fingering continue nonstop. But here Foss also pursues his interest in chance and improvisation. Both standard and experimental **notation** are used, outlining a variety of gamelike procedures that ensure, within limits, a different result in every performance.

Each player has a page of the Bach prelude and a series of detailed verbal and graphic instructions that tell conductor and players how to decide what fragments are heard and when. Much of the time, the conductor has no way to tell exactly what music will result from his cues. In Example 18.1, for example, performers must play the notated rhythm, but they themselves select the pitches from a Bach fragment of their own choosing. The original monophonic line repeatedly proliferates into garbled fragments, sudden outbursts, canonic overlappings, and volcanic sound masses. Foss's program note describes the desired effect as "torrents of Baroque sixteenth notes, washed ashore by ocean waves, sucked in again, returning . . . a Bach dream."

EXAMPLE 18.1.

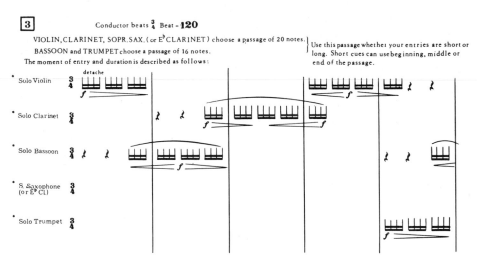

Lukas Foss: *Baroque Variations*, third variation

The ending of the movement is dramatically intense. At first the music's motoric energy winds down, becoming nondirectional, almost static. The rhythms are fragmented and askew, many of them now being chosen by the players; brief outbursts of Bach alternate with an ultraromantic cello phrase (itself a Bach fragment at very slow speed). Against a static backdrop, individual members of the orchestra play cryptic "games" with the material—a race between two flutes, for example, or the name JOHANN SEBASTIAN BACH spelled out (by xylophone) in Morse code. The quiet is shattered by a sudden burst of noise: rude percussion instruments (including trash can lids) playing ·in unpredictable fits and starts, garbled random fragments of Bach, and an obsessive repeated note E in the brasses (a violent exaggeration of repeated Es in the original Bach prelude, and a recapitulation of the "tonic" for the entire *Baroque Variations*). The texture grows still bolder, louder, and more insistent, and the repeated notes ever more manic, as the work advances to its angry conclusion.

Ultimately *Baroque Variations* is a music about music—past, present, and future. It is an attempt to confront the rift between the traditions deep within us and the inexorable forces of change.

Harrison Birtwistle: Punch and Judy

One of England's most imaginative composers, Harrison Birtwistle commands special àttention for the ritualistic, often static aspects of his work— characterized by one critic as having a quality of ceremonial "procession." He has made a careful study of Medieval techniques, and isorhythmic interplay is important to him. Many of his works involve the voice, text, and dramatic staging; more than a few are concerned with the retelling of violent, horrific myth.

In every one of these respects, *Punch and Judy* (1967) is revealing. For this one-act opera (scored for six soloists, five mime-dancers, a five-piece wind ensemble onstage and an offstage orchestra of trumpet, trombone, two percussionists, harp, and strings) Birtwistle and his librettist, Stephen Pruslin, envisioned the familiar puppet figure Punch as a mythic embodiment of remorseless evil. The murders he carries out, and his final redemption and union with Pretty Polly, are presented with a formality at once comic and chilling; by assuming an austere approach to **performance ritual,** Birtwistle transforms a traditional children's puppet play into a modern-day Greek tragedy.

Members of the cast periodically step out of their roles to function like a Greek chorus, reflecting on Punch's violent misdeeds. (The wind quintet, located in the onstage "puppet box," serves a similar function.) The mythic atmosphere is further intensified by religious and astronomical imagery in both staging and text. The very structure of the opera suggests ancient dramatic form, with a cycle of four "melodramas," each divided into a series of clearly stylized set pieces (and each ending with a ritual killing); moreover, much of the words and music are strophically arranged.

Birtwistle's music imbues the drama with a black sense of irony. This is often generated by a stylistic clash in **pitch logic** and **time,** particularly where intensely chromatic pitch material is combined with a caustic **parody** of traditional, occasionally folklike rhythm and phrase structure. Note the intensity of Birtwistle's highly stylized—but not minimalist—repetitions, perhaps reminiscent of Varèse (especially in the shrill use of upper registers), or of the starkly neoclassic Stravinsky of *Renard* and *L'histoire du soldat*. Materials are frequently layered into a **texture** that is richly innovative and complex, yet oddly familiar due to the element of parody.

The opening measures of "Punch's Lullaby" (Example 18.2) illustrate this. Punch serenades the baby for a while and then throws it in the fire. The voice and bass clarinet perform a tonally distorted nursery tune in

---

EXAMPLE 18.2.

PUNCH'S LULLABY

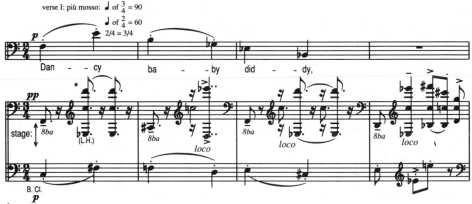

* The top line in these chords is played by the piccolo, and will sound 8va higher in performance.

Punch and Judy, Melodrama I ("Punch's Lullaby"). Music by Harrison Birtwistle, libretto by Stephen Pruslin

simple $\frac{2}{4}$, set against a skewed, waltzlike cross-rhythm in the other winds. Each of the two layers of activity is rhythmically straightforward, but when set against each other, they are harmonically and rhythmically in conflict. This and the sneering, singsong character of Punch's melody create a sinister air, a premonition of horror. The horror is realized as the words "dancy baby diddy" of the first verse become "bouncy baby burny" in the last.

Luciano Berio: Sinfonia

Luciano Berio, one of the first Europeans to break with serialism, succeeded in transferring his tape studio experience with collage to another medium in his *Sinfonia* for eight amplified solo voices and large orchestra. *Sinfonia* was composed in 1968, with a fifth movement added in 1969. The title is intended to reflect the most basic sense of the term's meaning—a "sounding together"—and the material to be sounded together is as diverse as can be imagined.

The text draws from three wholly unrelated sources: Part I uses brief, disjointed excerpts from Claude Lévi-Strauss's *Le cru et le cuit;* Part II, a tribute to Martin Luther King, Jr., passes isolated fragments of his name from voice to voice until the seemingly abstract phonemes gradually coalesce into the complete name: and Part III draws chiefly on passages from Samuel Beckett's *The Unnamable.* The fourth part is a sustained, vague echoing of the text from Part I, and the fifth part continues with the Lévi-Strauss where it was left off in the first, now layered and intermingled with refractory hints of all three texts.

Throughout, Berio improvises disjunct, freely associated words or sounds inspired by the verbal and musical context; it is here, ironically, that the disparate texts are unified beneath the surface, lending subtle significance to the work's title. For example, the French words *sang* (blood) and *eau* (water) are often taken out of context and juxtaposed during Part I. The latter forms a phonic association with the *O* of Part II's "O Martin Luther King," whereby *sang* becomes a veiled reference to the spilled blood of the black martyr. Later, in Parts IV and V, this relationship expands to "rose de sang" (rose of blood), an indirect reference to the fourth movement of Mahler's Symphony No. 2, where the German words "'O Röschen roth" (O red rose) appear. Since Part III is derived form the third movement of the same Mahler symphony, it implicitly joins this association among the other four parts. All these links are reinforced in Part V, as *sang, rose, roth* and *röschen* are splintered into individual phonemes (*sa, ro, rö,* etc.) that are continually interleaved.

Ultimately, however, the synthesis denoted by Berio's title is a musical one, and here too, a broadly eclectic mix of elements is brought together. In terms of **texture,** these range from whisper-soft a capella chords sustained by the voices (Parts I and IV) to the stratification of incongruously diverse vocal and instrumental activities (Parts III and V), the latter in itself being a reflection of the term *sinfonia.* The culminating synthesis comes in the finale, which builds on material extracted from the previous four parts, now reworked, reordered, and supplemented with fresh material.

A more remarkable integration—in fact, a historic instance of **parody**—occurs in Part III, the scherzo. Fragments of earlier pieces (Ravel's *La valse,* Stravinsky's *Le sacre du printemps,* waltzes from Strauss's *Der Rosenkavalier,* and other music by Bach, Beethoven, Schoenberg, Globokar, Pousseur, Debussy, and Ives, for example) form a fabric of free association, set against *another* scherzo, that of Mahler's Symphony No. 2. The Mahler excerpt is a lengthy one, at times played literally and at others disguised or attenuated; Berio treats it as a swiftly moving "''vessel'' on which the other fragments ride. At times the Mahler dominates the overall texture, and at other times it is overwhelmed by a barrage of quotations fading in and out, as though surfacing momentarily in a swift torrent.

Another level of collage is found in the *words* sung, spoken, whispered, and cried out by the vocalists. Although Berio's text centers on an excerpt from Samuel Beckett—from which we get the urgently shouted refrain, ''keep going''—there are also references to James Joyce, notations from Berio's own diary, and graffiti found on the walls of Paris during the 1968 student riots.

The **pitch logic** in the third movement revolves largely around the relationship between Mahler's scherzo and the other works quoted. The confluence of Mahler, Brahms, Berg, and Ravel in Example 18.3 illustrates this. The Mahler melody is reorchestrated, passed from the piccolo clarinet to clarinets 1 and 2, to violin group C, and to the piano right hand. The waltzlike accompanimental rhythm is left out at first, then filled in briefly by the lower strings, then dropped for a measure and finally picked up by the piano left hand. Overlaid on this are three measures of violin solo from the second movement of the Berg *Violin Concerto,* followed by three measures from the first movement, followed by four measures from the second

---

EXAMPLE 18.3.

Luciano Berio: *Sinfonia,* Part III

movement of the Brahms *Violin Concerto.* The bassoons then repeat a figure extracted from Ravel's *La valse.* A closer look shows that this is anything but a mere collage. The violin line from Berg, with its chromatically descending sixteenth notes, preechoes the longer, similarly descending line in the Mahler two measures later, which is then briefly accompanied by another more rapid descent in the violin line from Brahms. Hence, Berg and Brahms offer variation and comment on the Mahler. The Ravel figure in the bassoons resembles, and therefore echoes, an earlier part of Mahler's melody not shown here.

This is just one of countless instances in Part III where quoted fragments bear a rhythmic or melodic likeness to the Mahler. It is as though Berg, Debussy, Stravinsky, and all the others were improvising on Mahler, or vice versa. The **compositional process** of the movement, therefore, is one in which the Mahler *scherzo* provides an overall rhythmic and harmonic skeleton, fleshed out by Mahler's own melodic material or Berio's distortions of it and by its interaction with and reflection in material from other compositions.

Also shown in Example 18.3 is another characteristic touch: wry commentary from the vocalists. In this case, tenor I embellishes the Beckett monologue with "there seems to be a violin concerto," a statement corrected by alto II ("two concertos"). In measure 6 of the excerpt, six of the voices mimic the violin soloist's line with corresponding solfège syllables. The vocal ensemble's aloof role as commentator or observer can be viewed throughout *Sinfonia* in terms of **time,** particularly where voice parts are spoken: the words are temporally "detached" from the instrumental parts, being freely placed according to spatial context, whereas the instrumental parts are always metered. This and the use of rhythmic but unpitched vocal sounds require departures in **notation** like those seen in Example 18.3.

Berio's choices of borrowed music in Part III are based on more than melodic affinity; they have subtle connections to the work as a whole. For example, the choice of the Mahler scherzo, an orchestral expansion on Mahler's earlier song "St. Anthony's Sermon to the Fish," is related to the text of Parts I and V, which deal with water imagery in mythology. This relation is reinforced by Berio's use of Mahler's tempo indication, *fliessend* ("flowing"), as well as by both musical and verbal references to Debussy's *La mer,* Schoenberg's "Summer Morning by a Lake" from Five Pieces for Orchestra, Op. 16, and the drowning scene from Berg's opera *Wozzeck.*

Berio's deep involvement with Mahler is revealing, for Mahler was himself driven by a strangely moving eclecticism, and was acutely aware of history and style having reached a crossroads. This sense of historical crisis is intensified by the snippets of telescoped music history and the explosive, often angry, wall writings that pepper the text. Consider, too, the cryptic meaning of the repeated text phrase "Keep going" and the many musical fragments as aural "graffiti" of their own.

Mauricio Kagel: Staatstheater

Mauricio Kagels' *Staatstheater* (1970) derives its title from the Hamburg-ische Staatsoper, where it was premiered. The work requires fourteen solo vocalists, a sixty-voice mixed chorus, seven actors, five percussionists, a troupe of "nondancers" and assorted orchestral instrumentalists. One could plausibly call it an opera, since (apart from a wild assortment of unusual props) it relies on traditional operatic resources: soloists, chorus, dance ensemble, and ordinary looking costumes. Beyond these superficial aspects of **performance ritual,** however, *Staatstheater* defies all expectations. The performers exhibit bizarre and irrational forms of behavior to-tally and deliberately inappropriate to the conventional operatic stage.

At one point, for example, one of the protagonists stands before the audience with his face hidden behind a phonograph disc, which he claws furiously with a nail. In another scene, a man covered with drums walks about the stage while other members of the cast play on him with mallets. Elsewhere, one singer accompanies himself by honking horns with both feet; another musician fires at a tam-tam with a slingshot; and dancers perform calisthenics to a solemn a cappella vocal accompaniment. These are only a few of the antics with which Kagel blasphemes, lightheartedly but earnestly, the hallowed European operatic tradition.

Pitch logic and **sound color** in *Staatstheater* appear to be byproducts of a theatrical conception; specific pitch and rhythmic sequences are some-times called for, but these appear in aleatoric scenarios and gamelike pro-cesses whose sonic result is unpredictable and of little significance by itself. What *is* significant in this work is the visual, aural, and kinetic totality, and its hysterical, often violent assault on our habits of perception. In fact, Kagel himself described his creation as a "negation" of opera and other forms of music theater.

Staatstheater is subtitled "a composition of scenes" and consists of a nonstop concatenation of vignettes, arranged in nine sections. The sum total of these—one hundred minutes altogether—has little or nothing to do with traditional "plot" or narrative logic. Although **process** (at least with regard to the manipulation of sonic materials) seems equally distant, indi-vidual sections do have a certain method to their madness. Four of them, for example, involve lengthy sequences of "individual actions," each de-lineated on a separate page of score. (The first section, "Repertoire," calls for a hundred of these.) Some actions involve freshly devised props, such as a tabletop with metal coils that rests on a hunched-over actor's back as he drags the coils across the stage. Other activities are carried out with everyday objects (furniture, kitchen utensils, etc.), directing a high level of theatrical and acoustic focus to the utterly mundane.

Throughout *Staatstheater,* **notation** is predictably unorthodox, replete with verbal instructions, choreographic diagrams, and unique musical symbols. The excerpt in Example 18.4 maps out a short scene in which a performer uses two hands to crinkle parchment paper stuffed under the front and back of his shirt. The absurdity of the activity in question stands in contrast to the meticulous control over **performance ritual** (such as stage position) and **time** (the rhythm of steps and paper noises), all of which are precisely notated.

EXAMPLE 18.4.

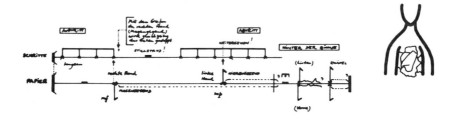

Mauricio Kagel: *Staatstheater*, "Repertoire"

© Copyright 1971 by Universal Edition (London) Ltd., London. All Rights Reserved. Used by permission of European American Music Distributors Corporation, sole U.S. and Canadian agent for Universal Edition London

Tom Johnson: Failing

Tom Johnson's *Failing* (1976), appropriately subtitled *A Very Difficult Piece for Doublebass*, typifies the composer's music in two ways. First, it engages the soloist in a gamelike **process**—in this instance, one that virtually guarantees failure, and leads inevitably, therefore, to an unpredictable outcome. Second, *Failing* entails a radical departure from conventional **performance ritual** by having the performer speak directly to the audience about the piece as it unfolds. In fact, the performer's ongoing description of the process in *Failing* is itself an integral part of that process.

Example 18.5 illustrates the work's underlying premise. In performance, the premise is articulated by the soloist's reading the text aloud while playing the notes written on the staff above the words. Johnson's **processes,** while not necessarily minimalist, resemble those of Reich and Glass in that they are always *audible*. His self-reflexive works are unique in that a composition, its performance instructions, *and* its program notes are identical.

EXAMPLE 18.5.

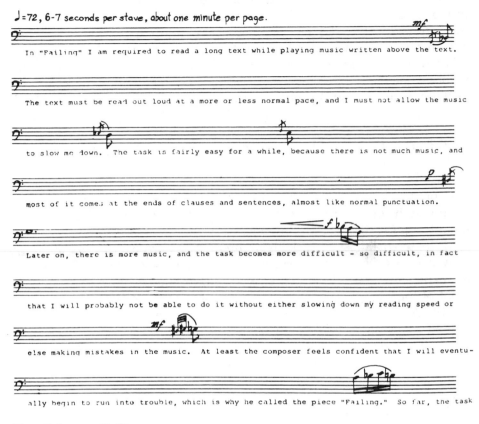

♩=72, 6-7 seconds per stave, about one minute per page.

In "Failing" I am required to read a long text while playing music written above the text.

The text must be read out loud at a more or less normal pace, and I must not allow the music

to slow me down. The task is fairly easy for a while, because there is not much music, and

most of it comes at the ends of clauses and sentences, almost like normal punctuation.

Later on, there is more music, and the task becomes more difficult - so difficult, in fact

that I will probably not be able to do it without either slowing down my reading speed or

else making mistakes in the music. At least the composer feels confident that I will eventu-

ally begin to run into trouble, which is why he called the piece "Failing." So far, the task

Tom Johnson: *Failing*

The composite **texture** becomes increasingly dense and more difficult to realize, until mistakes in either reading or playing (i.e., failure) become inevitable. The text provides continuous explanation and commentary on this activity; it also explores logistical and even ethical aspects of the growing performance dilemma. For example, the performer muses that no one in the audience can see the score, and in Hamlet fashion debates the consequences of "cheating"—all while playing virtuosic passagework on the bass.

Toward the end, as matters really begin to unravel, the player announces a new complication: although the notated music will go on, the written text is about to run out. Soon the soloist will be required to improvise a seamless continuation of the vocal monologue (while continuing to play music), further describing and commenting on his or her own activities. With no letup in the difficulty of the doublebass part, the uncertainties multiply and the piece ends in a state of crisis.

Though the composer notates specific pitches, rhythms, and other performance directions in detail, it is with the expectation that at some point the performance will deviate from the score in unpredictable ways depending on when and how the soloist "'fails." Like many of Tom Johnson's other works, *Failing* becomes a performance about the nature of performance—one that, in this instance, questions our conventional Western expectations of polish and predictability.

David Del Tredici: Final Alice

David Del Tredici made his first impact as a composer of highly chromatic, dissonant music. In a notable change, similar to that made by George Rochberg, he moved from his former stylistic position to a rediscovery of tonality—most significantly in an extended series of works, from 1968 to 1981, centered almost exclusively around Lewis Carroll's *Alice's Adventures in Wonderland*. One of the most controversial of these compositions—hailed by many and scorned by others as a brazen, counterrevolutionary endorsement of tonality and melodic simplicity—is *Final Alice* (1976).

Written for amplified soprano, orchestra, and a "folk group"(two saxophones, mandolin, banjo, and accordion), the work is structured somewhat like a one-act opera, with its primary text drawn from *Alice in Wonderland*'s last two chapters. Recitatives, based purely on Carroll's narrative, are taken mostly from the trial scene, while the five arias, using poems taken from or related to the *Alice* text, are presented as "evidence" to the court. Arias III–V actually have more to do with Alice Liddell, the real-life inspiration for Carroll's work. His deep affection for her is a subtext in *Alice in Wonderland*, and therefore in Del Tredici's music as well. Aria IV sets a popular nineteenth-century love poem, "Alice Gray," preceded in Aria III by an anonymous spoof on it from the same period. Finally, Aria V is an acrostic poem (the first letters of its lines spell Alice Liddell's full name) taken from Carroll's *Through the Looking Glass*.

Both Carroll's writing and Del Tredici's music draw life from the tension between simple, childlike innocence and the freakish world of dream and imagination. Often, **pitch logic** and **time** seem to be based on entirely traditional practice at first appearance, but then undergo a **compositional process** of layering and desynchronizing until individual lines and progressions become lost in a larger, more complex **texture.** This is what happens to the unaffected little tonal melody—an apparent **parody** of children's songs—that forms the central idea of the entire work. (Its major sixths dominate the music's fabric from the very beginning, even before the first vocal entrance.)

At the beginning of Aria I the little tune is presented with simple harmonic accompaniment in the accordion. (Example 18.6a shows the melodic line only.) Soon, however, it undergoes almost pathological distortions, as in Example 18.6b, where part of the melody is repeated incessantly ("But said But said But said" etc.). Within a few pages of score this repeated leap of a sixth has burgeoned, as though out of control, into a massive texture of leaping sixths involving the entire orchestra. Eventually (Example 18.6c, p. 384) the aria degenerates into pandemonium as the singer accelerates to a frantic pace while various sections of the orchestra try to accompany her, each with its own "incorrect" tempo, an ingenious gloss to the deformed logic of the sung verses.

Such ebullience and boisterous humor is typical of the entire hour-long work, which fluctuates continually between unadorned diatonic harmony and tonal chaos as chord sequences start out simply and then blur, collide, or unravel, either gradually or unexpectedly—all in keeping with the

EXAMPLE 18.6.

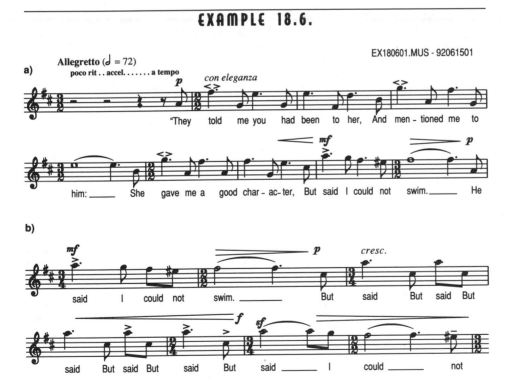

David Del Tredici: *Final Alice*, Aria I

sometimes charming, sometimes frightening, sometimes outrageous character of Carroll's words and pictures. The most poignant contrast of *Final Alice* comes in the last section, subtitled "Apotheosis." It begins with the Acrostic Song," a guileless melody of quarter notes and half notes, supported—at first—by an artlessly triadic accompaniment. At the song's end, the melody continues instrumentally, but its harmonic accompaniment gradually goes awry until the whole orchestra succumbs to a final moment of delirium. In a last gesture of Carroll-like whimsy, the composer leaves his personal stamp on the work by having the soprano count in Italian to thirteen ("tredici").

Paul Lansky: Six Fantasies on a Poem by Thomas Campion

Six Fantasies by Paul Lansky (b. 1944) is a landmark among works for computer-generated tape. Realized at Princeton University in 1978–79, it exploits digital *technology* to create an uncanny fusion of acoustic and electronic sound quite beyond anything heard before it. In creating the *Fantasies*, Lansky used a digital process for sound sampling and resynthesis known as "all-pole linear prediction." The voice of actress Hannah Mackay was digitally sampled as she read Campion's poem "Rose-cheek'd Laura, come." The samples were analyzed by a large mainframe computer and the results used to construct a program for generating and processing sound modeled on the behavior of her voice. When resynthesized, the voice gained all the virtuosity and versatility of the computer medium while retaining its human character and presence.

The six fantasies are entitled "her voice," "her presence," "her reflection," "her song," "her ritual," and "her self." Each is a unique musical reconstitution of the entire poem as read by Mackay. (Actually, the actress's rendition is heard unaltered in the sixth fantasy, but by then the inherently musical nature of her reading is fully apparent.) The poem itself is musical in more than just the acoustic sense, as the first few lines illustrate:

> "Rose-cheek'd Laura, come;
> *Sing thou smoothly with thy beauty's*
> *Silent music, either other*
> *Sweetly gracing.*
> *Lovely forms do flow*
> *From consent divinely framed:*
> *Heaven is music, and thy beauty's*
> *Birth is heavenly.*"

Except in the dissonant third and fifth movements, **pitch logic** is oriented toward a lush, often jazzlike tonality, a startling anomaly in the computer music repertoire. Lansky's treatment of **texture** and **sound color** is equally luxuriant, particularly in the first and fourth fantasies. While retaining a natural sense of diction, Mackay's words are multiplied and spun out into long, arching melodies and sumptuous, impressionistic chords that flow and shimmer with delicate shifts of timbre. **Time** is linked to the rhythms of speech, which are sometimes heard with little alteration, sometimes transformed into rather traditional rhythmic sequences, and sometimes stretched into slow, sustained passages.

In his program note, Lansky states that his aim was to transcend the distinction between speech and song. The *Six Fantasies*, however, go beyond this goal to bridge the gap between the human and artificial. The work provides a rare combination: creative imagination, an ear for sonorous beauty, and the cutting edge of technological innovation.

Laurie Anderson: "O Superman"

Although it eventually became a popular hit (number two on the British charts for over a year), Laurie Anderson's song "O Superman" (1981) was originally meant as a serious piece of experimental art and political commentary, in which a number of "characters" carry on a half-spoken, half-sung dialogue. As in Schubert's "Erlkönig," these characters are all represented by one voice. The text, which changes gradually from quirky humor to bleak cynicism, begins as a dialogue between the protagonist (Anderson herself?) and a phone-answering machine. A rather wistful plea recorded from "Mom"—"Hello, this is your mother; are you coming home?"—takes on an increasingly ominous tone: the recorded voice, somehow less innocent than before, now announces in matter-of-fact tones, "Here come the planes." The recorded message (is the voice still that of "Mom"?) has become a symbol for the military–industrial complex—mechanized, high-tech, and inhuman. Much of Anderson's art shares a fascination with the impersonal, disembodied voices of late twentieth-century culture: an airline pilot's voice from the flight deck, the digital voice in one's automobile ("your door is ajar"), and in "O Superman," the answering machine. Doomsday is announced in a recorded telephone message.

The song's approach to both **pitch logic** and **time** is minimalist with a steady ostinato pulse and repeated pitch drone continuing through the entire work. A digitized vowel "ah" (once more, the composer's voice) on middle C is looped to form an ostinato over which Anderson speaks or sings through a vocoder and a harmonizer. The digital **technology** allows her to modify her voice, at times splitting it into an electronic chorus of over- and under-tones. Her delivery remains coolly detached to the end, augmenting the sense of irony and alienation.

The harmonic world of "O Superman" consists of two electronically produced chords in continuous alternation: A♭ major and C minor, sharing the ostinato drone C. Beyond this surface repetition, however, there is almost constant change. First, although Anderson repeats the same melody over and over, she pauses freely within and between stanzas, so that the change between chords takes place at irregular intervals. Also, with each new stanza the accompanimental **texture** is subtly altered or expanded by added cross-rhythms, figuration in flute and synthesizer, timbral shifts in electronic processing of the voice, and, for the final stanza, a deep, resonant bassline. At the close, a saxophone-and-synthesizer motive takes over, gravitating inexorably to C minor. The work ends as it began, with the wordless vocal ostinato loop on the pitch C.

"O Superman" was meant to be experienced in either of two distinct **performance rituals:** as a record (consisting entirely of sound heard through speakers or headphones), or as a part of Anderson's two-day multimedia performance piece *United States* (premiered in 1983), a unique confluence of jazz, popular, and concert music that confirmed her prominence as a leader in experimental performance art.

Helmut Lachenmann: Mouvement (-vor der Erstarrung)

Helmut Lachenmann, born in Stuttgart in 1935 and trained in Venice under Luigi Nono, may be considered representative of a generation of European composers schooled in postwar serialism but concerned with other issues as well. The title of this 1984 work for chamber orchestra translates as "Movement (—before paralysis)." As that title suggests, the music is intended to convey meaninglessness and the numbing of one's perceptions and sensibilities in response to it. The instrumentation consists of five strings, seven winds, three percussion, and three "bell pianos" (each with a scale of electric bells). This ensemble is conceived as a machine—one that grinds on obliviously in a number of modes, described by the composer as "bowing," "fluttering," "throbbing," "rattling," and the like.

Ironically, this sense of empty activity is expressed through an astonishing display of **texture** and **sound color.** Except for the bell pianos and exotic array of percussion instruments, the instrumentation is traditional, but the sounds that issue forth thwart every expectation. Only a few pitches, chords, and rhythmic shapes are clearly audible; instead we hear whispers, rustles, whistles, clatters, and snaps, at times sparse and barely audible, at other times thickly layered in endless combinations.

For woodwind and brass players, unusual performance methods include slapping or rattling keys, blowing air (without pitch) through the instrument, and striking the mouthpiece or open bore with the palm. Percussionists are called upon to brush, scrape, and play on odd parts of their instruments. String players play on the bridge, tailpiece, fingerboard, and pegs (as well as strings) with a variety of minutely specified techniques. The graphic symbols and oddly shaped noteheads in Example 18.7 are typical of the nonstandard **notation** specially devised by the composer.

Performance ritual plays a large part in the work's hypnotic effect. Although the circumstances of performance—orchestral instruments in a conventional concert hall—seem ordinary at the outset, the actual performance—the timbres, textures, "choreography" of nonstandard performance techniques, and theatrical gestures—is foreign to our expectation. Lachenmann thus engineers an aural-visual paradox meant to jolt us to new levels of perception.

Henry Brant: Bran(d)t aan de Amstel

Because of his unique concerns with performance space, Henry Brant has created a number of works for specific physical locations (many of which do not lend themselves to duplication elsewhere). *Bran(d)t aan de Amstel* is one such piece, designed for the city of Amsterdam.

This four-hour extravaganza received its first, and perhaps only, performance on a day in June 1984. Given the unique circumstances of its execution, it could be considered an "installation," covering virtually an entire city. For *Bran(d)t aan de Amstel*, Henry Brant drew upon the resources of Amsterdam—in particular, its canals, bridges, and venerable churches (and perhaps the remarkable good nature and musical sophistication of its citizens as well). Four canal boats, each filled with twenty-five flutists and one percussionist, wended their way through the city along the river Amstel and adjoining canals. (With *d* added to the composer's name, the work's title translates from the Dutch as "Fire on the Amstel.")

As they played, the floating ensembles followed each other along a

---

EXAMPLE 18.7.

Helmut Lachenmann: *Mouvement (—vor der Erstarrung)*

© 1984 by Breitkopf & Härtel, Wiesbaden. Used by permission

ILLUS. 18.1.

Henry Brant conducting a boatload of flutists while
traveling down one of the Amsterdam canals

Photo: Pieter Boersma. Courtesy of De Ijsbreker,
Amsterdam

carefully predesignated route that passed bridges, churches, and other city
landmarks. Various ground-based participants were stationed at check-
points along the way—for example, a brass band at a bridge, ready to
perform as the boats passed underneath. These ground-based forces included three choruses, three wind bands, four hand organs and four carillonneurs in the bell tower of Amsterdam's famous Oude Kerke (Old
Church).

Brant had to consider problems of **performance ritual** and space never
found in the concert hall: the coordination of moving and stationary elements, the acoustics of city streets and neighborhoods, and the effect of
traffic and crowd noise on the ever-changing sonic mix. (A novel, and
perhaps unforeseen, aspect of the watery processional of musicians along
the canal route: other boats—pleasure boats, sightseeing boats, and the like,
unrelated to the musical plan—decided to join the parade.) For listeners,

the very scope of *Bran(d)t aan de Amstel* suggested many possible ways of experiencing it. Some city inhabitants were caught up involuntarily in fragments of the piece while going about their business. Others, who knew of the event, congregated at locations of their choice, generating a festive ambience as they waited for the boats to pass. Still others decided to follow the route, rushing from one checkpoint to another by tram, by taxi, or on foot.

Naturally, elements of **texture**—what portion or portions one heard, and from what blend of moving and fixed sources—also depended on the neighborhood or street corner one chose as a listening venue. At all times, though, Brant's skill in keeping various instrumental strata clearly etched and distinct from one another was obvious (an aspect of his great knowledge of instrumentation and **sound color**). Also important was the use of **parody** and quotation. Each choir performed its own set of American *Sacred Harp* fuguing tunes, each band had its own repertoire of Dutch marches, each hand organ cranked out its own assortment of nineteenth-century Dutch popular songs, and the carillonneurs played elaborate, Baroque-style variations on Dutch chorales. The floating flute ensembles played music composed entirely by Brant, but even these were based (though obscurely) on Dutch folk melodies. Although individual ensembles were coordinated, their overlapping juxtapositions were largely unsynchronized—an approach to **time** that, paradoxically, combines an Ivesian multiplicity and freedom (in moment-by-moment relationships) with carefully planned structuring of the event's large-scale duration.

The high point to all this was a "coda" employing all the boat groups and land ensembles (except the bell ringers), everyone having converged on a single location. Together with the din of excited crowds and auto horns, the result was a final, climactic collage—a modern-day synthesis of Handel's *Water Music* and Ives's "Putnam's Camp." All told, *Bran(d)t aan de Amstel* can best be described as music theater on a massive scale, a kind of multimedia urban carnival, seeming to unfold spontaneously but actually crafted and manipulated by a single creative artist.

PART IV

Issues and Directions

Notation, Improvisation, and Composition

In each of the following three chapters, we summarize our study of post–1945 music from a unique vantage point: national concerns, for example (Chapter 20), or recent developments within specific genres (Chapter 21).

The present chapter is devoted primarily to the various roles **notation** has played in the music of the second half of the twentieth century. It considers as well the changes that have taken place in the relationship between composition and improvisation since 1945.

Common parlance overstates the case when it equates the written score with the music it represents (as in "Where did I leave my music?"). Notation more properly considered, is a medium that facilitates the passage of music from the composer's imagination to physical reality. As a mode of communication distinct from sounding music, notation has assumed a variety of forms, reflecting the changing needs and purposes of those who write it and read it. Let us consider a number of these needs and functions, with special reference to music of our own century.

FUNCTIONS OF NOTATION

Communication with Performers

Whatever an individual composer's aesthetic philosophy, it must be communicated to performing musicians in order to be realized. Similarly, the unique physical and technical demands of a piece, or its expressive nuances, must be made clear to those who attempt to articulate them. One important function of notation, then, consists of *providing instructions to players.*

This may go well beyond simply telling interpreters "what to do." To perform the music of India or China, other considerations may be of far greater importance: for example, "how to think," or "which materials to use." In these societies, notation may provide an elemental framework upon which one improvises, or a detailed essay—similar to a poem or a philosophical treatise—to be studied in advance of a performance and that does not refer to specific sounds. Aspects of playing rarely accounted for within the Western tradition (subtleties of moving from one pitch to another or timbral changes affecting a sustained tone) may be the object of close notational focus, because they are more central to the musical language. In each case, though, notation reflects priorities and hierarchies.

Western concert music, particularly that of the Baroque through the Romantic eras, can be defined by *its* priorities: the subdivision of the octave into twelve equally tempered pitches, periodic rhythm (not only regular beats, but their geometric subdivisions), tight ensemble coordination among parts, and "formal" narrative moving in a single direction. In many respects, Western notation is ideal for stating these traditional values. It provides a visual, symbolic "picture" of sounds, to be read by performers as the music passes by (a feature not always found in other cultures) within the context of a known tradition.

In many ways, it resembles the Western "notation" of *speech.* In both notation and speech visual symbols represent individual sounds (phonemes), which are combined to create complex continuities.

During the late twentieth century, as we have seen, the language of Western music has undergone great changes. Increasing importance has been given to factors other than the mainstream of melody, harmony, rhythm, and meter; for some composers, the hierarchy of values has been rearranged so that the greatest attention is focused on density, articulation, register, dynamics, irrational beat placement, timbral gradations, or flexible options for continuity. Changes in notation have evolved to meet these new demands. The notation still tells performers "what to do," but reflects a shift in creative priorities and hierarchies.

What, then, does the notation specify? The answer to that question usually indicates what the composer chooses to "control." For example, Robert Ashley's *In Memoriam Crazy Horse* for large instrumental ensemble establishes a steady continuity—an overall **texture**—within which such parameters as timbre and register change. As seen in Example 19.1, pitches are not specified, nor are the textural possibilities controlled (or even suggested) in the notation. Change itself is uppermost in the composer's scheme, and this factor—dictated by passage from one quadrant to another—is controlled with precision and clarity. Each subdivision of the large ensemble (at least four players performing from a page similar to Example 19.1) creates a group sonority, which then undergoes gradual changes—of timbre, pitch, inflection, dynamics, and the like—as the players move through the quadrants of their individual circles.

In contrast with Ashley, however, Ben Johnston is quite concerned about pitch distinctions, to the point of notating intonation much more precisely than conventional notation allows. In his 1979 Duo for Two Violins (Example 19.2) Johnston indicates degrees of microtonal inflection with newly created accidentals, such as ↑, $\uparrow^{13}$, and ^{7} .

William Duckworth (b. 1943) uses **pitch logic** in an entirely different manner for his 1969 *Pitch City* (Example 19.3). In this work for any four wind instruments, he specifies pitch and note-to-note successions, but not register, rhythm, duration, instrumental timbre, or the precise synchronization of parts. Duckworth chooses to control mood, overall gesture, and large-scale continuity, however, by (1) insisting on quiet dynamics, (2) emphasizing sustained notes that last a full breath, and (3) requiring each of the four performers to follow a path from one of the corner F#'s (concert pitch) to the F# at the center. The result is a curiously "tonal" performance. In this example as in the others, then, the score, by communicating certain aspects of the performance to the players more specifically than others, reveals information about the aims of the composition. The composer may also wish to engender a certain quality of **performance ritual:** scientific precision, manic, volatile activity, or meditative stasis. Each of these might each call for a different set of notational conventions.

Communication with the Musical World at Large

One could communicate with performers solely by providing them with written instructions, verbal or symbolic, for physical action to be carried out on an instrument—that is, with a tablature. Though tablatures can offer admirable precision, they are by nature tailored to specific instruments,

EXAMPLE 19.1.

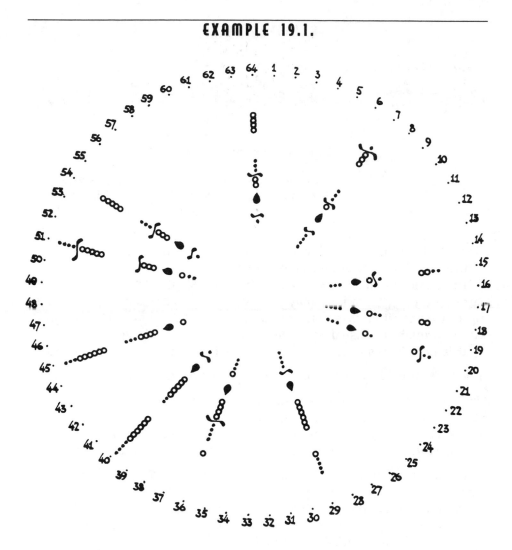

Robert Ashley: *In Memoriam Crazy Horse*

such as the guitar or lute, and thus may be nearly indecipherable for players of other instruments. The value of such a notation for musicians in general, and for posterity, would be diminished. To the degree that notation is "general" rather than physical action–specific, it provides a permanent record of musical experience (or at least those aspects that define "the work") for other composers, other performers, scholars, and future gener-

EXAMPLE 19.2.

Ben Johnston: Duo for Two Violins (first violin part)

ations. Notation thus can play an important role in the preservation of the culture—it allows communication with the future, in effect.

In certain Asian societies, where much music is either improvised or learned by rote, "notation" may consist of poetic essays on the materials appropriate to ritual occasions. In the European tradition, communication occurs through the visual, symbolic depiction of sound events.

It is not always necessary for the visual images to present the music directly; that is, ♩ *mf* does not *look* any louder or longer in duration than ♪ *mp*. The distinction is one of symbols; to interpret the difference between the two notes, one must learn a special code. By contrast, many examples of twentieth century notation attempt a direct "pictorialization" through vivid gestural graphics, proportional time schemes, and the like. The musical "meaning" of ⸙, when compared with ⸙, should be apparent to virtually everyone.

Paradoxically, much late twentieth-century music has become increasingly difficult to read from a score—that is, to hear internally from a visual study of its written symbols—for one of two reasons. First, music for unusual instruments, such as John Cage's prepared piano, may be notated with familiar symbols, which act as a sort of tablature telling the performer "which notes to play when," but giving no indication of the actual *timbres* and *pitches* that constitute the sounding music. Second, the notation of works involving chance, multimedia, or heightened performance ritual may present optional choices or control physical action only, rather than dictate fixed results. For instance, the score for Pauline Oliveros's *Sonic Meditations* offers, rather than pitches or rhythms, verbal scenarios for audience vocal participation. Robert Moran (b. 1937) uses graphics to notate his *Titus I* (1969), in which an ensemble performs on an automobile by striking it with hammers. Moran's diagrammatic scheme, again, functions as a tablature, specifying the locations on the car to be played (rather than the sounds they

EXAMPLE 19.3.

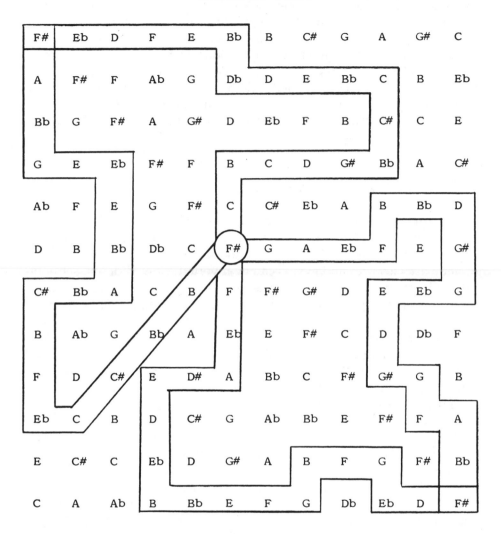

William Duckworth: *Pitch City*

make, along with melodramatic light effects and the choice of background tape to sound distantly throughout (a Wagnerian operatic excerpt).

Composers of the late twentieth century, then, have to face a problem unknown to earlier generations: choosing a notation. For a composer today, faced with so many aesthetic and stylistic options, notating the work is an integral aspect of the creative act. Lukas Foss writes, "Notation has to be re-invented with almost every new sound and new rhythm. I often notate my works three or four times before publication." The aim is for *precision*, whether in specifying pitches and durations or forming a list of boundaries and options for translating chance operations and improvisatory choices into sound. To quote Foss once again: "We must find the grammar, the vocabulary and the notation to make all the right possibilities available and rule out all the wrong ones. . . . My job is to notate as precisely as possible so that, if [the performer] carries out my instructions, the piece will *somehow happen of its own accord*."

An Essential Tool for Composing

Notation allows the creator to suspend time, to examine and manipulate materials, to discover or encourage relationships among materials, to compare passages with one another, to imagine sounds or relationships that do not yet exist. Gestures and events can be inverted, slowed down, set polyphonically against one another; effects can be calculated in advance, broken down to their most minute details, revised if necessary, and ultimately confirmed.

This particular aspect of notation, directed inwardly (to one's own "workshop") rather than outwardly (to a performer or scholar), need not depend on visual symbols. Its function can be accomplished by the manipulation of magnetic tape or a computer program. We can freeze time and musical gesture directly on tape, run them backward, splice and edit, or overlay detailed levels to build new textures and sonorities.

From the composer's point of view, then, notation provides one more important form of communication: *communication with oneself*. It permits an ongoing internal dialogue between the composer and the work, and also between the composer and a level of deep consciousness activated only when he or she is in the creative mode. For some composers, creative decisions are motivated by notation, that is, by relationships constructed directly on the page, rather than by sounding events imagined in the mind's ear. Other composers might regard such manipulation as excessively cerebral. But even they are likely to find that the sonic gestures they imagine or improvise are couched in *notational terms*—to the same degree that, in our everyday lives, we find it difficult to imagine objects, actions, or feelings for which we don't have *words*.

Finally, the activity of notating music can also be considered a mode of *performing*. The "performance" takes place on two levels of time: the actual duration—weeks, months, perhaps years—it takes one to produce a finished piece, and the "time" within the music. Musicians who have worked in electronic studios are familiar with the concept of "real time" performance. Those who notate music, whether with paper and pencil or by means of newer technology, often find themselves performing in "frozen time." This is one area where the worlds of *composing* and *improvising*—to be discussed later in this chapter—may meet.

A Visually Stimulating Object

A part from its function of conveying information about sounding music, notation may be an aesthetically moving object in its own right. In fact, scores by Cage, Crumb, Sylvano Bussotti, Cornelius Cardew, Earle Brown, and Stuart Saunders Smith have been exhibited as works of visual art.

Such notation may not only instruct but also excite the performer's imagination in unpredictable directions. Example 19.4 is a fragment from a 1959 solo piano work by Sylvano Bussotti (b. 1931), the *Five Pieces for David Tudor*. Many pianists may be overwhelmed by its commanding use of graphics; others may use the images as springboards for free improvisation. Bussotti's written symbols are only tenuously related to sound events or to piano performance. But the score is convincing on the level of sheer visual fantasy. By drawing upon traditional symbols and yet distorting them, the music is equally stimulating to the performing pianist *and* to anyone else viewing the score—and, paradoxically, in much the same ways.

The concept of musical score as visual artwork reverses the long-standing relationship of these two arts. In the nineteenth century many painters aspired to the condition of music (as the most romantic of the arts). Early twentieth-century artists found themselves equally fascinated by music, although for different reasons. Paul Klee and Wassily Kandinsky were inspired by musical subjects, Pablo Picasso and the cubists by musical instruments; abstract artists were drawn to the supposed clarity and non-representational state that they perceived in music. In the decades since 1945 the relationship between music and art has remained close. The composer Paul Paccione has noted striking similarities between certain visual styles and musical notations—especially the early graphic scores of Morton Feldman and Earle Brown as they echo the "gridwork" paintings of Piet Mondrian, Sol LeWitt, Josef Albers and Barnett Newman, or the grid "boxes" of the sculptor Louise Nevelson.

Other parallels between the musical and visual may come to mind: the love of palindromic symmetry in Webern and Messiaen, oddly paralleling that of many op and pop artists (Bridget Riley, Andy Warhol, Robert Indiana), and the relationship of steady-state dynamics—whether the understated quality of Feldman's constant *pianissimo* or Philip Glass's amplified *forte*—with the "color field" paintings of Mark Rothko. These connections are not necessarily revealed by the appearance of the musical scores. On the

EXAMPLE 19.4.

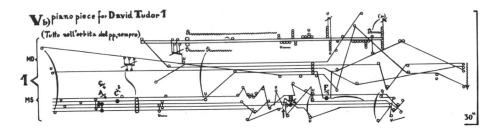

Silvano Bussotti: *Five Pieces for David Tudor*, No. 1, top system

EXAMPLE 19.5.

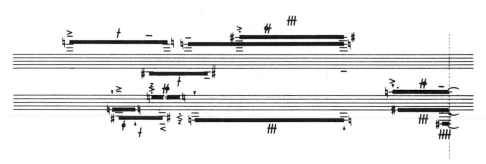

Earle Brown: *Twenty-Five Pages*

other hand, Earle Browne's indebtedness to Alexander Calder's mobiles is readily apparent to both the eye and ear.

Brown's *Twenty-Five Pages* (Example 19.5), like his *Available Forms* series, takes a "mobile" approach to continuity: it can be played by any number pianists from one to twenty-five, reading the pages in any order, either right side up or upside down.

Similarly, the spontaneous notations—impulsive, eruptive, and immediate—that dominate certain Cage, Brown, or Bussotti scores are reminiscent of Jackson Pollock's method of painting by placing his canvases on the floor and dripping (or casting, flinging, or pouring) paints on them, or the works by Yves Klein produced by having paint-covered models rolling about on the canvas. These and other 1950s experiments in "action painting" were, paradoxically, motivated in part by an attempt to bring the immediacy of real-time *performance* to the visual arts—moving (as were the Cage works of the same period) in the direction of theater.

The influence of a different "performance" art—*literature,* which forces one's eye to move about the printed page—can be seen in the early post-Darmstadt works of Pierre Boulez. The arrangement of "alternate routes" on the score of the Third Piano Sonata evokes the visual layout of Mallarme's poetry, pages of e.e. cummings, or the narrative discontinuities of Joyce. The sonata's score also resembles a road map, which is in its own way a kind of score (for "performance" by an automobile driver). In Malcolm Goldstein's *The Seasons: Vermont/Spring* a Vermont state map fragment actually does function as score. The score of Guiseppe Englert's 1965 *Aria* for timpani ensemble allows the performer to map out a route directly on the surface of the instrument, indicating, among other factors, the location on the drumhead for the articulation of individual passages and gestures.

A Reflection of Extended Performance/Timbres

Some of the most fanciful visual images in post-1945 scores are related to extended performance techniques for which there are no traditional symbols. Penderecki's *Threnody for the Victims of Hiroshima* (discussed in Chapter 12), calls for a variety of special playing techniques, each with its own written symbol, including playing between the bridge and tailpiece (↑), arpeggio on four strings behind the bridge (⁞⁞⁞), playing on the bridge (↑), and playing on the tailpiece (⌐). Other works asks for woodwind multiphonics, key slaps, and the like. Compositions for percussion may call for especially elaborate notation, since the composer may not only indicate a potentially vast array of sounding objects—and an assortment of staves, lines, and special symbols to represent them—but also specify (as Luciano Berio does for *Circles*) the exact physical placement of instruments.

New instruments, or familiar objects put to new musical uses, often suggest innovative symbols. Example 19.6 shows the shortwave radio part for Stuart Saunders Smith's *Here and There.* Performing this part requires the manipulating of dials and switches, changing settings, and adjusting volume controls. Starting at any corner, the performer reads the boxes in a

EXAMPLE 19.6.

Stuart Saunders Smith: *Here and There*, shortwave radio part

consistent directional way. The symbol ⟋⟍ is of special interest, since it specifies sounds appropriate to the radio medium (news, talk, or music).

Even multimedia installations may have a notated score. Any project that involves set construction, such as the placement of objects or electrical wiring, probably entails written instructions, detailing one aspect of performance: the steps necessary to create the physical installation itself. The second and more public "performance" may involve a written document as well. The notated directions for someone about to "perform" Max Neuhaus's *Drive-In Music* (see Chapter 15) are basically a set of driving instructions, complete with a schematic road map.

An Instrument of Control

The postwar split between proponents of "order" and of "'chaos" (see Chapter 7) was reflected in their approaches to notation. Composers who sought maximum control naturally favored notations designed to specify every conceivable nuance of performance; composers willing to relinquish degrees of compositional control extended decision-making powers—in varying degrees—to performers. On a different level, composers have chosen to control certain parameters of musical discourse (pitch, or rhythm) but not others. The question of control also may be considered in human terms: the degree to which one person inhibits or restricts the free will of another. (In this context, notation could be regarded as a weapon of political power, and musical performance as a political enactment; much of Cage's music is in fact motivated by this belief.)

Let us assume that the degree of control exerted by the composer over the performer (and perhaps over the listener as well) is politically benign. Even so, the issue of relative control—articulated by notation—is pertinent, especially in the open-ended artistic climate of the late twentieth century. For serial composers, music's subject matter—its content—is its network of carefully predetermined relationships. (In Charles Wuorinen's view, "composing is notating.") Consequently, every parameter is accounted for in the score, leaving no area of performer choice (or "expression"). For example, the Swedish composer Bo Nilsson (b. 1937) has carefully calibrated twenty different dynamic levels, from *pppp* to *ffff*, in his *Frequenzen* (1955–56) for mixed septet; each note requires a separate dynamic marking.

The performer who attempts such music may strive for a machinelike precision, realizing every one of the work's exact notational criteria. Ideally, then, each realization would be identical to all others, perhaps with a steely, hard-edged effect curiously similar to that of Conlon Nancarrow's player piano studies. Another, entirely different approach to supercomplex notation might, rather than suppress the human factor, exaggerate the idiosyncratic, even passionate aspects of music making, dramatizing the confrontation with near-impossible challenges and the prospect of failure. The music of Brian Ferneyhough suggests the latter approach; whereas a page of Babbitt may reflect a heightened sense of order and inspire a securely controlled performance, the score of Ferneyhough's Second String Quartet (Example 19.7) seems designed to test one's limits, challenging the player to skirt the borders of the uncontrollable. The music's ferocious intensity encourages a similar stretch on the performer's part. Although the score may seem overwhelming in its many minute measurements and relationships, the aural result is one of sweeping urgent, romantic, expressivity.

Few composers notate their work with Ferneyhough's extraordinary degree of detail. Far more common are notational formats that loosen the restraints on the performer, granting *limited freedom* through deliberate ambiguity and suggestions for alternative realizations. The works by Boulez, Stockhausen, and Brown discussed in Chapter 7 offer excellent examples of limited freedom with regard to *form*. Although moment-to-moment details of pitch, duration, dynamic level, and articulation are specified, the notation permits the performer to make decisions regarding *continuity* in each performance—indeed, it demands those decisions. *Rhythm and meter* are similarly made ambiguous by Earle Brown's use of proportional duration, which by treating horizontal movement along the

---

EXAMPLE 19.7.

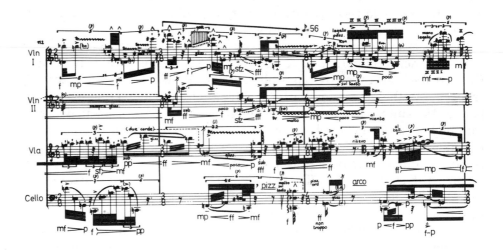

Brian Ferneyhough: String Quartet No.2

staff as an analogue of clock time (since each system represents the same agreed-upon time span) avoids reliance on a fixed pulse or referential beat. Similarly, *pitch* may be notated with relative specificity: register only (as in Morton Feldman's 1950–1951 *Projection* series), wide cluster bands to represent sound masses (Penderecki's *Threnody* or Ligeti's *Volumina*), melodic contours minus their noteheads , and a group of noteheads arranged in random ordering .

All of these notations, since they reflect a work's stylistic priorities, influence the psychological attitude that a performer brings to the music. A notational style inevitably sends a message, in essence, defining the performer's "job." Here are three such messages: (1) *You must articulate numerical truths with great precision;* (2) *You must make it clear that you are wrestling with overwhelming difficulties.* (3) *You are to project a spirit of carefree, improvisatory fluidity.* Perhaps this larger message, whatever it may be, supersedes individual symbols and their meanings. Though the two versions of Example 19.8 indicate essentially the same pitches and durations, each version would project a different intensity and value in performance.

Another area of limited freedom is that of *ensemble synchronization.* Certain notational devices allow individual parts to "speak" simultaneously, yet relatively free of rhythmic interdependence. In Example 19.9 from George Crumb's *Eleven Echoes of Autumn* (1966), two instrumental cadenzas (first violin and then clarinet) are presented in succession. Each is carefully detailed in pitch and in subtle nuances of rhythm and dynamics;

EXAMPLE 19.8.

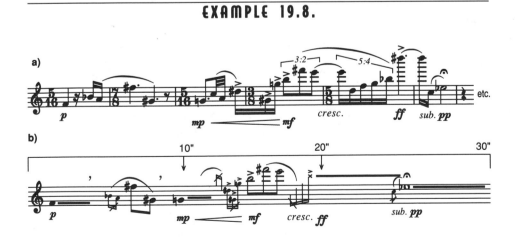

A melodic line notated in two ways

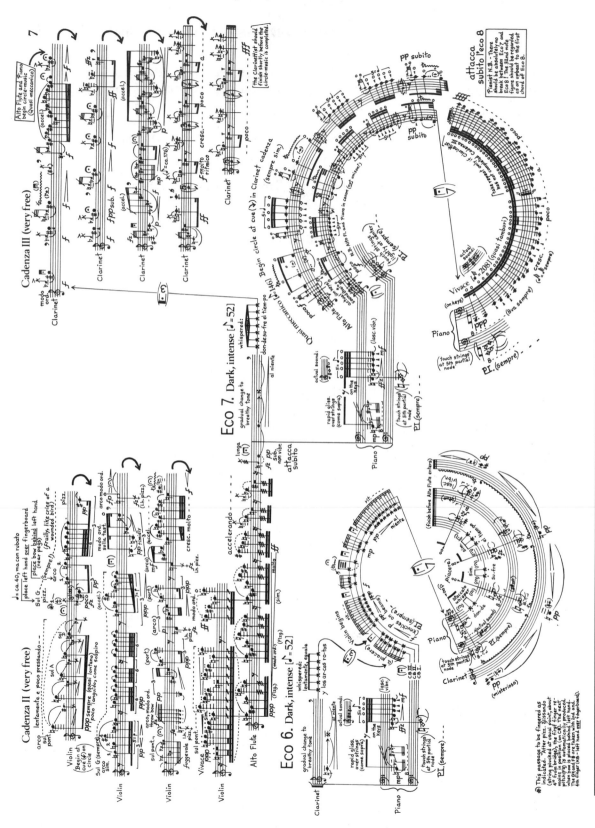

EXAMPLE 19.9. George Crumb: *Eleven Echoes of Autumn,* Echoes 6 and 7 © Copyright 1972 by C. F. Peters Corporation. Used by permission.

on the other hand, each cadenza is metrically free, unsynchronized with other parts. The accompaniment for each is notated in a circular format. This visual separation of polyphonic levels, which may recall the notation of Renaissance choral music, makes it clear that solo and accompaniment are *not* to be concerned about "lining up." The alto flute line begins as a series of gestures synchronized with the violin, then emerges from the violin cadenza to subside on a mysterious vocal whisper. During the clarinet cadenza, the alto flute synchronizes with the piano but not with the clarinet. The music evokes a spacious, timeless quality, unrestrained by adherence to a beat. Yet the notation is not all that free; instrumental entrances and exits are carefully cued and controlled.

A closed box containing individual note heads or brief gestures often functions as a fixed boundary within which improvisation or some other performance variable takes place. One such box is shown in Example 19.10; from Alvin Curran's *Home-Made* for soprano, flute, doublebass, and percussion; its length represents relative duration along a predetermined time line.

In Example 19.11, a page of his *Chamber Concerto II* (1977) for clarinet and mixed ensemble, Elliott Schwartz visually separates the two levels of an eclectic musical gesture. The rather tonal-sounding passage in traditional metric notation at the top of the page is performed simultaneously

EXAMPLE 19.10.

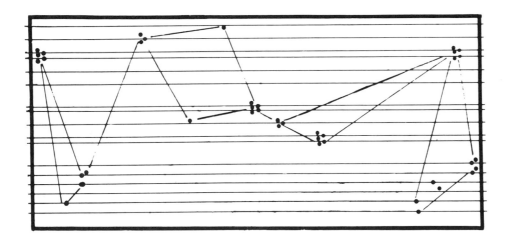

Alvin Curran: *Home-Made*

Reprinted from *SOURCE: Music of the Avant Garde* 1, no. 2 (1967). Used by permission of Composer/Performer Edition, Denton, Texas

EXAMPLE 19.11.

Duration of this page = 30 seconds

(through 7:15)

Other players: Each instrument plays the figure given below, in numbered sequence, as on page 11. After entering, repeat figure one or two times *ad libitum*, always *ppp*!

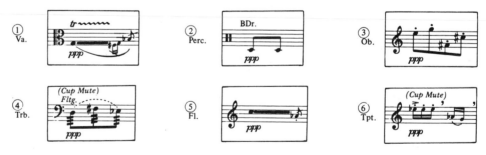

Cb. and Tuba silent for this page.

Elliott Schwartz: *Chamber Concerto II*

with the unsynchronized layered material below, the latter placed in boxes with instructions.

Eclecticism also dominates Example 19.12, from David Bedford's (1970) *Music for Albion Moonlight* for soprano and small ensemble. Proportional notation is combined with a line of clearly coordinated conductor down-beats (vertical arrows); similarly, indeterminate keyboard cluster and vocal cries are interspersed with traditional staff notation of pitch. (Note the vocal glissando carefully notated for a specified number of seconds.) At the opposite extreme—appropriately enclosed in a box—Bedford asks his players to improvise in response to the stimulus of a word ("Sklitter").

The examples noted thus far are still relatively controlled. Other works offer even *greater freedom:* in Earle Brown's *Available Forms* (see Chapter 7) many parameters—synchronization, texture, rhythm, pitch, and continuity—are decided on by the conductor and players. These options may be broadened when the notation is primarily "graphic," as in *Mobile for Shakespeare* (1960) by the Polish composer Roman Haubenstock-Ramati (b. 1919). The complete piece (scored for voice, keyboard instruments, and percussion) is contained on a single sheet, offering a variety of sound events (most of them notated with fanciful and ambiguous graphic symbols) and many possible paths for connecting them.

Similarly, the well-known *Aria* (1958) of John Cage contains no specific

EXAMPLE 19.12.

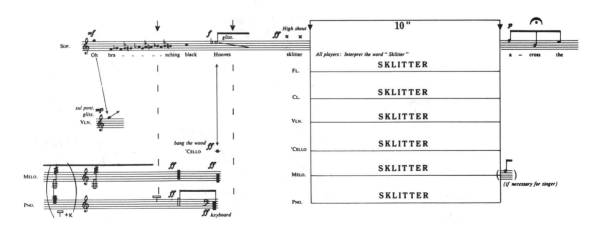

David Bedford: *Music for Albion Moonlight*

pitches, although each vocal phrase is notated as a general contour. (Five such contours are shown in Example 19.13.) A general melodic contour of this sort functions as an "ideogram," visualizing an entire concept rather than an "alphabetic" construction of component parts—that is, 🙂 rather than *F, A, C, E.* He therefore forfeits the opportunity to recombine and develop internal details (*FA, ACE, CAF*) in the grand tradition of Western art music. In another way, though, Cage's written instructions are quite specific: he uses *colors* throughout the printed score to denote a change in singing style, and has even suggested (but does not specify) some stylistic possibilities: blue for jazz, green for folk, brown for nasal, and so on.

A number of works by Cornelius Cardew use graphic designs to represent unusual combinations of freedom and control. Cardew's 1961 *Octet for Jasper Johns* consists of sixty symbols, each using familiar tokens—clefs, staff, pitches, numbers—placed in novel contexts. Each of the symbols represents a phrase, or even a complex passage, and each must be played in fixed sequence. A challenge for performers, apart from realizing the individual symbols musically, is to link them together to create a narrative thread. For instance, symbol 34, shown in Example 19.14, could be interpreted by playing all pitches as rapid four-note patterns, or by repeating whatever one had played in number 33 four more times, while incorpo-

---

EXAMPLE 19.13.

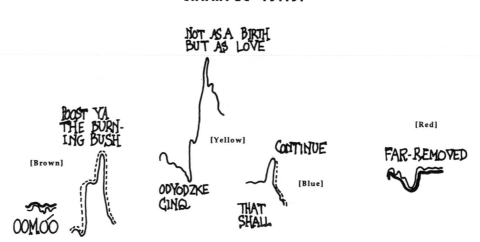

John Cage: *Aria*

EXAMPLE 19.14.

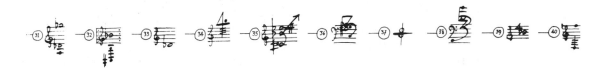

Cornelius Cardew: *Octet for Jasper Johns*

Copyright © 1962 by Hinrichsen Edition Ltd., London.
Used by permission of C. F. Peters Corporation

rating a high B tremolo as well. The assertive arrow in symbol 35 represents an unusual action performed only once in the piece, making a formal demarkation: Cardew suggests that listeners will probably recall the *Octet* as a piece where something surprising happened in the middle.

A similar concern for musical continuity, determined by visually ambiguous graphics, underlies Cardew's 1967 *Treatise* for an ensemble of any number of musicians. In *Treatise*'s 193 pages one finds many overwhelming, assertive, often brilliant graphic symbols. Although relatively few refer to specific musical gestures, all suggest vivid musical interpretations. Highly ambiguous, they force the performer to make choices. Such notation may suggest spontaneous improvisation, but, paradoxically, Cardew does not want his scores to motivate instant, reactive playing. Although he wants musicians to enjoy a strong sense of freedom, he wants them to base it on the implications of his notation—even to the point of writing out parts of their own. In this case, the notation is a riddle, a problem to be solved; the player's freedom lies in choosing from a multiplicity of solutions.

IMPROVISATION

For many improvising musicians, the *immediacy* of the performance experience is most important. Because improvisation is '"real-time creation," performers don't have the luxury of examining materials, editing their takes, or considering multiple possibilities. Their decisions are made while the music is in progress and *before an audience*. Guiding that decision making for most improvising musicians is a built-in stylistic compass: their familiarity with a commonly accepted "language." To a great degree, when, their improvisation is *controlled* by the comforting limitations of a style's boundaries. Jazz performers, Baroque continuo players, sitarists performing ragas, and soloists playing concerto cadenzas all benefit from this sense of context, tradition, and relative control. In fact, when we consider historical precedents and non-Western practices, controlled improvisation has been much more prevalent than the score-is-gospel approach of relatively recent Western art music.

With indeterminate and aleatory musics, however, the known contexts, precedents, and traditional languages of improvisation are largely missing. The emphasis on unpredictability—the absence of a ground plan—challenges the musician's resourcefulness and daring. Like other improvisers, one has to meet changing situations in full view of an audience, making decisions on the spot, revising goals, and putting accidents to creative use. But this activity is guided only by a bare dramatic premise, or perhaps has no guide at all—that is, no way to anticipate what the music will sound like. A high premium, therefore, is placed on risk taking.

All of these factors are multiplied when indeterminacy extends into *ensemble* genres. The addition of whims and wills—and accidents—other than one's own compounds the unpredictability that makes improvisation so attractive to begin with. Improvisation among friends and colleagues also heightens the traditional, chamber-music sense of performance as a form of social interaction. And while group improvisation certainly introduces new "dangers," it paradoxically also increases the margin of safety.

Just as improvisation as "real-time creativity" raises questions about the nature of composition, group improvisation as *collective* creativity encourages us to redefine the role of composer. The best of the new-music improvisation ensembles have certainly produced performances—many of them recorded—that can hold their own with the most inventive works of individual composers.

Not surprisingly, quite a few of these same ensembles have included important composers as performer-members. A brief list of those composers would include Cornelius Cardew, Frederic Rzewski, Alvin Curran, Jean-Charles François, John Silber, Lukas Foss, Larry Austin, Stanley Lunetta, Gordon Mumma, Alvin Lucier, Robert Ashley, and David Behrman. Many of these composers have brought their experiences in group improvisation to bear on their notated music. *Time Cycle* grew out of Lukas Foss's work with his improvisation ensemble at UCLA, and music by Cardew and Rzewski had similar origins in the Scratch Orchestra and Musica Elettronica Viva, respectively. The risk-taking aspects of improvisation have been translated into notated music; compositions that stress factors beyond the performer's control include Larry Austin's *Accidents* and Tom Johnson's *Risks*.

COMPOSITION

What, then, is the difference between *improvisation* and *composition?* The answer is not as simple as one might expect. *Notation* provides one clue. Notated music is composed in "frozen" time rather than "real" time. To reverse an earlier image, composition could be regarded as "slow-motion improvisation." Notation is the ingredient that allows the deliberate suspension of time.

Certain composers are especially adept at creating notated ensemble works that call upon the best instincts, reflexes, and sensibilities of group improvisation. Christian Wolff often sets up situations that coordinate subtle relationships and responses among the players. These relationships and responses become the subject of improvisatory game playing, intentionally designed to create unpredictable outcomes. In John Cage's words, each performer in a Wolff composition is like a "traveler constantly catching trains. He must be continually ready to go, alert to the situation, and responsible."

Wolff's *Duet* II for Horn and Piano consists of six sections, which may be performed in any order. Noteheads indicate duration: black notes are short, clear squares long, and clear circles variable. Lines joining two parts

EXAMPLE 19.15.

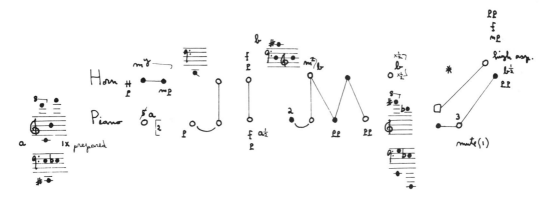

Christian Wolff: *Duet* II for Horn and Piano

reflect the nature of the ensemble relationship: simultaneous coordination, immediate response/reaction, or delayed response.

With knowledge of the performance instructions, we can begin to reconstruct the passage excerpted in Example 19.15. The pianist performs five notes from pitch source "a" (two of them simultaneously) in an irregular rhythm, indicated by the slash through the number 5. Meanwhile, since the players may begin together, it is likely that the horn player, using one or two preselected mutes, performs two notes. Immediately afterward the pianist holds a sustained tone, until a low concert D (its pitch inflected downward) is heard on the horn. Then after two rapid piano notes, the horn player, now using the other of the two mutes, sounds a single note chosen from pitch source "b."

At every moment, then, the two players are involved in a dialogue of alert listening, response and reaction. The score for *Duet* II confirms Barney Childs's observation that, no matter how indeterminate a given work, its *notation* (as a document that defines boundaries and hierarchies) is always fixed and invariant. The score also confirms Christian Wolff's belief in music making as "a collaborative, and transforming activity (performer into composer into listener into composer into performer." The activities of composing (including notation), performing, and improvising—separate yet inextricably linked—might well be considered related facets of this continuum.

Composers and National Traditions

20

As a social phenomenon, music reflects not only its time, but its place. Christopher Small has noted that taking part in a musical performance is "a way in which the participants affirm, explore and celebrate their sense of who they are." This awareness of identity is often rooted in history, geography, climate, folklore, religion, philosophy, cuisine, dance, and the like. Historically, such factors have played an important role in determining individual (or collective) style: the differences between Bizet and Brahms in particular, or between French music and German music in general. This is just true in the late twentieth century as in previous eras.

On another level, we hope this chapter will help dispel any notion that post–1945 musical developments have been restricted to Germany, France, and the United States. That would indeed be a provincial view! On the contrary, one can find provocative and exciting works of art, extraordinarily gifted composers, and first-rate performing ensembles in all parts of the world.

The phenomenon of nationalism, a major legacy of nineteenth-century romanticism (as well as nineteenth-century politics and economics) has shaped a major body of earlier twentieth-century music. Bartok, Vaughan

Williams, Sibelius, Debussy, and Stravinsky each felt a unique sense of identity—a special essence or "core" that they believed defined one's being as a Hungarian or a Finn or a Russian, exclusive of any other ethnic group. This sense has been especially important among peoples protecting themselves from oppression by outsiders and united by some mix of geography, language, and economic and political interests. (Historians have noted that nineteenth-century nationalism was primarily an upper-middle class intellectual movement, of little interest either to aristocrats or to the poorest underclass.)

The "purity" and exclusivity at the core of nationalist thinking is, of course, an illusion. When we consider musical figures of the past who are often thought to articulate national aspirations, we encounter many contradictions and paradoxes: Purcell's "English" art was fueled by French and Italian models; Lully, the giant of the French Baroque, was an Italian immigrant; Liszt, because he was brought up in Vienna, spoke virtually no Hungarian, while Sibelius knew no Finnish, since the language of educated Finns was Swedish. Such contradictions have increased in our own time, compounded by jet travel and the relative ease of studying abroad. Composers from many countries work at the IRCAM studios in Paris, or may seek out teachers in Princeton, Stanford, Berlin, or Rome.

In today's highly mobile society, then, and in the wake of this century's great political upheavals, many composers live far from their birthplace; their "roots" may remain intact, or become absorbed in a new nationalist context. To complicate matters further, compositional techniques and stylistic trends cut across state boundaries. Postwar serialism has touched every Western nation (although at different times and with varying degrees of influence); one also finds aspects of collage and style juxtaposition across a broad international spectrum. Similarly, interest in repetitive, gradual process has become international. The Belgian Karel Goeyvaerts (b. 1923), an influential figure since the early Darmstadt years, has become a major European proponent of minimalism; one also hears this technique in the more recent work of Stockhausen, and in that of Wolfgang Rihm, one of the better known of the younger Germans. In Denmark, we might look to the work of Pelle Gudmundsen-Holmgreen (a champion of the Scandinavian "New Simplicity" movement); in Hungary, to Zoltan Jeney and Istvan Martha.

Realistically, then, is it possible to claim that artistic nationalism still exists? Ironically, many creative artists feel strong ties to their original homeland when their home base is elsewhere. Whatever their place of residence, or their musical style, they find a way to demonstrate strong national or ethnic feelings. They may use folkloric or politically charged musical material, or socially conscious texts for vocal music. Other composers, influenced by political considerations, may choose certain genres or techniques: a preference for group improvisation (e. g., Cornelius Cardew, at one stage in his career) or a reluctance to compose concertos (like the Danish composer Per Nørgård, again at one stage of his work). Others who often worked out of political conviction include Frederic Rzewski, Hans Werner Henze, and Peter Schat. (Karel Husa's stunning *Music for Prague,* a classic example of music born of impassioned social consciousness, is discussed at greater length in Chapter 21.)

To illustrate the worldwide scope of new music, this chapter focuses on music from seven selected areas: Scandinavia, Eastern Europe, the Netherlands, Japan, Latin America, England, and Canada.

SCANDINAVIA

Since the close of World War II the Scandinavian countries (Denmark, Sweden, Norway, Finland, and Iceland) have been blessed with political stability and economic prosperity. Music is held in high regard as a cultural asset, and this great pride in the creative arts—which are backed by government funding—has resulted in zealous promotion of new music by way of commissioning projects, and radio and television exposure over the national networks. In each of the Scandinavian countries, a state-supported Music Information Center actively engages in the publication and recording of newly composed music. Cooperative ventures include the English-language magazine *Nordic Sounds* and the Nordic Music Days new-music festivals held at different sites rotating among the five nations.

Denmark

Although it is a peninsula, joined to Germany, Denmark has developed something of an "island" culture. As the most southerly of the Scandinavian nations, Denmark is closer to the European centers than to those in Scandinavia (Copenhagen is nearer to Hamburg, for example, than to Stockholm), and would thus theoretically appear more likely to be influenced by the cultural mainstream. In fact, Denmark has developed its own musical style—lean, direct, ironic, often eccentric, and deliberately "unfashionable"—independent of either Germany or the rest of Scandinavia. The influence of Carl Nielsen remains strong, and isolated aspects of his style are still heard in recent music: his distinctive approach to melody, his nonconformist use of instruments, and his unpredictable formal structures.

Serialism and the postwar "Darmstadt revolution" never took strong root in Denmark, perhaps because the Danes are suspicious of ideology in general, or—in the wake of World War II—have had difficulties embracing any Germanic proposals in particular. But a number of Danes have explored equally systematic approaches, though more individualistic and less doctrinaire, to composition. The "infinity series" of Per Nørgård (b. 1932) is designed to generate a continuum of pitches from a single interval—perhaps related to the system of "continual variation" developed by a senior Danish figure, Vagn Holmboe (b. 1909). Nørgård was the first Danish composer to acquire truly international stature in the postwar era.

ILLUS. 20.1.

Per Nørgård

Photo: Jesper Høm

His work is colorful, thought-provoking, iconoclastic, and bold; he often refers to music of the past, although for subtle associative purposes rather than shock value. (Nørgård's Third Symphony is discussed in the following chapter.) His exact contemporary Pelle Gudmundsen-Holmgreen (b. 1932) has moved in systematic directions of another sort: he is a leading exponent of minimalist process and the use of triadic building blocks, an approach often referred to in Europe as the "New Simplicity."

Danish independence of the continental mainstream has led to areas of postserial thinking, such as collage and stylistic eclecticism, well in advance of other European nations. In this regard Karl Aage Rasmussen has been an articulate and highly influential champion. His 1974 chamber work *A Ballad of Game and Dream* offers a crazy quilt of familiar tonal fragments, including tunes associated with children's games, or many overlapping textural levels, transforming the commonplace into something foreign and mysterious. Hans Abrahamsen (b. 1952) devoted his earlier efforts to the "new simplicity," but has broadened his expressive pallette in recent years. In his 1978 chamber septet *Winternacht*, Abrahamsen sets repetitive gestures against one another and is especially sensitive in his delicate transformations of simple triads—even, at one point, arpeggiating them to resemble the opening of Beethoven's "Moonlight" Sonata.

Poul Ruders is experienced at handling elements of collage, quotation, and music theater—appropriately so, for a composer influenced by Rasmusssen, Tippett, Berio, and Schnittke. Ruders's longtime fascination with the Middle Ages has led him to a synthesis of styles in which modal polyphony, extended pedals, and repetitive gestures are combined with a flair of broad, romantic breadth. A sure sense of expressive, even theatrical, gesture suffuses Ruders's music; in fact, he terms himself a "film composer with no film." *Corpus cum figuris* for twenty players, commissioned by IRCAM and premiered in 1985, offers the solemnity of organum, with resonant triads and open fifths inexorably moving across a sonic landscape gradually obscured by decoration and polyphonic layering. Its repeated low pedal pitches gradually accelerate to rapid ostinati and eventually to a virtuoso passage for multiple percussion inspired by African drumming.

Norway

In the late nineteenth century Norway offered one of the most striking examples of intense cultural "nationalism" in the person and music of Edvard Grieg. During the twentieth century, Norway was particularly slow to take up modernist ideas, partly due to Grieg's persistent influence and partly to the factor of geographic isolation. In bringing Norway's conservative musical culture closer to the postwar avant-garde, two figures, both born in 1922, have been prominent: Finn Mortensen and the Italian-born

Antonio Bibalo. Mortensen, at first strongly influenced by Hindemithian neoclassicism, has since gradually introduced twelve-tone technique into his work. Bibalo, who spent a number of years in London studying with the English serialist Elisabeth Lutyens before settling in Norway, has consistently worked in a free twelve-tone style.

An even more flexible use of modernist techniques can be found in the music of Arne Nordheim (b. 1921). Nordheim's 1982 *Wirklicher Wald* (soprano, solo cello, chorus, and orchestra), composed for the centennial of the Oslo State Conservatory, employs texts by Rainer Maria Rilke and the Book of Job centered on the transitoriness of human existence. The work is notable for its luminous, slowly evolving fabric of triadic references, reminiscent of Scriabin or Delius, offset by boldly angular, nontonal passagework of great intensity.

Norwegian composers of a later generation seem determined to surmount their perceived isolation. Three names have acquired international visibility: Åse Hedstrøm (b. 1950), now based in Stockholm: John Persen (b. 1941); and Olav Anton Thommessen (b. 1946). Hedstrøm's *Sorti* for string quartet is uncompromisingly hard-edged; she enjoys the tension produced by glissandi, sustained sounds produced behind the bridge, clusters, and other "noise" sonorities. Such moments alternate with passages of lyric stillness, setting up a curious balance. Persen, known for his political activity, was a leader in the Oslo "Artists Movement" of the 1970s; he is disposed, therefore, to see music as social paradigm. For example, he views the repetitive minimalism of his 1986–87 chamber sextet *Et cetera!* as symbolic of persistence, of the struggle of ideas to win acceptance. The point is made in a delightfully rude, irreverent, almost Ivesian way, with quirky rhythms and timbres suggestive of jazz.

Thommessen has attained prominence by winning a number of major international composition awards. His background is relatively cosmopolitan; as the son of a diplomat, he lived for extended periods in England and the United States, studied composition with Xenakis (at Indiana University) and Lutosławaski (in Warsaw), and acquired electronic studio experience at the Utrecht (Netherlands) Institute of Sonology. Perhaps as a consequence, his music is freely eclectic and antisystematic. Motives borrowed from other composers may figure prominently; his monumental orchestral work *A Glass Bead Game* (1983) draws on fragments of the Grieg piano concerto, the Verdi *Requiem*, and two Beethoven symphonies. These source materials—whether hints, snippets, transformations, or direct quotes—are set in unusual juxtapositions and surprising contexts, often on a canvas of late twentieth-century "cluster" sonority.

Sweden

During the immediate postwar years the Swedes proved more receptive than the rest of Scandinavia to mainstream European modernism. Karl-Birger Blomdahl (1916–68), Ingvar Lidholm (b. 1921) and Bo Nilsson set an example for younger composers by freely confronting the challenges of the Darmstadt revolution: serial pitch organization, chance, aleatory textures, and cluster sonorities. In particular, Sweden developed one of the major *electronic* music studios in the world (funded by the government radio network and based in Stockholm). During the 1960s and 1970s the Swedish Radio studio developed the genre, related to concrete poetry, known as "text-sound composition." Many composers from other parts of the world, including the Americans Amirkhanian, Appleton, and Dodge, have worked there.

Other organizations devoted to the avant-grade came into being during the early postwar period. Among them, the Culture Quartet, an ensemble of four trombonists including the composers Jan Bark and Folke Rabe, combined elements of free improvisation, jazz, and performance art, and *Fylkingen,* a society devoted to the furtherance of radical new music, often combined live and electronic forces in multimedia presentations. Three composers who developed their careers through Fylkingen and are known for their electronic music are Lars Gunnar Bodin, Sten Hanson, and Bengt-Emil Johnson.

Arne Mellnas (b. 1933) not only contributed to the Stockholm avant-garde, but also spent additional periods of study in Berlin, Paris, Utrecht, and San Francisco. Although his music reveals a sure command of many postwar techniques, the influence of Ligeti—one of his teachers—is evident in his use of controlled improvisation and unsynchronized, layered textures. Mellnas uses this method to create brilliant instrumental textures in his 1972 *Transparence* for large orchestra, a work reminiscent of Penderecki in its kaleidoscopic "wash" of ever-shifting instrumental mass.

Two active Swedish composers stand out among the younger generation: Jan W. Morthenson (b. 1940) and Daniel Bortz (b. 1943). Both are eclectic in their free use of simple triads, discordant clusters, and angular, atonal passages, often within the same work. Morthenson's *Strano* ("strange" in Italian) for woodwind quintet is a mystrerious amalgam of flitting, daring gestures, microtonal inflections, quiet sustained tones, digitally sampled woodwind sounds, and vocal cries by the players. Bortz's 1983 *Sinfonia 6* operates on a monumental canvas and evokes comparisons with Mahler for its deliberate confrontations of naively simple and impenetrably complex gestures, its use of the solo soprano voice as one element within a symphonic argument, and its unusual juxtapositions of massive orchestral weight and intimate chamber-music timbres.

Finland

This country at the northern tip of Europe faces the East as well as West; the capital, Helsinki, is nearer to Saint Petersburg, Russia, than to any city in Scandinavia. As recently as 1910, Finland was politically controlled by Russia, and nineteenth-century Finnish nationalism—of the passionate sort typified by Sibelius's music—was intensified by the constant threat of Russian subjugation. (It is understandable, too, that Finland experienced a unique sense of tension during the Cold War years.

The name Jean Sibelius (1865–1957) was synonymous with Finnish

ILLUS. 20.2.

Kaija Saariaho

Photo Credit: Marc Bezrat. Courtesy Finnish Music Information Center

music, even a decade or more after World War II. Twelve-tone explorations began only in the 1950s, and true "modernism" arrived with two composers of a later generation. Both Paavo Heininen (b. 1938) and Aulis Sallinen (b. 1935) explored serialism before moving on to more flexible hybrid approaches. Heininen studied with Lutosławski in Poland, Bernd Alois Zimmermann in Cologne, and Vincent Persichetti at the Juillard School in New York. Echoes of Persichetti may be heard in his Second Piano Concerto, solidly neoclassic in its driving rhythms and brittle textures. Sallinen works within the mainstream of expanded tonality and broad, romantic gesture. His 1987 Symphony No. 5, *Washington Mosaics,* for example, seems closer to the iconoclastic Scandinavian models of Nielsen and Sibelius than to the Germanic norm.

The first concentrated exposure to radically new music dates from the founding, in 1977, of the Helsinki group Open Ears. Two composers who have since achieved international prominence were among the first members: Magnus Lindberg (b. 1958) and Kaija Saariaho (b. 1952). (Another member, Esa-Pekka Salonen, has since developed a major career as an orchestra conductor.) Though neither seems remotely like Sibelius, their uncompromising, even willfully unsettling aesthetic stance and organic approach to form may strike the listener as characteristically Finnish. Lindberg's work is teeming with energy, admired for its explosive athleticism and brilliant orchestral color. (His *Kraft* is discussed in the next chapter.) Saariaho, like Lindberg, creates a complex overlay of many interactive strands to produce a highly sophisticated fabric. (Judging from the work of these composers, the Danish "new simplicity" has had virtually no effect on Finnish music)

Saariaho's background exemplifies the many-layered supranational art of the postwar jet age. After an initial period of study in Helsinki, she spent an extended period in Freiburg, Germany, working with the British composer Brian Ferneyhough (who has since relocated to San Diego) before moving on to a French residency at IRCAM. Like her compatriot Lindberg, Saariaho now lives in Paris. Basic aspects of her work can be observed in her *Io* (1986–87) for chamber orchestra, tape, and live electronics. Subtle alterations of timbre color extended held tones, trills, and tremolos; often, in fact, these states imperceptibly merge, so that a trill *becomes* a tremolo. As the electronic and acoustic forces continually exchange roles within a complex network, many component strands and gradual "phase shifts" combine to produce an intricate surface of great subtlety and expressive range.

EASTERN EUROPE

The twentieth century has not been kind to the countries of Eastern Europe. That region has seen major social upheavals, changing borders, the destruction of monuments to the past, and acute suffering during World War II. For many, the postwar years have been ones of economic hardship, political repression, and cultural censorship. Despite such obstacles, creative artists have continued to work—spurred on, perhaps, by their belief that the postwar reconstruction of culture is a mission of prime importance.

Social controls have often placed artists under special pressures as materials and expressive import confront the prevailing political systems. Among the Eastern European composers noted here, we find a substantial number of expatriates—more for political and self-expressive reasons than, as is the case in Scandinavia, a sense of cultural isolation. The existence of censorship, oddly enough, validates the *importance* of music in these countries: a recognition of the power of art. The authorities acknowledge this, because the citizenry takes art very seriously, much more so than in the jaded West. Ironically, this very belief in art's powers may have been confirmed by Eastern European developments during the twentieth century's final decade. The greater opportunities for political self-determination and open expression of national pride were first glimpsed in the gradual acceptance and eventual sanctioning of experimental, individual approaches to artistic creation.

Poland

Most music-lovers immediately associate the name "Chopin" with the word "Poland." Ironically, although this major Polish figure flourished during the early nineteenth century, certain aspects of his career would still apply to the Polish musical milieu of the mid-twentieth: the strong influence of French culture, an aversion to all things Russian, and a sizable community of expatriate artists making their influence felt from a distance. Prior to World War II, Karol Szymanowski (1882–1937) was well known for a body of music in which folk influences act upon an atmospheric, almost "impressionistic" style—not unlike a cross between Bartok and Ravel. During the postwar era Witold Lutosławski was the first Polish composer to rise to international prominence for his use of controlled chance in unsynchronized group textures. Significantly, Lutosławski, as had many of the Polish intelligentsia for over a century, settled in Western Europe. Similarly, Joanna Bruzdowicz (b. 1943) now lives in Belgium, and Andrzej

Panufnik (1914–91), who had resided in London since 1954, eventually became a British citizen.

Panufnik's music, often mysterious, solemn, and highly spiritual, creates a special intensity by way of repetition. Although his work may seem simple in its formal design and triadic pitch materials, the effect can be highly evocative, as in his 1983 *Arbor Cosmica* for chamber orchestra, its twelve brief movements flowering organically from the same motive. Joanna Bruzdowicz is more allied with the Schoenbergian, expressionist mainstream. Although she is most active on the French and Belgian musical scenes, there is a definite nationalist streak to her work. Her 1973 String Quartet No. 1, *La vita,* was conceived as an homage to Szymanowski.

A strong interest in new-music developments was manifested in Poland even in the earliest postwar years. Led by Lutosławski, and then Penderecki, the Poles cultivated a distinctive cluster-sonority approach to ensemble texture and orchestration. As early as 1957 an electronic studio, the first in a socialist country, was established by the Polish state radio. The monumental Symphony by Bogusław Schäffer (b. 1929), conceived as a notated graphic score for tape studio realization, is an outstanding product of that early electronic era; its 1965 realization by Bohdan Mazurek is no less impressive. Also benefiting from the brief relaxation of Soviet-style cultural repression in the late 1950s was the Warsaw Autumn, an annual festival devoted to the presentation of the latest international avant-garde music that quickly became a major forum for performances and the exchange of ideas. Among the founders of the Warsaw Autumn, two composers are especially prominent: Kazimierz Serocki (1922–81) and Henryk Górecki (b. 1933). Although both were early proponents of dissonant modernism, Górecki has since turned to a triadic, tonal, deeply meditative language—one of a growing group of Eastern European composers to do so.

Another link to international avant-gardism was forged when the composer-pianist Zygmunt Krauze (b. 1938) founded the Music Workshop in 1963. Basically a quartet of clarinet, cello, trombone, and piano, this ensemble became well known for its Warsaw Autumn appearances and tours of Western and Eastern Europe, performing works written for them by—to list but a few—Kagel, Nørgård, Feldman, Rzewski, Erb, and Nordheim. Krauze has held extended academic residencies in Cleveland and Buffalo and has also lived in Berlin and Paris. His style incorporates a variety of Western avant-garde techniques: collage, hints of minimalist repetition, and the use of folk instruments (such as bagpipe, fife, or hurdygurdy) side by side with electronic tape.

For his 1973 *Folk Music,* Krauze subdivides a large orchestra into twenty-one groups, each assigned a folk song or dance to perform. As all of the groups are instructed to play simultaneously throughout, the conductor's task is primarily that of controlling dynamics and balances, thereby bringing one or another group into sharp focus. In a more recent orchestral work by Krauze, *The Underground River,* triadic "ghosts" and pedal points appear amid kaleidoscopic flurries and cluster sonorities; at one point a slow Chopinesque passage in D-flat major can be heard against a tape of splashing water, bird calls, and other evocative nature sounds. *Tableau Vivant* for chamber orchestra is overtly political, a response to the 1981 imposition of martial law by the Warsaw government; in its fragmented use of the Polish national anthem and other layered references, the work is simultaneously somber, angry, and reflective.

The music of Tomasz Sikorski (1939–91) combines the clarity and repetitive quality of minimalism with a highly expressive intensity. His *Concerto Breve* for piano, winds, and percussion uses staccato flurries against clusters and rapid ostinati. *Other Voices* for twenty-four winds and gongs is more sustained throughout, creating an effect similar to Ligeti's *Atmosphères.*

Hungary

Musical references to Hungary extend back at least to the late eighteenth century Esterhazy court, across the border from Vienna, which supported Haydn. The nineteenth century saw the dominant figure of Franz Liszt: deeply committed to Hungarian social and political causes, and fascinated by the notion of applying Hungarian folk music (or what he believed to be such) to the concert stage. His sources, like those of Brahms's "Hungarian Dances," are questionable, perhaps derived from the Austro/Germanic view of Hungary as a somewhat "exotic" province. This view was radically altered early in our century by Bartók and Kodály, seeking out an indigenous national culture, and then (in the postwar era) by the striking innovations of avant-gardist György Ligeti (b. 1923).

It may be significant that Ligeti, who of all living Hungarian composers has the greatest international stature, has chosen to live in the West (Austria and Germany). Those who have maintained their residence in Hungary are not nearly as well known—in fact, not as visible as their Polish or Soviet counterparts. Their obscurity may be due to a relative lack of cohesion within the creative community; composers seem factionalized compared with their counterparts in other East European nations, and government support has reflected this unfocused state.

One of the most widely respected composers, György Kurtág (b. 1926), at first deeply immersed in the Bartók tradition, discovered Stravinsky and Webern while a student in Paris. Many of his pieces are small-scale, scored for traditional chamber groups (although one folk instrument, the cimbalom, is a special favorite), and worked-out in great detail. Kurtág's work is paradoxical in that its restrained, economical surface often erupts into romantic, even extravagant gesture. This duality is evident in his monumental cycle for voice and large ensemble (including cimbalom) *Messages of the Late R. V. Troussova* (1980), an impassioned setting of Russian love poetry. Comparisons can be made with Schoenberg's *Pierrot Lunaire* (twenty-one songs, constantly shifting instrumentation, from one movement to another, *Sprechstimme*) and to Webern's kaleidoscopic instrumentation. And beyond these, Hungarian influences, from Lisztian "thematic transformation" to the melodic and rhythmic inflections of Bartók, can be heard throughout.

Kurtág's colleague Sándor Balassa (b. 1935) is more interested in broader gestures, a wide range of timbral sonority, and grand sweeping designs. His 1971 *Iris* for large orchestra is broadly spaced, angular, and nontonal; its romantic rhetoric is reminiscent of Carl Ruggles or Roger Sessions. Balassa writes of the work, "Think of the human eye, the flower, the rainbow; all of them are called iris." The composition, then, is intended as a sonorous analogue to the organic, changing aspects of the natural world. Zsolt Durkó (b. 1934) is another composer with a penchant for large-scale, grand gestures. One of the best known of Durkó's works, the 1972 oratorio *Burial Prayer* for tenor, bass, chorus, and orchestra was composed for the centennial of the unification of the cities Pest and Buda; its text dating from circa 1200, is said to be the oldest surviving document in the Hungarian language. Durkó's setting stresses deep, sonorous pedal points and vivid colors, especially at the stunning conclusion—the fall of Adam, depicted by a virtual explosion in the orchestra and shouts and screams from the chorus.

Although cultural liberalization in the postwar decades progressed much more slowly in Hungary than in Poland, Hungarian composers have managed nonetheless to create a surprisingly eclectic and diversified scene. Rigorous pitch logic, and an extension of this logic to other parameters, typify the music of Andras Szollosy (b. 1921); his orchestral *Trasfigurazioni* (1972), for example, explores relationships between pitch and rhythmic series. At the other extreme, quasi-improvisatory minimalism, in the spirit of Terry Riley, can be found in the works of Zoltán Jeney (b. 1943). In 1973 Jeney cofounded the New Music Studio, a gathering of younger composers interested in the work of Cage, Reich, and other experimentalists.

Russia and Other Former Soviet Republics

Although rich in folk traditions, Russia produced virtually no indigenous art music before the nineteenth century. (The czars simply imported their music from Italy and France.) After the pioneering efforts of Glinka, two important schools had begun to take hold by the 1850s, one (Mussorgsky, Rimsky-Korsakov, Glazounov, and Stravinsky) more folk-oriented, the other (Tchaikovsky, Rachmaninov, and Medtner) more attuned to Western European models. After the 1917 Revolution, a compromise position was reached midway between the two philosophies: composers were encouraged to work in the grand Western forms of symphony, opera, and ballet—but within a populist context. As we now have come to realize, Prokofiev and Shostakovitch both learned to survive—with varying degrees of success—the challenges of accessibility, censorship, stylistic control, and the urgent need to communicate on a more personal level.

During the early postwar years, a number of Russian composers began exploring nontonal Western techniques; many of their efforts were performed only privately at first, and official sanction, essential to a composer's livelihood in the Soviet Union, was gradual. One such composer is Edison Denisov (b. 1929), whose music is strongly influenced by both Berio and Boulez. His 1964 *Sun of the Incas* for soprano and nine players, a setting of poetry by the Chilean Gabriela Mistral (the first Latin American woman to win the Nobel Prize for literature), vividly captures its text's furious intensity; in fact, that work provoked stormy debates within the Composers Union, where it was denounced as "modernist." Rodion Shchedrin (b. 1932) is an important figure of the same generation, with a spiky, often witty style that recalls aspects of Copland, Poulenc, and Hindemith.

An especially interesting figure who has become increasingly well known in the West, Sofia Gubaidulina (b. 1931) was a classmate of Denisov and Schnittke at the Moscow Conservatory. Shortly afterward she helped organize an improvisation group, Astreya, which fostered a fusion of popular and avant-garde styles and performed on Western, Russian, and Central Asian instruments. At one time her work was strongly criticized by the Composers Union; for conservative ears, her highly eclectic approach can be puzzling. For example, she describes her *In croce* ("On the Cross") for cello and organ as "a meditation on suffering." In this piece, gently arpeggiated, decorated triads are suddenly confronted by angular discords, clusters, and eerie *sul ponticello* slides. Unusual doublings and Mussorgskian chord successions add to the work's fascination.

During the final decade of the twentieth century, other republics of the former Soviet Union have begun to publicly articulate a greater sense of identity and autonomy. A number of important composers have been strongly identified with their republics. The Ukrainian composer Valentin Silvestrov (b. 1937), for example, was an early advocate of twelve-tone technique, graphic notation, and unsynchronized textural masses at a time when such devices were roundly condemned by Soviet critics. Giya Kancheli (b. 1925), from Tbilisi, Georgia, creates a music remarkable for its soaring, triadic gestures and an almost Medieval quality of modal polyphony. Kancheli's Third Symphony (1973) alternates slow, meditative passages for solo female voice with harsh, unsettling orchestral chords. A stirring climax—in which the chord series transforms itself into a commentary on

Stravinsky's *Le sacre du printemps*—eventually leads to the return of the vocal solo.

The Estonian composer Arvo Pärt explored an eclectic mix of serial and tonal elements in his early works; after 1968, however, his style began to focus on a single expressive state. The Symphony No. 3 is almost entirely gentle, modal, and consonant—like much of Kancheli's work, virtually Medieval in its stately sense of inner peace. In 1980 Pärt left Estonia, where he had been employed as a recording engineer for the state radio, and emigrated to Berlin; his career has been in ascent ever since.

Qualities in the recent music of Kancheli, Pärt and other Eastern Europeans—Gubaidulina, Panufnik, Górecki—may indicate an important movement in the making. The late music of Shostakovitch, particularly his final string quartet, provides a model; an urgent need to express religious feelings (at the close of an era in which such feelings were suppressed) provides a collective impetus. The music of these composers is couched in a language more consistently tonal, triadic, and consonant than any other of the postwar era. Its approach to repetition could be called minimalist, and its expressive intent mystical—even at times profoundly religious.

JAPAN

Not until after World War II, did Schoenberg, and other Western innovators became known in Japan. Once this happened, Japanese composers quickly adopted the latest developments, from twelve-tone technique and aleatoric methods to experimental theater and electronic music. In 1955 the national broadcast facility, NHK, opened its Electronic Music Studio, geared mainly toward *musique concrète*. Most significant, however, has been the assimilation of these advancements with music of national origin.

More than that of any other non-Western nation, Japan's culture fuses its old political, social, and artistic practices with modern-day trends of the Western world. Thus, enthusiasm for jazz, rock 'n' roll, and "classical" genres is equalled by devotion to the ancient traditions of *gagaku* (court music), Noh (ritual music drama), and folk music (with instruments like the koto, shamisen, and shakuhachi).

In the 1950s a number of groups combining Western avant-garde and traditional Japanese musics were established by such composers as Yoritsune Matsudaira, Toshi Ichiyanagi and Toshiru Mayuzumi. Toru Takemitsu and Joji Yuasa (b. 1929) have taken an especially provocative approach, often juxtaposing Eastern and Western elements without reconciling their differences. Examples are Takemitsu's *Cassiopeia* for solo percussion, gagaku ensemble, and orchestra (1971) and Yuasa's *Projection* (*Flower, Bird, Wind, Moon*) for eight kotos and orchestra (1967). Takemitsu's ethereal, other-worldly orchestral textures and Yuasa's Varèse-like clashes of instrumental densities serve as foils for the idiomatic gestures and timbres of native instruments.

Others in the older generation to have combined Japanese and Western musics are Maki Ishii (b. 1936) and Ryohei Hirose (b. 1930). Ishii places the two in bold apposition in his *Sogu II* for Western and *gagaku* orchestras (1971); this work is really two compositions played together, *Music for Gagaku* (1970) and *So* for orchestra (1971). On the other hand, in Hirose's Concerto for Shakuhachi and Orchestra (1976), soloist and ensemble function cooperatively; through most of the piece, a whispy orchestral accompaniment allows the bamboo flute's breathy attacks, rich overtones, and delicate melismas to stand in relief.

Some composers are more overtly European in their handling of texture, orchestral sonority, and formal design. The Piano Concerto No. 2 of Shin-ichiro Ikebe (b. 1943) has the sweep, color, and fervor of Messiaen, and his *Spontaneous Ignition* for orchestra is especially Stravinskian in its brilliant, driving ostinati. Similarly, the Piano Concerto of Teruyuki Noda (b. 1940) evokes comparisons with the hard-edged, virtuosic flamboyance of Martino, Davidovsky, or early Stockhausen.

Along with instrumental resources, Japan's heritage of distinctive vocal styles has also elicited remarkable works from this elder group. Perhaps the best known by Toshiru Mayuzumi is his *Nirvana* Symphony for men's chorus and orchestra (1958). The chorus's oddly pulsed incantations, low-bass clusters, and half-sung, half-shouted chant were inspired by Buddhist rites, while complex instrumental timbres were modeled on the sound of Japanese temple bells. In the *Requiem* for mixed chorus and orchestra (1977) by Akira Miyoshi, voice parts are sometimes sung, sometimes declaimed in frantic bursts or highly energized *parlando* lines, much like those in Noh drama. These take on a frightening intensity, set against violent eruptions of instrumental chaos.

Younger Japanese composers have also shown a fascination with their heritage, but have shifted its context. The modernist methods imported during the 1950s and 1960s are less influential now, while timbral nuance, static harmony, repetitive rhythm, and silence have gained importance. Much of their music reflects more directly the spirit of ancient sources, even when authentic instruments are not used. Exemplary of this is *Sen II* (1986) for solo cello by Toshio Hosokawa (b. 1955). Unorthodox techniques are used to create hushed noises, windlike moans, distant cries, speechlike inflections, and other effects. The elemental sense of mystery is enhanced by generous silences. Akira Nishimura (b. 1953) explores similar territory

ILLUS. 20.3.

Shin-ichiro Ikebe

Courtesy Tokyo Concerts Co.

in his *Navel of the Sun* for hichiriki (small Japanese oboe) and orchestra, slowly building from atmospheric microtonal clusters to vibrant sound masses. Not until halfway through the piece does the solo instrument enter with its extended, contemplative monologue. Both works reflect Japanese traditional music's linearity and emphasis on sustained, motionless sonorities.

The postmodern revival of tonality in America and Europe has its counterpart in Japan, with much recent attention on the works of Mamon Fujieda (b. 1955), one of surprisingly few composers there to explore digital technology. The traditional focus on stasis and repetition has also inclined some Japanese composers toward a process-guided minimalism related to Western practice, but deeply imbued with the nature-oriented mysticism of Eastern culture. Best known in this regard are Somei Satoh, Jo Kondo, and Akira Nishimura.

THE NETHERLANDS

For most concertgoers, the great heyday of Dutch music was the early Renaissance, when the "Netherlands style" of counterpoint, as practiced by Josquin, Obrecht, Ockeghem, and Isaac, dominated the late fifteenth and early sixteenth centuries. But it was hardly what one would call a *national* style. Some of these "Netherland" composers could be considered French or Belgian. Moreover, the style they perfected was rapidly assimilated into the Italian and then German cultural mainstream. This early instance of Netherlands *internationalism* is revealing in that some of its features still exist. Musical "nationalism" is not as strong an issue in Holland today as in other countries, partly because very little of its folk music has survived into the twentieth century, and, more important, because the character of the country itself—small, densely populated, multi-lingual, curious, tolerant, politically liberal, and cosmopolitan—would argue against any movement quite so parochial.

The extraordinary public and corporate support for the arts in the Netherlands has made it an important center for new music. Donemus, the national music information center, publishes, records, and promotes Dutch compositions throughout the world. The Gaudeamus Foundation sponsors international festivals for younger composers and new-music performers. The Icebreaker, a nontraditional performance space located by an Amsterdam canal, is known for its many festivals, symposia, and workshops. Finally, the Institute of Sonology—originally in Utrecht, now in The Hague—has been a major international center for electronic music since its inception.

A sign of the Dutch fondness for experimentation, quotation, and eclectic collage has been the role of Amsterdam as the center of the International Charles Ives Society. The surprising number of Dutch works created for unorthodox instrumental forces reflects not only the success of commissioning programs but also the presence in Holland of remarkable virtuosi specializing in less-common instruments such as bass clarinet, recorder, and guitar. Cultural liberality encourages Dutch musicians to make political statements through their art with a freedom Eastern European artists might envy. Significantly, very few Dutch artists emigrate to other parts of the world. Although individuals may feel dissatisfied, the Dutch hardly feel "oppressed," nor would they consider themselves "isolated" as do some Scandinavians. On the contrary, they are situated right at the center of the action, within striking distance of Paris, London, and Cologne.

Their history of world travel, trading, and colonization (particularly in Indonesia) has engendered a high degree of interest in non-Western cultures. Appropriately, they also produced one of the first major scholars in the field of ethnomusicology, Jaap Kunst. Ton de Leeuw (b. 1926) studied composition with Henk Badings and world music with Kunst. De Leeuw's travels in India, Iran, Japan, and Indonesia have had a profound influence on his own music. His 1974 *Mo-Do* for amplified harpsichord consists of many brief but intense movements, in the spirit of haiku, each constructed from modal fragments surrounding the central tonic, or *do*. Microtonal inflections, extended pedal points, decorative melismas, and drones create the fabric of his 1977 *Mountains* for bass clarinet and tape. In his program notes for this work, the composer refers to "echoes of folk music . . . eternal and not confined to any one setting."

A figure only slightly younger, Theo Loevendie (b. 1930), reached early prominence as a jazz clarinetist and began composing for "concert" performers only after 1968. He was also active in organizing a series of free informal concerts that brought a cross-section of music to people in schools, malls, churches, and streets. Loevendie, especially interested in the integration of styles, enjoys incorporating "alien music," as he puts it, into his language. The gestures, inflections, and timbres of jazz are crucial to his 1975 *Incantations* for bass clarinet and orchestra, while the *Six Turkish Folk Poems* (1977) for soprano and seven players evokes Eastern sources in its melodic contours. The songs are set against a series of ostinati, harmonically static but texturally detailed, rich with the shimmering colors of harp, celesta, and mallet percussion.

The middle generation of Dutch composers includes a group of five students of Kees Van Baaren (1906–70), the first Dutch twelve-tone composer. In 1966 they became known for their fiery political activism, especially their attempts to reform the programming of the then-conservative Concertgebouw Orchestra; their demonstration at a *Nutcracker* performance made headlines. Prominence of a different sort was attained with the overwhelming success of their group opera *Reconstructie* at the 1969 Holland Festival. The opera reinterprets *Don Giovanni* as an anti-imperialist, anti-American fable, with a Stone Guest in the form of Che Guevara and a brilliant musical fabric parodying Stravinsky, Mozart, Webern, Wagner, jazz, and rock.

Each of the five has followed a slightly different musical path. The more recent works of Peter Schat reveal a romantic, lyric thoughtfulness. In the spirit of other process-oriented (but antiserial) composers from the Dutch Willem Pijper (1894–1947) to the Danish Per Nørgård, Schat has devised a procedure for generating pitches, known as the "tone clock." Mischa Mengelberg (b. 1935) is known for his jazz performance, group improvisation with his Instant Composers Pool, and a body of eclectic, highly theatrical compositions. Jan Van Vlijmen (b. 1935) composes in a thoughtful, somewhat neoclassic idiom, as exemplified by the 1981 string quartet *Trimurti*. This work's three movements, effectively contrasted and balanced, are intended to reflect three great principles of Hindu philosophy: "light," "energy," and "darkness." Reinbert de Leeuw (b. 1938) is active as a composer, conductor, and impresario, having organized major festivals devoted to Satie and Schoenberg. His 1973 *Abschied* for orchestra is an important harbinger of the new romanticism, nontonal and dissonant throughout, with extroverted, impassioned surges projecting an atmosphere closer to Mahler than our own time. He describes the stormy fabric, which includes fragments of *La valse* and *Le sacre du printemps*, as a "permanent rage."

Of that group of five musical rebels, Louis Andriessen (b. 1939) has developed the strongest voice. His work still retains its youthful fire—a brash, aggressive, fearless, "in your face" quality closer to punk rock than to high art. Like Philip Glass, Andriessen enjoys the sheer sound of rock—its electronic timbres and high amplification—and he, too, has developed a language of high-energy, near-hypnotic repetition. His band of minimalism, however, stems from a different combination of influences: in Andriessen's case, rock music, street and protest music, non-Western ritual, and medieval polyphony. His 1977 *Hoketus* was inspired by a study of Machaut and the hocketing textures of Medieval music; it is scored for two identical and antiphonally separated ensembles, which alternate back and forth in their playing of harsh chords. There are no ingratiating timbres here, only the incessantly *fortissimo* steely sound world of amplified flutes; electric pianos, bass guitar, and conga drums. Example 20.1 indicates the source chord, from which both groups draw their pitches, and the pattern of alternations:

Andriessen's works for larger forces display a similar technique and aesthetic. His 1976 *De Staat*, scored for four sopranos (their text drawn from Plato's *Republic*) and large instrumental ensemble, includes ritualistic, insistent Stravinskian ostinati and resonant gamelan sonorities. For his 1983 *De Snelheid* ("Velocity"), Andriessen subdivides a large ensemble into three antiphonally separated units, each "led" by a percussive instrument, frequently at its own tempo. The resultant texture—sharp chords overlapping with each other, perpetual beats on the bass drum, woodblocks and tom-tom—is relentless in its high-voltage energy and its unvarying dynamic level.

Other younger Dutch composers include two students of Ton de Leeuw, Tristan Keuris (b. 1946) and Guus Janssen (b. 1951). Keuris has a sensitive ear for timbre, and his orchestral *Sinfonia* of 1974 is brilliantly colorful, often with the electricity, sonority and rhythmic drive of *Petrushka*. Fleeting references to tonal sources—an eclectic grab bag ranging from Viennese waltz to the blues—are curiously integrated. Janssen is well known for his jazz piano improvisations and for his minimalist compositions. His 1981 String Quartet No. 2, *Streepjes* ("Strokes") is dominated by deliberately limited pitch choices, similarly limited timbre (stressing natural harmonics), and vivid color contrasts, such as sudden *molto vibrato*.

EXAMPLE 20.1.

- the flutes play the encircled notes.

- the bass guitars play the lowest notes.

- the keyboard instruments each choose approximately the same chord from the given pitch material.

- the congas are tuned identically, both pairs in approximately a major second or a minor third.

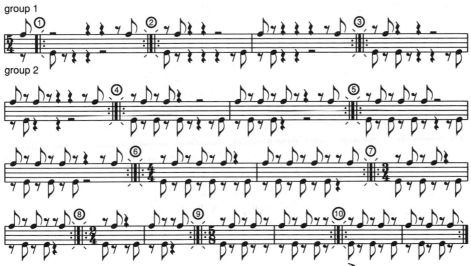

Louis Andriessen: *Hoketus*

Finally, Leo Samama (b. 1951), also active as a writer and critic, composes music with a cool, Stravinskian architecutre and a sense of the musical occasion as elegant and ceremonial. His use of vivid contrasts between bravura passagework and almost motionless calm is evident in two works for very different forces: *Monumentum pro Caecila* for string orchestra (1984), with a stark, dramatic harpsichord part, and the 1986 *Grand Slam* for solo accordion.

LATIN AMERICA

Although many North Americans and Europeans are inexplicably unaware of it, an active, vibrant musical life exists south of the Rio Grande. This milieu life is especially rich in its overlay of different traditions, not only the native Indian but the European. (As early as the sixteenth century sacred choral music by Victoria and other Spanish polyphonists was being performed in Mexico; similarly, there have been opera houses in Buenos Aires since the 1750s.)

The most important early twentieth-century figures built on this multifaceted heritage. Carlos Chavez of Mexico (1899–1978), like many other artists of his generation, responded to the highly nationalistic spirit that followed the 1910 Revolution. Chavez went beyond cultivated European techniques and materials, preferring a language of bold strokes, vivid colors, and native folk materials comparable to the brilliant murals of his countrymen Rivera and Orozco. His patriotic, nationalist sources include Indian ones, as exemplified by his 1935 *Sinfonia India* and the use of Aztec words in choral pieces. Chavez was also active as a conductor; he gave the Mexican premieres of works by Stravinsky, Schoenberg, Milhaud, Varèse, and others, founded the Orquestra Sinfonica de Mexico in 1928, and directed it for almost two decades. Another important Mexican composer, Silvestre Revueltas (1899–1940), who served as Chavez's assistant conductor, had a special flair for absorbing Mexican popular and folk music into his own style. By contrast, Julian Carrillo (1875–1965) had little interest in national materials, and focused instead on elegant microtonal divisions of the octave—what he referred to as the "thirteenth sound," indicating that his work had broken the intonational barrier of twelve.

Two other prewar composers—both deeply nationalistic—can be regarded as the equal of Chavez in international eminence: Alberto Ginastera of Argentina (1916–83) and Heitor Villa-Lobos (1887–1959) of Brazil. Early in his career, Ginastera developed a style that combined elements of folk music, urban Buenos Aires culture, and the European art tradition. The international side of his musical personality became more pronounced in the 1950s, as expressionistic, serial elements entered his work. During the '60s he directed the Latin American Center for Advanced Musical Studies, which brought Messiaen, Xenakis, Copland, Nono, and others to work with young Latin American composers; his operas *Don Rodrigo* (1964) and *Bomarzo* (1967) reveal great Romantic sweep, structurally and expressively akin to Alban Berg, and a sure knowledge of more radical postwar techniques.

Villa-Lobos was well known for his facility, prolific creative output, and insatiable musical curiosity (in each of these traits, very much like

Milhaud or Henry Cowell) and his success in merging the indigenous music of Brazil with European technique. His friendship with Darius Milhaud during the latter's residence in Argentina brought Villa-Lobos into close contact with the music of Stravinsky and Les Six. Claudio Santoro (b. 1919) is another notable Brazilian; a student of Nadia Boulanger, Santoro made ample use of folklore and popular music in his early work, then moved in the direction of "international" serialism.

Many younger composers, taking their cue from Santoro and Ginastera, have moved away from overtly nationalistic styles. Chief among them are three Mexican composers. Manuel Enriquez (b. 1926), whose background includes study at the Juilliard School, private work with Stefan Wolpe, and electronic experience at the Columbia-Princeton Center, directs the annual New Music Forum sponsored by Mexico's Ministry of Education. An influential advocate of the antinationalist position, he has created a broad catalog of works combining elements of serialism and graphic, aleatory notation. Hector Quintanar (b. 1936), a student of Carlos Chavez with extensive experience at the Columbia University and French Radio electronic studios, has employed graphic notation, free atonality, cluster sonorities, and extended performing techniques in his instrumental work; the brilliantly colorful *Sideral II* for orchestra (1971) is an outstanding example. Mario Lavista (b. 1943) is thoroughly comfortable with the international avant-garde, by way of early studies with Quintanar and further work abroad with Stockhausen, Pousseur, Xenakis, and Ligeti. Since returning to Mexico in 1970, Lavista has developed interests in group improvisation and the expansion of opera in directions of electronics and multimedia.

The most widely heard Argentine composers are strongly influenced by Ginastera. Antonio Tauriello (b. 1931) studied with the elder figure and worked with him on a number of opera productions. Tauriello has been active as an opera conductor (his credits include the Chicago Lyric Opera and New York City Opera). His 1968 Piano Concerto offers a highly expressive interplay of textural cluster blocks and controlled freedom in performance. Alicia Terzian (b. 1934) has special interests in the integration of live instrumental performance with electronic alteration, tape delay, lighting effects, and other visual and technological stimuli, as shown in her 1984 *Amores* for electronically modified strings and tam-tam; in addition, she is active as a new-music conductor and directs the Grupo Encuentros of Buenos Aires. Gerardo Gandini (b. 1936) pursues a dual career as pianist and composer; he originally studied with Ginastera and later worked in the United States and Italy. In his 1970 Fantaisie-Impromptu for piano and orchestra, Gandini creates a multilayered narrative in which collage, quotation (fragments of a Chopin mazurka), innovative timbral combinations, and aleatory textures play a part.

Younger Brazilian composers have followed the path of Santoro, rather

ILLUS. 20.4.

Mario Lavista

Photo Credit: Paulina Lavista. Courtesy of Cenidim, Mexico

than Villa-Lobos, in embracing the international avant-garde. The fascinating figure of Gilberto Mendes (b. 1922) may be seen as a model. Mendes's background includes study with Santoro and extensive work abroad with Boulez and Stockhausen. Judging from his music, however, the strongest influences on his creative development seem to have been Satie, Warhol, Cage, and the theater of the absurd. He delights in irony and satire, the extroverted gesture, indeterminacy, and visual and spatial surprises. Marlos Nobre (b. 1939), a student of Ginastera, is a rising international figure; his 1970 *Mosaico* for orchestra presents contrasted shifting sound blocks and a brilliant array of sound colors. Jorge Antunes (b. 1942) is one of relatively few Latin American minimalists. Originally a physics student,

Antunes came to music via the electronic studio and has developed so-phisticated techniques of working with multiple loops and ostinati similar to those of Terry Riley.

Despite the internationalists' disavowal of native materials, common stylistic threads still distinguish much Latin American music: the high priority given to timbral innovation, fondness for vividly brilliant colors, and textures that emphasize sonority over linearity. These unifying threads exist even though a number of prominent Latin American figures have chosen to reside in Europe, Canada, and the United States. Argentina alone has produced four such well-known artists: Mario Davidovsky (now living in New York), Mauricio Kagel (resident in Germany), Alejandro Vinao (living in London), and Alcides Lanza (based at McGill University in Montreal). Cuban composers form an equally impressive international roster. Aurelio de la Vega has been an important figure on the Los Angeles music scene, and two Cuban-born women—Tania Léon (now based in the United States) and Odaline de la Martinez (in England)—have achieved success in dual careers as composer-conductors on opposite sides of the Atlantic. All of these composers constitute an informal network supporting and promoting Latin American music around the world. For example, de la Martinez created the long-running Music of the Americas series in London, and the Mexican-born composer and pianist Max Lifchitz founded and continues to direct the New York concert series North-South Consonance.

ENGLAND

Nineteenth-century Germans referred to England as the "land without music," an unfortunately apt epithet. By the late nineteenth century, England had reached the low point of a musical decline that had begun with the death of Henry Purcell in 1695. The early twentieth century witnessed the start of a remarkable revival, led by Ralph Vaughan Williams and Gustav Holst. A vital component of this renaissance was the growing interest in folk music and the great art music (Purcell, Morley, Dowland, Tallis) of England's past. Perhaps as a result, young composers pursued a stylistic course embracing modal polyphony and the clear outlines of neoclassicism. The strongest foreign influences tended to be French rather than Germanic; during the period between the World Wars there was virtually no interest, other than that of Frank Bridge and his young student Benjamin Britten, in the Second Viennese School.

The Second World War brought a number of expatriates fleeing political oppression to Britain's shores. Their number included a handful of musicians—particularly Roberto Gerhard (who settled in Cambridge) and Egon Wellesz (at Oxford)—with Schoenbergian leanings. William Glock founded the forward-looking journal *The Score* in 1949, and in the late 1950s Glock and Hans Keller (another émigré) began to rebuild the music division of the British Broadcast Corporation into a leading center for the commissioning, performance, and discussion of advanced new music. The two heirs of Vaughan Williams as elder statesmen proved to be positive influences: Benjamin Britten for his flexibility and open attitude to the widest variety of musical stimuli, and Sir Michael Tippett for his intellectually challenging, tough-minded, and insatiable curiousity about vernacular, folk, and pop cultures of every sort.

The founding of new-music groups such as the London Sinfonietta and the Pierrot Players (later renamed the Fires of London) completed the transformation of London, by the early 1970s, from a relatively provincial outpost to the most exciting musical center in Europe. Although it is no longer preeminent (for many, Paris and Berlin have come to dominate the 1990s), London remains a vibrant, cosmopolitan hub of activity and an eclectic melting pot of influences. The *French* influence may be noted in the many British composers working in Paris at IRCAM, the number of British disciples of Messiaen, and the legacy of Boulez's directorship of the BBC Symphony Orchestra. The *American* presence is strong, primarily because of the Harkness Fellowships, which brought many English composers to study at such places as Princeton, Yale, San Diego, and Tanglewood. The influence of *rock* music is evident in David Bedford's collaborations with Mike Oldfield and Kevin Ayres, John Tavener's close association with the Beatles, and Tim Souster's connection to Soft Machine, Cream, and the Who. (For the first performance of the new-music ensemble Intermodulation, Peter Townshend lent his sound system.) The influence of *non-Western* music reflects Britain's increasingly multiethnic population, with its Indian, African, Mediterranean, and Middle Eastern communities.

Prominent among the first generation of postwar composers is the Manchester school—in particular, three important figures who came together at the Royal Manchester College of Music: Peter Maxwell Davies, Harrison Birtwistle, and Alexander Goehr (b. 1932). Theater works by the first two are discussed in previous chapters. Goehr, working within a lyric, Schoenbergian style of great breadth, has created a strong body of chamber, choral, and stage works; in his capacity as Cambridge professor he has also taught a number of England's most gifted younger composers. These Manchester composers and others of their generation, such as Tavener, Bedford, and Cardew, brought England to the forefront of the new-music scene by the late 1960s.

During the 1980s, led by the increasing influence of Brian Ferneyhough, the cross-Channel impact of IRCAM, and the rise of younger composers working in intricate, rigorously deterministic ways, the term "new com-

ILLUS. 20.5.

Alexander Goehr

Photo credit: Ahley Ashwood, Financial Times. Courtesy
Schott and Co., Ltd.

plexity" began to appear with some regularity. Complex musical rhetoric
is hardly new for Michael Finnissy (b. 1946), a friend and colleague of
Ferneyhough's for many years who, like him, did not win recognition in
England until he had achieved considerable success on the Continent. Finnissy's language often bursts forth with dense showers of pitch, eruptive
rhythms, and saturated textures. But it is also surprisingly controlled and
related, if perhaps obliquely, to the context of ritual tradition. His fascination for different musics covers a wide range: Australian, African,

Romanian, ragtime and jazz, Nancarrow's player piano rolls, Gershwin. Virtually every work of his involves aspects of parody/historicism.

Finnissy is a brilliant pianist, and many of his works involve athletic, supervirtuosic piano parts. Three solo works of the 1970s exemplify the range of his piano writing. In *Reels*, derived from the melodic patterns and ornamentation of Scottish bagpiping, individual movements alternate between extremes of loud (fast, dry, percussive) and quiet (motionless, gentle, resonant). Percussive attacks at the extremes of register are common. The syncopated lines and jazz bass of *Freightrain Bruise*, though dissonant and atonal, are intended as an homage to Erroll Garner, Thelonius Monk, and Art Tatum. The pitches of *Kemp's Morris* are based on a tune from John Playford's *The Dancing Master* of 1651; recalling the ankle bells of traditional Morris dancers, the pianist's knuckles have bells tied across them, while the piano sonorities also evoke distant bells.

Complexity of a different sort motivates the musical rhetoric of Jonathan Harvey (b. 1939). Early study with Stockhausen during the latter's most "controlled" period, further study abroad at Princeton, and association with Boulez at the IRCAM center in Paris have all reinforced Harvey's compositional approach, one of fastidious care in the initial choice of material and its working out. But the music itself projects not a hint of fussiness or kaleidoscopic fragmentation. For Harvey, "'discipline" can be viewed in the religious sense, as leading to transcendence. For example, in his 1985 *Song Offerings* for soprano and eight instruments, the text, by the Indian poet and philosopher Rabindrath Tagore, speaks of love, both spiritual and erotic, with urgent, breathless anticipation; Harvey's music, with its rich colorings and overlapping melismas, conveys this ecstatic sense perfectly.

The many British proponents of minimalism (or the "new simplicity"), include Chris Hobbs, Howard Skempton, and Michael Nyman. All are influenced to greater or lesser degree by Cardew, Feldman, Christian Wolff, antiestablishment rock styles, and a growing national tradition (begun in the 1960s) of experimental music for performance by children. Gavin Bryars (b. 1943) is best known for two programmatic works of 1969–71: *The Sinking of the Titanic*, based on the legends surrounding the tunes that the band kept playing as the ship went down, and *Jesus' Blood Never Failed Me Yet*, in which a tape-looped fragment of a Victorian hymn, sung by a down-at-the-heels Londoner, is gradually enveloped by a warm orchestral accompaniment. Both works are surprisingly gentle and quite moving.

Minimalist aesthetics may also be linked to a more extroverted, impassioned language. In the 1976 Viola Concerto of Simon Bainbridge (b. 1952), lyric, expansive lines emerge from repeated cells. His later *Concertante in Moto Perpetuo* and *Voicing* (both 1983) recall John Adams's similar efforts to create long, arching phrases as consequence of repetition. Steve Martland (b. 1958) has worked with Louis Andriessen in Holland and shares with

Andriessen (and with the American Michael Torke) a hard-driving, relentless, uncompromising sensibility. His *Babi Yar* for orchestra with rock guitars and percussion captures a sense of outrage at the infamous Nazi massacre near Kiev during World War II. *Babi Yar* opens with a sustained chord and holds this sonority against brutal piercing outbursts. At the work's gripping finale, the opening chord has been transformed to a quiet cluster, against which one hears tolling bells, gongs, and distant horns.

Given the model of Britten, the "new romanticism" has never lacked English supporters. In recent years, Oliver Knussen (b. 1952) has assumed a major role as a composer, conductor, and champion of new music. His opera *Where the Wild Things Are,* based on the famous children's story by Maurice Sendak, has a grand romantic sweep that underscores the staging ideally. Romanticism of a different cast colors the latest work of John Tavener. The flamboyance of *The Whale* has receded into a much simpler style, its expressive aims channeled—through the Orthodox church—into deeply religious terms. For example, his *Ikon of Light* for double choir and string trio, with its drones and pedals, may recall Pärt and Kancheli. Yet another aspect of romanticism can be heard in the music of Peter Dickinson (b. 1934), whose feeling for American music, extending back to his studies at Juilliard, has led him to an Ivesian view of simultaneity, collage, and stylistic transformation. His 1984 Piano Concerto is most evocative as various layers—atonal "new music," sweeping European symphonism, ragtime, blues—gradually penetrate one another, often uniting in a dreamlike blur.

Younger composers have their own approaches to romanticism. Judith Weir (b. 1954) delivers a broad range of expression, from tenderness to biting wit and irony, with a few bold strokes. She excels in dramatic music and has composed a number of minioperas, designed for simple staging or concert performance and built on traditional models. *The Consolations of Scholarship* (1985) for soprano solo and chamber ensemble is highly stylized and suggestive in the manner of Chinese opera: the lone singer plays all the roles, including that of narrator. Weir uses instruments boldly, often to double the rhythms of recitative in heterophony. Robert Saxton (b. 1953) bases many works on literary or philosophical imagery. His 1984 Concerto for Orchestra, influenced by Jewish mystical writings of the Kabbalah, portrays a journey through various stages of illumination, culminating in ultimate brightness. The music is dazzling in its colors and busy, complex textures. Although its chief generative force is a continual, rushing ostinato, added levels of melodic contour and rhythmic articulation establish a larger, broader pulse; Saxton also effects gradual changes in the ostinato sonority, analogous to the filter sweeps of tape-loop fades of electronic studios.

George Benjamin (b. 1960), like Saxton, attracted notice at a very young age; his studies include work with Oliver Messiaen in Paris and Alexander

Goehr at Cambridge. His 1982 *At First Light* for chamber orchestra is surprisingly secure for a youthful piece. In contrast with Saxton's elaborately decorated figurations, Benjamin prefers a greater efficiency, even frugality, in his handling of resources. But his use of register, dynamics, and instrumention produces surprising timbral richness, and dramatically convincing rhetoric. A later work for chamber ensemble and digital instruments, *Antara* (1987), was composed at IRCAM. *Antara* takes its name from the Peruvian panpipe; Benjamin uses two digital keyboards to produce electronically altered "superpanpipe" sonorities, within a larger context of microtonal inflections and abundant glissandi.

CANADA

Unlike Britain, Japan, or the Netherlands, Canada is a vast "stage"—a full continent in size—with a multiethnic, multilingual, multicultural population. In these respects, it resembles the United States, China, and the former Soviet Union. Canada is a very *young* country, younger in fact, than the United States as it became an independent nation a century later. With relatively little sense of history or tradition, it had a late start in approaching Western art music seriously. R. Murray Schafer, one of Canada's best-known composers, wryly comments on his country's attitude to High Art with the words, "I think there is a feeling that Europe in general represents culture, and that if God had intended Canada to have culture, Mozart would have been born there."

If "nationalism" can be identified in terms of *identity*, then it certainly exists as a major force in Canada, and on a number of levels. Many Canadians see a need to create an "identity" distinctly different from that of their neighbor to the south, the United States. (It is impossible to ignore the presence of the American mass media, and fears of being engulfed by "cultural imperialism" are quite legitimate.) Other Canadians may wish to confirm their nation's independence of Britain. And establishing a sense of identity *within* Canada is also complex. The nation is officially bilingual and bicultural, and great divisions continue to exist between the English and French communities.

Finally, one must consider other groups that comprise the total population: Native Americans and (as in the United States), an influx of immigrants. In fact, many important "Canadian" composers were born elsewhere: Oskar Morawetz (b. 1917) in Czechoslovakia, avant-gardist Udo Kasamets (b. 1919) in Estonia, Istavan Anhalt (b. 1919) in Hungary, James Tenney (b. 1934) in the United States, Harry Freedman (b. 1922) in Poland, and Bengt Hambreaus (b. 1928) in Sweden.

Government support for the arts in Canada may seem meagre when compared to the European norm, but seems positively enlightened when compared to the attitudes of Canada's southern neighbor. Generous funding was an important factor in Canada's early prominence in electronic music, as both the University of Toronto and McGill University set up influential studios in the late 1950s.

Canada's first composer to espouse European "modernist" technique was John Weinzweig (b. 1913), an early champion of twelve-tone technique. Harry Somers (b. 1925), who studied with Weinzweig and with Darius Milhaud, has developed a language that combines elements of both serial rigor and neoclassic transparency. In this and in his *Gebrauchsmusik*—music for previously neglected constituencies, music for the media, music based on ethnic and vernacular styles—Somers resembles Aaron Copland. He and Weinzweig are still important leaders and mentors, at least for what might be called (in this bifurcated nation) the "English" community. One of that community's major representatives, Robert Aitken (b. 1939), is an outstanding flutist and composer and the founder of Toronto's New Music Concerts series. His *Folia* for wind quintet (1980) offers a constantly shifting, polyrhythmic overlay of ostinati, in which an assortment of special effects figure prominently: trills, fluttertongue effects, singing while playing, glissandi, bent tones, changing vibrato speeds—all delightfully frenetic and virtuosic.

Perhaps Canada's most visible composer, R. Murray Schafer has had a thoroughly unorthodox career. Expelled from the University of Toronto, he settled in England before returning to Canada in the mid-1960s. His earlier music (such as the 1954 Concerto for Harpsichord and Eight Wind Instruments) is crisply neoclassic in style. While teaching in British Columbia, however, Schafer began to explore more experimental techniques. Influenced by the idea of Marshall McLuhan (a fellow Torontonian) and John Cage, he developed a fascination with sound and density, chance, theater, and graphic notation. He put these into practice by working with schoolchildren and composing works for school ensembles. Schafer's subsequent books on the presentation of new music in the schools, often in the form of classroom dialogues, are classics in the field of music education. Many of his own compositions can be thought of as extensions of his Socratic attitudes, designed to question—if not sabatoge—aspects of the Western concert tradition.

Schafer's 1970 orchestral work *No Longer Than Ten Minutes* (the title is drawn from a stipulation in his commission contract!) begins with no conductor on the stage, as all instruments enter on a staggered unison note. The pitch material then gradually expands outward in both directions as the conductor enters and approaches the podium (note the footsteps in Example 20.2). The end of the work is equally provocative; the conductor leaves the stage, and—against a sustained dominant-seventh chord played

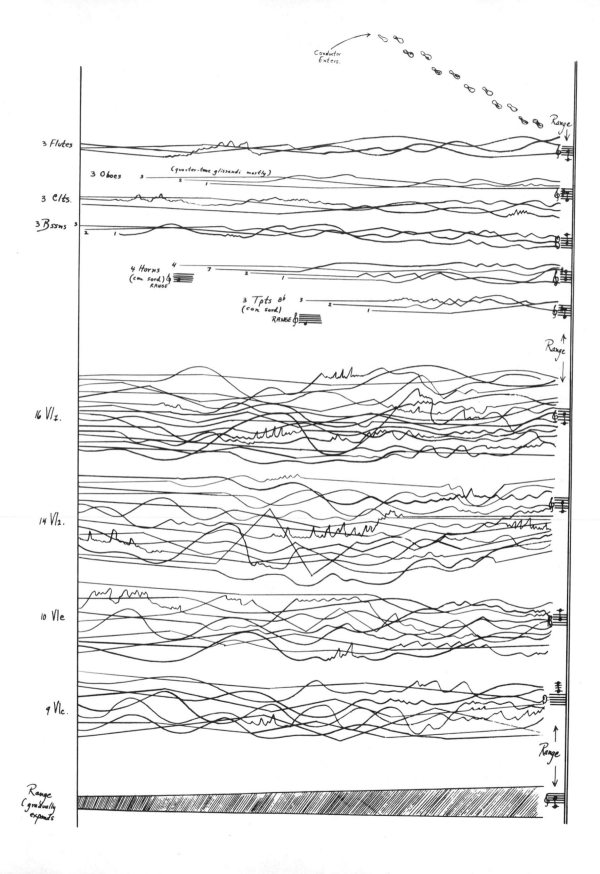

by a string quartet—we hear offstage woodwind fragments from the *next* work on the concert program. The dominant-seventh chord lingers, quietly but audibly, through the conductor's return to the podium, and lasts until the downbeat of the following piece.

Schafer's theatricalism has also manifested itself in his interest in the environment. He has written eloquently about the relationship between sounds and social structures, voicing his concern for the impact of industrial technology—specifically, the *sounds* of technology—on perception and sensitivity. In a related project, *Soundscape,* he has been actively recording and preserving the sounds of different communities. A number of Schafer's recent works are themselves conceived as total "environments." *Ra* (1983) is based on the Egyptian myth of the sun god's passage during the night. Its performance (including acting, dance, masks, and audience participation), lasting about eleven hours, takes place from sunset to sunrise.

The French community of Canadian composers has had its own mentors and leaders. Jean Papineau-Couture (b. 1916), twice president of the Canadian League of Composers, has long been considered the dean of Québecois composers. He was a student of Nadia Boulanger; the grace and clarity of neoclassicism abound in his music. Serge Garant (1929–86), more adventurous in his stylistic explorations, was in 1954 one of the first Canadians to compose tape music. His *Cage d'oiseau* for piano makes use of graphic notation and percussive sounds made on the piano lid. Gilles Tremblay (b. 1932), a former student of Messiaen and Stockhausen, works with contrasting textural blocks. His 1978 orchestral work *Vers le soleil* ("Toward the Sun") juxtaposes such elements as a sustained mass, a rapid rhythmic outburst, a "flock of glissandi," and a quotation from a Gregorian Alleluia. Their interaction and alternation moves the music forward.

The gifted composer Claude Vivier (1948–83) studied with Tremblay at the Montreal Conservatory, then with Stockhausen at Cologne and Koening at the Institute of Sonology in Holland. But his musical philosophy was shaped more intensely by travels to Iran, Bali, and Thailand. Vivier's style combines elements of the postwar avant-garde with ornate Asian melodic shapes, set against drones and decorated heterophonically. This duality dominates his *Siddartha* (1976) for orchestra; its forceful, direct opening gesture—an extended pedal note hammered out again and again, then held against increasingly elaborate figurations—returns as a hushed, quiet bass

---

EXAMPLE 20.2.

R. Murray Schafer: *No Longer Than Ten Minutes*

Used by permission of Berandol Music Ltd.

for lush romantic chord progressions, and finally subsides as series of repeated high notes on bells. Vivier's chamber sextet *Et je reverrai cette ville étrange* (1982) offers an even greater juxtaposition of styles, within the context of near-continuous monody—at one moment reminiscent of Québecois folksong, at another of middle Eastern melisma, all articulated by bells and gongs. The different scales and rhythmic patterns succeed one another quite naturally, with no sense of contradiction or inappropriateness.

Canadian music does not proceed from either a "British" or a "French" model, of course; such distinctions are largely superficial and ultimately limiting. The music of Alexina Louie (b. 1949) reflects many new directions—not only ethnically Asian, but Pacific coast—that may speak to Canada's cultural future. She received a traditional conservatory training, including advanced composition study at the University of California at San Diego with Pauline Oliveros, Roger Reynolds, and Robert Erickson. During her childhood and adolescence, she had shown little interest in her own Chinese heritage, but as a graduate student, began collecting Asian instruments and learned to play Chinese flutes and ch'in at UCLA. Asian techniques, such a pitch bending and heterophonic textures, and attitudes have subsequently influenced her compositions. A fascination with duality, contrasts of ying and yang, can be heard in her *Cadenzas* for clarinet and percussion, in which tightly integrated, dissonant passages are balanced by gentle, lyric gestures. Shimmering light and images of luxuriant foliage, against sustained pedal points, clusters, and triads, dominate her orchestral *Songs of Paradise*. *Music for a Thousand Autumns* (1983) for chamber orchestra reveals a dichotomy between its peaceful surface and the passionate intensity that lies beneath. Echoes of an ancient Chinese melody, originally written for the ch'in, are balanced in the finale by a steely, bravura piano cadenza. Louie notes that *Music for a Thousand Autumns* was begun just after Claude Vivier's life came to a tragic end. In her words, "the first movement is actually a call to Claude. His death made me think very carefully about the contribution of the artist to the world."

Pieces for Study IV: A Panorama of Works by Genre

21

We conclude with a wide-angle view of music composed since World War II—a varied sampling of works grouped according to four principal genres of the Western concert literature: *opera, concerto, chamber music,* and *orchestral music*. In past eras, a word like "opera" might conjure up a fairly limited range of expectations. By the end of the twentieth century, however, every such category now admits a host of possible approaches and concerns. We illustrate this range with a broad cross-section of repertoire.

OPERA

Philip Glass: Einstein on the Beach

To many, "opera" may seem a misnomer for Glass's *Einstein on the Beach* (1975). Superficially, it has all the necessary trappings: singers, actors, choruses (one large and one small), an "orchestra" (the six musicians of the Philip Glass Ensemble), acts, scenes, costumes, and stage sets. Beyond this, however, it diverges in many respects from any opera, traditional or contemporary, that predates it.

Einstein on the Beach lasts approximately five hours. Although there is no intermission, audience members are invited to come and go as they please, a novel variant on **performance ritual.** Many take that option, while others are too mesmerized, too transported by the sweep, scope, and sheer volume of the event, to leave their seats. (Those who do leave and return may find that very little has "occurred" during the interim.) *Einstein* may seem more akin to early-1960s "happenings" than to operatic tradition: on the surface, words, sounds, and images seem disjointed, fantastical, lacking any narrative logic. But on a more abstract level, they have a deeper psychological resonance, and all relate to a central theme: the figure of Albert Einstein and the many symbols—scientific, political, social, even musical—associated with his name.

Three primary images predominate in *Einstein on the Beach:* trains (a favorite analogy in Einstein's writings), a trial (symbolizing the moral test put to humanity by his discoveries), and a spaceship (suggesting the unknown futures opened up by his work). These and other nonmusical ele-

ILLUS. 21.1.

A scene from *Einstein on the Beach* by Philip Glass

Photo: Beatriz Schiller

ments were conceived and developed by the director and designer Robert Wilson, who has woven them into four acts of two or three scenes each, interconnected with five "knee plays." The stream-of-consciousness poetry spoken by the protagonists, sometimes forming a collage of indecipherable verbiage, includes contributions from actors in the original production. (One of these was Lucinda Childs, who also choreographed the opera.) Wilson's sets and staging and Childs's use of dance and movement, are perfectly wedded to Glass's music; the total effect is hypnotic.

It is *Einstein's* music, however, that has sparked the most controversy. Its relentlessly cyclical approach to **pitch logic** and **time,** unfolding over a vast time span, is emblematic of what some admire and others scorn in the minimalist aesthetic. Simple chord progressions and scalar patterns are repeated continuously for lengthy periods; most are transformed (sometimes swiftly, sometimes protractedly) by intricate but subtle rhythmic variation. Melodic and rhythmic cycles evolve through an additive and subtractive **process,** much as in Indian ragas. The plainly triadic harmony leaves one's ear free to become fully absorbed in these cycles, which are clarified further by audible numbers and solfège syllables (these are, in fact, the sole text sung by the choruses). Glass provides a succession of steady pulses, each serving as a background for gradually shifting ostinati and additive rhythms. The **sound colors** are brilliant (literally "electric") and constantly changing, as heavily amplified flutes, organ, different keyboard instruments, and voices move in and out of the busy yet curiously stately fabric.

The opening of *Einstein on the Beach* consists of three successive low tones (A, G, C) on the electric organ. (These tones have already been played again and again as the audience enters the opera house.) As the tones repeat, major triads are superimposed on them, forming a simple chord progression treated as a static ostinato "object." Each of the chords is repeated a number of times, and a small chorus articulates the chord series by singing the number of beats through which each chord is held. At other moments a chord series is arpeggiated in various ways, the duration of each chord gradually elongated or shortened by the use of additive techniques. The series illustrated in Example 21.1 is one of the most frequently heard progressions of the opera. This additive treatment of chord arpeggiation is a critical component of *Einstein on the Beach.* (The opera was composed around the same time as Glass's *Another Look at Harmony,* which incorporates a virtually identical approach.)

Although conventional plot is nonexistent, the drama has a definite dramatic focus in the figure of Einstein: scientist, kindly professor, humanist, amateur violinist, yet also the father of atomic energy. The "trial" that dominates so much of the ritual activity is surely related to Einstein's role in the development of the atom bomb. Note, too, that *On the Beach* was the title of Nevile Shute's 1957 novel (subsequently a film) about the

---

EXAMPLE 21.1.

Philip Glass: *Einstein on the Beach*

catastrophic aftermath of atomic war; similarly, a nuclear explosion is a central feature of the opera's final scene.

Oddly enough, the character of Einstein distances himself from the other performers by sitting midway between the action onstage and the musicians in the pit or by standing onstage but to one side, playing the violin—as did the actual historical figure—and observing the proceedings. (The solo violin material is drawn from the chord series in Example 21.1.) Other fleeting visual references to Einstein appear, disappear, and reappear with some regularity: a character drawing equations on an invisible blackboard, another smoking a pipe, still another sticking out his tongue (as the scientist actually did in a famous photograph).

Thea Musgrave: A Christmas Carol

Scottish-born Thea Musgrave (b. 1928), a resident of the United States for many years, has been successful at integrating advanced techniques into an accessible, dramatically convincing style. She is especially fond of weaving familiar quotes—often brief fragments—into complex textures, and of juxtaposing multiple layers of material against each other. In instrumental works, the effect of such gestures is Ivesian, and Ives was indeed influential in Musgrave's development, as her concertos bear out. But the same gestures are also ideally suited to stage music, where references, allusions, and intersecting events are often integral to the drama. It is hardly surprising, then, that Musgrave has had great success with her operas, especially *Mary, Queen of Scots* (1977) and *A Christmas Carol* (1979). The latter is her own recasting of the Dickens tale, with dialogue and storyline modified to suit her musical and theatrical requirements.

In *A Christmas Carol* Musgrave makes creative and dramatically poignant use of familiar resources: a plot well known to all (frequently using

Dickens' own words) and a literature of Christmas music drawn upon at appropriate moments. *A Christmas Carol*'s treatment of **time** and **pitch logic** is straightforward rather than experimental. Simple, transparent rhythms are the norm; a tonal center and associated scale are almost always present, though chromatically enriched and subject to the composer's own syntax of chord succession. The libretto unfolds along conventionally narrative lines, while soloists, chorus, and instrumentalists maintain a relationship well within the nineteenth-century European operatic tradition.

But Musgrave manages to evince a compelling sense of atmosphere from these materials; she is particularly imaginative in the domain of multilayered **texture.** Her opening music breathes the dark, damp air of old London, with fragments of "God Rest Ye Merry Gentlemen" adding irony to the dreary first tableau. Eerie cluster sonorities (both instrumental and vocal, the latter emanating from an offstage chorus), deep bells and gongs, and sharp motivic angularity are movingly contrasted, as in a multiple exposure, with distant caroling or snippets of a traditional English dance tune (at the Fezziwigs' party).

In place of Dickens's three Christmas ghosts, a single spirit leads Scrooge through past, present, and future. The spirit is wordless, making the role ideal for a dancer or mime, and it also assumes a variety of guises (a musician at the Fezziwigs' ball, a beggar, and so on), adding an Everyman theme to Dickens's story. Musgrave also specifies that certain pairs of roles must be sung by the same individual (e.g., Mrs. Cratchit and a charwoman, Marley's ghost and a rag-and-bone man). This decision seems motivated by more than the economics of opera production; ironic symbolism is equally important, perhaps in the spirit of Berg's *Lulu*. It may be that Musgrave's fine sense of **parody/historicism,** so obvious on the level of musical collage, is operating on a deeper level as well.

Other emotionally wrenching scenes of the Dickens original— Scrooge, for example, as a young man parting with his fiancée and as an old man confronting his own gravestone—are expanded in the libretto and underscored with an affecting mix of lyricism and harmonic tension. By the final scene, the opening fragments of "God Rest Ye Merry Gentlemen" converge into a full-blown, triumphal rendition, bringing the opera to a jubilant release.

György Ligeti: Le grand macabre

Until the late 1960s Ligeti was a central figure in the exploration of sound masses and densities in choral and instrumental writing. In subsequent works, however, his view of **pitch logic, time,** and **texture** shifted, focusing more on fanciful melodic lines, rhythmically erratic gestures, and the innovative treatment of individual instruments and voices. In *Le grand* *macabre* (1977) the result is a sometimes farcical, sometimes freakish score that powerfully reinforces the dark humor of the script.

Ligeti himself fashioned the libretto from a play, *Le ballade du grand macabre*, by the Flemish playwright Michel de Ghelderode. The story is set in Breughelland, and its central figure is Nekrotzar, a horrid specter who rises from the dead and proclaims the imminent destruction of the world. Among others in the cast are a drunken fool, a fat little prince, his court astrologer, a whip-toting nymphomaniac clad in leather, a Chief of the

---

ILLUS. 21.2.

Ligeti's *Le grand macabre* in performance

Photo: Enar Merkel Rydberg. Courtesy Kungliga Teatern
(Royal Opera), Stockholm, Sweden

Secret Police, a bird on roller skates (coloratura soprano), and two inde-fatigable lovers. Following much buffoonery, revelry, and political chica-nery, a comet appears in the midnight sky, finally signaling the end of all. The next morning, however, everyone awakens from a drunken stupor to find the world still intact; Nekrotzar slinks back into the grave, crestfallen and humiliated. As the opera ends, the amorous couple emerges after a long night of intimacy and bursts forth with a rapturous duet in celebration of love and life. One is left to wonder whether Nekrotzar was really Death incarnate or merely a trifling impostor.

The musical setting ranges from lush, poignant lyricism to vigorous, angular complexity to absurdly comical effects. Ligeti's caustic wit, aimed at both social and musical institutions (including opera itself), is felt from the very opening, which features a deft contrapuntal essay for twelve auto horns. Another sardonic touch is the pairing of Nekrotzar, a *Sarastro*-like basso profundo, with his drunken assistant, an implausibly high tenor whose part is punctuated with mutterings, squeaks, and hiccups. The wildly demanding parts of Prince Go-Go and the Chief of Police are both sung by high sopranos, adding to the air of dementia.

Musical **parody** is also present: in addition to brief quotes from the finale of Beethoven's *Eroica* Symphony and the cancan from Offenbach's *Orpheus in the Underworld,* there are scattered hints of Rameau, Schubert, Stravinsky, and many others. Often, the latter are woven into a subtle pastiche, a backdrop of familiar sound objects likened by Ligeti to pop art.

While other experimental operas of the 1960s and 1970s eschewed clear-cut, musically delineated roles and a meaningful storyline, these are all vividly present in *Le grand macabre.* To Ligeti, the abandonment of plot, character, and dialogue was a worn-out ploy of the 1960s. In this work he envisioned instead what he called an "anti-anti-opera," one that would renew as well as expand the operatic medium.

R. Murray Schafer: The Princess of the Stars

Schafer's *The Princess of the Stars* (1981) is in some respects a conventional opera: a drama whose dialogue and action are set to music, with the usual division of labor between singers, dancers, and instrumentalists. Neverthe-less, it remains a ground-breaking experiment in music theater in that it uniquely expands the limits of **performance ritual.**

For a venue it requires neither theater nor concert hall, but an outdoor hillside overlooking the waters and shores of a lake, located as far from civilization as possible. This setting is ideal for the work's story, drawn from Native American legend, in which natural forces play an important part. All participants, listeners and performers alike, must assemble at the

ILLUS. 21.3.

R. Murray Schafer's *Princess of the Stars*, performed at dawn at Two Jack Lake in the Canadian Rockies (1985)

Photo: Ed Ellis. Courtesy Banff Centre for the Arts

selected location during the darkest hours of the early morning; the opera itself then begins, just before dawn, with the singers and instrumentalists situated at water's edge, surrounded by members of the audience.

An unaccompanied aria by the Princess is heard from the opposite shore. Dancers and actors then appear from the lake's far corners, ferried in canoes and dressed in oversized, brightly visible costumes. As dawn breaks, they enact what Shafer calls an "archaic ritual." Canoes follow choreographed routes while their occupants perform large, ceremonious gestures and chant in a fictional language derived by Schafer from Native American dialects. These sounds and activities are accompanied by the land-based musicians and interpreted for the audience by a Presenter in mystic garb, who is carried about in a canoe of his own.

The story told is that of the Sun God's daughter, the Princess, who has fallen from the sky and been pulled into the lake by the Three-Horned Enemy. Wolf attempts to rescue her, aided by Dawn Birds who sweep the water aside with their wings. Wolf and the Enemy prepare to fight, but the Sun emerges from the horizon, drives the Enemy away, and commands Wolf to roam the world in search of the Princess. The Dawn Birds are ordered to freeze the lake and utter no song until he succeeds. (These and other plot details are loosely modeled by Schafer on Native American mythic explanations for natural phenomena—dew as stars scattered by the falling Princess, or winter migration as the silence of the Dawn Birds).

Schafer's revolutionary concept is in making the wilderness his stage. One of the *dramatis personae* is even drawn directly from nature: the Sun God is played by the sun itself. But beyond this, nature governs all the conditions—indeed, the very possibility—of performance. The sky, for instance, must be clear for the sun to take part, the lake must be calm for canoes to maneuver easily, and winds must be light for sound to travel.

The Princess of the Stars serves as prologue to a series of six equally extravagant theater pieces entitled *Patria*, begun in 1966. *Patria III: The Greatest Little Show on Earth* is also staged outdoors on a vast scale, taking the form of a carnival spread out over large fairgrounds.

Richard O'Brien: The Rocky Horror Picture Show

In previous chapters, space has not allowed us to consider the Broadway-style musical, nor has film been discussed except in a multimedia context. As a special case, however, we include Richard O'Brien's musical *The Rocky Horror Show* (1973)—and, in particular, its subsequent release as a movie, *The Rocky Horror Picture Show*—because the latter represents a startling and unprecedented phenomenon in music theater: a transformation of the Rock musical genre to the domain of audience participation.

To recall the plot briefly: an alien transvestite named Frank 'n' Furter from the planet Transexual, occupies an old mansion with a retinue of maniacal fellow Transexuals and several earthlings he has seduced or enslaved. They are joined on a stormy night by Brad and Janet, a newly engaged couple from late-1950s middle America who arrive looking for help with a flat tire. They end up losing their innocence instead; among those to whom Janet succumbs is Rocky Horror, an Adonis-like product of biochemical wizardry concocted by Frank 'n' Furter for his own gratification. The outlandish course of events, narrated by a ludicrously pompous criminologist, culminates in the destruction of Frank 'n' Furter and the return of his minions to outer space.

What makes this show exceptional is that the filmed version has spontaneously generated a **performance ritual** tradition of audience involvement, unintended (but enthusiastically welcomed) by the author/composer. Every Saturday at midnight, from the mid-1970s to the present, people from all walks of life in both America and Europe have flocked to screenings of *The Rocky Horror Picture Show,* many dressed like drag queens, Hell's Angels, ghouls, sci-fi aliens, or other characters in the film. Patrons also arrive with rice, eggs, tomatoes, and other objects, these being hurled at the screen in response to dialogue and action. (When Frank 'n' Furter proposes a toast to his dinner guests, for instance, it has become traditional to pelt the screen with slices of toast.) There is always dancing and singing in the theater aisles, often in remarkable synchrony with the film, whose choreography and lyrics have been memorized (after countless viewings) by many.

Much of the activity takes place onstage *in front of* the screen, where audience members mime or interact with what is projected behind them. (For instance, when Dr. Scott, a mad scientist, moves across the screen in his wheelchair, viewers sometimes attempt to race him across the stage in wheelchairs of their own.) The film, then, has become just one element—a cantus firmus—in a live multimedia show incorporating real-time stage action and intensive audience involvement. (All this has since spilled over into staged productions of the work, subjecting the cast to unforeseeable hazards and complications.)

At least part of this phenomenon was inspired by the infectious energy of the music itself. O'Brien's songs are a tongue-in-cheek **parody** of various pop genres, from early 1960s teen-idol music (Brad and Janet's love duet) to a hard-driving, Buddy Holly style ("Whatever Happened to Saturday Night") to a take-off on Jim Morrison ("Sweet Transexual"). The gospel-derived "chorus of thousands" sound is reserved for the show's jubilant refrain: "Let's Do the Time Warp Again." Like Galt MacDermot's *Hair* (1967), The Who's *Tommy* (1969), and Andrew Lloyd Webber's *Jesus Christ Superstar* (1971), O'Brien's musical demonstrates that the rock idiom is as capable as any of producing memorable tunes, striking harmonies, and a broad expressive range.

As one might surmise from our brief comments on these five works, the genre of music theater has been especially lively in recent decades. In one sense, of course, the idea of theater has pervaded virtually *all* postwar music. It is commonplace, in fact, for speaking, humming, physical movement, costuming, spatial directionality, or specific lighting cues to be incorporated into a new work for flute and piano or a string quartet. All of these might simply be considered part of expanded performance practice. This late twentieth-century penchant for the innately theatrical is compounded even further when one adds the extra dimensions of text, characterization, staging, and the great range of visual and sonic effects afforded by modern technology.

Minimalist repetition, digital sonic effects, ritual movement, and the creative use of performance space, for example, take on a unique power in such operas as *The Man Who Mistook His Wife for a Hat* by Michael Nyman, or Robert Ashley's *Perfect Lives (Private Parts)* of 1979. Style juxtaposition may be an ideal vehicle for wry commentary on the fragmentation of modern life—as in Leonard Bernstein's *Trouble in Tahiti* (1952)—or underscore much stronger social concerns. Opera has had a long history of association with social movements and political struggles. Such works as Anthony Davis's *X* and T. J. Anderson's *Soldier Boy* (both examining aspects of the African-American experience) or *Ghosts of an Old Ceremony* (1991) by Libby Larsen (subtitled "A Tribute to American Pioneer Women") continue in this tradition.

This is not to suggest that all postwar operas have been wildly experimental in style, or activist in content. A great many, on the order of Musgrave's *A Christmas Carol*, are designed to function within the post–*verismo* operatic tradition. Even here, though, composers delight in the use of dramatically powerful avant-gardisms, from cluster sonorities to tone rows to electronics. Opera composers of our time have also had the good fortune (or good sense) to draw upon a remarkable *theatrical* literature— important plays that have great musical potential. Significantly, postwar works based on material by Strindberg, Chekhov, Pirandello, and Yeats— Hugo Weisgall's *Six Characters in Search of an Author*, *The Stronger*, and *Purgatory*; Dominick Argento's *The Boor*; and Ned Rorem's *Miss Julie*—are by some of our most accomplished vocal composers.

CONCERTO

Here, too, is an inherently theatrical medium, although traditionally the drama in the concerto has been abstract: pitting instrumental forces against one other and differentiating them visually and acoustically by their placement within the performance space. Henry Brant's *Ghost Nets* for solo contrabass and widely antiphonally separated ensembles can be considered a latter-day extension of the Baroque concept. The contending forces of a concerto in the late twentieth century may represent different levels of technological "enhancement"—as with Olly Wilson's *Akwan* for piano, electric piano, amplified strings, and orchestral—or seemingly contradictory styles. William Thomas McKinley (b. 1938), who straddles the worlds of jazz and art music, easily reconciles such apparent mismatches in his *Paintings VI* for seven players and in his Concerto for Flute and String Orchestra. Tonal passages of great simplicity, abrupt dissonances, and outright theater all figure in the fabric of Michael Schelle's Concerto for Two Pianos and Orchestra.

Alternatively, one may view the genre as a study in weights and masses (a traditional approach) or—perhaps uniquely contemporary—as a *political* paradigm of class, role, and stratification. Per Nørgård, torn between both of these concerns, did not compose concertos for many years. Since 1985, however, he has created two works that focus on questions of balance in both senses: *Between* for cello and orchestra and *Helle Nacht* for violin and orchestra.

Finally, the concerto's nineteenth-century legacy is that of virtuoso showpiece. Today's extroverted approach to the theater of performance, along with a host of extended playing techniques, not only maintains this tradition but urges it in new directions. For sheer brilliance, it would be difficult to better Leonard Bernstein's Symphony No. 2, *The Age of Anxiety*, for piano and orchestra; Harvey Sollberger's *Riding the Wind I* for flute and chamber ensemble; William Kraft's Concerto for Four Percussionists and Orchestra and his 1984 Timpani Concerto; and Don Martino's Triple Concerto for Three Clarinets and Orchestra. For each of these works, the composer has had extensive experience in playing the solo instrument in question—in some cases, at a virtuosic level.

Charles Wuorinen: Second Piano Concerto

Charles Wuorinen has been a focus of controversy since his youthful rise to international prominence in the 1960s. Until his more recent period of procedural flexibility, his music was the product of rigorous serial practices affecting **pitch logic** and **time** on both smaller and larger structural levels, with elaborate intuitive embellishments on the surface. The Second Piano Concerto (1974) is constructed this way and exhibits the impenetrable dissonances and gargantuan complexities typical of the composer's pre-1980 compositions. It also reflects Wuorinen's own relationship, as a formidable pianist, to the solo instrument.

Technology plays a unique role in the concerto, which is written for *amplified* piano, a three-tiered speaker system, and orchestra. Speakers are placed next to the piano itself, on both sides of the stage, and at locations in the concert hall. As the work's single movement progresses, piano amplification is routed from one site to the next (or to all three) as directed in the score. The need to amplify the piano, both acoustically and spatially, stems from an unusual soloist-versus-orchestra relationship and the **process** it undergoes. In an ordinary concerto, ideas are developed equally and antiphonally between ensemble and individual. In this concerto, however, labyrinthian twelve-tone materials originate with and emanate entirely *from the piano*, while the orchestra's role is one of imitation and variation. The piano must therefore dominate the balance of forces.

An arch structure shapes the imitative process. At first, the orchestra echoes the piano's pitch and interval content (though not its rhythm) immediately. With time, however, there is an increasing lag in response, yielding a more traditional kind of antiphony between soloist and ensemble. By the end, the temporal gap is closed again, with orchestral sonorities doubling those in the piano.

ILLUS. 21.4.

Charles Wuorinen

Courtesy BMI Archives

Although notated in $\frac{4}{4}$ throughout, the *Second Piano Concerto* is propelled by incessantly changeable, unevenly constellated rhythms upon which a large-scale pattern of constant fluctuations in tempo is superimposed.

Sofia Gubaidulina: Offertorium

Prior to late-1980s *glasnost*, Sofia Gubaidulina was one of few truly innovative Soviet composers to gain international acclaim, pursuing what officialdom had once branded a "mistaken path." The work that assured her reputation was *Offertorium* (1980), a concerto for violin and orchestra based on the theme of J. S. Bach's *Musical Offering*. Gubaidulina subjects this melody to a compositional **process** from which a wealth of astonishing **sound colors** and **textures** issues forth. Densely intricate chromaticism is juxtaposed with straightforward rhythm and luxuriantly diatonic harmony, all coexisting within a single, convincing aesthetic.

Gubaidulina's use of **parody/historicism** is remarkable. The concerto opens with a multiple quotation: a statement of Bach's theme, orchestrated in *Klangfarbenmelodie* as Anton Webern had once done, but leaving off the final D (Example 21.2a). The three sections of the concerto, played without pause, constitute three forms of variations on this initial idea. During the first, Bach's theme "offers itself in sacrifice" (Gubaidulina's words), as subsequent restatements of it become increasingly obscured through rhythmic distortion, octave displacement, and submersion in the orchestral totality. Moreover, each restatement omits ("sacrifices") one or more notes from the beginning and end of the line. Every time the melody (or what remains of it) appears, the last interval still present is seized on by soloist or orchestra as a source of new melodic and harmonic developments. In Example 21.2b, the solo part derives from the ascending fourths (here inverted to fifths) while the orchestra continues with the descending chromatic motion so prominent in the theme. By the end of the first cadenza, repetition of the Bach has shrunk to a single, central pitch, F#, spun out by the soloist into a one-note rhapsody.

After a second section, in which ideas are drawn more freely from the Bach theme, the final portion of the work gradually reconstitutes segments of the melody from the intervallic weft generated by it. Only in the soloist's final cadenza, however, does the theme appear in the same simple and untruncated manner first heard in the orchestra, but by now it is transformed into its retrograde. Significantly, the soloist also has the privilege of intoning the final D, played in the violin's highest register, this represents not just the first but also the last D of the melody, missing from the original statement.

EXAMPLE 21.2A.

a)

Theme of J. S. Bach's *Musical Offering,* with Gubaidulina's Webern-style orchestration

EXAMPLE 21.2B.

Sofia Gubaidulina: *Offertorium*, first part

Used with the permission of G. Schirmer, Inc. (ASCAP)
on behalf of VAAP (Russia)

EXAMPLE 21.2B (continued)

b)

Brian Ferneyhough: Carceri d'invenzione I

Although not titled as a concerto, Ferneyhough's *Carceri d'Invenzione I* (1982) is a modern-day rethinking of the concerto grosso, scored for five winds, four brass, percussion, piano, and string quintet. The first in a series of works based on engravings by the eighteenth-century architect Giambattista Piranesi, its title means "constriction of invention" and refers to any creative **process** whose power arises from setting up strict, elaborately formulated limits and then surmounting them.

This notion is crucial to Ferneyhough's philosophy. In an interview he has related the work's title not to any desire to write illustrative material, but rather to an identification with Piranesi's approach to the creative act, especially "the way the materials relate to their formal constraints," resulting in imagery "hyper-loaded with expression, with explosive and implosive energy." In Ferneyhough's view, then, the engravings address his "central concerns . . . that all expression in art in some way derives from limitation." The *Carceri d'invenzione* cycle of seven works exemplifies this attitude on a number of levels, not the least of which is the challenge of generating a wildly diverse collection from a single body of material (a group of eight chords). Typical of Ferneyhough, the flowering of ideas in *Carceri d'invenzione I* spawns **textures** of staggering complexity, replete with intricately variegated pitch patterns, rhythmic shapes, dynamics, articulations, and timbral inflections. Built into the music is the energy and tension of players' efforts to render precisely that which is intentionally too exacting to perform without error.

Historically, the Baroque concerto grosso pits a smaller instrumental group, the concertino, against a larger one, the ripieno. In *Carceri d'invenzione I*, however, many smaller groups are all pitted against one another, and the groups change membership from one segment of the work to the next. At the outset, for example, piccolo, trombone, and piano form one group while seven other woodwinds and brass constitute another; in the next section the groups trade instruments and add new ones to form two new ensembles, while yet a third (a string quartet) is introduced. Each new grouping is assigned a transformation it must undergo (e.g., increase or decrease in density, registral span, gestural uniformity, etc.) Up to five independent layers of such processes are superimposed on one another, each with its own mix of instrumental **sound color.** The tutti sections serve as a ritornello, and ironically, this is where each instrument acts individually, dissociated briefly from group-defined activities.

A singular feature of *Carceri d'invenzione I* is the virtuosic requirement placed on the *conductor*, equal to the demands made on the other performers. With each regrouping, instruments are shuffled and rebracketed relative to others in the score, requiring a constant reorientation to the page for cuing purposes. Even more challenging is the treatment of **time.** Ferneyhough's phenomenally complex subdivisions and angularities in rhythm are made more so because they often occur within meters such as $\frac{5}{10}$, $\frac{3}{12}$, $\frac{9}{20}$, and $\frac{11}{24}$. Though unconventional, these are conceptually simple—a whole note can be divided by tenths as easily as by eights or quarters—but associated with constant changes in meter, an absence of pulse, and frequent shifts in tempo, they demand the most skilled baton work.

John Corigliano: Pied Piper Fantasy

While the traditional concerto is inherently theatrical, *The Pied Piper Fantasy* (1982) is expressly so, with extrovertly programmatic elements. John Corigliano wrote this work for the notoriously charismatic soloist James

John Corigliano

Photo: Toni Browning. Courtesy RCA Victor and
G. Schirmer, Inc.

Galway. To justify music that could exploit Galway's virtuosity and stage persona, Corigliano added his own twists to Robert Browning's poem "The Pied Piper of Hamelin," concocting a purely musical drama in seven interconnected "acts": "Sunrise and the Pipers Song," "The Rats," "Battle with the Rats," "War Cadenza," "The Piper's Victory," "The Burgher's Chorale," and "The Children's March." The two main protagonists are the flute soloist (the Piper) and the orchestra, which assumes a variety of roles.

   Pitch logic and **time** reflect Corigliano's typically audacious brand of eclecticism. Disparate styles, from simple diatonicism to tumultuous dissonance, are used to achieve the clever feats of tone painting with which different scenes, characters, and actions are depicted. Sunrise, for example, is portrayed by an arhythmic wash of ghostly instrumental effects that blossom into a delirious burst of orchestral light and color. Immediately following is the Pied Piper's song, whose gentle lyricism is entirely contrasting in idiom but emanates magically from what precedes it.

Yet another aesthetic is embodied by the rats' music, with its eerie and menacing squeaks, rattles, thumps, and scurryings, effected by attacking the highest notes possible, bowing or tapping on odd parts of the string instruments, and frantic execution of trills, glissandos, and random figuration. After the cataclysmic and cacophonous battle between the Piper and the rats (solo flute and orchestra), the chorale and march turn to a jovial and infectious triadic music, with a simplicity of rhythm (primarily in quarters and eighths) hitherto absent.

The last movement of the *Pied Piper* Fantasy is a multimedia event, complete with lighting, costumes, and audience involvement. The soloist, dressed for his role, breaks out a tin whistle and lures groups of young children out of the audience. They parade onto the stage playing their own flutes and drums, and are then led by the Piper down from the stage, through the concert hall, and out the doors—wonderfully effective levels of **performance ritual**. As their jaunty tune fades away, the orchestra gives voice to the townspeople's sorrow with a low, mournful echo of the Piper's song. (The two musics are not coordinated.)

The experimental playing techniques, improvisatory passages, and innovative **notation** in this work are called for in a tonal as well as nontonal context, a notable feature in many of Corigliano's works.

Donald Erb: Concerto for Contrabassoon and Orchestra

Until the late twentieth century, instruments like the string bass, tuba, bass clarinet, and contrabassoon were thought too eccentric and expressively limited to be featured in an orchestral concerto. Recently, however, concertos for such instruments have become more common and their idiosyncrasies have been welcomed. Donald Erb's *Concerto for Contrabassoon and Orchestra* (1984) is a classic instance of this composer's brash, iconoclastic, but highly communicative approach to the concerto. (He has written ten concertos to date.)

The single-movement work is divided into three parts in a traditional fast-slow-fast sequence. The close of each part is marked by a mammoth orchestral outburst. Between these sections are two harmonically similar, partly aleatoric transitions that build in **texture** and character to anticipate what follows. The final tutti is preceded by an extended unmeasured cadenza.

One motive shared throughout the work by both soloist and orchestra is a long glissando or chromatic scale, often sweeping or writhing through two or more registers. Erb's many variants on this one idea reveal his copious imagination for orchestral **color.** In one instance, the string section performs a prolonged glissando with pizzicato tremolando. In another, the woodwinds gliss down in continuous tremolos, the three trumpets gliss up with mouthpieces only, the lower brass skid down in fluttertongue clusters, and the strings slide up with tremolando clusters of harmonics, all simultaneously. At still another point, the strings skitter up and down chromatic scales *col legno*—using pencils! The aural impact of such events is beyond description. (See Example 21.3 for a typical passage.)

Each section of the concerto asserts a different relationship between contrabassoon and orchestra. In the first, brass and percussion attempt, but never quite manage, to develop a marchlike rhythm while the contrabassoon forms melismatic duets with bass clarinet and bassoon, later to be joined by tuba, harp, and electric piano. In the second section, subtitled "Night Music," the orchestra serves mainly as accompaniment to the soloist's now more lyrical lines, which are tinged with a sultry jazz feeling and end in a high register rarely attempted on contrabassoon. The third section is a scherzo in which soloist and orchestra finally work as equals, most notably when short, comical blasts of low sixteenth notes in the contrabassoon are mimicked and multiplied in the other instruments.

CHAMBER MUSIC

Chamber music is, by definition, intimate—an instrumental genre intended for performance by relatively few players in a relatively small space. It has traditionally been thought the ideal vehicle for a composer's most profound statements and most subtle timbral nuances. To a degree, those stereotypes still hold true in the late twentieth century; but one must ex-

EXAMPLE 21.3

Donald Erb: *Concerto for Contrabassoon and Orchestra*

© 1983 Merion Music, Inc. Used by permission

pand them to include ventures in music theater, multimedia, and interactions between live acoustic performance and electronic sounds.

The standard instrumental groupings are still of great interest to a significant body of stylistically diverse composers. Within the string quartet medium alone, one could explore the mobile, texturally fluid fabric of Earle Brown's String Quartet; the tighter, deterministic arguments of *Quatuor III* by the noted French composer Betsy Jolas; or the extended sonorities of Toshiro Mayuzumi's Prelude for String Quartet. Alfred Schnittke's *String Quartet No. 3* uses brief fragments from the past (Orlando di Lasso's *Stabat Mater* and Beethoven's *Grosse Fuge*) and a four-pitch motive derived from Shostakovitch's initials as springboard for a dizzying variety of contrasting stylistic overlays, from unadorned, triadic homophony to harshly dissonant counterpoint.

By the late twentieth century another chamber combination has begun to rival the venerable string quartet for primacy in composers' affections. This grouping of five players—flute, clarinet, violin, cello, and piano—is often referred to as the "Pierrot ensemble." To mention just a few works composed for this timbral mix: *Joan's* (dedicated to Joan Tower and the Da Capo Players) by Charles Wuorinen; Jonathan Kramer's *Atlanta Licks* (another of his works built on only six pitches); and William Albright's eclectic style-play *Danse macabre*. Richard Wernick adds soprano voice to the quintet grouping, thereby recreating the true *Pierrot* complement of Schoenberg, for his moving *A Poison Tree*, set to texts by William Blake.

We must note two other distinctive features of late twentieth-century chamber instrumentation. One is the ensemble composed of multiples of the same instrument, a veritable gold mine of unique coloristic possibilities. *B's Garlands* for eight celli by Martin Bresnick, Harvey Sollberger's Grand Quartet for Flutes, and a number of works by Gunther Schuller, such as his Quartet for Doublebasses and *Five Moods* for tuba quartet, are outstanding examples. Secondly, the human voice is appearing in chamber works with increasing frequency. For a wide range of styles, consider the florid gestures of Shulamit Ran's 1979 *Apprehensions* for soprano, clarinet, and piano (text by Sylvia Plath); the intensity of *A Solo Requiem* (1977) for soprano and two pianos by Milton Babbitt; Ursula Mamlok's *Stray Birds* for soprano, flute, and cello; and two luxuriant works by Bernard Rands: *Canti Lunatici* for soprano and *Canti del Sole* for tenor, both beautifully integrated with chamber ensemble.

Gunther Schuller: Abstraction

Abstraction (1960) was among the first of Gunther Schuller's many groundbreaking efforts to unite classical and jazz composition into what he calls "third-stream" music. The worlds of both art music and jazz are represented within *Abstraction*'s ensemble, the former by a string quartet and the latter by alto saxophone, guitar, drum set, and two string basses. The most advanced approaches to **pitch logic** and **time** appropriate to each group are employed—serial method in the string quartet, free atonal jazz in the other instruments. These approaches are, in fact, stylistically compatible, sharing a high level of dissonance, disjunct rhythm (freed from beats and bar lines), and the absence of themes or motives.

A compositional **process** brings the relationship between jazz and non-jazz elements to life. In the first and last twenty-two measures of the work, which are exact retrogrades of one another, both the classical and jazz factions explore the twelve-tone material together. Elsewhere, however, as in Example 21.4, the two groups diverge: the string quartet continues to pursue serial transformations of the opening tone row, while the other instruments become increasingly jazzlike in their behavior (with fascinating interplays of **texture**), until all but the guitar are improvising freely.

The saxophone leads the improvisation, and it was the pioneer sax player Ornette Coleman who inspired, premiered, and recorded this work. *Abstraction* is really an essay on his legendary playing style, with its fragmentary bursts of rhythm and color, cohering through a larger sense of shape and direction.

Samuel Adler: Seven Epigrams

It is generally assumed that music must break new ground or stand apart stylistically to have a significant cultural impact. In North America, however, the new works most often heard are probably the more practical, less exploratory ones so commonly programmed by high school, college, and amateur groups—especially wind ensembles—across the country. German-born composer Samuel Adler (b. 1928) has included many such works in his huge and varied *oeuvre*, works that demand skilled musicianship but are still within reach for players and listeners less seasoned in newer repertoire.

An exemplar of this is his *Seven Epigrams* for a sextet of woodwinds: two flutes, oboe, clarinet, bass clarinet, and bassoon. The seven succinct movements are marked "fast," "gently rocking," "quickly and very lightly bouncing," "very slowly and quietly," "quick march," "quite slowly," and "as fast as possible."

In spite of their brevity (the fourth movement is a mere seventeen measures), they offer all the richness of contrast their titles suggest while retaining a consistent, forthright approach to **pitch logic** and **time**. Although fully chromatic, melody and harmony have an immediate charm and lucidity, partly owing to a clear emphasis on just three intervals: the perfect fourth, perfect fifth, and minor second. The flute line in Example

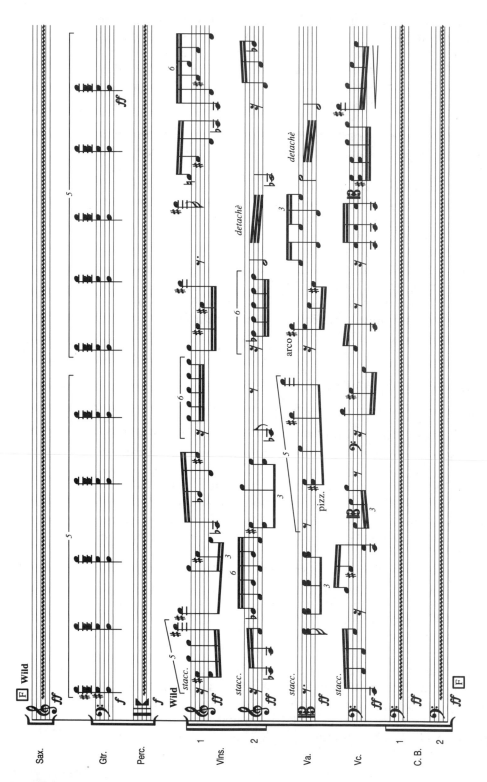

EXAMPLE 21.4. Gunther Schuller: *Abstraction.* Copyright © 1961 and Renewed 1989 by MJQ Music, Inc. All Rights Reserved. Used by permission

EXAMPLE 21.5.

Samuel Adler: *Seven Epigrams*, No. 3, flute part, and
interval reduction

21.5 shows one of many ingenious ways these are incorporated. The melody's fluid shape is derived from a double pattern of chromatically ascending fifths (diagramed below it), rhythmically and registrally projected in
various ways.

Apart from periodic meter changes and less common meters ($\frac{5}{8}$ and $\frac{7}{8}$),
rhythm is never obscure or lacking a pulse. Even occasional quintuplets or
septuplets are phrased beat by beat, posing little complication. Yet within
these constraints an inventive manipulation of patterns, gestures, and accentuation gives each movement a strong, expressive rhythmic personality.

George Rochberg: String Quartet No. 6

Rochberg's String Quartet No. 6 (1978) is the third of three "Concord
Quartets" (named after the Concord String Quartet, for whom they were
written). Two aspects of this work fascinate many listeners, both involving
parody/historicism. One is the bald juxtaposition of new and old languages (new and old views of **pitch logic** and **time**) from one movement to
the next. The other is the presence of extended passages—and in one instance an entire movement—that could plausibly have been written 150
years ago.

The first and fourth movements ("Fantasia" and "Serenade" respectively) are entirely atonal. The former has quirky yet incisive gestures that
recall Bartók, but with a brooding expressionism suggestive of Schoenberg.
The latter has the sparse, edgy dissonance of Webern's Five Movements for
String Quartet, Op. 5, or Stravinsky's Three Pieces for String Quartet. Set

against these, the other three movements seem transplanted *in toto* from another style period. The second movement ("Scherzo-Humoresque") is unequivocally tonal and centers on two ideas: a dotted motif with abrupt harmonic twists, and an airy, lyrical theme redolent of late Beethoven quartets (especially Op. 127, first movement). The third movement is a set of variations on Pachelbel's *Canon*, beginning and ending with an unaffected diatonic countermelody and passing through increasingly chromatic stages in between, at moments resembling late Mahler.

While the second and third movements are just eccentric enough to be distinguished from late eighteenth- or nineteenth-century repertoire, the fifth movement "Introduction and Finale," could masquerade as an undiscovered classic from the past (see Example 21.6). The slow, dramatic introduction could easily be attributed to Schubert. The G-major Finale has all the motivic, harmonic, and structural features of a sonata-allegro movement from the late Beethoven string quartets. Rochberg acknowledges his debt to history with fragmentary quotes from quartets by Mozart, Schubert, and Beethoven himself.

Were it not for subtle idiosyncrasies, much of this music would seem like brilliant forgery, each passage or movement equally adept in its chosen idiom. But when Rochberg chooses to imitate, it is out of a compelling personal necessity to reestablish meaningful, nourishing connections to the past, connections severed by a modern-day fixation on originality. In the

EXAMPLE 21.6.

George Rochberg: *String Quartet No. 6*, Finale

String Quartet No. 6, his "reapprenticeship" to the masters, particularly those of tonality, is an effort to reacquire the immense range of harmonic and rhythmic material they enjoyed—and the corresponding range of nuance and emotion.

Morton Subotnick: The Wild Beasts

From the mid-1970s to the present, Morton Subotnick has been a leading innovator in the interaction between live performers and electronic **technology,** both analog and digital. One product of his efforts is the concept of the "electronic ghost score," consisting not of music manuscript but of a magnetic tape and three sound-processing devices. The latter alter real-time input from the performers by (1) moving sound back and forth in stereo, (2) shifting frequencies up or down, and (3) shaping amplification levels. They are controlled by low-amplitude, high-frequency "ghost" signals on the tape, which cannot be heard by the audience.

The Wild Beasts, scored for trombone, piano, and ghost electronics, was inspired by an exhibition of turn-of-the-century French painters dubbed *les fauves* ("the wild beasts") by critics of their day. According to Subotnick's program note, he felt that subjects were depicted not as surreal but as normal objects viewed through an "unearthly" atmosphere in which "normal expectations of color and shape would not exist." Correspondingly, his idea was to present traditional instruments through "an unusual and continually transforming atmosphere," electronically conjured, whereby normal expectations of **sound color** and gesture would not apply.

The ordinary timbres of trombone and piano rarely prevail over the electronic effects, which often coincide with unusual sonorities in the instruments themselves. At the work's opening, for example, muted mutterings in the trombone are processed by rapidly wavering amplitude levels to form a bizarre and sinister monologue. Later in the work, massive chords and tremolos in the piano are transformed by pitch modulation into erratic, dizzying distortions. Throughout, the trombone contributes an especially varied repertoire of unconventional sounds: pedal-tone blasts, harmonic glissandi, fluttertonguing, and vocalizing through the instrument (hums, growls, exhalations).

In Example 21.7 Subotnick's visual sketch of *The Wild Beasts* outlines the interacting shapes of instrumental and electronic activity. The most striking and persistent interaction between performers and electronics relates to **time** and **texture**. Passages in the middle of the work involve strong, rapid pulsation in both instruments and electronics (amplitude and spatial location). The two pulse at asynchronous rates to produce a fibrillating, manically energized sound web.

EXAMPLE 21.7.

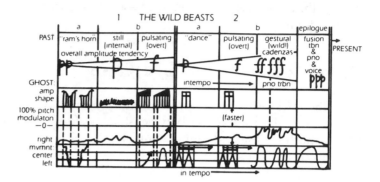

Morton Subotnick: *The Wild Beasts,* composer's pictorial outline

Used by permission of the composer

Ralph Shapey: Kroslish Sonata

For decades Ralph Shapey has been recognized as a forceful, unflinching individualist among American composers. During the 1970s and 1980s, when many others turned to a more accessible idiom, Shapey pursued his own rugged, adamantly dissonant course with redoubled energy. That style is very much evident in his *Kroslish Sonata* of 1985, a three-movement work written for and named after the duo of Joel Krosnick, cellist, and Gilbert Kalish, pianist. Like much of his output, though, this sonata has a gestural and structural lucidity that penetrates even conservative listening habits.

Pitch logic and **process** in Shapey's music are serially oriented, but with a creative latitude influenced by his teacher, Stefan Wolpe. The process behind the rhapsodic *maestoso* section that begins and concludes the first and third movements is immediately clear to the ear and eye. The cello plays a two-part phrase three times, with only slight variation; the piano's left hand accompanies this with a longer chord sequence, played twice with somewhat greater variation; set against this is a third sequence in the right hand, spanning the whole *maestoso*. (The piano part quotes from Shapey's own Double Concerto.) From the standpoints of **time** and **texture,** these three layers work much as in an isorhythmic motet: there is repetition within lines but a constant flux in relationship between them. In the fourth and concluding *maestoso,* this is transformed into an antiphonal scheme, with the now ornamented and rhythmically expanded cello part answered by more compressed, harmonically simplified lines in the piano.

Elsewhere in the *Kroslish Sonata*, other long-standing features of Shapey's music stand out with equal clarity, especially those relating to **texture** and **process.** Sharply outlined blocks of music, usually ten to twenty measures in length, have a somewhat static texture created by distinctive, cyclical patterns of rhythm and pitch. The monolithic exterior that results is enlivened by supple changes unfolding within it. Patterns or phrases in the *scordatura* cello part continually modify and realign themselves with those in the piano, which are also evolving (see Example 21.8). At certain points in the delicately hushed middle movement, the cello frees itself altogether from this process with expansive, quietly ecstatic interjections.

EXAMPLE 21.8.

Ralph Shapey: *Kroslish Sonata,* first movement

© 1987 Theodore Presser Company. Used by permission

ORCHESTRAL MUSIC

Peter Sculthorpe: Sun Music I

The orchestral *Sun Music I* (1969) is the first in a continuing series of *Sun Music* pieces by the Australian composer Peter Sculthorpe (b. 1929). Its austere but vivid aural landscape echoes the rituals of ancient culture, the mysteries of nature, and the sun-seared desolation of the Australian outback. The work's stark sense of clarity is partly a function of **sound color,** which in turn is clarified by **pitch logic** and **time.** The orchestra is made up of three instrumental groups: brasses, percussion, and strings. The timbre of each group is isolated through a distinct approach to pitch and rhythm, with corresponding differences in **notation.**

In the conventionally notated brass section, pitch and rhythm are precisely controlled; clusters, chords, and melodic fragments occur in brief, well-delineated cells, some of which are later repeated without being varied or transposed. In the percussion section rhythm is clearly defined, but pitch is usually obscured or indefinite. The string section uses primarily experimental notation and relies largely on contemporary devices not called for in the other sections, resulting in randomly fluctuating or indefinite pitch and rhythm. Included are quarter-tone clusters, unsynchronized glissandi, irregular tremolo, bowing behind the bridge, and striking the instrument.

Another defining element in *Sun Music I* is **texture,** which remains static and spare from beginning to end. There is little motion at any time; usually, individual notes or chords are simply repeated, and most sonic effects are merely sustained without transformation (see Example 21.9). Except during a climactic moment near the end, overlap between brass and string ensembles is minimal. The spectrum of rhythm and color is rich, but it unfolds slowly and at predominantly subdued dynamics, contributing to an air of timelessness and distance.

Karel Husa: Music for Prague

Karel Husa is a native of Czechoslovakia who moved to the United States in 1954. When he was commissioned to write a work for concert band in 1968, just as the Soviets were invading his homeland, the natural result was an outpouring of anguish and hope for Prague, the city of his birth. Versions of *Music for Prague* for both symphonic band and orchestra were completed in that year, and although the work was prohibited behind the

EXAMPLE 21.9.

Peter Sculthorpe: *Sun Music I*

Iron Curtain, it received over seven thousand performances in the twenty years that followed. It was a triumphal occasion, therefore, when Husa returned in 1990 to a newly liberated Prague, there to conduct his *Music for Prague* at a gala concert celebrating Czech composers.

In his foreword to the score, Husa cites three principal ideas that unite

---

ILLUS. 21.6.

Karel Husa, conducting one of his works in rehearsal

Courtesy of the composer

the work's four movements. The first is a fifteenth-century Hussite war song ("Ye Warriors of God and His Law"), a centuries-old anthem of courage and defiance among Czechs. Second is the frequent presence of bell-like sounds, representing Prague's hundreds of church towers and their ringing out in times of celebration and tragedy. Third is a dissonant three-chord motive, quietly stated at the opening but recurring later (Movements II and IV) in forceful, choralelike proclamations.

Symbolism is everywhere in *Music for Prague*. The first movement, "Introduction and Fanfare," begins with a piccolo solo, a "bird call" (Husa's words) symbolizing the rare moments of liberty Prague has seen in its long history. The adjoining fanfare represents for Husa a cry of distress, spreading urgently from the brasses to the entire ensemble. The second movement is entitled "Aria," and its continuous, tortuously chromatic melody (scored in richly doubled unisons) is a symbol of tragedy, as is the implacable tolling of percussion underlying it.

The third movement, "Interlude," is an extended rhythmic palindrome for bell-like percussion and suggests a calm before the onslaught. It is accompanied by an ominous, militaristic snare drum whose final, deafening crescendo brings on the massive, clangorous tuttis and insistent rhythm of the final movement, "Toccata and Chorale." Represented here is a battle between freedom and oppression, one with no clear outcome; the final chorale presents the Hussite song in bold, ensemble-wide octaves—but the melody is left uncompleted.

Through much of the work, **pitch logic** and **time** are rigorously organized, with nearly all melodic and rhythmic activity stemming from the Hussite tune. The first and fourth movements, however, grow to shattering climaxes in which the band or orchestra explodes into rhythmic and tonal chaos, notated aleatorically.

Per Nørgård: Symphony No. 3

In the early to mid 1970s, Per Nørgård became renowned in Europe for expanding familiar diatonic elements into vast, uncharted tonal realms. His exploration involved a compositional **process** based on novel approaches to **pitch logic** and **time.** Pitch material was derived from the natural overtone and undertone series (the latter an intervallic mirror of the former), generating strangely transparent tertian harmonies. Melodic sequences were drawn from this material according to a so-called "infinity series", uniquely formulated by Nørgård, and shown in Example 21.10. Rhythmically, all this was governed according to ratios of the Golden Section, a phenomenon related to the infinity series. These methods found their most extensive and elaborate application in the Symphony No. 3 (1975).

Apart from its theoretical intricacies, the infinity series has one simply

EXAMPLE 21.10.

A pitch scheme derived from the infinity series by
Per Nørgård

Used by permission of the composer

understood characteristic: it generates successively larger patterns from smaller ones, each layer identical in shape to the one that generated it. Thus, it can beget an entire movement in which every layer of activity, from the smallest melodic unit to a movement's overall form, is identically proportioned. This principle is played out most dramatically in the first of the work's two movements, and one can readily discern the stratified **texture** it engenders. Hierarchies of cascading, arching diatonic lines proliferate and overlap to build a gigantic, spacious tonal universe. Immense triadic formations swirl, merge, or collide like sonic galaxies, resonating the cosmological import of the methods that underlie them. A shimmering, otherworldly **sound color** prevails, often underscored by natural harmonics and untempered tunings.

The second movement, which adds a large chorus and a concertino choir to the ensemble, is equally monumental. Here, however, Nørgård focuses mainly on select portions of the series, employing short, varied thematic fragments to weave an opulent contrapuntal fabric of contrasting lines. In addition to meaningless syllables, the chorus takes its text from medieval hymns to the Blessed Virgin and from Rilke's poem "Singe die Gärten, mein Herz." **Parody** and collage play a part near the end, as amplified alto solo and piano emerge from a lush choral and orchestral tapestry with Schubert's *lied* "Du bist die Ruh."

Magnus Lindberg: Kraft

During the early 1980s the young Finnish composer Magnus Lindberg became something of an enfant terrible on the European scene, showcasing his own works with the wildly experimental Toimii Ensemble, which he had cofounded. This seven-member ensemble of assorted instruments, percussion, "found objects," and electronics became the core of Lindberg's otherwise massive orchestral score in two movements entitled *Kraft* (1985).

Kraft is a gripping and sometimes unnerving tour de force, overflowing with brilliant and utterly unorthodox displays of instrumental **texture** and **color.** Much of what Lindberg does is influenced by *musique concrète* and by Pierre Schaefer's system of classifying noninstrumental acoustic sources. Lindberg developed a like system of his own, yielding a cornucopia of earth-, fire-, wind-, and water-related sounds, elicited somehow from traditional instruments as well as nonmusical objects.

In *Kraft* the Toimii Ensemble is called upon for its special expertise in this domain, using nonstandard **notation** that sets it apart visually from the rest of the ensemble. (The parts shown in Example 21.11 are those played by members of Toimii.) Even so, the smaller group's rustles, caterwauls, explosions, and other effects are an extension of, rather than a contrast to, the rest of the orchestra's activities, which are more customarily notated

EXAMPLE 21.11.

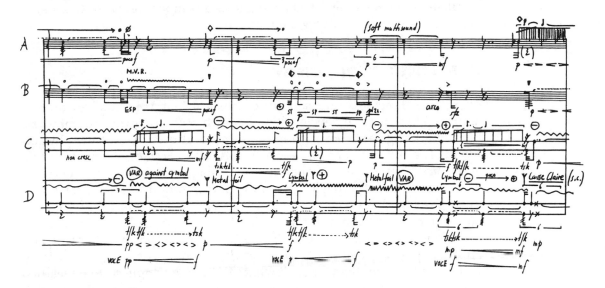

Magnus Lindberg: *Kraft*, Part I, solo parts

but of uncanny originality. (Both movements do, however, end with a quasicadenza for Toimii players.)

Kraft translates as "force" and refers to more than the work's sheer auditory power. Deeper forces propel the music from within, especially those of entropy and cohesion, which battle for supremacy throughout. The opening eruption, for example, seems to scatter sonic debris far and wide, but the subsequent period of inward gravitation leads to a quiet, homogeneous texture of briefly held tones. From there, a new episode of chaotic violence gathers momentum, but this time (near the end of the first movement) all parts congeal into concussive tutti chords, separated by moments of silence. The same pattern is expressed in **performance ritual,** as certain orchestral groups disperse through the concert hall and then return to the stage.

Lindberg's credo has been "Only the extreme is interesting," but the swings between savage complexity and luminous serenity in this work are not abrupt or arbitrary. Transition between extremes is often seamlessly protracted, partly the outcome of an involved compositional **process** for which Lindberg devised his own computer program. The use of computer in calculating density and texture suggests a comparison with Xenakis, as do other aspects of Lindberg's music.

Joan Tower: Silver Ladders

There is a directness and solidity of musical language, and an organic approach to structural development, in much of Joan Tower's recent work, revealing her great absorption in the forms and processes of the physical world. The titles of her works—such as *Amazon, Sequoia, Platinum Spirals,* and *Black Topaz*—often evoke "nature" images, including references to precious minerals (perhaps to honor her father, a mining engineer). More-over, she has described her musical perception in remarkably scientific terms, reminiscent at times of Varèse and his concern with "the intelligence in sounds." In Tower's words, "I was interested in physics, in cause and effect . . . paying attention to what an object does when you throw it, or when it falls, rather than telling it what to do. Then I applied what I learned to music. More important than melody were space, texture, height, register, color."

In *Silver Ladders* for orchestra (1986), the composer subjects straightfor-ward, almost elementary materials to an aggressively modern treatment. The work's provocative title hints not only at brilliance but a quality of singleminded directionality. Appropriately, its **pitch logic** is based primar-ily on two very simple resources, an ascending whole-step/half-step (or "octatonic") scale and the upward leap of a fourth (not clearly outlined until near the end of the piece). The scale motive generates inexorably rising lines ("ladders") that pervade the music, often pitted against other lines that descend or are fixed in register. Scalar motion occurs sometimes in massive orchestral unisons, at other times in intricate contrapuntal lay-ers, at still other times as the seed of more elaborate melodic shapes. The simplest scalar sequences are often the most explosive, made so by a glit-tering display of inventive instrumentation and by a driving rhythmic pulse that shifts unpredictably but is never obscured.

For Tower, the various kinds of **texture** in *Silver Ladders* are akin to metallic states (as the title suggests), ranging from solid mass, to molten volatility, to intricate filigree. Balancing the volcanic momentum that con-tinually reasserts itself are four solo passages (for clarinet, oboe, marimba, and trumpet) that reflect more gently on the scalar and fourth-arpeggiating ideas. The result is a composition that, while highly innovative, has evoked remarkable enthusiasm from concertgoers, even those usually unrespon-sive to new music.

*   *   *

ILLUS. 21.7.

Joan Tower

Courtesy of BMI Archives

It is appropriate to bring this survey of genres to a close with a few comments on the orchestra, if only because the orchestra (as an institution, as a sonic resource, and as an expressive vehicle) still symbolizes "classical music" for many listeners and composers.

As previous chapters have indicated, outstanding examples of post–1945 music do not necessarily have to be avant-garde. For some composers, the orchestral medium is important because of its link to the symphonic tradition—the rich sonorities and massive textures, the grand stage, the opportunity to make substantial statements within a known rhetorical format. A list of strong pieces extending that tradition would include Peter Mennin's Symphonies Nos. 8 and 9; Symphony *RiverRun* by Stephen Albert; David Stock's *Inner Space*; *Pentimino* and *Sanctuary* by Ezra Laderman; and Oliver Knussen's Symphony No. 3. Such works, conservative in the best sense, are also new insofar as they build on an expanded vocabulary of materials and a broader base of experience.

On the other hand, a great many orchestral works are indeed experimental. Some composers are drawn to the orchestra because its size makes certain timbral or textural effects possible, others because the concert stage setting presents a visual and theatrical opportunity. Others simply use the medium for exploratory purposes, to test their limits (and their performers' limits, and ours as well). Their experiments raise three issues. To begin with, no law forces us to define an orchestra along the lines of the traditional four families. A more flexible yardstick is needed to accommodate a sizeable body of music for large but highly unorthodox instrumental ensembles: *Under the Umbrella* (1976) by the Japanese composer Jo Kondo, for example, scored for twenty-five cowbells and gong, or Henry Brant's *Orbits* for eighty trombones, soprano, and organ (1979), or Gerhard Samuel's *What of My Music* for thirty doublebasses, soprano, and percussion.

Second, the orchestra's textural variety, density, and mass make it an ideal foil for electronic or computer-generated counterweights. In this regard, consider Larry Austin's witty, almost surreal *Sinfonia Concertante* (*A Mozartean Episode*) for computer tape and chamber orchestra (1988); Barbara Kolb's ingeniously balanced *Soundings* for the same forces; and the stunning *Verblendungen* for tape and large orchestra by Kaija Saariaho.

Finally, the modern symphony orchestra offers an unparalleled resource for innovation in the domain of **sound color**—indeed, a worthy rival for the synthesizer. By combining various instrumental timbres, registers, and virtuosic (or extended-technique) performance requirements, composers can achieve a brilliant palette of colors. Listen to Olivier Messiaen's *Des canyons aux étoiles* (1974), a glowing tribute to the vast spaces of the American West; John Corigliano's searing, impassioned Symphony No. 1; the sparkle of Libby Larsen's *Parachute Dancing* (1984); Donald Erb's *Prismatic Variations* (1984), with its auxiliary ensemble of tuned water glasses; and the provocative *Dare to Show That You Are a Lapp* by the Norwegian composer John Persen.

Music of the twentieth century's second half has proved to be remarkably rich, varied, witty, moving, rigorous, and challenging at times, hypnotic and soothing at others, occasionally terrifying, often quite beautiful, and always stimulating. There has never been a better era in which to explore the music of one's own time.

Select Bibliography

Twentieth-Century Music (general)

Griffiths, Paul. *A Concise History of Modern Music.* London: Thames & Hudson, 1980.

Hansen, Peter S. *An Introduction to Twentieth-Century Music.* Boston: Allyn & Bacon, 1978.

Morgan, Robert P. *Twentieth-Century Music.* New York: Norton, 1991.

Peyser, Joan. *The New Music.* New York: Dell, 1971.

Schwartz, Elliott, and Barney Childs, eds. *Contemporary Composers on Contemporary Music.* New York: Da Capo Press, 1983.

Simms, Bryan. *Music of the Twentieth Century: Style and Structure.* New York: Schirmer Books, 1986.

Stuckenschmidt, H. H. *Twentieth-Century Music.* New York: World University Library, 1969.

Vinton, John, ed. *Dictionary of Contemporary Music.* New York: Dutton, 1974.

Watkins, Glenn. *Soundings: Music of the Twentieth Century.* New York: Schirmer Books, 1988.

Whittall, Arnold. *Music since the First World War.* London: J. M. Dent, 1977.

Post-1945 Music (general)

Cope, David H. *New Directions in Music,* 5th ed. Dubuque, Iowa: William C. Brown, 1989.

Dufallo, Richard. *Trackings.* Oxford: Oxford University Press, 1989.

Griffiths, Paul. *Modern Music: The Avant-garde since 1945.* New York: George Braziller, 1981.

Smith-Brindle, Reginald. *The New Music: The Avant-garde since 1945.* Oxford: Oxford University Press, 1987.

The Loudspeaker Revolution

Benjamin, Walter. "The Work of Art in the Age of Mechanical Reproduction." Translated by Harry Zohn. In *Illuminations,* edited by Hannah Arendt. London: Cape, 1970.

Gumpert, Gary. *Talking Tombstones and Other Tales of the Media Age.* Oxford: Oxford University Press, 1987.

Hamm, Charles. "Technology and Music: The Effect of the Phonograph." In *Contemporary Music and Music Cultures,* edited by Charles Hamm, Bruno Nettl, and Ronald Byrnside. Englewood Cliffs, N.J.: Prentice-Hall, 1975.

Hitchcock, H. Wiley, ed. *The Phonograph and Our Musical Life: Proceedings of a Centennial Conference.* New York: Institute for Studies in American Music, City University of New York, 1978.

Kramer, Jonathan D. *The Time of Music.* New York: Schirmer Books, 1988.

Schaeffer, John. *New Sounds: A Listener's Guide to New Music.* New York: Harper & Row, 1987.

Stockhausen, Karlheinz. "Structure and Experiential Time." *Die Reihe* 2, Webern issue (1958).

"Order" and "Chaos"

Babbitt, Milton. "Who Cares If You Listen? (The Composer as Specialist)," in *Contemporary Composers on Contemporary Music,* edited by Elliott Schwartz and Barney Childs. New York: Da Capo Press, 1983.

————. *Words about Music.* Edited by Stephen Demski and Joseph N. Strauss. Madison: University of Wisconsin Press, 1987.

Boulez, Pierre. *Conversations with Celestin Deliege.* London: Eulenburg Books, 1976.

————. "Sonate, que me veux-tu?" *Perspectives of New Music* 2 (1962).

————. "The Threshhold." *Die Reihe* 2, Webern issue, (1958).

Brown, Earle. "Form in New Music." *Source* 1 (1967).

Cage, John. *Silence.* Middletown, Conn.: Wesleyan University Press, 1962.

————. *A Year from Monday.* Middletown, Conn.: Wesleyan University Press, 1967.

Childs, Barney. "The Beginning of the Apocalypse?" *Kulchur* 4 (1964).

De Lio, Thomas. *Circumscribing the Open Universe.* Lanham, N.Y.: University Press of America. 1984.

Kostelanetz, Richard, ed. *John Cage.* New York: Praeger, 1970.

Maconie, Robin. *The Works of Karlheinz Stockhausen.* New York: Oxford University Press, 1990.

O'Grady, Terrence J. "Aesthetic Value in Indeterminate Music." *Musical Quarterly* 67 (1981).

Rognoni, Luigi. *The Second Vienna School.* London: John Calder, 1977.

Stockhausen, Karlheinz. *Stockhausen on Music.* Edited by Robin Maconie. London and New York: Marion Boyars, 1989.

Van Der Toorn, Pieter C. *The Music of Igor Stravinsky.* New Haven, Conn.: Yale University Press, 1983.

Westergaard, Peter. "Webern and Total Organization." *Perspectives of New Music* 1 (1962).

White, Eric Walter. *Stravinsky*. Berkeley and Los Angeles: University of California Press, 1979.

Twelve-Tone Materials and Set Theory

Babbitt, Milton. "Twelve-Tone Invariants as Compositional Determinants." *Musical Quarterly* 46 (1960).

Forte, Allen. *The Structure of Atonal Music*. New Haven, Conn.: Yale University Press, 1973.

Kostka, Stefan. *Materials and Techniques of Twentieth-Century Music*. Englewood Cliffs, N.J.: Prentice-Hall, 1990.

Lester, Joel. *Analytic Approaches to Twentieth-Century Music*. New York: Norton, 1989.

Perle, George. *Serial Composition and Atonality*. Berkeley and Los Angeles: University of California Press, 1962.

———. *Twelve-Tone Tonality*. Berkeley and Los Angeles: University of California Press, 1978.

Rahn, John. *Basic Atonal Theory*. New York: Longman, 1980.

Smith-Brindle, Reginald. *Serial Composition*. New York: Oxford University Press, 1966.

Straus, Joseph N. *Introduction to Post-Tonal Theory*. Englewood Cliffs, N.J.: Prentice-Hall, 1990.

Wittlich, Gary E., ed. *Aspects of Twentieth-Century Music*. Englewood Cliffs, N.J.: Prentice-Hall, 1975.

Wuorinen, Charles. *Simple Composition*. New York: Longman, 1979.

Electronic and Computer Music

Anderton, Craig. *MIDI for Musicians*. New York: Amsco, 1986.

Appleton, Jon, and Ronald Perera, eds. *The Development and Practice of Electronic Music*. Englewood Cliffs, N.J.: Prentice-Hall, 1974.

Babbitt, Milton. "An Introduction to the RCA Synthesizer." *Journal of Music Theory* 8 (1964).

———. "Twelve-Tone Rhythmic Structure and the Electronic Medium." *Perspectives of New Music* 1 (1962).

Boom, Michael. *Music through MIDI*. Redmond, Wash.: Microsoft Press, 1987.

"Computer Generated Music." *Computer* 24, special issue (1991).

Davis, D. S. *Computer Applications in Music: A Bibliography*. Madison, Wis.: A-R, 1988.

DeFuria, Steve. *The MIDI Book.* Milwaukee, Wis.: Hal Leonard Books, 1988.

Dodge, Charles, and Thomas A. Jerse. *Computer Music: Synthesis, Composition, and Performance.* New York: Schirmer Books, 1985.

Ernst, David. *The Evolution of Electronic Music.* New York: Schirmer Books, 1977.

Hofstetter, Fred T. *Computer Literacy for Musicians.* Englewood Cliffs, N.J.: Prentice-Hall, 1988.

Howe, Hubert S., Jr. *Electronic Music Synthesis.* New York: Norton, 1975.

Keane, David. *Tape Music Composition.* Oxford: Oxford University Press, 1980.

Lansky, Paul. "The Sound of Software: Computer-Made Music." *Perspectives in Computing* 5 (1985).

Manning, Peter. *Electronic and Computer Music.* Oxford, Clarendon Press, 1985.

Matthews, Max. *The Technology of Computer Music.* Cambridge, Mass.: MIT Press, 1969.

Naumann, Joel, and James D. Wagoner. *Analog Electronic Music Techniques.* New York: Schirmer Books, 1985.

Roads, Curtis, ed. *The Music Machine.* Cambridge, Mass.: MIT Press, 1989. Selected readings from *Computer Music Journal.*

Roads, Curtis, and John Strawn, eds. *Foundations of Computer Music.* Cambridge, Mass.: MIT Press, 1985.

Schwartz, Elliott. *Electronic Music: A Listener's Guide.* New York: Da Capo Press, 1985.

Wells, Thomas. *The Technique of Electronic Music.* New York: Schirmer Books, 1981.

Whipple, Harold W. "Beasts and Butterflies: Morton Subotnick's 'Ghost Scores.'" *Musical Quarterly* 69 (1983).

New Approaches to Texture, Time, Sound Color

Bartolozzi, Bruno. *New Sounds for Woodwinds.* New York: Oxford University Press, 1967.

Boulez, Pierre. *Boulez on Music Today.* Cambridge, Mass.: Harvard University Press, 1971.

Bunger, Richard. *The Well-Prepared Piano.* Sebastopol, Calif.: Litoral Arts Press, 1981.

Cogan, Robert. *New Images of Musical Sound.* Cambridge, Mass.: Harvard University Press, 1984.

Cott, Jonathan. *Stockhausen: Conversations with the Composer.* New York: Simon & Schuster, 1973.

Dempster, Stuart. *The Modern Trombone.* Berkeley and Los Angeles: University of California Press, 1980.

Dick, Robert. *The Other Flute.* New York: Oxford University Press, 1975.

Edwards, Allen. *Flawed Words and Stubborn Sounds: A Conversation with Elliott Carter.* New York: Norton, 1971.

Erickson, Robert. *Sound Structure in Music.* Berkeley and Los Angeles: University of California Press, 1975.

Gillespie, Don, ed. *George Crumb: Profile of a Composer.* New York: C. F. Peters, 1985.

Harvey, Jonathan. "Brian Ferneyhough." *Musical Times* 120 (1979).

Kramer, Jonathan D. *The Time of Music.* New York: Schirmer Books, 1988.

Potter, Keith, ed. "Brian Ferneyhough." *Contact* 20, special issue (1979).

Reynolds, Roger. *Mind Models: New Forms of Music Experience.* New York: Praeger, 1975.

Schiff, David. *The Music of Elliott Carter.* London: Eulenberg Books, 1983.

Slawson, Wayne. *Sound Color.* Berkeley and Los Angeles: University of California Press, 1985.

Stockhausen, Karlheinz. "How Time Passes." *Die Reihe* 3 (1959).

Turetzky, Bertram. *The Contemporary Contrabass.* Berkeley and Los Angeles: University of California Press, 1974.

Xenakis, Iannis. "Elements of Stochastic Music." *Gravesaner Blätter* 18–22 (1960–61).

————. *Formalized Music.* Bloomington: Indiana University Press, 1971.

Multimedia and Extended Performance Ritual

Cardew, Cornelius. *Scratch Music.* London: Latimer, 1972.

Hansen, Al. *A Primer of Happenings and Time-Space Art.* New York: Something Else Press, 1968.

Husarik, Stephen. "John Cage and Lejaren Hiller: HPSCHD, 1969." *American Music* 1 (1983).

Hiller, Lejaren. "HPSCHD." *Source* 2 (1968).

Johnson, Roger, ed. *Scores: An Anthology of New Music.* New York: Schirmer Books, 1981.

Kirby, E. T. *Total Theater.* New York: Dutton, 1969.

Kaprow, Allen. *Assemblages, Environments, Happenings.* New York: Abrams, 1966.

Kostelanetz, Richard. *Conversing with Cage.* New York: Limelight, 1988.

———. *The Theater of Mixed Means.* New York: Dial Press, 1968.

Lucier, Alvin, and Douglas Simon. *Chambers.* Middletown, Conn.: Wesleyan University Press, 1980.

Nyman, Michael. *Experimental Music: Cage and Beyond.* New York: Schirmer Books, 1980.

Partch, Harry. *Genesis of a Music,* 2nd Ed. Madison: University of Wisconsin Press, 1974.

Performance Anthology. San Francisco: Contemporary Arts Press, 1980.

Schwartz, Elliott. "Performance in the Midst of Pluralism." In *Relativism in the Arts,* edited by Betty Jean Craige. Athens: University of Georgia Press, 1983.

Sumner, Melody, ed. *The Guests Go in to Supper.* Oakland, Calif.: Burning Books, 1986. Interviews with John Cage, Yoko Ono, Laurie Anderson, Charles Amirkhanian, et al.

Von Gunden, Heidi. *The Music of Pauline Oliveros.* Metuchen, N.J.: Scarecrow Press, 1983.

Young, LaMonte, and Jackson Mac Low, eds. *An Anthology.* Munich: Heiner Friedrich, 1970.

Minimalism, Historicism, and Postmodernism

Cole, Hugo. *The Changing Face of Music.* London: Victor Gollancz, 1978.

Gablik, Suzi. *Has Modernism Failed?* London: Thames & Hudson, 1984.

Glass, Philip. *Music by Philip Glass.* Edited by Robert T. Jones. New York: Harper & Row, 1987.

Grimes, Ev. "Contemporary Composers on Music Education for the General Public." Doctoral diss. University of Kansas, 1985. Interviews with Milton Babbitt, John Cage, et al.

Levin, Kim. *Beyond Modernism.* New York: Harper & Row, 1988.

Mertens, Wim. *American Minimal Music.* London: Kahn & Averill, 1983.

Potter, Keith, and Dave Smith. "Interview with Philip Glass." *Contact* 12 (1976).

Reich, Steve. *Writings about Music.* Halifax: University of Nova Scotia Press, 1974.

Rochberg, George. *The Esthetics of Survival.* Edited by William Bolcom. Ann Arbor: University of Michigan Press, 1984.

Rockwell, John. *All-American Music: Composition in the Late Twentieth Century.* New York: Knopf, 1983.

Schaeffer, John. *New Sounds: A Listener's Guide to New Music.* New York: Harper & Row, 1987.

Schafer, R. Murray. *The Tuning of the World.* New York: Knopf, 1977.

Schuller, Gunther. *Musings.* Oxford: Oxford University Press, 1986.

Schwarz, K. Robert. "Steve Reich: Music as Gradual Process." *Perspectives of New Music* 19, 20 (1981, 1982).

Small, Christopher. *Music, Society, Education.* New York: Schirmer Books, 1977.

Stockhausen, Karlheinz. *Towards a Cosmic Music.* Translated by Tim Nevill. Longmead Shaftsbury, Dorset: Element Books, 1989.

Young, LaMonte, and Marian Zazeela. *Selected Writings.* Munich: Heiner Friedrich, 1969.

Notation and Improvisation

Bailey, Derek. *Improvisation: Its Nature and Practice in Music.* Ashbourne, Derbyshire: Moorland, 1980.

Behrman, David. "What Indeterminate Notation Determines." *Perspectives of New Music* 3 (1965).

Cage, John. *Notations.* New York: Something Else Press, 1969.

Cole, Hugo. *Sounds and Signs: Aspects of Musical Notation.* Oxford: Oxford University Press, 1974.

Fink, Robert, and Robert Ricci. *The Language of Twentieth-Century Music: A Dictionary of Terms.* Schirmer Books, 1975.

"Forum: Improvisation." *Perspectives of New Music* 21 (1982–83), 23 (1985).

Karkoschka, Erhard. *Notation in New Music.* New York: Praeger, 1972.

Pooler, Frank, and Brent Pierce. *New Choral Notation.* New York: Walton Music, 1973.

Rastall, Richard. *The Notation of Western Music.* London: Dent, 1983.

"Report on the International Conference on New Musical Notation." *Interface* 4, special issue (1975).

Stone, Kurt. *Music Notation in the Twentieth Century.* New York: Norton, 1980.

Non-Western Influences and National Traditions

Behague, Gerard. *Music in Latin America: An Introduction.* Englewood Cliffs, N.J.: Prentice-Hall, 1977.

Craig, Dale A. "Trans-Ethnic Composition." *NuMus West* (1971).

Finnish Music Quarterly. Helsinki: Finnish Music Information Centre.

Foreman, Lewis. *British Music Now.* London: Elek, 1975.

Garland, Peter. *Americas: Essays on American Music and Culture.* Santa Fe, N. Mex.: Soundings Press, 1982.

Griffiths, Paul. *New Sounds, New Personalities: British Composers in Interview.* London: Faber Music, 1985.

Hartog, Howard, ed. *European Music in the Twentieth Century.* New York: Praeger, 1957.

Lang, Paul Henry, and Nathan Broder, eds. *Contemporary Music in Europe.* New York: Norton, 1965.

Lifchitz, Max. "New Music in Latin America." *Living Music* 7 (1989).

MacMillan, Keith, and John Beckwith, eds. *Contemporary Canadian Composers.* Oxford: Oxford University Press, 1975.

Malm, William P. *Japanese Music and Musical Instruments.* Rutland, Vt.: Tuttle, 1959.

———. *Music Cultures of the Pacific, the Near East, and Asia.* Englewood Cliffs, N.J.: Prentice-Hall, 1966.

McGee, Timothy J. *The Music of Canada.* New York: Norton, 1985.

McPhee, Colin. *Music in Bali.* New Haven, Conn.: Yale University Press, 1966.

Osborne, Nigel, ed. *Contemporary Music Review,* Japanese issue. London: Harwood Press, 1987. Includes essays by Toru Takemitsu and Joji Yuasa.

Partch, Harry. *Genesis of a Music* 2nd Ed. Madison: University of Wisconsin Press, 1974.

Rasmussen, Karl Aage. *Noteworthy Danes.* Copenhagen: Wilhelm Hansen, 1991.

Reck, David. *Music of the Whole Earth.* New York: Scribner, 1977.

Schwarz, Boris. *Music and Musical Life in Soviet Russia.* Bloomington: Indiana University Press, 1983.

Smialek, William. *Polish Music: A Research and Information Guide.* New York: Garland, 1989.

Swedish Music Past and Present. Stockholm: Swedish Institute for Cultural Relations, 1973.

Titon, Jeff, ed. *Worlds of Music,* 2nd ed. New York: Schirmer Books, 1992.

Tradition and Progress in Swedish Music. Stockholm: Swedish Institute for Cultural Relations, 1973.

Westbrook, Peter. "Alan Hovhaness: Angelic Cycles." *Downbeat,* March 1982.

Yasser, Joseph. *A Theory of Evolving Tonality.* New York: American Library of Musicology, 1932.

Select Discography

1. Composers and Audiences

Bartók, Béla. *Music for Strings, Percussion, and Celesta.* CBS MK-44707.
———. Sonata for Two Pianos and Percussion. CBS MK-42625.
Berg, Alban. Violin Concerto. London 411804-2 LH.
———. *Wozzeck.* Deutsche Grammophon Gesellschaft 423587-2 GH2.
Cowell, Henry. "The Tides of Manaunaun"; "The Banshee." PAN PRC S20-34; New World NW 203.
Debussy, Claude. "La cathedrale engloutie" from Preludes for Piano, Book 1. Phillips 420393-2 PH.
———. Nocturnes for Orchestra. Deutsche Grammophon Gesellschaft 415370-2 GH.
Ives, Charles. *Three Quarter-Tone Pieces.* Odyssey 32160162.
Mahler, Gustav. *Das Lied von der Erde.* CBS MK-42034.
Satie, Erik. *Gymnopédies.* London 421527-2 LH.
———. *Trois morceaux en form de poire.* Etcetera KTC-1015.
Schoenberg, Arnold. *Pierrot Lunaire.* Elektra/Nonesuch 79237-2-ZK.
———. Variations for Orchestra London 425008-2 LM2.
Stravinsky, Igor. *Le sacre du printemps.* Deutsche Grammophon Gesellschaft 415854-2 GGA.
———. *Symphony of Psalms.* CBS MK 44710.
Varèse, Edgard. *Density 21.5.* Sony Classical SK-45844.
———. *Ionisation.* Sony Classical SK-45844.
———. *Octandre.* Reference RR-29CD.
Webern, Anton von. Concerto, Op. 24. Chandos ABR 1046.
———. Six Pieces for Orchestra, Op. 6 Deutsche Grammophon Gesellschaft 423254-2 GC

2. Precedents and Influences: Music from 1890 to 1945

Cage, John. *First Construction In Metal.* MMG 105.
———. *Imaginary Landscape No. 1.* Avakian S-1.
Cowell, Henry. Piano Music. Composer's Recordings CRI ACS-6005 (casette).
Debussy, Claude. *Prélude a l'après-midi d'un faune.* RCA 6719-2 Rg.
Ives, Charles. *The Unanswered Question.* CBS MK-42407.
Messiaen, Oliver. *Quatuor pour la fin du temps.* RCA 7835-2-RG.

Schoenberg, Arnold. Suite, Op. 25. Denon CD-1060/61
———. *Verklärte Nacht.* London 410111-2LH.
Webern, Anton von. Piano Variations, Op. 27. Denon CO-1060/6

5. The Early Postwar Years

Babbitt, Milton. *Three Compositions for Piano.* Composers Recordings CRI S-461.
Bernstein, Leonard. Symphony No. 2, "The Age of Anxiety." CBS ML 4325.
———. *Trouble in Tahiti.* Deutsche Grammophon Gesellschaft 415253-2 GH2.
Boulez, Pierre. *Structures 1a.* Wergo WER 60011.
Copland, Aaron. Piano Fantasy. Delos DCD-1013.
Messiaen, Olivier. "Mode de valeurs et d'intensités." Musical Heritage Society MHS 1069.
Stravinsky, Igor. *The Rake's Progress.* London 411644-2LH2.

6. Pieces for Study I

Britten, Benjamin. *The Turn of The Screw.* London 425672-2LH2.
Cage, John. *Music of Changes.* Wergo WER 60099-50.
———. *Sonatas and Interludes.* Denon C37-7673.
Carter, Elliott. Sonata for Flute, Oboe, Cello, and Harpsichord. Elektra/ Nonesuch H-71234.
Foss, Lukas. *Time Cycle.* Columbia CSP AMS 6280; Contemporary Record Society CRS 8219.
Stockhausen, Karlheinz. Stockhausen Verlag CD1. *Kreuzspiel.* Deutsche Grammophon Gesellschaft 2530 443 IMS.
———. *Agon.* Argo ZRG-937; Wergo 50002.
———. *Threni.* CBS CMS 6065.

7. ``Order" and ``Chaos"

Babbitt, Milton. *All Set.* Columbia C2L-31.
———. *Composition for Four Instruments.* Composers Recordings CRI C-138.
———. *Composition for Twelve Instruments.* Son-Nova 1.
Boulez, Pierre. *Le marteau sans maître.* Ades ACD-14073-2; Turnabout 34081.
Brown, Earle. *Available Forms* II. RCA Victrola VICS-1239.
Cage, John. *Aria and Fontana Mix.* Time S-8003.
———. *Atlas Eclipticalis.* MODE 3–6 (4 LPs).
———. *Indeterminacy.* Folkways 2-3704.
Feldman, Morton. *Durations.* Time S-58007.
———. *Intersections.* Deutsche Grammophon Gesellschaft 139442.

Foss, Lukas. *Paradigm.* Deutsche Grammophon Gesellschaft 2543005.

Lutoslawski, Witold. *Venetian Games.* MUZA PNCD-041.

Martino, Donald. *Notturno.* Elektra/Nonesuch H-71300.

Stockhausen, Karlheinz. *Klavierstück XI.* Koch Schwann CD-310009 H1.

———. *Refrain.* Koch Schwann–Musica Mundi, CD-310020 H1.

———. *Zyklus.* Wergo, WER 60010.

8. The Electronic Revolution I: Tape Composition and Early Synthesizers

Antheil, George. *Ballet méchanique.* Phillips 6514254.

Babbitt, Milton. *Ensembles for Synthesizer.* Finnadar 9010.

Badings, Henk. *Capriccio for Violin and Two Soundtracks.* Limelight 86055.

Berio, Luciano. *Thema: Omaggio a Joyce.* Vox Turnabout TV-34177.

Cage, John. *Aria and Fontana Mix.* Time S-8003.

———. *Fontana Mix.* Vox Turnabout 34046S.

———. *Williams Mix.* Avakian S-1 (3 LPs).

Caine, Hugh le. *Dripsody.* Folkways FM-33436.

Carlos, Walter, and Benjamin Folkman. *Switched On Bach.* CBS MK-7194.

Davidovsky, Mario. *Synchronisms Nos. 1, 2, and 3.* Composers Recordings CRI S-204.

———. *Synchronisms No. 5,* CRI SD-268 (2 LPs).

Eaton, John. *Concert Piece for Syn-Ket and Orchestra.* Vox Turnabout TV-S34428.

Erb, Donald. *In No Strange Land.* Nonesuch H-71223.

Gerhard, Roberto. *Collage* (Symphony No. 3 for Electronic Tape and Orchestra). Angel S-36558.

Henry, Pierre, and Pierre Schaeffer. *Symphonie pour un homme seul.* Ades 14.122-2.

Hiller, Lejaren. *Machine Music.* Heliodor HS 25047.

Kupferman, Meyer. *Superflute.* Nonesuch H 71289.

Ligeti, György. *Artikulation.* Wergo WER 60161-50.

Luening, Otto. *Fantasy in Space; Low Speed.* Desto 6466.

Luening, Otto, and Vladimir Ussachevsky. *Concerted Piece for Tape Recorder and Orchestra.* Composers Recordings CRI SD-227.

———. *A Poem in Cycles and Bells.* Composers Recordings CRI SD-112.

Messiaen, Olivier. *Turangalîla-Symphonie.* CBS M2K-42271.

Posseur, Henri. *Rimes pour differentes sources sonores.* RCA Victrola VICS-1239.

———. *Scambi.* Mercury SR2-9123.

Powell, Mel. *Second Electronic Setting.* Composers Recordings CRI 227 USD.

Stockhausen, Karlheinz. *Gesang der Jünglinge.* Stockhausen Verlag CD3. Deutsche Grammophon Gesellschaft 138811 IMS.

———. *Kontakte.* Stockhausen Verlag CD3. Music and Arts CD 648.

———. *Studie II.* Stockhausen Verlag CD3. Deutsche Grammophon Gesellschaft 16133 (monaural).

Subotnick, Morton. *Silver Apples of The Moon.* Elektra/Nonesuch H-71174.

———. *The Wild Bull.* Elektra/Nonesuch H-71208.

Ussachevsky, Vladimir. *Of Wood and Brass.* Composers Recordings CRI SD-227.

———. *Sonic Contours.* Desto 6466.

Varèse, Edgard. *Déserts.* CRI SD-268.

———. *Poème électronique.* CBS MG-31078; Neuma 450-74.

Xenakis, Iannis. *Orient-Occident.* Elektra/Nonesuch H-71246.

9. Multimedia and Total Theater

Ashley, Robert. *The Wolfman.* Source Records 2, no. 2 (July 1968).

Bedford, David. *Spillihpnerak.* Finnadar 9007.

Berio, Luciano. *Circles.* Wergo WER 60021.

———. *Laborintus II.* Harmonia Mundi HMA-190.764.

———. *Thema: Omaggio a Joyce.* Turnabout TV 34177.

Cross, Lowell. *Video Laser II.* Source Records 3731-1 SR 19.

Crumb, George. *Songs, Drones, and Refrains of Death.* Desto 7155.

Curtis-Smith, Curtis O. B. *Unisonics.* Composers Recordings CRI S-388.

Dempster, Stuart, and Oliveros, Pauline. *Deep Listening.* New Albion NA022.

Druckman, Jacob. *Animus III.* Elektra/Nonesuch H-71253.

Erickson, Robert. *Ricercar à 3* for contrabass. Ars Nova/ Ars Antiqua AN-1001.

Erickson, Robert. *Ricercar à 5* for trombone. Deutsche Grammophon Gesellschaft 0654-084 (AR series).

Foss, Lukas. *Echoi.* Wergo WER 60040.

Holliger, Heinz. *Pneuma.* ECM 833 307-2.

Johnston, Ben. *Casta Bertram.* Nonesuch H-71237.

Kagel, Mauricio. *Transición II.* Mainstream (Time) MS-5003.

Ligeti, György. *Aventures; Nouvelles Aventures.* Wergo WER-60045-50.

Martirano, Salvatore. *L's GA.* Polydor 24-5001.

Mumma, Gordon. *Cybersonic Cantilevers.* Odyssey 32160158.

Oliveros, Pauline. *Horse Sings from Cloud.* Lovely LP VR-1901.

Reynolds, Roger. *Ping.* Composers Recordings CRI S-285.

Scott, Stephen. *Rainbows* (Part I). New Albion NA-009CD.

Stockhausen, Karlheinz. *Gruppen.* Stockhausen Verlag CD5. Deutsche Grammophon Gesellschaft 137002 IMS.

———. *Momente.* Stockhausen Verlag CD7 (2 CDs). Elektra/Nonesuch H-71157.

———. *Trans I* and II. Deutsche Grammophon Gesellschaft 2530 726 IMS.

10. Texture, Mass, and Density

Albright, William. *Organ Book I* and *II*. Gothic G-58627.

Babbit, Milton. *Composition For Synthesizer*. Columbia MS-6566

Becker, John. *The Abongo*. New World NW-285.

Berio, Luciano. *Chemins II b/c*. Sony Classical SK 45862.

———. *Sequenza I*. Chaves CD50-8005.

———. *Sequenza III*. Virgin Classics VC-790704-2.

———. *Sequenza V*. Bis CD-388.

———. *Sequenza VI*. Finnadar 9007.

———. *Sequenza IX b*. ADDA 581047.

Carter, Elliott. Double Concerto. Elektra/Nonesuch H-71314.

———. Sonata for Cello and Piano. Nonesuch H-71234.

———. String Quartets Nos. 2 and 3. Etcetera KTC-1066.

———. *Symphony of Three Orchestras*. CBS MT-35171.

Chihara, Paul. *Logs*. Composers Recordings CRI C-269.

Cowell, Henry. "Aeolian Harp"; "Sinister Resonance." PAN PRC 520-34.

Crumb, George. *Vox Balaenae*. New World NW-357-2; CBS M-32739

Dick, Robert. *Afterlight*. GM Recordings 2013CD.

Druckman, Jacob. *Valentine*. Nonesuch H-71253.

Erb, Donald. *The Seventh Trumpet*. Turnabout TV-34433.

Feldman, Morton. *The King of Denmark*. Columbia MS-7139.

Godfrey, Daniel. *Scrimshaw*. Spectrum SR-327.

Hindemith, Paul. Trio. Bis 57.

Husa, Karel. *Apotheosis of This Earth*. Golden Crest GC 4134.

Ives, Charles. "Majority." Etcetera KTC-1068.

———. *Three Places in New England*. Deutsche Grammophon Gesellschaft 423243-2 GC.

Kagel, Mauricio. *Music for Renaissance Instruments*. Schw HL 00211 (5 LPs).

Kondo, Jo. *Sight Rhythmics*. CP^2 11.

Ligeti, György. *Atmosphères*. Deutsche Grammophon Gesellschaft 429 260-2; Wergo WER 60022.

———. *Lontano*. Wergo WER 60045-50.

———. *Lux aeterna*. Deutsche Grammophon Gesellschaft 423244-2 GC.

———. *Requiem*. Wergo WER 60045-50.

Lutosławski, Witold. *Venetian Games*. Muza PNCD-041.

Messiaen, Olivier. *Chronochromie*. Koch Schwann CD-311015.

Nancarrow, Conlon. *Canon X*. ARCH S-1777; Wergo WER 168-2.

Oliveros, Pauline. *I of IV*. Odyssey 32160160.

Penderecki, Krzysztof. Capriccio for Violin and Orchestra. RCA 60370-2-RC.

———. *De Natura Sonoris*. Elektra/Nonesuch H-71201.

———. *Saint Luke Passion*. EMI 667-749313-2.

Reich, Steve. *Come Out; It's Gonna Rain*. Elektra/Nonesuch 79169-2.

Riley, Terry. *Poppy Nogood and the Phantom Band*. CBS MK-7315.
Rouse, Christopher. *The Surma Ritornelli*. Spectrum SR-327.
Schoenberg, Arnold. Five Pieces for Orchestra, Op. 16. Deutsche Grammophon Gesellschaft 419781-2GH.
Schuller, Gunther. Capriccio for Tuba and Orchestra. GM Recordings 2004.
———. *Five Moods for Tuba Quartet*. Crystal S-221.
Stockhausen, Karlheinz. *Carre; Gruppen*. Stockhausen Verlag CD5. Deutsche Grammophon Gesellschaft 137002 IMS.
———. *Zeitmasse*. Stockhausen Verlag CD4. Deutsche Grammophon Gesellschaft 2530 443 IMS.
Stucky, Stephen. *Sappho Fragments*. Spectrum SR-195.
Tavener, John. *The Whale*. Apple SMAS-3369.
Varèse, Edgard. *Arcana*. Sony Classical SK-45844.
———. *Déserts*. Composers Recordings CRI SD-268 (2 LPs).
———. *Intégrales*. Sony Classical SK-45844.
Webern, Anton von. Concerto for Nine Instruments, Op. 24. Chandos 1046.
Wolpe, Stefan. *Chamber Piece No. 1*. Elektra/Nonesuch H-71220.
Xenakis, Iannis. *Metastasis; Pithoprakta*. Chant Du Mon De LCD-278368.
———. *Nomos Gama*. Erato STU 71513.
———. *Polytope*. Candide Vox CE 31049.

II. Non-Western Musical Influences

Cage, John. *Cartridge Music*. Deutsche Grammophon Gesellschaft 137009.
Cage, John, and Lou Larrison. *Double Music for Percussion Quartet*. Hungaroton HCD-12991.
Chou, Wen-Chung. *Landscapes for Orchestra*. Composers Recordings CRI SD-122.
———. *The Willows Are New*. Composers Recordings CRI S-251.
Harrison, Lou. *Concerto in Slendro*. Desto CMS DC-7144.
———. *La Koro Sutra*. New Albion NA-015 CD.
———. *Three Pieces for Gamelan with Soloists*. Composers Recordings CRI ACS-6006.
Hovhaness, Alan. *Firdausi*. Grenadilla GSC-1008.
———. Symphony No. 21, *Etchmiadzin*. Crystal CD-804.
Hykes, David. *Hearing Solar Winds*. Harmonia Mundi 558607.
McPhee, Colin. *Tabub-Tabuhan*. Mercury MG 50103.
Milhaud, Darius. *Saudades do Brazil*. Angel CDC-47845.
Partch, Harry. *Delusion of the Fury*. Composers Recordings CRI CD-700.
Reich, Steve. *Drumming*. Elektra/Nonesuch 79170-2.
———. *Music for Eighteen Musicians*. ECM New Series 821417-2.
———. *Music for Mallet Instruments, Voices, and Organ*. Hungaroton HCD-31358.
Riley, Terry. *The Harp of New Albion*. 2CD-CEL-018/19.

———. *Shri Camel.* CBS MK-35164.

———. *Songs for the Ten Voices of the Two Prophets.* Kuckuck 11067-1.

Roussel, Albert. *Padmavati.* EMI DSBX-3948.

Takemitsu, Toru. *November Steps.* RCA Victor LCS 705L.

Ung, Chinary. *Mohori.* Composers Recordings CRI SD-363.

Wernick, Richard. *Kaddisch-Requiem.* Nonesuch 79222-2-J.

———. *Prayer for Jerusalem.* Composers Recordings CRI S-344.

Young, LaMonte. *The Well-Tuned Piano.* Gramavision 18-8701-2.

12. Pieces for Study II

Babbitt, Milton. *Vision and Prayer.* Composers Recordings CRI CD-521.

Berio, Luciano. *Visage.* Vox Turnabout 34046S.

Boulez, Pierre. *Rituel in Memoriam Bruno Maderna.* Sony Classical SMK-45839.

Cage, John, and Lejaren Hiller. *HPSCHD.* Nonesuch H-71224.

Crumb, George. *Ancient Voices of Children.* Elektra/Nonesuch 79149-2.

Davidovsky, Mario. *Synchronisms No. 1.* Composers Recordings CRI S-204.

Maxwell Davies, Peter. *Eight Songs for a Mad King.* Unicorn-Kanchana DKPCD-9052.

Penderecki, Krzysztof. *Threnody for the Victims of Hiroshima.* Conifer CDCF-168.

Schat, Peter. *To You.* Donemus/Composers Voice 6810 712.1 Y.

13. Collage and Quotation

Andriessen, Louis, et al. *Reconstructie.* STEIM Opus 001.

Bolcom, William. *Black Host.* Titanic Ti-175.

———. Second Violin Sonata. Elektra/Nonesuch 79058-1.

———. *Whisper Moon.* Folkways 33903.

Crumb, George. *Black Angels.* Elektra/Nonesuch 79242-2-P.

Foss, Lukas. *Renaissance Concerto.* New World NW-375-2.

Hodkinson, Sydney. *The Dissolution of the Serial.* Composers Recordings CRI S-292.

Kagel, Mauricio. *Ludwig Van.* Deutsche Grammophon Gesellschaft 2530014.

Maxwell Davies, Peter. *Antechrist.* L'oiseau-Lyre DSL02.

———. *Saint Thomas' Wake.* Louisville Orchestra LS-770.

Rasmussen, Karl Aaage. *Genklang.* EMI DMA 038 063-39267.

Rochberg, George. *Contra mortem et tempus.* Composers Recordings CRI SD-231.

———. *Music for the Magic Theater.* Desto 6444.

Schnittke, Alfred. Concerto Grosso No. 1. Deutsche Grammophon Gesellschaft 429413-2GH.

———. Symphony No. 5 (Concerto Grosso No. 4). Bis CD-427.

Stockhausen, Karlheinz. *Hymnen.* Stockhausen Verlag CD5. Deutsche Grammophon Gesellschaft 2707039.

———. *Kurzwellen.* Stockhausen Verlag CD5. Deutsche Grammophon Gesellschaft 2707045.

———. *Opus 1970.* Deutsche Grammophon Gesellschaft 139-461-SLPM.

Tippett, Sir Michael. *A Child of Our Time.* MCA Classics MCAD-6202.

———. *The Knot Garden.* Phillips 6500552+3.

Tower, Joan. *Petroushskates.* Composers Recordings CRI CD582.

Zimmermann, Bernd Alois. *Musique pour les soupers du Roi Ubu.* Harmonia Mundi DMR 1013-15.

———. *Die Soldaten.* Harmonia Mundi DMR 1007-09.

14. The Resurgence of Tonality

Adams, John. *Harmonielehre.* Elektra/Nonesuch 79115-2.

———. *Harmonium.* ECM New Series 821465-2.

———. *Nixon in China.* Elektra/Nonesuch 79177-2.

Argento, Dominick. *Six Elizabethan Songs.* Composers Recordings CRI C-380 (cassette).

Barber, Samuel. *Adagio for Strings.* Nonesuch 979181-2.

———. *Knoxville: Summer of 1915.* Virgin Classics VC7 90766-2.

———. Concerto for Piano and Orchestra, Op. 38. RCA 60732-2-RC.

Copland, Aaron. *Connotations.* New World NW-368-2.

Eno, Brian. *Music for Airports.* Editions EG EGS-201.

Górecki, Henryk. Symphony No. 3, *Sinfonie der Klagelieder.* Koch-Schwann CD-311041.

Harbison, John. *Full Moon in March.* Composers Recordings CRI S-454.

———. *Miribai Songs.* Northeastern NR 230-CD.

———. Piano Concerto. Composers Recordings CRI S-440.

———. *Ulysses' Bow.* Elektra/Nonesuch 79129-2.

Killmayer, Wilhelm. Sinfonie No. 2. Wergo WER 60116.

Menotti, Gian Carlo. *Amahl and the Night Visitors.* MCA Classics MCAD-6218.

Orff, Carl. *Antigonae.* Deutsche Grammophon Gesellschaft SLPM 138 717-19.

———. *Oedipus der Tyrann.* Deutsche Grammophon Gesellschaft 139 251-53.

Panufnik, Andrzej. *Sinfonia sacra.* Elektra/Nonesuch 79228-2.

Pärt, Arvo. *Tabula rasa.* ECM New Series 817764-2.

Penderecki, Krzysztof. Symphony No. 2, *Christmas.* MUZA PNCD-019.

Riley, Terrry. *A Rainbow in Curved Air.* CBS MK-7315.

Rochberg, George. Oboe Concerto. New World NW-335-2.

———. Piano Trio. Turnabout TV-S 34520.

———. String Quartet No. 3. Elektra/Nonesuch H-71283.

———. Violin Concerto. Columbia M35149.

Ruders, Poul. *Vox in Rama*. Bridge BCD 9036.

Satoh, Somei. *Birds in Warped Time II*. New Albion NA-009CD.

Schnittke, Alfred. String Quartet No. 3. Elektra/Nonesuch 9 79181-2.

Schwantner, Joseph. *Wild Angels of the Open Hills*. Composers Recordings CRI SD-497.

Stravinsky, Igor. *Threni*. Columbia ML 5383.

Tippett, Sir Michael. Symphony No. 4. London 425646-2LM3.

Wyner, Yehudi. Three Short Fantasies for Piano. Composers Recordings CRI S-306.

Zwilich, Ellen Taaffe. Chamber Symphony. Composers Recordings CRI SD-546.

15. New Views of Performance: Space, Ritual, and Play

Bernstein, Leonard. *Mass*. CBS M2K-44593.

Cage, John. *Cartridge Music*. ABT ERZ 1002.

Crumb, George. *Echoes of Time and the River*. Louisville Orchestra Records LS-711.

Dodge, Charles. *Any Resemblance Is Purely Coincidental*. Folkways FTS-37475.

Erickson, Robert. *General Speech*. New World NW 254.

Foss, Lukas. *Paradigm*. Deutsche Grammophon Gesellschaft 2543 005.

La Barbara, Joan. *October Music: Star Showers and Extraterrestrials*. Elektra/Nonesuch 78029-1.

Lucier, Alvin. *I Am Sitting in a Room*. Lovely Music LCD-1013.

———. *Music for Solo Performer*. Lovely Music VR-1014.

Stockhausen, Karlheinz. *Carre*. Stockhausen Verlag CD5. Schw HL-00214 (5 LPs).

———. *Mikrophonie*. Columbia 3211 0044.

———. *Samstag*. Stockhausen Verlag CD36. (5 CDs). Deutsche Grammophon Gesellschaft/Avant Garde 423596-2GH4.

———. *Stimmung*. Hyperion CDA-66115.

Subotnick, Morton. *After the Butterfly*. Elektra/Nonesuch N-78001.

———. *The Wild Beasts*. Elektra/Nonesuch N-78012.

Wolff, Christian. *Duet II*. Time S-8009.

16. Process and Minimalism

Adams, John. *Grand Pianola Music*. Angel CDC-47331.

———. *Phrygian Gates*. Music and Arts CD-604.

———. *Shaker Loops*. ARCH Records 1784; Phillips 412214-2PH.

Amirkhanian, Charles. *Just*. ARCH Records 1752.
Glass, Philip. *Akhnaten*. CBS M2K-42457.
———. *Music in Twelve Parts*. Virgin 91311-2.
———. *Satyagraha*. CBS M3K-39672.
———. *Strung Out*. CP² CP2/6.
Kramer, Jonathan. *Music for Piano No. 5*. Leonarda LE 332.
Ligeti, György. *Continuum*. Bis CD-53.
———. *Volumina*. Wergo WER CD 60161-50.
Reich, Steve. *Clapping Music*. Elektra/Nonesuch 79169-2.
———. *Different Trains*. Elektra/Nonesuch 79176-2.
———. *Tehillim*. ECM New Series 827411-2.
———. *Violin Phase*. ECM New Series 827287-2.
Riley, Terry. *In C*. CBS MK-7178.
Rzewski, Frederic. *Les moutons de Panurge*. Opus One No. 20.
Satie, Erik. *Vexations*. DECC 425 221-2DNL.
Schwartz, Elliott. *Dream Music with Variations*. Orion ORS 86499.
Torke, Michael. *The Yellow Pages; Vanada*. ARGO 430209-2ZH.

17. The Electronic Revolution II: Computers and Digital Systems

Austin, Larry. *Canadian Coastlines*. Folkways FTS 37475.
Birtwistle, Harrison. *Chronometer*. ARGO ZRG 790.
Boretz, Benjamin. *Group Variations*. Composers Recordings CRI SD-300.
Boulez, Pierre. *Répons*. IRCAM Records IRCAM-0001.
Chowning, John. *Turenas*. Wergo WER 2012-50.
Dodge, Charles. *Earth's Magnetic Field*. Elektra/Nonesuch H-71250.
———. *In Celebration; Speech Songs*. Composers Recordings CRI C-348.
Ghent, Emmanuel. *Phosphons*. Wergo WER 2022-50.
Harvey, Jonathan. *Mortuos plango, vivos voco*. IRCAM 0001; Neuma 450-75.
Hiller, Lejaren. *Algorithms*. Deutsche Grammophon Gesellschaft/Avant Garde 2543005.
Hiller, Lejaren, and Robert Baker. *Computer Cantata*. Composers Recordings CRI SD-310.
Machover, Tod. *Bug-Mudra*. Bridge Records BCD 9022.
Machover, Tod. *Light*. Composers Recordings CRI SD-506.
———. *Soft Morning, City*. IRCAM Records IRCAM 0001.
Melby, John. *Chor der Steine*. Centaur CRC 2045.
Subotnick, Morton. *The Key to Songs*. New Albion NA-012.
Vercoe, Barry. *Synthesism*. Nonesuch H-71245.
Xenakis, Iannis. *Metastasis*. Chant du Monde LCD-278368.

18. Pieces for Study III

Anderson, Laurie. "O Superman." Warner Brothers BSK 3674.

Berio, Luciano. *Sinfonia.* Ades 14,12-2.

Birtwistle, Harrison. *Punch and Judy.* Etcetera KTC-2014.

Foss, Lukas. *Baroque Variations.* Elektra/Nonesuch H-71202.

Johnson, Tom. *Failing.* Folkways FSS 37462.

Kagel, Mauricio. *Staatstheater.* Schw HL 00213 (5 LPs).

Lachenmann, Helmut. *Mouvement (—vor der Erstarrung).* Deutsche Harmonia Mundi HM 713 D.

Lansky, Paul. *Six Fantasies on a Poem by Thomas Campion.* Composers Recordings CRI S-456.

19. Notation, Improvisation, and Composition

Ashley, Robert. *In Memoriam Crazy Horse.* Advance FGR-5.

Austin, Larry. *Accidents.* Source SR-13.

Bedford, David. *Music for Albion Moonlight.* Argo ZRG 638.

Boulez, Pierre. Piano Sonata No. 3. Wergo WER-60121-50.

Browne, Earle. *Available Forms II.* RCA VICS-1239.

Crumb, George. *Eleven Echoes of Autumn.* Composers Recordings CRI S-233.

Feldman, Morton. *Projection.* Odyssey 32160302.

Ferneyhough, Brian. String Quartet No. 2. RCA AS-9006.

Foss, Lukas. *Elytres; For 24 Winds.* Vox Turnabout TV-534514.

Ligeti, György. *Volumina.* Wergo WER CD 60161-50.

Penderecki, Krzysztof. *Threnody for the Victims of Hiroshima.* Conifer CDCF-168.

Schwartz, Elliott. *Chamber Concerto II.* Composers Recordings CRI CD-598.

20. Composers and National Traditions

Abrahamsen, Hans. *Winternacht.* Paula Denmark 37.

Aitken, Robert. *Folia.* Centrediscs CMC 0482.

Andriessen, Louis. *Hoketus.* New Albion NA019 CD.

————. *De snelheid.* Donemus/Composer's Voice CV 8601.

————. *De staat.* Attaca BABEL 8949-2.

Bainbridge, Simon. Viola Concerto. Continuum CCD 1020.

Balassa, Sándor. *Iris.* Hungaraton SLPX 11732.

Benjamin, George. *At First Light.* Nimbus NI-5075.

Bortz, Daniel. Symphony No. 6. Phono Suecia PS CD 24.

Bruzdowicz, Joanna. String Quartet No. 1. Pavane ADW 7218.

Bryars, Gavin. *The Sinking of the Titanic; Jesus' Blood Never Failed Me Yet.* Obscure Records 1.

Denisov, Edison. *Sun of the Incas*. Melodiya C 10-18403-4.

Dickinson, Peter. Piano Concerto. EMI CDC7-47584-2.

Durkó, Zsolt. *Burial Prayer*. Hungaraton SLPX 11803.

Enriquez, Manuel. *Ritual*. Forlane UM3568.

Finnissy, Michael. *Catana*. Etcetera KTC 1096.

———. Piano Music. NMCD002.

Gandini, Gerardo. Fantasie-Impromptu. Louisville First Edition LS-714.

Garant, Serge. *Cage d'oiseau*. Radio Canada International ACM 12.

Gubaidulina, Sofia. *In croce*. Koch-Schwann CD 310 091 GI.

Harvey, Jonathan. *Mortuos plango, vivo voco*. IRCAM 0001; Neuma 450-75.

———. *Song Offerings*. Nimbus NI-5167.

Hedstrom, Ase. *Sorti*. Aurora ACD 4961.

Hirose, Ryohei. Concerto for Shakuhachi and Orchestra. Sony Classical 28AC 2026.

Hosokawa, Toshio. *SEN II*. Fontel FOCD 3225.

Ikebe, Shin-Ichiro. Piano Concerto No. 2. Camerata 32CM-87.

———. *Spontaneous Ignition*. Camerata 32CM-110.

Ishii, Maki. *Sogu II*. EMI C063-02-257.

Janssen, Guus. String Quartet No. 2. Donemus/Composer's Voice CVCD8701.

Kancheli, Giya. Symphony No. 2. Melodiya SUCD 10-00129.

Knussen, Oliver. *Where the Wild Things Are*. Arabesque Z-6535.

Keuris, Tristan. *Sinfonia*. Donemus/Composer's Voice CVH1.

Krauze, Zygmunt. *Tableau Vivant*. MUZA PNCD-113 (CD).

———. *The Underground River*. MUZA SX 2741.

Kurtág, György. *Messages of the Late R. V. Troussova*. Erato 2292-45410-2.

———. *The Sayings of Peter Bornemisza*. Hungaraton HCD 31290.

Lavista, Mario. *Ficciones*. Forlane UM3568.

Leeuw, Reinbert de. *Abscheid*. Donemus/Composer's Voice CVH1.

Leeuw, Ton de. *Mo-Do*. Radio Nederland BFO A-13.

Loevendie, Theo. *Six Turkish Folk Poems*. Stemra 6812.901/06.

Louie, Alexina. *Cadenzas*. Centredisques CMC-CD 2786.

———. *Songs of Paradise*. CBS SMCD-5080.

Martland, Steve. *Babi Yar*. Factory FACD 266.

Mellnas, Arne. *Transparence*. Phono Suecia PS CD 22.

Morthenson, Jan W. *Strano*. Phono Suecia PS CD 26.

Mayuzumi, Toshiru. *Nirvana* Symphony. Phillips 9500-762.

Miyoshi, Akira. *Requiem*. RCA Victor SJX-1085.

Nobre, Marlos. *Mosaico*. Phillips/UNESCO 6833-177/8.

Noda, Teruyuki. Piano Concerto. Camerata 32CM-58.

Nishimura, Akira. *The Navel of the Sun*. Camerata 32CM-110.

Nordheim, Arne. *Wirklicher Wald*. Norwegian Music Productions NCD-4910.

Panufnik, Andrzej. *Arbor Cosmica*. Elektra/Nonesuch 79228-2.

Pärt, Arvo. Symphony No. 3. Bis CD-434.

Persen, John. *Et cetera!* Aurora ACD 4961.

Quintanar, Hector. *Sideral II.* Louisville First Edition LS-714.

Rasmussen, Karl Aage. *A Ballad of Game and Dream.* Danish DMA-038.

Ruders, Poul. *Corpus cum figuris; Manhattan Abstraction.* Point PCD-5084.

Saariaho, Kaija. *Io.* Finlandia FACD-374.

———. *Petals.* Neuma 450-73.

Sallinen, Aulis. Symphony No. 5, *Washington Mosaics.* Finlandia FACD 370.

Samama, Leo. *Grand Slam.* Radio Nederland BFOA-13.

———. *Monumentum pro Caecilia.* Babel Attacca 8844-2.

Saxton, Robert. Concerto for Orchestra. EMI CDC 49915 2.

Schafer, R. Murray. Concerto for Harpsichord and Eight Wind Instruments. Radio Canada Internatl Programme 193.

Schat, Peter. *Serenade for Strings.* Babel Attacca 8844-2.

Sikorski, Tomasz. Concerto Breve; *Other Voices.* MUZA SK 2857.

Takemitsu, Toru. *Cassiopeia.* EMI C063-02 257.

Tavener, John. *Ikon of Light.* Gimell CDGIM 005.

Thommessen, Olav Anton. *A Glass Bead Game.* Aurora ACD 4927.

Tremblay, Gilles. *Tracante.* Radio Canada Internatl ACM 12.

———. *Vers le soleil.* SNE 523-CD.

Vivier, Claude. *Et je reverrai cette ville étrange.* Artifact 002.

———. *Siddartha.* Centredisques CMC-CD3188.

Weir, Judith. *The Consolations of Scholarship.* Novello NVLCD109.

Yuasa, Joji. *Projection (Flower, Bird, Wind, Moon).* Denon OW-7842-ND.

21. Pieces for Study IV: A Panorama of Works by Genre

Corigliano, John. *Pied Piper* Fantasy. RCA 6602-2 RC.

Erb, Donald. Concerto for Contrabassoon and Orchestra. Leonarda LE 331.

Glass, Phillip. *Einstein on the Beach.* CBS M4K-38875.

Gubaidulina, Sofia. *Offertorium.* Deutsche Grammophon Gesellschaft 427336-2 GH.

Husa, Karel. *Music for Prague.* CBS MK-44916.

Ligeti, György. *Le grand macabre.* Ades 14.122-2 (4 CDs).

Lindberg, Magnus. *Kraft.* Finlandia FACD 372.

MacDermot, Galt. *Hair.* RCA 1150-2 RC.

Musgrave, Thea. *A Christmas Carol.* Moss Music Group 3-MMG-32 (3 LPs).

———. *Mary, Queen of Scots.* Moss Music Group MMG 301.

Nørgård, Per. Symphony No. 3. Danish DMA-077.

O'Brien, Richard. *The Rocky Horror Picture Show.* Rhino R21S-70792.

Schuller, Gunther. *Abstractions.* Atlantic 1356.

Sculthorpe, Peter. *Sun Music I.* Odyssey 32160150.

Shapey, Ralph. *Kroslish* Sonata. New World NW-355-2.

Subotnick, Morton. *Wild Beasts*. Elektra/Nonesuch N-78012.

Tower, Joan. *Silver Ladders*. Elektra/Nonesuch 79245-2-ZK.

Webber, Andrew Lloyd. *Jesus Christ Superstar*. MCA MCAD2-10000 (2 CDs).

Who, The. *Tommy*. Rhino R2CD-71113.

Index